The
Wyeths

1974

The
Wyeths

The Letters of
N.C.Wyeth, 1901-1945

edited by *Betsy James Wyeth*

Gambit   *Boston*

1971

"Portrait of 'Babe'" (1909), page 304, by kind permission of Mrs. Stimson Wyeth.

The endpapers for this book are reproduced by permission of the Houghton Mifflin Company, Boston.

Color plates by Henry N. Sawyer Company

To all who brought forth the writing of these letters and
in so doing gave us the man who wrote them.

CONTENTS

LIST OF ILLUSTRATIONS

ILLUSTRATIONS

Illustrations

ILLUSTRATIONS

COLOR PLATES

ANDREW NEWELL WYETH I
(April 29, 1817–April 13, 1900)
married May 4, 1843
AMELIA H. B. STIMSON
(April 5, 1818–February 22, 1891)

AMELIA ANNIE
(Jan. 4, 1846–Oct. 6, 1903)
married April 8, 1869
JOHN BARKER
(July 15, 1845–June 20, 1932)

ANDREW NEWELL, II
(Feb. 2, 1853–July 29, 1929)
married Dec. 21, 1881
HENRIETTE ZIRNGIEBEL
(Dec. 25, 1857–Aug. 11, 1925)

NEWELL CONVERS I (N. C.)
(Oct. 22, 1882–Oct. 19, 1945)
married April 16, 1906
CAROLYN B. BOCKUS
(March 22, 1886)

EDWIN RUDOLPH
(Dec. 5, 1886–Aug. 2, 1960)
married Dec. 25, 1913
CLARA LOUISE MOELLER
(Jan. 14, 1889)

HENRIETTE
(Oct. 22, 1907)
married June 28, 1929
PETER HURD
(Feb. 22, 1903)

CAROLYN
(Oct. 26, 1909)
unmarried

NATHANIEL CONVERS
(Oct. 24, 1911)
married Jan. 16, 1937
CAROLINE PYLE
(March 5, 1914)

PETER WYETH
(March 22, 1930)
ANN CAROL
(April 9, 1935)
MICHAEL
(Feb. 13, 1946)

NEWELL CONVERS II
(Nov. 14, 1941–Oct. 19, 1945)
HOWARD PYLE
(April 22, 1944)
NEWELL CONVERS III
(Oct. 13, 1946)
ANDREW NATHANIEL
(June 28, 1948)
JOHN BOUND
(March 15, 1950)
DAVID CHRISTOPHER
(Sept. 16, 1953)

SUSAN ELIZABETH
(Dec. 28, 1847–Sept. 20, 1934)
unmarried

HARRIET CONVERS
(July 21, 1855–March 1, 1923)
unmarried

NATHANIEL
(May 29, 1889–Oct. 27, 1954)
married Dec. 25, 1909
GLADYS POND
(Oct. 17, 1888–Nov. 15, 1966)

STIMSON
(May 29, 1891–June 13, 1970)
married June 18, 1923
CONSTANCE TWIGG
(March 31, 1899)

ANN
(March 15, 1915)
married Oct. 26, 1935
JOHN W. McCOY
(May 11, 1910)

ANDREW NEWELL III
(July 12, 1917)
married May 15, 1940
BETSY M. JAMES
(Sept. 26, 1921)

JOHN DENYS
(Aug. 18, 1938)
ANN BRELSFORD
(Sept. 26, 1940)
MAUDE ROBBINS
(March 9, 1944)

NICHOLAS
(Sept. 21, 1943)
JAMES BROWNING
(July 6, 1946)

Chapter I

THE SETTING

By way of an introduction ...

The majority of these letters, written by N. C. Wyeth, were saved by his mother, Mrs. Andrew N. Wyeth II. She died in 1925, and on the death of her husband, in 1929, the box of letters was passed on to N. C. Wyeth's youngest brother, Stimson, who lived across the street from his parents' home in Needham, Massachusetts.

On various visits to his Uncle Stimson, Andrew Wyeth had read enough of the letters to realize that they contained a rich source of information on his father's life, and shortly after N. C. Wyeth's sudden death in 1945, Andrew Wyeth sent for the correspondence and turned it over to an old friend of his father's, who intended writing his biography. This biography was never written, and in 1948 the letters were returned to their sender.

At the end of a long day in his studio, Andrew Wyeth often pulled out a letter at random from the box and read. I have no memory of ever reading through a single one of them. Then, in 1960, Andrew Wyeth's brother-in-law, Peter Hurd, expressed an interest in writing his father-in-law's biography, and the big box was once again sealed up, and sent off to him in New Mexico. Mr. Hurd, under pressure to keep up with his own busy career, never had occasion to uncrate the box. In January 1965 I became for the first time deeply involved in N. C. Wyeth's work. A large retrospective show of his art was scheduled for the opening of the new William Penn Memorial Museum in Harrisburg, Pennsylvania, the following October. We selected from books, dating as far back as 1907, pictures we would like to include in the exhibition, but were at a loss at locating some of the originals. Perhaps, we concluded, the correspondence would provide some clues. So Mr. Hurd read-dressed the crate, and one snowy morning in early February it arrived at the express office.

I helped open the crate and remember being astounded at the number of letters it contained. That very day I started reading them. Day after day I read. And by the end of May I knew that I had come across a personal document of unusual richness—one that traced the author's evolution from an exuberant, naive student of drawing to an artist able to give eloquent expression to a maturing perception of his own nature, and that of the world around him. In my enthusiasm, I seized every possible opportunity to read one of the letters aloud to whoever would listen. And it was with reluctance that I left them behind when we departed that summer for a five-month stay in Maine.

When the N. C. Wyeth exhibition opened in Harrisburg on October 13, a few passages from the letters appeared in the catalogue; and as I walked through gallery after gallery of his work, I recognized a major artistic talent and a man of major human dimension. I also knew that my husband, Andrew, had always been aware of these truths and was almost alone in his knowledge of them. It was, I think, at that evening opening in Harrisburg that I made up my mind to pay back a debt long overdue.

I was very young when I first met N. C. Wyeth, only seventeen. He seemed to me then a force to be challenged and overcome. I married his youngest son when I was eighteen, and together we lived under my father-in-law's shadow. "The old days" were continually referred to: golden years, when the five Wyeth children were growing up together. And as I overheard these reminiscences, it was as if life itself had come to a finish, all excitement in living had gone, nothing new remained but the horror of World War II —and memories of past Christmases, past intimacies, past voices. I rebelled with all my being. The little schoolhouse my husband and I lived in, owned by my father-in-law, I repainted in the brightest colors I could dream up. And when "Pa," as we called him, came by each morning to deliver the mail, I could sense his disapproval. I knew that he and I would never really come to know each other, and between us stood his son, deeply devoted to his father and stimulated by the vitality of his young bride. Ever so gradually we built our life together. "Pa" was left out. I was almost pleased when he failed to understand some of my husband's early attempts at tempera. Indeed, he could hardly, I felt, be expected to; he was bogged down in the *past*. Then one bright morning in Maine a neighbor came knocking at our door with a telephone message: "Call home immediately!" I can even now hear the calm voice on the other end of the line from a million miles away: "Pa was killed an hour ago." If I could just once say to him, "I'm sorry!" Perhaps this was my motivation while I worked on the manuscript: reading, xeroxing the entire correspondence on a rented machine set up in our home, rereading everything, gathering together all the family photographs and the reproductions of N. C. Wyeth's work, and editing the final selection. I knew him for six years, but I never understood him until now. Forgive my foolish heart.

Newell Convers Wyeth was born in his parents' home on the outskirts of Needham, Massachusetts, on October 22, 1882. His father, Andrew Newell Wyeth II, had built the house a year before for his bride Henriette, née Zirngiebel, whose parents lived in a house directly next door to the young couple.

Grandfather Zirngiebel had arrived alone in America in 1855, carrying letters of recommendation from the University of Neuschatel, Switzerland, where he had received a degree in horticulture. After a brief period of employment in New Orleans, he accepted a position as director of the Harvard Botanical Gardens, whereupon he sent to Switzerland for his wife and purchased a house in Cambridge, Massachusetts. The Zirngiebels had two sons and one daughter, Henriette, born Christmas day, 1857. French was spoken in their house and on many occasions Swiss relatives gathered in costume to honor the country they had left behind. Near neighbors were the Andrew Newell Wyeths, who had three daughters and one son, Andrew Newell Wyeth II, born February 2, 1853.

The Wyeths were an established family in Cambridge. Nicholas Wyeth had arrived in Cambridge from England in 1645. Through the following generations, Wyeths attended Harvard College, took part in the Boston Tea Party, fought and fell in the American Revolution, traveled West and helped set up Fort Hall on the Oregon Trail, shipped ice from Cambridge's Fresh Pond to the Indies, prospered as farmers and married other New Englanders. On December 21, 1881, young Andrew Newell Wyeth, New Englander, married Henriette Zirngiebel, daughter of French-Swiss parents.

Instead of staying in Cambridge, the groom chose to live near the town of Needham. Perhaps this was to please his young bride, feeling she would be happier living near her parents, for John Denys Zirngiebel had resigned his position at the Botanical Gardens and moved to Needham to carry on his experimental work in horticulture, building long rows of greenhouses and flower gardens. His new son-in-law, who had his own grain business in Charlestown,

Massachusetts, purchased a few acres adjoining the Zirngiebel property. These are the acres, the houses, the fields gently sloping to the Charles River N. C. Wyeth knew so intimately while growing up with his three brothers.

In 1925 he wrote, "My brothers and I were brought up on a farm, and from the time I could walk I was conscripted into doing every conceivable chore that there was to do about the place. This early training gave me a vivid appreciation of the part the body plays in action.

"Now, when I paint a figure on horseback, a man plowing, or a woman buffeted by the wind, I have an acute sense of the muscle strain, the feel of the hickory handle, or the protective bend of head and squint of eye that each pose involves. After painting action scenes I have ached for hours because of having put myself in the other fellow's shoes as I realized him on canvas."

The Wyeth family, 1902. Standing, left to right: Convers, Edwin and Nat. Seated: Stimson, Mrs. Wyeth and Mr. Wyeth.

6

There was one nagging problem. Young Convers disliked school and spent his time drawing. His mother knew that he had fixed up a corner of his bedroom where he could go to draw, far from the disapproving eyes of his father. The situation grew tense when Convers' studies became neglected. His father decided that the only cure for the boy was to send him to Vermont for a year's hard work on a farm. Mrs. Wyeth came to her own decision. One day she carefully selected a group of her son's best drawings and took them into Boston for advice. Returning home encouraged, she persuaded her husband to give Convers a second chance. He was sent to the Mechanic Arts School in Boston to learn drafting. Graduating in the spring of 1899, he convinced his father that more training was necessary. Borrowing money from his father for each step in his schooling, he next attended the Massachusetts Normal Arts School. It was here that an instructor, Richard Andrew, saw qualities in his drawings that suggested illustration. He encouraged Wyeth to choose the career of an illustrator. Next came the Pape School of Art in Boston, with summer instruction under George L. Noyes in nearby Annisquam. The winter and spring of 1902 found Wyeth studying under the illustrator, Charles W. Reed. It was here that the young artist, Clifford Ashley, home on vacation from the newly opened Howard Pyle school in Wilmington, Delaware, convinced Wyeth that Pyle's was the best school in the country for illustration, and besides, the tuition was free if, after a trial period, the student was approved by Howard Pyle. Wyeth sent a group of drawings with a letter of introduction and purpose. The long-awaited reply from Pyle finally arrived. On October 18, 1902, Henriette Wyeth waved goodbye to her son in Needham as he walked down the drive and disappeared beyond the spruces. The next morning when the *Colonial Express* from Boston arrived in Wilmington, Delaware, the tall, husky New Englander stepped down onto the station platform with his future before him.

During the forty-three years that followed, N. C. Wyeth poured out his hopes, disappointments, joys, sorrows—his life—in letters to those back home in Needham, and, after his parents' death, to his widely scattered family.

The WYETHS

In editing this collection of some twelve hundred letters, I often omitted whole pages or an entire letter. Sometimes only a paragraph appears, often the complete letter.

My deepest appreciation goes to the Wyeth family for trusting me with the original letters and for so generously allowing them to be shared. After I had read and reread this massive correspondence, something N. C. Wyeth once said lingered in my mind, "It's interesting how far a man can see from home."

B. J. W.

Chadds Ford, Pennsylvania

N. C. Wyeth ink drawing, 1901.

Chapter II

LEAVING HOME

*"If I could only be near you folks and the
animals and still be near Mr. Pyle."*

I[*]

This letter was written when N. C. Wyeth was eighteen. He had been sent to Annisquam, Massachusetts, for a series of art lessons under George L. Noyes. Among the students were Sidney M. Chase, Henry J. Peck and Clifford W. Ashley. In the fall of 1901, Clifford Ashley left to study at the Howard Pyle School of Art in Wilmington, Delaware, and it was through him that Wyeth first heard of Howard Pyle's classes. Sidney M. Chase and Henry J. Peck were later to become Pyle students as well.

Annisquam, Massachusetts
July, 1901. Sunday

Dear Mama,

Well I'm having a great time but of course I'd like to see you all. It's so lively here that it takes a little of the homesickness away. It cost me 1.94 cents for grub this week including things such as clam fork, dish towels, fish lines, etc. Oh! 54¢ more that I forgot to count in.

To-day I washed draws stockings face towel jersey night gown (did same last Wednesday). I haven't missed a morning cleaning my teeth combing hair etc. (HOW'S THAT)

Made the best sketch in ink to-day. S. M. Chase (not the fat one) was here today with his father. Ashley went to Craigville last night in a hurry. Received a letter and hustled off.

---

* N. C. Wyeth was throughout his life an idiosyncratic speller. Naturally enough, this trait was most flagrantly exhibited in his early years, though throughout his life he persisted in introducing a hyphen into such familiar words as today, tomorrow, together and tonight (to-day, to-morrow, to-gether, to-night), and he often preferred to write recieve instead of the more conventional receive. The editor has chosen to retain the author's spelling, punctuation and stylistic inconsistencies—as far as the need for absolute clarity permits—in the first fifteen letters. Thereafter, spelling and punctuation have been altered to conform with general usage.

Words in brackets are those introduced by the editor. Editorial deletions are not indicated.

The WYETHS

Newell Convers Wyeth was the eldest of four sons. He was born October 22, 1882. Edwin Rudolph, nicknamed "Ed," was born December 5, 1886. Nathaniel, always called "Nat," was born May 29, 1888. Stimson, affectionately called "Babe" while he was in his teens and later called "Stim," was born May 29, 1891.

Annisquam, Massachusetts
Night before fourth, 1901

Dear Ma,

It's been like the 4th since I came down here. Everybody is firing revolvers & fire crackers and at night the boats in the harbor are firing fire works.

I have made 2 pencil drawings 1 water color and 3 oils (2 that are good)

Tell Ed to run hard and start <u>quick</u> and tell him to let me know how 4th races come out. Tell Nat that theres lots of cat boats, Sloops, Schooners, skinning dishes, half raters, dorys etc. down here. Tell Stimson not to throw away the slow match and hold the fire cracker the 4th. Have used mouth wash steady (a good thing.) Tell papa am not spending much (no more than [can] help).

3

Annisquam, Massachusetts
July 16, 1901

Dear Papa,

We've just finished our dinner of bacon and eggs. I started work at 5.15 this morning and stopped at 10. I took an extra lesson this morning, but of course can drop out of any lesson after this. What do you think of taking a couple extra lessons making 12 lessons. It depends, if I see that I can do all right alone I won't go outside of the 10 lessons. If you don't want me to take more lessons all right because I can get along all right.

4

Leaving Home

Annisquam, Massachusetts
Monday morning, 1901

For Papa,

My money is holding out well but am going to take 2 extra lessons this week. I've taken 9 so it leaves only 1 for the week. I think I'd ought to have 3 a week any way. I took 2 the first 2 weeks making four, then I took 3 lessons in the mornings of last week and 2 in the afternoons making 9 all together. I have now $11.00 $5 of this towards tuition and $6 for other things as: wrent for boat $1.50

next weeks living ex.	2.00
boat fare	.40
75¢ for expressage	.75
odd carfare	.25

You can make a check out to Mr. George L. Noyes.

5

A walking trip was a much planned-for yearly occasion with the four Wyeth boys. On this trip a close friend, Ned Lawrence, from their hometown, Needham, Massachusetts, went along.

Webster, Massachusetts
April 7, 1902

Dear Ma,

Made Webster this afternoon at 2.30. The scenery has been grand all along especially from Worcester to Webster 17 m.

We got to Framingham Sat. afternoon at 4.30, stopped with Neds Uncle (fine man) at night. Started Sunday morn at 8.30, reached Westboro (Dr. Millers) 4.00 and were kicked out. (fussy old people) Made our way to Shrewsbury (18 miles) then took electric to Worchester (7 miles) and put up at Neds cousin. Would have walked to Worcester only t'was to late.

Started for Webster at 11.30 Monday reached Webster 2.30 Bad country so took electrics from Worcester. Walked balance to Webster 5 or 6 miles (easy day Ned had belly ache so that accounts) 20 mile walk to-morrow to Sturbridge, thence to Warren 25 miles more when we finish.

Good walking weather but bad sketching weather (no sun

Had a row on Lake "Charqoqqoqoqoqqmanchauggaggaggagunga-
maugg" (Fine)

6

[Postcard]
Sturbridge, Massachusetts
April 9, 1902. Tuesday, 12.45

Dear Pa,

  Reached prettiest village yet. 15 miles. Started 8.45. Cloudy weather.
Writing this in an old country store.

7

West Warren, Massachusetts
April 12, 1902

Dear Ma,

  Got to our winding up place at 6.30 PM Tuesday. Reached here
ahead our schedule. Walked from Webster to Brimfield 25 m.
Hows that Didn't get wet abit.

8

*The spring before N. C. Wyeth joined the Howard Pyle School of
Art, Charles H. Davis instructed him in landscape painting at Davis's
studio in Mystic, Connecticut.*

Mystic, Connecticut
May 4, 1902

Dear Mama,

  Arrived at 4 o'clock. Fine country and fine boarding place so far.
We've just had supper.

  This is the time table:

> Beans ala brown bread
> Corned beef
> Picca-lillie
> Bread—Cake—Cookies
> Tea

Walked around and picked out subjects (Good) Saw Davis and was glad to see us.

Will start work to-morrow morning if weather permits.

9

Mystic, Connecticut
May 7, 1902

Dear Mama,

Have tackled two big cow subjects 18 × 22 including New England barn yard scene.

Am going to try a large pasture scene (fine subject) We certainly have good board. I'd be satisfied with less to eat. But when you see it on the table and are paying $6 a week why it seems as if you'd ought to eat it.

Good crit from Davis to-day. We are working every minute from five to 5.

I'll tell you this trip is pulling me out of a big hole, have gained 100 per cent in my painting all ready, I *think*. Am getting strong sunny effects.

10

[Postcard]
Mystic, Connecticut
May 15, 1902

Dear Pa,

Will be home Sat. night on the 5.48 train to Spring St. with my trunk. Can one of the boys meet me at Spring St. with the team.

11

For eight years Howard Pyle, the great American illustrator, had been on the teaching staff of Drexel Institute in Philadelphia, Pennsylvania. Anxious to form his own school, he experimented in the summers of 1898 and 1899 with an art class at nearby Chadds Ford, Pennsylvania, selecting ten of his most promising Drexel students. The students, freed from the academic restrictions of a city art school, made such marked improvements painting from nature that Pyle resigned his position at Drexel and opened the Howard Pyle School of Art in 1900 at Wilmington, Delaware. During the summers the class returned

15

The WYETHS

*to Chadds Ford. No tuition was charged, as Pyle felt this would give
him a wider range of students to choose from.*

*The young student applying for admission submitted samples of his
or her work, and was later subjected to a personal interview. If Pyle felt
the student's work showed promise and his character was of a serious
nature, the student was accepted on a trial basis. He was expected to
pay for his own board, art supplies, and studio. He would be allowed to
sit in on the Saturday night composition classes where a work done
during the week by an "advanced" student would be selected by Pyle
as the basis for his weekly criticism.*

*The two young fellow students mentioned below were Clifford Ashley
and Henry Peck from the Annisquam days.*

N. C. Wyeth the week he left for Wilmington, Delaware.

Wilmington, Delaware
October 19, 1902

Dear Mama,

I reached hear ¾ of an hour late (7.45). The city is quaint
as you said and now while I am writing this the side walks are
lined with "white" ladies and "colored" ones also washing their
front steps and sidewalks.

16

Ashley fixed his room all up in great shape. Hung my pictures around and put a big stuffed dummy in the doorway besides taking a pear and putting it in the bed.

Ashley and Peck went to Chads Ford and won't be home till 8 o'clock this morning.

The doorway of the room has a big sign over it with "Welcome" on it. One of my pictures (Onion's barn) has a thermometer on it. 90 degrees. I think I shall like the place better than I expected.

You can address me 907 Adams St. for a couple days. Will you please send sketch book when you have time and everything that's in it.

12

Wilmington, Delaware
October 26, 1902

Dear brothers,

Was very glad to here from you and to learn that our colony of animals are getting well taken care of. Nat, please take good care of "Bud". She's too fine an animal to let go. When you ride keep your knees *tight* when you can do that incessantly you'll be a good "sticker." Ed—I haven't seen your name in the paper yet for making any "gains" but expected to see a head line some time saying

Wonderful	Marvelous
Wyeth Kicks	N. Wyeth rides
A Coal	5 min.
" " " " " "	without
" " " " " "	falling
Super Human	once
S. Wyeth	" " " " " " " " " " " "
watches cow	
1 hour & a Half	

Now "babe" be sure and clean your teeth or they'll get rusty; but the next time you write, write in German.

13

Philip Hoyt was another student.

[Postcard]
Wilmington, Delaware
October 27, 1902

Dear Mama,

Hoyt wants me to ask you to put my boxing gloves in the box. He thinks he'd like to try it. Heard Mr. Pyle's first criticizm this morning it was fine. I made a mistake. My address is:

N.C. Wyeth
No. 4 East 4th St.
Wilmington, Delaware

14

A student became a full-fledged member of the Howard Pyle School of Art only after he had passed successfully through a trial period of study. He then moved into one of a group of studios adjoining Pyle's own, where the teacher could keep a close eye on the progress of his pupil's work.

"Uncle Gig" was Henriette Z. Wyeth's brother, Agustus Zirngiebel.

813 Adams St.
Wilmington Delaware
October 27, 1902

Dear Mama,

I've got a perfect little room. The room is $2 a week. As to the studio, for light it's one of the best in town (an old photographer's studio) 50′ × 30″. The fellow is a typical Yankee named Hoyt. He's from Vermont. <u>Perfect Habits.</u> Shrewd and as economical as possible.

I had to get an easle of course and Pyle could get a $25 one for 12.60. Hoyt says Don't ye dew it! Make it. He made a slendid one for himself, lumber (hard pine), iron fixings and all cost four dollars or a little less. Now it's quite a piece of mechanism and needs a cabinetmaker's skill to make one so I bought his for five dollars and he's making himself a new one making a few improvments (which is to his great delight). The rent for that fine studio is $4 a month. Note (models only 20¢ an hour.)

I met Mr. Pyle Sat. morning. One of the most pleasant men I ever met. He's stern but open hearted. Just think, he built an $8000 studio just for the "boys" as he called them. He says, "I do this for them because it continually opens up new things to me. Besides it keeps me down to simple drawing which is at the bottom of any body's "success".

He said he was very sorry that I did not come earlier for my work was very practical and looked promising (I have faint prospects of working for Sat. Eve. Post already). Mr. Pyle is about 6 ft. three inches and has a terrible strong face, very square jaw and very wide between the eyes. The fellows are the finest set of fellows I ever met. All six footers but Ashley. Mr. Pyle seemed pleased to think that I had a collection of "arms" and advised me to have them all sent down. Could you get Uncle Gig to make a case and send everything I got in the line of arms and relics. It won't cost much.

I think that after half of the year is over I'll be able to get some work. Just think "Harpers Monthly", "Harpers Weekly", "Colliers", "St. Nicholas" Christmas numbers are to be illustrated all through by Ashley—Peck—[Harry E.] Townsend—Hoyt (by the way a "Plugger") [E.J.] Cross and "Pyle". These are all pupils of Pyle.

How is Nat getting along with the Pony. Tell him to *please* take good care of him. I'm just dead gone on that pony and if you'd have to get rid of him it would upset me entirely. Don't worry about my character. I *couldn't* go wrong in this crowd.

15

Wilmington, Delaware
October 30, 1902

Dear Mama,

Yes, I have all my clothes sorted; the dirty ones in a laundry bag I bought and the clean ones placed in my spacious bureau drawers. My pants are laying flat on the shelf closet and my jackets and coat are hanging up.

Have made 3 compositions unsatisfactory to myself. It's such an abrupt change that it will probably take me a week or so to get my hand back again.

It's Hallow'ene night Friday. They make a great time of it here. They have parades and balls all night.

Tell Papa my money's holding out all right. Have got my easle, a dandy too. Hoyt has a fine camera and some day I'll take a picture of my rooms etc.

16

Wyeth is confused as to the location of the house Howard Pyle rented at Chadds Ford. It is still standing on Route 1, a mile east of the village next to the well-known Lafayette Headquarters. For years it was known as Lafayette Hall. Washington's Headquarters is closer to the village by a quarter of a mile.

The name Pape refers to the founder of the Eric Pape School of Art in Boston, Massachusetts, where Wyeth was a student in 1901.

Chadds Ford, Pennsylvania
November 3, 1902

Dear Mama,

I didn't write before because I knew I was coming down here to stay over Sunday and would tell you about the place.

Mr. Pyle lives at Chadds Ford until the middle of Nov. and then moves to Wilmington for the winter, so now we have to come down here Sat. night to the composition lectures.

It's almost fifteen miles from W. but only 10¢ carfare (steam).

Regular price is 60¢ but Mr. Pyle got a student's pass from the road. So the reduction. The country is elegant, very hilly, almost mountains, and very picturesque. The houses are made out of either stone or brick, and not a stone wall is to be seen.

The house the boys have is a large brick mansion on top of a hill surrounded with large trees (which are still green), at one time Gen. Greene's headquarters. It's massive, each room having a huge fireplace, the windows being high with heavy paneling. The walls are hung with about 4 or $5000 worth of Mr. Pyle's originals. He let them have them as long as they wished.

They have a large orchard of fine eating apples of all sorts, grapes and peaches galore. They also have a large icehouse well filled. They get all this for $100 a year. We arrived here about 6 o'clock last evening. The house was lighted up by a couple of fellows who are still working down here, and every fireplace had a roaring fire in it which was certainly cheerful.

After partaking of a lunch put up by Mrs. Simpers (our grubber) we straggled along toward Mr. Pyle's house about a mile distant. Reaching the house we walked around the spacious porch (an old colonial mansion, at one time Washington's headquarters, it's situated on the Brandywine River). We saw through the high windows a sight which impressed me much. There was Mr. Pyle reading, his face of great character intently bent on a book, and flocked around the rest of the table were five of his children reading or drawing and on one side Mrs. Pyle with the youngest child in her lap and at her feet a cat and dog lay asleep. Mr. Pyle has never been away from Mrs. Pyle one night since their marriage except once and that was 2 weeks ago.

The composition lecture lasted 2 hours and it opened my eyes more than any talk I ever heard. It makes Pape look shallow. I could not help to tell you what he said. As to my composition (which was a load of hay stuck in the marsh, the horses urged by the men, one of the men at the wheel, the horses pulling to their utmost), Pyle, I am glad to say, mentioned the fact that the action was good. He told me the first thing where I had trouble, and what I had in mind to do but did not hold to my first idea. He seems to read one's mind. After the lecture we were invited to play ping-pong and in a short time we trudged home.

Tomorrow I start on a subject for *Harper's Weekly.* That is I'm going to try it. I'm doing it on my own hook, but of course Pyle is going to criticize it and when he sees I'm doing it for publishing he will help me all the more. The subject is "Spring Moving." A couple of old skinny horses attached to a load of household goods, stuck in a muddy country road, and men with their shoulders at the wheel and one lacing the horses. Magazines want subjects that need nothing to explain them.

As to my guns, never mind. Pyle lets his pupils have any of his costumes or guns whenever they are working on subjects.

All the fellows went in swimming this morning. I did not and will not until next spring in the Charles. I was in the Halloween costume parade, over 2000 in parade. I rigged up in one of Hoyt's farmer costumes with cowhides.

17

Wilmington, Delaware
November 6, 1902

Dear Mama,

Mr. Pyle wants us all to work with the intentions of painting sometime and when I get far enough along in my training of composition and drawing I'm to start in color also. He says we'll have to illustrate wholly in color within 10 years because they're getting so they reproduce color very accurately. It's Mr. Pyle's 50th birthday next March and he is going to give us a dinner and present us with a Pyle medal. It seems that lots of artists use Mr. Pyle's name when they go to publishers and after March 1st no one can say they are with or had been with Pyle unless they have a medal (foxy stunt). Every one of your letters has some sad story to tell, this time it's the disposal of the "poor old quackies." Isn't there any possible way of saving the poor tame birds? It really made me cry to hear that they were to be killed. I am so attached to all our birds, horses and cows that I miss them almost as much as my relations. I wish and sincerely hope to see everything I left behind when I come *home* in the spring. Be *sure* and keep old "Jack." If I could only be near you folks and the animals and still be near Mr. Pyle.

Leaving Home

18

Wilmington, Delaware
November 10, 1902. Sunday evening

Dear Mama,

I raised a "whoop" when I heard you had saved the ducks and wish them and Jack good luck. I've struck another subject that Mr. Pyle likes better, and that is a couple of horses breaking through the ice on a lake during ice cutting. He told me to work that one up instead of the "Spring Moving." I'm going to work some more on that old "Turning the Steer" picture of mine and show it to *Sat. Eve. Post.*

19

Frank E. Schoonover was a member of that first class chosen from Pyle's students at Drexel Institute to go out to Chadds Ford in the summer of 1898.

Wilmington, Delaware
November 12, 1902

Dear Mama,

I have a couple of subjects ready to take to the publisher and next Tuesday Hoyt and I are going to Philadelphia and New York. He is going to take me to and introduce me to the art editors of *Ladies' Home Journal, Sat. Eve. Post, Success, Harper's Weekly* and some others I don't know.

Mr. Schoonover, Mr. Pyle's strongest pupil (an independent artist now), likes that cowboy–steer drawing of mine and advises me to show it. He thinks someone will take it. I hardly expect work from the publishers 1st trip, which by the way has never been done, but if I do, I'll jump the Brandywine.

How are the animals? All my past years' life with those animals seems to me like a dream now. To think that I was and am the owner of a pony seems like a myth. Poor pony, how is she, and how does Nat handle her? The gentle beast won't do him any harm, I know. How is old crow? I can hear his old grumbling and growling now. I hope he lives through the winter.

Stanley Arthurs, Howard Pyle and Frank Schoonover in Pyle's studio.

20

Wilmington, Delaware
November 16, 1902

Dear Mama,

I've been drawing all day. I got to hustle a composition to take to N.Y. Tuesday. The title is: "A friend in need is a friend indeed." It is a farmer with a two-horseload of wood on a pung stuck on a bare spot. A fellow with a milk wagon has fastened his horse on front and is pulling the farmer's load onto fair going. [It] will show my ability to draw action if nothing else.

Hurrah! Mr. Pyle said in the last composition class that I was showing great progress. He says that I'm still weak on horses and will have to study them a great deal more. I'm glad he told me what he thought, which will certainly make me study them.

Those apples were great! I could shut my eyes and imagine myself home when I was eating one.

We had the composition lecture out to Chadds Ford Thurs. and I walked out alone. It was terribly hot but I managed to get there in 2¾ hours. Distance 12½ miles. 'Twas good exercise. The roads out here (in the country) are very sandy and excellent for horseback riding. I don't know how many times I wished I had the pony. I certainly envy Nat and wish he would exercise her more.

Mrs. Griffith (the old lady) does my mending and is glad to do it free. I patched my light pants last night and did a good job. I wear those weekdays. Just the thing for the studio. I've cut myself down to a hot roll and a cup of coffee for breakfast.

21

Wilmington, Delaware
November 23, 1902. Sunday afternoon

Dear Mama,

I have decided under Mr. P.'s advice to wait a little while before going to N.Y. He says if you can possibly afford to wait it will be better for you in the end.

22

Wyeth remained interested in horses throughout his life. When he left home, his polo pony, "Bud," was put in the care of his younger brothers.

Wilmington, Delaware
December 10, 1902

Dear Mama,

Oh! Those photographs!!!

I was simply taken off my feet! The group is certainly fine and you all looked natural but yourself. Of Grandmama! The most natural picture I ever saw of her.

Nat on the pony—is fine. "Old Bud" looks chunky and plucky with his winter coat on and Nat proudly sitting for his picture being very careful to "toe in." I can't seem to believe that I ever rode a little "beaut" like that.

It seems as if I'd read a book—very, very interesting—telling of a boy's life in the country and it had impressed me greatly. Somehow I feel as if I'd lived here for years and that in Needham (the land of liberty) was an ideal of mine and so it is.

That calf picture I've looked at with an enlarging glass and have picked out lots of detail that set me wild to see the old place again.

25

I can imagine the calf pulling at that cold grass, which I suppose was the greenest on the place, not stopping to look up, not even at the camera so interested was he in his belly.

Now for the surprises! Papa on a pony! I was thunderstruck. I never imagined that he would come to that. Does he ride any? Still Papa looks as composed and confident as if he had played polo for years.

"Papa on a pony!"

The pig picture was fine also, but it made me sorry to know that probably piggy was in heaven when I was gazing at his portrait. Stimson looked a grain upset. Perhaps he smelt the pig. Old quack was fine, but where was the other one. Is he alive? I sincerely hope so.

I wish I were so I could earn a living now. I know that there are three more to prepare for life and it makes me feel that it's not right for me here spending money and Papa standing "down there" in cold and rain earning it for me. I'm glad you sent the picture containing Grandpapa. The old place looked natural.

26

Stimson, old quack, Papa and pig.

23

Wilmington, Delaware
December 14, 1902

Dear Mama,

I've held off as long as I could and now I'm going to say I want to come home Xmas. Every one of the 15 fellows have gone or are going. Mr. Pyle is trying to get us low rates on the Colonial express and if he can, can I come home?

24

Wilmington, Delaware
January 2, 1903

Dear Mama,

Well, I reached here Tuesday night at 10:30 safe and sound. I had a tramp through New York and called on many publishers. I got a large illustration to make for *Success,* in fact, have it well along now. It represents a surveyor in the Rocky Mountains surveying in a perilous place. He is perched on a fist of rock hanging over a canyon of terrible depth.

25

813 Adams St.
Wilmington, Delaware
January 5, 1903

Dear Mama,

I finished the bucking horse today. It simply knocks the other flat! I hope Curtis Pub. Co. will accept it. I think from now on I can easily support myself. I don't think I shall have to ask you for more money unless *Success* and Curtis Pub. Co. are slow in paying.

26

According to tradition, the figurehead referred to below had been stored in the barn at Needham. It was a memento of the privateering days of Captain Job Wyeth, N. C. Wyeth's paternal great-grandfather.

Wilmington, Delaware
January 8, 1903. Tuesday night

Dear Mama,

Well, I'm more than pleased at receiving an answer stating that I was to have the figurehead. I told Mr. Pyle about it and he seemed so pleased that I know it would have been a great disappointment to him if I had failed to get it. I want to say that I hope that no one has disturbed or will disturb any of the color. Don't let anyone clean it or deface it, will you? Cause all its value is in the old worn color and its old dilapidated state. I brought the drawings to Phil. and N.Y. Tuesday. I received no new work as yet (but some promised) but am glad to say that *Success* was more than pleased with my work. It will appear on the 3rd page of March *Success*. They didn't tell me the price but I'm certain of getting $30 anyway. The *Post* went wild over my cover and gave me $60 for it. Give my love to Papa and tell him of my little success.

27

Located in the neighboring town of Dedham were the Karlstein Polo Fields. As a young boy, N. C. Wyeth found the action of the games irresistible. His first drawings from life were of the polo ponies, and he often picked up pin money by selling these drawings to the owners of the horses.

Wilmington, Delaware
January 26, 1903

Dear Mama,

I went to Phil. yesterday and spent all morning at the "Zoo" which is the finest I ever saw. Made some sketches and studied the wolves carefully as I am painting them now. We went to the annual exhibition in Phil. Supposed to be the best exhibit of the year anywhere. Was not as well satisfied with it as Boston Art Club exhibits but saw some very notable work by Sargent, Whistler, Alexander and Winslow Homer.

Felt pretty blue today as I am not at all satisfied with the progression of my picture. Besides there was quite a snowfall and there were lots of sleighs out; all this made me more than homesick. It wouldn't take much to have made me take a trip home. You spoke in your last letter about me not coming home at all. Intend to come home for 6 weeks or 2 months anyway this summer.

Mr. Peck wrote a fine letter and I am happy to say is greatly attached to the horse. I've given up that scheme of bringing the horse down and, by the way, Mr. Peck spoke a little like "horse dicker" in his letter.

Now don't try to sell her for me or say anything about it to him, but let me know what you and Papa think if I talk horse trade with him. Now again I want to thank you and Papa for all you have done for me. I realize that I'm not a fellow of much knowledge and have lots to learn, but what I have was born in me as I'm sure I didn't acquire much at school. I think I have enough logic and tact in me to make up for a deal. I notice that the bookworms and literary fellows lack a vital quality in their work. To be sure, they get subtle meanings into their pictures; they get them mysterious, quaint, showing great imagination acquired from reading, but the public have opened their eyes and realized that you don't have to go back into the Colonial and old English days to get "pretty" pictures and stories but you can find them in nature amongst animals and amongst the people who are still living close to nature, such as the Canadians, Cowboys and even the Indians, Woodsmen,

Trappers, Fishermen, Hunters, etc. The best of books are written on subjects close to nature or nature herself.

Of course I'm in a position to get the cream of ideas and it has untangled my mind a great deal and I now believe I'm on the track of a clean, deeply interesting life.

I don't suppose I should talk so confident of myself and talk like a "swell-headed guy" as I might have to call on home again for help, but I felt like explaining matters and so have blundered through it.

When I thank Papa I don't want him to think that I mean it for the money as that is only secondary to his great kindness he has shown me in every way and the great faith he has had in me from the beginning.

I don't know what started me to write this, but I was bound to finish it out and hope you will live to read my signature.

28

Wilmington, Delaware
January 29, 1903

Dear Mama,

Have just received a letter from Mr. Leland of Dedham, Mass., and he wants to try the pony for 3 days and offers me $75 for him. Now I intend giving Mr. Peck first choice and if he wants him for that amount, why I'll let him have it.

Now I'll do the business part of it and will write Mr. Peck my offer and then after receiving a quick reply from him will find out if he has any faint idea about horse buying. Meanwhile I will drop a line to Mr. Leland striking for a little higher price and when I receive his return letter will probably have heard from Mr. Peck and will write him, Mr. Leland, a final letter.

29

Wilmington, Delaware
February 27, 1903

Dear Papa,

Wednesday I went to N.Y. but had no luck in obtaining work but have the promise of some a little later. Meanwhile a great surprise was in store for me at Wilmington.

Howard Pyle standing on the porch of his studio.

I was asked to Mr. Pyle's house yesterday as he wished to see me, and as near as I can remember this is what he said: "Wyeth, I've been watching your work very closely and I see you have a great deal of talent but what you need is knowledge, that is, you have not had a good training and thereby no foundation. The man that you have studied with has filled you with ideas and put the right spirit into your work, but he himself, I can see, has had no training. Now, I'll give you the chance, seeing that you are determined and I know will make good use of your time, to enter my school and study with me for one year. I feel that I can teach you a great deal in that time and am positive that it will be of *great* value to you. But meanwhile you will have to drop all other outside work for publishers and devote your entire attention to what I think is your most important work in preparation for your future art. Now consult your people and tell them as near as you can what I said. I want you to start Monday morning and from then on you are a member of the Pyle school."

It's a good deal to ask of you (but there are no tuition fees, and it will not cost me anymore or not as much as it has right along). I intend to work for *Forward* Saturday afternoons and Sundays and in that way 'twill lessen expenses a good deal for you later.

30

An important part of a student's training was to draw directly from a plaster cast. These casts were often heads of famous people, or of a hand, arm, or foot.

Wilmington, Delaware
March 2, 1903

Dear Mama,

Am now ready to start in with Mr. Pyle tomorrow morning at eight. My appreciation of your and Papa's willingness to let me take my own course cannot be expressed in words. When I come home in April I'll find a place for the pony or sell him.

He [Mr. Pyle] found that I have not had much drawing from the cast and I'll have to draw ½ day every day for awhile from them.

I think 'twould be a nice plan to write a short "to the point" letter to Mr. Pyle and thank him for his great interest in me (if you feel so inclined, but don't praise me any on your life).

31

Wilmington, Delaware
March 5, 1903

Dear Mama,

Well, everything and everybody is in a stew just now as Mr. Pyle's 50th birthday comes off tomorrow night. I don't know but what I've told you, but he is going to give us a big dinner tomorrow night inviting only us fellows and Mrs. Pyle. There will be twenty-three of us all told and the immediate class (including me, I think) will receive H. Pyle buttons.

He told me today that he has regretted that he did not take me in the class at first and tells me that my future is a future of positive success, as I have great determination which is *sure* to win. I only tell you this to show you his faith in me. I am drawing in charcoal from the cast, and certainly making a thorough study. He was surprised at my first drawing (as I told him I never drew from it to speak of) and said lots of good things about it. Don't think I'm getting swelled-headed, because I'm not. I only want to give you the particulars, which goes to show in which direction I'm going, front or back. Please thank Papa for me and keep your share of it for your unflinching generosity and the great faith you all have in me and someday I know I can repay it one way or another.

I received a letter from you yesterday dated about Feb. 20th. It was addressed Wilmington, Mass. and so took quite a ramble before it reached here. My address is:

N. C. Wyeth
907 Adams St.
Wilmington, Del.

Please remember me to all and hoping all exceedingly well. P.S. Am more than glad that the pony is disposed of for awhile anyway.

32

Wilmington, Delaware
March 9, 1903

Dear Mama,

In spite of the rain I made as truthful a sketch as I ever painted and will send it home when perfectly dry. It's a picture of Mr. Pyle's Studio and a small portion of ours.

Well the grand dinner came off very successfully Thursday evening and I'll tell you it will be a marked point in my life; I really never went to anything so impressive as that. I don't know but I told you about the "Loving Cup" we presented to him. (It cost $92.) That meant $4.40 from each fellow. I did not hesitate paying as it will only occur once. The inscription on the cup was—

Howard Pyle
Presented by his Wilmington Pupils
on the occasion of his
50th birthday
1903

There were about 30 of his pupils there and Mrs. Pyle. It was a corking dinner served with wine (of which I did not partake). There were a number of toasts drunk: to Mr. Pyle—Mrs. Pyle— Mr. Peck—and as Mr. Pyle said, "to the baby of the class"—meaning me. I think that was quite an honor, don't you? I, with a number of others were presented with H.P.S.A. Buttons. They are beautiful; will show you in April. There is a little piece of black and white ribbon on each one which was obtained in France especially for these pins. The pin is red and gold standing for clean and beautiful color, in other words "painting," and the ribbon stands for illustrating in black and white.

33

Wilmington, Delaware
March 16, 1903

Dear Mama,

Mr. Pyle has given me an ideal subject to work on; the subject is "Indian Summer." It's a hard one as I'm not aesthetic enough to tackle a poetic subject. But that's what I lack, Mr. P. claims, as he thinks my work too brutal and also that I'm not "subtle" in my work—that is, for instance, if I'm drawing a man and a horse falling off a cliff, I'd have him on the way down into the deep chasm, man and horse in the air, or something to that effect; now he says to have the horse still on the cliff but make the horse look as if he was going to fall and that will make the observer say, "Oh! I wish that man would hurry and jump off!" or, "Why don't that horse jump to one side!" etc. See! he wants me to leave more to the imagination. On the whole I think I am getting along pretty well, but Oh! My! what a pile to learn!

How is Grandmama and Jim! Regards to Lena and all the animals.

34

Wilmington, Delaware
March 30, 1903

Dear Mama,

I have been mending my pants which, I am sorry to say, are almost impossible to mend anymore. The only pair of whole breeches I have are my black ones and of course I have to save those for best.

The *Leslie's* job is a "corker." The full-page illustration is the picture of a man that is shot in the back and his horse is going like h——; he is reeling in his saddle but keeps a hold on the pommel and thereby sticks.

35

Although N. C. Wyeth was known as "N. C.," any student from the Howard Pyle days always called him "Losh." The name originated in an attempted cover-up. Mr. Pyle frowned on all swearing. One day Wyeth's cuff brushed against his wet canvas and just as he was on the verge of saying "gosh," he caught sight of Mr. Pyle entering the studio door and quickly exclaimed, "Losh."

Wilmington, Delaware
April 6, 1903

Dear Mama,

I talk so much of country life and also of the rotten, intolerable city life that the fellows have gotten me down for a "country lad" and I am generally known now as "Losh."

36

[Postcard to his mother]
Wilmington, Delaware
April 7, 1903

If there is a boat to Fall River Sat. night I'll be on it. HURRAH!

37

Howard Pyle expected the summer students to make their own living arrangements and to pay for their quarters and meals. Wyeth and his fellow students rented rooms in a farmhouse overlooking the Brandywine Creek on Route 1, about two miles west from where Mr. and Mrs. Pyle lived.

Wilmington, Delaware
April 28, 1903

Dear Mama,

[On] Sunday, Peck, Ashley, Townsend, [George] Becker and I went out to the Ford [Chadds Ford] to look for a place to live. We found one. A large old house with about ten rooms. She agrees to board us for $3.50 a week. As to the rooms we can have those for nothing. They are elegant ones, all with 4 and 5 windows each. The food will be plain fare but wholesome.

My *Leslie's* work is nearly done and Mr. Pyle has seen it. He liked it very well and said he would give a good deal if I would stop all outside work for a year and asked me to try and arrange it to do so. Well, the money that I will get from *Leslie's* will keep me a good while and when that's gone Mr. Pyle might decide to let me work outside.

38

Wilmington, Delaware
May 13, 1903

Dear Mama,

Oh! I'm having a struggle with my art. There is a great deal more to it than one thinks. In the class we are having facial construction which is terrible hard. I have great trouble in keeping or getting originality into my work. Last night in the composition class Mr. P. said that my work was fanciful and not based on real fact as I usually take Western or Canadian subjects.

People can talk about art being a "dead cinch" but they are mightily mistaken. Its grind, grind, grind all the time, from early until late.

Chapter III

SUMMER SCHOOL

"This country is much like New Hampshire in miniature."

39

Across Route 1 from Washington's Headquarters was an abandoned mill. Howard Pyle rented this mill to provide extra studio space for his students.

Chadds Ford, Pennsylvania
May 22, 1903

Dear Mama,

I bet you can't strike within 10 m. of where I am at this minute—.

I'm in the topmost room of a large, three-story, old-fashioned, stone country house on one of the highest hills in Chadds Ford.

I am now located, or rather was last night, for the summer. Of course we go in every day for awhile (that is to W—) until we get the Old Mill ready to work in.

I guess the lantern leaks and so got oil on the paper.

Well good night and good luck to all.

40

N. C. Wyeth's maternal grandparents were still living when he wrote this letter. "Grandpapa" was John Denys Zirngiebel, "Grandmama" was Henriette Zeller Zirngiebel.

Chadds Ford, Pennsylvania
May 25, 1903

Dear Ed,

This morning Schoonover, Townsend and I took a "— of a walk" through the country. We started by following a wandering brook almost to its source. On the way we spied numerous fish and birds that I never saw. We scared up an eagle hawk [turkey buzzard] that was fully 15′ from wing to wing. To tell the truth, when he went up it was as if a whole tree was rising from the ground.

Oh! Say, but you're a lucky "geezer." Until you've had to live away from home as I have and on top of that not self-supporting,

Henriette Zeller Zirngiebel and John Denys Zirngiebel, N. C. Wyeth's maternal grandparents.

you'll not appreciate your good fortune in being able to acclaim your knowledge around <u>home</u>. I'll tell you there is a great sight more to that little work "art" than one could possibly imagine.

Of course when I was home I'd knock out a picture of a horse in a few days and get 40 or 50 dollars for it, but that was the shallowest art a fellow could possibly do. I sold those because they were likenesses (somewhat) of a man's favorite horse and there being nobody around doing such things it was a novelty to the few who bought them. Now I could not have kept that up for a year; the market among my friends would be filled and with the "bum" (if I may call it so) training I had gotten would not have enabled me to improve fast enough to make customers wish for more of my paintings. I'll tell you, Ed, Papa's a lucky man not to have any others studying in my line.

Don't let athletics run away with you as you may see in nine cases out of ten [it] doesn't amount to a row of pins. What you want to do is to slowly but steadily get ahold of the simple facts of nature by reading and observing and also get all you can from

40

Grandpapa, who can probably give you more practical knowledge than lots of professors, and then when you come to the science part it will come easy. This is also true in art. I've lived in the country, closer to nature, among animals, etc., and have learned and observed lots of little, seemingly little, things that have helped me in my final scientific study. Write compositions and stories of your wanderings in the woods and when you can, send one to me. Do as John Burroughs does. If you can get some of his books and read them they are wonderful.

You've got a most interesting future before you if you wish to make it so and I wish you all possible success.

41

Chadds Ford, Pennsylvania
June 19, 1903

Dear Mama,

I know I will paint something that will tell someday. Just give me time. I've fully decided what I will do. Not altogether Western life, but true, solid American subjects—nothing foreign about them. I have no enthusiasm to see Europe except perhaps the homes of my people and a mere curiosity to see the country, but nothing deeper.

We had a big argument the other night in which I took up "That we should work for the benefit of American Art and that there are just as great subjects here to paint."

My work lately to a certain degree has gone to pieces. I'm having difficulty technically and also with my color. But I can see myself that I have gone ahead and more so lately in the thinking part of it, which, after all, is the "big thing." Mr. P. prophesied that such would happen but in due season I would pick up and be so much the better for it.

This afternoon Henry [Peck] and I took a deuce of a cross-country walk which has inspired me with ideas. A walk like that is as good as hard study once in a while.

42

Chadds Ford, Pennsylvania
June 22, 1903

Dear Mama,

Well, this ends quite a successful day to your "burden." This morning was composition lecture and "gee whiz" you would think I was the only pupil (in quality) he ever had. I'll not get a swelled head by any means, cause I don't get those blowups as often as I might. For the last 6 or 8 months I've been devouring all books possible on American Indians, Trappers, Cowboys and Backwoodsmen of all sorts and am now fully decided to take up that branch of art. It interests me more than anything else.

My composition today was two boy Indians, naked, cautiously climbing up over a rock which looks over a deep black hole of water at the sharp turn of a winding brook. Everything is dark save two bright glimmers of evening sky which are shown through the dark mysterious woods which form the background. One of the Indians has a fish spear uplifted, ready to dart it into the transparent water upon any trout that happens to be lurking there; the other boy, by a gesture made by the one with the spear, is told to "keep back." I tried (and evidently did) to get the primeval feeling in both figures and landscape.

All my best work that is vital work has been of that nature and I intend to stick to it.

Am just finishing Catlin's book on American Indians and if I can hold his knowledge in my head I'll have a big part of my Indian study learned.

I was much surprised over that Tibbet's letter and I'm positive I made no agreement about dog picture. I think it's a game of his to get some money for that saddle, so to save trouble will write to him for photo of his dog and make a little painting for him.

43

Located less than a mile east of the old mill was the spacious house, Lafayette Hall, that Howard Pyle rented for his family.

N. C. Wyeth witnessed the lynching of a Negro outside of Wilmington, Delaware.

Summer School

Dear Mama,

You asked as to my routine of work, well: for all days but Sat. and Sun. we get up from 6 to 6:15, breakfast at 6:30, "Slick up" room and write letters and do odd jobs until 7:30, walk to studio (Old Grist Mill) about 1 m. distant, start work from model

The old mill, Chadds Ford.

8:00 and work until 12. Home to dinner and spend rest of the day on landscape, supper at 5:30 to 6, go swimming, play ball till dark and from then on *read or write*. Bed 10:30. Sat. we spend as we wish; I usually work on landscape. Sundays—Comp. class 9–11, home to dinner, fool around until 3:00 and thence up to Mr. Pyle's and play tennis, ping-pong, sing or anything we care to. Mr. P. joining in all the sports.

As to the excitement [lynching], I'm out of it, but I saw it all, hoping never to be as unfortunate as to see another like it. Nobody knows I saw it but the fellows I was with, and [we] wish to keep it quiet. The thing haunts me now.

44

"Mr. Taylor . . . has got his grass down."

Summer School

Dear Mama,

We are all invited to spend the Fourth with Mr. Pyle and expect a big time. He is just like Papa in that score, very patriotic and enjoys the Fourth as much as the boys.

Mr. Taylor, the man that owns the place where we live, has got his grass down and is having excellent weather to make it. Down here they cut it in the afternoon, going around shaking out a few thick wads of hay, and do not touch it again, beginning to cart it in at noon the next day. I don't understand cause it actually goes in green.

He [Mr. Pyle] has been asked to write an article on the school for *Harper's Monthly*. There are to be 8 pages of illustrations by the students as examples of the work. I don't know as I'll be represented as my work is undeveloped in comparison with some who have been here 4 or 5 years. I'll try for it just the same.

45

Chadds Ford, Pennsylvania
July 5, 1903

Dear Mama,

Thus have I passed two of the most pleasurable and satisfactory days of my Penn.–Delaware life. It seemed as though Mr. Pyle felt as if he couldn't do enough for us. Yesterday [William J.] Aylward, [Herman] Pfiefer, Peck and his brother, Hoyt, [Herman] Wall and myself went up to Mr. Pyle's from a kind invitation extended to us last week. We reached his house about 8 A.M. immediately starting to celebrate by firing off cannon crackers, day fireworks, balloons, etc., which we supplied in great profusion. The racket lasted until noon when a luscious dinner was put before us, including wines, ginger ale (of which I partook), two kinds of ice cream and confectionary. We then sat down to a game of "Fan-Tan"—Mr. Pyle joining in, running over with fun and witty remarks. About three o'clock we again started the bombardment until about seven; then we ate a delicious supper. We then went out on the spacious porch where Mr. Pyle gave us an interesting talk winding up with an account of his failures and successes up to the present time. Everybody then trotted in the house where Mrs. Pyle played college songs, etc., all joining in the singing. (There were a number of young ladies there too.) After the singing, being about 9:30, all departed but Aylward, Wall, Pfiefer, Cross and myself and we played "The Black Queen" with Mr. and Mrs. Pyle until 11:30; then Mrs. Pyle went to bed and the remainder played until 1:15 when we partook of ginger ale and ice cream and finally wound up at 2:00 with a short, exceedingly interesting talk on Gen's. Grant & Lee, comparing their abilities.

We returned home and slept until 6:30 and then about 8:30 walked up to Mr. Pyle's to attend Comp. lecture which was the most interesting one yet heard. After the lecture Mr. Pyle drew me aside and told me to hitch up the "span" (which are a fine pair) to the carriage, and for four of us to spend the day (taking our dinner) driving through the country, which we did, getting back at 5:30 driving 25 m. (I drove). We covered all the ground that had seen action during the "Battle of the Brandywine," seeing all its historical points and relics. Arriving home to Mr. P., he then gave us a vivid description of the battle and all the minute details and anecdotes, which was the finest discourse I ever heard. With a hearty handshake we then bid good evening to the finest people I ever met and finer than I ever expect to meet. I'm now ready to tumble into my cot and dream sweet dreams of that which is impossible for me yet to realize. With great and sincere love to you and Papa will say good night.

46

Chadds Ford, Pennsylvania
July 10, 1903

Dear Mama,

My breeches came all right and they will be of great use to me now. Thanks much. It's as hot as the deuce here and wheat harvesting is at its height. We can get no models as all the inhabitants (women and all) are busy.

47

Summer School

[To Ed]

Dear brother,

Your most interesting account of that successful trout-fishing trip aroused a passion in me to take a similar expedition, which I took at the first opportunity; the fish did not accumulate in my borrowed fishing basket as they did in your case, but nevertheless I enjoyed the ramble across country in many other ways.

Last Friday morning I got up about 4:30 A.M., having overhauled my tackle the night before (a fine trout-fishing outfit belonging to one of the fellows), also procured a bait box of choice worms and a bunch of cold roast beef sandwiches, cheese and early apples. I made off after a hearty breakfast, my mind full of "dreams" of a fish basket lined with cool grape leaves and wet grasses enveloping a bounteous catch of bespeckled trout.

This country is much like New Hampshire in miniature, full of winding brooks, splashing and sparkling over stones and rocks, winding its way into dark mysterious woods, there flowing along with a somber stillness as if resting after its merry dances down the hills, then out of these like a burst of enthusiasm continuing through the sunlit fields and pastures on its way to the mother stream.

I had no luck, but did not care in the least, as I was attracted more and more by the beautiful effects of nature, which were made very dramatic having been the identical "fighting grounds" on which was fought the "Battle of Brandywine." I would sit for half an hour at a time in some beautiful poetic spot which bore the scars of an earthworks thrown up by the Americans or "Redcoats," thinking of the wonderful contrast between the bedraggled, ragged, blood-stained soldiers of Washington, and the clear, pure, cheerful babbling brook till at last my imagination made me almost believe that I could see a Continental soldier lying down beside the brook, drinking of the cool water, the perspiration dripping from his tense face, and around his head a soiled, redstained kerchief falling half over his eyes. I became so carried away that I got up in search of relics, which of course was useless, but nevertheless my enthusiasm spurred me on to hunt and hunt. Using up my time in this way 'twas about two o'clock before I ate lunch, which I devoured with a great relish.

I then retreated toward home straight across country, passing many picturesque, almost primeval-looking bits, arriving home about four o'clock.

Capping the climax I watched the approach of an awe-inspiring thunderstorm, which broke upon us in torrents of rain.

That night I went to bed early amid the din of the soft pattering of rain, quickly dropping to sleep while flashes of the day's thoughts and journey were quickly passing through my mind.

48

Chadds Ford, Pennsylvania
July 16, 1903

Dear Mama,

Just after taking a most beautiful and charming walk down the Brandywine meadows and pastures. [George] Harding, one of the most enthusiastic admirers of nature, accompanied me, and we are now "chock-full" of enthusiasm and feel perfectly capable of painting a masterpiece (at the present time).

On our travels we came upon a huge oak overhanging the river, with a black woods forming a background, when in the profound silence of evening a large white (snowy white) crane rose from the bank as silent as death slowly disappearing from sight. We finally got up and started for home across the pasture, which was soggy and wet, when we suddenly heard a roar and thudding of hoofs, and what should we see but a huge bull making for us not 20 yds. away. We turned and I fell; Harding made it across a pond in the pasture, going in up to his waist. When I finally got on my feet after much difficulty I also made my way across the pond. We then sat down and roared at the sudden change of our thoughts, immediately before thinking of the quiet, poetic beauty of nature and its charms and then running for our lives.

Nothing unusual has happened except that at this minute there is some tall swearing going on downstairs as the result of a trick played on a couple of the fellows. Crumbs and horsehair in their beds, water instead of oil in their lamp, no can (chamber vessel), and all their clothes in knots. I didn't do it, so there!

"Mrs. Turner's place" was a large Victorian serpentine stone edifice that sat on the high ridge of land behind Washington's Headquarters. It had been built shortly after the Civil War as the elaborate summer home of Mr. and Mrs. Joseph Turner. They called it "Windtryst." Mrs. Turner had died on June 20, 1903, and her son by a previous marriage, Archer Randolph, was occupying the house with his children.

Chadds Ford, Pennsylvania
July 21, 1903

Dear Mama,

I was invited out to dinner and thence up to Mrs. Turner's place for the afternoon. The Turners are the bluebloods of the County. A son about my age invited me horseback riding with him. I eagerly "took him up." The outcome was that this morning at 4:30 I was spinning along at a good rate on a stylish horse, in (my old favorite) a McClellan saddle. We rode for about 1½ hrs., getting back for breakfast about 6:30. This fellow's name is Randolph (the grandson of Mrs. Turner). He knew nothing of riding and was telling me awhile ago about his going to buy an English saddle for $35. I advised him to get an old (new) McClellan army saddle, which to my surprise he got, much to the satisfaction of his uncle, who is a well-known "Rough Rider."

From this lucky "advice" I won the favor of his uncle who is here from the West at present, and now will probably have "a whack" at horseback once in awhile. "There's nothing like *luck*."

Nat is getting to be quite an auto-mo-billy-goat, isn't he? Only tell him to keep a level head and not try to straighten any telegraph poles.

50

Chadds Ford, Pennsylvania
July 24, 1903

Dear Mama,

I've finally struck a keynote in my work this summer. To my surprise, a pleasant one I assure you, Mr. Pyle informed me that my picture, a new one I've just started, is the biggest one (in idea, composition and thought, although not in size by any means) that has been painted by any of his pupils of the present and past. He says if I work it out right he will surely use it for the "School Article" in *Harper's* next winter. Now if that pipe dream will only come true I'll be happy.

Well, the 2nd of August (a Sunday) is approaching nigh and I'll tell you there are not many happier than I to think that I'll spend a whole month at <u>HOME</u>.

Chadds Ford, 1903.

51

Chadds Ford, Pennsylvania
September 3, 1903

Dear Mama,

We have a Negro model up at the mill, which makes a fine but very hard study. Mr. Pyle seemed surprised at an improvement in my work, naturally thinking that a vacation would tend to hurt it (he don't know how I "did art" when home I guess).

I am wearing the blue shirt and it is just fine. The weather is not warm and the weight of it is right. We are having corn here but Oh! what corn. It is fully 16 inches long and the diameter about four inches, not any exaggeration. Tough as the deuce, it's simply the yellow cattle corn they grow for the mills to grind into meal.

52

Chadds Ford, Pennsylvania
September 5, 1903

Dear Mama,

I received the welcome box Friday evening safe and sound, together with your letter which bore such sorrowful news of the passing of "Old Tom" the faithful. I actually cried when I read your vivid description of his departure from this world and if there is a heaven he certainly deserves to go there. It's a very funny thing that when I was home last I remember looking at him one day and thought to myself, "I'm afraid I'll never see you again old boy," and it happened. He's been a good old horse, hasn't he? I suppose Papa will ride up with Grandpapa from now on and I can imagine Nat and Ed contemplating their good fortune secretly. Goodness, I'd love to have a chance to go to the Needham station mornings, but I may sometime.

53

Chadds Ford, Pennsylvania
September 7, 1903

Dear Mama,

Cool, clear as a bell, exhilarating day preceded by a terrific thunderstorm and young hurricane yesterday. With all this to make one feel "up and doing," I myself feel blue and somewhat discouraged. To speak plain my *Success* work was not satisfactory, that is I'm going to work over and make changes in several of the pictures— I knew it! You see I had no one at home to act as a competitor, which means of course competition which we get down here in great force. I'm awfully sorry I undertook the job as it practically did me no good under the condition.

Last night we had a house dance party up to Mr. Pyle's. 'Twas a big affair, special trains arriving from Wilmington, etc. I couldn't dance and so expressly for the occasion I sprained a ligament in my thigh. I couldn't dance of course with a bad "peg." Don't let it leak out.

My composition this week is a big affair. I imagine I'll get "sat upon" but there's one consolation in that by the (sat upons) you learn. I made it in oil, "black and white," and about three feet by two. The subject: unloading a circus from the trains early in the morning—am much disappointed.

I want to say the last thing that I'm not built for [is] society "flim-flams," and the more I attend these high social functions the more I'm disgusted with them. My next letter will be a treatise on society, so look out.

54

Chadds Ford, Pennsylvania
September 15, 1903

Dear Papa,

I'll tell you the weather is fine and the air full of the odor of dying corn. The corn is about ten and eleven feet high everywhere and I've seen ears two feet long and more. They're just starting to cut it and it makes a fine sight on these steep side hills, especially in the light of these golden evenings we are having. In another month I'll be 21, am sorry to say. It makes me feel small when I think of your early career. I wished mine had been as practical. Mr. Pyle predicts my art is to be a great financial success, which I sincerely hope it will.

This fall weather makes me think of home more than ever. It's a season of the year that impresses me more than any other. It gives one sort of a melancholy feeling, at least it does me. It must be fine now just as the leaves are starting to turn and the mornings are snappy and cold.

55

Chadds Ford, Pennsylvania
September 21, 1903

Dear Mama,

Don't worry about me not looking decent, as I look as good if not better than anyone else. Hot days I wear a blue shirt and breeches (not overalls). Cold days I wear reg. shirt, with both shirts I wear, as all the rest do, a hdkf. around my neck. Changed my underwear three times last week. How's that! Undershirts thankfully received!

56

Chadds Ford, Pennsylvania
September 24, 1903

Dear Mama,

You know we have a dog (setter). It's the mascot of the crowd but seems to take to me. It was bred from the finest hunter within a hundred miles and through a friend we got her. The trouble is she is a "slut." She is the most intelligent dog I ever saw. She is now about 5 mos. old. We've had her three mos. out of those five. She went with us today and put up 12 or 14 different quail— exactly as well as a trained dog. She inherits her mother's instincts, no doubt. Now if you can get Nat to pack up my gun, that is take it apart and wrap bags (grain) around the separate parts so that the barrel won't jam, and wrap protective stuff around it all and send it:

> N. C. Wyeth
> Chadds Ford
> Pa. C.O.D.

I'll be more than pleased. I probably won't go out more than once or twice but it will be worth it. "Lots of quail," tell Ed.

57

Chadds Ford, Pennsylvania
September 27, 1903

Dear Mama,

Have just finished a big fat dinner. I wish I hadn't eaten so much. I'm growing heavy again and it's <u>got</u> to be stopped.

Well, I haven't heard from *Leslie's* yet so will have to beg more money and this time for clothes. I need new clothes now as my others look quite done up.

As to that *Harper's* article. Mr. Pyle has just signed a contract for one year with *Harper's*. Meaning that he will work for them entirely. He will probably make about thirty drawings during the year for them @ $300 apiece. So you can see that's a total of $9000. He'll probably not write the article on the H.P.S.A. until after the year of the contract expires.

58

Chadds Ford, Pennsylvania
October 3, 1903

Dear Mama,

Did Papa get all the apples picked up in Cambridge, and how many did we get from the trees at home? Missing this fall at home is just like missing something of my life. Nobody knows how I used to enjoy that season at home. I hardly know myself; it's a feeling that can't be put into words. Of course I'm enjoying it down here too, but in a different way, not as much in a spiritual way as I did home, but from more of a *real* artist's standpoint—his anticipation of subjects suggested by nature that he might paint in the future, when capable of expressing himself; his thoughts of the future in general and best of all—pleasant memories of home, which are always painfully enjoyable.

Today ends up our model work; for three weeks we are going to paint the fall landscape and nothing else. I'm very glad as we haven't had much outdoor work this summer. They are all to be sketches. As Mr. Pyle calls it, "An Art Holiday." Letting us do anything we want in any way we want at any time we want.

Last Saturday night we went up to Mr. Pyle's and acted out "Mrs. Jarley's Waxworks." I was Narcissus. There were about 12 different characters and together with the extraordinary witty remarks and description of the characters as they were brought on the show was a success. Mr. Pyle laughed until he cried. Peck was "Columbus" and he was capital.

59

Chadds Ford, Pennsylvania
October 8, 1903

Dear Mama,

Well, I've been sketching a good deal this week and have turned out some of the best things I've ever done. I never realized how much indoor imaginative landscape work would help me. Today however I didn't do a thing. I went to the mill this morning and started to work ('twas too cloudy for outdoor work) and [the] Randolphs came down with a young lady friend of theirs and wanted me to go riding. I was in my painting clothes with farmer's straw hat on and of course refused to go. They were in their best rig with a new span of horses. They finally persuaded me to go after much coaxing. I bet I looked funny in amongst so much loud "calico." Nevertheless I went and on top of that "took lunch" with them spending in all about 6 hours in their company. Say it's a great thing to be an artist as they seem to lay all peculiarities to his "artistic temperment."

Don't be afraid I won't bank on that, but if people like to recognize or in other words are bound to find "artistic temperments" in a "guy," you might as well take advantage of it—they'll think none the better for you if you don't. Was up Sat. night to dinner—Sunday noon to dinner—Tuesday night to dinner and this noon to lunch. Guess I'll stop paying board and live on my friends. But withal, my work goes on the same with once in a great while the above experience.

Last Sunday I sent the 5th of a series of Indian drawings into the Composition class. Mr. Pyle says:

"You've got some fine subjects, Wyeth, and the thing you'll have to do will be to go and live with the Indians. You have the physical make-up to live by their customs and habits which would be a great help to your work."

I was glad to see that he recognized my "speciality," so to speak, and will feel free to follow it up.

60

Chadds Ford, Pennsylvania
October 15, 1903

Dear Mama,

Mr. Pyle is moving into town now and I suppose he'll want us to come in, but we are all going to beg to stay out here until Nov. 1st. We are all sketching to beat the cars and some of the best work of the year is being turned out. I had no idea how much I had learned this summer until now; it certainly is telling in my outdoor work.

Now I'll tell you. I have a camera here (Pfiefer's) and some plates. I'm going to take a number of pictures of the mill and the house where we live, the center of town, etc.

I have no faculty for writing letters. I can put down sentences of facts but a letter that requires subtlety of handling I'm way off. I often realize how far behind I am in the literary world—but there are a number of fellows here way up in that line that I wouldn't exchange my ideas and thoughts for double their talent. They are narrow-minded as the devil and not in the least versatile.

61

Chadds Ford, Pennsylvania
October 19, 1903

Dear Mama,

One of the most perfect days I ever have experienced. Saturday morning Mr. Pyle's team drove down to the house to fetch both me and all our summer sketching to his house. We went. After placing himself (Mr. Pyle) in an easy chair, we, in turn, exhibited our work to him. He was the happiest man I ever saw after he finished gazing upon our works. And to my keen pleasure he turned around and congratulated me upon my summer's work and told me that *mine* was the strongest—most practical and on the whole the best of all. He then ranked [Thornton] "Oakley," Harding & [Alan T.] True respectively. Now I don't tell you this to brag or anything else, but I feel so happy that I have to tell someone and of course 'twould not do to spring it around here.

Furthermore we had an exceptionally fine lecture today, although my comp. wasn't up to snuff. Now intermingled with this glorious climax of the summer's works was a grand finale in the Chadds Ford social sphere. You know the Saturday evenings were spent in a social way at Mr. P.'s; well he told us fellows to get up something of an entertainment (something rich and rare) for the last Saturday evening they will (probably) ever spend at the Ford. *We did it.* He said he'd sanction anything we did. It was in the theatrical line being a burlesque on vaudeville. The program was as near as I can remember as follows. In fact I'll enclose a facsimile of a program—

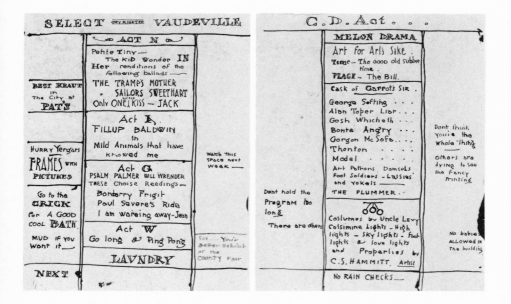

Now as you see by this program "Petite Tiny" was your humble servant. I sang two pieces of music with my voice pitched high and gave an imitation of "Dan Daly." The feature was my dancing which took down the house. (We had a fine stage, scenery, etc., and a large audience.) This feature turned out to be one of the hits of the evening. I had on a straw bonnet, with streaming black hair (real wig), my face painted to kill, eyebrows darkened and lips reddened, etc. My exceedingly low neck powdered and pants' guards on my arms for bracelets, with white gloves on also, a pink waist and mosquito netting, exceedingly short skirt that flared out almost straight, my blue underdrawers for tights reenforced with swimming trunks, a new pair of tanned stockings on with a pair of old sneakers bearing a large rosette with a bell on each sneaker and pink ribbons on my knees with bells. Thus I appeared. I'd describe all the others but it's too much work. The "gist" of the "Art for Art's Sake" was a burlesque on the class this summer. Each fellow taking off the other, making "awful swipes" at everybody—that is in the pun line. You can probably guess who is who in the program. Cross took off me as Losh Whicheth and I impersonated him as Bonte Angry as his real name is "Monte Cross." Peck took off Gorgon McSofa (Gordon McCouch) and True took off Thonton, his real name Thornton Oakley (his mother always calls him "Thonton"). 'Twas a great success.

Today a friend of [the] Randolphs was out and had a camera. He wanted a picture of Mr. Pyle but Mr. Pyle would not be taken alone so took [Samuel M.] Palmer and I, putting his arms around both of us.

This is the last week at the Ford and I'll make the best of it. Then back to Wilmington where I hope before I leave again I'll be doing illustrating galore.

62

Chadds Ford, Pennsylvania
October 22, 1903

Dear Papa,

In answer to your ever thoughtful wishes I can say that my birthday was a grand success from start to finish. The day was perfect. I went to Philadelphia early in the morning and spent a large part of the day in the galleries. The pictures were fine and best of all I could well appreciate pictures that before were blanks. You can't realize how gratifying it was. Late in the day I went to the zoo where (as it is always the case) I enjoyed it much.

Chadds Ford, Pennsylvania
October 22, 1903

Dear Mama,

Oh! what a big, round, pretty, and luscious cake; an excellent example of your birthday cakes. All the fellows wished me to tell you, "You sure can make cake" (it's a western phrase and means a great deal). It's all gone but a small piece which I'll eat when I'm alone, then I can fall into the grand thoughts of home and all particulars connected with making the cake, etc.

From Mr. Pyle's advice I went to Philadelphia yesterday morning to see the big foreign exhibition en route to St. Louis exhibition. It was grand! I'll make some of the best things yet—you'll see!

We pack up tomorrow and leave, possibly forever, dear old Chadds. I can earnestly say that this has been (speaking as to advancement in my work) the most successful year yet passed. As Mr. Pyle often says, "Periods of hard struggle are big stepping stones to success."

Chapter IV

HOWARD PYLE

"Mr. Pyle is at the bottom of my present standing, and without him I'd have missed the biggest *part of my life, and* the thing *is something I can't explain."*

My room at Mrs. Swayne's
Wilmington, Delaware
October 26, 1903

Dear Mama,

I'm a day late, and why shouldn't I be? Have been packing and unpacking since last Friday and not settled yet. The stuff accumulated so.

The studios are practically settled and I'm crazy to get hold of a brush and start the model work. I never attended an exhibition that so thoroughly aroused my ambition and inspirations to work. I feel *now* as if I could paint a masterpiece. Time will tell.

Ashley, Schoonover and [Stanley] Arthurs are getting up a Studio dance, getting out printed invites, etc., which demand dress suits, etc. How glad I am. Oh! what an elegant time *we* will have! BOSH!!

You've probably seen my *Success* picture (Nov. number) and my *Leslie's* (Nov. number). Both came out fair, don't you think?

I'm experiencing last year at this time over again. The same feelings, inspirations, the same mystery of it all and it's hard to believe that I'm in such close touch with the master (H.P.) and his hand. Last year I was looked upon as a green, unexperienced newcomer but now I've been through the mill of hunting for work, getting it and having it published. That seemed to be the initiation they put me through, both with Mr. P. and students. I'm under the bed clothes now and shall stay there until it gets too hot, then I'll don my own clothes and walk the floor alone.

65

Wilmington, Delaware
November 5, 1903

Dear Papa,

Oct. 22nd was my 21st birthday. I feel deeply this epoch in my life, when a fellow should cease from being wholly dependent upon his parents, especially when he has three equally high-aspiring brothers on the verge of jumping into the scientific world. This means expense. Now this is not "gas" written for the purpose of making me appear "very wise and thoughtful" and in that way gaining your confidence, etc., etc., which would be like to entice you to further your generosity. I want to pay back from this date all I receive from you (starting Nov. 1st).

Last night I went up to Mr. Pyle's city residence to help him hang a few choice pictures. We finished the job very satisfactory (it took until 12:30) and what do you think he presented me with? —an original (black and white) of a pirate fight on board ship. One of the best illustrations, a good many say, he ever made.

66

Wilmington, Delaware
November 9, 1903

Dear Mama,

Well, yesterday was a large day with me, that is, in size.—Saturday Mr. Pyle called me in and asked me if I'd care to go to church with him; the result was that Peck, True, Townsend and I accompanied him and his family to church. We then took an hour's walk. After dinner I decided to walk to Chadds Ford, so at 2:30 I started— making it (12½ miles) in 2¼ hours. There I met the Randolphs riding. There were already five in the team and I piled in on top. We took an hour's ride and then met Peck and Aylward at Chadds Ford Station. I left them there and we three went up to [the] Taylors and had supper, paying a visit to "Madam" (the dog), etc. We then went up to [the] Randolphs and stayed until 10:30, passing an excellent evening (probably our last call). We three then walked back to Wilmington, reaching there at 1:30. Twenty-six or 27 miles is pretty good for a day's walk and my feet feel as big as a house.

Now for a bright bit of news. You know the dance [that] occurred Friday eve.? Well, it was a very formal affair, so dress suits were in line. That of course put me out. Mr. Pyle found that I was not going, so Friday morning called me in his studio and presented me with a *brand new* dress suit which cost him $80. He wore it once in Boston while delivering his lectures and that's all. I went down to the tailors to try it on and see that there were no changes to be made and "by Gingoes" it fit better than any suit I ever had on or ever expect to have. I attended the dance and had a fine time, although I only danced 2 dances.

67

This letter refers to the death of N. C.'s grandmother, Henriette Zeller Zirngiebel.

Wilmington, Delaware
November 11, 1903

Dear Mama,

I have just received Papa's letter bearing the sad news, which struck me like a thunderbolt. I've thanked God that dear Grandmama's illness was not long, which was not only better for her but for you. Mama, I can't write anything, it's impossible. You know how I feel. She was one of my best friends in the world and I never loved and admired a person more.

68

Wilmington, Delaware
November 29, 1903

Dear Mama,

I am fully decided as to the line of work I shall do, and *will* do it when I've learned to draw and handle my mediums. The *great West* is the place for me, including Mexico. It has never been painted except by Remington and he has only pictured the brutal and gory side of it and not the sublime and mysterious quality of those limitless plains and their heros. Well, I must keep on dreaming, dreaming, hoping against hope that I'll soon see *that* land of mighty.

Mr. Pyle is in Chicago and we are left for a whole week to battle alone with our troubles, and when we feel blue we'll have no kind and powerful guardian to come in and cheer us up.

In your last letter you mentioned the family plot, which I must say sounded strange and absolutely out of place. I can't realize that and will not absolutely believe it until I see it.

Wilmington, Delaware
December 4, 1903

Dear Mama,

Yesterday afternoon we had a dancing master come to the studio and give us lessons, which cost 65¢ apiece. So now I know something about dancing, and one more lesson will fix me up. I'm in the "Virginia Reel" in the show, which is one of the attractions, and in a quartet also. The "Reel" is [a] pretty lively affair as we are all peasants and have to make things more than lively. My costume is short, loose, green velvet trousers, "bandage leggings," low brogans with big buckles, white peasant shirt, scarlet sack with sombrero and scarlet kerchief. They have sold about 900 tickets at $1.00. It takes place Monday and Tuesday nights. [Frank B.] Masters is in it and takes the cake.

I ache all over as if I'd played a game of football. Have just completed the best study I ever did. Mr. Pyle has not seen it as he is still in Chicago. He arrives here Sunday.

I don't know just what day I'll be home just now, probably the Monday before Xmas.

70

Wilmington, Delaware
December 14, 1903

Dear brother Nat,

Nat, I never before gave you credit for possessing such a sympathetic nature; I never thought you saw things from a sentimental standpoint until now. I read more in your letter than you really wrote; it was similar to a book of brief notes that meant pages to me. You look at things of life in about the same way I do. Don't by any means ever affect sentiment, but where you find yourself thinking sentimental thoughts never be ashamed of it, *as often is the case.* Never be afraid to express them openly and frankly; you'll never regret it. Your beginning to express your inner thoughts is exceedingly promising and hope to hear *more* from you in the future.

71

Wilmington, Delaware
January 8, 1904

Dear Mama,

I'm 12 hours late in writing, but why shouldn't I be? Radical changes have been made in the school. Townsend is fired—McCouch is fired—leaving only *six* fellows in the class. I have been changed from my former studio into Peck's and Ashley's. Therefore there are three in each studio. The rent has of course gone from $5 to $8.33⅓, but that means we will be steadily supplied with work.

Mr. Pyle was much adverse to my painting my picture in sunlight, but I was bound to do it and have stuck to it against his wishes; but now that I'm pulling it out I can see he is pleased that I did stick to it. If I make a success of it, so much bigger the victory for me. If I fail, woe betide me.

72

It was on this sleighing party that he first met his future wife, Carolyn Brenneman Bockius.

Wilmington, Delaware
January 9, 1904

Dear Mama,

Mrs. Swayne got up a sleighing party for tonight so will probably go. 'Twill be a fine evening for it, cause the sleighing is good and it's warm. My sweater will act tonight.

73

Wilmington, Delaware
January 10, 1904

Dear Mama,

How time does go! It don't seem an hour ago that I sat down to read one of Robert Louis Stevenson's books and now I find that I've been reading steady since 2 P.M. without intermission. I just looked in the glass and my gorry! I look like a bleary-eyed old soak!

The WYETHS

Went to church today as usual and heard a good sermon, but next Sunday I intend to go for the first time to my own church. I met a Miss Bockius the other day and she being a Unitarian asked me to go. I accepted with pleasure.

Yes, I am enjoying the dances, but I'm afraid there is a tendency in them to lead a fellow out of his track and it's hard to get back again.

74

Wilmington, Delaware
January 29, 1904

Dear Stimson,

While a high wind is busying itself carrying off men's hats, embarrassing the fair sex, completing the unfinished task of ridding the trees of their stale foliage and cutting up the devil in general, I'm sitting back in a large chair enveloped in a long bathrobe, red woolen slippers on my feet (my toe sticking out of one), disheveled hair, wearing a woebegone expression with a pipe in the middle of it. I can almost imagine myself looking like a second-rate Sherlock Holmes, complete in everything but acuteness of mind.

In my immediate surroundings there isn't a place that I can possibly rest my eyes and feel easy.

Out of the window? Nothing but a detestable city park, dead and dull, the concrete walls twisted so absurdly that it makes you dizzy to look at them. A man will come along, his child stumbling after him. The child is yelling, trying in vain to attract his disinterested father's attention—the father turns toward the child, but instead of answering the little chap's eager question, he blows his nose with his fingers and after much delay he puts on the finishing touches with his handkerchief—he starts on his way unheedful of the bawling kid who has fallen flat, groveling in the muck.

75

Wilmington, Delaware
February 10, 1904

Dear Mama,

Everything dates from the fire now! What I saw, heard and went through cannot be told in words.

Monday morning at ten o'clock Mr. Pyle telephoned to *Collier's* to inquire as to the school going to the Baltimore fire as correspondents. They answered yes, by all means. 11:01 we were on the train speeding toward the burning city. We were all excited as to what we should do, methods of obtaining special passes, etc., and to add to this we could see for 25 miles the smoke from the fire, boiling and rolling up over the peaceful and quiet landscape. This set our enthusiasm so high that we were hardly controllable. Our trip down was taken up with dividing money, supplies furnished by Mr. Pyle amounting to $210 and also dividing paper, charcoal and various sorts of material brought along by Peck. We arranged a plan of attack which could not be properly accomplished without passes, and thanks to Mr. Pyle, who furnished us with letters from *Collier's* with an additional note written on them by him, which after lots of valuable time lost in "red tape" enabled us to procure these passes.

Having reached Baltimore at 2 P.M., we made our way to the court house and separated; it was not until three that we were within the fire lines. It was a condition made by *Collier's* that we had to have sketches in New York by 12 o'clock or not at all. Therefore we had to have sketches finished and at the depot (at Balt.) at six o'clock. We had beforehand appointed True as a delegate to be sent to *Collier's.*

The WYETHS

I'm afraid we were (the H.P.S.A.) not made for newspaper articles because I am ashamed to say amongst the ten that went down we turned out but seven sketches instead of twenty. Mine, it was voted by the crowd, was the most successful one and am glad to say that *Collier's* liked it the best, but then that isn't saying much.

Now that tells what we did or rather had to do. Now here's what we saw—

As soon as we reached Baltimore, Oakley and myself paired off and made a mad dash for the courthouse and after some delay, above mentioned, we received passes from the chief of police.

We lost no time in swinging under the ropes and soon we were enveloped in smoke and lost in ruins, a sight that I will never forget in my life.

After wandering through this horrible picture of ruin and destruction we, after much difficulty, wound our way out. We saw hundreds of subjects but all big ones, so after a consultation decided to make one good drawing apiece rather than numerous mediocre ones. We found an old Jew shoestore where we made our drawings. My subject you'll probably see in *Collier's*. I had to make it in an hour, so you can't expect much.

I was sorry I didn't make more (of course I didn't have time) because *Collier's* was hungry for them. I was disappointed in the work as a whole and I think the H.P.S.A. lost a chance to make a big hit. After True was seen off we again turned our faces toward the raging fire. We had nothing to eat as there wasn't an eating place in Baltimore. But we were now confronted by another obstacle. Passes were all void after 6:00 and you couldn't see much outside the lines. Our train didn't leave until about 2:00 in the morning so what should we do? We made a rash move. After maneuvering around for about an hour we found a little alley unguarded, so we entered. From there we wound our way on in darkness, stumbling over all sorts of merchandise, clothing, wire and clutter burning and smouldering, and finally reached a 10- or 12-story building entirely gutted and dripping with water. We entered and after much floundering and slipping reached the other side which was open to the center of the ruin.

Ten minutes after we left that building (the National Bank, I found out afterwards) the whole thing collapsed, which sounded like the roar of an explosion from the bowels of the earth.

70

The sights I saw from now on I cannot describe—everything aglow
—immense high walls balancing and swaying like sheets of paper
in the stiff wind, which was continually sweeping over the place,
whistling and moaning through these Pompeian towers, huge pieces
of tin flapping and banging on the tops of these towers like the
wings of some colossal bat, while all around us were explosions and
bursts of green flames darting out from under tremendously large
piles of bricks, barrels of oil exploding and covering acres, hissing
and splattering like huge serpents when they struck water. In the
midst of all this "hell" you would see a burst water main spouting
high in the air, and above in all the ruins you could spy myriads
of gas jets burning and blazing, often blown out but instantaneously
lighted by the terrible heat from the stacks of white hot bricks
underneath.

Through all this the six of us wandered (the other three—Peck,
Pfiefer, Masters—being afraid) alone and undisturbed until 11
o'clock. We now had to be very careful in escaping from the
clutches of the guards as there was a fine for entering, so winding
our way to the waterfront we found a skiff and cutting the rope
landed safely at the lower part of the city.

The city is under martial law and it looks like war, I can tell you.
Troops of cavalry rattling through the streets, militia guarding all
public buildings and pacing to and fro along the firelines with
orders to shoot if anyone passes. They are retaining strict measures
as there are millions in the vaults under the ruins, which might be
easily looted in that scene of frenzy and excitement.

I am happy to say that I have one of the best subjects in the
world to paint. The "Battle of Concord" at the "Old North Bridge."

Well, there's a lecture in a few minutes so will stop.

76

Wilmington, Delaware
February 16, 1904

Dear Mama,

I haven't lived in this world at all for the last two days and when
you learn the reasons you will not blame me. I was approached with
the subject of "War Correspondent" by Mr. Pyle yesterday while at
dinner with him. He asked me, "Would you care to go to the

Russo-Japanese War as correspondent for *Collier's?*" I jumped at the chance like a starving dog at a bone. I answered yes, by all means. He instantly telephoned for a messenger and sent a telegram to *Collier's* to call him up on the phone early Monday morning. He meanwhile planned my trip, what I should take, do, etc. I'll tell you my enthusiasm was at its height this morning, but it was shattered like thin glass when they said, "Two weeks too late, would have been glad to have gotten him then (meaning me) but it's too late."

I have fallen back to earth with a thump! Oh! if I'd only known, a chance of a lifetime!—a trip around the world intermingled with thrilling experience!—an eye opener! Well, this dream is over and there's one consolation—I'm glad H.P. thinks I'm capable of being a war correspondent.

Oh! *Collier's* gives the crowd $200 for work.—Expect check tomorrow and when all expenses are paid will probably get about $35 apiece.

77

The "people in despair" were Mrs. George Bockius and her daughter, Carolyn. The sick man was George Bockius, the former's son.

Wilmington, Delaware
February 21, 1904. Sunday evening, 8:00 P.M.

Dear Mama,

I'm now deep in a successful picture of how the embattled farmers stood and fired the shot heard round the world.

I never enjoyed making a picture more in my life. I have finally identified myself with every character, entering into each man's character until I almost know how he would talk—laugh—and act.

To begin with I have endeavored to grasp the significant meaning of this battle. Here these half-civilized frontier farmers, their mouths full of oaths and Connecticut rum, standing here in their old weather-beaten clothes, laying the foundation for a great nation. Just think what it means! My point of view is from the "Britishers'" positions looking into the faces of these grim farmers who are nervously waiting for the English to fire first. Every one of them tense with anger and excitement, shuffling and grumbling, anxious to plug the redcoats in front of them.

The last five hours I pray may never be duplicated! The night is a howling, wet, unearthly one, black as ink. With the wind and rushing water it is deafening, a strong suggestion of hell.

It being my duty this evening to make a call, I ventured out intending to stay out 20 min. or so, confidently expecting a very pleasant chat. I reached the house and on entering found its people in despair. I knew instantly it was sickness for as soon as I entered, continuous groans and screams met my ears, followed by a rumble and thump of furniture overhead. The helpless people (the mother and daughter) were of course glad to see some man and instantly told me that the son (about 23 yrs. old) was strangling because of a heavy bronchial cold and in his anguish was thrashing around the room.

All of a sudden a window opened which meant that in his hysterical struggle for air he had made a dive for one. I rushed up the stairs and there met an appalling sight. He was hanging by the open window writhing and yelling, his hand clutching his breast, but when he saw me he made a jump for me. I stood still and caught him around the waist and made toward the bed and after much trouble untangled myself from his frantic clutches. His strength failed him and every breath inhaled sounded with a stinging hiss combined with a metallic rattle—more like some devilish machine than like a human body.

After numerous futile attempts, I finally reached a doctor by phone and fortunately he lived near and arrived in due season. It was now about 11:45 and I made toward a drugstore for medicines upon which depended the sick man's life. The power-supplying lights were gone and all was total darkness, and feeling my way I slowly reached a drugstore. I rang the night bell for fully five minutes and was then answered (through the tube) in a way which meant that the druggist would not come down. After pleading with the cuss for an unnecessary length of time in my uncontrollable state of excitement, I threatened to break in the door, which was heard by a policeman. He quickly appeared and, sensibly listening to my story, ordered the druggist to come down or he threatened arrest. The druggist was soon fulfilling his duty in a very deliberate manner, grumbling and muttering all the while. I slopped back to the striken house and delivered my goods and made toward my little cot in a peculiar state of mind, I can tell you. Thus ends a poor synopsis of my little adventure which was a good lesson to me in this way— "Take care of yourself." Let us hope the poor fellow survives.

78

Wilmington, Delaware
February 26, 1904. Friday

Dear Mama,

I'm still wrapped up in my Concord picture much to my satisfaction, as it is hard for me to keep up my enthusiasm for a long period.

Last night a dance was given in our studio and our own personal friends were invited, there were but 6 couples and I can tell you we had a glorious time. The first time I ever said such a thing about a dance.

We've started on model work again, half days, the other half on illustration, of course. I'm not at all sorry that we have come back to a little study, as I'm in sore need of it.

We are all very busy in preparation for the banquet March 5th. We've hit upon a novel scheme. It is this: We are all to attend the banquet in costume (unbeknown to H.P.) representing his many characters he has originated and made famous. Each one will give some appropriate toast or song. It is a good deal of trouble but we're going to make it a time of his life.

79

Wilmington, Delaware
February 27, 1904. Sunday

Dear Mama,

The word *Sunday* is extremely inappropriate as a name for the seventh day in this part of 'the land. Slimy, cold, wet, dank, thick air, heavily laden with diseases, foul to the core. Even the drinking water after these heavy rains is oily with debris, alive with germs causing two-thirds of the populace to be weakened and helplessly laid low by acute attacks of the dysentery. Hardly a square can be passed but what one is told by that silent message, the "Crepe," that Wilmington is accountable for one more soul.

While writing the above I kept continually hearing a peculiar noise not unlike a muffled thump of a bass drum. It sounded weird and uncanny and added much to the discomforture of the day. It became more distinct until I was certain it must be a drum of some sort. I raised my window and looking out saw a small army in black slowly approaching, their black heads bobbing up and down like so many corks on a choppy sea. I comprehended at once, as the scene is not an uncommon one in these parts.

A colored peoples' lodge were escorting their dead comrade to his last resting place. I watched them slowly approach up the paved hill and when within half a block the accompanying band burst forth with a doleful funeral march that echoed and resounded in the narrow brick-walled streets causing a terrible congested confusion of music which was heartrending in itself. All this added greatly to the uncivilized nature of the ceremonies.

They all walked with their hats off and heads hung, scuffling and stumbling along, some in step, a number with crutches, some engaged in conversation, gesturing and laughing to suit their pleasure.

What if a thing like that would happen in Cambridge, Newton or any of the towns? Would the people tolerate? *No.* But here it seems in its place; it seems to be adopted to the surroundings. It's perfectly harmonious and nobody questions or objects to it!

There is not another day in the week that I feel the significance of the above conditions here in Wilmington, but Sunday is a day that one sits still and contemplates. You spoke about stockings. Oh Yes! "my kingdom for stockings." I hope Papa's cold is improving and hope it won't turn into asthma. It's bad business!

80

Wilmington, Delaware
March 7, 1904

Dear Mama,

The Banquet! That's all you hear talked about—that's all we're thinking about or all we have thought about this last week. "It" occurred last night and I can vouch it was one of the liveliest affairs that ever stirred up this dead town for many a moon. It was not only lively but exceptionally unique and original and moreover strenuous.

Our plan was, as I have probably told you, to represent, to the

extent of our numbers, the principal characters originated and pictured by Mr. Pyle during his illustrious career, such as pirates—
soldiers—Robin Hood characters—wise men and numerous characters originated by Mr. Pyle, as—Sinbad—Munier—Little John, etc.
There were about seventeen of us costumed out absolutely correct
in detail and color and it so happened that each stature was utilized
in such a way as to fit their characters absolutely. What more could
you ask?

It was the finest set of characters I ever saw together and not only
that but every fellow acted his part during the evening.

Mr. True was toastmaster and the only one in full dress. He called
for Mr. & Mrs. Pyle and escorted them to the studios, which had
been elaborately decorated by us with bunting (red, yellow, black
and white) Japanese lanterns and flowers. They arrived about 8
o'clock and found the hall (studio) entirely devoid of humanity.
True seated them and started apologizing for us fellows being late
when lo! a red and gold curtain rose, displaying a gorgeous gold
frame containing a striking resemblance of Robin Hood. It completely phased Mr. Pyle and amid enthusiastic applause from our
small but mighty audience we were exhibited one by one, each taking some pose easily recognized by its "maker."

We then burst into the room chanting and singing, the various
armor-chains and trappings clattering and clanking, making it an
impressive entrance. Mr. Pyle was so overjoyed he actually threw
his arms about us in his wild ecstasy, followed by a wonderful speech
which will be remembered by us all. Then followed the dinner, and
a rich one it was—all the waiters were in colonial costume and with
the mountainous candle chandeliers, lanterns, flags, stocks of guns,
swords and relics it made a beauteous display.

During the dinner a number of appropriate and witty "toasts"
were made, ended by a long and serious one by H.P. which will no
doubt inspire every fellow to exert all his powers and energy to do
his best in the future.

At eleven-thirty and after a few songs, the "banquet proper" was
dismissed and then followed a scene that should be put down in
the annals of history—one humorous and at the same time dramatic.
It sounds like tales of "Old Heidelberg" to repeat last midnight's
exploits.

At the given signal we ran every waiter (ten) out of the house, then we finished the bounteous supply of victuals—ice creams—drinks, etc. Then, unbeknown to me as to how it started, there was a rush and crash and two bodies of fellows clashed together, about 9 on a side, each wielding a huge sword striking right and left; every light was extinguished and one could see nothing but continual splatterings and sunbursts of sparks caused by the clashing steel. Becker's sword was wrenched from his grasp and hurled through a window, followed quickly by Ashley's. Becker and Ashley retreated to safe quarters and viewed this weird production, each one sure that somebody's head would be smashed. This kept up some twenty minutes until fellows dropped out from sheer exhaustion. They all dropped out but Pfiefer and me and the battle royal continued for five minutes under strenuous conditions. I had a broadsword and wielded it with all my might and he had a cavalry sword and did the same. Amid cheers and yelling we fought until by a lucky stroke I broke his sword at the hilt, sending the blade with a br-r-r-r-r-r across the room. Thus ended the duel and the wonderful part was that nobody was seriously hurt.

Not satisfied with this, a mighty tug of war was started and when deep in this game a nonparticipant emptied the contents of a bucket containing not the cleanest water.

Mr. Peck was the miscreant but was easily overpowered and I can vouch he knows more how the "water cure" might feel than any other fellow in the crowd. All of a sudden amidst the confusion, the ever-grinding hand of "Grandpa" [James E.] McBurney was raised in protest and told us of our sins—it was 1:15 Sunday morning. We carried our tails between our legs and sneaked home to dream wild dreams of Hell and War.

I arose about 9:30, stiff as a board, and after a vigorous wash and rubdown was restored *to my normal* condition. But Oh! the studios!

Talk about Destruction, Desolation, my heavens! It certainly looked like a dissipated old hole. It looked as if it had been raided by some army, and moreover one part of it looked tragic. In one corner was a broken sword and near it and on its blade was blood and a little to one side a bloody rag. The funny part is nobody knows who spilled the blood. The roll will be called tomorrow.

Today I rigged up again the same, with the exception of a fake putty nose, and had three photos taken which I will positively send when printed.

N. C. Wyeth as Little John.

81

Wilmington, Delaware
March 21, 1904

Dear Mama,

After hustling for three quarters of an hour I finally have squatted myself in a Penn. R.R. car to be whisked to N.Y. where I will fondle the puppet of fate scandalously.

I worked all day yesterday and succeeded in putting my final touches on my "Concord" picture. You may ask why I rushed so. Well, Arthurs came back from N.Y. Sat. night with news of a possibility to make a drawing for Scribner's Pub. Co. Now if I get a stand-in with those people it will mean a good deal.

78

*Frank Schoonover, encouraged by Howard Pyle, had made a pro-
longed trip to the Hudson Bay region of Canada. Pyle believed that if
a student displayed a deep imaginative affinity for a particular locale,
his work would greatly gain—in authenticity and understanding—from
his firsthand acquaintance with the life and landscape of the place.*

Wilmington, Delaware
March 25, 1904. Thursday night

Dear Mama,

I suppose you wonder why I have not written. To begin with, my
trip to New York was a gratification, and in a certain sense I might
say the spirit of the trip was mighty pleasing.

My Revolutionary picture went with a rush and was liked much
by all the art editors who saw it. My heading for *Leslie's* was liked
very well—so much for the deliverance of ordered work. Now for
Scribner's. I actually refused two full pages and this is why. Mr.
[Joseph] Chapin (by the way one of the finest outspoken and polite
men I *ever* met) told me the facts and it was that this story he
offered me had to be done quickly and well. It would need a great
deal of understudy of costume, customs and character. I read
the story right there and considered the matter seriously and my
verdict was not to take it for my own good. Mr. Chapin seemed
well impressed. He finally found a Russian story, which he had not
read, and if the story is anything like what he thinks it is he'll give
it to me.

Now I think that's pretty promising for the foremost art editor
this side of the Atlantic to say to a fellow who is making the initial
trip of his advanced art career.

I spent two days in N.Y. visiting numerous art exhibitions which,
I am glad to say, encouraged me to quite an extent. Remington's
show was fine—it was vital and powerful although most of his
pictures were too gruesome to allow them to become living works
of art. He's too insistent on showing mangled bodies, wounds, etc.
Nevertheless the exhibition impresses you and convinces you that
Remington had lived in that country and was telling something—
you could not say that about any of the other exhibitions as they
were absolutely shallow and meaningless.

The lost boy has returned! Schoonover. He came back tonight hale and hearty. Stouter, stronger, with face shining like a squaw's and the color of bronze. Happy, enthusiastic, talkative—good and vital signs which promise excellent results in the way of pictures and story. He brings with him the terrible and pitiful tale of Leonadis Hubbard's death from starvation, which he himself narrowly escaped on his last trip. This trip will be the "setting up" of Schoonover for years to come, both physically and in character.

83

Wilmington, Delaware
March 31, 1904. Wednesday

Dear Home,

I have settled down for a hard grind. Now 'tis easy to guess what has inspired me. Schoonover has just got back with his toboggan, snowshoes, traps, furs, skins, moccasins, guns and, above all, his sketches. His return has meant a great deal to me. It inspired me to work and work hard with a similar result in view. Naturally I was very enthusiastic, which pleased Mr. Pyle, and from that Mr. Pyle has developed an idea that it will be a comparatively short time when I can do the same thing in a different part of the country.

84

Wilmington, Delaware
April 11, 1904

Dear Mama,

Hooray! Zip! Boom!!! About forty-eight hours and I'll be on my way toward the one place, Home! I'm so worked up over it I can't realize what it means, and for two whole weeks!

No going to the city once except to Cambridge. Don't tell anybody I'm coming home.

I've worked hard and strung up to the highest pitch of excitement by Schoonover's return, books I've been reading and a marked advance in my work (don't take this for self-praise). I'll live two weeks of the life of the free. Mr. Pyle is at the bottom of my present standing, and without him I'd have missed the biggest part of my life, and the thing is something I can't explain. It can only be explained on canvas and I'll do it, you'll see.

85

Wilmington, Delaware
April 16, 1904. Friday evening

Dear Mama,

I have worked hard on the fatal picture that held me back a week from my long-anticipated home visit.

I didn't realize until last night that I had not written you as to my new creation on canvas. I passed in a composition entitled "The Moose Call." One Indian on a lake in the moonlight calling a moose. Mr. Pyle liked it exceedingly and strongly advised me to remain and while in the spirit of it to finish it right up and take it on to New York where he feels sure I will sell it and that I can surely obtain work by it.

86

Up until now, Wyeth had been illustrating magazine stories. This commission for Charles Scribner's Sons inaugurated his career as a book illustrator and his long relationship with Scribner's. The book was Boys of St. Timothy's *by Arthur Stanwood Pier.*

Wilmington, Delaware
May 23, 1904

Dear Mama,

Wednesday I was in New York. My Russian "sketch" was satisfactory and [I] was told to go on with it, but besides I got a book to illustrate (3 illustrations) from Scribner's so will be busy for quite a spell. The illustration I am now at work on is a football picture, "Hurdling the Line." I have a boat race to make also and the third one I haven't decided on my subject.

87

The Turner estate had been sold, and Howard Pyle never again held summer classes at Chadds Ford.

The WYETHS

Dear Mama,

Yesterday I spent some money on a pleasure. I hired a horse and "run about" and drove to Chadds Ford in company with Miss [Etta] Boulden. The day was superb and the country was paradise. I visited all my acquaintances, all expressing their sincere sorrow that we were not to live with them this coming summer. I can tell you they are no more sorry than I am. We went out about 9 A.M. arriving there about noon and had dinner (prearranged) at the "Lafayette Headquarters." We put up the horse in their huge barn and made off on foot across country. Visited the "mill," studying the many scrawls and sketches on the walls, which brought back associations I shall never forget. It seemed such a terrible pity to see Mr. Pyle's former home closed and barricaded. I had the keys so made a tour of inspection of the place. It seemed as if it were a house of the dead. All was dark and damp and bare. A few of his famous paintings still hanging on the walls, a few books on the shelves, the tennis outfit in the closet, the old piano and a few other things which all reminded me of the happy times spent there last summer. It seemed so queer to go into that house and not hear the voices and romping of children, or not see Mr. Pyle standing in the doorway beaming all over with joviality. The beautiful lawn and tennis court are all overgrown with lush grasses and weeds, with a few hens of the neighbors leisurely feeding around the porch.

The same with [the] Randolphs', desolate but beautiful. Situated on a high hill overlooking the rolling, billowing hills for miles, perfectly quiet save for the bark of a distant dog or the lowing of cattle on the distant pasture land. Beautiful flowers choking up around the porch as if they were striving to be seen by familiar faces.

The old mill with its same rattle and scrambling voice, the same sighing rush of water through the "wheel." It made me feel queer, almost heartbroken and *very* homesick.

88

N. C. Wyeth's courtship consisted of frequent canoeing trips on the Brandywine Creek.

Dear Mama,

Who said "birch bark canoe?" For heavens sakes, get it; they are getting more scarce every year. Tell me if it is in its natural condition and its length. Get Nat to make a sketch of it.

Quite an account of Grandpapa but he deserves better—very badly written and I wish they'd keep my name out of their blooming "yellow jacket" of a paper. People will think the paper belongs to the family.

Carolyn Bockius on the Brandywine.

89

Wilmington, Delaware
June 19, 1904

Dear Mama,

I have sent the second of my Scribner's book illustrations. The first procured a very desirable answer from the publishers. The second picture was sentimental and I was not successful with it. The next is the "boat race," Hurrah!!

90

Howard Pyle borrowed the Civil War cavalry outfit to use in illustrating a story for Harper's Magazine, *"The Non-Combatants," by Robert Chambers.*

Wilmington, Delaware
June 26, 1904. Sunday

Dear Papa,

A day filled with dead, sickening heat, absolutely impossible to keep cool.

I'm all at sea as to the doings of the farmer—it seems funny to hear of you haying, because not having seen any such work being done this season it seems extremely early in the summer for it. I'll tell you sincerely and honestly that this is positively the last summer I'll ever stay in any kind of a city. If it were not for the close application to my work I could and would not endure it. I can easily understand why you travel every morning and night twelve miles to enjoy the freshness and life of the country. I hope soon you'll not have to go in town at all.

Mr. Pyle is still using Mr. Reed's cavalry boots, etc., to great advantage, having three or four Civil War pictures to paint.

91

Wilmington, Delaware
July 8, 1904

Dear Mama,

Mondays always develop some sort of news in relation to my work, as it is composition day. Well, I passed in a picture that won a good deal of applause from H. P. It was "The Prophesy"—an Indian standing on a rock that commands a view of the surrounding country. His pony stands by him, head hung low, unconscious of all around him, and on the other hand the Indian (a medicine man) intently gazing at the huge rolling clouds. I have pictured in these clouds huge war horses and warriors racing across the sky, just as the Indian sees them. I have drawn in great detail the surrounding country with its lakes and rivers. Mr. Pyle called it a powerful picture.

92

Wilmington, Delaware
August 12, 1904

Dear Mama,

Today was a day of jot for me. I have at last graduated from the class and after tomorrow I launch forward "full force" into illustrating and painting. Mr. Pyle notified me today that I had probably finished my model work forever, so here goes!!

93

Wilmington, Delaware
August 14, 1904. Sunday

Dear Mama,

How often have I lingered over that poor little group of photographs procured on *that* walking trip with brother Nat. Nobody knows what sentiments transpire in my mind, what inspirations alternately rise and fall as I identify myself again with that snatch of ideal life placed upon those meager bits of sensitized paper.

I'm almost afraid at times they may do harm. At times I'm in such mental conditions that it would take but a very little to set me off—out—away from all these nauseative and depressing circumstances of life. Mr. Pyle is the only *solid rock* that keeps me here and to that I will cling as long as I see fit.

I've been away from home nigh onto two years now, and even as important as the two years have been to me they seem to be a side issue attached to my life. I could go right back home now, I'm sure, and fall back into the old routines, as if nothing had happened. That feeling will always cling to me until I die.

94

Wilmington, Delaware
August 23, 1904

Dear Mama,

Yesterday was an extremely strenuous day for me, I can tell
you. I feel it. We started at six in the morning to paddle up to
Chadds Ford. The river is running quite high and very rapid and
to go fifteen miles it took us from six until two in the afternoon.
Taking an hour for lunch we returned shooting hazardous dams
and rapids, only overturning once, which nearly cost the life of
Arthurs. After about a six-foot drop into a wild rapids the canoe
overturned (my birch bark canoe); going on down stream at a terrific rate it left me behind, but as luck would have it, it got hung
on a rock. All this time Stanley was caught underneath. After quite
a struggle I reached him and pulled him out. He showed good
pluck and shot three other dams fully as bad. The trip told on us
all but I certainly feel as if I could paint "Shooting the Rapids" now,
introducing a good deal of realism and local color into it that I
would have otherwise missed.

95

Wilmington, Delaware
August 28, 1904. Sunday evening

Dear Mama,

You seem to be a might skeptical as to your capability of imparting
your feelings in relation to nature and the way you interpret it.
I understood perfectly all you suggested.

As I have before mentioned, I think our views of certain things
are very similar, which makes it possible for us to understand with
a greater meaning a mere suggestion. It is like a crude sketch that
might be made upon an inch of space—it means a thousand and one
things to its author, but to one of a different mind, of different
temperament, its meaning is dead and void. Of course we have lived
very closely for many years, which has enabled us to study each
other's nature—moods and the characteristic ways of expression;
this faculty (if you can call it so) of course we will never lose, no
matter how changed opinions and ideas may become, the same,
underlying facts will always be there.

Wednesday I received a letter from the *Saturday Evening Post* stating that they wished to see me in regards to illustrating a "Western Story." The same day I spoke to Mr. Pyle in regards to a trip to Cheyenne, Wyoming, to witness the "Annual Busting Contest." He seemed very enthusiastic over the project and urged me to take it but suggested that I consult *Scribner's* about it and see if it would not be possible for me to make a couple pictures of it and write (with H. P.'s help) a short article. Well, I immediately sent to Denver to inquire about the "Contest," etc. Well, Saturday I made my way to Philadelphia to see the *Post*. I got the story, "a beaut," and the same day invested in a few pieces of useful costumes (mostly cavalry and equipment) and upon my return found a "poster" awaiting me—on it was the following:

Frontier Sports—Aug. 30 & 31—Cheyenne, Wyoming

Mr. Pyle (this shows how thoughtful he was), upon receipt of the poster and knowing I was away, phoned to *Scribner's*, but with no avail, as all official men of the house were gone, so the "project" fell through. Mr. Pyle always looks upon the bright side of things and says, "Well, next year at this time you will have established a solid name as an illustrator and thereby gain more prestige in a matter of this kind." And I think he's right.

Nevertheless I'm booked for Western work this winter and feel, if it is possible, that I must make a trip there in October. I'll have the money and will *take* the time and am sure I will benefit greatly by such a trip.

96

Wilmington, Delaware
September 9, 1904

Dear Mama,

Mr. Pyle thinks it an excellent plan for me to go West for a month, so I immediately wrote to the Smithsonian in regards to the ceremonies carried on by the Utes of Utah. I have planned to go in October, which is a likely month for Indian Festivities. Meanwhile I spoke to Chapin about such a trip. He took much interest in it and wants me to come to him with any material I may gather before going anywhere else.

The WYETHS

Mr. Pyle suggests that I make three or four pictures with a facing page of text for each picture. It's *just* the kind of thing I've been wanting to do ever since I can remember and I can't realize that at last my time has nearly arrived for such work.

97

Wilmington, Delaware
September 11, 1904

Dear Mama,

Well, you may say that the eve of my departure to the land of "promise" and of many dreams is near. To think that in probably a month I'll roll up in a blanket miles away from civilization under the clear and cold dome of stars, with a pack mule and horses picketed nearby, with only an old guide by my side, why I can't believe it and *won't* until it is proven.

Mr. Pyle has had for some months past a very bad toe (big toe) and yesterday he had the toenail cut completely out by the roots. It of course necessitated his taking ether but even then the surgeon feared a struggle from such a powerful man, so H.P. called on me for help. It was a struggle, I can tell you. Of course I had the advantage of position in holding him down but even then I had to strain every nerve and muscle to fulfill what was expected of me. The operation was a nasty one and one I shall not forget and am mighty glad it's over.

Well, enough of that.—I had quite a confidential talk with Mr. Pyle the other day and was made very happy and very much encouraged by a statement he made. He said he had more confidence and faith in me than anyone he ever had and predicted that [I] would become a painter of renown. He thinks I have got the roots and fundamental ideas of his, which he claims will be the foundation of any successful artist, and says he will back me up in anything I undertake. He wants very much to get Schoonover and me into one studio as he thinks we will aid each other in a number of different ways. He thinks I obtain a broader and bigger grasp of facts of life and put them on canvas in a vigorous way, which is a physically vigorous way, while Schoonover puts more time and thought to minor details, which count very much in the make-up of a successful picture. In this way we would influence each other in the weak points of their [*sic*] art, thereby in the end strengthening both.

The photograph N. C. Wyeth gave Miss Bockius as a keepsake before he left for the West.

Chapter V

TRIP WEST

"Here I am in the great West, *and I'll tell you it is the great West."*

98

Dear Mama,

Had good luck. Chapin is evidently much interested; secured transportation for me both ways and letters to friends of his in Chicago. Have got to hustle out Sat. morning. Should have gone today but hadn't time to pack. Things look bright and favorable now, and if I don't succeed it's *my* fault and no one else's. Everything seems strange down here for the place is practically deserted, nearly all the fellows being away.

Bought a new trunk and dress suitcase—old one weak in several places. Got a good one for $3.50, trunk for $4.50—

The next line you'll hear from me will be from Buffalo, then Chicago.

99

Alan True's parents lived in Denver, Colorado. They were very cordial to N. C. Wyeth on this Western trip, securing passes for him to enter and live on the Indian reservations and also providing him with board while in Denver.

[En route]
September 25, 1904

Dear Mama,

As I start this note we are looking out over the west end of Lake Erie, so you can see I'm not a great ways from Chicago. The ride thus far has been long and tedious. I have a longer one from Chicago to Denver but the country will be entirely new to me, which of course will add interest to the trip. I was disappointed in the Hudson River scenery, although the Catskills were very fine. My route carried me up the Hudson to Albany, thence straight west through Schenectady, Syracuse and to Buffalo, then along Lake Erie to Toledo through Cleveland to Chicago. In the latter place expect to meet Townsend and remain with him overnight, as it will be impossible for me to get passes to Denver until Monday morning.

My last talk with True developed more than I really thought he had arranged for me. I don't know what I'd do if it weren't for his people.

The country we are speeding through now is very uninteresting, as it is nothing but flat, half-developed farm country. What crops of corn there are are *poor* and from what wheat that is still out I should judge it was a flat failure this year.

100

Denver, Colorado
September 29, 1904

Dear Mama,

Here I am in the *great West,* and I'll tell you it *is* the great West. After 54 hours of riding I reached Denver Tuesday night about 8:30. The ride as soon as I struck Nebraska was most interesting, but from New York to Iowa was simply terrible. Nothing but low flat prairie land full of bogs and sunken streams, dirty nasty little towns surrounded by poor farms of no importance and between these settlements nothing but grass and sky.

But gradually I caught glimpses here and there of the life of which I have dreamed. First I saw the adobe shack or mud hut made of sods; these are scattered on the limitless plains, 30 and 40 miles apart; sometimes around these dwellings would be a woman in a sunbonnet watching the train pass, or a pony standing by the door patiently awaiting its rider, but usually these places were lifeless.— For a whole day we rode through the plains at the rate of 60 miles an hour, so you can imagine how much of this country I saw.

Once looking ahead from the car window I made out a cloud of white alkali dust; of course I thought it some windstorm or possibly a stampede of cattle, but soon a black speck appeared and upon coming nearer it proved to be an old stage coming across country. It set me wild! The old driver up in the box with his high sombrero, a long bullwhip in his hand, blue shirt and vest, white kerchief around his neck, high-topped boots and all literally covered with this white dust. These things continually appeared, thus keeping me in a frenzy of excited expectation. True's people have treated me royally. Without them I don't see how it would have been pos-

94

sible for me to have got along. I leave Friday night for the plains. I go to a place called Deer Trail in the train and there get a horse and ride 45 miles to the Hash Knife ranch where I expect to actually take part in the roundup, which happens in a few days.

Up to date I have spent only about seven dollars since I left New York and that for grub and traveling necessities. But today I blow in my largest expense and that is for my outfit: saddle, bridle, pair of blankets, boots, spurs, breeches, chaps, slicker (rubber coat) and saddle blanket. This will reach up about $55. I have an experienced cowpuncher who has offered to pick me out a good saddle, which is a very serious and important acquisition.

You have <u>no</u> idea of the wonderful hospitality of these western people—an easterner can't understand it until he has really experienced it, and I am experiencing it in its best form.

I expect to stay on the plains for a couple of weeks, then back to Denver and then up into the mountains in what they call Routt County, which is the wildest place in the state.

I am gratified to think that my conceptions of the West were about right. In fact I feel perfectly at home here. All but with the cowpunchers; they are very quiet and reticent, but after a time when [they] find who you are and what purposes you are in their country for, they are sociable and willing to impart all the information they can.

The WYETHS

This is the only time in his life that N. C. Wyeth kept a diary. Excerpts are included here in chronological order.

[Diary, *September 30, 1904*]

Left Denver 8 P.M. and reached Deer Trail, Colorado, about 10 P.M. Slept at "Hotel." Met Mr. Martin, a sheepherder, and rode with him to his ranch two miles east and took dinner. With the additional company of "Dutch Lou" continued on our way east to Jack Stuart's sheep ranch; distance, 18 miles.

There slept in "bunk house" with "Dutch Lou" and "Bill Taylor" (an English herder).

101

Deer Trail, Colorado
October 1, 1904

Dear Mama,

Well here I am in the heat of a desert. This will be the last you'll hear of me for a few weeks or more as this noon I leave this God-forsaken handful of houses for the plains.

I landed here last night about ten o'clock. I expected from descriptions to find quite a village but, by the gods, all there is is a station, saloon, combination hardware–dry goods–groceries and postoffice store and a group of half a dozen dwelling houses, but with an abundance of corral and cattle sheds. The mud here is terrific, the result of a heavy rain these last two days.

The hotel was a ramshackled, old one-story building run by a widow with two children; the breakfast consisted of fried pork, fried potatoes, hot soda biscuits and coffee. I am now waiting around for a sheepherder to pull out to a ranch 19 miles from here, which will bring me that distance nearer to my destination. At this place I'll get my horse and ride alone about 25 more. I expect to get there tonight.

There is an old herder in here that has been on a 3-day drunk. He comes in from a distant ranch about twice a month to make up for lost time. The saloon is typical with its card tables, low ceiling and those big tin lamps. In fact the impression I have received is not unlike that which Wister describes in *The Virginian*, lacking to a certain extent the interesting characters.

Saloon, Deer Trail, Colorado.

It all seems as if I'd seen such places before, although I never have. It's probably because I've identified myself so closely with the life that I know to a certain extent what to expect. This trip will be a good test of my grit and endurance and is a good preparatory one for the mountain trip later. You can see nothing as far as the eye can reach but prairie and sky, a limitless and pathless expanse.

My rig is blue shirt, corduroy breeches, hightop boots, belt and pistol, spurs, quirt, good saddle and bridle, blankets, rubber coat, paint box; and camera completes my outfit.

Thus I shall pass into the land of sun and sky.

[Diary, *October 2, 1904*]

"Dutch Lou" started west, back to Martin's ranch, with 1300 lambs. Found out later that he was lost; went 12 miles north out of his way.

Continued my weary way east on a green colt to Andy Middlemist's, accompanied by a Swede ranchhand named "Ericson." Had dinner at Andy's with Bill Simpson, Old Jim, Kid and a ranchhand. Waited for Elroy Gill but finally about 2:30 P.M. made my way alone. Reached Gill's Ranch (RG) about sundown.

Met Henry Gill, but boys were not at home. By the way, while at Andy's, Bill Simpson jewed my $1.00 pipe from me; he gave me his with some tobacco. Met Elroy and Mark.

[Diary, *October 5, 1904*]

Fine clear morning. Took Gill's light "rig" and pair of "roan mares" to return "Jack Stuart's" colt. Stayed at Jack's overnight, slept with "Scotty," the best sheepman in the country.

Left next morning, Oct. 4th, for Gill's. Reached Big Beaver Creek and found that big box wagon was stuck in narrow trail, loaded with grain and square piano. Luckily they had left a spade, so spent next two hours and a half digging and widening trail.

Jack Stuart in his bunkhouse.

I pulled rig through the "creek" by hand and went on. Missed my trail and went 20 miles out of my way. Reached Andy's at noon, took dinner and there met Gill in search of me, thinking I was lost. He remained there and I took his saddle horse and went on an "Antelope Hunt" with "Date" Middlemist (expert cow-puncher).

We ran into a wild bunch and after firing half a dozen shots without success, I left "Date" and went to Gill's ranch. Gill got home the next night bringing along a fresh quarter of beef, something we were in much need of.

Wrote letters Oct. 4th, did nothing else, but feel almighty blue.

· 102

RG Ranch
Limon, Colorado
October 5, 1904

My dear Mama,

Out of the west window, plains; out of the east, plains; out of the north window, plains; out of the south, plains.

Forty miles from the nearest town, eighteen miles from the nearest neighbor, and here I am alone in a mud or, as they call it, "adobe" shack. The three men have gone three miles to a "crik" after a load of hay, and I'm left alone to write.

Saturday, Oct. 1st, I wrote from the town of Deer Trail, and from there my story starts.

As luck would have it, after I unfortunately discovered that it was impossible for me to obtain a horse, I ran into a sheepherder who was going to drive eighteen miles nearer to my destination to a large sheep ranch to receive 1500 lambs, so I piled bag and baggage into his "rig." This was just after a heavy rain and the roads were "heavy." We left Deer Trail about 9 o'clock and reached his own ranch (en route to the former sheep ranch I spoke of) about noon, where he fed me. Here a "ranchhand" joined us, and with his "bed" (everyone carries his bed with him here) made quite a load for a small rig. We reached the sheep ranch about sundown. This ranch is owned by a Scotch man named Jack Stuart, a tall, thin, highly complicated fellow with clear blue eyes and exceedingly keen. He at first refused to let me have a horse to complete my journey because I did not openly admit I could ride and besides was an Easterner, but finally agreed to let me try one of the "broncs" (an unbroken pony). His "gentle" horses he was saving for the "round-up." So the next morning we all went down into the "corral" and saddled a colt. I had not given him to understand I could ride much so I had no reputation to live up to, but when I did get on the "bronc" I managed to "stick" alright although the horse did "pitch" a bit. The result was I gained the Scotchman's confidence and he let me take the horse. I reached the Gill Ranch (or as I headed my letter, RG) Sunday night safe and sound.

Gill's Ranch. Left to right: Elroy Gill, N. C. Wyeth, Andy Middlemist.

Monday Mr. Gill let me have a two-horse "rig" to take back the borrowed horse and to get my luggage, which I had left there. I returned yesterday experiencing quite a predicament at a gulch called the "Big Beaver." There a huge ranch wagon had got stuck with a heavy load right in the middle of the trail which was only wide enough for one wagon. Rather than stay in the middle of the desert for no knowing how long, I proceeded to dig the passage wider, which took me almost three hours. It was hard work but a good experience. I have a couple photos of the "predicament" so I hope sometime you may see what I was up against. This proposition delayed me so that I had to "grub" at the last ranch before Gill's. There I found Mr. Gill thinking that something had happened so came out in search of me. This stopping place is what they call the "Hash Knife" ranch (the name is derived from the appearance of their brand("⭥").

Gill is a great talker and got so interested that he stayed at the "Hash Knife" all afternoon. Meanwhile I went out hunting "antelope" with "Date," one of the cowboys in the ranch. We ran into several herds but got no shots at them. Got home late last night alone on horseback. Mr. Gill has not got home yet so I guess he is still talking.

The "roundup" starts next Sunday and for two weeks I'll be on the trail with them. That will be hard work for me but will do me good.

I have learned many things that I should never have known had I not "traveled west," but am agreeably surprised to find that I *did* hit a few things right.

[Diary, *October 6, 1904*]

I did my first work of the cowpuncher. Elroy and I went out and rounded up about 300 head of cattle, counting calves. We started at 7:30 A.M. and were in the saddle continually until 5:15 that afternoon. After rounding up the cattle we proceeded to cut out the RG's. These we herded and drove into Gill's big pasture. During this "roundup" we "worked" 6 square miles. Proclaimed by Elroy himself to be a big day's work.

Got my first bad spill into a gulch. Fell down a bank 20 ft. Horse hurt his leg, me, my arm. A little sore that night but well in the morning.

[Diary, *October 7, 1904*]

Got up very tired at 4:30 and drove team to Limon 42 miles after coal and lumber. Had dinner at McCully's (Mac's) on the way and reached Limon about 4 o'clock.

There loaded the two wagons with 4600 lbs. coal and lumber. Had supper at the "Hotel." Elroy was being bumholed by some insurance agents. They took him to the saloon a couple of times—tried to interfere for his sake but got in trouble; all were a little wild with whiskey and thought better to keep out of the way.

[Added Oct. 9] I found out later that they "pulled his leg," as he called it, for $80. Went to bed early but Gill did not turn in until past midnight—full.

Started back to the ranch morning of Oct. 8th about 6:30, had no dinner for either horses or ourselves.

Reached the ranch about 8 P.M. in terrific storm after several breakdowns and mishaps.

Ate a big supper and then to bed.

[Diary, *October 9, 1904. Sunday*]

Did my washing and cleaned guns, then proceeded to make a few color sketches of the adobe house, etc., and found that I had neglected to bring *white paint,* that meant that I was unable to do any sketching on the roundup.

"... proceeded to make a few color sketches of the adobe house."

3:30 P.M. started with horses for Andy's—horse ran away with me on the way. Pitched a bit—had supper at the "Grub wagon" and then enjoyed some good singing by the new school marm— very pretty too.—Bill Simpson favored us with some Scotch songs. Good—I sang too.

The feature of the evening was the cutting off of Elroy's whiskers —eight men got him down and Katy Simpson cut off one side of his "sideburns"—he got almighty mad.

After a feed of prunes went to bed in Andy's barn.

[Diary, *October 10, 1904*]

Got up at sunrise to prepare for the start.—Charlie Barret herded and drove the horses, about 125 head, into the "corral." Then the fun started—the horses were wild and the roping exciting. After the men got their saddle horses I attempted to rope mine.—I picked out a horse and lo! got him first throw. I felt very proud, especially as a "puncher" was looking through the bars at me, but my pride fell when he said—"Hey, whose horse yer hooked?" I looked and found that I mistook the brand. I then tried for the right horse making about 25 throws before success rewarded me. Skinned three fingers, which proved to me in good form why "cowpunchers" wear gloves.

No excitement in starting except that Brennan's horse pitched almighty hard. Took two photos of the outfit and then all were off!

Reached "Jim's Canyon" about noon. Punchers started a "shooting bee" using prairie dogs as targets. Bad shooting. Had grub and helped cook with dishes.

About three o'clock new men started to come in, making a total of about 28 men. Joe Mager and Walter Brennan and myself went to the neighboring bluffs and rolled rocks down into the canyon. Good Sport—raced back, cheered by "punchers" assembled around "Grub wagon." After supper all gathered around campfire and talked.

Great excitement in camp! DT boy's horse comes in riderless, but no rider appeared. Detachment of six sent out in search of lost rider. Stirrup leather broken and some claim they see signs of blood on his hind feet. All evidence points to a bad result. Never-theless the punchers are shooting craps and enjoying themselves generally.

Jim's Canyon.

[Diary, *October 11, 1904*]

Sleep sound but am aroused at an early hour (about 4 A.M.) by calls, boisterous expressions of sorrow, and intolerable cursing—a weird sight by the light of half-moon.

A boy's body brought in by two horsemen, rolled up in a yellow slicker. The bad omens of the previous night proved only too true. The horse had thrown the boy and had kicked his head to pieces.

The effect of this calamity on the "punchers" is strange. All are reticent and act as if they were greatly provoked. The innocent horses have to take it. The roping in the "corral" is harsh and cruel—the "cinchs" are pulled and buckled with a fiendish ferocity, and as each rider mounts he digs his horse with his spurs and uses his quirt relentlessly until the horse actually squeals.

The horse herd has been taken out around the point of "Cheyenne Look Out." The punchers are standing around in groups, talking, or rather mumbling. A faint shot is heard from the direction of the horse herd; all seem to know what has happened as if it had all been prearranged. The "outlaw" horse had been shot; even the owner, who was then in camp, hardly raised his head. In pairs the cowpunchers silently rode away to start their work for the day.

The victim's body was strapped to a "gentle" horse and was led away by the owner.

I expect tonight will develop all points of detail as to how the boy was killed where he was found. I am anxiously waiting to hear the detailed accounts, which I think will develop some very dramatic descriptions.

There has been a high wind and cold at that. The skies are clear as crystal.

Dutch Lou, Date and Tug Simpson related in a very few words the circumstances that led up to the finding of Harry Ziddle's body. Date spoke—

"The moon was shinin' like it was day.—God it was sure bright. We loped up 'Hash Knife' trail 'till we got to 'Big Beaver,' then Andy and Chub swung north onto 'Deer Trail' and we fellers followed out the 'Hash Knife.'" Here was a long pause to relight pipes; all was absolutely silent with the exception of a few muttered curses from the intent listeners.

"Of a sudden Tug wheeled—he seen a hat. By God and it was Harry's; not fifty yds. further a wooden stump and right 'long side—Harry—That's how we found him—."

No one made a single comment, and as the fire slowly died the "punchers" dispersed one by one to their blankets.

All were up at sunrise, the horse herd swung in at the same time, the same pounding of many feet, the whistling of ropes shooting through the dusty air and in ten minutes the camp was deserted save the cook.

Went on the circle—started 6:30, returned 11:30 off to the bunch, 12:30 returned at dark—chapped everybody in the crowd but me. Lord help me tomorrow night.

Started out 6 in the morning and rode till 12:30.

Had bad time with 300 cattle going through Rattlesnake Gulch.

Gill put up exciting performance with "bucking horse" this noon. He's sure a rider. Cut cattle all afternoon—built big fire out of cotton wood logs in the evening, but "turned in" early. It was no use because five of the boys dragged me from my warm blankets and gave me a tremendous drubbing with a pair of hard leather "chaps."

My hide was so sore that I slept little—I also had a bad foot—the result of a kick received from a horse.

[Diary, *October 14, 1904*]

Middlemist creek water made all sick—left for the "Hash Knife" after mail—a forty-mile ride and with a sore foot 'twas not pleasant—no mail there so continued on to Gill's 15 miles further—still no mail so on to Linden 25 miles further—80 miles in 12 hours and I felt sore.

[Diary, *October 18, 1904*]

Foot worse but had to ride about 10 mile circle for Gill's horses. Had to cook big supper for four men (4 insurance agents). They and Gill talked all night, I slept. Insurance agents didn't leave until noon of Oct. 16, then Gill and I left for "Scotty's"—52 miles. Reached there at sundown after trouble getting through the "Big Beaver."

Mrs: Robinson bathed my foot and said I had broken a bone in it—she worked over it about an hour, which helped it mightily. Bought an old time saddle and left with "Bob" the boy for Agate, Oct. 17, left Agate 11 P.M. for Denver. I look almighty shoddy, but it can't be helped.

[Diary, undated]

The time between Oct.18–Nov. 6 was spent in Denver, Colo.

There I rented room 626 in the Charles Bldg., Corn. 15th & Curtis. Completed four pictures.

103

Denver, Colorado
October 19, 1904

Dear Mama,

Well here I am in *Denver,* back from the "Roundup." I have spent the wildest and most strenuous three weeks in my life. Everything happened that could happen, plenty to satisfy the most imaginative. The "horse pitching" and "bucking" was bounteous. This was because the horse herd consisted mostly of colts—something unusual. The spills and mishaps were numerous and fierce and one very dramatic thing happened which I shall make use of and that was the death of one of the cowboys. He was thrown and kicked to pieces. The circumstances connected with this incident were most weird. This story I shall relate to you when I come home Xmas.

For 9 days I was in the saddle from 5:30 in the morning until dark, with a half hour taken out for noon "chuck." It is a steady strain on a fellow's physical endurance and not only that, but it keeps his nerve and grit in constant use to their limit. Nevertheless it's a grand training, well worth all the privations and hardships. I only wish I had such a training when I was younger. I find that I have the physical end of it, but my nerve and grit foil me at certain times. I've done things these last few weeks that I'd never dreamed I could have accomplished, but when the example is set by 20 or 30 reckless, half-wild men the same spirit is bound to catch all.

I was never as well in body and mind as I am at present and I feel just like work. I have enjoyed a big room in one of Denver's buildings for a studio in which I am going to live and paint for a month or so. I have subjects enough to paint and they might keep me busy for some time.

My future plans are then to go to the Navaho Reservation and live with the Indians. This Reservation is in the South so will have warm weather. We had hot weather on the plains, with only one rain. Today we had a snowstorm and quite a good one too.

I saved all the rattles off of rattlesnakes I have killed and have fifty-two.

104

Denver, Colorado
October 22, 1904. Saturday

Dear Mama,

Today I went to a big "Bronco Busting" contest, which of course was fine. I got into the arena amongst the riders by telling the manager I was to "write it up."

One of the features of the afternoon was a Negro who threw a *wild steer* with his <u>teeth</u>. It's a fact! The man, or animal is more like it, is built like an ox. Enormous shoulders and a terrifying face.

He gets on a horse and dashes after the steer, throwing himself off the horse onto the steer going at full speed. He then, after a terrific struggle, succeeds in sinking his teeth in the poor steer's nostrils and with a powerful wrench hurls the brute to the ground. The scene is brutal and seems almost superhuman. It arouses the audience into the highest pitch of wild excitement. With all this do you wonder how I can sleep? Such is the life here.

I have started and nearly completed my first picture. I was afraid after so long away from a brush that I'd lost my grip, but I have improved in my color from the rest. The subject is "Roping in the Horal Corral."

I have thus far got a good bit of cowpuncher costume and wish you could see me in my angora chaps on a bronc. You wouldn't know me.

105

Denver, Colorado
October 27, 1904

Dear Mama,

Well I'm hard at it and am having, I dare to think, fairly good luck with my work. I have already completed two big paintings and am on with the third. Upon completion of the fourth I'll hie myself to the Navaho Reservation where I will spend the remainder of my time, probably until the 18th of Dec., then home!

Thus far I proclaim the trip a *success*. The experience I have gained has been enormous and covers a good deal of ground. I am perfectly well, the only mishap being a broken foot. Was kicked by a horse the last day of the "roundup" and have now discarded the "crutch." I can paint now, thank goodness, standing up. Thanks to a tight riding boot and spur strap, my foot was not deformed, although it started to knit before I reached surgical aid.

106

Denver, Colorado
October 29, 1904

[To Allie Leonard of Needham, Massachusetts]
Dear Al,

This country is wonderful, Al, and to suit *you* it is chock-full of game. Even I, my own self, succeeded in dropping an antelope. I have the pretty little feet as a remembrance of that sparkling and crisp morning when the shadows of our horses were still long and thin, and of the crack of the 45–90 Winchester, which sounded muffled and dim on that broad expanse of plains. How white the throats of that bunch of six antelope looked against the brown prairie, and the way they all but one "lined" it off until they were mere specks against the horizon. 'Twas a happy and proud tenderfoot that slung that fresh meat over his saddlehorn, I can tell you.

The above is a mere incident that happened between times. To explain all, I worked for the "Hash Knife" outfit. I had fully intended to sketch, that is accompanying the outfit as a guest, and watch the proceedings from the "grub wagon" so to speak, but on reaching that country and finding that it was an easy matter for me to obtain my "string of horses" (each man has to have six or seven horses), I decided to bust right into the work of the cowpuncher. It took all my earnings, $8 per week, to pay for the horses, so I came out even financially, but the experience and knowledge I have gained of that particular life is unlimited in value to me.

Everything happened in the way of excitement on that roundup that possibly could, it seems. A stampede (very unusual these days) in which one of the cowpunchers was killed (thrown from his horse and got hung in the stirrup and had his head kicked to pieces), and numerous spills, in which I participated in one of the worst, but escaped unhurt except my wind knocked out. Otherwise all went well until the last morning of the roundup. I was in the corral trying to rope one of my mounts when a d——d pinto pony kicked me in the ankle. I could hardly walk on it and when I reached the home ranch found that I had broken a bone in my instep.

Oh! I was going to close, but I had an experience yesterday that I must relate and one that really inspired me to write to you. I took a trip from here into the foothills of the Rockies (which are really mountains) to a little mining town named Golden. Upon reaching there by railroad I could not resist the temptation to take a short walk up into the mountains. I had nothing with me but my sweater as extra protection and after five hours of steady climb, reached the top of one of the lower foothills. It was actually *hot* when I left the little town in the valley, but upon reaching the first heights I immediately put on my sweater. Well, I gazed onto the next mountain and that was covered with timber—the one upon which I was [had] nothing but rock, rattlesnakes and soapweed, and near the top it was white with snow.

The sight immediately brought back the two weeks of paradise you and I spent in dear old New Hampshire. It made me think of those mountains we tramped over, of the frozen brooks, the dense firs, the cracking of the cold and the ring of our guns that so often echoed through the woods in vain. Yes, those few thoughts of the past actually drove me, against my wishes, on to mount that next gigantic mound and experience once more that pleasure of climbing up a snowy hillside, and I did. I had my Colt 41 so tried a number of shots, but without success, at coyotes and one wild cat. From below the timber looked not unlike that which we went through, but lo and behold! when I reached it they were enormous pines, seventy-five to a hundred feet high and scattered a hundred feet apart. Well, I reached about two-thirds the way up and saw the sun was getting dangerously low, so hurriedly retreated. But it was dark in no time and I can tell you I had reached the regular trail, so felt safe to a certain extent, but it was almighty cold and I did not care to spend the night there.

Well, d——d if I didn't meet a man way up in that God-forsaken place making his way to a small timber camp of his. I was of course invited to share his comforts such as he had and then I spent the night. It was sure cold as we had a hard enough time keeping warm in the cabin. I left the old woodsman a sketch of his "shack," which seemed to please him and now I'm here again in my studio.

107

Denver, Colorado
October 29, 1904

Dear Mama,

Talking about a snapshot. Of course, on the plains I was the only one that could manipulate the camera so I'm in none of the pictures but one, and that's not much account. But about four days ago a photographer I met up to the "Busting Contest" got interested in my work and, knowing that I had a good "outfit," came down to the studio and took a couple of photos of me in the rig I wore on the plains. He posed me so I'm afraid they will look a little affected.

N. C. Wyeth "... a little affected."

108

Denver, Colorado
November 3, 1904

Dear Papa,

Well, this is on the eve of my departure for the "lonely lands"—
the land of the Utes and Navahos. For a little over two weeks I have
enjoyed painting as I never did before. I was "chuck-full" of genuine

eagerness and enthusiasm to paint, and I think the results show it. I think the four pictures, which are now completed, show an advancement over my other work even though they are among the first full-color subjects I ever painted.

Of course the color in the West is magnificent and cannot be touched with paint and brush. I have made every effort to get all the brilliancy of the country without exaggerating. Mr. Pyle will no doubt give me good crits that will pull me out of my difficulties.

I have had a great many cattlemen and cowpunchers for critics, and I'll tell you they helped a great deal. My pictures, I can vouch now, are authentic and true to life. Nobody can call me up on that part of it although technically and in color they might be bad. My subjects have been:

1. "Roping Horses in the Corral"
2. "A Bucking Horse in Camp" (Billy Hill)
3. "On the Circle" (driving cattle through a gulch)
4. "Around the Grub Wagon" (evening effect)

[Diary, *November 5, 1904*]

Steiner took them [the pictures] and is to exhibit them for two or three weeks—promises me a write-up.

[Diary, undated]

Nov. 6th left Denver for Durango. Reached the latter place the evening of Nov. 7th after marvelous ride through the Rockies.

Made arrangements same evening to take stage to Farmington—about 70 miles. Great excitement over election.

See my first Indians in the native country.

109

Durango, Colorado
November 7, 1904

Dear Mama,

Thank goodness! I have struck one more P.O. and will make use of it by dropping you a line. En route I had to go through a big part of New Mexico. Tomorrow I take the stage for Arizona to the Navaho Reservation. There I shall make my headquarters with "Navaho Bill," an old Post trader. I have to go about 40 miles in the stage and the rest of the way alone on horseback.

Durango is a little mining town located in the heart of the tremendous and awe-inspiring Rockies. It all appears like a dream. It is election night and one street is crowded with miners, cowpunchers, and stealing around amongst these men, like cats crouched beneath large gaudy blankets with their feathered heads sticking out of the top, are hundreds of Indians. They are as silent as foxes, wearing beaded moccasins and dangling from the right hand usually is a quirt all colored and decorated. It is all wonderful to me and I'm so anxious to get out on the street again amongst them, I can't write.

"See my first Indians in the native country."

I've got to make arrangements with the stage now, so good night and good-by till Xmas.

The WYETHS

[Diary, *November 8, 1904*]

Start 7 P.M. for Farmington. Sit on a box with the driver—change horses twice. Reached Farmington 8 o'clock the same night after tedious journey.

Pass through many small villages of Mexicans and a few Indians. Lots of goats. Follow the Rio Los Animos bottom all the way.

Great excitement at Farmington over election returns. Stop at Allen's Hotel and arrange with him to drive me to Simpson's—30 miles into the desert.

Nov. 9th ford the Rio San Juan with great difficulty.

Allen relates many early experiences, "Punchin' Cattle" in Texas —"B.F. Springs."

Reach Simpson's Trading Post 1:30, Nov. 9th.

Very cordial welcome.

Meet the noted "Navaho Bill." Spend the afternoon watching the Navahos trade. They give me a mud hut all by myself. Fine fireplace, lots of Navaho blankets and good bed—well fixed. Nov. 9th bum around the post watching Indians—taking photos, sketch, etc., pull sheep.

[Diary, *November 10, 1904. Friday*]

Make sketch—watch Indians chop wood all afternoon.

[Diary, *November 11, 1904*]

Make five studies from Indians. Ride 8 miles to Navaho "Hogan" and sketch Indian blanket weaver—unload four tons of hay in the afternoon and arrange with an old Indian to buy a horse. Am planning a three-week trip cross-country into the Reservation.

[Diary, *November 12, 1904. Saturday*]

Made color study in the morning—bought three ponies and sold them again making $5.00—unloaded big load of produce.

Slept in Hogan with 5 Indians. Gambled until two o'clock. Lost $5.50. Ate horsemeat for first time. Slept well until 6:30.

Trip West

Canon Gallegos, New Mexico
November 13, 1904. Sunday

Dear Mama and Papa,

It seems as if I were in another world, stranded from all my friends and relatives, although I have *staunch* friends here. It seems as if I were stranded here, in a strange land amongst a more strange people. And to speak plain I *am* strange.

This morning I awoke a poor man. All I have in "this" world now is my horse, saddle and bridle (and these are good) and a few sketching materials and my camera.

Last night I slept in a Navaho "Hogan" (a mud hut) with a dozen or more Indians. "We" gambled until 2 A.M. during which I lost $2.00. From 2 until 6 I slept soundly. A day previous (for *safety*) I deposited at a nearby government post, 22 miles (at Muddy Springs, N. M.), all I had with me, and as luck would have it a bunch of Mexicans on the night of the 10th bound and gagged the "Trader" and "cleaned out" all the cash, including mine, taking a total of $350 to $400. I am over [number missing] miles from any railroad with but one horse, so you can see I *am* stranded.

Now *don't* worry. I'm out for the experience and it's sure coming my way. Nobody from Needham can help me because it would be *foolish* to forward money. I would never get it. The country is full of thieves.

Inside of an hour I start with a posse in a hunt for these damned Mexicans. It is no doubt useless, but the "Trader" (a Mr. Taylor) is much wrought up (so am I for that matter) and is bound to proceed. We will have two Indian guides besides three or four of us.

I expect to return to this post inside of two weeks. There is a position now open for a mail carrier and messenger to ply between Muddy Springs and Fort Defiance, Arizona, on horseback, a distance of 85 miles, and I have got it. In that way I'll earn my way out of the country. I'll also sell my camera when I have used all my film.

Luckily I have a return ticket from Durango to Denver and also one on the stage from Farmington to Durango. Look on a map and I think you can place me.

The loss of my money will be a great drawback in the matter of collecting costumes. I'll pick up all I can anyway by trading, etc.

This is where I am writing now, my eyes are full of smoke but it's *very* warm. This morning it was about zero but you wouldn't know it, the air is so dry. I have eaten "horsemeat" for three days and thrive on it.

This country is as desolate and wild as it *ever* was. The Indians are very hospitable and perfectly harmless nevertheless.

There is one thing—I can't get Indian photos very well. They have a superstition about a photo that makes it a serious matter to

Interior of a hogan.

take one. For instance, the first one I took from the observation car on the way to Durango. We stopped at the Ute–Apache Reservation station and a group were at work nearby. I took a "snap" and "by gorry" I was scared for a minute. They surrounded the car, talking and gesticulating in the wildest manner, every now and then cursing in "American." It was so cold that I was the only one on the Observation Platform and felt a little uneasy, I can tell you, but in a very few minutes they quieted down and went back to their work. I'll have a photo taken of myself and outfit on the mail trail.

I have had very little time to sketch although I have made 8 or 10 Indian heads in pencil and a couple in color. The only thing I can do now is to keep my eyes and ears open, and *one* rule that is well to follow (Keep your mouth shut). That I have found is absolutely essential in this part of the world. I don't believe I have spoken fifty words a day since I've been here. With the Indians it's all sign language and there is very little talk among the whites. One who talks is not liked.

An Indian is to take this letter with a sack full of others about 128 miles to Farmington, N. Mexico.

117

The WYETHS

[Diary, *November 13, 1904. Sunday*]

At last, a calamity! Mexicans (about five) raided Muddy Springs Post and stole over $500, including $85 of my own money—great excitement—scores of Indians around ready for the manhunt.

10:30 A.M. Arranged to go with two men and an Indian guide to trail Mexicans—started 10:50 after hearty meal. Borrowed 30:30 Winchester from Cambell (surveyor).

Struck Mexicans trail at noon.—Dinner of cold beef and coffee.

Lose trail in Rio San Juan—windy.

Reach village of Navahos 7:30—cold and tired—sleep poorly. (8:30 same night)

Had hard day—went without dinner and returned to Nav-Hogans sundown—no success. Talk of giving up hunt, hoping two parties had better luck.

[Diary, *November 16, 1904. Wednesday, 12* P.M.]

Hunted for Mexicans until sundown with no success. Reached Muddy Springs Trading Post 10:30 P.M. after intensely cold ride—bright moon.

[Diary, *November 17, 1904. Thursday, 4:30* A.M.]

Luckily I own my outfit, including fairly good horse. Will be able to earn $1.25 a day above horsefeed—as mail carrier and messenger between Fort Defiance and Reitz's Trading Post (Two Gray Hills). Distance about 100 miles to be covered every three days. Will have to sell camera.

Will start on trip today.

[Diary, *November 17, 1904. Later*]

Started 6:30 A.M. with Indian Guide for Reitz's Trading Post—was told I could make the trip before sundown, but instead of the distance being 50 miles, it proved to be from 72 to 75. Slept in an Indian Village (4 Hogans) so almighty crowded and buggy that I decided to sleep outside. Had only a sweater and saddle blanket. Slept until one o'clock—then built a fire which I kept going until sunrise. Terribly cold. Had ½ pound of crackers. Small can of veal loaf and four apples to last for four meals. Traded a pocket knife for red Navaho garters.

Ate very hearty when I reached the post.

[Diary, *November 18, 1904*]

Started about half hour after sunrise and completed journey about one o'clock. Was never so glad in my life to see white people.

Start for Fort Defiance in the morning.

Almighty tired and a little sore.

Traded during the day a blue flannel shirt for a blanket, also a red silk bandana for 3 goatskins and one sheepskin. Have not pawned or sold camera yet. Expect to pawn camera later.

[Diary, *November 19, 1904*]

Horse too tired, so lay over until Monday morning. Freight for Reitz from Joe Wilkes 14 miles—two loads of flour.

[Diary, *November 20, 1904. Sunday*]

The first day of rest for a long while—do nothing but sleep and eat. Take a few pictures.

[Diary, *November 21, 1904*]

Start 6:30. At 1:30 P.M. complete 35-mile ride to Moore's Trading Post. Reach Ft. Defiance 8:50 after a hard, tedious ride.

John B. Moore's Trading Post, 24 miles from Ft. Defiance, is on the line between New Mexico and Arizona in the foothills and within a mile from the Churchill Range. Good water and lots of grass. Good buildings. Big store, well stocked. P. O. Crystal, New Mexico. Horse is tender-footed behind, and will have him shod tomorrow here at the fort.

To keep their long hair from falling over their faces, the Navahos often tied a scarf, called a bandy, around their foreheads.

[Diary, *November 22, 1904*]

Back to the Two Gray Hills—52 miles. Picked up saddlebags, bandy and old robe. Expect old saddle trade for pocket knife.

[Diary, *November 23, 1904*]

Back today to Fort Defiance. Made new friends. Bought photos to be paid for upon my return to Denver.

[Diary, *November 24, 1904. Thursday, Thanksgiving*]

Hard ride to the Two Gray Hills. Cold as hell.

The WYETHS

[Diary, *November 25, 1904. Friday*]

Nothing eventful happened. Make trip back to Ft. Defiance with new horse.

[Diary, *November 26, 1904. Saturday*]

Back to Two Gray Hills.

[Diary, *November 27, 1904. Sunday*]

Again to Fort Defiance (heavy mail).

[Diary, *November 28, 1904. Monday*]

Heavy wind and lots of sand blowing. Takes two hours longer than usual to Two Gray Hills.

[Diary, *November 29, 1904. Tuesday*]

Again to Ft. Defiance—expect to give up job in a couple of days. Have saved 8 dollars which I expect to invest with returns from horse sale in Indian costume and a few blankets.

III

Old Fort Defiance, Arizona
November 29, 1904

My dear Mama and Papa,

Thank goodness! I can and will arrange to be home Xmas if nothing radical turns up.

Start for Two Gray Hills, New Mexico in a few minutes with mail—about fifty miles. Have made the trip seven times. Hard life! but it seems to agree with me.

[Diary, *November 30, 1904. Wednesday*]

Back to Joe Reitz's.

Have bought two blankets and two quirts for $3.

Have my eye on two others, also a string of beads. Found an old bandy.

[Diary, *December 1, 1904. Thursday*]

Once again I struck the trail and I vow that one more round trip will conclude my weary travels in these damned sand hills! Very heavy mail for tomorrow and it looks like a storm.

[Diary, *December 2, 1904. Friday night*]

Sure enough a drizzling rain and almighty cold. Took cold yesterday.

[Diary, *December 3, 1904. Saturday*]

My last trip! Thank God.—But now for a hard 120 mile ride back to Simpson's—Canyon Gallgos.

Heavy snow and the trail almighty dim. Drifting badly.

[Diary, *December 4, 1904. Sunday*]

Reached Reitz's about 10 P.M. after very hard trip for the horse. Will start tomorrow for Simpson's. Can luckily make camp with a surveyor's outfit at the Choco Canyon.

[Diary, *December 5, 1904. Monday, Ed's birthday*]

Slept fine with Phelps Dodge R.R. outfit after hard trip. Horse played out. Met Winningsted (Old Canadian Pacific surveying engineer). Gave me good material.—Hope to start early and hope to at last complete my journeys across this desert.

112

Muddy Springs, Arizona
December 14, 1904

My dear Mother,

December fourteenth!—that glorious day!—What a pleasure it was to turn my face homeward, to follow once more and for the last time the winding trail that disappeared in the blinding rays of the *eastern sun*. What unbounded joy it was to know that in a comparatively short time I would be with my people again in my own dear home.

Instantaneously I felt reluctant to leave those brutal and rugged mountains, the dry, scorching plains, to abandon for good that long dim trail that lay over the sandy desert like some big lazy snake asleep in the sun.

How I hated to leave those Indians and how I shall miss the many long silent evenings spent with them in their "hogans," seated around a flaring pile of crackling piñon listening to the low plaintive moan of the wind as it swirled down the canyon.

The life is wonderful, strange—the fascination of it clutches me like some unseen animal—it seems to whisper, "Come back, you belong here, this is your real home."

N. C. Wyeth on the trail.

Chapter VI

MARRIAGE

*"I shall stand by this girl my life throughout,
and nobody can ever stop me."*

113

Wilmington, Delaware
December 29, 1904

Dear Mama,

Back again at the old stand! Ready to "butt in" with the ferocity of a tiger after a most delicious and "scathing" criticism. Never mind he. has set me on the right track and tomorrow I'm off! Clear the road!!

He liked much the picture "Driving Cattle through the Gulch" and not quite so well the scene around the campfire. The others are too much "Remington," he claims. He has already started me on my writing "A Day with the Roundup"—good subject and I think I can do it.

The same old place and even now as though I had never been on the trip as far as time is concerned.

114

Wilmington, Delaware
January 1, 1905

Dear Mama,

Last night I went out to dinner—to the Bockiuses'—and saw the old year out. We fired a large brass cannon at 12 sharp and it blew to pieces, miraculously doing no damage. They make a great deal of New Year's here and the noise all night resembled not a little the Fourth.

Not many of the fellows are here as yet but probably will pile in tomorrow. I'm up for composition for tomorrow night and if I don't make a hit, it's all up with me.

Phoebe Pyle [Howard Pyle's daughter] is back "just for Xmas," so they say. She got fat while in Europe. Mr. Pyle makes a fool of himself over her, I think. Society has certainly got him by the pants.

Wilmington, Delaware
January 9, 1905

Dear Mama,

I have been floundering around in my writing, and don't know whether I've done anything or not, which is extremely unsatisfactory, and Friday my "properties" came and those set me wild —again. They are better than I had anticipated.

H.P. has not seen them yet but expect to show them to him to-morrow.

Today True and I spent the biggest part of the day fixin' up the studio and I'll tell you it looks grand. To stick in a room *now* and write is an utter impossibility. I'd like to "wallow" around in the Indian blankets, saddles and cowpuncher outfit all the time; they still smell of smoke, of alkali, and horse just enough to set me wild.

Alan True and N. C. Wyeth in their studio.

By the above "ecstasies" don't think I meditate another trip, for I say no! I want money now and I'm going to knuckle right down and get rich(?) no, but seriously speaking, it's the "devil" to feel broke, to have to depend on somebody else. I owe Papa almost $500 and nobody else. How happy I'll be when that is paid off. It means only about 5 pictures—*whoop!*

I'll knock hell out of everybody down here when I get started 'cause I *can* do it and *will*. Just wait till I get on my fat —. A studio by myself is all I want, then I can thrash 'round, cuss and yell to my heart's content. I'm chuck-full of everything now but money. Great health, good ideas and stuffed with enthusiasm. It's my whole life now to show you, Papa and my own brothers what I can and will do.

Winter? None here—just like early spring—March. I am invited out to dinner next Sat. evening, very formal.—I'm goin' to bust it up—even if I lose my "social standing."—I can bust anything now.

116

Wilmington, Delaware
January 15, 1905

Dear Papa,

I blame **Mr. Pyle** a good deal for my wild state of mind this last week or so, but I've acted somewhat independently, which has rather pleased him. Once more he shows in his interest in me that he has confidence of my future, which is the best and most wholesome encouragement he could give me.

It may seem peculiar that I have written to Mama, then to you, but I realize now that the letter to her must be rather wild and rattly so am trying to sandpaper the rough edges down with this one—I mailed hers previously.

117

Wilmington, Delaware
January 20, 1905

Dear Mama,

The skys are brightening, the light glow of success is gradually throwing its soft light on my path. May it continue.

After Frank [Schoonover] had written and sealed a letter to you

127

he kindly told me all about the letter you wrote him. I'm glad you did—and I hope you can believe him if not me.

His answer to the question in regards to my relations to a certain young lady was right, perfectly right.

Now, Mama, *please* have faith in me—to be sure I am in love with Miss Bockius, but I pride myself with a level head. I am no fool. Do you think for a minute I would do anything rash? What can you expect? Here I am down here, I am 22 years old. I am working just as hard as God will allow me, I do *no* running 'round as do some—my mind is well centered on my work and plenty of that to do. Here is a young lady of great sensibility—of inspiring thought, one strongly appreciative of art, of nature and in many ways of my mind. She has taken a sincere interest in me and my work and it helps me to accomplish what I hope to do for *you,* for *Papa,* for my *brothers.*

Carolyn Bockius at the time of her engagement.

I shall stand by this girl my life throughout, and nobody can ever stop me. Over a year ago I met her and as to success? Last year was not very bad was it?

I'm not going to write much to you in regards to this matter, only a few facts, but you may trust that I am cool and have my head—you may think me rather deliberate.

This summer you have got to come down, you and Papa if possible. I have lots to show you and can keep you interested a week surely. Mr. Pyle intends to go to Europe so you want to come before he goes. He'll probably go in late summer.

118

Wilmington, Delaware
January 20, 1905

Dear Papa,

I was mighty glad to have received a letter from home.—I have been neglected, I can see, as a matter of punishment, and it *has* been punishment. Nobody has written for over a week and I feel the loss terribly.

119

Wilmington, Delaware
January 22, 1905

Dear Nat,

I have come to the conclusion that I shall never be satisfied—my mind is ever bent on the life other than that in which I am living. When in the trackless wilds of the plains I was thinking of home, of you, of all my home people. But when I got back I dreamed of the "Indian," the "Puncher" and their homes, their country. And so it is—now, ever restless, uneasy. But I *will* control myself.

I am afraid I am selfish. I love my art better than anything, anyone else in the world, but there is where it is unfortunate to be an artist. It is a sacrifice for the sake of art, but at times I feel guilty, downright guilty.

Why do I leave home two or three days before the time set every visit? It is to get back at my easel, to mingle again with my fellow workers. It is something I shall never overcome, I know. To one who loves his home as I do it is the single *curse,* if I may so express it, of the profession.

Mama told me of your toboggan—it set me wild. How I enjoyed those few crazy trails on Stimson's skis. A sport so tame in comparison to the life I had just left, but it thrills me through when I recall those vigorous tumbles in that keen air, the freedom and the fervent unrestrained yells.—I'd like to die under such conditions.

When you have anything you think would be of interest to me, write me. I'm always looking with intense interest and hunger for little glimpses of the life at *home.*

Now this P.S. keep to yourself—it is rather a graphic description of yesterday's (Sunday) doin's.

The crust is like glare ice but rather billowy and skis on such a surface are rather hard to manage. Well, Schoonover, Ashley, Arthurs and myself went out in the country to slide down Penny Hill (a long steep one). Well, there was a crowd there, and when they spotted the skis they all became very much interested.

It was up to me to coast—and I did. At first trying the less steep places, growing bolder and bolder although every time taking a worse tumble. At last I tried the steep place. I got down to the cart path safely but there my skis crossed and I dove through the air about 15 or 16 feet by *actual* measurement and what's worse have broken a ligament in my right shoulder. I can control my hand but cannot in any way control my arm. I have to lift my arm around like a piece of wood.

120

Wilmington, Delaware
March 3, 1905. Friday, 6:30 P.M.

Dear Mama,

Tomorrow is inauguration day [Theodore Roosevelt] and I have just decided to see it. [Harvey T.] Dunn and I have arranged to go on the 12:50 tonight (round trip $3.50) and have sworn by oath not to spend a cent more. We have a haversack packed with canned beef and crackers and will carry blankets and sleep out of doors if we decide to stay Sunday. I thought like this—I'm so near Washington it would be a pity to miss such a sight. Five hundred Indians in the parade, lots of cowpunchers, Filipinos, scouts, etc.—a grand sight!

121

Wilmington, Delaware
March 6, 1905

Dear Mama,

I thought at first we were fools but I find that the thousands of people we bluffed in Washington were the "fools."

Friday night Dunn and I came to the conclusion to don "cowpuncher" togs and "do" Washington, so 10 minutes after our decision we were off. Upon reaching Washington we immediately searched out Headquarters of the 125 cowboys who were going to parade. We found them in the "Metropolitan" Hotel on Penn. Ave. and "butted in." They were extremely cordial and learning that we were way from New Mexico and South Dakota immediately dispatched orders to save two "mounts" for us. The result was that Dunn and I were in the "Inaugural Parade" and were enthusiastically cheered by the million-and-a-half people. Not only that, but we were treated to a big dinner and were invited to the reception of Roosevelt, but that was impossible owing to the only thing that blighted the day. Dunn's horse, while rounding the sharp corner near the White House, slipped and fell on him so that he could not walk on the foot at all, and again we thought that the crowd might wax reminiscent and that would be liable to expose us. So right after the parade we "light out" for home, tired but heartily satisfied.

The inauguration of Roosevelt I shall never forget. What fools some mortals are!

122

[Postcard to his mother]
St. Georges, Delaware
March 14, 1905

Just for the sake of diversion, Peck and I have "set out" across country. We are now following the towpath along the canal into Maryland. A two-day trip—fine weather—quaint towns—exceedingly fine trip thus far. Will drop postals along the way—headed for the Chesapeake Bay.

123

Wilmington, Delaware
April 21, 1905

Dear Mama,

Last Saturday night our studio was *looted* and some $75 or $80 worth of stuff was taken in the way of properties and, as it happened, all but one article was mine. After a vigorous and tedious hunt we finally located the stolen goods in a "pawn shop." The thief is still at large however.

The unpleasant part was that I had three different fellows arrested on suspicion but they all provided an alibi. The consequence was that I had a hand-to-hand encounter with one of the fellows, but thanks to a fortunate blow, succeeded in "vanquishing" him.

On the other hand I have successfully completed my *Harper's* work and will deliver them Tuesday, having delivered another *Post* story yesterday for which they paid me well and with another story to do.

My Western pictures I shall at once tackle and by May 5th shall be home. I intended to have them done in time to take to N.Y. with the *Harper's* stuff but am having some trouble with the "corral" picture so shall return from N.Y. Tuesday night and finish it, as I said, by May 5th.

To see me flying around you wouldn't think I was the same lazy lump that I was at home. It's great to be busy.

124

Studio
No. 1305 Franklin St.
Wilmington, Delaware
May 5, 1905

Dear Mama,

Harper's sent me another story (Western). You can't imagine what satisfaction that gives me.

Studio
Wilmington, Delaware
May 18, 1905

Dear Mama,

Reached Wilmington in time for the lecture, just. Yesterday morning I got to work on the *Harper's* story and have nearly finished my first picture.

As luck would have it I've had the studio all alone as both True and Oakley are in N.Y. My, but it's just heaven! Mr. Pyle opened up today in his old-style way of talking and it was like a breath of cool, fresh air on a hot desert.

126

Wilmington, Delaware
May 22, 1905

Dear Mama,

Today Miss Bockius and I spent the day in the country. I packed the grub and cooking utensils and we ate dinner and supper in the woods. Had a most enjoyable day.

127

Wilmington, Delaware
May 26, 1905

Dear Mama,

Now for startling news!

There is quite a shake-up down here amongst the fellows in regards to location for the winter's work, the result of which is that Schoonover, Arthurs, True, Oakley and I have to get out and it is to our great advantage. A Mr. [Joseph] Bancroft, a wealthy manufacturer of this city, is going to build four new studios for us on a most desirable location. Swiss Chateau style with glass house attached for sunlight painting, shower, bath and numerous improvements. It is going to cost him considerable but being a strong patron of art (American) he is much interested in our welfare, thus his generosity. Tonight decides whether he is cocksure of doing it and 'tis hard for me to wait an answer.

Schoonover takes one, Arthurs another, Ashley and Peck the third, and True and I the fourth. True will not stay over a year, probably, so eventually I shall have the studio which just suits me. Oakley moves to Phil. and has his studio there; so much for him and I wish him luck.

128

Wilmington, Delaware
May 30, 1905

My dear brothers,

Another year shot to pieces! and four quarts of good ice cream I'll bet!

Three cheers! ! ! ——! ——! ———!

Edwin, N. C., Stimson and Nat.

134

Above you have the portraits of the "Big Four"—in size at least, and may it be that someday our achievements become equally as great. That someday we shall rise up and above *all* classes and that the competition for supremacy be between us alone.

Now to you, Nat and Stimson, I extend my heartiest wishes for your success, and may you both retain your good health of mind and body, and with these pitted against this mighty world *win out* mid deafening applause.

129

Wilmington, Delaware
June 9, 1905

Dear Mama,

My eyes are now *perfect,* thank goodness! Tomorrow morning I'm going down to see that fool *Elligood,* the man that nigh ruined my eyesight and cut a goodly hunk out of my pocket book. I was eventually treated by Dr. R.S. Moon of Philadelphia. His prices were good but his treatment better. But how fine it is to see! Why I was actually blind before. I don't wonder my pictures have always lacked finish.

Sunday Miss Bockius and myself came down from the "Ford" in my canoe, which I recently repitched and tarred to *my* great approval. I make it a point to spend every Sunday in this out-of-door recreation, usually with "Miss Bockius," and find that it helps me through the entire week.

Again I am hearing very favorable comments upon my work from Mr. Pyle, I am happy to say. I feel that to regain his confidence is to win a double victory.

130

Wilmington, Delaware
June 13, 1905

Dear Mama,

I could hardly believe the words in your letter of today concerning a proposed trip to Wilmington—just think, you and Papa. Well, I'm just thrilled to death and to me it will be the event of the year!

I have told Mrs. Swayne and she is ready for you. I have not told Mr. Pyle of your coming yet but will tomorrow.

135

The WYETHS

Of course I want you and Papa to meet Miss Bockius and her mother. I know you shall like her. She's a very timid girl and rather shy, thank heaven, so don't be hard on her. I told her you were very critical. Wasn't I right?

I shall arrange one day for a trip in a carriage out through the "Ford" and that surrounding country. It will please both you and Papa; you by the quaint romantic atmosphere that hovers about it, and Papa by its picturesque farmlands and fertile valleys.

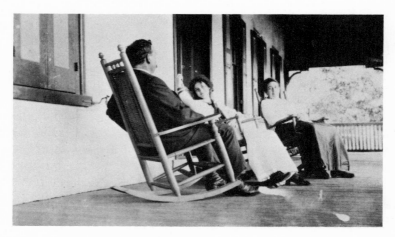

Mr. Wyeth, Miss Bockius and Mrs. Wyeth at the Chadds Ford Hotel.

131

Wilmington, Delaware
June 21, 1905

Dear Papa,

Well I hope you reached home safe and sound, no worse for the trip. I got back in due season for the lecture and found it had been postponed so am glad we made no arrangements to take that in. My business call in N.Y. was a very successful one in regards to making pictures for art stores, and shall take it up on condition that Scribner's does not object.

Wilmington, Delaware
July 10, 1905

Dear Mama,

My *Post* drawings are off and a *Harper's* picture nigh completion unless some unexpected difficulty looms up. Today I worked
until this afternoon and then about 4 o'clock Miss Bockius and
myself went out in a buggy to "Mount Cuba." This little spot is
another diamond dropped in this part of the country. You approach it passing through wide rolling fields until of a sudden,
like a miniature "Pikes," a knob of a hill protrudes above the general level of the country. But your attention is soon drawn from
this fascinating "lookout" to a precipitous roadway that seems to
drop from beneath your horse's feet. The horse zig-zags his way
downward until you feel almost entombed in a sarcophagus of
hills and foliage; it seems actually dark.

Wedged in the bottommost corner of this valley still works an
old sawmill, and near to it a little red schoolhouse, and beyond a
grist mill—and what more could you want?

133

Wilmington, Delaware
July 14, 1905

Dear Mama,

Well—first thing—I want to know if you would be willing
to let Carolyn stay with you a week or so! She's got to go away
for a short time at least, and as all her relatives and friends are
either sick or in Europe she necessarily has to stay at home.

Her home is not one for her—there is too much turmoil, the
household is *not* harmonious, and she is very sympathetic and it
tells on her. She has to work hard and that keeps her in, and that
is just what she shouldn't do. Now I have mentioned this idea to
her and naturally she rebels, thinking it too forward, etc. But you
will enjoy her and she will cause no trouble at all; in fact she is
the easiest person in the world to get along with.

Now if this seems agreeable to you and you think it right, please
let me know or drop a few lines to Miss Bockius including a sort
of invitation. Say nothing of what I have said.

134

Wilmington, Delaware
July 23, 1905

Dear Mama,

To begin with I want first to thank you for so kindly an invitation to Miss Bockius. You don't know how I appreciate the fact. I know what it means for you to open your generous and ever-kind heart and take into your life another confidante—one, a stranger to you, but thrown into your path, as it were, by a son.

This congenial reception of yours coming to pass has melted away the one and only barrier I was at all doubtful about, and I can't thank you enough for it.

The girl has made me appreciate you, Papa and my home far more than ever before.

The poor girl is crazy to visit you and I *know* it will do her a wonderful amount of good in *every* way. She is one with her arms open to drink in all the good to be had, and is hungry for such a life and to mingle with the *real* people she most certainly will find "at home."

She is timid—but her mind is alert, and although she may seem rather backward to comprehend and moreso to put into immediate practice, she will store it in her head and shall make good use of it later.

Her character training has been superb but her practical training (except in money matters) has been somewhat slighted.

This "discourse" may seem rather strained and unnecessary but I feel as if I must say something.

She expects a great deal from my brothers for I have placed them all on the highest of pedestals, not for effect but because I <u>most</u> sincerely believe they are the best and <u>cleanest</u> and most high-minded set of brothers I ever saw, and I've seen and studied many.

135

Carolyn Bockius's first view of the Wyeth farm in Needham was from the Charles River. Nat Wyeth met the young couple in a canoe and paddled them down river to the landing at the Wyeths' property.

138

Marriage

Dear Mama,

Tomorrow we start at 6:30 A.M., so you'll see us about 5:30 tomorrow evening.

Oh! say, I want one of the boys to meet me down the river where it leaves the car track—you know, just before you go up Lynch's hill. I'll telephone from Boston the time we shall be there. It will be rather novel to come home that way.

Did I tell you Mr. Chapin has taken my pictures without even seeing them?

The boatlanding on the Charles River, where Miss Bockius arrived for her first visit to the Wyeths.

136

Wilmington, Delaware
August 6, 1905

Dear brother Nat,

Ah! Nat—it is late, yes very late, but I am bound to write you a few lines, because a little thing came to my notice just now that drives me to do it.

Just as I was sliding things back into my desk, stacking books and papers back into their places, I chanced to handle an old letter addressed to me in Stimson's handwriting. On the back of it were a few crude sketches of a pen representing a horse–a buggy–a trunk –two feet–rain. Even so roughly drawn, you haven't any idea what that little sketch meant to me. It brought back that little snatch of home-life that I so enjoyed around Xmas and it brought back keen, intensified pictures of you in your rough, wholesome dress, un- daunted by the cold and wet, cheerfully driving a brother and his trunk to the station, crowded into the top of the buggy, holding the slimy reins, spitting on roughened hands to relieve that dry grit that is so uncomfortable—oh! yes, I know, I remember every bit of the detail.

And how just this incident arouses and stirs my affections for home into white heat. How I would like to see you, talk with you, it would do my soul good.

Well, soon I shall—how soon I know not.

137

Wilmington, Delaware
August 8, 1905

Dear Mama,

You don't know what immeasurable pleasure and satisfaction it gives me to have her [Carolyn] up there with you all—it's *great,* and I'll tell you I appreciate it.

138

Despite the fact his fiancée was visiting his parents, N. C. Wyeth joined in on the yearly walking trip with his younger brothers to Ver- mont.

Marriage

Wilmington, Delaware
August 8, 1905

Dear Nat and Stimson,

Please measure exactly the length and width of your feet at the longest and widest parts, and send measurements to me. Anything you can suggest that I have forgotten—do so. The list I have made is sifted down to absolute necessities—trusting however (in which there is no doubt) that we vary our "menu" once in awhile with fish–frogs' legs, etc., I shall try and provide the blankets–ponchos (rubber blankets) and moccasins.

Also I shall invest (sh!) in a Stevens (32) pistol rifle in place of a larger one. Babe will carry that. You (Nat) get hold of any kind of a revolver, for protection, and I'll carry my "Colt." With these three we are ready for game, dogs or fish.

Get yourself matchboxes and a small compass (which are inexpensive). I'll get two more of those big fishermen's knives, like I have, for you and Stimson (they close up). Carolyn can tell you about them.

Let me hear from you when you are ready with *suggestions*—

—The "One-Man" Outfit—

Compass & matches
Blanket
Poncho
Sweater (no jacket)
Extra suit of underwear
Two extra prs. of socks
Watch
Large knife
Large handkerchief

One "Firearm"

A suggestion—soft felt hat (med. brim)

—moccasins—

outfit to be equally divided—
   3 tin plates—forks—spoons—cups—pails

frying pan—bacon fork
1 folding candle lantern (candles)
1 AXE
fishing tackle
mosquito solution

Bacon
Pork
Pancake Flour
Sugar
Salt
Coffee
Tea
Soup Tablets

139

Wilmington, Delaware
September 3, 1905

Dear Mama,

Mr. Pyle is fine! So is everybody. Mr. P. is very enthusiastic over my success and it seems last Monday night he talked to the class about it. He said that the only way to write was to write yourself and *not* bring it to him. So you see I won that point. He wants me to make something of the trip we took to Vt.

Well, I got here OK Saturday and got to work yesterday. Our new studio shall at last be started Wednesday!!!

140

Wilmington, Delaware
September 7, 1905

Dear Mama,

I'm in my new room! and it is grand!!!

Three big windows—two of which look out over the reservoir, right over toward Mr. Grant's place; no houses either side of us; quiet, unpaved street and no electrics. And the people are great—a Mrs. Taylor (about 50) and her husband.

My work is well along—I have just finished a great picture of

"Kit Carson" and H.P. thinks it one of my best pictures. The second one (a panel) is about 3 ft. long and a foot high, of a prairie schooner "en route." The latter I have just layed in with considerable success. Am working hard and steady as I have an awful lot to do. The *Harper's* story, as you know, and Schoonover is stuck with an Esquimau story and wants me to help him out with it—I shall.

141

Wilmington, Delaware
September 25, 1905

Dear Mama,

I have finished and sent the two *Harper's* drawings, which I completed with considerable success, and have started one of the two Esquimau drawings for the Sunday mag. Then next the *Post* work. Have you seen my two pictures in *Harper's* this month? *Bum* reproductions! This month's magazines are quite well filled with H.P. students' works.

Schoonover frontispiece in *Outing*
Wall in *Metropolitan*
Aylward in *Scribner's*
Mr. Pyle, Arthurs and myself in *Harper's*.

142

Wilmington, Delaware
October 1, 1905

Dear Mama,

The *Post* have just sent me the last of a series of three articles on "Hudson's Bay Company" and I have to have all the drawings in by Nov. 1st. It's an important article and they are paying me well.— For the Kit Carson drawings I received $275, which is d——d good for any magazine. If they pay me as well as that I shall do my best work for them; and too, the subjects they offer are the best, just what I want—and 1st-class authors too.

I have just completed a huge picture of the Cree Indians trading over the stockade with the early French, for the *Post*. It's in full color and H.P. says it's one of the most realistic pictures ever done

in the school. You might know how I feel. Oh! if I only had time
to paint what I have in my mind. I'll do it some day.

143

Wilmington, Delaware
October 5, 1905

Dear Mama,

The Kit Carson drawings are creating quite a stir at the Curtis
Publishing Co., as I saw today that they had them all framed in
gold and hung on exhibition down in their big hall. They were the
only pictures on the wall of deep red plush, and I tell you they look
pretty well.

Today they told me that Emerson Hough had just completed a
trip through the West in their interests and he shall have a series
of stories (a good many) shortly, and that I shall do my best for
them. The *Scribner's* work ought to give a boost after it appears.

I am going to suggest a series of Indian pictures to the *Journal*
(*Ladies' Home*). That is, such subjects that would be appropriate
—Navaho weaver, wedding ceremony and the like.

There is so much to do that I don't know where to begin. It
seems as though my letters, ever since I came down here, have been
one long string of talk of how fine I am doing—I don't want them
to be monotonously so because, you know, "all sunshine makes a
desert." Of course I only tell you of results. It's useless for me to tell
you of my troubles in producing results, for those to you would
seem trivial and insignificant. All I can say is I have plenty of that
and even then I get my work out much quicker and easier than
anyone else down here. Mr. Pyle seems much pleased with my work
of late and tells me I'm on the right track.

I've felt terribly homesick lately and try to stave it off by thinking
of all the good fortune I'm having, but it's no use. The "Fall" has
got the hold on me; it means that three years ago this month I left
home.

144

Wilmington, Delaware
October 16, 1905

Dear Mama,

The *Post* are wild over the stuff I've done for them of late.
They have just had an exhibition of it this last week. I went up to

see it—some 15 drawings—all framed in gold and hung on deep red velvet. The papers in Phila. had quite an account of it, but was unable to get copies as I knew of it too late. They (the *Post*) want me to stick by *them* and one big magazine (such as *Scribner's*), and they say they will stand by me as they appreciate the fact that I want to *paint*.

They said they would restrict me in no way and that I could make my pictures any way I pleased. Now Mr. Pyle comes into the scene. He had a long talk with me Sat. afternoon, which lasted far into the night, in which he expressed great desires, or I had better say requested me, to quit illustrations and to paint. Although I remember all his arguments in its favor, I couldn't begin to tell you in writing. The result is that I am starting today to spend half of my time painting and the other half illustrating.

145

Wilmington, Delaware
October 23, 1905

My dear Mama,

I have kept rather by myself these last two or three days as I have had a lot of reading to do, and besides, Carolyn is away so did not spend today in *the open* as is usual. Being thus alone, I gave myself to meditation. The result was *homesickness,* and to cap it all came that "box." That dear old box that reeked of odors that told inexhaustible stories. Even the pasteboard around the cake made me walk again into the "other room" and open that closet door to find "one of those clothes boxes on the top shelf," and then sure enough, sticking out from the overloaded shelf, would be an old "Shuman" or "Continental Clothing Store" box perhaps that would drop at your feet at the slightest touch. Yes, and that partly dried grass. I can see Papa now, raking it up, down by the barn or perhaps by the currant bushes where he had cut it with the scythe that morning. And too, I know how you made that grapejuice and how you tested it in the making and just how the kettles and things set around on the kitchen table over by the sink and on the back of the stove. If I cared to tire you with my writing I could describe every movement in minute detail.

It darn near made me cry, those flowers—those told a great and profound story, one I can't express. Twenty-three of them there were. And let me congratulate the one who packed the box.

And to you, Mama, the cake is delicious. It was so good I wanted everyone to taste it so I have *a little* left. *Thanks to all.*

Well, let me think that those pinks came from Grandmama and Grandpapa. Do you remember how we used to celebrate our birthdays together, with the same ice cream?

146

Wilmington, Delaware
October 29, 1905

Dear Mama,

Mr. Pyle has gone to Chicago today to lecture, etc. Enclosed you will find a photo of him. The cast is a head St. Gaudin's gave him. He had a photo taken of it so as to use it in an illustrated lecture in Chicago and Milwaukee. He considers the piece of sculpture (original study for the figure of "Victory" on the Sherman Statue, N.Y.) a masterpiece.

I am working in his studio this week and it's fine to be alone. The only thing is that my work does not seem adequate to the surroundings. The result is a continual keen disappointment.

147

Wilmington, Delaware
November 5, 1905

Dear Mama,

I just learned of Grandpapa's sudden shock. It dumbfounds me. Please let me hear by telegram every day, charges paid at this end. Don't fail!

148

Wilmington, Delaware
November 27, 1905

Dear Mama,

Tonight I was in Mr. Pyle's studio for about 2 hours during which time he gave me one of the best talks I ever heard in regards to work. He is at work on a mammoth battle picture some 10 × 20 ft. for Indianapolis capitol—gets $7000 for it.

Don't miss getting *Harper's*—H. P.'s fine pirate pictures, also fine Aylward in *Scribner's*—also Peck's in same number—Oakley and Schoonover in *Century*—Wall in *Metropolitan*. H.P.S.A. well represented—eh?

149

Wilmington, Delaware
December 1, 1905

My dear Mama,

Last Monday I attended Phoebe Pyle's "Coming Out." It was a grand affair. All the celebrities were there for miles around. Teddy [Roosevelt] and his wife sent enormous bunches of carnations and American Beauties. As a bit of detail—Phoebe had on a $500 dress. You wouldn't guess it. She is to "come out" in Boston and Washington this winter some time. Get tickets early and avoid the rush.

I'll tell you I admire these men that do so many things at once, more and more. Here I am working and working with lots to do of course, but I cannot seem to accomplish a thing on the side. I come over here of an evening with drawing material or a book perhaps, intending to draw or read, and by gingo I get so darn sleepy I tumble into bed and know nothing until daylight. There's piles and piles I'd like to do but can't seem to.

150

Wilmington, Delaware
December 5, 1905

Dear Mama,

I got that paper containing Grandpapa's photo and the obituary. I shall be very glad to make that painting and will do my best with it. I could almost paint one from memory. I'll try and have it by Xmas.

Well, it won't be many days before I start for home. Just think, 20 days and it's Xmas. Gads!

151

This second trip west to Grand County, Colorado, was sponsored by Outing Magazine *to obtain material on mining engineering.*

A railroad was in the process of being built through this remote country. *Always interested in new experiences, N. C. Wyeth rode the work train. The fireman became ill on the way so Wyeth pitched in and took his place, thoroughly enjoying stoking the fires in 20-degrees-below-zero weather.*

[En route to Chicago by train]
February 21, 1906. Wednesday

Dear Mama,

Well, my trip is over!

Short—but *Oh! My!*

It has been a grand and glorious trip full of incident and, consequently, interest.

All was most elaborately crowned with practically a gift of some most valuable Indian costumes.

I took a flying trip up to Colorado Springs to see Mrs. Krebs' son who is out there for his health. She begged me to visit him, and so I did. Well, yesterday I returned to Denver and proceeded to call on a curio dealer by the name of Kohlbergh. I never go there until the last thing as his prices are usually steep and his costumes are so good that I am liable to sink money there that might be of more value a little later.

Well, yesterday I called on him. We got talking and do you know he got so interested in my work, etc. (in fact he aided Remington a great deal) that he invited me to his house. It all resulted in his giving me three or four valuable trophies, including a huge painting painted by "Crazy Horse," chief of the Indians in Custer's Battle. The painting is of course symbolical, and some 10 × 12 feet in size on coarse cotton cloth. It is a wonderful curio, painted in beautiful Indian colors.

The picture has no perspective or distance, but simple, individual drawings of Indians and soldiers in hand-to-hand encounter. It is very noticeable that there is not a dead Indian on the picture, but plenty of dead U.S. soldiers, and all the soldiers that *are* shooting (and those are few) are shooting *wild;* but almost every Indian *is* shooting and with perfect marksmanship. Crazy Horse—evidently— had very little use for the U.S. Cavalry. In fact, he pictured them with a great deal of contempt. Down in the lower righthand corner is a crude map of the "Battle of the Little Big Horn" (Custer's Battle). "Crazy Horse," by the way, personally killed Custer.

I have "Crazy Horse's" beaded vest too—it's a beaut! Well, to cut a long story short, I bought a dozen of the finest Indian properties I ever expect to get or see, for just the price Mr. Kohlbergh paid the Indian for them. I've got one thing that he said he had only seen and owned one other like it—a hollow tree drum or big tom-tom.

It stands about 3 ft. high and about 2 ft. through.

When you hit it, it makes the thrills creep up your spine, it sounds so much like the *"Indian."*

Well, in fact, I've got three tom-toms, all different and from different tribes. Sioux, Pueblo and Apache.

I got a valuable squaw dress, 3 Indian saddles (one like the one I sketched in Cambridge).

I got another pair of beautiful buckskin leggings, a Mexican sombrero, a Sioux silver belt (silver discs), a Navaho panela (very valuable) and two Indian Traveaux trunks—a rawhide folding case they make, highly decorated, some 3 × 5 ft.

On my trip to the R. R. Construction Camps I picked up some corking *mackinaw* coats and pants, also a suit of leather, with more character and history than anything I've got.

These mackinaws are these big, highly colored, plaid coats lumbermen and woodsmen wear.

My outfit consisted of a corduroy cap with earflaps, a black leather sheepskin-lined coat (a peach), corduroy breeches, high lace boots, camera, suitcase and no shave. I carried a sweater, which I was thankful for many times.

Well, to go on with "Kohlbergh"—I found out *afterwards* that he was a great friend of True's, and that it was not unusual for him to take a fancy to a fellow and help him in remarkable ways—and so he helped me. I have a chance to make a goodly sum through him by letting him sell Indian sketches, etc., in his store.—I have promised to do so and *shall*. He is on the lookout now for Indian headdresses, buffalo robes, etc., for me which he will give me at the price he pays for them, *and he's a Jew too!* Me for the *Jews* after this. I went to dinner with him too. He is a prominent churchworker in Denver and a rich man. He is thought a great deal of too.

Well, I have tons I could tell you and will when I take a trip home.

Now I shall hit for Wilmington. My work is somewhat congested now on account of this trip; it will necessitate 6 pictures in 6 weeks.

I received your letter yesterday, thank goodness, and I must say, notwithstanding the unpleasant things that are taking place at home, your letter was *most cheerful*.

You don't know how good that makes me feel; it gives me a new and bright look at facts of life again.

I don't know why Carolyn has not written to you but will soon know why. I got a letter from her also yesterday in which she says she is very well, etc.

We are just crossing the Platte River, Neb.

You probably notice how bad this writing is and at times how much worse it grows? Well, when it's almost readable the train is at a standstill and when it's nonreadable it's moving.

I started from Denver last night, Tuesday, at 10 P.M. and will not get to Chicago until Thursday morning, 7 o'clock. If we are on time I'll get the 10:30 A.M. train for N. York and reach there Friday about noon, and Wilmington that night. That makes a two-week trip to the day. I shall mail this letter in Chicago.

Mrs. True and all wish to be remembered to you and only wish that she could meet you.

Gol! I wish Papa could take a trip with me; I'd take his waistline down a few points, I *know*.

Congratulate *Stimson* on his algebra, will you please? I reread your letter a little while ago and discovered a mistake of mine. I read in your letter that Stimson got 100% in al(1), but on the next line I saw 'gebra.'

I gave the Trues an untrue account of it. If undue congratulation came for him just put them right, will you?

Well, I guess I've written all that will go in one envelope.

Give my love to Papa and the boys and inflict the duty of letter-writing upon them—also ask Papa to drop a line. My address for the next little while will be 1305 Franklin St.

152

Wilmington, Delaware
March 1, 1906

Dear Papa and Mama,

I had written and sealed this letter but could not send it without adding a few more words in response to some things that were said in recent letters.

Many times have I lain awake thinking of you all at home, and trying to imagine what you were thinking of. It may be that I have not led up to the fact of marriage with enough tensity [sic] or enough purpose to satisfy your minds that I am really acting for the best. But after thinking things over I can see very well how you have all been shut outside of my life (or mine out of yours) and how sudden, certain happenings of my life have reached your ears without much forewarning. But I must confess that I did try to emerge the idea of marriage into your minds as gently as possible, and one means of mine was to work like the devil and to accomplish everything that was placed before me. This I have done to a certain degree. Now comes, I must admit, a *final test*. But as I have written in letters two years old—"Wait and you'll see."

Now here is a question in my mind. Is it to be such a test after all? I don't believe it is anywhere near as hard a test as that of the one, two, or more years before the final step. After April 16th I'll have a home, a home located in the heart of my working atmosphere, a place to retreat, a place that is my own, one of rest, cheer and contentment. It's no need of me to tell you what that means to a man.

I can feel also what it must mean to you both to have me married, away from home, like a stranger or a distant friend. But it would actually taint my life to have any such ceremony as the usual custom runs. I want to sort of melt or emerge into this new life; I don't want to feel that I've made a terrific jump that must needs sever me from my old home ties and thoughts to make room for new ones. And that's what a wedding would do for me.

As for Carolyn, she is just the girl I want, and I couldn't find a better one in *a thousand years*.

I know I have the confidence of Papa and I'll do my level best to win Mama's!!

153

Wilmington, Delaware
March 5, 1906

My dear Mama,

Mr. Pyle came from New York yesterday (where he has spent 4 or 5 days) and for the first time looked upon a picture I started Sunday (the "Chief's Burial"). He went all to pieces. That is he went simply wild over my result, telling me that it was the biggest picture ever painted in Wilmington, not excluding his own work. He says that New York editors are agog with appreciation of my late work and they claim that I'd ought to make some big pictures sooner or later.

Tuesday I received an "art editor's" letter from *McClure's,* signed Howard Pyle, and I can tell you it looked strange. His letter was worded in that same sing-songy way that characterizes all editors' letters. He evidently has got into the art editor atmosphere.

We are at a standstill for a few days as our house will not be vacant for 2 or 3 days. Then it is to be repapered and painted as we wish it.

Well, Mama, why don't you ever mention my future, give me a few hints, or to Carolyn?—Say something for heaven's sake. Anybody would think that I was ostracized from your thoughts. I think you treat me, or us, rather cold and in a very unsympathetic way. You were in love once (I hope) and were married, and if you didn't receive sympathy and attention during that period, I'm mighty sorry. Nevertheless, I want it and I think you should give it to me. Just because I'm going to get married a few months earlier than you think I'd ought to, that's no reason why you should act so cold. We both want and need you as a mother and look forward to it if you will only give yourself up to us.

Think it over please.

154

This last studio that N. C. Wyeth occupied in Wilmington was located at 1515 Rodney Street.

Wilmington, Delaware
March 11, 1906

My dear Mama,

I'm all "moved in" and have the finest looking studio in the bunch. I've got my late "Western things" and wish you could see them. Everybody is wild over them, especially H.P.

155

The first gap between teacher and student seems to have appeared when Howard Pyle became art editor for McClure's Magazine. *After Pyle accepted this position, he apparently felt confident that he could persuade his best students to do a great deal of illustrating for the magazine. This pressure seems to have bothered N. C. Wyeth.*

In preparation for their coming marriage, the young couple papered, painted and furnished their rented house located at 1331 Shallcross Avenue, Wilmington, Delaware.

Wilmington, Delaware
March 23, 1906

Dear Mama,

Mr. Pyle is anxious for me to contract half my time with *McClure's,* but I shall *most decidedly* stick out against it. It will tie me down too much, that is it will limit my chances of picture making as it will bind me to illustrations. Of course he claims that I would have the rest of my time to paint, but I want to be seen in the different magazines and, besides, it would sacrifice all my chances for trips for *Outing.*

I completed a picture today (Indian standing in the woods beside a little brook) that totally eclipses anything I ever did. I feel almost like running home to show it to you. The color is very different and I know it would appeal to you. Everybody says that I have "found myself" at last and that I had ought to do big work.

Well, the house is being fitted up with fresh paper, etc. Carolyn tends to that almost wholly. She has remarkable taste and is very businesslike. The way she gets after the workmen would make you smile. I'm working *hard* and will work harder. I'm simply *crazy* to accomplish certain of my ideals and shall fight to the finish.

156

Wilmington, Delaware
March 26, 1906

My dear Mama,

Mr. Pyle is plum daffy over my picture of the "Burial" and got so put out because I intended to publish it that he put his foot down with a crash and refused to let me do anything else than to paint it big, in size, for exhibition. He "guarantees" that it will win me medals and admission into the "National Academy" and insures me that if I paint it as he thinks I can, it will win me great fame.

Well—don't that take your breath away? He said all this and ten times as much before a crowd of people and it embarrassed me much.

I'll have to substitute another one in its place for *Outing*. I have an endless number of subjects and so it's an easy matter.

157

Wilmington, Delaware
April 7, 1906

My dear Mama,

To begin with, Carolyn and I are very busy fixing up the house. She is there quite a bit and I put in all my spare moments outside of my "working hours."

The house is coming superbly and when it is complete I know I'll be restless 'til you and Papa see it. The "mission rooms" interest me more perhaps than any other part of the house: they are the living room (no parlor) and the dining room. I have designed the whole thing myself. Of course it's not half done, but it is coming along fine. To carry out the idea thoroughly I have had made some diamond-shaped lattice frames that fit into the windows. What little woodwork there is in the room has been finished up beautifully in dull weathered oak to match the furniture. Sage green burlap runs to a plate rail 26 inches down from the ceiling. Above the plate rail the paper is yellow buff; the rail itself is weathered oak also. From the center hangs a mission lamp. The table is very heavy mission and circular. In the same room is a sideboard, a serving table, six chairs, and underneath a big Navaho rug, black, white and gray.

The livingroom is lighter—that is, not quite so severe. The furniture is mission, to be sure, but the carpet or rug is sage green, the wallpaper ecru, with a light ceiling. Quite a heavy oak molding down about 20 inches. The hall is simple cartridge paper, varnished floors with a strip of carpet. The second floor is all matting and the bedroom is "colonial" to the slightest detail. No gas fixtures, but brass candlesticks, all solid mahogany. I got a small table for Carolyn that goes in that room. It's a rare pattern and one you would go positively wild over. I'm trying hard to have it duplicated for you. I have not heard yet, but I can probably do it.

The one other room we have furnished upstairs is furnished with wickerwork and a big couch which can be opened, with a large compartment for clothes, etc. This room shall be sort of a sewing room or upstairs living room. The other bedroom we will furnish a little later. The colonial room is painted in white with beautiful colonial wallpaper. The windows were furnished with folding shutters on the inside, which makes it very quaint. The bathroom is in white enamel with *imitation tile* paper. The kitchen is neat and inviting and we got the stove from the people who were there. They are going to board so we bought it cheap.

"The furniture is Mission, to be sure."

Well, you can see it all when you come down this summer.

Tomorrow I will finish another of the Indian series which Mr. Pyle likes better than any. An Indian boy spearing a trout.

Today I faced Mr. Pyle with my final decision in regards to the

McClure contract. It was as I said t'would be—a refusal. I made a very logical and reasonable stand and *for once* he saw my position and agreed with me that I was in the right.

Mr. Pyle told me how much they wanted me and that I must talk with him about some sort of an agreement in June. So things will rest until June.

He told me today as sincerely as he ever said anything—that I was the only man in the United States that can do the work *McClure's Magazine* wants.

That sounds preposterous, don't it? But let them think so and I'll do my best to keep quiet and saw wood and live up to the calling.

Now I haven't told only one other person about that statement, so don't think that I'm swelled-headed.

The fellows were surprised that I stood out against H.P., but I believe that Mr. Pyle thinks me stronger for it—especially as no one else ever did such a thing.

158

Wilmington, Delaware
April 10, 1906

Dear Mama and Papa,

Well, I am up to my neck in work, and with all the hurry-scurrying around between hours I have started and nearly completed the fourth picture of the "Solitude Series."

Gee! it's pouring in so (the work) that I hope something won't *bust*! It's hardly understandable; I never spent such a strenuous month in my life. But I feel in "bang-up" condition and equal to every bit of it.

It won't be long before I, or "we" I should say, will meander towards Needham. The last of June at the latest. I've got to work hard until then, and then I think I'd better take a layoff for a week or two. I'm going to try and work a little at home perhaps.

I'm awfully glad you are going to send flowers—I think that's fine.

We shall be married in the little Unitarian church by Rev. Bowser —he has preached in Needham when Mr. Allen was there. Mrs. Bockius and George will be there and that's all. Seven-thirty Monday evening.

Wilmington, Delaware
April 13, 1906

My dear Mama,

The next time I write a long letter [it] will be written on a "mission desk" at 1331 Shallcross.

I wish you would please send that box (Home box). I'll feel much hurt if you don't. It means a lot to me to have <u>you</u> do those things. Don't let the fact that others are doing likewise discourage you. I'll think an awful lot of it. Carolyn says she feels the same way about it too.

Chapter VII

OFFERS AND COMMISSIONS

"Every day letters pour in for work, many of them great offers."

*N. C. Wyeth and Carolyn Brenneman Bockius were married April
16, 1906.*

Wilmington, Delaware
May 1, 1906. Saturday night

My dear brothers,

It's a long, long time since I've addressed a letter to you, isn't it—
in fact to any of you three. Well, I think you may excuse me this
time, 'cause as you know I've been "busy a plenty" these past weeks,
yes, *months*. Not but what I may have had time to sit down and
scratch off a line or two, but you know as well as I, that to write a
letter means to sit down in a real serious and thoughtful mood and
say something that's *worthwhile*. Now I don't wish to intimate that
my letters are always "worthwhile," nevertheless I do my best
whenever I attempt it.

My writings are usually very disjointed and the reason is this—
that I have an almighty lot I want to say and I haven't the necessary
knowledge of English to warrant my composing my thoughts fluently and with ease, but I guess you can make them out—at least
do the best you can.

Many times each day my thoughts run to Needham, dear old
town, and to you boys. The first thing, I wonder what you are doing;
then unconsciously my imagination evolves something—Nat perhaps
half on his head, twisted under somebody's machine, his legs and
ample buttocks protruding, his feet shod with an old pair of Papa's
square-toed shoes perhaps, an old pair of gray pants torn *somewhere,*
and a dirty, greasy jumper, the pockets sagged with the weight of
auto junk, with a bunch of ragged "waste" bulging out from the top.
If you could see his head it would resemble a storm-tousled chrysan-
themum, his light, ragged hair fairly greasy, his face shiny with
perspiration and with a streak of something black drawn from his
nose across his chin, or a splotch across his eye. That's Nat, the old
son of a gun, with a few cuss words thrown in.

Now Ed walks into the yard—his shoulders thrown back with a

certain air of pride and dignity—wearing a light topcoat and a few books under his arm. He doesn't turn up the back steps but passes straight down back of the barn to the "hotbed." Perhaps he lingers there a minute, perhaps not. He scans the river and the surrounding country carelessly and turns back to the house, casts a casual remark to Nat perhaps—civil but disinterested.

He directs his way into the house, places a few peanuts or a piece of chocolate in Mama's sewing basket and then quietly retreats to his room to study.

It's almost evening. The old spruces loom up big and mighty against the evening sky. The stillness is gently broken by the liquid note of a robin, perched on the uppermost limb of the old grapevine tree snugged against Gran'papa's barn. If you should listen carefully you might possibly detect a slight movement in the stable, but all else seems to be still. Suddenly you become aware of footsteps along the walk, 'round front of the house. In the dim light the figure finally appears and turns down the walk—his head the least bent, a green bag slung at his side. His gait is loose and shambling. He plods down by the steps and disappears into the dark square of the barn door. You may overhear a few gentle words of sympathy, softly imparted to the cow. The henhouse door rolls open and then shuts; the footsteps become audible again and the figure emerges from the "dark square," his head still down and still that shambling gait. He slowly climbs the back steps, lingers at the top to watch the flight of a crow, southward bound. He watches it until it becomes a part of the evening sky. It has grown dim and you feel, rather than see, him on the steps.

The whole pantomime was profoundly impressive. It foretold the future of the lad—simple, full of meaning, something that reeked with the spirit of nature.

I have caught the spring fever for fair. For two or three days I've felt good for nothing. You have to expect those feelings sometimes I suppose, but it always scares me 'cause I feel as if everything had slipped from my grasp.

The "Solitude Series," tell Mama and Papa, were very enthusiastically received.

Well, soon I'll (we'll) see you all, and we will raise hell the Fourth, won't we? I say "soon," for 8 weeks will pass like wildfire.

Mr. Pyle is clean off his trolley these days. All worked up over the *McClure's* business.

161

Philadelphia, Pennsylvania
May 3, 1906

My dear Mama,

I'm writing this in the Broad St. station, Phil., en route to Atlantic City, to the big publishers' dinner to which I was invited. Pres. Roosevelt is supposed to come—Mark Twain and other notables.

It's the biggest thing ever given in Atlantic City—at the Marlborough-Blenheim Hotel.

162

Wilmington, Delaware
May 7, 1906. Thursday evening

My dear Mama,

It's four or five days since I wrote you—but time slips by so I can't seem to drop a line in "on time." The last note I believe was written in Broad Street Station—what followed that writing was great!

We reached Atlantic City about 4:30 and spent the two hours between then and "slickin' up" time paroling the famous boardwalk. We had automobiles at our disposal, but it being so late we made no use of them beyond riding from the station to the hotel (about 1000 yards distance).

The Marlborough-Blenheim is a wonderful structure of peculiar design—most elaborate furnishings and enormous in size. As a detail: our room (Schoonover, Arthurs, True and I) had hot salt water, cold salt water, hot ordinary water, and cold and ice water; the faucet of the latter was actually frosty all the time. Two big bathtubs with beautifully tiled floors, walls and ceiling and immense looking glasses. The towels were the finest and many of them.

The bedroom proper was extravagant to the extreme, canopied beds, massive dressers and dressing tables, all sorts of lights in all sorts of places.

It would kill me to sleep in such a room two nights in succession.

The dinner was grand! When I say grand I mean not the "Menu" but the associations and the way the whole program was carried out. Not a moment was lost, every minute some new interest presented itself.

N. C. Wyeth, Stanley Arthurs and Frank Schoonover in Atlantic City.

I was fortunate enough to sit by Louis Mora—a painter (decorative) of renown, a Boston man. His conversation did me all sorts of good; on my left sat a man of not much account, at least I found him so. The rest of the names you can find in the table list in the enclosed book. Shreyvogel and I hit up quite an acquaintance which resulted in a most interesting talk. I had a corking chat with Grover Cleveland and he gave me some fine advice. Edwin Markham (the poet) seemed profoundly interested in my work and talked at quite a length to me about it—so did Dr. Henry Van Dyke and others. Gov. John Wise of Virginia perhaps interested me more than anybody on account of his unique and picturesque way of presenting facts. My talk to him was rather short but chuck-full of meaning. Met Paul Morton (Life Insurance Co. president) and all of the New York illustrators.

It was indeed a great bonanza for me, I can tell you.

It was especially gratifying, especially as quite a few artists of note asked to be introduced to me! WOW!! and the remarks that usually followed were exceedingly complimentary, I can assure you.

163

Wilmington, Delaware
May 11, 1906

My dear Mama,

Isn't this aesthetic writing paper? I feel rather cramped, which is not inducive to good letter writing. Well, to begin with—it's d—— hot! and it's been so all day—nevertheless I finished a pirate picture which I think is very successful.

This pirate, "Bartholomew," has escaped from prison where he was to be hanged; he made his way for two hundred miles through dense woods and terrible tropical swamps. At last after many days, he came upon a big white sandy beach; there he came across an old hulk half-buried in the sand. He managed to pull out of it a couple of old rusty spikes and from these he wielded out, with a big stone as an anvil and a smaller one as a hammer, two crude knives. The last few words embody my subject—good?

Now I'm to start three pictures for *McClure's* which are to appear as important illustrations in the famous November number I believe—I say "famous November number" because that is the first number that H.P. is to supervise and arrange.

Now the last week has hatched out a scheme I hope may be carried into execution. It's this:

About the middle of June I hope my work will be completed up to a certain point. Now I want to do a set of pictures at home—that will necessitate my packing up a few bits of costume and also lugging John Cummings (my trustworthy model). I'll have to have him for about two weeks perhaps, although *I'm* arranging to stay a *month.*

Now is this plan *feasible?* John's a good sound Irish fellow that I've had for several months; he is gentlemanly in his crude way and *clean* in every way.

I s'pose we could arrange in some way to let him sleep with one of the boys, and Carolyn and I to have the spare room.

Now if this can't be done, why say so. I make one condition however—I shall do nothing of the sort unless you have help of some sort. I want to do this badly. Let me hear soon. I shall pay the model's traveling expenses and board at home, but pay him nothing for posing; it will be sort of a vacation for *him* you know. He's a fellow that has been only a few miles out of Phil. and it would be quite a treat for him to see Mass.

I got a bully letter from Nat. It was just chuck-full of Nat and nobody else—simply told, and bubbling over with meanings I know perfectly, and enjoyed. I'll write to Ed, Sunday, that will be *one* around. Tell Papa I don't forget him by any means and that he should share all the letters. I know he understands that, but it's nicer to mention it at any rate.

Work as usual seems to be pouring in, but it's really foolish for me to accept the work as I can paint plenty of my own subjects.

Your wishes that I paint certain subjects shall certainly be carried out—someday *you'll see;* I'll paint a big decoration embodying that great spirit of the primal solitudes.

But *once* in awhile I must paint a "bloody" one as a foil for the other extreme. I don't believe a fellow can be considered masterful unless he tackles those extremes and is successful in both; one is bound to be food for the other.

Your letter was a *fine* one. It reached us, accompanied by Nat's, and they were both read and highly appreciated before breakfast. Don't think we get up late—the point is the mail is delivered at 7:20.

I'm preparing already for my homework by having canvases stretched, etc. I'm wild over the scheme.

Carolyn is going to write tomorrow but nevertheless she wishes to send her love to all and her appreciation of the last letters.

164

My dear Mama,

Well—this has been another loud week. Full of opportunities, some of which I am trying hard to realize.

Mr. Pyle blew in like a whirlwind last Saturday and presented me with the leading article for *McClure's* for the coming months, or rather the months following August. The subject for the first installment is "A Montana Hold-up." I have already started it and it's most surely the strongest thing I ever did of its kind. Arthurs said, "It's the most original thing you've done in a long while." That meant a great deal to me from *him*. I have to finish the picture by Thursday, so you see I have to hustle. I started Monday morning to lay it in (a huge canvas), and finished the "lay-in" by 12 o'clock.

Then Mr. Pyle telegraphed for me from N.Y. and I had to leave immediately. That broke into the "spell" of the pictures terribly. But I went and met S.S. McClure and received an order for an "Indian Cover." "An Indian playing on a reed, and in a canoe at moonrise," to represent Indian summer, you know.

My heavens, things are coming in so fast I don't know which way to turn. Every chance seems better than the one preceding it.

I don't know just how I'm going to turn out all I've got on hand.

I received your letter today and was glad you will allow me to bring my family—my model man—and my model—girl.

165

My dear Mama,

This has been rather a half an' half week with me—Monday in N.Y., Tuesday morning painting, loafed in the P.M. Spent Wednesday in the country—loafed Thursday, but today laid in my picture of a "prospector" for *McClure's*.

By Jove! I'm beginning to believe that illustrating is as hard as any other work with the exception of, perhaps, shorter hours. I've stuck to it pretty steadily outside my western trips and I'm starting to feel it.

I'm looking forward with great pleasure to my visit home and am in hopes of arranging for June 15th. I have this picture I mentioned and two other illustrations for *McClure's* before I go.

I shall endeavor to complete three western pictures for *Scribner's* while home—these are due July 15th—then by August 1st I shall have to have an Indian cover done for *McClure's*. By Oct. 1st I have to have 4 pictures for *Outing*—3 for *McClure's* and another cover. I don't pretend to remember the other stuff to follow.

166

Wilmington, Delaware
June 11, 1906

Dear Mama,

Well, as usual I have something new to tell. Mr. Pyle has made me a pretty fine offer which I will accept (in writing) this afternoon. The agreement is that I shall devote 30 weeks of my time out of one year to *McClure's* for $4000 starting no later than July 15th. And furthermore they do not prohibit me from working for other magazines (a restriction that I fought against). You see this gives me a good living and also gives me time to paint, which I most certainly will do.

We are making ready to start for home next Friday morning, which means that Saturday morning finds us in Needham.

The model John will not come until I'm ready for him.

167

Wilmington, Delaware
June 15, 1906

Dear Mama,

Mr. Pyle is a busybody, you know, and tomorrow he returns from N.Y. and he *might* want me to make a full page by Sunday or *something* foolish.

If anything *does* delay us (which is improbable), I'll telegraph. So don't let telegrams frighten you.

168

Wilmington, Delaware
June 22, 1906

Dear Mama,

This has been an almighty wearisome and sad day for me. My head is in a whirl and in this condition Mr. Pyle expects *so much* of me.

I knuckled down this morning at 8 o'clock and managed to make a "lay-in" which is not altogether satisfactory to me. Tomorrow I hope will pull it out. I'll do my best to make home the Fourth.

169

Wilmington, Delaware
July 2, 1906. Friday night

My dear Mama,

This week has gone past like lightning.—Really, I never experienced such a "fast" week in my life. I've bent *every effort,* poured every bit of my inner self into my work this week, endeavoring to reach a much higher plane in my work, and secondly to satisfy Mr. Pyle in his wish for a "big" cover design. I have, I am positive, reached a higher plane, according to those opinions about me, including Mr. Pyle's. I would like so much to have you see the picture. It's one of an Indian chief with his right hand up, palm forward showing friendship. He is on his mustang with his feathered lance across his saddle.

The week has been very individual. I know I shall always remember it because it has been one of intense seriousness of purpose and more or less of a victory for me.

170

Wilmington, Delaware
July 15, 1906

Dear Mama,

Tell me, how does Papa talk in regards to me, my methods, theories and ideas of all things pertaining to life and living? I have a vague notion that I'm a little strange and peculiar to him. Tell me.

The WYETHS

"Uncle Deny" was John Denys Zirngiebel II, Mrs. A. N. Wyeth's older brother.

Wilmington, Delaware
July 30, 1906. Monday

My dear Papa,

It has been on my mind for some time to write to *you*, but in every instance I found my time too limited to write anything other than the regulation newsy letter, and really I wanted to say more than that.

Whether or not my way of thinking has been changed by different environment or whether I simply approach subjects of discussion differently than you do with precisely the same result in view—

I know I have been misunderstood in one or two cases. This failure of mine to make my arguments comprehensive (if I may call them arguments) have resulted, I am sure, in making me appear (to you and Mama and possibly the boys) conceited and too assuming, perhaps a bit overbearing. I'll tell you I am mighty sorry to leave such an impression.

The unassuming quality is one that has been in my favor from the time I started out alone, and to lose that one, redeeming feature of my personality in my own home is a great and painful loss to me.

As I have no one to "exploit" my character, I'll have to do it myself. Even that is a little assuming—well perhaps it is—but I'll resist from singing praises to myself and shall restrain myself from dwelling upon any good qualities I may contain.

I am an enthusiast, pure and simple. A strength to my art but at the same time a great weakness; impractical, erratic and many times unreasonable. These qualities at once lead me into good, bad and indifferent circumstances. In conversation I am liable to exaggerate or overstate; the same in my pictures. Restraint will be my salvation, if I am strong enough to maintain it.

And too, the atmosphere here with Mr. Pyle tends toward the philosophical, which leads us all into a deep and involved study of human nature and character. That state of mind leads a fellow into a never-ending train of thought, so involved and so subtle at times that, unless he is talking with a person who understands his ways of thinking and his ways of expressing, he is liable to misapprehend.

Offers and Commissions

Practical ideals and *artistic* ideals are as foreign to each other as black is to white. They are of <u>equal</u> value (*in their proper places*) in their relations to life and living. But if a boy is naturally gifted with the "artistic ideal," be it either in art, music or writing, he should be guided into it, placed into its atmosphere unhampered by too much practicality; the latter will come from *necessity*.

The fellow with the ideals or, in other words, with the "temperment" can be flattened into insipidity if inoculated too strongly with the practical. The fact is he absorbs only the hard, unsympathetic version without enjoying its admirable qualities, and right here let me say that Uncle Deny is a *mighty* good example of the treatment.

Now the above is what I wanted to say the day we talked and the day you disliked what I said concerning ideals.

The ideals of good, straightforward, honest, wholesome, kind, practical living fills a most important place in this world and are every bit as good and enjoyable as the artistic ideals—but one is as different from the other as sky is to earth.

172

This letter was written to his fellow student and lifelong friend, Sidney M. Chase. Philip Whitney was a Howard Pyle student.

Wilmington, Delaware
August 2, 1906. Tuesday night

Dear old Sid,

Chase, you cut out the finest chunk of time to be sick in, possible. Mr. Pyle has been on a terrible rampage for the last three months (caused by high life in New York, and the magazine). He's just about to "come about" again and soon we all hope will drop back into his old form. Of course I can't kick. The next four numbers (*McClure's*) will demonstrate why. I have promised to sign a contract to give half my time to *McClure's* (am not restricted from other Mags.), but unless things settle somewhat I'll not do it.

Your berth is ready for you in the front studio and we'll all be *damn* glad to see you back. When will it be?

[Philip] Whitney's back—ragged, fat and sassy—Schoonover's West for *McClure's*, and the rest are pluggin'.

My vacation was knocked in the head. I only got six days at home and no opportunity for any more until next summer.

The WYETHS

Wilmington, Delaware
August 3, 1906. Friday night

My dear Mama,

My! how I would like to drop in now for a long stay and have some good chats with you; and I would talk cool and collected too, because now I have made up my mind to do it and <u>will</u>. It has made a big change in me already: in fact the power of restraint I am trying my best to acquire in my conversation, in my moments of meditation and in my work.

Your appeal to me to make quieter pictures instead of the "brutal" kind has taken a firm hold of me and from now the balance of my pictures will be of <u>your</u> liking.

Every day new emotions, new feelings, new appreciations come to me, and how contented it makes me feel to know that I can detect them in you, in other words to know that they all came from you to me directly. Your letters have helped me more to appreciate _your_ true feelings than anything else and I wish you would write more. They are so out of the ordinary, not so much in their actual words as in their suggestion.

From the first time you said, "Oh, I wish you wouldn't make all your pictures with so much action." (It was when I was making a picture of a horse running away with a tip-cart, and also on some sketches of a calf running away with a boy.) Ever since you said those words I had a strong underlying feeling that you were _right_ and you _were_. Someday you will see me paint a big picture, perhaps a decoration of a very quiet and remote subject—it will never be a picture of action.

My next cover for _McClure's_ is an Indian Hunter standing ankle-deep in the water with a wild goose over his back, a bow in his other hand, looking up at a V of wild ducks passing over his head. He stands by some low marsh grass and the moon is just rising.

I have already started the picture and Mr. Pyle thinks it is the straight and most poetic thing I've done.

There is a large-sized squabble going on in New York between _Scribner's_ and _Recreation_ and I am one of the chief factors in the case.

It seems that a fellow by the name of "Figaro" has actually copied my "corral scene" and sold it as an original painting to *Recreation,* who, in turn, have published it as a cover for this month. In the table of contents they have credited "Figaro" with the cover, and not only that but he has openly stated that I copied his picture as he made his in 1902.

Today he had the audacity to call me up personally on the telephone from N.Y. and charged me again with copying his picture. Of course he has no case whatever, but *Recreation,* I have come to the conclusion, are paying him to perjure himself for their benefit as it means money and reputation to them.

Mr. Pyle is very much perturbed by the affair as of course he saw me paint the picture. The fellow (Figaro) has wonderful *nerve* to try to bluff a thing through like that and the New York magazines are quite excited over the affair.

Now Mama—please tell me how you are and just what your condition is. I think and think and *think* and sometimes get so worried I have to quit work. Nobody tells me just how you are. I'm going to take a run up home the very next time I'm in New York, so don't be too surprised if I blow in some day. I'll try to do that pretty often now, as there is no excuse why I shouldn't.

Keep me posted on the boys and their "doings." Schoonover just returned from the West with all sorts of materials and costumes.

174

Joseph De Camp was an artist of the American Impressionist school and taught at the Museum of Art in Boston.

Wilmington, Delaware
August 10, 1906. Friday night

My dear Mama,

Mr. Pyle has sent in his resignation to *McClure's*—which was prophesied by all magazine men before he actually took office there. His reasons for his leaving are very many and intricate; the magazine's reason is just one big fact—that H.P. is not the man for the place. He is too impractical, too radical in his views, and too perceptible, and over all he has *no* business sense.

Of course this all results in my overthrow as far as the *contract* goes.

"It's an ill wind that blows nobody good."

It's what I prepared for and expected and to tell you the truth I'm tickled to death. The stringent obligations I was under was like a millstone around my neck. Not the obligations to *McClure's* so much, but to Howard Pyle. He followed me around like a shadow requesting me to hustle out other peoples' work to make room for his and actually asking me to shirk their work so as to give *him* more time. He blinded me by keeping me enthusiastic and interested —I can see now that he manipulated me about like a puppet. And it is only now that I have come to the full realization of facts. I have heard indirectly from the N.Y. publishers that "we fellows" have "no sense of obligation" and it is now I see that my future depends on the magazines and not on one of them. Mr. Pyle has been using me for his personal betterment and yesterday I told him so.

I did it for my own good, for my own future good—Schoonover took the same stand, and so will True.

The offer to True was made with great certainty, in fact he got True to believe at one time that it would be only a matter of *hours.* And what happened! Poor True prepared himself for the event and got rid of his obligations in the way of stories he had to illustrate, waiting, waiting, waiting until the thing has just simply sloughed through.

Mr. Pyle had no more idea of placing True as art editor four days after he suggested it than he had to fly. True is broken up and I'm sorry for him.

Schoonover's case is different.—He went West with the idea from Mr. Pyle that his expenses were to be paid by *McClure's* of course.— Schoonover's bill amounts to $2000, including traveling expenses, photos, etc. For the material he got for the magazine it's very reasonable, but do you know that H.P. would <u>not</u> OK the itemized bill (and he had written receipts for every expenditure) until Schoonover actually settled the thing by *law.*

Now back to me.

He has crowded these cover pictures in on me until I have made two more than I counted on, which has eaten up my time terribly, so much so that if conditions had remained the same I would have had to complete 10 pictures (all feature pictures) within five weeks.

I balked!

I was under strong obligations to *Outing* (the pictures for the article for which I took the Western trip) so I simply threw over the big Xmas story for *McClure's*. It was a blow to H.P. as it will look bad for him to be withdrawing his pupils from the magazine as he is leaving, but I've followed out his words to a *letter* until now, as you know, and now for my own good I've made a stand!

And *oh!* how relieved I feel. Actually I feel like a new man. Just think, I have five weeks now to make five drawings for *Outing* and I'm going to make some rippers.

Mr. Pyle surprised me indeed when he told me today that my stand was justifiable and that what I said carried a good deal of weight.

There is one point however that I've got to square up. He has told *McClure's* that the reason that I refused to do the story was that I did not care to be connected with the magazine as long as he (H. Pyle) was not identified with it, and that I didn't care to have my work appear with inferior illustration. That's damn bad talking you know! and if that's the kind of blunders he has made I don't wonder he has resigned.

Well, it's all blown over and, as I say, I feel like a "newborn babe."

I am seriously considering a series of New England farm life pictures.—Isn't that more to your liking? All of them reposeful and full of poetry.

Tonight I am writing to Joseph De Camp for advice.—I am going to try and arrange some study under him next summer. This is absolutely the last summer I'll spend in Wilmington.

175

Wilmington, Delaware
August 17, 1906

My dear Mama,

This week has been full—full to overflowing with agreeable and disagreeable happenings—mostly disagreeable. It all resulted in a flying trip to New York yesterday which was exceedingly satisfactory as far as I was concerned but disgusting as far as H. P. is concerned. I'll go into no details whatever about the affair as the whole thing is nauseating to me. I'm going to talk no more about these matters to no one.

I feel as though I'd like to shake myself like a dog just from the water to rid myself of Mr. Pyle and his present influence.

He has won the grand distinction of being a *"notoriously selfish overbearing hypocrite"* and I agree with them [*sic*].

He has given me invaluable training up to this point, but now that he has degenerated into something incredible, it's my duty to myself and to everybody else, to "break away." I'm afraid the latter is impossible as I have no other studio to go into.

If you could only see how I'm situated. A favorite with him I am still, but he is leading me down the wrong path now. If I could only tell you how I feel and my surrounding atmosphere at the studio. If it wasn't for Carolyn I'd go clean off the handle. Yes my work is improving with all the fuss, but when I think what I might do under better conditions, in a healthier atmosphere.

If I only had money enough saved I'd seek the country immediately and there I am positive as I live that I could paint great pictures. I feel like damning everybody down here; they all look alike to me, now. I seem to stand out alone with my ideals against everybody—at least they don't stand with me. But thank heavens I've got Whitney of *Outing* (grand fellow) with me strong, also Chapin and Russell, and that's all I want. I'll show people soon that I've got no limit to my ability and I'm going to leave these fellows in a cloud of dust.

P.S. I wormed back into somewhat the same spirited writing but I couldn't help it. I've felt this way for a week and I'm just about played out. Whitney is my inspiration and one of the sincerest friends I've got.

176

Wilmington, Delaware
August 24, 1906. Friday night

My dear Mama,

At last the spell of terrific hot weather was broken today by a severe rain and easterly winds—so cool in fact that the fellows had small fires in the fireplaces at the studio. This weather has had a very bad effect on me, making me feel inanimate and at times disagreeable, but notwithstanding these drawbacks I have turned out the best picture I ever painted. It's a moonlight scene in the West. Eight miners digging through a 14-foot drift during intensely cold weather. This completes the second one of a series for *Outing;* the first one also is very successful but hardly up to this one.

"I have turned out the best picture I ever painted."

I was very sorry for having written such a nasty-tasting letter last time and will *never* do it again. But it's like when you swear to relieve yourself. Letters are dangerous and I mustn't forget that the impression made by them lasts unto the end of the week or until you receive my next letter.

Oct. 10th I go to Kansas City to take in the stockyards. I set that date because that is when the big rush of cattle come in from the West. This is another trip for *Outing*. He (Whitney) wants me to take at least one trip a year for him. I will also go to the Chicago stockyards. This will be a timely subject, eh?

177

177

Dear Mama,

It's Friday night and I've just returned from a bunch of the fellows who have been serenading this section of the town. I was and am in stocking feet, and, do you know, although I ruined the stockings, it felt fine to wander through the grass and over the fields without shoes on.

Tomorrow Carolyn and I are going to Bushkill, Pa., with Schoonover and his people. It's to be their eventual home and they are up there now. The place is very wild and is situated in the Pocono Mountains (a part of the Blue Range). Even the old fur trader comes down through there every fall to buy up the furs from the local trappers and hunters. It's the place where Frost (A.B.) got all his bewhiskered types. His old studio over the grocery is still there. Black bear are plentiful ten miles back in the hills and red deer (a small variety) are numerous, so numerous that they are a nuisance. Beaver and marten abound in the many streams and lakes. The Pocono Range is covered with a *virgin* forest.

All this is within 2¾ hours of N.Y. City; to locate it on the map, find Delaware Water Gap (on the upper Del. River) and follow the stream up north for about 12 miles and you have it.

We leave tomorrow morning at seven, but I'm going to go down to the P.O. and ask for my mail earlier so that I'll get your letter. I'd hate to wait until Monday for it.

178

Dear Mama,

Schoonover, Dunn and three other fellows had a miraculous escape from death Saturday last. They were riding in an auto going at 40 miles an hour clip—when both front tires exploded—the machine skidded into an iron bridge rendering them all unconscious and almost (within six inches) cut Schoonover in two. His arm is all smashed up, his left fortunately. The rest are O.K. except for the shaking up and nervous strain.

179

Dear Ed,

It was with *great pleasure,* pleasure, that I read in Mama's letter of your initial lecture and heartily congratulate you for it.—You're the first one in the family who has attempted professional teaching. You will find it of the most inspiring pleasure and you will doubtless gain much from the work.

In our work here I have done more or less criticizing and I find that when I have helped someone I have helped myself doubly. It crystalizes your own thoughts and drives you to strike for something better. May you have all sorts of success and may you *always* hold your *dignity*.

180

My dear Mama,

When I think of it, it seems an age since I last wrote *you;* at the same time it seems but yesterday.

Friday I leave for the "West," which means that this week has been a continual hustle; everything seeming to accumulate and happen the last few days—as is always the case.

I don't know as I reported to you about my last *Scribner* pictures (the Civil War series of two), but anyway a good thing can be told twice. They were *very* enthusiastic over them, intending before they saw them to reproduce them in black and white in the Xmas number, but upon being so agreeably surprised at the color, they concluded to publish them in the January number in full color, and what's more, Andrews (the best platemaker this side of the water) will make the engravings.

All this "tickled me to death" as the whole scheme was an experiment; in other words the work resembles my past work in no way except in perhaps dramatic statement. I made the radical change for the better, I knew, and when my efforts were corroborated by men like Chapin [of *Scribner's*], Whitney [of *Outing*] and Burlingame [of *Scribner's*], it made me feel very gratified.

It would be useless to tell you on paper just what my changes constituted, but I think you will understand better when you see the results. I will find myself working on pictures very much longer than I used to, which means not so much income, but what of that, if only someday I can be called a *painter!*

I have, since the delivery of the *Scribner* pictures, completed an *Outing* picture, illustrating a Lawrence Mott story of Labrador. It is a fight, and indeed ferocious, between two fishermen on a wharf, but so restrained that it will be liked even, I think, by you. I have endeavored to get the spirit of the fight in the elements of nature about them rather than in the "fighting action" of the men; in other words I tried to infuse a dreadful, ominous feeling into the landscape instead of relying upon physical expression.

Now for the trip—all I can tell you is where I intend going—what I shall see or do I know not until I'm on the grounds. I can tell you what I hope to do in a few words.

I want to see and experience if possible the life in connection with the stockyards—driving, branding, unloading, loading cattle—to watch the progress of big cattle sales from the auction stand, to study the characters that must teem in such a place—cattle kings, outside investors, cattle bosses—cowboys and the like.

I have got to write an article, also, which shall be "An Impression" as the Roundup was. I have no right to treat it otherwise as I shall only see a week of it.

I shall also try to see a little of the Nebraskan and Missourian ranch life—which will be, I hope, this time of the year embodying harvesting, thrashing, etc. I also will try and get down to New Orleans on a "Packet Boat," one of those "stern-wheelers," you know, freighting cotton and molasses manned by "niggers," who in turn are manned by slave drivers with black snakewhips. The latter experience is doubtful as I have got to return in time to turn out some important work for *Century*.

I think I have a very interesting trip before me and the best part of it is that I am "commissioned" and don't have to worry as to whether a magazine will take the "stuff" or not.

I'm glad the box pleased you, only wish I had more to put in it. Money, for instance. Not that you need it you know, but the mere sentiment of "sending money home." I know if you were in need of it I could support the whole "outfit," but I'm too anxious to do things and accomplish things to save much money. Now, for instance, I sunk quite a bit of money in my new colors which were necessary to make the desired change in my work, but see what came of it—? I swerved my work in such a direction that may win me the name I want—at least it showed me how far I was from the ideal and big work, which alone is worth heaven knows how much. You'll see.

You see in this work a man is directed to different efforts by the mere change of the wind perhaps. His mind becomes so sensitive that the least thing changes his course of thought. Sometimes for the good and sometimes for the bad. In this case for the good undoubtedly. That's the way I'll live, at the same time plying every bit of common sense and practicality I own. It's not Papa's fault if I haven't got it, is it?

Give my love to Papa and the boys and tell Nat I'll send the check tomorrow for his tuition, and tell him I hope to hear as good reports of his schoolwork as in your last letter.

May Stimson and Ed both have luck "shooting"—and may your pen slide easily, and tell Papa when his pen slips well to drop a line.

181

While in Washington, Wyeth paid a visit to his first cousin, Harry Barker. This letter ends with the hint that Carolyn Wyeth was expecting her first child in January.

Chicago, Illinois
October 14, 1906. Sunday evening

My dear Mama,

I think we (I mean all country-breathing people) are the most fortunate people living—at least among the fortunate ones, when I see the way the millions of people live and pass their life. I have had occasion today to walk through the worst part of Chicago on the way to the Stockyards, and I must say that the slums of New York or

Boston do not in any way *compare* with this town for filth and absolute vileness—not only in their surroundings, but in their immoral atmosphere.

On the "east side," as they call it, live two-thirds of the population —not a full-blooded American amongst them. Mingled in with these peoples' homes are innumerable "bad houses" with the significant "red light" flaring dreadfully. Under these very lights the children play; within a near proximity of these *houses* the younger generation are born and brought up. I loathe to think what all this means in the future. Rotten, rotten, *rotten!* is all I can say and think about it. The only fit places to live and sleep are right in the pens with the cattle in the stockyards—these are comparatively clean, at least the associations are better.

Today, Sunday (although you would never guess it as theaters, saloons, ballgames, etc., are in full swing), I went to the Art Institute galleries here where they have a very choice collection of modern pictures and some old masters. I was feeling blue and this rather stirred me up to my work again.

I then went to the stockyards and located all the places of interest, so that when the work began I would know just where to go.

Fortunately I struck it just right as tonight, about 9 o'clock, 9000 cars of cattle come in from the West—including all varieties of cattle from Texan longhorns to N. Dakota white faces. So in a few minutes I start for the "yards" to make a night of it, watching the unloading by electric light. It will be intensely interesting and dramatic.

The yards cover one square mile, divided off into thousands of small yards thirty feet or so square, each connecting with the other by gates and chutes. Above this tattoo of fencing are walks elevated on trestles from which the buyers and sellers view *the* cattle. From these elevations I shall witness the spectacles.

A million or more of cattle will pass through those yards *tomorrow,* unloaded first, then sorted, some to the slaughter houses, some to eastern markets on the hoof and some back to the ranges for breeding purposes. Besides all these cows, there are horses, sheep and hogs to watch go through the program; so you see I have plenty to draw my material from.

I shall go through Armours, Swifts, and Hammonds also, which will be very interesting. There are *great, great* chances and my results ought to amount to something good!

I spent three hours in Washington with Harry—we went down to his boat and had quite a chat. He's the same old "Hal" and won't change in a hundred years! He gave me a very earnest appreciation of the fact that I got married and feels very much disappointed that he didn't do so earlier. He thinks it's too late now as he has grown into a rut, "a selfish rut," he calls it.

Thank God I'm N.C.W. and that there is a Mrs. N.C.W. and may there soon be a little N.C.W.

182

The Midland
Kansas City, Missouri
October 16, 1906

Dear Mama,

I believe this is the dirtiest city God ever created—it beats Chicago. I landed here this morning and shall spend a couple of days at the stockyards here.

I have given up the proposed Montana trip because my time will not allow it. It would take just a week to simply travel to Billings, Montana, and back and *that* uses up more time than I've got. I shall probably strike Wilmington about Monday evening.

I've got lots of material and look forward to writing an interesting account of it. Well this is just a note to let you know my whereabouts. Write to Wilmington cause I don't stay in one place long enough to get letters.

183

Studio
Wilmington, Delaware
October 24, 1906

My dear Mama and Papa,

How many things that box of cake, pears and violets brought back to me—its very odor ravishingly suggested Needham and home; I stood over the box and just dreamed in its aroma for a few moments and in that time thought of many joys and pleasures and a few sorrows. The very deepest sorrow was that I should probably never enter into the life that box depicted!

The cake was and is better than it ever was and the pears seemed more delicious and the violets claimed the same spiritual pathos in their delicate odor as ever. The note acted as a golden key to it all.

Postals from the boys and letters from you and Papa made me feel very happy and I want to give you all my hearty thanks.

I am back at work but am having considerable trouble with it at present. I intended to write you all a long descriptive letter before this, but while my work is in a precarious condition I can't get up any enthusiasm to do so.

184

The painting, "Fishing for Sturgeon," was later published by Scribner's *magazine under the title, "The Silent Fisherman."*

Studio
Wilmington, Delaware
November 2, 1906

My dear Mama,

I'm writing this letter under the soft light of the candle. We are just completing a supper of oysters and I feel full! The coffee tastes fine.

I'm going to walk with Schoonover tonight by the light of the full moon. Last night True and I walked about 10 miles and it was glorious.

Monday I went to New York with a picture for *Century* magazine which was very successful. I landed a big commission from *Scribner's,* one with *Century* and one with *McClure's.* They all want sets of pictures like the Roundup set only different subjects of course. When I returned I found a request for covers for *Ladies' Home Journal*—a firm offer to illustrate a Western story (book) from Chicago publishers, and a reserved order from the Cream of Wheat people for an advertising picture of Western life. I am at work on a big picture for the academy exhibition which is already *sold* to Mr. Krebs. I expect to get about $350 for it besides reproduction rights from *Scribner's.*

"Fishing for Sturgeon" is the subject.

I have a few more minutes so will add a few more impulsive sentences. My work is taking a new and stronger stand and I feel very much encouraged.

Nat spoke about being home Thanksgiving. If possible Carolyn and I will come up for a couple of days, but you see it's so near Xmas that we may not. You see it's your anniversary the 23rd and I want to be there and also stay over Xmas day, and two trips within 20 days is a little too much. Write and tell me which you would rather have me do.

185

Studio
Wilmington, Delaware
November 9, 1906

Dear Mama,

Last night I started a letter to Ed but was "switched off" by the noisy arrival of a bunch of H.P.S.A.'s endeavoring to serenade us. I joined them later and so forgot to finish Ed's letter.

This week has been a very busy one for me, expecially in the thinking line. I have started my painting subject for the Academy exhibit and my feelings have been running high and low at a great rate.

It seems to me that I'm growing awfully sensitive to conditions about me. Even down to the placing of my chairs and paraphernalia, or the arrangement of curtains. I think it's because I've been thinking so much of my work that it's starting to tell on my nerves.

It's a big undertaking this painting—it means much more than I ever thought. Mr. Pyle is boosting me in great shape. He seems to have taken a sudden interest since I've actually started to paint.

Every day letters pour in for work, many of them great offers. I'm painting my Cream of Wheat ad of a "bucking horse"—an old story isn't it?

A peculiar thing happened three nights ago. I dreamed of Grandpapa's funeral—not a detail missing, as it happened the following day was exactly like the fateful day a year ago. It made me feel peculiar all day.

186

Studio
Wilmington, Delaware
November 16, 1906

Dear Mama,

Another week gone! But to some good I can gladly say. I finished

a "bucking horse" picture for "Cream of Wheat," and now I'm well
on with the second, "The Mail Carrier."

Carolyn comes over to the studio about every afternoon around
4 o'clock—she is here now and is *extremely* enthusiastic over the
picture. Her opinion I value highly, not from sentiment but because
she really is a very good critic and has helped me many times.

I never saw a girl change so in my life! (I suppose it's because I
never had the chance.) From a young fly-away girl into a *real* wife
and mother. From morning until night it's either planning work—
sewing—or something of the sort, and every night, and sure as
clockwork, she carefully pulls out every little garment which she
has made and talks about it and then carefully lays it back. My,
how tender and sweet she is during those moments, almost spiritual.
I always thought that there must be something *really* grand in being
married and not until now have I begun to find it out.

187

En route to New York
November 28, 1906

My dear Mama,

How I would like to continue this journey straight on to Needham! If only to drop in for the noon hour—not that I'm hungry
or that I'm starved, for Carolyn feeds me well, but just to complete
the family circle you know. How much that dear old New England
custom of "family reunion" means to me—I shall always regard
that with my tenderest affection and reverence. After this year we
shall make it a positive custom to come home for Thanksgiving.
I'm only sorry that we could not establish it this year.

I received your most interesting and cheerful letter just before I
took the train—I read it on the way down to the station and passed
it to Carolyn. We both got down to the "Market" about 7 o'clock
in order to buy the turkey—cranberries—celery—nuts—raisins, etc.,
before I left for N.Y.

As we walked down the line of country wagons backed up to the
sidewalk—exhibiting long rows of beautifully dressed turkeys, chickens, ducks, geese, bunches of white crisp celery, homemade mincemeat, cottage cheese, butter, coleslaw, great yellow pumpkins, pop-
corn, and to cap it all, nice clean linen bags with ready-mixed
plum puddings ready to steam; when I saw all this I remarked to

Carolyn how you and Papa would enjoy looking all these things over. The old country people calling their wares, chattering crowds of buyers with an occasional squawk of a hen or the startling gobble of a turkey—it is all so quaint and homely, almost ideal. On one corner stood an old farmer and his wife selling big luscious mince and pumpkin pies—he had on an old sailor's reefer with a red scarf around his neck, an old muskrat skin cap on—corduroy trousers with cowhides; she had a homemade knitted hood with a great green bow on top that stuck up like butterflies' wings, a deep green shawl with great monogram initials in the middle of the back in deep orange, rendered in elaborate scroll, rather a short skirt of gray, and on her feet were great huge overshoes—they were both standing on a mat of padded carpet to protect them from the cold, damp sidewalk. Their wagon was backed up nearby, filled with a goodly reinforcement of pies and fruit cakes.

They were selling out fast.

I talked with them and found that they started 1 o'clock last night from "Beaver Valley" in order to procure a good stand.

How interested you would be in those country folk who still, in some places, cook in the open fire, and how Papa would enjoy talking to the old farmers who are carrying on really neat and successful farms.

My trip to the "Big Town" is a hurry call—that is, Mr. Mapes of the Cream of Wheat Co. telegraphed for me to run up and see him at the Waldorf-Astoria. He is the owner of that famous cereal co., and is a man of immense wealth. I have just completed two pictures for him, $250 each, which he is immensely pleased with. While in Chicago and Kansas City he followed me around with letters and telegrams inducing me to come to his home—make my headquarters at his club, the use of his autos, etc. But that did not attract me very much as I was interested in things of the *cattle country*. And I knew too that my duty was to *please* him with my work. I was confident of the latter because I had seen things he had obtained from other men which he liked, and they weren't very good.

And I did please him and he appreciates it and has duly overlooked my probable indifference to his lavishing invitations.

Now that he is satisfied I don't care what he thinks of *me*—he is a businessman and when he finds a man who is of value to him, formalities, etc., *go to the winds!*

WHERE THE MAIL GOES CREAM of WHEAT GOES

I haven't told you people at home in detail what I have been doing. You may think I have, but I haven't.

I have been painting, painting for exhibition—and thus far have failed! That is to say I put three months' work on a picture that has proven a failure—three months more may pull it out. It's a big Indian subject "Fishing for the Sturgeon." It's an extremely simple one, but Oh My!

188

Offers and Commissions

I am beginning to see in the dim distance what *real* painting means. I can see now why painters have to struggle and starve. To accomplish what I have (and I call it an accomplishment) I have given up all my other work. I had to, to do anything. I wrote the magazines not to tempt me with stories for three months and they didn't. *Outing,* who owed me considerable and whom I counted on for funds, put me off unfortunately until Nov. 15th. That's the *"hell"* of working for *one* magazine. You have to depend entirely upon them. But now the 3 mos. is up I have received a landslide of stories and all good ones too. So now I'll go back to work. The trial at this painting has given me a wonderful insight and has driven me into far better work. The thing I finished for the Cream of Wheat created quite a sensation in the Wilmington circle and I hope to make my work progress steadily from now on. It has been a hard rub; Carolyn has boosted me in great shape, always cheerful, always comforting. No one knows just how hard I did work, but I think you will see the advance in the pictures I have just completed and in my work from now on.

I am not trying to write a "self-pitying" letter, but I know you are all sincerely interested in my closest endeavors. The fellows do not know just what I've been doing, in fact they have not seen this picture or even been in my studio.

I have determined upon one thing for certain—there isn't a fellow down here that will ever paint! unless he takes a "horrible brace." Dunn comes nearer than anyone. By jove, how I look forward to the work, how I wish the days were twice as long, the nights twice as short. I'll show you though in *only a few years, you see!*

Ed, from what I can understand, is booming along in good serious form and tell him to concentrate his every effort on his profession. I don't like to hear of his uplift in social life of Needham especially —that don't count, and too I wish Nat wasn't so popular and handy; it's fascinating and enjoyable but not productive. Tell Babe to build huge castles in the air and then try to climb up to them, tell him to think a lot and be *philosophical* above all. The time will come when he will do big things if he keeps his mind clean and well balanced.

Now give my heartiest Thanksgiving greetings to Papa and the boys, with the biggest share for yourself.

188

Studio
Wilmington, Delaware
December 7, 1906

Dear Mama,

My cover for the competition [*Ladies' Home Companion*] is completed after three weeks of arduous labor. Mr. Pyle kindly assures
me that I will land one of the best prizes and would not be at all
surprised should I ring in one of the 1st there. That of course is the
verdict of an enthusiast, so you can't count on that much. I know
one thing, it's the best thing I've done and very conscientiously finished. I hope to bring it home with me so that you can see what it
looks like.

I shall be home either 19th or 20th. Sid Chase and I are planning
to go up together, which will make it very pleasant.

I've got about 'steen things to paint before Xmas but will try to
do them.

189

Studio
Wilmington, Delaware
December 14, 1906

My dear Mama,

Let this be a short note because by this time next week you'll
know more than I could write in fifty letters.

I never hustled so in my life as I am at present—I received new
inspiration or desire to try the last straw and put my picture through
for the exhibition. I feel pretty blue about it at present but hope
that during the next five days I can execute wonders.

The subject is so subtle—yes, so damned subtle that I can't seem
to put power enough into it without spoiling it. I have very little
confidence in its passing the array of judges (six best artists in
America), but it will at least give me an idea where I stand.
P.S. On the following page is a story H.P. told me today.—I
think it's good.

An Englishman hired a valet whom he always called "Piles."
" 'Piles' do this, 'Piles' do that, etc."

190

One day a friend asked him, "Why do you always call your man *'Piles'*? Is that his name, pray tell me?"

"Aw, no my good fellow, <u>no</u>, only don't you know—he's such a bloody hass!"

190

Wilmington, Delaware
December 19, 1906. Tuesday night

Dear Mama and Papa,

You say startling! That doesn't half explain or half express the surprise. Just think, no discomfiture to speak of before one o'clock the eventful morning and not an absolute realization of things until 4:30. Surprise! Why, a bolt of lightning from a clear sky wouldn't be it.

And yet with all the *"foretold disaster"* gathered here and there, the event was one of the easiest and simplest that could ever take place.

Although Carolyn had been quite active up to within a couple of weeks, the cause was perfectly natural. Simply this, that nature was good to her and arranged her presentation early to prevent possible hardship. I had a specialist list things that might have been involved and I take his word for some good and so pass it on to you as <u>truth</u>!

The baby is doing splendidly, perfectly and beautifully formed, with lots of hair and a fine-shaped head.—They all claim it resembles me absolutely and I agree with them inasmuch as its eyebrows meet and its ears are of the A.N. and N.C. type, with a forehead exactly like Stimson's. Naturally she is small, weighing only five pounds, but oh! my, what a lusty voice.

Carolyn is perfectly well, and even has color in her cheeks. The past three months she surprised everyone the way she gained in weight: 133 lbs. five weeks ago; she has been out in the air a great deal, which I think accounts for her present condition.

We have a trained nurse (homeopathic) from the city hospital and she will receive the best possible attention. Of course the next two weeks means a great deal but things as they are now seem exceptionally well.

I am sorry that I have established such a precedent of extreme optimism that you cannot believe my uttered words. But thank God,

I am optimistic and how sorry I am that more people haven't the same weakness.

Of course underlying all of this novel and exquisite gratification I feel extremely sorry that I cannot be home the 21st. Carolyn wanted me to go, but to come home in a few hours. Well, I was advised to stay, being the only man in the house, tending to fires, etc., being so important at present. I know you realize and appreciate my position and feelings. It is useless for me to write further upon this subject now but will drop you a line Thursday night.

I was rather sorry that you did not drop a line to Carol, as she looked for a note from you in every mail and seemed very much disappointed this A.M. especially. I did not show her the note I received but simply told her of the pleasanter parts, keeping your thoughtful apprehensions to myself.

How does everybody take it? Here it has created quite a stir. The house is so full of flowers and plants sent by friends that we have absolutely no place for them.

Ashley and Peck donated our old wooden porridge spoon used at Annisquam, tied with a big pink ribbon and properly inscribed:

Presented to "Henrietta Clifftine Wyeth" first child and daughter of Mr. & Mrs. N.C.W.

In memory of the many good old puddings and pastries stirred cooked and eaten at the cottage "Squam." signed

Henry J. Peck
Clifford W. Ashley

By the way, as previously agreed, we decided if it were a boy to name him Nathaniel and if it were a girl "Carolyn," so the latter is the case.

With all this I have at least pulled out my Indian picture after over two months' work and shall send it to the exhibition. It will be quite an event here as it is the first picture to be tried from this place. I hope I am successful. Another remarkable thing is that yesterday and today I accomplished the result.

There is a thing I want to ask Papa or anybody that is interested to try and think of some place within reasonable distance of the house where I could rig up a studio—that is—put in a skylight about 6 × 6 feet and have floor space amounting to about 20 × 25. Has Mr. Morse any unused building? If I can get such a place I would make a long stay at home in the summers. I wouldn't want the studio at home, but apart where I would be alone. Ask the boys to think it over.

Now I'm going right on with a big story for *McClure's* and when that is completed will take a run home. There will be no break in my work, only Xmas day and possibly only half of that.

As the express this time of the year is slow, I want you to watch for a box which ought to be there before Friday and another before Tuesday.

Carolyn sends her love to you both and only wishes she could see you.

191

The children who helped to brighten Christmas were Carolyn Wyeth's brothers and sisters. Elizabeth was one of her sisters.

Wilmington, Delaware
December 23, 1906

Dear Mama and Papa,

We lost our baby Friday morning about eight o'clock. It all transpired like one beautiful dream—but now that it is all over we must think and act philosophically—and we have.

Dear Carolyn bears up wonderfully and from the minute her heart was almost broken she steadily acquired her normal control and now she seems to bathe in one perfect halo of beautiful thoughts and of wonderful inspirations. The sacrifice has been tremendous, but how it has lifted us and too, how much nearer together it has brought us.

Let not this letter be one of morbid sorrow, let it be one that contains the message of spiritual uplift. How much akin to the beautiful is sorrow.

Carolyn is very well physically and will sit up tomorrow.

I buried the little girl today in Mt. Lebanon cemetery (a little country cemetery beside an Old Quaker Meeting House in Rockland on the Brandywine near Chadds Ford), a beautiful secluded spot, one where Carol and I had often stopped to read the quaint inscriptions there and to walk through the quaint walks of boxwood.

Don't let this spoil your Xmas for I'm going to make it as cheerful and pleasant for Carol. The children will be here and we will have a tree.

Tomorrow I will send my box to you and of course am very sorry that you will not receive it for Xmas. The few things will be labeled. The picture from *McClure's* is for Papa. You have probably received that by this time.

Mrs. Bockius and Elizabeth are here and join Carolyn and I in wishing you all a *very merry* Xmas! Especially so from Carol and I.

Chapter VIII

THE COUNTRY

*"As time goes by I seem to be drawing closer
and closer to the quiet 'domestic' farm life."*

"Aunts Hat & Sue" were Harriet Convers Wyeth and Susan Eliza-
beth Wyeth, maiden sisters of N. C. Wyeth's father. They lived in the
old Wyeth homestead at Cambridge, Massachusetts.
Louise Barker was a first cousin on the Wyeth side.

Wilmington, Delaware

December 24, 1906

Dear Everybody,

The box has gone! and here is an index to its contents and to the
respective owners.

Carolyn's pictures number three—one to Mama and Papa, one to
Aunts Hat & Sue, and one to Louise Barker.

The portraits of Grandpapa and Grandmama are for Mama, with
apologies for Grandmama's as it is unfinished. Later I shall want
it back for more work. The fruitcake and pudding is from Carolyn
and the pudding is from Mrs. B. [Bockius]. (Steam well before
using.) The Western pictures are labeled on the back—Elizabeth
sent Mama the collar case—and Papa the calendar—she made both.

Stimson gets the Dumas books and Ed the book on gardens, Nat
The Motor for one year.

I think that covers all. When the box comes please be exceedingly
careful in removing the cover as glass is immediately under it.

The original I hope Papa has already received.

May your Xmas be a merry one—with love from us both.

Wilmington, Delaware
December 28, 1906

My dear Mama and Papa and brothers,

With mingled joy and sorrow we spent Xmas, and we both *must*
say that the biggest part of the day's pleasure was furnished by the
arrival of the case containing the letter and various articles from
Needham.

Xmas morning we had all the children over here and they livened things up in great shape. Carolyn had dolls for them and enjoyed presenting them immensely. They were here all morning talking and laughing, which kept the house in right good Xmas spirit. After they went Carolyn sat up for the first time and she and I had dinner together. It was the first time she had had much of an appetite and I'll tell you she enjoyed it. We had turkey and fixings with a delicious custard pudding one of the neighbors sent in.

Then about 2 o'clock when we were all alone the box came, and I'll tell you we surely enjoyed it. Carol insisted that I unpack every bit of it in the bedroom and such a keen delight it was, that we carefully pulled every nail and patiently untied every knot. We examined every scrap of paper in search for home "signs" and "trademarks" until everything was carefully opened and inspected. I guess we acted like hungry children: not that we are starved by any means but it seemed actually delicious to get things from Needham.

That shawl is exactly what Carolyn wanted, and she wants to know if you made it. And that chair! You couldn't have sent anything that I could appreciate more than that. I remember it so well that it brings back hundreds of things near to me. Anything to do with Grandpapa is almost sacred to me; his personality is a constant study and inspiration to me. It seems as if I know him better now than when he was living.

The flowers of course were very expressive and meant more to me than their material beauty, but Carolyn enjoyed them also. The apples we smelled before we opened the box, they were so fragrant.—Carolyn has eaten three already and proclaims them the kind she loves!

I need not say that the photos [letter continued] *enroute to N. York Dec. 29, '06* were a big surprise and a most satisfactory gift.

The one of Papa is a *corker*. I don't believe I ever saw a more faithful portrait, and too his expression is so genial and contented —a quality very eminent but rarely portrayed in his photographs. I must say I like the one of you and Stimson *unframed*. It is admirable of both. Perfect character studies, which is more than one usually gets. I have seen you look just like the other one, but the expression is so incidental or perhaps unusual that I like it less. Babe is *fine* in both but I favor the unframed one still.

The "old man trio" has caused considerable interest and well it may. I'm mighty glad to get ahold of that picture. Tell Stimson I guess he knows what I want. And that frame of Nat's workmanship couldn't be more appropriate, could it? It's remarkable how well he worked out that seal. Was that border a "stock design" or was it original with him?

Tell Ed that his book could not have been better chosen and the autograph makes it much the more valuable. I have read it aloud to Carolyn already and we found it very quaint and interesting. I'm sorry I don't know more about Dover, it is so rich in interest.

The Cambridge gifts were as usual, beautifully dainty and useful. These we will write to them about.

I think I have memorized all now and if I haven't, just remember that it has just slipped my mind for the present.

Our box I hope reached you with nothing broken. I put a large valuation on it for protection. They handle a thing of that sort much more carefully.

I am delivering a picture to *Century* today that should have gone up last week. I have lots of business calls to make so shall use up the whole day.

Give my love and thanks to everybody.

We received our respective letters yesterday and Carolyn has read hers I believe half a dozen times. It is indeed a beautiful and comforting letter. I took the liberty of showing it to True.

My letter too is one that I will always cherish, one that is full of sincere love and encouragement.

194

In closing this letter, Wyeth refers to the fact that his second cousin, Marguerite Holzer, "Gritly," had made a bound three volumes of the letters that he addressed to his family between 1901 and 1906.

Studio
1305 Franklin Street
Wilmington, Delaware
January 4, 1907

My dear Mama,

You have been very generous in your letter writing, both in their volume and in their bountiful appreciation of tokens and other things. No one has appreciated them more than Carolyn, which of course gives me the greatest pleasure.

Your "great" letter in two parts (to Carolyn and I) was so complete that it has put me at my wits' ends to answer it. And then in addition there came two other letters from Papa and Ed that flooded the flowing bowl of completeness. I shall not attempt to answer them in detail—that would be folly—but I shall offer one *great big* thanks! for the big part everybody home has taken in covering up our grief. It was all done so naturally and unconsciously too, which makes it the more valuable.

The great sorrow has been to me one of the greatest things that ever took place in my life. It has lifted me out of a chaos of semi-serious work and an admixture of immaturity, and placed me on a pure high plain of intense and deeper thought.

Of late months my whole work seemed to be culminating toward a new restraint and quietness that I hardly understood myself. I seemed to be awakening to more serious and remote things; I started to love the facts of life that were more subtle and consequently more delicate.

In short I seemed unconsciously to be preparing for some radical happening; the latter has given me new impetus which I hope may result in something that you can be really proud of.

If I only knew that my letters were someday to reach a library shelf in book form—I surely would have been more discreet in my statements. How I hope that Gritly bound them with smoked glasses covering her eyes.

195

Wilmington, Delaware
January 13, 1907

My dear Mama,

I sailed in last Wednesday and started a whopper of a Cream of Wheat picture—one Stimson would go wild over—"An Esquimaux Half-breed" on top of his dog sledge of freight, protecting himself from a pack of wolves, late afternoon on a great frozen lake. Incidentally, there is a case of Cream of Wheat amongst the canned goods and flour. The title is "The Yukon Freighter." The picture is about five feet high and three feet wide; I completed it today.

I haven't heard anything about my Academy Picture and have only slight hopes of its being accepted. Let us pray!

Wilmington, Delaware
January 18, 1907

Dear Mama,

The week has been one of the usual hustling kind and nothing to speak of has happened except that the Academy has turned down my "Indian Picture."

Of course I feel keenly disappointed but I more than half expected to have it turned down. The Academy received 2500 canvases and accepted only 220 out of the lot, so I do not need to feel terribly hurt. There is one big satisfaction, and that is that I have broken the ice and I'm sure I'll never let another year go by without at least sending one picture.

The next disappointment I expect will be the return of the *Ladies' Home Companion* cover—I think I have perhaps a little more chance of doing something there then I had at the Academy, although there are 1200 contestants from all over the world.

One satisfaction is that they are both saleable subjects and I can dispose of either of them at goodly prices.

Nothing can discourage me as I know too well the deficiencies in my work. How I hope the time will never come when I shall feel satisfied. To reach the goal of one's ambitions must be tragic. And another thing I hope is that I will always be able to judge my own work with a sane and unprejudiced mind.

197

Wilmington, Delaware
January 25, 1907

My dear Mama,

This Friday ends a week of intense suffering—mental suffering I may add. I have on my hands a big story which I am illustrating for *McClure's*.—The pictures to begin with are a great disappointment to me; secondly the story is so confounded strong that it makes my efforts appear terribly weak. Next in line I visited the Academy exhibit and there saw some really great work by Gari Melchers. He is of foreign extraction but eminently an American who hails from Detroit. (See *Harper's* for Feb.) These pictures are so wonderful that they have caused me to realize my inability to paint a real big picture. My arguments with *myself* are long and wearisome. They involve theories that are not writable by me at least.

After all this vivid and intense introspection I have determined upon a course that takes *nerve* above all, concentration and a long hard fight.

I want to be a *painter*. I respect illustration but now realize keener than ever before the terrible rut I'm in. A dangerous one too. I shall continue illustrating by all means, that has its commercial value, my bread and butter. But I want to be able to paint a picture and that is as far from the realms of illustration as black is from white. Illustration is built up on superficial technique, pet receipts of effect and *everything* that's artificial, besides always containing a literary meaning and expressing some melodramatic incident.

I want to paint a picture with nothing but a soul, with nothing other than a spiritual meaning and I'll do it.

To do this I've got to cut down my remunerative work. I'm going to make a proposition to *Scribner's* to give me at least $300 worth of work a month—that will give me about enough to live on and to keep up my insurance.

I then will have plenty of time to do their work well and enough extra time to paint, or rather prepare to paint.

I have got very severe plans made in detail pertaining to my personal behavior in regards to my art. It's going to be a year of stiff hard labor.

Don't think me discouraged with my present work but please look favorably upon the fact that I'm striking for a higher, yes, the *highest* plane of art.

198

The Wyeths had spent a week in Needham.

Wilmington, Delaware
February 23, 1907. Friday night

Dear Mama,

I found many telegrams and letters here urging on my work but, thank heaven! I am in a position now to ignore the publishers rush calls and they know it. At the same time I can't help complying with their wishes if it is possible. I have nigh completed two pictures since Tuesday.

The *Ladies' Home Companion* cover design did nothing for me— the subject was not quite suitable they said. It's funny, but do you know those disappointments are *not* disappointing; it acts as a stimulant for me. Wall landed $500 third prize and I'm almost as glad as though I got it. His cover was not very good technically but a bully idea for the magazine. I shall dispose of mine elsewhere. I have two other offers for it already.

Let me say a word about Carolyn. I never saw the girl more elated and satisfied with a visit. She talks and talks about you and Papa (family harmony appeals to her above all, and well it may). She said one thing that was worth the whole trip to me, and that was "I feel as though your mother was my mother too!" Well that just took my breath away because that's all I wanted. Didn't you feel nearer to her than ever before?

We had a very nice trip back and all in all it was as pleasant a week as I've had for a year. One reason why I enjoyed it too was because I was under *nobody's* thumb; I even said, "To hell with the publishers" for seven whole days.

199

The poem Wyeth referred to was "Back to the Farm" by Martha Bianchi. Four illustrations in full color and eight ink drawings for it appeared in the August 1908 issue of Scribner's.

Wilmington, Delaware
March 12, 1907

Dear Mama,

I am particularly overjoyed at the present time with my prospects for the summer. Never could a fellow have more to anticipate than I have.

My summer's work embodies all that is the highest class of illustration; so high in fact that all there is left for me to do is to make it overreach itself with the quality of my work if possible; and I believe I can do it.

To cap the climax of all the beautiful subjects I've got to do, came a beautiful poem from *Scribner's* of which I enclose a copy. I want everybody to read it—more than once too!

For this poem I am going to make a series. And I'm going to make the finest things I ever did or anybody else either. I've got the whole summer before me and that is all I want.

Isn't that one of the richest poems you ever read? This ought to strike Papa's deepest heart string.

Enclosed are four or five photos I took with my new camera out around the Chadds Ford country. Titles on the back.

Also there are a series of photos entitled "A Glimpse of the Frontier" enacted by Messrs. *Dunn, True* and *Wyeth.* Taken out back of True's studio.

"A Glimpse of the Frontier."

200

Wilmington, Delaware
March 29, 1907

Dear Mama,

Scribner's are my strongest backers and they are the top notchers too. I certainly am fortunate and shall do my level best to make myself a valuable adjunct to the magazine. They practically monopolize my summer's program with that farm series and an Indian sheep-herding series.

I've driven out to Chadds a number of evenings this past 10 days, and it has aroused my feelings to such a point as to make me feel exceedingly homesick—the country strikes home—it is a homelike country! sympathetic and so pastoral. It has made me wonder and marvel, lately, why I should have been blinded by *Bushkill*. Bushkill is fine! but it hasn't the barnyards, the waving grain, the great fields of corn—it hasn't the great piles of corn in the fall with scattered pumpkins and little piles of golden ears—it hasn't the neat white farm buildings and cattle.

Of course there is lots it has got—primitive woods, dark velvety pools, mysterious brooks and waterfalls, great hills and valleys and wonderful backwoodsmen characters. But as time goes by I seem to be drawing closer and closer to the quiet "domestic" farm life, so to speak. That which embodies poetry and rest. I'm just beginning to love the farm and *home* life of the country.

The spirit of wandering and adventure is mainly a desire of the past.

Another thing! I don't believe any man who ever painted a great big picture did so by wandering from one place to another searching for interesting material. By the gods! there's almost an inexhaustible supply of subjects right around my back door, meager as it is.

I have come to the *full* conclusion that a man can only paint that which he knows even more than intimately, he has got to know it spiritually. And to do that he has got to live around it, in it, and be a *part* of it!

I feel so moved sometimes toward nature that I could almost throw myself face down into a ploughed furrow—*ploughed* furrow understand! I love it so. The conventional humdrum life is so shallow and meaningless—it seems no more than existing!

Now this summer you and Papa have *got* to come down—I'll pay the fare if that bothers. Come out to Chadds Ford—I've got a horse that you and Papa can drive and an easy rubber-tire carriage.

Now about the boys, tell me when they can come and I'll send a ticket.

I shall leave my studio about the 1st of May so as to get out to the Ford before the planting is over.

201

The Randolph place, with the "tower room," was the home Mr. and Mrs. Turner had built called "Windtryst." It was destroyed by fire September 11, 1914. The estate was sold and being farmed by a Mr. and Mrs. Pusey Taylor when this letter was written.

Wilmington, Delaware
April 5, 1907

Dear Mama,

Dunn and I have just returned from a most charming day at Chadds Ford—"charming" sounds rather flat for me, don't it, but that's just what it was. We cooked dinner in Hoffman's valley near a beautiful little brook and it was simply *great!*

Well, we have arranged everything at the Ford for the summer. I have got the old mill for *nothing* and Carol and I have a "tower room" in the Randolph place on the hill, which also has the tower just above it which is as large as your dining room. This is open on the four sides with wonderful vines crawling all over it. The view therefrom is wonderful.

Now this is just the place for you and Papa to come to. Lots of room and a fine place to grub (at the Washington Headquarters).

202

Wilmington, Delaware
April 8, 1907

Dear Mama,

Well, my whereabouts and doings are comparatively insignificant now to the great proposition that confronts you in the case of Nat.

It may be silly for me to discourse on the subject, but I cannot help reiterating some of the few things that have transpired in my mind since reading your last letter.

I have always been *peculiarly* interested in Nat, why, I don't know, unless it is the fact that I have been closer to him than to either of the other two, and also perhaps, because I have always found him so sympathetic, honest and appreciative, which constitutes a quality very rarely found in the modern boy or even brother. I in no way mean by the above statement to depreciate the qualities of Ed and Stimson, for they have their admirable sides too; but *you* know, *humanity!* and sympathy! are so beautiful, satisfying, I may say sumptuous and rich and *rare*.

He is so gentle in his friendship, understanding, and in his work so unobtrusive; but still behind that there lies a great masterful power ready to strike when the time is ripe and ready, and may heaven forbid *anybody* from interrupting his progress!

I have yet to learn whether my marriage has helped me or not. I have cleared the first hurdle because I possessed a supreme confidence in my ability (which perhaps bordered on conceit). I am losing that boyish effervescence which buoyed me up, and now all things rest on a rock-bottom of fact. I know I shall succeed because of my love and appreciation of nature and of truth. Nothing can foil that, but idleness or dissipation.

I refer to myself to show the two different natures—Nat is so different; he lacks that bubbling enthusiasm that helped me so much. His is a deep, soulful nature that should get well on its way before the physical matters of the world should bother him.

Tell Nat, for me, to keep his ideals to the front and to keep his eyes pinned to them.

There is no satisfaction in running a race unless one has that great throbbing desire to *win!* How pleased is the man who wins a second or even a third prize, but how *Supremely Happy* is the man who captures *First!*

203

Wilmington, Delaware
April 16, 1907

Dear Mama,

I'm going to ask a favor of you people up there, and it is this.

Next week sometime, either Tuesday or Wednesday, probably, Carolyn and I are going to N.Y. I shall deliver some work and then we shall turn around and enjoy a few things in that great city which should not be missed—one of them is the play "The Great Divide" (Western, which has led the big critics to pronounce it the first American Classic) *and* the wonderful "Hippodrome." The world's greatest stage, where they show a complete Western frontier town and where the 6-horse coach drives in hoopeetalick, Indian fights, dances, etc., by 150 real Apaches and Sioux. I can't describe the thing except that it is as near the real impressive fact as anything could *ever* be. Now all this would set any one of the three boys *wild!* and the favor I ask is to let *one* of them off for three days. Send him to New York City and I'll take care of him from then on, expenses and all. We will see those two shows, ride the length of Fifth Ave. on top of a "bus," etc., in order to see the town, and then come on to Wilmington where I want to show (the fortunate one) Chadds Ford and entertain him at 1331 Shallcross before we close up for the summer. Then I'll load him on a "flyer" for Boston with "Keep in Cool Place, *Perishable!*" tied to his lapel.

Now if ever you wanted to do anything for me why just carry out this plan of mine in some way. It will be worth a hundred dollars. *Break* the hard-shell rules and regulations for *once!*

Yes, I have got a horse temporarily until I find a good saddler.

As Carolyn cares very little for driving, I shall probably get a saddler only. Then watch me drop great lumps of superfluous fat in the roads.

Now I wish I could get a couple prints or reprints of Grandpa and Grandma Wyeth. Ask Papa about them, I'll pay.

Hang on to every photo of the family you've got; how fine they are after years go by.

204

Wilmington, Delaware
April 19, 1907

Dear Mama,

Your letter and the preceding telegram were indeed joyful news to me, for I was very much afraid that puritanical rules would prevail. Am more than glad to learn that Nat can prolong his stay.

From the minute he sees me he is at my mercy!

Tell him *not* to trim up but to come in the rough. I don't want it to be a "visit to distant relatives," just sort of a "drop in" affair.

I only wish the whole outfit were coming!

Now tell Nat not to miss the boat, for I'm looking forward to the minute I see him.

205

New York City
April 25, 1907

Dear Mama,

Well, Nat is here strong!

We found him at 7:45 waiting on the wharf. He had already taken a ride on the "hoss-cars" and had struck up an interesting acquaintance with the Irish driver.

206

Chadds Ford, Pennsylvania
May 3, 1907

Dear Mama,

Here we are, located at Mrs. Taylor's at Chadds Ford.

Well, how did Nat get home and how did he enjoy himself? It was so easy to entertain him as he has that wonderful natural ability to interest himself *in everything.*

He blew in on me like a fresh, invigorating sea-breeze; he seems to have given me a new impetus, and I think that is because he was so appreciative. I think sometimes that "appreciation" is about all a fellow needs to boost him along in the right direction.

207

Chadds Ford, Pennsylvania
May 17, 1907

Dear Mama,

The warm rain is dripping, dripping, dripping—that soft gentle drip that comforts one into a peaceful drowsiness. The lush green leaves are sodden with the wet.

Midst this haven of gorgeous nature the old mill slumbers—its huge oaken wheel is stilled forever, its great spacious bins are empty with only the faint odor, as that of old rose leaves, to tell the tales of harvest and plenty.

And within this mill I am working! On either side the hills roll back into beautiful and limpid horizons and to the east and west stretches a great peaceful meadow with its winding brook and willows, its cattle and its larks.

A gentle and silent valley but at one time the scene of a great and bloody conflict between men.

Of course my news is confined to a smaller area of land and also to a smaller variety of interests now, so you can't expect anything more than a general knowledge of what I've been working on etc., etc.

We get up very early—we go to bed in a similar way. Carolyn sews mostly and gets brown (very). I paint mostly and dream (a lot).

I have lately accepted a commission from Houghton Mifflin to paint a picture of "Hiawatha Fishing" (from Longfellow's "Hiawatha"). They wrote to H.P. and he referred them to me. I couldn't help accepting such an opportunity.

Middle row, left to right: Nat, Carolyn and N. C. Wyeth.

Chadds Ford, Pennsylvania
June 7, 1907

Dear Mama,

Well, the past month has been one of the "revival of energies" so to speak. I have determined and have got well started on a plan of action that is one of the most serious I have ever contemplated, not excepting a *thing*.

It has been *absolutely* evident to me the past six months of the uselessness of clinging to illustration and hoping to make it a *great* art. "It is a stepping stone to painting," so says Mr. Pyle—but I am convinced that it is a stepping stone backwards as well, which will in time leave you in that most unsatisfactory position of "a good illustrator, but he has *done* his best work."

Now I'll tell you why. To begin with, an illustration must be made practical, not only in its dramatic statement, but it must be a thing that will adapt itself to the engravers' and printers' limitations. This fact alone *kills* that underlying inspiration to create a thought. Instead of expressing that inner feeling you express the outward thought or imitation of that feeling, because a feeling is told by subtleties and an engraver cannot handle such delicate matter.

Mama, the argument is really such a strong one that this raw, inadequate statement of it seems ridiculous! To confirm that which I believe I *should* do have been many letters and words from different people in regards to the *Outing* pictures. I have not only heard from individual people, but three of the biggest magazines have sent congratulations, *Scribner's, McClure's* and *Collier's*. That is saying a good deal because the magazines as a rule vie with each other and show so much professional jealousy that they usually say *very* little.

In every case have they mentioned the *poetry* that I succeeded in getting into the pictures and *not* the effect or action—I consider that a big victory!

This Hiawatha picture is about finished after four weeks work on it (and I'd like to put about four more into it). It has thoroughly stirred up in me the desire to make that poem a life work—that is to work and work and work on a series of decorative pictures embodying that *American classic* "Hiawatha," and sometime I may place a commission to decorate a public building with it. Could any subject be more appropriate?

Of course this is "shooting high" indeed, but what of it—no one can aim too high!

The article on Agassiz contained something in it for me that the author probably never imagined he got, and that was the way in which he told Agassiz's great *courage!* It made me feel weak and insipid and I believe it has given me an impetus that I'll never lose. If you know of a good book on the life of that *great, great* man please let me know.

And when you wrote to me about his daughter, was it?, who spoke of Grandpapa's being Agassiz's great co-worker, it made me thrill and it explains to me perfectly that Grandpapa really enjoyed life as more ought.

209

Chadds Ford, Pennsylvania
July 1, 1907. Saturday

Dear old Sid,

That incessant drip, drip, drip of the rain always inspires me to take up my correspondence. Your postal was indeed a reminder —it brought back our trip up there together as keenly and as vividly as any description: the station at York Beach, the stage ride, fishermen, the forlorn summer cottage with its cold mattresses and uncomfortable-looking beds, with the miniature snow drift on the window sill—and the cream puffs.

That particular trip is exceptionally significant to me, Sid, and I'll tell you why.

I visited the place with my mind made up absolutely to arrange details for the summer; I foresaw just what I would do. Everything seemed just right in my mind—wonderful country and above all, most congenial company, company whom I respected and knew was a benefit to me. But for the very first time in my life, Sid, I had to recognize a *something* back in my mind that in turn recognized the fact that Ogunquit was not the place for me—the physical character of the country battled with my subconsciousness; I felt immediately the craving for the very quiet and pastoral country, an atmosphere that, as I have come to find out, fit dreams of my early boyhood: of the meadow brook, of the big willows, of plowed fields,

212

of hay cocks in the burning sun, the smell of cows and the calls of the barnyard.

Never have I appreciated nature as I have in this phase—I have enthused over Colorado's mountains and Arizona's deserts. I have been profoundly impressed by the great canyons with their torrents and falls and I have watched hair-raising struggles between men and horses midst wonderfully picturesque surroundings, but never have I felt the real story of nature as I have *this summer!*

The past few months have been an awakening, and I almost feel proud of it!

And, Sid, I believe you have had a great deal to do with it and earnestly hope that sometime I can do half as much for you. That sermon of restraint which you so constantly preached to me shall always cling to my memories as one of the most valued of teachings. And this is a country of "restraints." Everything lies in its subtleties, everything is so gentle and so simple, so unaffected.

210

A fellow student of the Pyle school, Howard E. Smith, was also spending the summer at Chadds Ford.

Chadds Ford, Pennsylvania
July 3, 1907

Dear Mama,

This is the eve of the "Fourth" and I feel as though in some way I should be connected with you people in the celebration. Here, you might think it a Sunday evening except for a few colored lights I have already set off. Smith and Carol and I walked down to the Ford this evening to make a few meager purchases, which we did— half a dozen sky rockets, two dozen Roman candles, some Bengal lights and *a* mine. Of course we hadn't much to choose from but it was fun picking them out and discussing which would be the better purchase, etc.

To tell the truth I feel like celebrating good and hard, and I'll tell you why.

Monday I brought my first farm picture in town to Mr. Pyle— and it created a sensation, to speak honestly. Not a *startling* sensation, thank heaven, but it astonished everyone, even down to certain ones who were always prejudiced against my work.

The fellows told me (after the interview with Mr. Pyle) that when I put the picture up before him his face turned red and perspiration came out on his neck in little beads. He put his arm around my neck and gave me a great, affectionate squeeze—and he couldn't say enough in favor of it. He said that it was the first *big* note ever sounded under his teaching. He told me he was proud of the picture.

Somehow, it has surprised everyone! They all seem dumbfounded that I could handle an extremely subtle and gentle subject in a realistic and vigorous way, and now I feel more confident about the reality of it, because the country folk, farmers mind you, have all liked it and have picked out every big feeling in it—late afternoon, quietude, the clear cool brook, the majesty of the pigeons circling down onto the barn, the peculiar sadness in the farmer-boy's face, what he is thinking and oh! myriads of things have they found. Oh! how anxious I am that you should see it—I am more than anxious because I believe it's the very thing you have always wished me to paint. In the picture I think I have at last got that feeling of lonesomeness which you feel when you look at a Swiss mountain picture with its beautiful valley and village and perhaps its crystal lake.

211

Chadds Ford, Pennsylvania
July 12, 1907. Thursday

Dear Mama,

I am so glad that you enjoy with me the success I have had with my farm picture. I am deep into the second one (of the hay field) but see before me a long concentrated battle. It is a big subject and it might be that I shall start it again. A young girl about eleven years old giving a fellow a drink from an old pitcher—the fellow is resting on his scythe and drinking, in the middle distance are two other men working—they are on a hill overlooking farm buildings and surrounding hills—a hot sun floods over everything.

212

Chadds Ford, Pennsylvania
July 19, 1907

Dear Mama,

I spent yesterday within the brick confines of Wilmington, which,

214

although full of interest and movement, was very wearing and tedious—particularly as it was terribly hot and humid.

My errand in town was to show Mr. Pyle my second picture, which still again aroused his enthusiasm and won his respect and compliment. He made a remark which in itself was ample return for my effort. He said, "It shows how unqualified a teacher is to always judge what is the right and what is the wrong course for a fellow to pursue." Furthermore he added, "It has been a very pleasurable disappointment to me to see the way in which you have pulled yourself through a crisis."

Perhaps you remember that six months ago my enthusiasm for Mr. Pyle and his teaching dropped very decidedly. I never told you why for the simple reason that I didn't know myself. But now that I feel once more confident of my abilities I can look back and see clearly why such relations existed.

When a fellow is groveling around in the dark, searching for something upon which to base good healthy principles, and then the man who has always brought him the proper stimulant ceases to do so and moreover creates a discouraging atmosphere, should not his instincts drive him away just as smoke from burning sulphur would drive him into clear, pure air?

How many times he told me that he doubted my real ability to even paint a big picture because he felt sure I was in the clutches of commercialism and technical facilities. Even allowing for his impulsiveness, that did not relieve my mind of such a terrible foreboding.

And now that I "impulsively" left his immediate environment for the peaceful and pure country, I am able to do my own thinking in an atmosphere not polluted with the minds of all the fellows besides *his* powerful influence.

I'll never forget a thing that [Henry W.] Ranger said, "the man who passes up beyond the level of an art colony or above the teachings of a certain school is the one who goes out by himself and does his own thinking and solves his own problems."

I do not wish in the least to intimate that I feel on the "higher plain," but I *do* believe in the *principle* and congratulate myself upon the fact that I really appreciate its meaning and have actually tasted slightly of its benefits.

My! what weather we are having! Hot and humid! Rattling thunderstorms daily, cloudbursts and *all* that constitutes variety in weather conditions.

From the hill ("Fox Hill," as I call it, having found at least six homes of the Reynard on either slope, all with young ones, and Fox Hill is where we live, thank heaven) the country rolls back like some great billowing crazy quilt: patches of tender green corn interspersed with squares of ripe yellow wheat and the rich succulent greens of the woods. Great voluminous clouds boil up from hot, quivering horizons, blossoming in great bunches of ominous rain clouds. How about the effusion of words! It's great! It's a sight that Papa would revel in!

I got a fine letter from Mrs. Elizabeth Custer—wife of the famous Indian fighter—in regards to those Solitude pictures. She considers them the best example of the interpretation of primitive Indian life that has been produced and has placed them amongst her most valuable historical collection of papers and pictures, which she expects will be passed down through generations of the Custer family.

I shall certainly write her and maybe sometime shall have the pleasure of meeting her.

Your letter was indeed a pleasure to me. Your confidence in me has always been evident, consequently an inspiration. I shall make the greatest efforts to maintain that confidence, which is nearer to me than anything else in the world, and hope that *sometime* you can fully realize your predelictions.

Please let me hear as to your plans for a trip to Chadds Ford!

213

Chadds Ford, Pennsylvania
August 20, 1907

Dear old Sid,

By Gad—it was *bully* to get your letter! It blew in as fresh and breezy as old Ogunquit.

I'm glad that you have harvested costumes and fisherman's paraphernalia. That sort of thing *cannot* be overdone. The least thing, usually so commonplace on the grounds, becomes so extraordinarily vital and interesting when brought into the studio. The fragrance from a piece of kelp should inspire big things.

O Chase! how I love life, nature and all things that grow.

I speak as though I had never appreciated and loved life and nature before, which is not true; but I'll tell you, Sid, the fact is we've been confined to the studio too much, too incessantly—we hadn't time to contemplate nature; all we contemplated were the technicalities of picture building and thereby missed the great underlying impulses of *nature,* and that impulse, I believe, can only be derived from close association with the things you love.

I think that our movement this summer has been one of the biggest and perhaps the most radical thing that has ever happened in the Pyle school, and from what I hear it has excited much favorable comment from the fellows and also from Mr. Pyle.

I know that the preceding "spiel" is awkward and ungainly, but I rely upon your insight to read between the lines and to shape things up coherently for yourself. I have lots bubbling over that I would like to say, but this letter contains some of the frothiest foam only.

214

Elizabeth Jeffreys Guss, "Aunty Guss," and her maiden sister, Anna Jeffreys, "Aunt Anna," lived at Washington's Headquarters.

Studio
1616 Rodney St.
Wilmington, Delaware
September 12, 1907

Dear Mama,

It may surprise you to know that I have just moved in town for the winter! It's like this—last Monday the water on the Taylor place went out of commission and for how long, God knows! I was very much afraid to stay, this being the month that we have to consider (in regards to Carolyn). You know that this is the last of the eighth month and if anything *should* have happened out there without the convenience of *water!* say the *least* numerous minor preparations that are all so important, it might have been very serious.

The past summer has been a glorious one for me and I reckon these 5 months probably the most valuable time spent since under Mr. Pyle's teaching.

I believe that to build up one's character is to build up his work, whatever it is—a sort of a process of elimination of the weak points. This is an aged theory I know, but they spring up fresh and new with some particular vital meaning every once in awhile, it seems to me.

At least I have an honest, and unprejudiced idea of what my true goal *should* be! and that is something I acquired at Chadds Ford.

I have started the fourth and last picture (cultivating young corn, with a little chap riding on the horse, tightly gripping the brass knobs of the harness, his dad trailing the cultivator with the rope-lines around his neck—an old white horse you know, patiently plodding up the side of a hill, with a big stone barn in the immediate background to the right, and a view of the soft spring landscape to the left with winding roads, woods and river, and a distant farm house).

As a parting word let me say that we have found some friends in Chadds Ford that we have formed a great affection for, Aunty Guss and Aunt Anna. Two old Quaker ladies who have filled the vacancy of grandmothers most adequately.

Aunty Guss and Aunt Anna.

They made Carol's summer continually pleasant and their home seems almost like my own. I shall never forget them.

215

Wilmington, Delaware
October, 1907

Dear Mama,

Yesterday something took place in one of the studios that I have been waiting for, for a long time. Dunn has on his easel the *biggest* start on a picture ever perpetrated in Wilmington. I don't assume that my opinion is infallible, but the subject and its rendering exactly coincide with my ideal of what a big picture should be.

I say that I have been waiting for it; and by it I mean that I have been looking for that spirit in work that is competitive with my ways of thinking. His effort has set my blood tingling, he has done me unestimated good, and if he will just hold himself and not become conscious (which is his great weakness) he will do *everyone* good who will have the privilege of seeing the picture.

I've got the place at the Ford and I look forward with all my eyes to next summer when I can have you and Papa and the boys on the hill with us. By Jove, you will enjoy it!

216

Wilmington, Delaware
October 7, 1907

Dear Mama,

To New York and returned! A trip that embodied all that is grand and encouraging!

Mr. Chapin received the pictures with more enthusiasm than ever before, and he passed me a compliment that is hardly discreet for me to tell to anyone outside those who are intimate. He told me that no magazine had yet published a series of pictures that contained the *quality* and *refinement* that I showed in the "Farm Series."— That was enough! He said other things, but that was the most he could say and the most I could ask. It's the ultimate compensation.

Of course, his opinion is not infallible; at the same time he is a man of sound judgment and *always* means what he says, and never says more than is necessary.

The WYETHS

It's needless to say that I am very much pleased—not exactly happy because toward the end I became morbid and discouraged over what I *didn't* get into the pictures, and besides, H.P. gave me very little encouragement when he saw them last week. The fellows were astounded at the cold, indifferent reception he gave me and they seem disgusted with his actions.

Now, however, I feel cooled off in regards to H.P.'s seeming indifference and feel myself above that sort of thing and will tolerate it. Not that I assume any bigger ideals than those which he has, but I know that he lacks consideration for a fellow who is serious, and he is subject to whims and prejudices.

217

Wilmington, Delaware
October 16, 1907

Dear Papa,

I've got an hour or so waiting for some canvas to be sent out from the store downtown and as I have just received your letter, and besides I feel so much like going into the country this afternoon, I'll just drop a line in regards to that place I am going to take.

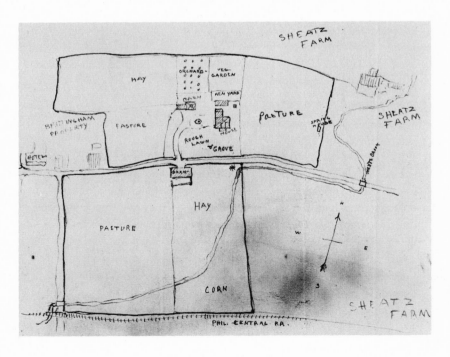

The Country

Enclosed you will find a rough map of the buildings and their general layout. Perhaps if I say that where I have put the star* on the map is the turn in the brook where you and Mama and Carolyn and I went and washed up and the very spot where I took your pictures with Carolyn high up on the fence, it might straighten things out in your mind in respect to location, directions, etc.

The farm to be sure is of a good size, 45 acres; but when you consider it you can readily see that it is not a particularly good *farm* in the farm sense. The plots east and west of the house marked "pasture" are stipulated in the lease *not to be broken.*—The reason is that they are both steep slopes, and during the frequent *heavy* showers the earth is washed in great quantities into the village on the west side and into the spring house on the east, thus seriously interfering with the water supply and pump. Now the largest piece of ground (s.w. of the house) is pasture also and I shall not bother it. The two hay fields I shall take good care of and shall probably plant the patch (5 acres) with corn as it is low and unfit for anything else. The orchard is large and also a big space for vegetables. I will only use what I need and probably put field corn in the remainder, if field corn don't interfere too much with the sweet.

Really, the yard, embodying the house, henhouse, barn (which I will use for studio), grove and rough lawn constitute more land in proportion than I have shown so incorrectly in the plans. The lawn cannot be mowed with a lawn mower (thank heaven) but the people who were there this year went over it twice or three times with the horse mower, which kept it looking neat. The grove is a corker and has pines, maples, oaks, cedars and some chestnut trees in it and not too near the house. That is it don't crowd onto it, about as far from the front porch as our spruces are home.

I think I can manage it all right. Of course I can't expect to run it so as to make much from it, and only expect to get vegetables (summer and winter) for the house and enough hay and corn for a good cow. In this way I can save a great deal. Mr. Taylor or Sheatz are both willing to take the hay and corn land on shares. Whether or not I'll do that I can't say until I consider it more carefully. However, I am going to pay much less rent than in town, and as we proved this summer it is much less expensive to live there, particularly as my work keeps me at home, and last but not least, look what I will have about me! I can't begin to tell you (as you must realize to a certain degree) how valuable it will be to me.

The little barn just west of the house is now a carriage house—square and about 28′ x 22′. So you see there will be little for me to do but to sink in a skylight, and besides it's a four-slope roof to a cupola and one roof is exactly north. The walls are 2-foot through and of stone.

"The little barn just west of the house."

The barn down on the road, possibly you remember it, is of stone, with mows and cow stable (for twelve I believe) in the cellar. There is also one cow stable and horse stall in the same building with the studio—running water in both barns.

With all this I think you had ought to try and get down next summer, after your farm is running good, to straighten me out (I don't doubt but you smile when you read this and say "That's no joke!"). However you must come. It's a spick-and-span place and still rustic too. The view is magnificent and the water fine.

Well, I guess I've given you enough of this, but I thought it might interest you and help you to locate and know just where the place is and about how it looks.

Mama has a sketch Aylward made once 5 years ago—sunlight and amongst trees. That's the house.

Carolyn is in fine health and very expectant. She eats like the deuce and has a never-ending appetite. She smiled broad at your letter and what you said about being a grandfather.

I don't like to think of you as getting old, but I do wish with all my heart and soul that you will be a granddad very soon.

218

Wilmington, Delaware
October 18, 1907

Dear Nat,

Seems to me that I am doing considerable letter-writing home this week, but each one has been prompted by preceding letters from home, so I guess I'm not the only one that is writing. And then again my thoughts are continually with you all, and there is always a little consolation you know in sitting down and having a little chat with one of you—on paper.

"Personal Advice"—*that* made me laugh! I am so glad you didn't open that letter to find it filled with "ways to become famous" and "how to succeed in life" and great, wise discourses on the "philosophy of life," etc. I rather imagine that you heaved a sigh of relief when you scanned its contents, eh? At any rate if you do get *harangues* like that from me take them for what they are worth to you, and consider the deed better than the word.

Your letter was as fresh as usual and you told lots you were not aware of, as is usually the case in your letters. My only wish is that you would write *oftener*.

You are indeed right when you say that a man needs congenial surroundings (congenial in effort, I mean) to bring out his best work, and what is more than that, he needs *keen mental competition,* particularly during the building-up and developing of his intellect, whether it be mechanics, business life, nature study or art. To associate with men eminent in their work or to associate with them through their books is absolutely necessary. The latter, I believe, is almost as good, because in their works or results, whether it be a book, picture, or a finished piece of mechanism, you get the condensed and highest qualities of the man's efforts, therefore evading all of the man's personal weaknesses both in mind and character, which is bound to make one lose respect, and which ultimately affects your confidence in his ability. When you lose confidence in a man's ability you *cease* to reap benefits from him—I think you will agree with me.

Your reason for favoring automobiles and their construction in preference to other things seems to me perfectly legitimate and your stand is well taken, but I am glad to hear you say that you could easily direct your interests if the opportunity arose. I think that's a big step to be able to say so. You probably remember a little discussion we had on the subject once.

Well, Nat—sail right into your work at the N.A.S. [Normal Art School] and you will be bound to be heard from. *Any man* who sincerely and honestly works, and has particular ability in that work which he undertakes, is bound to come out *on top!* Don't you worry, but just *put things through!*

219

"Home" to N. C. Wyeth's grandmother Zirngiebel was always Switzerland.

Wilmington, Delaware
October 20, 1907

Dear Mama,

I seem to be working myself into that "frenzied happiness" that can hardly last—I am almost afraid. These few days seem to be the zenith of a year's pleasure of *living*. It also seems to come just in time for me to feel that great profound day—the 21st, and I can remember Grandmama as well as though she were in front of me. How the autumn symbolizes her character and life. How her yearning soul, yearning for *home,* seems to be told in the mystical haze that veils the landscape, that wonderful home-calling atmosphere of dying nature.

Oh! it's useless for me to try to talk in this way, but my heart yearns, in some way, to impart those innermost feelings. How I hope you can understand even a *little* of what I am trying to say.

I am so glad a "box" is coming. If it did not I would feel it strongly. I never want you to miss that if you can help it, it means a great deal to me—you know I left home on the 19th of Oct. and that box always coming down about that date has a great symbolical meaning to me.

I hope that sometime you will find out Carolyn's real appreciation of those little things that you do—she *loves* them! If nature only permits her to have and *keep* that for which she is *living* and for what I am *longing* this will be one of the happiest homes in existence.

I've got two or three business letters to write and after that Carol and I are going over to the studio and build a rousing fire in the fireplace. I'm going to smoke and dream and she will read, I guess.

Give my love to all—I should like to remember my own birthday a little bit by thanking you and Papa for giving me life—and that with both's help I have been made to love and rejoice in it.

220

Wilmington, Delaware
October 24, 1907

Dear Everybody,

My mind is not my own about now, and I don't suppose it will be for some days to come, and I guess you can all account for the reasons.

The event of my *25th* birthday is now indelibly stamped upon my memory and if all promises hold true to their being, I shall always have a *personal* reminder of the occasion.

Everything happened and came off so beautifully! The day of the 21st Carolyn showed some signs that afterward proved to be symptoms—not that there was any pain, for there wasn't, only an unusual heaviness, and not at all until 11 o'clock did labor start—and it was all over at 12:45. Absolutely no unnecessary pain and as normal a birth as could possibly happen.

The baby is particularly strong (I've got this directly from the doctor, so my enthusiasm is amply justified) and her yell is lusty to the extreme. The babe was put to the breast just one hour after birth and pulled and pinched so hard that Carol made many faces therefrom! I may add that this morning (it's now about 5:45 A.M.) the nurse tells me that the milk has arrived in goodly quantities, so now the hungry little "gink" can be satisfied.

Next I must tell you her name. We have chosen the two names from her grandmothers and for the sake of "Euphony" have arranged it thus: "Ann Henriette Wyeth."

Am I not right that "Hattie" was derived from the original Henriette? I am very much ashamed to acknowledge that deficiency in my knowledge of my own mother's name, but I can't for the life of me ever remember of ever seeing your name any other than "Hattie."

One hour and a half have elapsed, although it sounds as though it were arranged to order, so that I could tell about it, you know. I have been walking the floor with "Ann Henriette." The remarkable thing was that she had been yelling like the devil for about half-hour straight and the instant I took her in my arms she "closed up" completely and stayed so! It pleased me, I can tell you, but I guess it's a bad reputation to have, isn't it?

Carol is very well, except that she hasn't had all the sleep she needs on account of the baby. However I guess she can make it up today all right. She was extremely pleased at your quick reply and recognition and asked me to send her love to you all.

It pleased me very much this morning when she talked long and with very much detail how fine it would be to go "up home" Christmas. The nurse and doctor both said that if everything goes as well as promises there is no reason in the world why we shouldn't go. It would be *grand,* wouldn't it!

Now that birthday box—by Jove, it was fine! It was as precious to me as though it had been filled with rich, costly presents. Oh, my, *more so* because it has given something far beyond that which wealth could buy. The smell of the box was enough!

Carol insisted that I take the top boards off down in the kitchen but not to *touch* another thing until I placed it on a chair beside her bed—and so I did.

The letter on top with *Convers* on it was greedily opened and

226

fully absorbed before another thing was touched. Then followed the flowers that to me meant so much—that is a phase of "the box" that I hoped you wouldn't forget, and you didn't. They were as crisp and fresh as you could wish, and the great breath of "spices" that filled the room as soon as they were disturbed was remarkable. They seem as bright and fresh as ever, this morning, and I shall keep them until the last faint aroma leaves them.

Then Papa's "Buauro Boss?" [Beurre Bosc] and the apples and Cambridge pears are delicious—more than in their taste. Carol is glad that the pears are still hard so that in a week or so she can have some of them.

Aunt Hat couldn't have sent *anything* that could be more appreciated, and she gave such profuse apologies in her letter to me too, which, by the way, I consider *one* of the finest letters I ever got.

Then *last!* The cake with a "reputation."

After I took all the other things out and peered down into the scented gloom of the box I beheld that which symbolizes more than anything else, my birthday. It seemed to sleep in a golden languor, as the rich odors of nuts, spices and sweets exhaled from its plump jacket of icing. Stimson wrote "a cake fashioned by Mama's hands" and that is what strikes me deeper than anything else. The 25 nuts and the "squeezed" blood red barberries were not missed—and then the taste—it's needless to say anymore—great!

No, nothing was missed—from Nat's careful printing on the box to the bottommost clod of packing within it.

As to myself—I laid in a picture the eventful day and will complete it today, so you see I am somewhat collected. I can concentrate there seemingly—I suppose it's because the subject demands such contrary attention to that which I show at home that it makes it easier.—It seems to be rather a source of wonder to the fellows that I can do it. You know I painted my best picture of the Solitude pictures during the "marriage siege."

Chapter IX

AT CHADDS FORD

"And then to Chadds Ford!"

Wilmington, Delaware
November 1, 1907

Dear Mama,

First of all, Carolyn is perfectly well and was up yesterday for the first time, also up today, and tomorrow will be allowed to walk around. The baby is doing fine!

She was so pleased over the selection of names and besides she suggested and insisted that the baby be called Henriette, and pronounced in the French—the way Grandpapa used to call Grandmama, you know.

222

The students of Howard Pyle were Harold Matthews Brett, E. Roscoe Shrader, Percy Ivory, Herbert Moore, and Howard E. Smith.

Wilmington, Delaware
November 4, 1907

Dear old Sid,

Your leaving Wilmington is a hard blow to a number of us who have so seriously counted on your wholesome and well-balanced influence.

There is nothing of much consequence I can tell you, as everything seems to be very quiet—*except Brett*—he's in Arthurs' studio at present. Dunn is working on some illustrations and intermittently on a *painting* which I think is *big*. Pioneer girl twisting grass for fuel—perhaps you saw the start. It is really coming along fine!

Shrader is back and at work, doing the Norsemen's shipbuilding subject for Moore. The latter is still in *Chicago* and expects, I believe, to be there a couple of months, from reports.

Ivory is back with plenty of *good* costume and chuck-full of Mexico.

Smith is hiking around getting the plumbers at the "can," to be put in your studio—so Brett can stay within his own premises—Smith's article "went!" and he is happy. Have not heard much about it yet so can't say more. He's "tickled" and relieved, I can tell you. He made three or four nice sketches during the last few weeks.

As for me—I've started my "painting" too. Have been working on it some three weeks. When it gets along I'll photograph it and send it up. "The End of the Day" suggests the subject perhaps.

Well, this news may strike you as being a little light and commonplace just now, but I believe you will like to keep in touch with things in Wilmington, and if you say so I shall make it a point to keep you posted.

223

Bancroft Studios
No. 1616 Rodney Street
Wilmington, Delaware
November 4, 1907

Dear Mama,

Of course I have been pretty well tied down in town for the last three or four weeks, but from the north windows of the studio I can look out upon a long bank of hardwood trees that are still dense with the richest bronze, golden foliage you ever saw. In places a great tall tree stretches its long gray arms above the mass with only a few fluttering leaves left to tell the tale of summer. It seems to me that *just beyond* that bank of trees lies that stretch of country that I love, and the nodding tree tops are forever beckoning, beckoning.

As I grow older, each season as it progresses becomes more beautiful than anything I ever saw, and then as it merges into the following one my emotions and loves seem to run still higher until at times I feel as though my sense of appreciation *must* break.

Yesterday I wrote an article for the *N. Y. Herald*. I was invited to contribute on a certain question and gladly did so because the idea appealed to me. Whether it will be accepted I know not, as I was a little late, and too, it may not be good enough. There is a movement in N. Y. City to have the Metropolitan Art Museum set aside a gallery for the best example of illustrations. As I understand it, the men at the head of the museum are not at all in favor of it, so the *N. Y. Herald* is publishing opinions by ?eminent? illustrators and painters and of course will only publish the favorable comments.

The funny part of it is that H.P. was telling me in great glee that he was asked, as a dean of American illustration, to contribute and took it upon himself to assume that his opinion was all that was asked for. Well, he read me his "sour grapes," sarcastic, wholly undignified article with great importance. I did not receive my invitation until the next day so was innocent of any false play. Well, I have got a chance to air my views, that do not at all agree with his, and on the same sheet. I hope that luck favors me.

224

The John referred to was John Cummings, the model, employed by Howard Pyle for his students.

Bancroft Studios
Wilmington, Delaware
November 6, 1907

Dear Mama,

Everything seems to be going superbly; the baby sleeps all it should and eats like the deuce. She is extremely healthy and strong and a *"fine looker"* according to the "Wimmen folks."—I don't know they all look alike to me. I know, however, that she has good lungs, looks very healthy, and has rings of fat around her neck and wrists and a big wad on her bottom.

Tell Nat that John has been working about three days a week in the Wilmington Garage and is also taking a complete course on "Gas Engines" in the Correspondent Schools in this City. I encouraged him, as he is really too alert and too useful to stand and pose all day long, and besides when I go to the Ford I shall not want him. He is the same old faithful, but now that I have got into my work so deeply I can't tolerate anybody talking or acting in any way free about me, and we have become so familiar that it is impossible and too late to draw the line now. Thus a change will be better for me.

225

Bancroft Studios
Wilmington, Delaware
November 10, 1907

Dear Mama,

Yesterday I purchased a baby carriage. I have bought it probably a little early, for outdoor use, but Carol wanted it downstairs so that she can use it as a "downstairs crib." By the way, where is the old one we all used—I suppose there is nothing left of it? Are there any of the old things we used left at all? Highchair or anything? Would like to own something of that sort.

I have completed a *Post* story and this morning I started one of the "Aerial Warfare" pictures for *Scribner's*. I am still working on my painting, of course, and I am gradually pulling it out, I believe. Everyone likes it immensely.

Your letters have all been so rich and full and weighty that I don't wonder that you feel the need of a rest. I shall write just as often, of course, and if my letters ever have too much in them just tell Nat to "close me up" a bit. Perhaps a safety-valve on my writing spirit, registered to low pressure, would be a good thing.

226

N. C. Wyeth's mother was a highly emotional person. On her doctor's advice, Wyeth was asked to not write her such intense letters.

Bancroft Studios
Wilmington, Delaware
November 10, 1907

Dear Papa,

Received your letter yesterday and write in answer to ask you about this letter-writing proposition. You see, I got a letter from the doctor in which he asks my cooperation in that I will not write to Mama, but to the rest of the family. In today's writing I have followed out *your* suggestions—that is, to write just the same.

I shall try to keep my letters *down* in temperament and spirit and that may eliminate the real cause of her mental nervousness. You see, it's awfully hard for me to restrain the thoughts that are deepest in my mind, particularly when I write home. *There* it is that I confide my innermost feelings (except to Carol of course), and it is from there that I receive my real and most valued consolation, sympathy and appreciation; and when all my feelings and thoughts are caged up from everybody else for a week at a time, there necessarily comes a "blow-off" in my letter home.

It might be well to ask Mama for the letter I have just written to see if it is "within bounds" before she reads.

227

Dear Mama,

Last night I heard Paderewski, and never have I *ever* enjoyed music so much! Even now it seems incredible to think that what I heard was rendered on a piano and by one man—it was marvelous!! *Not* in a technical sense at all, but the wonderful, wonderful feeling with which he interpreted the music.

Friday night—I started this letter last night but I had to take charge of the baby until 12:30—she's been doing a whole lot of bawling this last 24 hours, in fact that's just what she's doing this minute.—Now she's stopped—for only a minute, I guess—there she goes!!

Well, my work has been pretty confining both at the studio and at home, so have very little else to tell you. My picture seems to be very much liked by all the fellows, which fact is intensely stimulating—I haven't showed it to Mr. Pyle, but will as soon as I feel it is on its last lap. Today I scraped out the face of the character in the picture—one that I have worked on for over six weeks. It used to be that I would not have the *nerve* to do such a thing, but I am happy to say that I feel perfectly free to paint on this picture all winter, if necessary, to reach the proper result.

228

The new Howard Pyle student was William V. Cahill.

Dear Mama,

Thanksgiving's over and nobody is the worse for it in *this* house. Henriette celebrated by keeping me up walking until about 1:30 this morning. Too much turkey I guess. She tipped the scales today, 10 *lbs.*, so you can see she is doing well. It's pretty hard to realize that she belongs to *us* sometimes, particularly while I am at work in the studio and suddenly remember just how things are.

How anxious I am for you to see her and hold her, and Papa too; I've *thought* and *thought* about it, and the best of it is that in all probabilities it will all be realized in three weeks or so. We shall take the sleeper direct to Boston and then to Needham station. From the station home I intend to get a hack from Eaton's—if you or Papa have other suggestions, let me have them. I do want a closed carriage however.

In spite of *hard times* and the fact that most of the fellows here are idle (as far as ordered work goes), I have *Scribner's*, *Century* and *Sat. Evening Post* hot on my heels.

Cahill, a fellow who recently joined the colony, is one from a clique of *painters* in N.Y. From amongst the *big men,* [Childe] Hassam, Birge Harrison, H.D. Murphy, John Alexander, etc. He has great ideas and theories that seem and are diametrically opposed to *illustration*, but undoubtedly of a very high class in respects to real painting.—He has been coaching me on my big picture. He is extremely anxious that I should get it into the Academy this year and predicts that it will take well and sell quickly. He asked me how much I was going to ask for it and I said $500. He laughed (and I thought that he meant it too much) but this is the figure he said would be a nominal price, $1500.

Not being used to the "painting prices" and "painting world" it looks exorbitant to me, but he trotted out a list of prices of the last exhibition and I see that it really *is* nominal.

229

Bancroft Studios
Wilmington, Delaware
December 3, 1907

Dear Sid,

I suppose that peaceful old Haverhill is blanketed in white tonight as we are here. It is a remarkably beautiful storm and makes the country appear positively "New Englandy," which by the way reminds me of certain beseeching passages in your recent letter. In regards to them, let me tell you something.

My grandmother was born in the mountains of Switzerland. When twenty-three years of age she tore herself from all her people and the quiet romantic little dairy home to follow my grandfather to America. Dropped into the heart of Cambridge, Mass., among strange people, unable even to speak a word of their tongue, she lived for three years. Then it was, in 1867, that my grandfather purchased a lonesome bit of land in the outskirts of Needham and on the Charles River, and here my dear old grandmother almost pined her heart away for her home and people in the Swiss mountains. During this pitiful condition of mind she gave birth to her only daughter—my mother.

Here, prenatal influence asserted itself. Her longing soul became my mother's inheritance. I can read it in her every letter, in her eyes and in her voice. It has always impressed me profoundly, and I in turn have inherited that strange love for things remote, things delicately perfumed with that sadness that is so exquisitely beautiful.

Among those misty gray hills of Chadds Ford, along the stretches of those succulent meadows with their peaceful cattle, in those big sad trees and the quaint and humble stone farmhouses tucked underneath them, there is that spirit which exactly appeals to the deepest appreciation of my soul. To me it is all like wonderfully soft and liquid music.

And to go further, I want to tell you that when my mother visited that country two years ago it nearly overwhelmed her. To this day she speaks and writes about it. It struck a responsive chord in her soul too!

My yearnings for home and New England are from the *heart*, but my love for that quiet, pastoral country, so supremely remote in spirit, if not in fact, is from my soul.

I suppose, Sid, it's folly for me to attempt to write these things, words seem so inadequate and meaningless, but I just couldn't help it. I only dare to hope that I can commune these feelings to you in my work—sometime.

I would never have ventured to write this sort of letter to anyone but you—it would be foolish. I know *you* will *try* to search its meaning.

Enough of this.

The work here in Wilmington seems to be running about the same, a little more commercial perhaps. The latter fact jars me considerable.

Smith is doing some interesting illustrations for *Harper's Mo.* and is also carrying along a subject picture which I have not seen. Shrader

237

is painting the "Viking" picture; Moore is still West. Dunn isn't doing much of anything at present, it's nearing his wedding day you know and he is rather unsettled. Arthurs is completing his "Old Boston Post Road" pictures and so far they are coming fine! Schoonover was gambling at "Monte Carlo" when we last heard from him. Peck is still sighing and painting a little. Brett is busy.

230

Bancroft Studios
Wilmington, Delaware
December 3, 1907

Dear Mama and Papa!

Carol will write I suppose tomorrow but I must drop a line to tell you how much we value the cup you sent to our baby. Nothing is more suitable! and well do I remember the battered one that I used to throw around—I can remember using it out in the yard and under the old shed between the house and barn where the dirt used to be rather sandy and soft. I can even remember the shape. Wasn't the handle a butterfly's wing?

231

Bancroft Studios
Wilmington, Delaware
December 8, 1907

Dear Mama,

Well, we've heard so many words of warning from every side that, notwithstanding the doctor's, "I don't see why not," we have finally decided after considerable debate not to risk taking baby up home Xmas. Of course that deprives us of the same trip. It's needless pain for me to dwell on that fact but will hasten on to try and smooth over the disappointment with another plan. Papa partly suggested it in his Saturday's letter and I am enlarging somewhat the suggestion.

Can't you possibly arrange to come down right after Xmas, say the Friday or Saturday after? You must! I'll send you your ticket both ways with extra enough for a stateroom which is $3, I believe, and then surely Papa will be willing to pay for whoever might come with you.

It's *just* the right time to come, everything is going fine, lots of my work here to show you, all kinds of accommodations at the house and *everybody* anxious to see you!

I want you here before we break up to go to the country.

I don't see how it is possible for me to come up alone *at all* because you see Mrs. B. [Bockius] is alone with all her children and work. Eliz. is away living with her aunt, and Hilda, the next oldest girl, is the only help she has, and George is on his back with bronchitis (the main support of the family), and so you see I can't depend on any of them to stay with Carol, and I *can't* leave her alone!

Just think! Get into your stateroom at 8 o'clock in the evening and I'll meet you at the train in Wilmington at 7:30 in the morning. Don't let anybody "palm" you off into those damnable sleepers!

232

Bancroft Studios
Wilmington, Delaware
December 14, 1907

Dear Mama,

P.S. Enclosed is an article, *N. Y. Herald,* to which I was asked to contribute. The article explains itself. Mr. Pyle and I were both asked, but his was such a nasty fling at the Museum directors that they would not print it. I think myself that he took a very unwholesome view of it; I read his contribution before it was sent. Kindly save this as it is the only one I have.

233

Bancroft Studios
Wilmington, Delaware
December 24, 1907

Dear Mama,

Xmas is closing in fast, and when I think that New Year's day is only a week off it makes the time simply *evaporate!*

It is extremely mild this evening, in fact it is summery! But in strong contrast to the mellow atmosphere, there stands at my left just outside the open window, with its fragrant branches sticking inside the room, our Xmas tree. Heavy rains drenched it in our backyard last night, and today John made a stand for it and put it under cover on the front porch to dry out. The wind is blowing up from the west, deliciously fresh and will probably get cooler tonight.

I have been very busy with my work and some Xmas shopping and will welcome the relaxing trip home. Tonight Carolyn and I are going downtown, just to mingle in the Xmas crowd, and I am going to look into the time tables and see if I can't make better time by changing in New York to the Grand Central instead of taking a through train. If so I shall telegraph the exact time I am due at Back Bay. Let Babe notify the telegraph operator to telephone the message down, or to notify Crossman's store or some such place.

The trip home is a great big event for me and involves many-sided feelings.— First I am happy that I am to go, secondly I am sorry to leave Carolyn and the baby, thirdly I can't realize that you are actually coming back with me. The latter is the great redeeming feature to both Carolyn and myself.

Boxes will pass one another between Needham and Wilmington somewhere.

234

Wilmington, Delaware
January 22, 1908

Dear Mama,

The half-past-six whistles are blowing and it is still quite dark, so between now and daylight I'll write a few lines.

My work is pushing me terrificly, which has worried me considerable the last few days, and which resulted in rather a poor night's rest last night—however I feel like starting in fresh this morning and hope to accomplish something. The instant publishers press me for time, that minute I go to pieces. Last Saturday I got word that *Century* wanted their picture ahead of time—well, that was crowding some, then, on top of that, yesterday the *Post* ripped *3 weeks* off my time, making it compulsory that I get in three drawings in four days. Then to cap it all, John was called up to Philadelphia last night and will have to spend the day there with his dying aunt. Of course I am sorry for him, but damnit, today I wanted him beyond words! —and now the baby is crying!

Unfortunately yesterday I got quite a scare. Of course Ed did not think, but you know he enclosed that sensational clipping with Nat's photo—well, that is the first thing I looked at when I opened the letter, and when I read in glaring type that "Five Skaters Die in Icy Waters" and then glanced down and saw *Nat's* picture I actually almost keeled over. It was hard for me to open the letter but when I saw that Ed started out by telling me how you enjoyed your trip I immediately revived—but by gawd!

Nevertheless, the incident and the unfortunate way in which it impressed me clung to me all day, and does now. I felt like flying up home and giving Nat a good hug! It was just as though he had been dead and was resurrected.

I am glad that Nat got the poor little cuss out and I know that if anyone had the courage to do a thing like that it would be him.

Now that sketch (of the artist), the postals and baby's photo I want to send all together so patiently wait until all are in readiness.

We continually talk of your visit, particularly Carol.

235

Wilmington, Delaware
March 6, 1908

Dear Mama,

Scribner's just bestowed another grand chance upon me in the way of a poem. The poem deals with the spirit of an old canoe in the northern waters. The last four lines of the five verses will give you the gist of the entire poem:

> While in memory's haze I live the days
> That forever are gone from me,
> As I rot on the marge of the old portage
> With grief for company.

Scribner's seems to know what I like. They sent me an engineering story which calls for a picture of a surveyor clinging to the sheer wall of a canyon. The latter picture I must complete in another week.

And then to Chadds Ford!

I wrote Ed day before yesterday and enclosed carfare both ways. If he can do it I certainly would like to get him down before we leave Wilmington. That only leaves two Sundays, as the 16th we start to pack.

Oh! George B. [Bockius] was over last night—no, Wednesday night, and I showed him Nat's blueprint of his auto. It took the fellow clean off his feet. I never heard him ever praise anything before, but he couldn't say enough about that drawing. He said it was exceptionally professional and worthy of a much older man of experience.

236

Wilmington, Delaware
March 9, 1908

Dear Mama,

You can imagine how things are rushing and stewing when I tell you that the creation of a picture for *Scribner's*, preparing for a wedding, and getting things together to *move* are all on the go at the same time.

Thank heaven! the picture I mention, the "Locating Engineer" has come *very* easily, and I think is quite a striking illustration, comparative to my other work of course. That ends my four years of illustration in the city of Wilmington, and I confidently and eagerly want to say that this move will mark a big change in the quality of my work.

Perhaps I have mentioned it before, but I have written two or three long arduous letters to you that have never been sent—yes, they've been torn up; simply because I couldn't embody the things I wanted to say. I have made, what would seem to anyone else, radical changes in my attitude toward art and its real meaning. The reason that I consider this winter "eminent" is because I have done all my thinking *alone* and have built up a new and purer foundation (purer, in that it is entirely *my own*) upon which to build the work of the future which I long for so intensely that it is painful to wait.

Recently I have been re-reading Hamilton Wright Mabie's essays on "Nature and Culture," "Weeks & Days," etc., and in one *Essays on Work and Culture,* on page 149, Chapter XVI, starts a talk on concentration, which I wish for my sake you would read. "Concentration" and the following two chapters on "Relaxation" and "Recreation" are *superb!* and will do you untold good!

I want you to know how I feel and what I intend to work for. —"Concentration" embodies my thoughts in very concrete form and in exceedingly understandable form.

Last photo taken of N. C. Wyeth in his Wilmington studio.

237

Wilmington, Delaware
March 16, 1908

My dear Sid,

Well, Carolyn is upstairs packing this minute and I've got to join her just as soon as I finish this note. This week will be one of worry

243

and work. We will certainly be greatly relieved when all our stuff is safely stored in our new home. You see it's all got to be teamed out (about six big loads); to freight it would mean crating the whole business and handling it four times.

I have solved two or three problems this winter that I feel have put my mind on a restful basis, which seems to me is necessary before one can accomplish. I have come to one *conclusion*, and that is painting and illustration *cannot* be mixed—one cannot merge from one into the other. The fact is you have got to drop one absolutely before attempting the other, because the viewpoints of the illustrator and painter are so entirely different.

I shall illustrate for at least five years more and throw my whole soul into the work, and then I hope to have funds enough ahead to allow 10 good solid years of painting. If I can't grasp something in that time I shall start again. Meantime I shall study nature as closely as possible, that is to be very observant and to associate with it as much as possible, to learn to love and appreciate its moods, to study its trees and skies. I hardly expect to be able to commune with nature as I should, until I can drop *all* commercialism; to paint only for *myself*, not even for exhibitions, until I feel established.

I hope sometime to be able to throw off *all* that conscious feeling that I am painting for magazines or exhibitions or *anything* or *anybody*. That condition of mind, I am firmly convinced, *must* be attained before one can religiously paint, and one can hardly say that it is possible to work definitely for such a condition of mind; it is more a case of living simply and naturally, and so sincerely that you unconsciously eliminate the inferior qualities of your nature. By the way, Sid, I have just got hold of a little pamphlet *As a Man Thinketh* by James Allen (not James Lane Allen). It's one of the most wonderful essays I ever read.

Say, I didn't intend to "string out" so upon what *I think* is right, but I only wanted to show you upon what lines I've been thinking and what I intend doing. If I could only have a day's talk with you! I think you would help me mightily! You gave me a wonderful boost once and I think you could do it again.

Under separate cover I am sending you a photo of Carolyn and the baby.

Well, this is my last letter to you under the above address; in a

week we will be in our new home. Try to arrange a trip to Chadds
Ford sometime this summer.

Carolyn Wyeth with Henriette.

238

Chadds Ford, Pennsylvania
March 24, 1908

Dear Mama,

Well—here we are! in the second story S.E. room of the Chadds Ford Hotel—awaiting for Millers to move. We have a *glorious* room, even if it is in a hotel! Our windows overlook the broad sweep of valley that runs up to the old mill and beyond; the trees scattered through it are just showing the first signs of spring; that haze that envelopes the tree forms caused by the first bursting of the buds hangs like a wonderful gauze over all.

Although it is mild, a high March wind is whistling around our windows—it is a mournful wail and makes me think of two things, Harris School and the "Story of Kennett"—rather an odd combination stirred by the whistling wind, but it distinctly suggests both to me.

To go back a week—when Ed was down to visit us in our little home *that was*. His visit did me *worlds* of good! and my only wish was that he could have made it a longer one. I spent a particularly fine morning with him, when we walked out to the tower and rambled down through the rocks to the river and followed its course home. For the *first time* I caught that spirit from him that I have always hoped and felt sure was there. A deeper love for growing things than simply their practicality and the scientific element.

Although he talked a great deal on "specie," "genus," and "family," he showed clearly his inner love for growing things and also their *beauty*. How he marveled over the trees, their uniformity and character, and the fellow just longed for those hills that we could see from the tower, and I can honestly say that I never saw them *more* beautiful than on that morning. I believe it was partly because he was so appreciative that they seemed more beautiful to me through his sympathies. You know, I enjoy a landscape *much* more if I am with one who looks at it from a *"pure"* standpoint, than when I am with one (an artist for instance) who looks at it with a half-commercial eye—that is he (the artist) immediately adapts it to his canvas, to be admired and bought by someone, he gloats over its possibilities to bring him fame and fortune. I *know* that is how 99 out of a 100 do look at nature, and there is the rub! I pray many

246

times that I shall always love *nature as a refined*, sensitive layman would, and not as a "nature-faker" would love it!

This is getting away somewhat from my letter I guess—but to get back; Ed is in the right track and all he needs is the right environment, and if he can't find associates wherever he locates that are the right kind, he would be better off alone. And that is what I tried to impress upon his mind. To choose his companions *discreetly*, to hold his dignity. I am anxious that he gets a room alone where he can read, and write his letters, for I believe that in writing the *right kind* of letters a fellow crystalizes many good thoughts that otherwise would disappear like morning mists.

There goes our dinner bell! Back again with a full belly!

All our furniture is out here and up at the house, I am glad to say. With all the previous good weather I was afraid lest we "get soaked" —but we chose three fine days to move in and now there is nothing to worry about now in that line.

I got a whole diagram from Ed about vegetables, when to plant, how, etc. There's a fine patch all fenced in and we anticipate "big truck."

239

Chadds Ford, Pennsylvania
March 28, 1908

Dear Mama,

Well, there's enough to write about—lord knows! Uncle Gig has been here! He blew in Wednesday night about 8 o'clock—great surprise! and he stayed until this morning. We made most of his time, and blest with the finest weather, he has left with a mighty fine idea of this country. He was carried away with it!

The evening he came, we talked until 12—we were up at 6:30 and took a walk over to the creamery, around the meadow and back, then after breakfast Carol, Uncle G. and I took quite an extended walk over the hills back of the town, returning at eleven, and from then 'til one I took him away up the valley and over the western hill through Pocopson, Birmingham, near Dilworthtown and back the "Crik" road. The afternoon he and I spent walking around and up by Lafayette's Headquarters up over their hills to Taylor's and down to Washington's Headquarters (where we paid "Aunty Guss" and "Aunt Anna" a call), down through the old mill and back to supper—a short walk after supper and a few yarns in the saloon and we all went to bed tired and sleepy.

The day was ideal—it was windy and great armies of fleecy clouds scudded across the sky, painting the hills with ever-changing colors and shadows. It was very balmy, in fact we got quite burned.

I can't begin to tell you how I know he enjoyed it, except to remark that he enjoyed the *simple things*—the call of birds, gurgling brooks, the trees, the violets and dandelions that are just peeping out, the soft warm grass, the soaring buzzards and the historic quaintness and neatness of the farms; even to genuinely enjoy sitting on the spacious hotel porch when the walks were over and to say "My God, this is what I *like!*"

After all the years he has spent "having a good time," going here and there to dinners, theaters, picnics and parties, it's remarkable and agreeably surprising to see him long to get back to nature, to seek the simple, natural things and to honestly and heartily enjoy them. It has done me worlds of good—and with all his weaknesses (and every *last one* of us have corresponding weaknesses as bad, and in *many* cases a darn sight *worse*) he has that redeeming feature, given to him by Grandpapa, I suppose, appreciative of *simple, wholesome* things. What a pity that more people haven't that quality. There is *always hope* for a man who has it, and although he may not leave a bank account, he has enjoyed the short life given him and has helped other people to do so, besides. And, pray tell me, what else is there to live for!

To leave Uncle Gig— I spent the morning in my garden "spading up." I have manured the patch which is about 65 by 125 feet and have about ⅓ forked in. There is still the cornpatch, however, about half that size, which I shall leave until next week. I hope to finish this job tomorrow—it's pretty hard on my gut!

The farmers predict a cold snap soon.

Our stuff is all in the house, so I really don't worry any as far as that goes, but I should hate to see all the trees and shrubs nipped.

Oh! it is possible that Uncle G. will come down next week to help us settle. He certainly would be a good one, wouldn't he?

240

At Chadds Ford

Dear Mama,

Well, by Jove! I don't know what the devil I'd have done if Uncle Gig hadn't turned up when he did. He's put in three days of stavin' hard work and has accomplished what I thought almost impossible! To begin with he has laid two rooms of matting, put up three stoves, unpacked 5 barrels of crockery, etc., and two boxes of lamps, bric-a-brac, etc., and numerous other things.

But do you know, we are pretty well straightened out inside, and inside of a week we will be all fixed.

He's a corker! that fellow; we have had some mighty fine talks, and by Jove if he had had the proper opportunities when he was young he would have made something big out of himself.

How much he has inherited from Grandpapa!

241

Chadds Ford, Pennsylvania
April 9, 1908

Dear Ed,

Such a marvelous spring—beneath, on every side, our hill drops down into great, warm meadows with sparkling glints of brooks, and above them, big gauzy clusters of willows crowded with flocks of blackbirds. The distant hills, ruddy with red maples, fade off into the dreamy haze of spring, punctuated here and there with dazzling white farm buildings. It's useless to try to describe it, in fact it's almost painful to do so, because I would like so much to have you here to enjoy it with me.

Your visit (which I am so thankful you were able to make) has meant more to me than you can imagine. Although the time was short, I read between the lines, so to speak.

Uncle G. has of course given me quite a vivid picture of your surroundings and work, and judging from it, I should think that you have a mighty good start! Dig at it! Throw yourself into your work! Shut your eyes to *time* and think of your *future!* Make everything you do a foundation stone to the final, great structure, whether it's shoveling shit or planning a "Pagoda." And bear this "last but not least" fact in your mind—think of it always! Don't for God's sake let any *friend* or friends interfere with your progress.—Suffer your loneliness and make companions of your *books! Sacrifice* the small things for the *great.* Clench your fists and *make* yourself <u>strong</u> in character and you will be strong in *purpose* and superior in results. It's *hard,* but what is *good* and *great* is *always* hard. Don't weaken at crucial moments!

Looking down from the Wyeth house onto the village of Chadds Ford.

242

Chadds Ford, Pennsylvania
April 13, 1908

Dear Mama,

Smith and Cahill are out here and at work, but for some reason I don't feel at all sympathetic with their method of approaching their work. They have come like hunters with guns over their shoulders, to "shoot landscapes" and nothing more. They talk of "beautiful brooks," "lovely trees," "wonderful skies," "bully atmosphere," etc., etc., but *neither* has an iota of appreciation of the deeper significance of growing things, of the *mystery* of nature, of its *deeper* meaning. To me, their appreciation of nature seems aesthetic but foundation-less.

I sincerely pity them and undoubtedly they pity me with my "responsibilities." Without the latter, a man is like a boat without a ballast, and they (like the boat without ballast) are flipping like eggshells across the surface of the water, and how they can arrive at any solid ground without *smashing* is more than I know. Time will tell, however.

243

"Hilda" was Carolyn Wyeth's sister, Hildegard Bockius.

Chadds Ford, Pennsylvania
May 25, 1908

Dear Papa,

Well, we all certainly hope that everything turns out favorable in regards to your arrangements for a trip "south!"

Yesterday we made ice cream for the first time and I believe it's the first time I've turned a freezer for 5 years or since I left home. It brought back old "churnings" on the cistern-top, I can tell you. I remember once when Joe McGilvery came over and helped churn for some celebration.—I think it was the time when you had those large tents set up back of the barn, and had all those Cambridge people out!

Well, to get back to ice cream—for once we made it so rich we couldn't eat it. I got cream at the creamery—thick as butter—for 20¢ a quart—so I thought we would spread ourselves and get 2 qts. cream and mix with a quart of milk and 3 qts. of strawberries (and by the way they are only 3 for a quarter *now*). We've got a six qt. freezer, and *by damn* if it didn't swell and fill the can up! First time I ever got really *stuck* on *one* saucer of ice cream!!

We called in a number of friends but have not got rid of it yet. Even *Hilda* proved incompetent!

Now Papa, keep me posted just when we may expect you.

244

Dear Mama,

It's really been too hot to accomplish much. I've done comparatively little practical work but have worked out of doors, that is
on outdoor studies quite a good deal, and can really see rapid improvement in that direction. Although I am, of course, extremely
inferior, in landscape *particularly,* I have surprised myself somewhat
in the way I am grasping certain truths in my close nature study.
I have spent considerable time on the study of an apple-tree trunk
with surrounding detail, intent only on putting down as close an
imitation of the thing as it is possible. This study alone has encouraged me immensely as it is a radical departure for me and is the
result—not of natural ability, spontaneity, or luck—but *good solid*
study!

I have come to believe that the thing for me to do is to start right
at the bottom, to build up a solid foundation of knowledge—a close
knowledge of *nature,* to get right down to facts as they exist.

With such preparation (as I hope to achieve) there is no reason
in the world that one can't keep on growing the rest of his life. I
mention this because so many men reach the height of their achievements in early or middle life, and from that point they decline and
live the rest of their lives in torture. What *they* produced was the
result of gifted ability, spontaneity, etc., etc. They had no need for
hard study in their early days; they could produce better without
that "encumbrance." *But* when at last "the fires of youth" left them,
their *ability* left them and they became stranded, with no rock-
bottom of knowledge to refer to, nothing upon which to rebuild.

My work has been more or less the result of enthusiasm and
spontaneity and not so much the result of hard work. People say to
me sometimes, "You must work hard and fast to turn out so many
pictures." Yes, I do work *fast* but not *hard!* Everything has come
easy to me and Oh! I am so thankful that I can at least judge *myself*
in the true light. The next proposition is to put the idea into *action!!*

I drive myself into the heat to sketch and into the studio to
work when I had much rather sit on the porch and read or smoke.
That's all well enough, but I want *work* to become a habit, some-

thing I can't shake from me, and not something I have to urge myself to do. I was always sensitive to competition and a little bit now would help me get into the traces.

Baby is almost free of her rash.

The butcher was here this morning and he weighed her, 19½ *lbs.* Pretty good, eh! She is *so* alert to everything that to *me* she puts every other baby I ever saw in the shade. We will see what her grandfather's verdict is!

"I have spent considerable time on the study of the apple tree."

245

Chadds Ford, Pennsylvania
May 29, 1908

Dear Nat and Babe,

All my surplus energy has slowly and surely dribbled out of my system today in the form of good old substantial, odoriferous <u>sweat</u>; consequently I find myself with emaciated mind, empty stomach and lost manhood this evening; *therefore*—you are both *deprived* (sarcasm for *relieved*) of any pretentious birthday epistle. In fact I found that I had barely strength enough to make out the check for $5. I'm sure if I'd been less fatigued I could have reached a higher denomination.

For the life of me I can't recollect your ages—only know that you are both still young and fair-looking and with prospects. I can't wish you anything better, unless it is *health* (and it's not worthwhile to mention that to a Wyeth, God bless the name). So what can I say?

I've managed to cover a couple of sheets with bullshit; *anyway,* I only wanted to use this paper to protect the most valuable "enclosed" from curious eyes.

You can only cash it *once!*

With best wishes from us *both!*

P.S. You get a Stevens-Duryea, Nat, and Babe can buy out Mama's interest in the "Marine Paint Co." *Keep the change.*

Chadds Ford, Pennsylvania
June 20, 1908

Dear Mama,

The past two weeks mark the first period of time that I have resolutely stuck to a certain idea, in regards to my work. I have come to a *definite* conclusion that *no* one knows what I am really striving for and that *therefore* I shall *not* suffer the humiliation (for it is humiliation) of showing my work to *anyone*. I refer particularly to my *studies*—not to my illustrations. My work now is primary work—crude, chaotic, uninteresting! I am striving to express things that no one knows but myself—if I *could* explain and describe these intangible things, why, I *wouldn't paint,* I'd write and lecture, I would be an author of essays and stories, in short I would be a literary man instead of an artist. I am striving for knowledge, just plain, solid, intimate knowledge: I am *not* making pictures to be looked at, anymore than a musician carefully tuning his instrument wishes those meaningless sounds to be called expressive harmony. My studies now mean nothing to anyone else—so *why* show them? It is a bitter pill for me to swallow, because I have my impulsiveness, my enthusiasm, my natural desire to please, and my craving to hear from people whom I respect that I am gaining ground, to battle against—and I'll tell you it's hard.

Carol knows my resolutions and is heartily in sympathy with them, and I can say, even in this short test, she has saved me twice from attempting to break my resolution. She accomplished the task with the usual woman's cleverness by embarrassingly reminding me of my resolutions while I was in the act of going to the studio with friends. I hope she can keep up her courage (and maybe if you just tell her quietly in a letter that you know of my resolutions and that you feel that she could be a great help to me in that direction, it would encourage her beyond measure).

I'll tell you, Mama, no one knows or can they even faintly realize just what a struggle it is to achieve real distinction in painting (I do not mean *popularity,* understand, but a distinction in personality of work). If I had had as clear an outlook on what one has before him in art, five years ago, as I have now, I am afraid the discouragement would have turned me to other paths.

I have *never* fought, I have never *worked* (this is an *honest, un-affected* statement made in *no* whining voice, with no idea of solicit-ing remarks of sympathy or praise)—I have *not*—and that is all there is to say about the matter! What I *have* accomplished has come easily, impulsively and what is more to my sorrow, *quickly*. When I look back onto the last four years I can hardly believe that it was myself that produced that flashy, superficial succession of work.

It is as though I had been working out on a sunny hill with the winds blowing and great cumulus clouds lifting and passing over my head, with the world stretched out at my feet and disappearing into everlasting distances. *Now* I feel as though I were in some deep, mist-laden valley, searching vaguely for a path that will lead me to the great towering peak that faintly shows its ragged head through the haze. I feel almost hopelessly strange. Everything seems so far beyond my reach—so intangible! With everything said, I know vaguely or in other words I can *sense* what one ought to attain and therein lies my hope, my excuse for living!

Work and *patience!* Therein lies success, therein lies my weak-ness!

247

The "Indian Sun-Dance" series never appeared in McClure's. *Two of the illustrations were published in black and white for the second edition of* Reminiscences of a Ranchman *by Edgar Bucher Bronson in 1910.*

Edmund C. Tarbell (1862–1938) and Frank W. Benson (1862–1951) were at this time among the foremost exponents of the American Impressionist school and were popular as teachers.

Chadds Ford, Pennsylvania
June 30, 1908

Dear Mama,

It's about 5:30—another one of the many wonderful days we have been having this past month. It's hot and dry, although outwardly the country does not show it in the least. The greatest manifestation lies in the exceedingly dusty roads, and then you hear the farmers talking about "dry-rot" in regards to potatoes; otherwise everybody is pleased because it is such excellent harvest weather.

Tell Papa that Dr. [Arthur] Cleveland (that's the big dairy farm we visited one afternoon and walked up through his corn, oats, and clover fields) well, I was up there last night and they have got in 65 acres of the finest hay you ever saw! They have about 70 acres more to handle and expect to put it in in at least 10 days if the weather is favorable.

That field of timothy and clover between the house and the spring house got in in wonderful condition; in fact only about two loads of the three fields cut got wet and that was only a shower. There are about 18 tons (according to average judgment about the village) in the barn and that is the small half. I am anxious to see the rest go through with the same luck.

Today the men are expected down to put in the concrete dam and new raceway. I shall be very glad when this is completed—we will be all fixed then in every respect. I've got a fellow lifting the sod out near the flagpole for a strawberry bed. I shall get the plants and set them out in a few weeks, in so doing we will have berries next season; I am also planning on rhubarb plants and asparagus. I have just put in three rows of late corn and a new batch of lettuce and radishes. Our first peas were done for two weeks ago and the next lot are coming in now. Also stringbeans, they will be fit to use by Sunday. I also have a third lot of peas on the way (about 4 inches high now) and have got 2 doz. of the finest tomato plants in bloom that you ever saw. The latter of course are rather late because I didn't get them planted very early. Lima bean poles are entirely covered with the vines and I have already snipped the runners in order to throw the strength into the beans. Beets, onions, turnips, etc., etc., abound, and I'll tell you we're just living on vegetables.

From *vegetables* to *art*—Have really put in some licks and feel better in every way for it. When I talk of all the gardening, one would think I hadn't the time for my work, but do know the more I do, the more I have time to do. I get into the swing of things and accomplish far more than unsystematically jumping from one thing to another. Yesterday afternoon I laid in a big landscape with thunderclouds, 4 × 5 feet. The day was hot and it took the starch out 'n me, I can tell you. I haven't looked at it this morning yet so can't tell you how it looks. I can't trust my yesterday's impression of the result. I am at work on the last *Post* drawings for the Convict story and will feel greatly relieved therefrom. I have done some

257

very poor work for that story, and simply because I was not in sympathy with it. I shall then start on the *McClure's* "Indian Sun-Dance" series.

I feel at times on the verge of something worthwhile in my painting (not illustration), and *know* that if I had two years in which I could devote my time almost exclusively to close concentrated study of nature that it would put me on my feet and on the road to superior work—work that I feel is the only kind worth doing. I do want to accomplish something in my lifetime that will stand for posterity, that will last and be respected and do good. Therein lies the only reason on earth why I should be given the talent to paint, and it will be a shame if I can't develop the *best* that is within me. There is True, poor fellow, who, I can't feel has the ability, and falls right into the chance I would give my life for. Money! He's been left *money* enough to enable him to study for *years!* and what does he do the first thing but plan a trip to Europe. Knocking the underpinning out from under him the first start-off.

It's a shame! He hasn't the strength (artistic) to go over there and still hold what personality and individuality he might have. He will be caught in the whirlpool of the powerful influences then and come back *somebody else*. He'd ought just to *study* (and there are just as good teachers in drawing and painting here, Tarbell and Benson for instance), *study, study, study,* that is the thing—then after one knows nature thoroughly and intimately, he will find in her that which he wants to express, he will find phases that he *never saw before. Now,* as it is with *all* of us young fellows, we paint things because some other artist has made them beautiful to us through his interpretations, and not because we originally perceived those beauties ourselves.

248

Chadds Ford, Pennsylvania
July 25, 1908

Dear Mama,

What hot weather! It has taken the starch out of me, although I have managed to put in the biggest part of every day in the studio. I've got the first "Sun-Dance" picture under way, although I am having some trouble getting it into shape (no more than I should, however). Babe has posed for all the Indians and you may realize how well he does for them. Just the *color!* Just the *figure!* And just the *spirit!* I am only sorry that I shall not have him for the others, and if it were possible I should manage to get sketches from him while he is here, but I haven't formulated my other pictures definitely enough yet to know exactly what I would want.

My, how that fellow has developed! His appreciations of music are really remarkable for so *young* a fellow, and one who has not come in contact with much *good* music.

How glad I am that he don't taboo *good* music. Anyone who *does* (those who call it "classical") I am genuinely sorry for; they lose the sense of the *highest form* of *emotional expression*. Music is as necessary to a man as writing or painting, as meat and bread are to the body.

249

Chadds Ford, Pennsylvania
August 1, 1908

Dear Mama,

Ask Nat to inspect this rough sketch of a patent gate opener and fastener which has very recently been invented by his illustrious brother, Stimson Wyeth. The idea is really a very neat and compact affair—and what is more it is rustic, consequently picturesque. It is shaped out of hand-hewn oaken strips with wooden pivot pegs, and from the gracefully carven lever pivoted at the top of the stationary post there drops a rawhide strip to the latch. It pleasantly reminds one of the man who built a chicken coop from the inside and therefore shut himself in.

It is easily made, taking no less than the greater part of three days in which to construct it.

Last night we had Cahill, Smith and his brother down to supper. Rachel made us up a fine meal as usual—Lima bean succotash, roast lamb and potatoes. Babe made 4 quarts of the finest lemon sherbert I ever tasted and with a "damn-you Tessie" coffee for a windup; we left the table in the finest of spirits. Then followed an evening of music (angelus) and I must say 'tis a long, long time since I have enjoyed music as much. The "tout ensemble" sympathy accounted for it, I guess. They all seemed *so appreciative*—Grieg, Mendelssohn, Chopin, McDowell, Beethoven and Meyerbeer reigned supreme!

The last piece I was sorry I played; it was Chopin's funeral march. He [Babe] was keyed to such an intense pitch of sensitiveness after two hours that it struck him excessively strange, heavy and weird, and the poor fellow went to bed with spirits somewhat dampened and dreamed of coffins in dark rooms and dim candles all night.

Well, I glory in his temperament! I predict that, if he can prevent his acute sensitiveness from overpowering him to the extent that he would become *morbid,* he will do great work.

250

Chadds Ford, Pennsylvania
August 8, 1908

Dear Mama,

I have completed the first of the "Sun-Dance" pictures, which I can honestly count as one of my best, in rendering at least (the subject is necessarily illustration, which hurts it). I have also got the second picture well along with about two days' work on it to finish up. This one I believe is the best one of the two. Much broader in subject and more subdued color also.

Today I took a photo of Babe as "The Virginian" and then we made an Indian wig of hemp à la Nat and dyed it black. Tomorrow morning I shall take some pictures of him in Indian costume before he goes tomorrow at 11:15.

251

Chadds Ford, Pennsylvania
August 15, 1908

Dear Mama,

You will have to excuse a short note. It's about quarter of three and I've got to get to my sketches. I've got two started, one from about 3:30 to 5:30 and one from then until 7:00. Studies of a row of haymows—beautiful subjects. This is my third day on them.

I have also got my third Indian picture well underway and had ought to complete it in three days anyway. It is, I think, one which will be liked by the magazine at least. A Sioux medicine man delivering a prayer of appeal to the sun, asking that the (then disappearing) buffalo be returned to their country. He is surrounded by a ring of buffalo skulls, with Indians sitting back of him and big mountains looming behind all—very sunny!

252

Chadds Ford, Pennsylvania
August 16, 1908

Dear Babe,

Talk about thunderstorms!!! The one we have just had, the past hour and a half, makes the one that blew in the day you were here look like Aunt Hat doing fancy work on the front lawn.

About four o'clock I went over back of Sheatz's barn to make a study of some haystacks—it looked a trifle threatening in the south and it *did* manage to pee a bit, but it didn't bother me with my work. All of a sudden I noticed a peculiar livid yellow striking on Taylor's hill (I was facing east); I turned, and just over the brink of a big bare hill behind me I saw a long black edge of a cloud—black, as I never saw it before. I continued with my sketching for a few moments, but was forced to stop on account of the yellow that gradually slid down Taylor's hill and transformed the entire background of my picture.

That *yellow* puzzled me! I could see nothing but black behind me, so packing up my paint box, I struck out for the top of the hill.

What I saw looked truly unnatural: a clean, straight, vivid strip of burnished-gold sky—positively *metallic,* which reflected a gorgeous glow of gold-bronze over the western slopes. The hills appeared as though one were looking through stained glass at them—so intense was the light.

It looked forboding! So I struck out for home.

The black cloud grew to tremendous proportions, its upper edges tattered and wisplike. The yellow streak remained the same—a blinding garish light. The distant hills started to deepen into wonderful inky purples and the foreground looked green—a *poison* green, and the buildings in the village stood out hard and edgy like toy blocks, painted yellow, red, white and blue. Little people started to run back and forth, pigeons darted like white specter-spots against the black sky, cattle and horses looked impatient and walked nervously about. Suddenly, the distant trees changed from their deep sodden green into silvery greens and whites, the whole landscape seemed to awaken with a shudder. One could hear a soft rush, as of distant water; gradually it grew louder and louder and without warning the wind was upon us! Dust flew! Fallen leaves sailed high in the air like live things, trees swayed and bended, the grass flattened to the ground, and above all, great mountains of purple and black clouds hurtled through the sky. The distant band of yellow became darkened like tarnished brass. Peal upon peal of low, rumbling thunder trembled the air and in the distant sky the fork lightning streaked to the earth in fantastic tracings.

What followed I can hardly describe! A pandemonium of wind, rain, livid flashes of lightning and thunder that cracked in quick succession. The air flared with treacherous bolts that seethed and crashed like hellish serpents and the house trembled and shook in the tumult. One's very head became dizzy and the walls of the house seemed to melt in the livid flashes!

The rain poured down in sheets and it was as dark as night.

This continued for three-quarters of an hour without abating. Gradually the western horizon lighted up dully and the good sunlight shown through the still-pouring rain, making it look like bronze, getting brighter and brighter until the sky scintillated with the golden drops of rain.

I don't know that I ever felt more grateful to the sun in my life! After such a terrifying storm! to go out onto the open field (and I had Henriette on my shoulder) to look down upon the shining valley with its river and broad quiet meadows, and the cows peacefully feeding, the fresh green grass sparkling with the wet, the fragrance of soaked earth in the air—how grateful I felt for it! Not that I feared my safety through the storm, but to witness such a mighty and terrible battle of nature, and then to see her come up serene and smiling!

And Henriette seemed to understand too!

Even as I write this letter, distant rumblings and occasional dull flashes I can still see from the window by my desk.

Today's storm was strange all 'round. A cool fall day to begin with, and then it came very slowly at first and the comparatively small black cloud seems to have accumulated to an immense size in a very short time—and it hung incredibly *low!* It seemed as though it must have almost touched the tops of some of the hills. I think that's why we got such an electrical display—we were practically *in the clouds*.

Well, it's pretty hard for me to tell you how I miss you!

It got to be mighty natural to see you 'round, and I almost felt at times that you belonged here. Although I did very little work during your visit I feel and know that it did me lots of good; I feel that way *always* when any of *my* family are around me. For one thing, your unusual interest in the meager music I had here, your soul-felt interest I may say, repaid me alone!

253

Herman C. Wall, a Howard Pyle student, lived briefly in Chadds Ford with his wife.

Chadds Ford, Pennsylvania
August 17, 1908

Dear Mama,

The day is beautiful! and reasonably cool too! I've just turned four quarts of "Babe's Lemon Sherbert" for the benefit of Mr. & Mrs. Wall, a Mr. & Mrs. Wishart and their two children, Margaret and Hilda, and possibly Smith and Cahill (most likely Smith)—not forgetting Carol, Henriette and myself.

Tell Babe that the last two Saturday's B.B. games—double headers both days—were peaches. Yesterday's I did not see, but when I went down about 6:30 for kerosene (no sun so could not work on evening sketch) I saw quite a commotion over by the fence where the crowd sits and soon discovered that there was a fight going on. It seems that Sellers Hoffman's brother was scorekeeper and at the end of the last inning a discussion arose, advanced by the opponents (Lenni) who were beaten 4 to 0, that they had another inning coming to them. The scorekeeper was besieged and questioned. It was all down in black and white, absolutely proven beyond question, when one of the Lenni players, a big strapping buck, called C. Hoffman a *"liar."*— Ca *wonga!* (accent on the ong) Hoffman struck him between the eyes and he dropped like a lump of meat. The Lenni crowd closed in and Sellers Hoffman dove into them *all,* turning them upside down, right and left, yelling, "Go home you dirty skunks!" and many other things, altho he did not swear *once.* And they went. One sustained a broken finger, another a cut in the back of his head, and a third, the fellow who caught the scorekeeper's donation, was taken to Dr. Green's drugstore and there was administered hot drinks, headache powders, ice, etc., etc., by Sel' Hoffman himself. But the town slept quietly last night save the braying of the gray mule over at the hotel.

Tell Babe also that Chadds Ford were beaten all round the day he went. The young B.B. team beaten 9–7.

The old   *" " " "*   3–2.

The Quoit team beaten by 12 points, and those twelve were lost by Newn Arment, the wheelwright.

254

Chadds Ford, Pennsylvania
August 22, 1908

Dear Ed,

First let me tell you how glad we all are that you are coming.

If Nat would only get a hump on and invent a "friction drive" or a "double-ended, non-halation, anti-cosnichtianlodalyiaise differential gear" or something or other and get coin enough together to glide the steel rails to Chadds Ford, the whole damn family will have been here, and I only wish he could come with you—however, I suppose that pleasure will have to be deferred.

Well, old root-digger! I understand that you passed a lemon to the Dago who thought he could wrestle.—I'm proud of you, my boy! And you bet your sweet life I'll stand around when you're down here—only when you're safely on the train, out of my reach, I'll stick out my tongue at you—so there!

Well, to "get serious" I *will say* that we are having ideal working weather.

Carol is sitting beside me and she asked me to tell you that she is particularly glad you are coming. She anticipates lots of flower-gardening next spring and has yards of advice to ask of you.

255

Chadds Ford, Pennsylvania
August 28, 1908

Dear Mama,

We have just had supper, and while Hilda and Carol are cleaning up the dishes I will write a few lines.

The past three days have been extremely stormy! a strong, wild, nor'easter'. The wind has howled around the house like mad and the rain has beat terrifically against the windows. But we have been cozy and warm—Hail to the *fireplaces!* Carolyn was made to see in the past three days how cozy a country house *is* during a storm. The dancing, crackling fires have been so cheerful and even the baby seems contented sitting before them.

This evening before supper, just as the dark was closing in, we were lounging before the sewing-room fireplace and we were talking about your visit here in October. How you will enjoy this place! from the great spread of the Brandywine valley and its hills, to the snug cozy open fire of an evening. The month is a glorious one here. The foliage will not be so highly colored perhaps, but it will be a golden russet and russet greens with the pale yellow of the linden and the dark bronze greens of the pin oaks, and over all a mystical gauze of opalescent haze that makes the country look as if it were suspended in vapor or floating in wonderfully luminous water—so intangible! so elusive in its spirit! Great fields of stacked corn with nugget-colored ears lying in heaps, and here and there great round pumpkins—you know!—just what one reads about and seldom sees.

The past week has just reeked with the autumn spirit. Even the large crop of windfall apples seems a perfectly proper harvest, so cool and sharp has been the weather.

Yesterday afternoon I spent picking up apples (it is a pity too, so many on the ground). I picked up about 5 barrels, some of the finest Baldwins, Smokehouse and Snow apples you ever saw, *but all bruised!* These will be taken with many others I didn't pick up to

265

the Pocopson cider press tomorrow with three 45-gallon whiskey casks. These I expect will come back full, according to general judgment. Of course the cider will be good for a day or two but immature apples do not make a lasting cider so it will all be vinegar. It costs 1½ cents a gallon to have it pressed, which makes a cask of 45 gals. (with $1.50 price of cask) and costs about $2.18 a barrel.

It had ought to make mighty good vinegar, and if you think it worthwhile I will freight home a barrel.

This afternoon I started out in the drizzle to sketch—the country was beautiful! But I did more walking than sketching. I started about 1:30 and finally started a sketch at quarter of five, so you see my ramble was quite extended. The sketch was successful I think, and one I hope to do on a larger canvas; at six I made a second sketch but had to hurry on account of fast-fading light, consequently got poor results.

The baby's cheeks have been continually pink, *very* pink, from sitting in such close proximity to the open fires the past few days. Considering the fact that she is in the throes of teething she is re-markably well. Her face is growing more expressive every day—it seems to me that she has changed in the past week. She understands now when you ask her to give you what she has in her hand—she promptly passes it to you although at times very much loathe to give it up.

256

Chadds Ford, Pennsylvania
August 29, 1908

Dear Mama,

Although the "weekly letter" has only been written a few hours, I can't resist starting another on account of the rather sudden, or perhaps better, unexpected actions of Smith and Cahill. I learned yesterday that they both intend to leave Chadds Ford the last of October—one for New York, and the other for Boston and never to return.

This naturally surprised me a great deal, because both have been so loud in their admiration for the country and both had expressed, so definitely, plans to remain here.

The seclusion I have so often talked to you about is at last to be realized, and October will be the month for me to start my *real* fight under conditions which I believe are what they *should* be. The break from the fellows will of course be felt, more or less, socially speaking, but this I can easily replace if I keep my mind nourished with good reading and persistent work.

Cahill's sudden change (sudden to me) has weakened him in my estimation. His principles are undeniably good; he has taught me many things for which I will be everlastingly grateful, but I am sorry to see him apparently forget some of his most vigorous resolutions of last spring, resolutions that were based on solid ground, that if carried out would lead him to better things, I *know!* His idea of getting out into a country to develop *himself,* to throw himself into Nature's arms as it were, and there *study* her and seek in her that which belongs to *him alone.* This resolution embodies a number of problems that require persisting to the end—unending hard work, good simple living, continual reading of the best and the consistent avoiding of all associations that are not helpful!

Now he yearns for the companionship of the many; he is homesick for the diverting associations which he so loudly denounced a year ago—he decides that he wants to paint "street scenes" and that in the summer the seashore is the only place to paint, that he must get into the "line" of the exhibitions, to place his pictures in them and "get started." He claims Chadds Ford an unmerciful climate to work in, he calls it God-forsaken, and hurls at it many mudballs, that it is too far away and that one knows nothing of what is going on, etc., etc.

He forgets however that under precisely these conditions, only in many cases much more remote, the very masters whom he worships worked out their problems. They did not have to walk Broadway to know what was going on—but they *worked* and did things, they accomplished their resolutions!

To be sure the summer was exceptionally hot—but what about the men in the fields? They worked, and for mighty small pittance too! Can't a fellow who paints pictures in the coolest spots, under shady trees or in open doorways or by cool brooks—shouldn't he work at least half of every day? But no—according to Cahill the heat makes him listless, dopy, good for nothing; he lacks inspiration and zest—yes, but he said in the spring that he wanted to study, study, coldly and cruelly study—that inspiration was unnecessary for what he wanted to do for the next three years! (And upon this was based one of those blasting arguments of last spring.) The trouble is, he doesn't *love* this country and has not even tried to do it. He has gazed at her as a visitor would or what's better, a *real-estate* dealer, cutting out fragments here and there that would sell.

And Smith—as I told you, *never* his own master but easily influenced and guided by others. Cahill has taught him to be dissatisfied with this country in the face of the fact that Smith has told me many times that this country outshone any other *he has ever seen!* and many other things as foolish.

He intends to study with Tarbell and Benson this winter—this is a good thing for him if he does not allow that school of painting to take him up bodily and spoil what little personality he has in his work. But it's a good thing and I would like to do it myself!

So it goes! I feel, however, that I have my eye on the right track. I have had this financial proposition made very clear to me, which means that I must accumulate enough ahead for 8 or ten years living —*then* paint!

Howard Smith by his easel, Chadds Ford.

So I have started! I am trying to instill into the minds of the magazine editors that I want subjects that are *local*, subjects that I can paint honestly and conscientiously; in this way I can study and accumulate, and *then*, when my bank book thrives sufficiently, I shall *paint*—but not until then is it possible.

257

Chadds Ford, Pennsylvania
September 5, 1908

Dear Mama,

I have spent the last two days in New York.—I delivered the "Sun-Dance" pictures, which, judging from the praise tendered me at *McClure's*, I should feel in one sense pleased with the result. They were apparently liked very much, which was corroborated by their decision to publish them in the Xmas *McClure's*.

Included in my New York debauche was a ticket to Belasco's presentation of that cynical, queer and clever Hungarian play "The Devil." George Arliss, an English character actor, headed the list and it was quite good—but rather tedious to me on account of its superfluous intrigue—not a healthy sort at any rate, but I'm not sorry I saw it.

I don't know that I have ever been more lonesome than I was that night bumming around alone—between 4 and 8 in the evening there is absolutely nothing to do. Business offices closed, too dark to see pictures—nothing but to kill time—it came near killing me!

If I could write verse—I should write one on "Bread"—"Mrs. Eaton's Bread," but as that is beyond me I can only offer humble thanks and a request for the receipt. (Or can it only be made in Needham?)

And paint rags!! By the great horn spoon! I can wipe up the earth now! When I turn quickly and glance into the box, I sometimes think I catch a glimpse of Papa in his nightgown, then Mama half-dressed, or Eliza perhaps. Then the bed clothes make me feel like lying down, but I have to forget that. Carol raided the box the first day and swiped a big cloth for cleaning, but *no more*—I've hid them!

258

Chadds Ford, Pennsylvania
September 25, 1908

Dear Mama,

It's about quarter of seven and Carol is still asleep and Henriette is beside my desk sitting in her highchair, playing with a cigar cutter and a "Koh-I-Noov" pencil. How long she'll be contented I don't know—at any rate I'll write as long as she sits quiet.

Aylward reached here Wednesday noon and stayed overnight, leaving on the first train in the morning. I don't know when I have enjoyed a visit more, from an "outsider" so to speak.

Let me say here that yesterday, following Aylward's departure, I managed to start a picture for *Scribner's*. It's the first time in many months that I really have taken a vital hold of illustration and I can feel it in my bones that the entire set is going to be a jump ahead. My sense of color I know is improving (it is a remarkable sensation to me, as I never had it before, to actually *feel* color combinations, to unconsciously fit color harmonies to your temperament); it has been that my color was all receipted, so to speak; I made the sky blue because we naturally suppose it is so, I made sunlight yellow, because H.P. first told me to, I made distances blue and shadows blue because other men did it, etc., etc. Of course I haven't entirely shaken the *disease* yet, but I feel that in the course of a few years my color will be my own.

The floor is littered with every unbreakable article I have on my desk—rulers, pencils, watercolor brushes, Stevens pistol, cigar cutter, leather cigar case, pocketbook, watch fob, spectacle case, and duplicates of many of them. I guess she's getting a trifle hungry, so will hie myself to the table and oatmeal. Carol still nurses her, but we feed her too.

259

Chadds Ford, Pennsylvania
September 28, 1908

Dear Nat,

Well! The way the country is changing costume is miraculous— only I don't like to see it go so rapidly. Last night, for the first time since August 16th, we had rain and it has continued intermittently—but just now the wind is high and leaves are sailing through the sky like crazy birds.

It is wonderful how thin the trees have grown in their foliage since yesterday. It is noticeably so around the house, or rather in the house—it is so much lighter, so light that the rooms actually look garish.

My studio is completed for the winter (except for a stove) and I consider it better in many respects to any one of the studios in town. The place is entirely sheathed on the inside, besides heavy papers underneath—a new floor over the old one and new heavy doors, that clamp practically air-tight, with windows in them. My working light is perfect, and it should be that my work hereafter improves to do justice to the surroundings.

Chapter X

ILLUSTRATIONS AND PAINTINGS

"I am steadily grasping the significant and essential facts that go to make up the foundation for painting."

Wyeth was working on a set of four illustrations to accompany an article titled "A Sheepherder of the Southwest" that he wrote for Scribner's January 1909 issue.

Chadds Ford, Pennsylvania
October 9, 1908

Dear Mama,

My pipe's full and alight and I'll write as long as she burns! Supper is over; Carol and the baby are in the sewing room, and from the noise the latter is making I should judge "sleep's the thing." There they go upstairs and now I suppose the poor little kid will have to cry herself to sleep—that's the only way we can do it.

I have found it difficult not to go out and spend these enchanting days in the fields with my canvas and paints; in fact I managed to paint something in the way of a landscape in spite of rush work. A moonlight! I know you would not recognize it as my work, it is so restrained and yet strong and appealing. (My cloak of modesty is *off* for the present, understand.)

Together with this I am carrying on the "Sheepherders." The one I said I had "signed" in my last letter has been painted twice over since.

The second—a "Mexican Greaser" watering his herd is a striking composition and has unusual opportunities to develop. It will be hard on account of the herd of sheep in the foreground, reflections in broken water, etc., but believe that I can pull something better than usual out of it.

261

Chadds Ford, Pennsylvania
October 16, 1908

Dear Mama,

Yesterday the law lifted from poor bunny. It really made my day rather sad—working in my studio and hearing the incessant firing on every side with the mingled yelps and cries of the dogs as they slaughtered the poor rabbits. On one hand I was trying in my weak way to show my appreciation of living nature on canvas, and on the other hand a hundred men and boys [were] destroying her willfully, within easy hearing. I suppose it will be the same today.

Of course it is a long time since I have killed an animal, and I am rather surprised at myself to see how radically different my viewpoint is. To show me a dead animal (one killed for the sport's sake) seems almost to the point of being revolting, not mentioning the feeling of contempt that wells up within me for the man who killed it.

Well, to change the subject—I have completed the first two of the sheep pictures and shall send them along right away in order that they can go ahead with the work of reproduction. The third I shall start today (a moonlight of "herder" by small fire, smoking, with bunch of sheep around him).

I've had quite a siege with these two but have pulled them out into quite individual pictures. One would hardly recognize them as mine, so different is the color arrangement and general technicalities. My article is coming comparatively easy. I am not worrying about the English—or its form, etc. They (*Scribner's*) will straighten that out.

Aunty Guss and Aunt Anna have been down since Wed. morning helping Carol with flannel waists, petticoats, a couple skirts, flannel nightgowns, etc.

Yesterday morning Aunty Guss wrote a postal in answer to one she got the previous night. I carried it to the P.O. It was very brief and I couldn't help reading it. I found it so interesting and quaint, and so characteristic of the good woman that I memorized it with intention of sending it to you—so here it is:

Dear Esther—

We will be at home on Saturday. Come if thee can but leave thy headache at home.

as ever thy friend
Elizabeth

Fourth day 10th month.

262

Chadds Ford, Pennsylvania
October 19, 1908

Dear Nat,

This has been one of those "homesick days," a day that is peculiarly empty—hollow, so to speak—when one talks, his voice sounds miles away. I worked hard all day, but after four o'clock my grasp of what I was doing suddenly left me; the bottom seemed to drop out of everything so I quit! I wandered about aimlessly, positively unable to fix my interest on anything.

Tonight however, after an early supper, I took Henriette and we had a grand walk up the bank of the river to Brinton's meadow, and home. She talked and chattered all the way, and although my arms got somewhat tired, I felt like walking forever with her. The cool evening drove us homeward and here I am brimful of homesickness, ambition, resolutions and God knows what else—and the little tired kid is sound asleep upstairs in her crib.

What a wonderful thing life is—how exasperating! how beautiful! How hopelessly entangling is one's mind! What a maze of sentiment, emotion, love, depression, inspiration, discouragement, hopefulness one passes through in just a few hours. It seems so *never-ending*, so tiring and hopeless at times that I wish I were one of the peaceful old cows I see browsing on the green hillside—or a bird perhaps, they seem so carefree.

It seems to me that if one's work were going well, or simply, properly directed, that it would solve this involved state of mind, and one would think clearer, with more directness and show greater strength and steadier advancement therefrom. Somehow, since I have been made to see the limitations of illustration and to recognize the unlimited power of painting, I have no honest care for the former. I *have* to do it of course, and therein must lie the secret of the trouble I seem to be having to straighten out my mind.

Somehow it seems to me that unless one can work for the *best*, there isn't much satisfaction working at all. I know this is a very impractical statement for me to make, but it's from the heart and there is no evading it. I do my best to throw my spirit and enthusiasm into my magazine work but *for the life of me*, it is only nickle-

277

plated—it wears off, ere the picture is done. As I say, if the work was "on the road" to bigger things, but it *isn't!* But now I'm going to plead for subject matter from the magazines that fits the country about here so that I can work from *Nature!* If I can get them to respond, I'll feel as though something was won!

Pencil drawing for haystack picture.

How I did enjoy a little study I did of a group of haystacks! I *loved* them before I got through and I have an affection for the picture too! It is not a remarkable picture in *any* way, but it is truthful, it is not "*faked*"; there are no horses running, kicking and snorting all over hell in it, there are no scenic mountain passes, raging torrents, soaring eagles or boiling clouds in it, just three or four silent haystacks, such as you and I would like to have slid off of when we were kids, and above them, arching over them, *so conveniently*, two or three rum-cherry trees! And along the foot of these stolid stacks runs an old cart-path speckled with sunlight.

That picture I really and truly loved to paint! The *one* and *only* picture that was supremely delightful to do! I shall give this to Mama and Papa Xmas.

263

Chadds Ford, Pennsylvania
October 23, 1908

Dear Mama and everybody!

It [the box] came Wednesday afternoon, and that evening, about dusk, I built a rousing fire in the fireplace, and with the baby in her go-cart on one side and Carol on the other we slowly and carefully "unpacked." You never saw anything like it! the way that Henriette seemed to sense the pleasure and excitement of unpacking "hidden treasures." Her little hands twisted, opened and shut faster than ever, and she said petty, petty, petty, to everything produced.

Tell Papa that the corn crib is *full* to the *roof* of the finest big corn you ever saw. I'm almost tempted to send home a box of sample ears, and that is only half you know. The stalks I have sold, with the exception of a few which I have retained to batten up cold places around the house.

We are all ready for winter—studio and all. Stoves are up, coal in, wood in (by the way I struck a bonanza in wood; a fellow who has a sawmill sold me slab-wood: *great hunks*, including big knots of oak, chestnut, hickory and beech, for 60¢ a two horseload. I've got one boxstall entirely filled (six loads) and the woodshed with another load in it. Later I will have four cords of sawed wood stacked up by the henyard; thus I paid 4 dollars a cord—sawed and delivered, mixed wood, but mostly hard, and with 5 tons of coal we feel prepared for the worst. I myself look forward to it!

Well it strikes me that between the "Needham Home" and the "Chadds Ford Home" we have kept the mail lines *hot* this last week!

264

Chadds Ford, Pennsylvania
November 13, 1908

Dear Mama,

Well, the rush is over! I've written my narrative of 5000 words three times, making 15000 words between Saturday last and Wednesday afternoon.

I have not heard how they liked the article or whether they will accept it (maybe not); however, I expect a telephone connection with Mr. Chapin between now and the time I end this letter and I may be able to give you the tidings—good or bad.

As I sit at my desk the low sun is shining on "Washington's Headquarters." With all the leaves off nothing obstructs a clear view of the place except a thin network of bared trees. Taylor's "mansion on the hill" also stands out gray and somber (one would hardly guess the kind of people that live in the house, judging from the distant view). The country is all new! You see this is really the first time I ever stayed in Chadds Ford to watch just this season of the year. One would hardly recognize the country, it seems so much bigger, one can see so much further. Back of us on a great bare hill, Mr. Sheatz has turned out eighty young steers. They wander back and forth over the dry brown grass in groups or perhaps huddle up in the lee of the worm fences. It really is a grand sight; their deep red coats all wooly and ruffled and the ocher field as a background. From my studio windows I can see them through the bare, bleak orchard and if painted with simple fidelity and truth would make a powerful "November" picture.

It's been right cold here going down to 26 with a high wind. An inch and a half of ice on the hens' water pan tells the story and I noticed tonight that the ice I dumped on the ground *yesterday* morning seems not in the least melted.

Just heard from Chapin—"Article *bully!* Went without a hitch!!" My last picture goes tonight—*the sheepherders and story* (hanging fire for four years) *is finished.* No one knows how good I feel.— I worked hard over the pictures, and Friday (a week ago today) I received a telegram telling me that "text" should be in *that day.* Saturday at six I was at it until that night at 10—all day Sunday,

Monday, Tuesday and Tuesday night until 12, then Wednesday I copied it for the final time, and off on special-delivery Post. My *second* story, for the best magazine in the world! of 5000 words, written in 4 days!!

265

Chadds Ford, Pennsylvania
November 28, 1908

Dear Mama,

The day of Thanksgiving is over—and we are truly thankful (not that it is *over* exactly), but we were brought to a sudden realization what it really means to be thankful, yesterday morning.

Katie, Carolyn and Hilda were all busy with the dinner—decorating the table, etc., when Henriette bit off a large piece of apple from a rosy Baldwin she was playing with. I was at work in the studio when suddenly Hilda rushed in and told me that the baby was choking. When I reached her she had fainted from the want of breath.—Katie was doing her best, hitting her back, etc., and Carol was wholly unstrung. I remembered what you did to me over the bannister and grabbed her by the feet and shook her violently. It proved successful and the apple skin fell to the floor. It took some time for her to get around again—but oh! how thankful we felt the rest of the day—and will *always*.

Well, to turn the subject to something more cheerful and appropriate to the day, let me say that we had a most enjoyable and sumptuous dinner. The Aunties were here and so were Cahill and Hilda. Katie served up a delicious dinner.

Your letter I read just before we ate. It was certainly a well-written and appropriate letter and everyone enjoyed it—but Hilda. She said "I swear on the *Bible* that I didn't take that cake," much to the *shocking* of the Aunties.

(Sh—sh—To solve the mystery—*I* took that cake last summer and ate it piece by piece in my studio.)

Well, Katie's grunting and wheezing around me here lifting "mission chairs" and cleaning up the room after the "fracas." So I'll have to *vamoos!*

If you really want to know what a distinguished son you've got, living in Chadds Ford—peruse the magazine article in the fore part of *Scribner's* for Xmas. It'll do your soul good—and my head *bad*.

The WYETHS

A close friend of N. C. Wyeth during his boyhood years was his second cousin, Henry Holzer. Violet was Mrs. Wyeth's maid.

Chadds Ford, Pennsylvania
December 5, 1908

Dear Mama,

I have spent the past hour pouring over that book of home photographs and you may well believe that I feel the irresistible desire to write you a letter in consequence. Whenever I feel homesick I fly to that precious book—why I do it I know not, for invariably it leaves me in a much more depressed state of mind—a sad longing, a keen and impossible longing for the past.

It is a peculiar fact, but do you know that photographs have always aroused me to the depths of my feelings? There is something in them that suggests the infinite—they bring to my mind, for the moment, almost complete realization of the profound meaning of life, enshrouded in a glow of deep, tragic red. Why *tragic*, I don't know, but for some reason or another *anything* that I appreciate keenly and profoundly is always sad to the point of being tragic. Whether it is a lone tree on a hillside bathed in the fading light of the afternoon sun, or the broad stretch of a green meadow shining and sparkling after a shower, or be it even the birds joyously singing in the spring trees, or merry children going to school—it is all so sad, because it is all so beautiful—so hopeless.

But those photographs! How every *detail* burns my soul!

Take the one—the view from the "Stone Bridge" up the river. Onion's meadow on one side, Lyon's on the other, and between, the long majestic curve of the river leading up to the dark, massed spruces on the "Avenue." And just clearing the dark tops of the spruces, its silhouette spotted against the sky—the windmill!

To *think!* existing *in this very photograph* are *all* things that existed that day, *seen* and *unseen*. Beyond the trees are concealed the greenhouses, the old house, our house—*imagine* how it was!

It was Sunday—Edwin and I were with Henry. It was before noon. The day was gray and warm, there were soft velvety breezes that would come and go, throwing patches of blurred ripples across the placid stream.—Oh! I can remember so distinctly that warm, limpid day as though it were yesterday!

And *beyond* those trees, those dark, massed spruces, Grandpapa in his shirt-sleeves and brown straw hat, out along the hotbeds

"Grandpapa . . . out along the hotbeds."

perhaps—just looking. And Grandmama bustling around the kitchen with "Mary Finland" preparing the Sunday dinner—and across the way "over to Hattie's"—*you* know how it was! Papa delving into the many things he so enjoyed doing on a Sunday morning—you with your morning's work and the care of Stimson, and Nat tagging around after Violet.—Oh! it's no use to go further. I guess I have

283

lived that day's life all over many times while studying that picture. And I get a long, distinctive, vivid story out of each picture in that book.

It is so fascinating! More than that, it is a pleasure *sacred* to me. If it is depressing, it *is* at least uplifting and purifying. After an hour spent that way I am lifted entirely out of the usual vagaries.—I feel *better, purer* and *more determined*.

I don't know why I write this way—but as I said, it was *irresistible*. You may not get the drift of what I am saying; it is hard to put it in words; it lies so much deeper than is possible to write or say. However, I think this subtle appreciation runs in the family.—I think Stimson has it and if he were away from home he would feel as I do.

The day has been dull and heavy; the skies have threatened snow since early morning but tonight they have cleared and now they are fairly *crackling* with stars! I put in a good round day in the studio and tomorrow I hope to finish the picture. "The Prophesy of the War Cloud" is its title.

After much consideration—balancing wisdom and expediency carefully in our minds—we have decided to board Cahill for the winter. It is not entirely an unselfish idea, for I believe the fellow can give me invaluable help. He will work in the "Lodge Hall" at the Ford, which has kindly been *loaned* to him, but will sleep and eat here.

I have used all arguments to stay him from going to N.Y. and mixing up with the crowd again, and finally prevailed upon him. I believe the fellow needs a chance to try himself out but has heretofore been too restless and experimental, moving from place to place, changing one theory for another, etc.

He has learned to love this particular country with an affection I thought at one time he did not possess. He is deeply interested in the romantic side of it, too, which shows that his interest runs deep. My argument was that he should give himself a chance, that is now that he is identified with the place, stick to it and make some use of it. To be deep-rooted in a country is all-essential I believe.

The baby is hale and hearty and full of the devil. Yesterday Carol went to Phila. and left H. in my charge. I painted with her on my left arm for about four hours. She was asleep on my shoulder most of the time and when not asleep she was running and laughing.

She seemed very amused at my brushwork. Carolyn returned in good spirits and *not* tired, so I feel that she is improving, although you can still play "Annie Rooney" on her ribs.

We are looking forward with great eagerness to your arrival. Rumors are afloat that the first of the year will start you southward. Am I right? Let me hear.

267

Chadds Ford, Pennsylvania
December 7, 1908

Dear Mama,

Work looms up gigantic before me and I can see a winter of incessant plugging before me. I shall endeavor to do more and better than ever in order to satisfy my ardent desire to paint outdoors from next spring until winter. It will be necessary to sacrifice many pleasures and anticipations. I have spent a big part of the summer on work that has brought me no remuneration, and considering my plans for the summer, I feel it necessary to economize and save time wherever I can. I have two handsome commissions for the winter besides many other opportunities which I shall endeavor to handle. I am steadily grasping the significant and essential facts that go to make up the foundation for painting, and it is this that I am striving for. It is a long tedious journey, and my lack of patience is the one obstacle I have to contend with.

My work in its present state is meager, weak and lacking in the slightest maturity; I thank God I can see its shortcomings, and thank Him again that I can appreciate the good in other men's work.

I feel sorry that a letter of a recent date should have been taken as a critical one. In a sense it *was,* but mainly it was simply a desire on my part to unload a bit of philosophy that I've had in my brain for a long while.

Although I know that both you and Papa have been very lenient the past few years and not in the slightest over-anxious to get us *earning money,* that spirit *has* been apparent years back, and I believe was more or less inoculated in Nat in spite of the fact that he was told not to worry, etc., etc.

My outburst was sort of a subconscious, occult feeling I have had in regards to the thousands of youths who are prematurely loaded onto the world and only a precious few of whom ever succeed. I blame commercialism for it all.

268

Dear Mama,

The day was replete with all the pleasures and happiness of Xmas; the weather was glorious, the white hills sparkled and the skies vied with the snows in their brilliancy.

Many, many times during the day my mind flew to the Christmases of the past, to our dear customs which were always so faithfully followed—to the curtained sitting room concealing hidden treasures from peering eyes returning from the Sunday School Celebration; the restless night in bed, the early, feverish dressing; the final call to *come down*; and *then*—the lighted tree, shining and sparkling; the coincident four sides of the table for the four brothers, heaped with gifts; the pervading fragrance of balsam; the delicate aroma of ginger cookies!

And now it is *I* who is establishing that very custom, in all its ever-important details, in a new home and country. May I always be as successful as you and Papa were, and bless *my* family with fond recollections of the past.

It will always be remembered by me as the really *first complete* Xmas in *my* household.

I told Ed of a dream I had one night.

I was working in my studio—the day was rather murky and there was a deep slush on the ground.

In the quiet I heard, coming up the road from the village, the tramp of horses and the yells and curses of men; the medley of voices grew nearer and louder.—I became concerned, as it sounded threatening and foreboded evil. Rushing to the back window of the studio I gazed out through the mist down toward the big barn, and there I saw indistinctly a writhing mass of men and horses slowly and laboriously making their way up the hill toward the house.

The slush and slimy mud was deep, the horses were mud-splattered and lathered with sweat—steam arose in clouds. On each side were great red-faced men beating the poor beasts with cudgels and spiked poles. Through the dense sweat-steam I made out a huge van not unlike a Conestoga wagon. It wobbled drunkenly and creaked and whined under its apparently weighty load.

I waited———

As they approached, a little hump-backed, queer-looking man bounced out of the wagon and rushed toward the studio. I met him at the door, and in a dry gibbering voice he announced a shipment of written matter from Needham.

They were *delayed* and *miscarried* letters, letters from *Stimson* to *myself! Thousands* of them! Since then I have prayed mightily for forgiveness—forgiveness for all the naughty things I've said about Babe's *not* writing.

But my God! what if it had been true—how could I have deciphered all those letters!!

269

Chadds Ford, Pennsylvania
January 8, 1909

Dear Mama,

Tonight it looks like a storm again; this morning it was as clear as a crystal and yesterday it *snew* a bit. By the way, yesterday was a red-letter day. The hotelkeeper, Mr. Stackhous, asked me awhile ago if I would object to his using my name on invitations to a fox hunt. That is—he wanted to "drop the fox" at our barn in order to make the invitation a little more dignified. You see if he were to say, "Fox dropped at the Chadds Ford Hotel," it would be taken immediately for a "booze party"—thus his request. I gladly granted it of course, and it was a grand affair. They had over 200 dogs and some forty riders—men from all over the countryside, as far as 25 miles away. The fox was a beautiful large male of the red variety and was as large as *Tommy* the Beagle. Its brush was a corker! Carol was honored by the Hunt voting to let her let the fox go, but she was too timid and the day was very cold and stormy. So I did that part. The dogs were penned in our barn, by the road, the night before, and when the time came to let them loose, they were simply *wild!*

After the fox was let loose for at least 15 minutes the signal was given for the dogs. The hooks that held the great double doors were loosened and the pack tore out of the barn like mad. Their own impetus sent them across the road up toward the house, which threw them a little off the trail, although previous to letting them out I had dragged the canvas bag which contained the fox between the point I released him and the big barn door. They scattered in all directions until one of them caught the scent on me, he let a terrific bay, and then the pack tore toward me from all directions. Anybody would think I'd have been eaten alive but as each one reached me they would bay and turn away; finally they located the trail and away they went in a great mass. There were hundreds of people watching the dogs and riders off and they cheered and cheered. The riders left in hot pursuit and for a long time we watched them wind in and out, up and down the hills until they finally disappeared. But all afternoon one could hear the distant baying of the pack.

It was all extremely picturesque as they were all farmers (many Quakers). *Some* fine horses but mostly were skates (comparatively speaking), but they all *could jump*. No one had riding boots that I remember of—they mostly wore felt boots or rubber boots. The one insignia which did prevail was the cap.

270

Chadds Ford, Pennsylvania
January 18, 1909

Dear Mama,

My N.Y. trip, 'tis needless to state, was full of interest to the point of bursting. For the first time I took advantage of the Salmagundi Club of which I have been a member for over a year. There I met many of the painters whose names and work have been so familiar to me in the exhibitions.

This club is situated on 12th street just off of Fifth Ave. It was once the home of Rogers of "Rogers Group" fame. (You remember the group we had of the boy watching his dog going down a rabbit hole with his horse standing by him? Done in plaster? Well, that's a "Rogers Group.") Besides its being his studio where he did his modeling it was his elegant home. With a few alterations and additions it was changed into apartments suitable for a club, with library, gallery for exhibitions, billiard and pool room, card rooms, etc., etc., besides a spacious grill room where members can get the very best meals at cost (so for 60¢ one gets a meal that would cost $1.50 to $2.50 at a high-class restaurant). The Club also has rooms (only six) that a fellow can make use of for a small sum. I'll tell you it fills a terrible vacancy that I always felt in N.Y. when I had to spend a night there.

In the face of the fact that I spent two most enjoyable evenings there, it proved to me *conclusively* that the city is *no* place for any artist to work, young or old. I do not refer to the men who dissipate, or to dissipation, but simply to the too-close contact of sensitive personalities, which is *bound* to breed dislikes and disrespect, and which is often the underlying impulse that brings out a man's inferior qualities unless he holds himself in severe check. In art, personalities don't count for much anyway. So often the inner-man is concealed by a crude outer-man, and oftentimes he does his listeners more harm than good, and shatters the respect others had always had for him. Although I was most favorably impressed by the men of note whom I met, I could feel that with too-long club acquaintanceship I would soon begin to disregard them.

Oh! by the way, I went to the German Contemporary Exhibition at the Metropolitan Museum and found it interesting but very disappointing. They are certainly miles behind America in landscape (in regards to refinement and spirituality), and as to their figure work it is *too* striking, *too* vehement in technique and color, and decidedly morbid, melodramatic and sentimental in subject. Notwithstanding, it was mighty instructive, but proves beyond all doubt to the minds of the critics that Germany strikes no such high note in painting that she does in music. Holzer's photos of people seated with flowers and leaves in their hands and dishes of fruit at their feet exactly symbolize what one finds in the weaker part of the German pictures. They are representative and I am truly surprised at the comparison of the Art of an old people with that of a new—it is decidedly in favor of the new. Among the people at the Exhibition I saw Pres. Eliot [of Harvard] and his wife. I also chanced to hear a few remarks he had to make about a very weird and repulsive picture painted by one Franz Stück—not complimentary I assure you.

271

Dear Mama,

After the N.Y. debauche it has been rather hard for me to settle down to do work *that counts*. I have no end of work to do and it is only the question of doing it and getting it out of the way. It is so hard—the desire to paint landscape pulling one way and the necessity to illustrate pulling the other.

As I write, the last rays of a deep-rose sun are striking on Washington's Headquarters. The trees are a soft glowing red—the little snow that is left, a gray, silvery color, is lying in thin streaks across the fields, and the distant hills are bathed in a pink gray mist softly melting into the sky.

The cat is in the foreground playing with a half-live field mouse.

And isn't it mild? But the farmers all fear that the worst is to come. While I was down to the store this morning I heard them

"While I was down at the store this morning . . . ."

relating their experiences during the blizzard of '88—it was interesting and very dramatic. You and Papa must remember it well.

272

Dear Papa,

We intended to keep it secret, but I can't; this week the baby suddenly struck out to *walk* and now she's going all about as big as life—it is comical to see her. She wears a gray smock, a facsimile of the one Mama got from Carol Xmas.

Well, Papa, the wheel has made another turn, hasn't it? Although one wouldn't guess it to look at you. Accept the heartiest wishes and *many* happy returns of the day from Carolyn and myself.

273

Dear old Stimson,

Today is one of those letter-breeding days, black and stormy, the wind whistling and the rain slashing, comfortable and cozy in the house, fires crackling and books or music at hand. And speaking of music, that's the very thing that has stirred me to write this afternoon. Recently I purchased half a dozen new pieces—cradle songs, lullabies and serenades by Schumann, Schubert or Liszt.

They are the very pieces I heard when I was a kid—Uncle

Deny on the violin, Uncle Gig on his flute, Mrs. Lehman on a
Sunday or perhaps one of the Holzers. Then there was an old woman
who used to play those little German and Swiss folk songs *so* well,
I forget her name. She worked for Grandmama about 12 years ago,
I should say.

The very thing that lies deepest in my thoughts about this music I
cannot express, but it is all about home—over to Grandpapa's—
sighing spruce trees, the big maple in the springtime, the place
where they used to dump broken flowerpots at the foot of the
avenue, the tame squirrels that ate out of Grandpapa's hands, the
pumphouse, old Lizzie.—If I'm painting and want to express an
emotional thought, mystery, great spaces, profound skies, silence
or the like, I fly to my dream-thoughts of *home* and there I find a
bottomless well of inspiration—a longing that grows stronger and
deeper every day.

God damn it, it drives me almost *mad* sometimes; it seems as
though I could fly, and overtake the *past* that is vanishing so rapidly. And then the river in the spring with the whistling blackbirds, the flooded meadows, the alders along the banks, the boat
and the water lapping against it—all when we were young, when we
didn't care, when there wasn't competition, struggle, worriment—
money, diplomacy, and a *career* to look after. And what is this damn
nuisance we call *career?* I wish one's talent—one's *life* wasn't bartered
and sold like so much cabbage; it makes me sick and weary.

274

Chadds Ford, Pennsylvania
February 20, 1909

Dear Papa,

It undoubtedly seems strange to you to hear me say that the
very source of my livelihood (and a good one it is too) is the very
thing that is standing in my way. All that I have done in the
past, all that I could do in the future (in illustration) would be
utterly forgotten in a preciously few years except by a few friends
and relatives perhaps. It is my purpose to create pictures that will
last, like the works of men like Michelangelo, Raphael, Millet, and
scores of others. These men are taking as active a part in the develop-

ing of this country *today* as Roosevelt, as Taft, as *any* contemporary; their work will *always* have that power, because it is *great!* and *uplifting!*

I am fighting for the best opportunities, I am trying to fit myself into the things that will do me the most good—in other words, I am experimenting—the man that grows is *always* experimenting.

Therefore that is one reason that I have been impractical and not far-seeing. People have already told me, "You certainly have the courage and nerve to turn down a successful career to try for something else." They invariably say, "something *else*," not "something higher."

Now, Papa, kindly take the time to ferret out the real underlying meaning of the above. I have *always* felt that you have never quite understood me, rather because I never expressed myself clearly, and partly because your life has been one of *facts* rather than *intangible* hopes.

Therefore—I am going to *drop* illustration. But before, of course, I shall have made all arrangements for a livelihood.

I have already spent a day with Eric Pape in New York and have talked matters over very satisfactorily.—I shall teach in his school two days a week morning, afternoon and evening class—8 months in the year. For this I shall receive $1200 with a probability of more. The rest of the time I shall paint, paint, paint. I shall have a studio in Boston, shall have my models, will have criticism from De Camp if possible (the idea of studying at the Museum and teaching at Pape's school could not be thought of, as it would give his school a black eye to do such a thing, and then J. De Camp's teaching is just as good as Tarbell's, if not better).

Of course, with your permission it is our happy intention of living at home and sharing expenses, which of course will make it astonishingly cheaper for us to live than it does now. Carol and Mama will get along so well and I feel that one is a boon to the other. I *know* that Mama will be a Godsend to Carol and the baby at any rate.

I have signed no agreements as yet but in all probability will arrange everything so as to start in on the fall term at Pape's.

As for me it is like a "Resurrection" to think of reversing the old home life that I felt at one time had been swept away from me forever. To be with you and Mama and Stimson again is beyond any happiness I ever dared anticipate—but I can see it now on the horizon.

And poor, lonely Carol is so looking forward to it. The isolation out here for her mind, which naturally craves uplifting society, is a little too much.

275

Chadds Ford, Pennsylvania
March 17, 1909

Dear Mama,

The baby is as lively as a bunch of steel springs and is doing more *stunts* and more talking than ever. Last night Carol and I were enjoying her antics just before going to bed—we had taken off her dress—even her diapers. Well, she was a comical sight running around the warm room with just shirt and shoes on. Finally Carol asked her to go over to her drum-shaped music box (the one with the wire handles), which was lying on its side, and sit down on it. By Jove! if she didn't go over to it and slowly back up to it and cautiously sat down. *Then* she betook a strained expression, grunted a few times and I'll be darned if she didn't do a job right there! It was the funniest thing I believe I ever saw!! You see she thought its shape resembled a pot somewhat and being in that "*mood*" thought that's what Carol meant. We will humor that little trick—only—we must teach her the difference between a music box and a wicker chair.

By this time you may have heard from Nat that once more I shared his bed and board. I found Nat in fine spirits with a week's time schedule which would bring him $23.50. We talked Sunday night until after 12 and the rest of the night I dreamed of Henriette, much to his amusement—getting out of bed, lighting matches trying to locate her, and finally, picking up a bunch of Nat's dirty laundry and going to bed with it perfectly satisfied.

With Pape I made better arrangements than ever—arranging to teach two days in the week and an hour's work on Saturdays for $50 a week making $1600 for the year of eight months.

Last week I painted a picture which I called "The Pay-Stage." *Scribner's* bought it quick and pronounced it the very best I ever did for them. You see, one never knows when he is doing something good. Chapin claimed it far superior in color—much surer and masterly in technique, and stronger than usual in dramatic meaning.

Houghton Mifflin has given me a New England ms. [*Susanna and Sue*, by Kate Douglas Wiggin] for which I am to make 10 pen-and-inks similar to the *Scribner's* things I did. I shall finish the first one today.

Let me outline my trip to N.Y.—it was quite eventful. From Philadelphia I took a chair car because I intended to do some sketching on the way. The car proved to be full of theatrical people (people playing in Phil. and going to N.Y. over Sunday). Directly side of me sat David Warfield of "Music Master" fame. Before long we opened up an intensely interesting conversation which lasted until we got to Jersey City.—I was then introduced to William Gillette, whose company I enjoyed going across the ferry.

On the way back on the W. 23d ferry a big rangy, sinister-faced fellow came along—big black slouch hat, leather vest, black coat, thin bowed legs and a white silk handkerchief stuffed around his neck. He cast his black eyes at my hat a couple of times and once at *me*, rather deprecatingly. Finally he sat down near me and it wasn't long before I broke the ice and we were off! The fellow proved to be the sheriff of Virginia County, Montana, in search of a horse thief whom he had already caught in Trenton. He had been in N.Y. conferring with the N.Y. police chief and was on his way to Trenton. Well, the tales that followed during dinner on the Pullman which I treated him to were astounding. He showed me his new Colt-44 to the astonishment of diners and conductors. Had a unique time, I can tell you, and with hearty invitations to come out to 'ginia City the first chance I can get and a promise of a "big time," I left him.

276

Dear Mama,

We are all sitting on a blanket spread out on the warm ground down by the brook, within a few feet of the place where you and

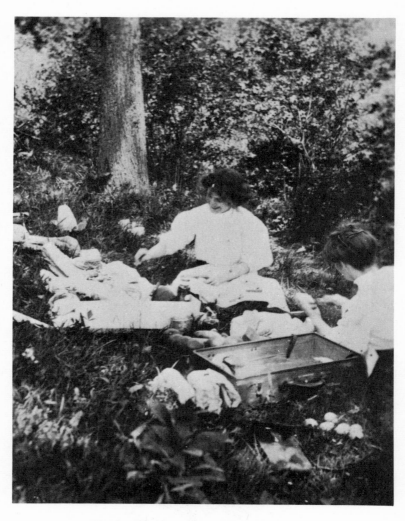

Carolyn Wyeth and her sister, Ruth Bockius.

296

Papa, Carol and I "washed up" the day of the memorable drive to Chadds Ford, four or five years ago. We did this yesterday too.

I have erected a large, practical stone fireplace on an "island" just below the point where the brook leaves the road, and yesterday we broiled a delicious shad, had corn, baked potatoes and coffee. It was great!

This morning, as it was my duty to read over a book manuscript (for which I am to do the pen-and-inks), I lugged along a blanket, a pad of paper and the "galley proof sheets," and settled myself 'long side the brook to read. *Glorious* is no name for it!

Yesterday I got a *mighty* cheerful letter from Papa. One that made me feel good all day—his suggestion of seeing us in a few months, made all by himself too, was a *pleasure* to read.

The wind shifted a few minutes ago and is blowing from the *east*—that's not just what we want today as it is a little raw—how remarkably quick the change!

2 P.M.

Just at the end of the last paragraph a fellow came plodding along with a broken-down motorcycle. I passed him a casual question, "What's busted?" "I don't know" was his answer. He stopped and he started over his machine verifying this thing and that thing until he had tested about everything. Just at this point I happened to remember a little incident related by Uncle Gig in relation to Nat and a poor fellow who was flat on his back under a "busted" machine on Dedham Ave. The owner had taken everything apart, adjusted it afresh, but seemed unable to remedy the fault. He'd been working an hour or so in the hot dust and Nat had been looking on for a few minutes and casually put in the remark, "Are your wire connections OK?" "By God I never looked *there*," answered the fellow. It had never occurred to him to look in the simplest place for the trouble. Like the fellow who loses his glasses and suddenly finds them pushed back on his forehead.

Well, so did *I* come to the rescue—so did *I* win a *second* batch of laurels on Nat's lightning philosophy and witty reasoning. This *poor* cuss (see how patronizingly I say it?) also overlooked his "wire connections" and sure enough found a plug broken off one of the batteries. He went on his way rejoicing! You had ought to have seen me look on—silently, but oh! so *knowingly*, as he unfitted and re-placed a thousand bolts and nuts and then to mention, offhand-like,

297

"How about your connections?!" Oh! Me! what a pleasure it is to be confident, sure and then to feel superior—I deigned not to look at the poor fool as he disappeared up the road.

Enough of this!

We cooked dinner à la mode on the kitchen stove—fried eggs, bacon and cocoa.

The clouds have now shut in pretty close—we expect rain. The dear old fireplace will wait—we expect many a good meal from those piping-hot stones.

277

Chadds Ford, Pennsylvania
April 5, 1909

Dear Mama,

A glorious day—but we all feel a little sad. Poor old Peer died last night.—Although I am more or less sad because I was so attached to the dog, I am more sad that such a stalwart, healthy, happy animal should have to leave this glorious life for the sake of an idiotic notion of damn fool man.

I was given the puppy with a string tied to him, i.e. that I should promise to return the dog when the time was ready to have his *ears clipped*. So last week it was done.

Had I known what atrocious butchery it is to do the thing, the dog would never have left this place—however, I was assured by the owner (a millionaire damn fool—a typical milk-brained *sop*, the kind whose hardest labor it is to serve tea in the afternoon) that it was a *small* matter, etc., etc.

The dog left me, a great, powerful, healthy pup—good natured, happy and with lots of sense. I remarked as I took him to the train, "I wonder if he will come back the same old rollicking pup?" He didn't—last Wednesday he returned—a thin, battered and bloody spectacle, his great fleshy ears trimmed to the head—all plastered up with springs in his ears to make them "point"—I was ashamed of it, I couldn't look anyone in the face as the poor wretched animal followed behind.

I nursed him carefully; he failed steadily. He slowly made his way into his box and layed down for the last time. This morning we found him dead.

I really feel bad—I can't bear to see an animal's life sacrificed unless it is absolutely necessary—the cruelty placed on such good dumb beasts, such as poor Peer had to take, is an outrage. Nothing less than a licking, within an inch of the brute's life who perpetrated the act, would be what he deserves.—I have written him and told him what I think! He's supposed to be a choice bit of "Wilmington Social Life" but he's not fit to be at large.

I may not be a good dog or any kind of an animal disciplinarian, but by Jove! I do get attached to them to the point of *real* affection.

278

Chadds Ford, Pennsylvania
April 20, 1909

Dear Sid,

The winter has been glorious in its many, diversified, intellectual pleasures.

And as for the teaching at Pape's, I am enthusiastic and I know I will enjoy the work. I feel that I can awaken an interest there and do some good; all I teach will be fundamental, a striving for *truth* and not mannerisms. The exaction of good drawing demanded of me is bound to do me good. As you know I did very little life drawing, and know damn little about the figure—the constant association with it will familiarize me with it.—I am sure the good will counterbalance the harm. Pape promises *positively* to leave me alone.—I have outlined my methods and he believes in them.

My reasons for not illustrating I explained as best I could in my other letter; I have apparently failed to make them clear. They are conclusive as far as they concern me—to read the lives of masters, from Angelo down, confirms me—and to listen to the writings and talkings of our *best* contemporary men confirms me—the underlying quality of *every* great work is truth, and the magazines of today, with their commercial spirit, their limitations of picture production and their price limitations make it *impossible* for a man to *paint pictures* for them. A *successful magazine picture* is essential, one adaptable to limited reproduction facilities is essential, a reasonably small payment is essential. One is limited in every direction; to paint, he must paint what he feels and to paint it as he wants to, and spend what time he needs.

If you were a poet, could you sit down and compose a poem on a given subject—yes—but what would it be? Would it compare to the real abstract inspiration that leaps into your soul? Would it constitute the great art? No, not by a damn sight, and you know it. And if you were continually writing commercial poetry, would not the continual constructing of poetry, the habits of expression, the fitting of this meter or style to this sort of subject, or the fitting of that meter or style to that sort of subject get you into a receipted way of doing things? Would it not be difficult to write a few pure lines naturally, unaffectedly, without a tincture of receipt? Can a poet write real verse with an idea in his mind where it is to appear and how will it impress people or will the editors like it? *No,* a thousand times *no!* All this I have felt for a couple years; I find that it is being reaffirmed on every side, past and present; it is the basis of all the past true art. Our lives are short; it is up to us to clear away as much of the interfering dead wood as it is possible, as soon as possible. The trouble is, Chase, we have always associated our minds with those of illustrators, *not* painters; we have such a different viewpoint that at a first glance the painters seem entirely wrong—it is our duty to investigate. They have investigated us and have perceived our limitations, and it is our solemn duty to listen to what they have to say.

The same love, the same enthusiasm that goes to make illustration, goes to make painting—the one is born into the world under limitations that choke and distort and soon die—the other is born full and free as the air; if it ripens it will stand as a perfect expression of those loves and will last forever. The difference to me, Chase, is so pronounced, the stumbling block of illustration so apparent, that I can't see how it is that *you* don't see it. I can't believe that I could be the *exception,* to keep on developing my illustration and eventually *paint.* It has killed them *all;* [Edwin] Abbey is the best, he has come nearer to it—but his pictures are *far* from being paintings in the true sense—they will always live as pictures of history—but not as Chavannes, Millet, Constable, Whistler, Monet, Velasquez, etc. Abbey is an illustrator on a large scale; you feel history and incident, and some character, in his pictures, *never* music or emotion.

Well, Sid, old boy, I'll ring off! Try to understand what I'm trying to say.

My model is waiting for me.

279

Chadds Ford, Pennsylvania
April 23, 1909

Dear Mama,

The great danger with me, I write on impulse—I never know what I'm going to write about, and so when my pen hits the paper, I just simply ramble—just the way I talk I guess.

I have often likened my letters to one of these toys you wind up and set on the floor—sometimes it will go in a true circle, but mostly it will whirl around once and the second time it will smash into a chair leg, turn upside down and go like hell, spinning out its strength, making a great racket but *doing nothing*. So it is, I get wound up, smash into a subject, make a whole lot of noise and *say nothing*.

The above fault embodies one of the greatest weaknesses I have to contend with. *Restraint*. If I could do things calmly and deliberately I would accomplish far more than I do. Mr. Pyle said from the beginning, "Wyeth, *Hold your Pegasis!*" (Guess that don't spell Pegasus, but you understand.)

280

Chadds Ford, Pennsylvania
May 5, 1909

Dear Mama,

No! I haven't settled with Pape yet, but I anticipate little trouble in making him see my way. He is tying me down too close, i.e. he restricts my studying with an instructor during the summer months, which, if I had so agreed would have practically jeopardized all my chances to obtain knowledge, except from *him*, and I have an idea that one can get precious little of healthy instruction there.

281

Chadds Ford, Pennsylvania
May 7, 1909

Dear Mama,

Hasn't it been hot? Eighty-six all day, and the same for the past

301

two days. Our apple blossoms are all falling, and our backyard is literally covered as with new snow. I am sorry to see them leave us so quickly. Carol has been in the garden pulling radishes—she got a nice mess, tender and sweet.

The place is wonderfully beautiful just now—it kind of makes me hold my breath when I realize that we are going to leave it—I don't believe there is a more beautiful spot in the world!

I have just completed Thoreau's book.

It may be, in the course of two weeks, you will see me home on a flying visit. I intend to do so before I annex my signature to that "restricting contract" of Pape's. I have no one to talk the matter over with here.

I hope that neither Papa or you will lose your patience with my apparent unsettled state at present. No one but myself realizes what a serious matter this coming change is and what bearing it has on my *future*. The matter of moving, i.e. breaking up here and settling with you of course is a serious undertaking in itself, but it is trivial compared to what happens to myself and my art; primarily it is *that* that I am making the change for, and it would be exceedingly foolish not to arrange the *best* that can be arranged.

282

Chadds Ford, Pennsylvania
May 15, 1909

Dear Mama,

At last! I have on my easel a picture that embodies a quality which I have never before obtained—*Music!*

I feel that I have just touched the very edge of something which I have thought many times was perhaps completely out of my reach—this slight taste of that supreme achievement in painting, suggestion, has given me great encouragement and confidence, and although I know that years will pass before I shall be prepared to say any words of importance in this branch of my art, I feel a great sense of relief to know that it is possible.

My intense sense of realism—which has often run to brutality in my illustration, that quality which has made people say in spite of themselves that my "illustrations were paintings" has led me into such a scrutinizing light, as it were, that I am unable to close my eyes (that have always searched for telling detail and facts), and to *feel* my picture out with more vagueness, simplicity and suggestions—i.e. to embody in my picture an *abstract* spirit.

In this one I have an Indian seated in the rocks, moss and ferns, piping on a reed—by him there trills a small brook, splashing over the rocks and eventually pouring out into a shallow pool—behind him is a large birch with smaller saplings.

The entire foreground is in the silvery transparent shadow of a spring woods and the background shines in that warm yellow-green sunlight that sprays through young foliage. It is *realistic,* and there is the Indian and his reed, the splashing brooklet and rocks, etc., but when one looks at it he forgets the realism, he is removed from the consciousness of looking at a realistic picture and thinks of nothing but the spirit of spring. That's what I *want* the picture to inspire when it is done!

Just give Babe a nod that we want to be remembered to him, don't bother him anymore. I am hoping that he can get down here this summer as he did last. Tell me, can he do it? I want to enjoy once more his company in this country before we leave it.—My God how I *love* it, too! With all there is to look forward to I can't help feeling that it is going to be hard to *break away.*

"Babe," 1909.

"Winter," 1909

Chapter XI

FAR FROM NEEDHAM

*"Like a bolt of lightning from a clear sky,
there comes every once in awhile profound
memories and visions of home."*

Dear Mama,

I have something to say—it is ten o'clock but I must say it! I am forcibly struck by an impression, in some way I must give it expression—my pen is handy, the window is open and it is cool, so here is my method. I'll send it to *you*—I must send it somewhere—I don't want to keep it. Look it over and throw it away!

It is a still hot night. As we sat on the porch earlier in the evening, listening to the thousand mysterious voices in the grass, in the trees and hedgerows, we were startled by the long white flash of an automobile searchlight darting along the meadow road below us. It pierced the night with a merciless glare, painting the roadway, the fences, grass and trees with cold, glaring and unnatural colors.

We watched the huge machine as it slid toward us swiftly and silently, its searing light boring its way through the darkness, until to our surprise and *consternation* the shaft of light swung its great arm into our driveway and slowly moved up the steep path. As it followed the curve toward the house, the blinding light was turned full upon us—we felt positively abashed, to be suddenly placed in that brazen glare which seemed to search out our very souls with microscopic minuteness. The sudden change from silent, soulful reverie in the dark into that harsh, garish flame seemed almost to the point of being revolting.

Common courtesy demanded that we meet our friends, whoever they may be, and to treat them as cordially as possible.

The conversation that followed proved to be entirely in keeping with the great trembling car that throbbed with suppressed power, and the rank nauseating odor of gasoline which it emitted. We talked automobiles and prices, speed and endurance, roads and distances. Not *once* did our minds turn to the wonders of the great mysterious night that enveloped us, the deep vault of the heaven with its thousand twinkling eyes, or the arching trees that hung above us exuding the lush fragrance of spring. These were forgotten *utterly*.

Finally, and without once leaving their luxuriant seats, they said good-night and left us. The car shuddered violently and with much coughing and wheezing it turned about. Once on the road it settled down into a humming purr and soon disappeared over the hills.

The occupants have reached their homes by this time, some fifteen miles distant, within thirty minutes as they had planned. They shot through the night like an arrow, veils fluttering, coats and hair blowing. The night's pleasure with them has passed—they have ridden miles but they have no remembrances of their outing other than fleeting recollections of fantastic blurred objects, a vague sense of the vibrating machine. Their faces tingle with the rush of air that had beat upon them, they think only of their *next* ride and how much farther and faster they will go.

Now for reflection!

Here we are—the three of us. The baby is sleeping peacefully in the cool hammock under the trees, Carolyn is resting likewise in another hammock slung on the porch. I am at my desk by an open window. Without, the sounds of the night insects gently reverberate through the still air; from the distant meadow floats the soft trilling chorus of a thousand frogs; from under the wall by the cellar window comes the louder chirp, chirp of the cricket. Above us the stars hang in the trees like tiny lanterns, and between the larger openings of the branches the infinite depths of the heavens suggest those great intangible secrets of the universe.

I have taken a belated walk into the garden. The low rows of peas lay long and shadowy as though asleep; the gaunt bean poles stand like sentinels across the head of the patch; and beyond, in great protecting mounds, rise the vague towering forms of the apple trees.

How grand it all is! How I reverence it! How it makes me revolt against that unwholesome, empty and selfish life lived by just those people with whom we parted company two hours ago. I deplore the great mistake they are making; I am sorry that they are missing so much—I can't help pitying them!

I hope this is understandable—it is quite late and my mind may be dull. However, I'll fold this up and slip it into an envelope and seal it—I won't look at it again.

With all said and done, this impression is so strong that I can almost cry—for *what,* I don't know, perhaps it is because I'm so glad and so sorry.

Mama, you're a staunch *backstop* for all the vagaries of the impulsive minds of us boys, otherwise I wouldn't send this.

However, I feel relieved having let off superfluous steam; I hope you can relieve yourself of this outburst as easily.

284

N. C. Wyeth was illustrating a poem titled "The Moods" by George T. Marsh. The four illustrations appeared in Scribner's *magazine, December, 1909.*

Chadds Ford, Pennsylvania
May 29, 1909

Dear Babe,

I have completed two of the Indian series for *Scribner's,* which, by the way, having been seen by True and Ivory [on] Sunday and Harding yesterday, were pronounced way and beyond my past work; in fact one of them, "Spring," they consider almost entirely in the light of painting.

My plans for the fall have been uppermost in my mind of late. I have considerable correspondence with men whose opinions I am bound to respect. They are all inclined to drive me away from the teaching idea and therefore I feel less inclined to undertake the job. At present I feel that I must retrench financially, enough so that I can say *to hell with* everybody, for 6 or 8 years. Then I can do as I damn please—and *paint, not* for ammunition companies, but for *myself!* It takes more courage than I've got to go to a man of money and arrange a business proposition, which would be to borrow the *necessary.* Businessmen are too wrapped up in material things to *begin* to understand the processes of a man's art. There is risk in everything to be sure, but it's astonishing to know that painters as a whole are far more successful in the end than businessmen.

285

This letter refers for the first time to the "absent member," the child expected in October.

The WYETHS

Dear Mama,

Yesterday, i.e. last evening, I put in all the rest of my planting, which utilizes every foot of my two truck patches. To enumerate: third planting of corn, fifth of peas, some bush lima's, late-summer turnips, fifth of radishes, fourth of lettuce, and another batch of large onions for scallions.

Never have I seen a garden flourish as this one has this spring. *To think* that Sunday we will pick our first peas, good full-grown ones too! Last night we had our first mess of beets, and had we believed it we could have had beets a week ago. I planted some of the latter very thick to use as greens and we are all of the opinion that they will beat spinach.

My potatoes are just blossoming, and I find they are weeks ahead of any about. I only wish I had about 10 acres in instead of 12 short rows.

In the art line, things have been humping along quite as successful. This morning I completed another ammunition picture, one which has occupied my attention for some days. I have also got my third Indian picture "Winter" under way, which I think promises to be one of the best.

Carolyn is very well and surprisingly energetic. I'd hate to enumerate all the stuff she has made with her needle this spring.— She has just come into the room so will see if she will tell me—12 pairs of Henriette's drawers (tucked), five nightgowns for the baby, three dresses for the same, four flannel petticoats and two sacks— four dresses and two sacks for the absent member. Besides helping Aunty Guss with two afternoon dresses. She is laughing because I'm writing this and thinks it foolish—but it's a pleasure for me to blow *somebody else's* horn once in awhile.

I forgot! we are all exercised over "hidden treasure." An old colored fellow who lives about a mile from here, and one I have often interested myself in, insists on there being "a heap of treasure" in a certain spot on this place. The tales he relates about the wartime history of this place are harrowing and worthy of being written. The fact is he claims that he has waited years to find the *right* occupant of this house who would be worthy of the treasure. *I* am <u>it</u>! So you see why it pays to be genial and an easy mark. So we have arranged to dig out this treasure this summer sometime during the full o' the moon, cause 'tis *then* that the treasure would be nearest the surface of the earth. Besides, I must get one more person into the scheme because as we dig within a marked circle, one has to stand outside of the hole while two dig and when one is to be relieved, the one outside steps in as the other steps out, thereby keeping the "rymath" (I found out later that he meant "rhythm"). I thought 'twould be fine if Babe would be here in order to take it all in. The reason that I'm following it up is just for the fun of it. It's bound to be weird and there might be some interesting material to use in writing.

Well, I expect 10 days or so will find us home. The minute I finish the next picture, "Winter," we will start.

286

Chadds Ford, Pennsylvania
June 8, 1909

Dear Mama,

Today I am not, as is usually the case, under the spell of the day. My mind is too much diverted by the work on my easel, which far surpasses any past results, and what is more, promises a new opening, infinite in possibilities of development.

I am truly elated over the way my work is progressing; I am walking only-on-the-high-places at present.

My last picture, "Winter," is proving itself the best of the set in many ways, a condition perfectly agreeable, for what is more encouraging than to feel that the last thing is the best? My abilities seem to have no limitations at present—I hope this spirit will last—it embodies self-reliance and confidence which are two essentials in painting, a point wherein I am liable to lose poise.

287

Chadds Ford, Pennsylvania
June 11, 1909

Dear Babe,

Like a bolt of lightning from a clear sky, there comes every once in awhile profound memories and visions of home; not of the home proper just at this particular moment, but of the life as we lived it in its entirety.

The WYETHS

It may be perfect folly to waste the time writing, or rather, *trying* to write about such abstract matter, but I must let off steam somewhere, and as the cost is only 2¢—why not?

The main theme of this afternoon's visions lies in one very strange, and to you, intangible detail.

A fresh breeze blowing through the pine boughs, along the river somewhere—most likely through one of those big pines up at the oaks. The point of view seems to be from the ground. I lie on my back looking up at the heavy green foliage of needles slowly lifting and lowering against the bright but somewhat gray sky; I watch the changing shapes of light as it breaks through the moving branches; the beauty of the tree's construction losing itself in the deep shadowy dome of green fascinates me. The great mystery of earth and sky, the profundity of the infinite depths shining between those swaying branches impresses me and like soft exquisite music the lap-lap-lap-lap of the rippling river reaches my ears. My whole soul is atingle! My imagination is on fire! The universe towers in my mind a great overpowering mystery. The significance of the tiniest speck of bark on the pine tree assumes the proportions of the infinite sky; my brain almost bursts with the effort to really appreciate the meaning of *life,* of *existence!* I reach a pinnacle of thought and my mind collapses—I watch the swaying tree and I hear the lap-lap-lap of the water—I thank fate that I was brought into this life—I ardently promise, with all my soul, to do my best, to make my short life of use, to add an infintesimal might to the world!!

288

Chadds Ford, Pennsylvania
July 1, 1909

Dear Mama,

Today I started at work in the studio and have had a very successful day. Layed in the last Indian picture, "Summer," with sky effect that Babe and I saw at the bridge.

The two weeks home did me lots and lots of good; I enjoyed everything in the highest sense. Although I loafed, my mind seemed always on a high level, and that, capped with the visit to Concord, will afford me much valuable inspiration for many a month.

289

Chadds Ford, Pennsylvania
July 6, 1909

Dear Mama,

I don't know what did it, but since my trip home I have a far bigger and broader outlook on things. I mean my attitude toward nature seems decidedly stronger and more definite. Somehow I feel that after reading Thoreau, becoming thoroughly inbred with his magnificent attitude toward nature, and then going to the very spot he loved and knew so intimately, I feel that it has intensified *my* attitude. That trip to Concord was invaluable to me, and besides the pleasure above mentioned, I know not when I have enjoyed an excursion *externally* as I did that one.

I hope that the next time we come home that some such trip can be taken again.

290

Chadds Ford, Pennsylvania
July 16, 1909

Dear Mama,

Yes, Wednesday I went to N.Y. with my last picture. "Summer" was the subject. The poem was written by Marsh (the one who wrote "The Old Canoe," you know) [and I] did a superb job with it. Four verses called "Moods"—Spring (Song), Summer (Hush), Autumn (Waiting), Winter (Death). To me they strike a big note and I was decidedly enthusiastic over them.

Give my love to Papa and tell him that all but one field of hay is in the barn, beautifully made and of fine quality—that at present there are about fifty head of cows in the lower pasture and in the mowed field between us and the village, and that the farm is rented out for next year too, for which I am glad. The wheat hereabouts is all in and day and night one can hear from some direction the puf-puf-puf of the threshers at work.

291

Chadds Ford, Pennsylvania
July 19, 1909

Dear Mama,

I have just come in from the studio after two hours spent on Babe's portrait! I want that it will be a good likeness and will be worthy of a space on the wall at *home*. In succession I want to paint the portraits of the entire Wyeth household, providing I can get each one to stay long enough to do it.

292

Chadds Ford, Pennsylvania
August 2, 1909

Dear Mama,

In the kitchen we have at last installed a veritable "Bridget"— Bridget Connie is her name. She has a rich brogue, thick as cream, and an unhealed wen on the right side of her forehead, big as a peach. However she's the "yes Marrm" type and apparently very clean—she walks with a sailor's roll and crooks her arm like a prize-fighter. However, she put up a bully simple dinner fit for a king, and now if she doesn't hit the booze bottle she's OK.

293

Chadds Ford, Pennsylvania
August 7, 1909. Sunday afternoon

Dear Mama,

Outside, a damp misty gray light is filtering from out a threatening sky. The foliage hangs limp and soft like dampened paper. The very birds seem to fly sluggishly through the oppressive atmosphere and their calls seem dull and muffled in the thick air—but no rain! The brief storm of over two weeks ago only exasperated; the heavens seemed to tantalize the earth as a man would worry a thirsty dog with a wet sponge. At the present moment the sun has burned through a thinner level of the clouds and is spraying the hills with a liquid gold; a wagon is coming down the road by Sheatz's Lane and the dust is almost motionless behind it, hanging in thick yellow billows, floating on the heavy air in a compact mass.

I have reached a point in my work, where, to make the most of what is significant, *truly* significant, in my nature, my power or whatever you wish to call it, I must turn into the one right path and forsake for good that other diverging and ever-narrowing pathway which always ends in a *blind alley.*

My ardor for *practical* work has been replaced by the desire for a bigger and *lasting* achievement, and there is no swapping back again if I should have to die for it.

If ever I needed help I need it now, and whoever will do it will profit handsomely, not only in worldly wealth, but more (and particularly if it be my own blood), because I feel confident that within me there lies a higher power that, if given the chance of expression, will be a worthy reward.

My request is of course to borrow money—enough to provide me with the simplest wants for five years beginning next spring, thereby starting with a clean slate after the extra expense of the autumn event. My work will consist of persistent study from nature; landscape, figures, portraiture and still life. I shall indulge in practical work only so far as I can dispose of the serious work finished, be it to *Scribner's* or otherwise.

To mention in brief the important expenses—my rent for house and studio combined, under the present subrenting (which is signed for two years more and in all probability as long as I stay here) is as reasonable as it is possible to make it anywhere: $23.50 a month. My life insurance is $209.50 a year, fire insurance $12.50 a year, with the average expenses of living, which have greatly diminished since living here. Furthermore there would be many smaller things where we could economize.

The sum I have figured on, as small an amount as possible, and still one which would be adequate (for a sum not adequate would be as bad as nothing) is $5000. This money I could pay interest on and in due time refund in proportion to my earnings.

This concludes the proposition. I have not expressed any one part of it in flamboyant terms, but it is serious, it is deep meaning, it is as significant an effort of expression as it is possible for me to give you.

If I can find some response to this appeal I will not only feel eternally thankful, but will recompense the helpers and the world with my deepest and most serious efforts.

294

Chadds Ford, Pennsylvania
August 15, 1909

Dear Mama,

I hope that the above portrait(?) does not imply anything im-modest, but I really *did* feel a little picturesque sloshing through the middle of a mile and a half of brook.

This morning (Sunday) dawned bright but soon clouded over until the sky seemed *stuffed* with gray opaque clouds; by ten o'clock it was dark and threatening—much to my delight. . . .

I struck for the brook in Sheatz's meadow. Its clean, shallow waters and the gravel bottom proved too enticing. So stepped in, leggings, sneakers and all, and followed its winding path to its source, or at least to the spot where three distinct springs joined, making a large dark pool which overflowed and ran west to the Brandywine.

To plod along through clear, shallow, fast-running water, minnows darting either side of you at every step and frogs plunking in—sort of punctuating your steps—and then, as it happened with me, to scare up a feeding blue heron, and at intervals, disturbing the same pair of sandpipers that kept just so far ahead, gave the stroll a certain wild, remote character.

I do not know that I ever felt more.

I must admit of a certain guilt, however: to cloud the waters with ruthless strides, to mark with every step an ugly hole in that beautiful, flat, clean bottom seemed to me wicked—I felt more like a trespasser than ever before. Those thoughts marred the pleasure not a little until I started to retrace my steps for a little way and was mightily pleased to find that the swift stream had completely effaced the ugly scars, and that the minnows still darted past me and just as many frogs "flipped" into the brook.

295

"Grandpa" was N. C. Wyeth's grandfather, Andrew Newell Wyeth I.

Chadds Ford, Pennsylvania
September 1, 1909. Thursday evening

Dear Babe,

What a glorious day this has been. It has reminded me many times of the "call of that blue jay over by the nut tree," and then, to go with it all, came Mama's letter, distinctly sad in character, which more than kept my heart full all day.

The wind howled around my studio since morning. The half-door which I keep closed creaked incessantly, sounding exactly like a turkey hen calling—not because of this did I let the door continue its song, but because it brought back a little detail which is fastened in my memory like a jewel. You remember the door that lifts with weights before that spacious cold storage closet over to Aunt Hat's? It is behind the stove—*you* know. Well, years ago, I guess I must have been no older than ten or eleven, we all went to Cambridge the day before Thanksgiving (of course to stay over the feast day). Well, as I was fumbling around in that treasure drawer in the flower room, between the kitchen and sitting room, Grandpa called to me and said, "Listen to the gobbler we are going to eat tomorrow," and with that he slid the above-mentioned door in such a way as to produce just that peculiar cluck that turkeys make. I was just young enough to be impressed by the mystery of it, which was more impressive perhaps because I was always aware of Grandpa's scrupulous honesty in everything, and therefore considered his remark with greater weight.

Andrew Newell Wyeth, N. C. Wyeth's grandfather.

Ever after and even now I look upon that door a little furtively—it always makes me hark back to those raw, late fall days when we went to Cambridge—the tin ostrich in the tin cart with a man sitting in it; the fly that would buzz by working it back and forth; the white, time-worn dominoes; the little glass-covered puzzle in the red box, "Pigs in Clover," it was called, with the bewildering isles through which one must guide the quicksilver; the "tiddlywinks" and the myriads of nicknacks and games that crammed that drawer to its capacity. And then that sort of a straw-basket boat with a red enameled lining which was always filled with nuts on that day. And I'll bet you a dollar you will find everything I have mentioned all there, and in their very same places.

Oh! that creaking door made me think all day. If I started to completely record my memories of this particular subject, the morning would find me still plying the pen.

That annual Saturday when I used to make the journey for our four barrels of apples—all the hundred details connected with the trip. Old Tom, the light express, the yellow blanket, the wagon seat with its folding back, the hook where one hung the reins. The pungent aroma of apples spiced with a basket of quinces; the paper bag of Seckels given us to eat on the way; the sagging of the heavy wagon in contrast to the light, springiness of the morning's ride; the muddy roads into Watertown, the Chestnut Hill Reservoir; the long monotonous and rough stretch between Newton Highlands and the Falls with always that pleasing sensation when we suddenly came onto that big suggestive sign, "Master and Wells," and then that restful feeling when we struck the downward slope of Webster Street after leaving Highlandville. And once I remember we stopped for Sutton's milk.

If I let myself go too long and too intensely in this way I reach a point of *desperation* almost—to think that they have *gone* and that every minute makes them farther away. It makes me *wonder* that I have been able to throw myself into *this* life so thoroughly and so deeply.

Tonight is one of those times when I would like to be suddenly transplanted back into my home.—I can fit myself so vividly into the very day, hour, and minute of the life and details that always take place at just this time of year.

My God, my eyes fill up when I think of the rain beating against those old windows at school, running down those large panes in blurred streams. The boughs of those scraggly pitch pines waving up and down like the stiff, awkward gesticulating of an old woman. And then the wind—how it did use to whistle through those loose doors and large keyholes! and suddenly! the entry door of the "boys' entry" would bang open and quickly following the inner door would slam back—for an instant papers would fly and then the teacher would venture into the intruding gale to close the door. I can see her now, hair blowing back from her forehead, squinting, and with a determined frown, force the door closed; then asking "Bennie" to go out and "shut and bolt" the outside door. He would squeeze through the grudging door space made by the teacher and we would hear a loud bravado *bang!* as Bennie slammed the door to with a vengeance—returning with a smile lurking around his mouth telling of a little fun concealed in the overvehement duty. My, but don't these things crowd my mind tonight? How I love to think of them.

Well, I must stop this sort of writing, it must get tiresome to read so much of it.

Some may think that I write too much *stuff*. But it is, I find, a great relaxation to do this, and furthermore I believe it does me much good, in this respect: when I write I think of only the best that is in me, that which is worthy of being read by another. It may not be worthy, however, but it speaks of my better self, at any rate. Another thing—writing sort of ties my day's work with my night's rest, it keeps up the momentum as it were. I say this not only for writing, but reading and music too. These three things I find are filling in more and more of my spare time. Nevertheless I shall always make a decided effort to spend a big portion of my "spare time" with Carol and the baby, which I think goes to make up the most vital part of my education.

Last night we had a roaring fire in the fireplace which we enjoyed like a new toy. It was really quite sharp outside and it felt decidedly comfortable. The feeling of fall was intensified by the prolonged calls of three foxes which we could hear while lying in bed. I was a bit scared for my pullets (31, all of my own raising, although hatched in stolen nests) but find them "intact" this morning.

Tomorrow morning I wish you were to be here; I shall drive to Wilmington, starting at seven, with Jenkins' team, to fetch back a secondhand chest of drawers in which to store sheets, towels, etc., now packed in trunks. I shall go down the "Crick Road" and you know how glorious it will be. I shall go alone.

296

N. C. Wyeth was referring in this letter to his request for a loan of $5000.

Chadds Ford, Pennsylvania
September 6, 1909

Dear Papa,

I received your letter this morning and will answer it immediately before Ed arrives. I understand matters perfectly and have no reason to think that you haven't acted prudently in your conclusions. I have always had slight knowledge of your affairs, otherwise I probably would never have written on the subject.

Your advice is practical, but not adaptable—your interpretation of my particular case is still wrong, but even if right and you were as convinced and sure as I am myself, I take it that my plan is impossible for you to meet.

I will endeavor to pull out in some way, however, and if I am successful in the bigger and better undertaking I am positively sure the results will justify my present actions.

I am decidedly sorry you couldn't have taken a run in on us last month, but you won't miss another year if we have to cage you up and ship C.O.D.

With thanks for your letter and love from all to all.

297

Chadds Ford, Pennsylvania
October 15, 1909. 6:30 A.M.

Dear Mama,

I got to talking with Carol at the conclusion of the last paragraph, which lasted until I was sleepy, so will conclude this letter this morning. The wind blew up a rain storm—everything is soaked and dripping outside. I am glad, for we need all the rain possible for our springs—if we don't get considerable before the ground freezes we'll have trouble with water.

The subject which interested us so much was in regards to a trip to Europe. Yesterday, while working, I was thinking out in the simplest words a method of explaining just why I do not care to go (yet), and I was discussing all this with Carol.

I think I can make it clear.

First, just what is painting, *true* painting? Nothing more or less than the result of a man's love, respect and knowledge of *nature*—

321

in short, his attitude toward her. Secondly, what real value can a painter get from looking at other mens' masterpieces? Only *one true value* exists—*inspiration*! To obtain a bit more is obtaining something *not* your own, to go a step farther than the *spirit*—the *message* of a picture means that you are imbibing the man's personal *methods*, or in other words, the artificial part of his art, *his* means to *his* end. To do this throws *your own* personality into the profound risk of being adulterated with another's.

The sole big value in painting is individuality; all the rest— method, technique, color, drawing, etc.—are accessories—these are simply props to support the big expression.

Now for me or any other very immature student to turn himself loose amongst the best pictures in existence is taking a great risk. A fellow who has anything in him is very susceptible, it is his strength and weakness at the same time. He will unconsciously absorb the artificial (besides the exalted) from masters' work and unconsciously adapt it to his own work. Will not this infect his personality—his individuality?

I feel that I am learning what to avoid and shall do all in my power to protect my individuality. I have yet to acquire it, by forgetting, gradually, what my illustration has taught me.

So now, after the glamour of that remarkable invitation to go abroad has worn away, I look at my inability to accept the kind invitation a god-send. This is truly the way I feel. I will probably not be tempted again in such a manner, at least for a number of years, and *then* I shall be ready to go.

It makes me shiver to think what a trip of that sort would have done to me.

Bridget has went!! Housecleaning is all over and we are enjoying our solitude.

298

Chadds Ford, Pennsylvania
October 19, 1909

Dear Mama,

Carolyn is in remarkable spirits concerning the approaching event. It is wonderful to me the way in which nature slowly and surely converts a mother's mind in face of pain and possible danger.

I mention this in a very perfunctory manner perhaps, but in reality it is something that has stirred my deepest feelings and respect all summer.

299

Fred Miller and George Salter were workers in Mr. Zirngiebel's greenhouses.

Chadds Ford, Pennsylvania
October 22, 1909

Dear Mama and *All,*

What a day this is! How many impressions have flashed through my mind, from the moment I started the nails from the painted boards of the "home box," until now that I hear a wild wind blowing and can see myriads of dead leaves darting and tumbling through the air like live things! No one knows! Even if I *have* tried to explain in the most detailed manner to Carolyn, I know she can't understand—*no* one can!

It has all, these wonderful strange memories, flitted before my mind against a gray mysterious background of sadness; and once, when at last I picked the bunch of pinks from the bottom of the box, I came upon that spray of arbor-vitae, I could contain myself no longer. Whoever placed that bit of green in the box had little idea what a vivid world of the past it would bring into my mind. *Never,* in all my reminiscent moods have I been so vividly transferred into my past life. Never before have I been so deeply moved—*way down deep*—it touched a spot so remote in my feelings, impossible to describe, and almost *tragic.* Why, I don't know. Spasms went through my whole body—a vague infinite appreciation of the terrible fact that the past is *gone,* gone *forever!* And with this feeling a vivid panorama of my life at home moved before my mind. I could hear all the noises peculiar to our home—the squeaking and trembling wheeze of the iron pump under the spruce trees by the "propogating house"—the rattle of the tin cup as it was dropped on its chain—I could hear the crunch of steps coming down our gravel walk and someone pulling the barn door closed with a low rumble and a thump—and then those ever-sighing spruce trees, sounding like the rush of distant water or, as I used to think, the wind whispering to itself. But greatest and most *painfully* vivid, brought

323

back by that green emblem, was the sight and smell of the *old* potting shed, the one near where the iron pump stood; the one with the slanting runway which led one up along the dangerous chasm, wherein stood the brick boilers, and into the *upper* house. I could particularly remember it on a rainy day or during early spring when the snow was melting, leaking in big drops into the loam on the potting benches, or into holes worn in the dirt floor. And at intervals the rushing sound of snow sliding off the greenhouses, terminating with a tinkle of the many icicles broken off at the eaves, and the final soft thump as the snowslide struck the ground.

And somebody suddenly bursting in the door, bare-headed, with a basket of cuttings from another greenhouse—Fred Miller or Salter perhaps—with Uncle Gig always standing around smiling and making remarks.

Empty "Dills Best" boxes in the windowsills and the blue paper and tinfoil packages of "Winner" smoking and chewing tobacco thrown about.

All this, with the silent thoughtful figure of Grandpapa appearing and disappearing, his head bowed, his peculiar listed walk and the rhythmic thud, thud, thud of his wooden shoes. I must stop! I could keep on *forever* it seems to me. How I enjoy it—and how painful it is!

Well it all came to me in a *bunch* last night after I had opened the box.—I was swept off my feet, absolutely!

It seems a trivial matter now to mention the articles one by one, because the thoughts behind them mean so much more to me. However, let me thank all in behalf of Carolyn and Henriette, too, for the magic box. The poor little kid was so excited while I was opening the box that she actually cried. She seemed to sense the significance of the occasion. Her attitude last Christmas during the same ceremony is brought to mind. I am positive that she is sensitive to the atmosphere about her, particularly when anything unusual is to take place.

The box was received in the dark, I took pains to keep it right side up, I opened it as I received it—therefore is the reason why the "green token" was on the bottom. Everything was in *fine* shape. The cake, as usual, is *superb!* It has a distinctive flavor that no other cake can possibly have. A birthday cake to taste right to *me* must be made in Needham, by my mother, packed in a homemade box; and it must be snugged into one part of the box with various articles about it; it must be flavored with a smack of "lady finger" apples and the spicy odor of a few pinks. It must be shipped on a two days' journey to "ripen." Then it is *right*!!

I feel so happy, yes, so *proud* to know that I love, sacredly, these little simple ceremonies. They mean more to me "than the meeting of the Allies in Paris." And I feel so contented to know that this spirit will always live in all of us. I shall do my best to create it in my own children—if it can be created.

This has been a glorious birthday. I live in hope, Mama, that someday your *courage,* displayed 27 years ago today, and your faithfulness will be rewarded—I shall do my best.

300

Chadds Ford, Pennsylvania
October 27, 1909

Dear Mama and Papa,

I seem to be making up for the deficiency left by Papa. Another girl! Think of it!

Well, I'm not disappointed even though my preference said *boy*! As old "Hack" Brittingham downtown said, "It takes a boy to *get* a boy, but it takes a *man* to get a girl."

Carolyn is getting along particularly well; everything perfectly normal, with an exceptionally easy birth. Got nurse and doctor here just in time.

Predictions made three years ago of the disaster that would likely take place at these times always keeps me in terrible suspense until it is over—the relief is almost worthwhile the painful period of worriment.

We have named her (my request) Carolyn. It was the chosen name for the first one, and as long as this opportunity has come along to perpetuate the name, I must take advantage of it.

Now Mama, *you* know *your* program now. The nurse may stay four weeks, according to how Carol feels, however don't wait that long. Carol is continually asking me to tell you to come as soon as you see fit.

The baby was born 4 o'clock afternoon of 26th. October is sure an eventful month for me!

301

Chadds Ford, Pennsylvania
November 3, 1909. Wednesday

Dear Mama,

Carolyn and the baby are doing particularly well! The doctor sees no reason why he should call again until the 10th day— Carolyn's first day to sit up. The baby is decidedly different than Henriette. She's a sleeper, which as you say, is fortunate. In regards to her looks—it's a wonder that I hadn't spoken of that in my last letter. She is a *dead-ringer* for *Nat!* To me the likeness is *laughable,* and I am sure you'll agree. She is just as well formed as Henriette— a shapely round head, a good forehead, a fatter nose and a little larger mouth than No. 1. She is very fat and has good lungs. Her eyes are dark, although they may change, and her hair is black—at present writing.

302

Chadds Ford, Pennsylvania
November 9, 1909. Monday afternoon

Dear Mama,

I laid in one of my best illustrations for *Century* this morning while Henriette busied herself lining out the coal in a double row completely around the studio. I sacrificed a pair of rompers, a clean face and hands for the sake of quietude.—I rather enjoyed it for she was singing about Papa, Mama, baby, "suppy," "dinny," etc., in variegated tunes—it was cheerful!

Fine weather, but everyone is concerned about the winter's water supply. If the hills freeze up as it is now, there will be lots of water *hauled,* I can tell you.

303

Chadds Ford, Pennsylvania
December 13, 1909

Dear Mama,

There's a wild old nor' easter' blowing in tonight—rain is coming down in torrents. In fact it's been storming so all day. Last night brought quite a heavy fall of snow but of course it's all washed away now—every trace of it.

Everything's going along in fine shape! Saturday my glass house was not only completed but the curtains were all up (Aunty Guss and Anna were here all day Thursday and sewed on 30-dozen rings). I can't possibly tell you in words what a wonderful improvement that addition has made. The light effects I can get are remarkable not only in variety but in quality. It is truly an incentive to do better work to have such a superb place to do it in.

Saturday night I built a rattling good model stand $6' \times 6' \times 5'$ and $3'$ high. I put casters on it which makes it very handy to move around.

304

Chadds Ford, Pennsylvania
December 27, 1909

Dear Mama,

I don't know which is the most important item I have to talk about—Nat's marriage, the snowstorm or the nonarrival of the box. The latter I hate to mention; I feel more sorry for you than for us. It has made me think a whole lot. No, we haven't received it—it has been sent on a wrong journey. The poor flowers worry me.

Next—the snowstorm. I have not been ten feet from the door. A seven foot drift right out back of the kitchen door and the bathroom window all but suffocated in one. No trains since Xmas night until tonight and I doubt if this will be so. What a wonderful Xmas!! What appropriate weather.

Was called to N.Y. Friday and met Conan Doyle. Am to paint three pictures to illustrate important writings of his to appear in Aug. *Scribner's*. He suggested that I do them. Also loaded up with lots of other work.

Chapter XII

THE SEASONS

"Now is the season to dream of one's hopes, to build those castles high in the clear brittle air—and then, to jump for them."

Dear Folks:
 ~~Happy~~ *New Year! from*
all !!

Chadds Ford, Pennsylvania
December 30, 1909

Dear folks,

Happy New Year! from all!!

Well this *is* winter, in dead earnest. More snow than Chadds Ford has seen for many a year, and yesterday was recorded as the coldest day for fifteen years—so you see we are *going some*. I also see that we are supposed to have 30″ of snow on the level, which is likewise, *going some*. However, that strikes me as being very conservative. Why, we have to get up on chairs to look out of the window—I've taken photographs.

306

Chadds Ford, Pennsylvania
January 21, 1910. Friday

Dear folks,

Raining like the devil—water running off the hills in torrents.
The "Crik" is *way* up and one can hear continual shooting along its
banks—a slaughter of the poor muskrats that are drowned out of
their homes. (Skins worth $1.10 apiece accounts for it.)

All are perfectly well—babies free from colds, etc. Made my very
best landscape on Wednesday—feel elated. Lots of practical work to
do.

It's five o'clock, Henriette is just emerging from her nap in the
hammock hung beside me. Has slept since 1:30. Must feed her
oatmeal before mailing this note, so good-night.

307

Chadds Ford, Pennsylvania
January 28, 1910. Friday night

Dear Babe,

A hissing storm of wind, rain and sleet is writhing and twisting
itself out in the darkness. The moaning wind and an occasional
seething against the black windowpanes fills me with awe, and a
certain *dread,* this particular evening, due to the final summing up of
a mysterious tragedy that took place in Chadds Ford over two years
ago.

I must tell you about it. The tragedy itself is not out of the
common, compared to the many that take place, but underlying *this*
one, I have felt from the beginning a certain terrible, unrelenting
force—the force of *Nature*. Nature is kind, but she can be unmercifully cruel with an indifference and unconcern that is terrifying!

In the month of February, two years ago last night, one Joe
Lynch, a hard-working farmer, was swept from a small bridge near
Brinton's Mill during a terrific freshet. The drowned horses were
found, tangled in their harnesses, and the light buggy was picked
up some months later about eight miles downstream, with a solitary
leather glove wedged between the racker-plate. Lynch they could
never find.

332

His stricken family struggled on, bearing, besides their grief, various and fearful tales told by undiscriminating people of how his body must be clinging under some nearby bank, clutched by the gnarled roots of a sycamore or linden, floating and swaying, rising and falling in the current. This ghoulish thought pervaded the country around. The Negroes became much affected by these tales and superstitions and ceased to fish along the banks. Even the white farmers talked furtively of the specter which in all probability was near at hand. Old conservative Benjamin Ring was known to prophesy that the body would yet be found under our very nose!

Two summers and a winter have passed. This, the second winter, entered with a vengeance on Xmas day, which, as you know, has continued almost without intermission. In consequence the old Brandywine has been completely demoralized; its banks have been racked and torn; many of its great trees have pitched forward into the torrent and its misshapen course is fringed with heaving barriers of thick, dirty ice. At intervals this ice has clogged the waterway, inundating the surrounding lowlands, submerging roadways and fences, filling barnyards and cellars. The big meadows just below us have been transformed into a vast, desolate jumble of enormous blocks of ice, lying helter-skelter, stacked up against trees or standing on edge in long rows resembling encampments, and here and there great mounds of smaller ice, ground and crushed, blocking the railroad and highways. These ice fields have their attraction, however, in that many fish are imprisoned in isolated pools, and these fall easy victims to any who wish them.

And so, last Sunday, Max Loper, an old bent colored man, worked his way through the icy labyrinth on Pyle's meadow, filling a grain bag with the choicest of fish.

Now it happens that a crude-oil pipeline passes through the lower end of this meadow and when the tremendous force of ice gouged the ground it tore away a full section of pipe, causing a nasty leak; and on this same day, a little knot of men were busily mending the break when they heard a distant, dismal shriek from amongst the ice. They were concerned and started an immediate and systematic search. In half an hour they found, doubled up in a hollow behind an ice block, old Max Loper, his bag of half-live fish flopping around him, and Max staring with wild fascinated eyes at something, something concealed in a small ice cave. The old colored fellow appeared

333

stunned—he sat huddled like a wax figure. The men followed his gaze and were startled to behold a headless skeleton with felt boots still clinging and a skeleton arm with a leather glove on the hand.

For days this awful thing was laid out in the "Quoit Club Room" where any and everybody inspected it at will. The talk of the village was Joe Lynch, the felt boots, the glove—the perfect feet within the boots, the fleshy hand within the glove and the seal ring imbedded in a swollen finger. The village became polluted, a morbid atmosphere pervaded the very hills.

"The talk of the village was Joe Lynch . . . ."

Today was the funeral—a *public* funeral! Carriages filed past the house in steady numbers and tonight they filed back.

Nature did her work oh! *so* slowly, so deliberately; and now she will complete it with the sanction of her children.

As I sit here near the window, listening to the mournful storm as it sweeps over the hills, I can't help but feel it a fitting epilogue to

334

this tragedy. The moaning and whining of the wind, the angry spasmodic rattling of the windows bespeak still other sinister contemplations of Nature.

308

Chadds Ford, Pennsylvania
February 25, 1910

Dear Mama,

This has been a fine clear and cold day—not sympathetic to me, however. I dote on gray, misty, days and *revel* in what other people call *nasty* days. I love rain.

Tomorrow they drop a fox at the Headquarters—supposed to have been dropped Washington's birthday but postponed on account of the weather. Expect a big crowd, I guess. I want to make a couple of photos if I feel like attending.

Aunt Anna has her teeth! She's Aunt Anna no more—she's an ad for a dentist. Had long letter written to Stimson on certain thoughts that came to me on Cleveland's Hill at sunset but did not send it. Am tired of hearing myself *talk*. *Do* is the thing, *not* talk.

309

Wyeth was preparing to illustrate "Through the Mists" by Arthur Conan Doyle. The story with illustrations appeared in the November and December 1910 issues of Scribner's *magazine.*

Chadds Ford, Pennsylvania
March 4, 1910

Dear Mama,

Today follows two days spent in the cities. On Wednesday to Philadelphia and yesterday to Wilmington. To the former to purchase a summer dress for Carol, the first in two years, and to the smaller city to continue my research for material to be used in the Conan Doyle pictures. Therefore, today, following the seven hours spent with the Saxons, Britons, Huns, Romans; shields, sea axes, spears, cudgels; helmets, plumes, fibulae; galleys, keels and lateen sails, my mind sees little more than a kaleidoscopic pageantry of the above—all confusion! However, I am beginning to feel on speaking terms with those hairy Saxons, and when I walk up stairs my legs bend stiff with bronze kneecaps and shin guards, and I duck my head in the doorways lest I knock my shining helmet to the floor.

And out of doors it is so beautiful! It's a pity to pry into ancient graves and let their sinister secrets blind one to the pure, wholesome beauty that lies about us. And still, if these pictures I am to paint were to be done as they *should* be, that very spirit which lies about us in such profusion should be their main interest and soul—they should not be *historical, damn* the word, but should symbolize humanity and the world, allowing the details to sift in as only ordinary and commonplace garb, to designate the *season* of man's development even as the changes in the trees denote the development of Nature's seasons.

My solitary interest (I mean soul interest) is in trying to do just this. If I fail in this particular—I fail altogether. If I succeed I will feel a better illustrator for it. I dare not conjecture the result.

As I am sitting here, the light new-fallen snow is visibly disappearing. The air is apparently balmy and soft, yet the glass still registers below freezing. The blackbirds are hopping amid the leaves, throwing them this way and that, intermittently bristling their feathers in effort to make that rusty squeak. Is not their song an appropriate one for the earliest bird? It is so much as though the winter had rusted their lungs and "vocal cords" and they were the first to limber up for the summer. It is an interesting fact, too, that as the spring progresses their song becomes softer and sweeter. It reminds me of a joke I saw recently, accompanied by a picture of a man bundled in blankets, soaking his feet in hot water and mustard, barricaded on his left with cough-cure, salve and other medicines, and on the other with a great pile of handkerchiefs. His nose was very red and dripping, and so were his eyes. He was crooning this beautiful line to himself: "Cub gedtle sprig, ethereal bild'ess, cub!"

Perhaps that's what our blackbirds are saying.

Last week I heard the frogs (no, only *one*) peeping, down near our spring house, and night before last too; and then it snowed yesterday.

That's the way it goes—the road to higher work looks clear and pleasant, the skies appear warm and alluring, the grass even starts green under your feet and then, of a sudden—it snows! However, if you listen carefully some spring harbinger can always be heard. That's it—*if you listen!*

It's nearly mailtime. In brief I'll say that the rompers you sent couldn't have fit better—they were taken off this noon for the wash so you see they have done service right from the beginning. They are fine and make her look exasperatingly cute. The appealing advantage is the right of way one has to her business section which avoids disastrous delays.

310

Chadds Ford, Pennsylvania
March 18, 1910

Dear Papa,

Here's a little farm—a gem!

The snug little stone-and-plaster house is beautifully located on the road from Wilmington as it makes its final turn into Chadds Ford. A sloping pasture runs from the back of the house up to a clump of great oaks from the roots of which oozes a delightful spring never known to have gone dry. To one side of the house, some seventy yards, is a frame barn, on Grandpapa's order, fitted for the housing of three cows and as many horses, also shed room on either side. The place comprises some 20 acres of fairly good land,

337

excellent for chickens. A beautiful brook purls by the house and through an orchard of twenty or more trees.

As a paying farm I guess it is not much, but as a home it is everything a man could wish for. The rent is but $12 a month, so its price must be moderate.

I don't know just why I should talk thus of this place—but yesterday I spent most of the afternoon within its confines and was much impressed with its possibilities—I thought of many things, I can tell you.

The owner of the "little farm," John McVey.

338

The Seasons

Chadds Ford, Pennsylvania
March 25, 1910

Dear folks,

The glass registers 80—there is a stiff breeze but, oh, so soft and warm. Henriette's out in the garden playing in the newly turned loam, and Carol is reading *Old Curiosity Shop* on the front porch. The baby is asleep (part of the time). I have just returned from an utterly unsuccessful afternoon spent on a landscape. It seems at such times that my craft had forsaken me entirely.

As I mentioned, I believe, in my last letter, I went to N.Y. My sketches were received at *Scribner's* rather half-heartedly. I feel soused in cold water at present. Unfortunately, this scheme is a pet idea of the literary editor, Mr. Burlingame. The result is he is attending to the art end, too, which makes it disagreeable for me. He insists upon *literary* pictures—that's my weakest point (thank heavens), therefore when I show him sketches embodying big abstract but *moving* emotion, he balks and demands the story-telling, descriptive picture.

I shall say no more about it; such details must bore you all.

How wonderfully and powerfully the call of *home* with the little family and Chadds Ford appealed to me. The trains couldn't go fast enough. As we finally coasted down into the valley, then only did that tightening iron band around my head relax.

At present I am reading my seventh volume of Thoreau. The very richest of his thoughts I have struck yet. *Familiar Letters*, edited by Frank Sanborn. Wonderfully appealing, and brings one in closest touch with Thoreau as a fellow man. The book interprets a side of the philosopher which most biographers have purposely avoided, apparently to intensify their conception of the man as stoic.

Familiar Letters tells you how interested he was in the house cat, and what tenderness he showed for his home people and his few friends. The letters are full of genuine pathos, not because they are pathetic, but because they are so tender, and so sincere.

Even in moments of intense grief, when he lost his favorite brother, "John," his child friend, "Waldo" (Emerson's oldest boy), and his own father, his letters are so wholesome, so hopeful and uplifting, that one feels the more, perhaps, his profoundly deep grief.

"The little family."

Sometimes I believe I do not fit this life, this busy, bustling life. It does not allow me time to think, to expand, to grow naturally, slowly, healthfully. At times I feel as though I would walk over one of these hills into a secluded valley and lie down, and there remain to grow slowly, oh, so slowly!

To come in contact with men who talk money, who want to buy me by piecemeal, and in searching for the best they get the worst, because they push and prod, they are disrespectful. They consider you a cog in their clattering machinery, and they drop a dirty check into your bearings that you will run the faster.

340

312

Chadds Ford, Pennsylvania
March 27, 1910. Sunday P.M.

Dear Mama,

Today—Easter, we celebrated for Henriette with a present of two live rabbits. Yesterday afternoon I built a really good and strong box and pen.

Just now H—— is asleep. She is quite attracted to the habit of taking a book to look at before she drops off to sleep. Today she took a catalogue of "art prints" including "old masters," etc. I sneaked 'round to the desk window from where I could get a good view to watch and listen to her solitary conversation. She is getting so now that she involves the people in the pictures in a sort of story; very simple, it is true, but nevertheless the principle is there. Suddenly she came upon a portrait by Velasquez of some knight—she said "My, *my,* my! Aunt Mama!!" And it does look like you too, a very great deal.

Henriette is here now, in my lap, and says, "Make a rabbit." She wants "Aunty Luke's" house too! and a "*chookie!*"

I didn't tell you that we have another (collie) puppy. A corker!

313

Chadds Ford, Pennsylvania
June 13, 1910. Monday morning, 6:30

Dear Babe,

Yesterday I took a memorable walk and I must record it. I saw many *new* things, received so many new impressions; yet it was the same old walk—a path I have almost *worn* to "Sugar Loaf," and the more I follow it the more I am inclined to do so.

The day was very solemn; a heavy misty atmosphere smothered the earth. It had the effect of magnifying objects. A tree in the middle distance looked vague and huge; the ones in the foreground fairly towered and made me feel for the instant, awestruck.

The aspect of nature everywhere struck me as being very unusual. Even as the house lost itself in the heavy atmosphere behind me, I felt suddenly *alone*, absolutely alone in the world. I tried to sense that New York, Boston, Needham lay before me somewhere in

"The Ford"
Monday morning

the interminable distance. I could not do so. The idea of sound
penetrating that dank leaden air seemed almost an impossibility.
The rustle and swish of the wet grass against my boots seethed
unusually loud, the noise being so confined. A bell might have
sounded like the click of two stones underwater.

As I approached the ravine, that memorable valley where you
lingered over the dying embers one summer's night, those gaunt
ragged trees smouldered through the haze like great gibbets, their
grotesque arms flung out on either side. From the top of one of
these flew a number of large birds. They were swallowed in the
black air and I was left to guess what species they were. They
circled back to my right; I could barely discern blurred spots moving
swiftly, and could hear a faint whir of wings, but that was all.

I seated myself in one of the two big oak logs, which you may
possibly recollect, near the red corn-barn. Everything dripped with
the congealing mists. To my right, hidden in the deep grass
spotted gray-yellow with fading mustard flowers, I could faintly

hear the gurgle and silvery tinkle of a brook. It sounded muffled, like the frozen brooks when you hear the water racing under the ice.

The wind was east, yet I could feel a soft damp draft coming up the valley from the south. I sat attentively for some time in that muffled silence. Now and then the landscape would grow perceptibly lighter, then darken again, and I knew that behind the mantle of fog great wet clouds must be moving. Gradually the lighter periods became of larger duration. Suddenly I was startled to actually see the gray vapor move in a body toward the north. In five minutes old "Sugar Loaf" loomed grand and majestic. There was still a haze, but the group of trees at its summit could easily be counted—and then, as though in boisterous indignation, a flock of crows on the peak of "Sugar Loaf" started a tremendous calling and crying. They were robbed of their seclusion by the lifting fog.

Column after column of gray cumulus clouds sailed majestically toward the north. The legions of clouds continued their silent flight; sometimes it would darken, accompanied with a sharp silvery shower; then the sun would burn a new brilliant shaft of blinding light through the wet.

314

The murals that Howard Pyle completed so quickly were for the Hudson County Courthouse, Jersey City, New Jersey.

Chadds Ford, Pennsylvania
July 4, 1910

[To his parents]

I seem to accomplish so little in spite of my desires. I am under a continual upheaval and incessant movement of thought. In short, my desires seem to be racing out of all proportion to actual results. To still more intensify my thoughts and dreams the trip to Mr. Pyle's studio added abundance. I have been continually mauling the event over and over in my mind, coming always to a desparate conclusion. "If I could only do what I can *feel!*" This thought is one reactionary perhaps from, "What a pity to throw away such an opportunity." This latter in regards to Mr. Pyle's 70-ft. decoration which was *completed,* completed, I say, in *one month* and a *day*

—and he brags about it! I can only write in brief that the picture is no decoration—not even a good illustration, that it is terribly unfinished and ill-considered from an artistic standpoint. No thought, of the higher quality, was attempted on the canvas. A shell of *delineation*, absolutely nothing else. Not even good drawing! I must stop. No! I am not overcritical, nor am I criticizing from an assumed standpoint. I know what I say is true; I have pride and belief enough in my own interpretations and discriminations to feel certain that I am right in denouncing the work. Denouncing is a hard word. If Pyle had done his best (which would mean at least something as good as his past achievements) then I would use a less harsh word. To begin with, Schoonover and Arthurs are painting the decoration *for* him to considerable extent. Now this is permissible providing they carry the work only through the preliminary stages, and then the master, in seclusion with his *whole soul*, waves his magic wand and lifts the mass of rudimentary paint and masses into *living, virile* or personal expressions. Yes, it hurts me, if painful thoughts hurt at all. My heavens!!

315

Chadds Ford, Pennsylvania
July 8, 1910. Monday

Dear Mama,

Friday I finished my Conan Doyle pictures.

I'm ready for a run into Virginia to consult Miss [Mary E.] Johnston of *To Have and To Hold* fame. Tomorrow I leave for two days in N.Y. with various errands of business nature which will occupy every minute. I shipped the C.D. illustrations on the first train this morning to an Artists Packing and Shipping Co. to unpack and take to *Scribner's* on Wednesday at ten o'clock, when I will be there. The pictures were too bulky to send to the *Scribner's* office in a packing case. I hope they will be received as my best work.

I've got a beautiful scheme, I believe, which I shall offer to them (*Scribner's*). A series of decorations of pastoral material symbolizing: "The Wind," "The Rain," and "The Sun," and "The Moon."

[Letter continued]

July 11, 1910. Thursday

I returned from N.Y. last night after two days filled with a

344

remarkable variety of impressions and one or two unusual experiences. My pictures were received at *Scribner's* with great enthusiasm, particularly the last one, "Invasion of the Huns."

Scribner's gave me another ms.—a story by a Miss [Dorothy] Canfield—and have asked me to go ahead with my new scheme, which, however, will not be used until a year *Xmas*. With my four Civil War pictures and two covers for *Popular* I am quite satisfied to receive no more orders.

The unusual experience, made more so by a marked coincidence, I shall only tell in brief; it is too disagreeable even to mention.

Our train ran down and killed two men, just the other side of Trenton. I sat in the smoker, the first car, and when the cowcatcher struck the poor fellows it threw them high and to one side. The result was one of them went by my open window; it seemed not three feet away. This impression was sickening, but what made it worse was the fact that our train was backed amidst the frightful remains of these men, and we, in the first car, were called as witnesses to certain facts, therefore having to wallow 'round in this frightful tragedy.

This was not all. Coming home yesterday, darned if we didn't strike *another* man within three miles of the same spot, cutting off a leg and injuring otherwise. This time I was not called upon, but the shock was even worse than the day before, owing to my already sensitive condition. The quick, sharp blows of the engine whistle and the air brake send the shudders through me. This first occurrence upset me for the day, and I did my errands in N.Y. in a kind of a haze.

I found the babies in good shape when I returned, and Carol too.

316

Chadds Ford, Pennsylvania
July 11, 1910

Miss Mary E. Johnston
Warm Springs, Virginia

My dear Miss Johnston,

Your suggestion to pay you a visit to talk over the illustration of "The Long Roll" is most agreeable and I write to arrange a date convenient to you.

345

I heartily anticipate the work before me and consider it a distinct advantage to consult the author before undertaking the illustration— a privilege never before experienced by me.

317

Chadds Ford, Pennsylvania
July 21, 1910. Thursday

Dear Babe,

I leave for Virginia today.

I hope the usual weekend letter will come in to Carol. It's funny that a little trip like this should concern us so, but I'll tell you, *one* night away from these babies is enough, but *five*, think of it! I hope the distraction will be great.

318

Warm Springs, Virginia
July 24, 1910

Dear Mama,

I promised myself that I would write to you from this marvelous little Virginia mountain town, but find that it takes considerable more than mere mental "promise" to fulfill my vow. My time has been filled to overflowing with variety. (I find more and more that *impressions* constitute the value and pleasures of any trip—*sight-seeing*, I hate the word! it means nothing in reality; it should be named sight*feeling*.)

Until I left "Virginia Hot Spring"—a resort, I was depressingly disappointed in almost everything I saw, except the novel bits of picturesque scenery—cabins, etc. The moment I got into the stage to this place I regarded the subtle change. I emerged from the commonplace atmosphere of a modern resort into a truly remarkable one of the *old* South. To suddenly drop into a community of the old South's best families, to hear still the conversations and discussions relative to the War, to walk and talk with a dozen veteran captains and colonels of the Confederacy, to see their families, children and grandchildren about them—*all* with that romantic picturesqueness of character so strangely southern—and to watch the fervent and tense interest which the sons and daughters, the grandsons and granddaughters showed in every word uttered by the venerable soldiers has been my remarkable experience. I am truly living in the past! The great sombre Alleghenies loom above us and symbolize mute testimony of the struggle. To me they seem a most fitting monument to the past history of this tragic state—Virginia.

As I sit now in my little quaint room, I can feel the spirit of Jefferson and Lee, who both slept in the very bed I used last night and who have no doubt written on the same table, as *nothing* has been changed. Both their names appear on a registry in this room— and lo! mine is added. (Methinks both will turn in their graves.)

To have the old servants, some who were here during and before the War at your service, to have them brush your clothes as you put them on in the morning, to remain at your beck and call always, to talk pleasantly and intelligently of the "Homestead," as they call this place, and all its history—always courteous, never leaving you without a low sweeping bow, has completed the illusion.—I am in the South, and the threats of War are brewing over the mountains.

The "Homestead," called on the map "Warm Springs," is an old, old aristocratic resort of the Virginians mainly, although Georgia, the Carolinas, Louisiana and Tennessee have sent their quota of high-bred countrymen for years. Before the advent of the railroad the stage route was its only means of connection with the larger cities— Staunton the nearest, some sixty miles away, over terrific mountain roads and passes. So you see, the aristocracy were intent upon isolation. Of course the springs which have miraculously cured thousands of cases of rheumatism, gout, etc., were a strong attraction and still are.

It is a little settlement comprising a hotel and some two dozen colonial cottages of various kinds—that is, some are mere rows of sleeping rooms, others are more of the grandiose with huge porticoed fronts and enormous double porches. The hotel itself is built in this plan and is a truly impressive building. Surrounding this entire group, interspersed with magnificent linden, maple and locust trees, is a high white fence with a great gate at the entrance alongside of which is a tiny cabin in which sits the gate keeper—a little black porter named "Queen Ester." Pennies are tossed to him by all who enter or leave. As you approach in the coach the great gates are swung back and you are ushered in with a magnificent sweeping bow from "Queen Ester." The stables are handsome with some forty saddle horses and coach horses. A mountain brook, cold as ice and flashing across a white, stony bottom, races by the entrance—it comes directly from the great mountain that rises almost straight up for 1000 feet.

Miss Johnston, approaching middle age, of an intense nature and one of those true heroines of the old South, has impressed me exceedingly. My visit with her has been decidedly helpful and as she is heartily in sympathy with the *way* I *want* to illustrate her book, she intends to use pressure to induce the publishers to let me have my way. This is worth much to me. Her ideals are *very* high, which has kept me well up—however, in some instances I have aided her, I believe in seeing the true light. This reciprocation in itself has made the trip well worthwhile.

We have taken two long drives: one to the summit of Warm Springs Mountain, before mentioned, and one to an enchanting mountain torrent ten miles away. In the windings over the mountains I have seen considerable of the country. The view from "Flag-Rock" (a Civil War signal point) was simply overpowering! I cannot recall that I have ever been so profoundly impressed. The great sadness of the scene will always stay by me. These mountains are *tragic! Never* in the Rockies was I ever moved so strongly.

Well, with all this which I have so briefly suggested and my thoughts of the little family so far away, you can partly appreciate the state of my mind. As I looked northeast over those never-ending ridges and for the moment realized that *somewhere* there rested the little home in Chadds Ford, and farther on—just a little farther, I could imagine the tips of the big spruce trees that Grandpapa planted; it near made me break down. I never have been so moved by my surroundings.

I found it an ordeal to leave home for the trip. Only a suggestion would have turned me back. I left from Philadelphia through Wilmington, and as we sped past the single pair of shining rails that curved away to Chadds Ford, it made me *sick*.

I don't know whether I'm a weakling and have no force, or whether the development is in the true direction. I believe the latter is the case. Pray let me think so anyway.

One gets a fresh view of himself in strange surroundings, and therein I am profiting. My confidence in my chosen direction of activity is enhanced. I feel surer than ever. The big suggestion, however, is *work* and *work harder*—time is short.

At present a thunder storm is rolling down from the mountains north of us. The clouds suggest a deluge. Had I extra clothes with me I would hie myself to a neighboring hill to watch it. Wouldn't Babe go wild over this! The sheep and cow bells are ringing constantly in the distance and from far comes the occasional blow of the supper or dinner horn—some mountain dweller calling her own.

319

Chadds Ford, Pennsylvania
July 26, 1910

My dear Miss Johnston,

One of the most enjoyable and truly impressive trips I have ever experienced has ended! Although the period was brief, impressions so crowded into my mind that it is difficult now not to think of the three days in Warm Springs as a very substantial period spent in Virginia.

We descended into Hell, 103 degrees, on Monday morning, only an hour late. Here I remained over three hours to visit the Corcoran Gallery, where it occurred to me I had seen a Jackson portrait. A glaring sign stuck in the lawn read "gallery closed," which nigh turned me into a fit. However, I appealed to the janitor, and through the kind persuasion of a "special permission" copyist, I was allowed the run of the building.

I found the portrait, which I would judge was a very truthful representation. Its conformity with the photographs I have seen seemed exact, and as it was a three-quarter length, the gauntlet and saber were in evidence. His hair agreed with your conclusion, brown inclined to auburn, with a tendency to fluffiness. His hands, however, were probably idealized.

In due course a "Rodin" book should reach your sister, Elizabeth, by express, which I hope she may further enjoy. His remarks on the "antique" I believe are valuable to us all.

320

Elizabeth Shippin Green was a student of Howard Pyle. N. C. Wyeth, although he uses her name below in a somewhat irreverent manner, admired her gifts as an illustrator.

Chadds Ford, Pennsylvania
August 10, 1910

Dear folks,

There is not much to tell.—The babies are all well. Little Carolyn seems disposed to "Elizabeth Shippin *Green*" but we are not going to dose her for it. Carolyn is pretty well, but feels the hot weather dragging on her a little I imagine.

321

Nathaniel Wyeth, "Nat," had married Gladys Pond of Needham, Massachusetts.

The map accompanying this letter is interesting as it clearly traces N. C. Wyeth's walk with his brother and also includes the same intimate area that years later N. C. Wyeth's son, Andrew, would use in painting after painting. Red Barn became the Karl Kuerner farm. Little Africa became "Mother Archie's Church," and J. Hamer's small farm eventually passed to Adam Johnson's ownership.

Chadds Ford, Pennsylvania
September 6, 1910

Dear old Babe,

We are alone—and I'll tell you, it's darned lonesome! Nat and Gladys left us, as planned, last evening on the seven o'clock. They reach Dayton, if all goes right, about noon today.

The reaction is starting—I can feel it. I shall in all probabilities wander about the place without much direction of travel or thought for a couple of days, perhaps less. The past six weeks has placed another notch on my gun.—I always have and always will consider those periods when we can get together as being important, mutually so, I hope. They are distinctly different in every way from any other happening during the year. The combination of brotherly affection and earnest endeavor is something that cannot be matched and my only hope is that these occasions will be repeated at least yearly as long as we live.

The three remaining days grew in their importance regarding Nat. Owing I believe to his physical improvement and becoming *acclimated*, as it were. I'll tell you when a fellow has been doubled over a drafting table for a year with that incessant procession of gears, transmissions, bearings, etc., passing through his mind, and besides such a location as Dayton, [Ohio], (geographically and spiritually), it is no easy thing to suddenly adapt oneself to entirely different surroundings (geographically and spiritually).

I believe if Nat were located here, say for a month, his true identity would return. The novelty, if one can call it so, of visiting a brother for the first time with a young wife is likely in itself to upset a sensitive nature, such as Nat's is.

At any rate, the last two days, Saturday and Sunday, showed a big change from the pleasure standpoint.

Saturday it rained hard! (something unusual). In spite of which Nat and I took a long walk, starting directly after lunch and returning about 5:15. Our course led us over spots familiar to you, with many stops and tarries to inspect this and that. A half-hour visit with Pearson Barnes was very edifying (he was in charge of "Little Africa" for the day) and then a half-hour with Jake Hamer, the old colored fellow on the hill, proved interesting.

The letters placed on various spots I shall explain:

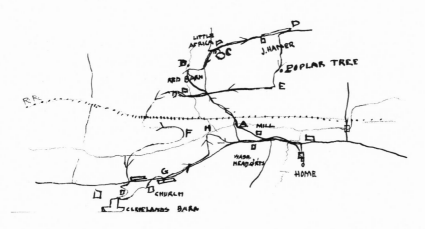

A. We cut across the mill pasture.
B. We slipped into the woods near the "red barns" that I could dispose of a burden.

C. Is where we held our brilliant consultation with Pearson.

D. Just above J. Hamer's where we looked at the view up the valley.

E. Another view from heighth near poplar tree.

F. A circle around in pasture where we hoped to kick out a rabbit or two—no luck.

G. Repaired to church shed to avoid extra heavy downpour. (Dotty chicken not there.)

H. Nat inspects old dam breast in Turner's meadow and enjoys a dump.

We returned with our pockets full of plums, Seckel pears, and apples and found Carol sewing and Gladys lying down asleep.

Yesterday we decided (about an hour before we started) to take the nine o'clock train to Kennett Square, thence by electric through Lenape to West Chester where we would take dinner at the old "Green Tree Inn." We did this, much to our delight. Carol, Gladys, Nat, babies and all. A chicken dinner and a "siesta" on a broad second-story porch in old-fashioned hickory rockers—and then Nat and I walked around the town, much to his pleasure, as he thought it the nicest little town he ever saw. We visited two garages, inspecting Maxwells, Chalmers—Detroits and Studebakers, and ended up in hiring a chauffer to drive us home to Chadds Ford, which was accomplished in twenty minutes. We arrived home about 3:30, prepared a supper of bread and milk, apple pie and boiled corn (very tender), and the time had arrived that they should pack. Nat felt pretty bad that he should have to return to Dayton—a place that I find he literally hates. He anticipates an opportunity to come east during the coming year—I hope he gets it.

322

The Shaw Memorial is a bronze bas-relief, by Augustus Saint-Gaudens, that stands in the Commons, Boston, Massachusetts.

Chadds Ford, Pennsylvania
September 17, 1910

Dear Mama,

It's just seven o'clock. We had an early supper of green corn—fritters, and tea; spent the hour of sundown and afterglow out of doors, and at dark, watered the flowers and ferns. The "things" are in off the porch and Carol is now upstairs with the children putting them to bed (no nap for Henriette today, and the baby seems ripe for sleep). So I anticipate a quiet evening with Carol before the open fire, which I can hear crackling from way in here at my desk. I am immersed in Lewes' biography of Goethe, and Carol is in the midst of *Oliver Twist* and his troubles.

The *boom* of yesterday's sunrise brought the autumn! So it seemed. Never have I witnessed such a sudden change, not only of air but in the outward aspect of nature!

A sort of withering, chilly wind swept over us from early morning till late last night. The trees have shrunken most perceptibly, and their foliage has *condensed*, as it were, into tufts of leaves. Our maples were full and *bosky*, like huge compact bouquets—today they are broken and ragged, with punctures of light showing through them. This evening in the light cool breeze, their leaves rustled dry and papery. The fall is here! I have detected its stealthy approach on certain days since late July, but it bounded in and landed square on two feet while I was sleeping.

Simultaneously, that yearning to ramble through the woods and fields is felt. *Now* is the glorious season, wherein one enjoys to the utmost the walk into the garden to gather the last of the corn, to pick the *final* and most delicious morsels in the way of beans, tomatoes, lettuce, radishes, beets and a few apples.

It is a remarkably subtle thing, this exquisite pleasure. One must be *unconscious, humble;* one cannot or *must* not anticipate—simply sling a basket on your arm and walk forth, aimlessly, into that treasure patch, into the orchard, across the lawn—*anywhere*. There is a multitude of things to discover—even a particularly young ear of corn with its silk still pale thrills one with a certain yearning and praise for the memories of summer, together with the more strident forebodings of blowing snow and shrieking winds.

Now is the season to dream of one's hopes, to build those castles high in the clear brittle air—and then, to *jump* for them. Still, I believe one feels, as a reaction perhaps, his inabilities and weaknesses more strongly than ever.

Practically speaking, I am preparing myself for the Civil War Series, which interest me greatly. Today I made a careful copy from a photograph of "Stonewall" Jackson and followed it with a number of other imaginative sketches of his head in various positions. The idea is I wish to familiarize myself with his features so that when I start on the final painting of "The General" I can idealize him and yet retain an unmistakable likeness.

The opportunities in this subject are great—but we will see what we can do. The next, "The Battle," will also call for much meditative study.

I am so anxious to lift these pictures out of the glutted market of the *usual,* the *standard-war-picture* type. I want that they will appeal to the *emotional* senses, rather than the "play-acting" mind. The interest in them should *first* be the *tragedy* of *war,* then the pictorial element.

The wonderful *Shaw Memorial* is so perfect in this respect, in spite of the very distracting detail of a white leader and colored troops. One gazes on that relief from first to last with a full emotional appreciation of *War.* Only for fleeting seconds can one observe the incidental details, as interesting as they are. Providing, of course, that one looks upon this production with a sympathetic and receptive eye and mind.

One cannot separate from the whole any *one* detail in this sculpture and call it beautiful—it is only beautiful in its relation to the unit, the complete expression.

It would be just as foolish to pick out a certain movement in music of Beethoven, Tschaikovsky, Grieg, and play it over, and call it beautiful. It can be *interesting*, ever growing less and less impressive until it becomes *tiresome*. Robbing it from the "ensemble" has depleted its meaning entirely. Its relation to the *whole* gives it its *beauty.*

So with writing, let the flow of expression always tingle of the one big thought that inspired the writing. Keep your details true but *subordinate.*

323

James Jenkins worked as a handyman for the Wyeths.

Chadds Ford, Pennsylvania
September 19, 1910. Sunday night

Dear old Babe,

After ten days of pondering, scheming, and experimenting, only an hour ago I placed "Stonewall" Jackson in a glory of shot and shell—in pencil. *But I have it!* even though rough and obscure in bewildering criss-cross lines and smudges.

The past hour, as a fitting aftermath, I have listened to Elman, Caruso and Kreisler (an even more remarkable soloist than Elman). The hopes, glories and anticipations that crowded through my mind, not only relating to myself, but to *you*, almost drove me to tears for relief. I have turned to the pen instead. Mayhap this medium will transform my painfully aspiring attitude to one of disgust—it often does. I feel my shortcomings more keenly when I write than at any other time. I believe that is why I resort to writing so much. I come face to face with myself, as it were. To set down a belief, which, like a resolution, never fails to intensify, to bring into greater relief, one's failure to live it.

I often look with considerable envy upon such men as old "Jenkins" here. A man of no intellect, patient, and in most ways happy. His lack of understanding makes whatever his troubles may be *less* painful. He trudges here in the morning, crossing the pasture with his pipe alight, the low sun and long shadows transforming the cool, wet field into a paradise. He knows not this to be sure, yet there is an unconscious contentment shining in his face that tells the tale. His light meandering duties carry him over every part of this grand old hill during the day; his old horse as friend and assistant gives him keen pleasure, and at night, with a last look at the well bedded and fed, old "Chance," he trudges home—pipe alight, the low sun and long shadows again working magic. His little house over the hill, snug and homelike with one window peeping over the slope, and a faint blue skein of smoke rising from the chimney.

I have all this and *more*, yet, how I would like to *relax;* be content with a wheelbarrow, a rake, an apple basket, a pipe.

No! we can't do it, and yet, *this* is exactly what we are eager to interpret. Constable, the English landscape master, well said, "Oh! had I but the mind of a child and the abilities of a man!"

As I expected, the letter is coming to nothing; just a fragmentary expression of *yearning*. My letters often remind me of the effect one gets when listening to a phonograph. One suddenly lifts the needle and then says, "Well, the rest isn't very good, that's why I stopped it."

324

Chadds Ford, Pennsylvania
September 24, 1910. Friday

Dear Mama,

This room (where my desk is) has been transformed into the coziest room imaginable. My saddles and paraphernalia I have oiled and cleaned and hung in the attic. The clothes, costumes, etc., are packed in mothballs in trunks, easy to get at; they are far better off in that spacious attic. The room is now our sitting room, with big clock, table and lounge moved into it. We will now enjoy this big stove this coming winter. The other room is fitted out with a large "cage," that is, a stand like my "model stand," only better made, with a high fence of close mesh wire around it, and carpeted with tightly stretched "denim." Thus we will keep the baby out of drafts and various articles of hardware out of its stomach. I made the "cage" as we call it, and am proud of the job; it is on ballbearing casters and is easily moved. *"Plated"* with green "denim" around the bottom. Carol has experienced her first sense of relief in months.

325

This letter reports the first symptoms of the disease—poliomyelitis— that was to leave Henriette's right hand permanently damaged.

Chadds Ford, Pennsylvania
October 3, 1910. Friday

Dear Mama!

Time is a thousand times too short, and paper thousand sheets too few to tell you how I am feeling at the present moment.

With this is mingled my concern and care of Henriette who has been sick for three days. Temperature, and stomach upset—nothing bad as yet, except that she has not put a thing into her little stomach for two days. She acts bewildered and needs constant attention. I will be happy when she is all right again. I hate beyond words to see a child ailing—it is pathetic.

326

Dear Papa,

It was mighty good of you to let Mama come down and we appreciate it. I'll tell you it meant a whole lot to me to have her here—it seemed to balance everything.

Henriette is in fine shape constitutionally, big appetite, fine color etc. Her right arm is still limp however. Of course she can move it and hold light articles, such as paper, pencil or even a spoon, but cannot manage it well enough to use. She sleeps well.

If I were the "batty" kind I'd go on a bat, out of pure pleasure over her recovery.

327

Dear Mama,

First, I hope your trip home was pleasant and undelayed. Second, Henriette is showing further signs of rapid improvement—her thumb actually in use, handling her scissors with apparent ease. Her appetite is just as ravenous and her patience just as remarkable.

The doctor called this morning and marveled still more at her speedy recovery but still insists on her confinement, less the turpentine cloths, which is agreeable to us all. He gives her two weeks more in her room and then claims all danger of contagion past. Last night she slept better than any night yet. "Backit" [biscuit] is still all the rage. Two for this morning's breakfast, one after a good dinner this noon, and two this evening with a call for more; but when I went up with the "second order" she was fast asleep.

Tonight's mail brought news that makes me feel particularly pleased. From Houghton Mifflin (Mr. Scudder). The letter tells the tale:

Dear Mr. Wyeth,

It is a wonderful piece of work and will create a sensation wherever it is shown.

It was a great opportunity and you have risen to the occasion. You may have done better work but I have not seen it.

When I came back from lunch this afternoon I found the box waiting to be opened. The picture has held me by its powerful presentation of a great man and the longer I look at it the more I see to admire.

The atmosphere has the same quality as your "Hiawatha's Fishing."

The luminous quality is remarkable. The effect of the halo about his head will suggest *St.* Stonewall to his admiring Southern friends—

I hope you will hold it at a good round price and not sell it to the first bidder.

We shall make a poster of it and send it broad cast.

Sincerely yours.

W. S. Scudder.

It has made me feel mighty pleased, I can tell you. I felt that the picture had dramatic strength, and I am glad my surmise is verified.

Received a note from Miss Johnston enclosing six or eight snapshots of Warm Springs. If my longing for that place continues, I shall make an effort one of these days to spend a little while there with the whole family. It would be a wonderful place to paint.

Well, I hope letters as cheerful as this one will leave Chadds Ford often. Little Carolyn is in great shape.

328

Chadds Ford, Pennsylvania
October 26, 1910. Thursday

Dear folks,

Although it's 11:30—half-hour before dinner, I have at my elbow a goodly hunk of Mama's cake!

I am just in from the studio where I have left a complete "lay-in" for my battle picture. I succeeded in getting good strong movement and if I can keep it, the picture will attract. With the least cause I could report very enthusiastically about the start I have made, but the week's fight with my work kind of knocks the spirit out of me. This is the sole reason why I have not written—no spirit. Without this I am *nil!*

However, even this should not excuse me from an answer to your kind letters and full box! I enjoyed them all as I always do—with very deep pleasure. It made me feel all over again those dearest of possessions—our childhood. I think the apples did it as much as anything else; then the cake brought up more recent visions, covering the period while I have been away from home.

(I can hear Henriette taking her third day's exercise—walking.) It's like starting all over again. It is really pathetic to see her own ability to walk improving, as she is quite rapidly, when one remembers how particularly sure she always was on her feet six weeks ago.

Henriette got over *40* postcards. Aunt Hat sent her a cute little doll, and Hilda sent her a book. I got her a dollhouse, one with a cardboard front, with porch, etc., real windows, and a chimney on top. I placed it on the sewing table the night before, after she had gone asleep. About 6:15 just as the dawn was brightening she woke me with a rather startled, "Wha's dot?"—pause—"Wha's *dot*, pa-a-aper?" She saw the silhouette of the roof against the window. I said, "I don't know, what *is* it?" Quick as a flash she replied, "I guess dat's Aunty Guss house, wif a *post* on't." (The house has a chimney on it.)

Little Carolyn's birthday today. She is thriving wonderfully and is getting to be a regular milk fiend.

329

Chadds Ford, Pennsylvania
October 29, 1910. Friday evening

Dear folks,

I say evening—it's only four, but the skies are so murky that I am using a lamp. Cold icy rains and some snow have been cutting us to pieces for the two days and nights past and bids fair to howl through the night coming. It is dreadful! Coupled with the bare, stark trees and brown hills my mind has not been my own. I feel lonely and uncomfortable. Although the house is comfortable and warm, the moaning wind and the rattle of rain and hail against the windows makes me shiver. Last night lying in bed beside little Henriette, the pangs of homesickness blended with the reproachful attitude toward myself kept me awake half the night. The wind howled, shutters banged, and the great trees creaked and groaned outside like all possessed. Work has been impossible, and today I plowed through some thirty chapters of the Civil War. Horrible! I know tonight will be one of nightmares, moaning winds, and dead men.

330

Chadds Ford, Pennsylvania
October 29, 1910

My dear Miss Johnston,

Pardon my long delay in answering your kind note—the one with those bully photographs!

Your letter reached me just at the conclusion of four weeks' terrible suspense. My oldest little girl, a strictly healthy and robust child, was suddenly struck down with that dreaded disease "Infantile Paralysis." It came suddenly. In eight hours the child could not move. But now it is nearly over and she is well on the road to (so the specialists think) complete recovery.

Meanwhile, I made every effort to concentrate on "Stonewall" Jackson. The picture suffered in technical fluency; in other respects it was more successful. Houghton Mifflin Co. seemed quite pleased at any rate—I wonder about you! They may send you a photograph but kindly postpone your judgment until you see a *truer* proof. The falsity of values in the photograph make an entirely different thing of it, even to distorting and changing the facial expression. The man's head and the horse's head were painted in warm glowing colors which on the camera plate took black, etc., etc.

At present "The Battle" is well on its way toward completion. I am enjoying it very much.

How I do appreciate your affectionate regard for that wonderful little settlement! That mountain country took me by storm—I have never gotten over it! I am waiting for the day that I can pack up and with my little family invade that spot again; not to look around simply—but to *live* there and *paint,* and to drink in great draughts of those silent peaks that lean and crowd against one another—such everlasting grandeur I never before appreciated.

Two weeks ago a supplement to a New York paper printed a series of "Social Activities at Virginia Hot Springs." Amongst the photos was old "Flag Rock" covered with *society.* Shameful! It really hurt me to see that glorious, *profound* spot covered with tawdry bonnets, champagne bottles and bloated men. Through the groups one could catch glimpses of those three great peaks. It made me feel sad.

I was sorry when I read you were to leave. I know how you must have felt.

Kindly give my best regards to your sister, Elizabeth. Trusting that your next note, if you will give me the pleasure of one, will tell of swift, pleasant writing!

331

Saturday night

Chadds Ford, Pennsylvania
October 30, 1910. Saturday night

Dear old Babe,

Now I shall start some sort of a letter and will try to finish it.—I have made the effort twice, both unfinished letters lying here on my desk. One starting, "The wind is lashing the trees"—and the other, "I have just returned from a moonlight ramble." But in both cases I was too dull in the head to "continue to a finish."

The day has been one of those crackling kind—noisy and blustery. A cold wind swept the hills from sunrise to sunset. My studio sang the first strains of that long winter song—the wind whining through the cracks in the big doors. In the house all sat cozily about the fires, the bright sun pouring in the windows, the wind-tossed trees throwing moving shadows on the warm carpet. These are the days that suggest coming winter, bare barren winter with its white fields and gray skies. How one appreciates the stores of wood in the shed, vegetables in the cellar, preserves in the closet, and warm coats in the attic. It strikes me that Nature casts this mantel of dreariness over us, that we may enjoy, to the fullest extent, our harvests. I have always felt that in the southern countries where all is sunshine and warmth the year round—how much they miss! What anticipations they know nothing of. Neither do they know the comfort of a blazing fire—of the peculiar flavor of nuts on a winter's night—nor of the still woods in winter and the patches of shining fields—of blowing snow and glistening ice. Oh! it's all *great!!*

All is going so well in the house here. Henriette is improving rapidly and will soon join us on the lower floor. Carolyn, Jr. is thriving—so big and healthy! Carol is well too; always busy, always planning.

In the studio I am playing a very important part in a "fight to the death."

The "Rebels" successfully charging a Union breast-works. The picture, as a dramatic statement, is my very best—in other qualities, I shall wait until its completion.

[Letter continued]
November 2, 1910. Tuesday afternoon, 4:00 P.M.

Well!—things have taken *another* turn—Nat comes home! Got his letter this morning. I guess he is tickled to death—he'd *ought* to be. We all know how he loathed that country, and how he longed to be back East—and then to be able to locate so near home! Well, I'm glad! That's all I can say. We may all, or rather, *I,* may drift into Massachusetts some fine day with my little family, and then the home state would hold its own once more, as far as the Wyeth family goes.

Chadds Ford
Pa

Chadds Ford, Pennsylvania
November 2, 1910

Dear Mama,

Have spent a very satisfactory morning on my third Civil War picture—"The Spy." I believe, in real power, it is the best of the three! I shall in all probabilities complete it tomorrow.

"The Battle" has already been shipped and I am waiting anxiously to hear how it was received. You will, no doubt, get a chance to see these as they will put the originals in bookstore windows. When I'm home Thanksgiving I shall see Mr. Scudder and ask him to post you just when and where they will be shown. I am anxious that all of you see them. The pictures will show me at my best in many respects. Technically, no; but in serious, and (to considerable extent) realized effort; they are vastly superior to any illustrations I have ever done.

The WYETHS

It is hard for me to get any one of my fellow workers to commend my late work above my old, but I *know,* as certain as daylight, that my present work is built on firmer ground, has far more depth of meaning and comes nearer to painting than my early work. This attitude of my friends only goes to prove that their greater interest lies in *clever* work rather than in the more considered and thoughtful kind.

It is so satisfactory to do illustration for a house such as Houghton Mifflin. They are far more deliberate, more thoughtful and careful in their judgment of pictures. Instead of being disappointed that a picture is not brilliant technically, they look deeper to find out whatever the artist may have tried to say. So in my "Stonewall Jackson"— they appreciated its dramatic intent, although I must confess it was poorly painted. (There is talk of this picture being bought for the Richmond Historical Museum.)

This is a dull November day, but *glorious* nevertheless. Outside the window I hear the neighbor's chickens scratching in the dry leaves. This side of the house is protected from the wind, and it looks comfortable out there—I'd like to be with them! There is something so fascinating kicking around dead leaves.

Henriette is very lively and well in the daytime, almost entirely well on her legs and her thumb getting stronger too.

Collier's Weekly published an article on the new findings made in Infantile Paralysis. The article is highly worth reading, and shows the caution that one should take. The disease is now pronounced strictly *contagious,* and only ten per cent of the patients recover *completely!* So we are *very* fortunate, more so than I had thought, with Henriette—although to be sure she has not fully recovered as yet. I massage her arm every night with alcohol and sweet-oil. In this article I learned that massage is simply to keep the affected muscles alive until the deadened nerves take up their functions once more. I never realized the importance of massage before.

The *flaming day* ahead of us is [the] twenty-first—the night of the twenty-first! It is our plan to travel on the Colonial Express by night, that the ride will be restful rather than a strain on the children.

Unless sudden work prevents, we shall stay perhaps two weeks, with the permission of the grandparents! I have never been so anxious to get back into New England again. This time of the year too!

Tell Papa that the turkey stunt will have to go by the boards. Of course I could get turkeys enough, but my idea was made up mostly of sentiment—to get one from the Cleveland farm. As it stands, their fifty-one turkeys are sold to a dealer.

The cider jug I dared not send, owing to the strike of expressmen in N.Y.—It would have exploded before reaching Needham.

333

"Town Meeting Day," written and illustrated by Sidney M. Chase, appeared in the November 1910 issue of Scribner's *magazine.*

Chadds Ford, Pennsylvania
November 9, 1910

Dear old Sid!

Since reading your "Town Meeting Day" I've had it in mind to write, never thinking it would be this late day; but you know how it goes!

You may have heard through Smith of the serious time we had with little Henriette this summer—or *fall* rather. Infantile Paralysis. The name is enough. There is no need telling you further.

This period knocked out a couple months for me of course, and this together with a trip through Virginia left little to my summer. The season departed leaving me near empty-handed so far as accomplished work goes.

Early in the summer I painted three pictures illustrating a series of stories by Conan Doyle. Now I am at work on the material gathered in the South. A series of Civil War pictures for Houghton Mifflin Co. The story of the confederacy from the southern viewpoint by Mary Johnston.

As Shrader put it in a letter just received, "The Brandywine School is well represented this month in the magazines." *Harper's, Scribner's, Century*. Smith's came out remarkably well. He has "caught on" to the Boston methods rapidly, no use in talking! It is refreshing to see such clean, well-drawn illustrations in *Harper's*.

Now to be critical—I feel no *passion* in his present work, except for a certain technical efficiency. His sense of the picturesque and his knowledge of details all go to make up interesting pictures, but they lack ardour, *emotion;* in other words *individuality*. A man can never express himself individually upon another man's vehicle of expression. Passion lies in the *personality* of the brush stroke, not in the *craft* of the brush stroke. Pictorial patchwork of the most excellent execution is not valid unless executed individually.

I have come to realize that artistic expression only exists as a serious and valuable possession insofar as one makes it his *own*. We have such a remarkable example in Homer. He knew light and shade, values, drawing, etc., in common with others. Further than that, *all* he *possessed* was distinctly his.

Now if Smith, for instance, had taken from the Museum just those "truths" without the mannerisms, he would have taken all that legitimately belonged to him. He may grow out of it in time, but I'm of the opinion if he does it will be into something else—another mannerism. It takes vigorous strength of will to say no! to a powerful influence. It is so easy to follow a blazed trail and so hard to strike out into a trackless wilderness.

In my own case, I am making headway, very slow headway. I do not show it in my illustrations, although I believe them to be healthy in that they are experimental—that is, I have not tied myself down to method but am always seeking new fields, new vehicles of expression.

I have done a great deal of landscape the past year, and it is in this that I show some progress.

Incidentally I have had two offers or invitations to exhibit. Macbeth of Macbeth Galleries in N.Y. wanted me to let him have three during the summer, and the Marshall Field Galleries in Chicago were very enthusiastic to give a one-man show there. But I declined both. You may think me foolish. It would take several sheets to explain myself, so I won't try it. In a nutshell, the pictures would not have represented me truthfully. No two are alike hardly; they are all experimental. I got a little good out of each one, but not *one* contained to any degree accumulative power.

Now these sketches of mine are almost laughable in their *dissimilarity*.

Here I am, as usual, talking about myself. Kindly pardon the "thousand eyes!"

334

The Seasons

Chadds Ford, Pennsylvania
November 14, 1910. Sunday

Dear Sid,

It's just shutting in dark. The wind is whining about the north windows and a faint seething of wet snow can be heard against the panes. From my chair at the desk here, I can dimly make out a solitary light in Washington's Headquarters. At times the light vanishes as the straight driving snow thickens—then it shines again, twinkling. The cozy room is conducive to a "heart-to-heart" talk with a friend— you for instance, and a good pipe. Next best—paper and pen. So here goes! In advance let me thank you for your time.

It is hardly ever, when I make a criticism, I do not suffer periods of self-reproach. Simply because of *my own* infinite shortcomings. My suggestions, relating to your "Town Meeting Day," I do not feel so bad about. My criticism of the story was *incidental;* it was *trifling* compared to the *big movement* in your creation. My allusion to your pictures was different. With one *sweep,* I criticized them more or less severely. I was honest in my intention; but *now* I realize that I should have been more explicit, therefore less harsh.

In your story I read, "No word was spoken as they jolted off over the frozen ruts, past the black patch of hemlocks, and turned into the road for home." Here is marked simplicity! In one brush stroke you have told a *triple* emotion—the silent men, the cold, still country, and the moving sentiment of the road toward home. The elimination of detail, of useless half-tones and superfluous shadow is perfect. One reads this passage with a thrill!

When the master paints a portrait, it is not the wrinkles or the play of intricate shadows and reflections across the face that impress; it is first, that prime statement of *light,* flooding a countenance. Secondly, the character.

We have many examples of remarkable character portraits, but darn few that combine those two qualities in the order I named. Rembrandt, Vermeer, Velasquez present this profound combination in almost everything they did. It is the reason why we stand awe-struck before their works.

Here is a quotation: "A great artist is known by his omissions."

But the point I bring is this. With less in your pictures you would tell *more*. Not less figures understand, but less insistence and confusion of detail.

Now regards selection and treatment of subject. I contend that illustration should carry the higher emotional expression; that it should not serve in the capacity of descriptive text to the detriment of bigger feelings. Your hand-line fishing picture was a big picture besides being the very best of an illustration. *There* was an emotional picture coupled with the subordinate interest of character and picturesqueness.

In the colored picture of the "friendly greeting" the incident *compels* attention; it is dominant. It was undoubtedly meant to be. As an artist (not a writer) you should confine yourself to the true function of an artist—to interpret the *primal* attractions of *life itself*. —The essential details may sift in as accessories. Your "lobsterman" was impressive—why? It is needless to explain. Not because of the lobster traps and old clothes—mainly—because of the elemental surroundings and conditions primarily. And didn't that illustration add dignity and power to your story? Did anyone feel the lack of *coincidence* with certain lines in your text? Could that picture have been spared better than the fish-weighing one?

An artist who senses the deeper meanings in Nature should express that understanding of her—subordinating the variations of the picturesque and details. There are many who have not the power to feel the profundities and consequently build their expressions on skeletons, as it were. Many such works are interesting, but how lasting? How important?

You may argue that your function is to illustrate as you do. But I do not agree when I look at "Hand-line Fishing" and "The Lobsterman."

Thus endeth the first lesson!

335

The family had just returned from a three-week visit to Needham.

Chadds Ford, Pennsylvania
December 10, 1910

Dear folks,

Trip uneventful—no! We made fine connections which makes it

decidedly eventful! Children caught no more cold is our belief, although it's hard to tell exactly. Henriette slept straight through, but Carolyn was quite restless.

Everything in good shape here! Have already investigated house scheme, etc., and find a much more fitting place up at the Turner place—the west side of the 2nd floor. Three rooms, bath, and plumbing in back room adaptable for kitchen. The mill thrown in.

Well, I must hustle this in the mail. Love to all. Thus ends a *glorious* three weeks!!

336

Chadds Ford, Pennsylvania
December 29, 1910

Dear folks!

Christmas is over—and yet it *isn't* over—the glamour of it all still fills the house. The odor of the fir-balsam permeates every room; the smell of second and third-day turkey is still with us, and the every-now-and-then toot of a tin bugle or the tumble and clatter of blocks keeps Xmas morning fresh in our minds. And what a morning that was!

We were up at five thirty. While Carol dressed I got the fires up bright and warm downstairs. (Oh! what a sensation it was to come downstairs in the dark, the air heavy-laden with the aroma of the tree, and that new smell of the presents lying about, and to feel around the dark room for a match, conscious of that glittering tree in the corner, the faint dropping of a "needle" or two striking a tinsel ball with a tiny ring)—it was all so mysterious and beautiful; it brought back the same tingle of excitement which we all felt at home before the door of the sitting room was opened.

Then, just as Carol awakened Henriette, I thumped and banged around in the hall in my stocking-feet, rocking the whole house almost, and Carol whispered to Henriette to listen to Santa Claus. *Well,* if you ever saw a child awake and on her toes quicker than that little snipe! you've got something to talk about. I rang bells, blew horns and made tramping noises.—I got excited myself and felt the illusion just as keenly as she did, I'll bet! Carol admits she did herself. Then, as a careful bit of effective work (I had bought a corking long-whiskered mask with peaked hat combined), with the hall lamp dimly burning, I bobbed up the stairs and peered through the palings at the top of the landing. Henriette dressing in the bathroom saw me! Well, I can't for a minute express just how she looked and how she acted! It was glorious!! She was laughing and crying both, and between them she managed to pipe out a timid, "Hello Chris!"

Well, the climax was reached when at last all three—Carol, *little* Carolyn and Henriette came down the stairs and I met them at the bottom, rigged out in my costume, squatty and distorted, handing Henriette a filled stocking, and bowed myself out of the dim hall, onto the dark porch and shut the door. The rest went in to view the lighted tree, and I joined them as soon as I could slip off my duds.

The effect on Henriette was what I wanted it to be. It all astounded her, and I know she will never forget it and her remembrances of her first impression will give her many, many pleasant hours in later life.

My own feelings, while going through this pantomine, I can never express in words; but they will always be clear in my mind, and will add to the already long, long list of dear remembrances that continually parade through my vision. My antics were carried out with such seriousness and enthusiasm, that at times I felt like *bawling;* and then again I felt unreal, as though I were someone else, or crazy—or something! I can't say! I only know that underneath it all, the great truth that I was a *father,* acting this all out for my *own* family seemed fantastic, a *dream!* Sudden realizations of the fact however were what made me feel the pangs of past childhood. This is what made me feel like *bawling*—I wished that I could be a child again with Henriette.

The usual excitement prevailed. Henriette discovered one ornament after another on the tree, which she remembered were there a year ago. Little Carolyn was fascinated with the flickering lights and colored tinsel. She was the first, however, to discover the new toys on the floor, and in short order put everything to *use!*

I glory in a certain victory brought to me this Xmas! One I *never* expected. Two people—my own dear wife and the other, my very proper Aunt Hat, *both* recognized my one dissipation—my *smoking* proclivities. The first honored me with fifty delightful cigars; the latter, with a beautiful copper ashtray with a *cigar holder* attached! Now! all ye minions who proclaim smoking an evil—*list* to the precedent—the art of smoking has been *honored!* It has been elevated to the dignified position as a legitimate and perfectly proper thing to do in a "Wyeth" household!! All ye who do *not* smoke descend to the cellar that ye may not pollute the heavenly scented air!

337

Chadds Ford, Pennsylvania
January 27, 1911. Friday

My dear Miss Johnston,

I am about to paint the fourth and last picture for the first volume of *The Long Roll*—"The Lovers." The meeting of Colonel Cleave and Judith Cary, in Chapter 19, is to furnish me the material. And now I ask you for a little additional aid in regard to costume.

Judith has left the hospital. What would be her dress? And what sort of outside wrap and bonnet would she wear this spring afternoon—if any? And please say a few words about her hair and face.

And Colonel Cleave—would he wear a cavalryman's jacket or a coat with skirts? A sash? A soft hat with braid?

I find that the selection of his costume is so much a matter of choice. I think it better for you to decide.

338

For a brief period while their new house was being built, N. C. Wyeth moved his family to Windtryst.

Chadds Ford, Pennsylvania
February 7, 1911

Dear Sid,

At present we are preparing for a slight change. I have given up this farm, which has gone up in price, and we are removing to the "hilltop" where you and your mother and father visited Carol and I. There we have a corking "apartment," of three large rooms and a bath with all conveniences, and the mill, second floor, is being

371

transformed into a big studio with an eighteen-foot skylight. All, including apartment, for $120 a year.

The studio is something I should have gone into anyway, my present one being too small for work.

Just now I am negotiating for a small piece of land on "Rocky Hill" where I shall erect a small quaint cottage, for I must provide a place that I can come to at anytime in later years. My attachment to this place is beyond words, and although there are other important matters to be considered, I must, for the sake of my work, make myself comfortable in this grand valley.

Mrs. Wyeth walking over the new land they had bought.

Chapter XIII

HIS CORNER

"I'm totally satisfied that this is the little corner of the world wherein I shall work out my destiny."

339

Dear Sid,

Have just accepted a commission from Scribner's to handle "an elaborate edition" of *Treasure Island!* The gods have smiled upon me!!

340

Dear folks!

I'm very much ashamed of my negligence—the week slipped by unmercifully fast—in fact, I hardly know one end of a week from another these days, which the rest of the letter will explain and fully justify my remarks!

The weather is nothing short of *gorgeous!* Made doubly so by tantalizing snow flurries and miniature blizzards, then suddenly bursting into genuine spring weather—all in a day!

The tawny hills all about us speak volumes. The sunny sides of rocks are warm and comfortable; at their bases, one can see the green actually breaking through the warmed mold; and in the protected swamps, the skunk cabbage "horns" are up four to six inches. Bluebirds abound, and robins have been about for a month.

Work abounds! and it is coming easily too. Have just completed an "allegory" of summer and have started one of autumn. Both farm subjects. The Houghton Mifflin Co. sent a letter brimming with praise for the *War Time Lovers*—so that is done. With numerous ideas of my own, several definite commissions for sporting subjects, and *Treasure Island,* my summer is enshrouded in hidden pleasures (and no less, hidden struggles too, I suppose). But damn it! I believe I look forward to fights now—it adds zest; it's like putting sand on the track!

Furthermore, I am feeling like a *man* now! I have bought the most glorious sight in this township for a home! No buildings, but a stunning location, exceptional water, the most enchanting, purliest, and most musical rock-bound brook flowing through it you can imagine—a handsome grove of black walnut trees, a wood lot (around the brook) of oak and beech, a hill looming up back of the "house sight," crowned on one side by a glorious ledge and nut trees, and a surrounding field of 8 acres of the very best land, besides the section chosen for our house of 4 acres, and the lower field (clear and tillable) of 6 acres—18 in all.

I paid $2000 for it—and to have the deed in my hands gives me a new reason for living!

The property lies on the crest and north slope of so-called "Rocky Hill," almost directly opposite where we are now. Papa and I touched the east end of the property the day we walked through Atwater's young orchard. Babe knows the little brook. It lies due east of the schoolhouse, in fact between the school and Atwater's orchard.

Thus culminates a deal I tried to put through a year ago. I'm totally satisfied that this is the little corner of the world wherein I shall work out my destiny. Later on, if the success of my work justifies it, I look forward to a summer cottage in New England—but here, I must acknowledge my soul comes nearer to the surface than any place I know.

It won't be long before we build. The dreams of years will at last take shape before another year has passed, I hope. As I look through the fat envelope of sketches of plans made in the past, I find that fundamentally they are the same. Extremely simple in arrangement and very moderate in size. Nat has at present my last drawings which embody pretty much the scheme—only I have changed from frame to brick—it is more durable, will cut the winds, and cheaper; and with white trimmings and green shutters and big chimneys, I shall perpetuate Bayard Taylor's spirit in architecture! It will be a place you will all glory to visit—this will be one of the crowning glories—to have you *all* enjoy it, as another *home* to come to!

The history of the sale is an interesting story which can better be told on the spot sometime. The deed is clear and the land is mine, *mine,* mine! When I first set my foot upon it last Wednesday as *owner*—the thought ran through my head, "This experience is a sure antidote for *Socialism!*" My heavens! how wholesome and hearty I felt!

The children are in prime health—*no* colds, and eating like beavers! Carolyn is floating around in space, as buoyant and enthusiastic as a chicken in grasshopper season!

I retain my studio ($30 per annum), but of course we move up in the Turner house soon. Although you may not understand it, even this is a pleasurable anticipation. Oh! damn it, we're optimists, I guess, that's all. (But who wouldn't be an optimist?)

341

Reference is made in this letter to the possibility of a mural decoration being commissioned. These murals were completed for the Hotel Utica, Utica, New York, and have since been removed.

The two sisters, Aunty Guss and Aunt Anna, are moving from Washington's Headquarters to the town of West Chester, eight miles away.

"On the Big Hill"
Chadds Ford, Pennsylvania
March 30, 1911

Dear Mama,

It seems an age since I wrote—and I guess it is! Well, if you'd seen me ambling up and down stairs with trunks, beds, bureaus and pianos!—lounging on a big moving-wagon, in old clothes and a tough-looking hat, lounging with a real swagger—*proud* of the opportunity to stretch my stale muscles, proud of the chance to be, for a short five days, a hard-working laborer (combined furniture mover and teamster). Yes, I did it all myself with the exception of half a dozen heavy articles—stoves, piano, angelus, Victrola, etc.

Jenkins, as it happened, moved on identical days—so with a heavy team from Stackhous and a large wagon I tackled the job alone. It was great! and I thoroughly enjoyed it. And now to cap it all we are all settled in our new quarters—the *coziest, simplest* and most *delightful* little apartment you would ever care to see. Carol is delighted! which means me too!

Today we started in on our housekeeping alone. Three delicious simple meals, eaten with quiet unmolested pleasure in our sunny little kitchen in the tower, are ample compensation for our move.

You may judge from what I say that I do not regret leaving the old place? I *do,* decidedly. I went there this evening to pack a few odds and ends in the loft of my studio. It was showering steadily;

the eaves of the old house dripped, the trees dripped, and the tin gutters sounded with that plaintive internal trickling—the windows stared blankly and a few chimney-swallows circled around the abandoned chimneys. It all sounded like sobbing—the house and trees quietly sobbing, and the birds hovering about the big empty house, as though in sympathy with its loneliness.

I wondered what it was, 'way down within me, that made me feel bad, and I concluded that it rested upon one fact—that no longer would Henriette run and play around the big yard, or pass in and out of the great green shadows from those trees. That is what struck me deeper than anything else. She had become used to the place—she knew where the violets first appeared (she had visited the patch up in the orchard a number of times this winter in great anticipation); its paths and byways were a part of her tiny instinct; she could run to the "stoodio" at her pleasure. All these things are taken away from her, and she must begin over again.—That's what makes me feel bad.

With little Carolyn, I feel different. She is not so deeply rooted as yet, and it makes slight difference to her where she is, provided the bottle and her Mama are at hand.

And Carol? The house was *so large,* so *hard* to keep warm and cozy in the winter, that it was beyond her to get the pleasure she craved out of it—that of housekeeping. It was a burden. We always anticipated that with little changes and additions, such as we could do without much expense, we would finally render the house what it should be—homelike, comfortable, and in shape to be reasonably easy to care for. We succeeded in a degree in making it homelike—but otherwise we failed. In the summer it was fine in every respect.

Carol's burden is my burden—that's all I can say. With her feelings, I began to see too, with all my professional work coming on, that I had too much on my hands, besides the expense of extra help. And so we are here! Under *greatly* reduced expense, and happier in every way.

What has made this recent and unusual work of mine doubly enjoyable has been the strongly contrasted thoughts continually flitting through my mind: visions of the stunning work I am about to launch out upon—*Treasure Island*. I fully believe that this five days' "recreation" has stimulated my imagination remarkably—at least my vision is decidedly clearer, and I can see my pirates passing before me in almost real flesh and blood—mostly blood!

My trip to New York—whence came the "sweets," was highly successful, and left me *boiling over* to get at my work. Chapin at Scribner's was highly pleased at the scheme I had laid out for a pirate book and, "Anticipates," as he puts it, "that the outcome will be my best work yet." I trust his prophecy has some meaning.

To further crown the procession of opportunities comes a possible commission that climaxes my career thus far—one I hope that may be the beginning of many like commissions.

Friday, Delos Johnson (of the famed "Johnson Brothers," hotel builders—"Ten Eycke" in Albany, "Knickerbocker" in N.Y., etc.) comes to see me here to talk over the mural decoration of the big "grille room" in a luxurious hotel to be built in Utica, N.Y. Thus far, the proposition is to reproduce the four Indian pictures ("Summer," "Autumn," "Spring" and "Winter") *life*-size on the walls of this dining hall. I can say no more now. It looks like a big chance for me, if I understand his letters right. He had Maxfield Parish and Remington do his other work, so I feel very pleased to think that he is really after *some* quality.

I shall know more on Friday and well let *you* know right away. I am almost afraid to talk about it, fearing it will vanish into the thin air. It's a chance that many men have waited *their lives* for and never got.

It may interest you to know that Edwin Abbey strongly recommended me to handle *Treasure Island*. He is a close friend of Charles Scribner, and through Chapin I learned this agreeable news.

I'm so full of startling news and thoughts (startling to me at least) that I am aware that my pen is missing lots of things which would interest you. You must excuse me this once however.

I just received a hearty letter from Nat—full of fire and health— more his own true self in it than I detected in him personally last summer.

It's mournful to see the Aunties packing up. It's breaking Aunt Anna up considerably, and I am almost afraid of results.

She is by far the most sensitive one of the two, and she feels it, leaving the very village where she was born, to spend the rest of her days in a town. I can't help but blame Aunty Guss for it. She is rather impulsive, and is, I believe, a little carried away by the idea of living *in a town*, where she can *go* more.

She is going to miss her garden, her porch, and all the other advantages of the country, which has had so much to do with her good health. Where they go, they have *no* porch nor any yard to *speak* of. Right on a paved street! We feel deeply sorry to lose them, and more so because we believe it a serious mistake.

I have on my desk, blueprints of our house plans, which I will send in two or three weeks for you all to see.

Papa's enthusiastic letter made me feel good! I was also pleased to note that *sentiment* has got the upper hand of practicality—in that he wishes we had *not* left the Harvey place this spring. Only a matter of $530 in expenses, that's all! But I'm glad he values the sentiment that high. That's what I've done all my life through, thus far. I've paid heavy money penalties for sentiment and have not yet regretted it.

Even *now*, economy is more the result of "fate," for in so changing our home I sought greater contentment. I suppose if it were to *cost* me $530 more instead of less—I'd do it just the same!

Such a damn fool am I (but I question whether I am or no).

Henriette has by no means forgotten anyone "up home," as she calls the place where "Aunt Mama" and "Aunt Papa" lives. She is wearing the rompers you made her still.

342

Chadds Ford, Pennsylvania
April 17, 1911

Dear folks all!

I am perfectly aware of my delay in writing you a "long letter"— but heavens knows where the time goes! Oh! I know where the time has gone; perhaps I should put it, Heaven knows why the days aren't *longer!!* The weeks are slipping by "unbeknownst," as John Cummings would say. Not until this morning did I realize just how much I had accomplished; but when I started to pack my work of two weeks, and to hunt boards and nails for said packing, it dawned upon me that to complete four huge pictures in two weeks was going some! Well, I did, and I am proud of them, which is more to the point. Not satisfied of course—but then, one can be proud and not satisfied. Isn't that so?

Yes, the cover design, the decoration for the book lining, the title page, and one illustration [for *Treasure Island*]. These had to be hustled through in order that Scribner's could get out a "dummy" book for their salesmen.

Now for the remaining twelve illustrations, which must be completed by July 1st. Between times, in fact right away, I shall start a magazine story for them of two full pages and about four vignettes. These to be done May 15th. Also a *Century* story, a picture for the Forbes Company, and one for a private party (a sportsman) in Connecticut. With all this comes my mural commission—but I've lots of time on this.

It's no use in talking; it's great to be rushed once in awhile. Once I get up an impetus, I can work with both hands, painting a blood-curdling pirate fight with one, and with the other, an infant sucking its mother's breast!

And sleep and eat? Why do you caution! My lord, I honestly wish that my appetite would subside—and I sleep eight and nine good long hours.

343

Chadds Ford, Pennsylvania
May 26, 1911

Dear Mama,

All in fine shape—work going fine—*some* rain—cellar wall completed—studio foundations under way.

Will write good letter Sunday to you and Boys!

Twenty gallons a minute of the finest soft water—51 degrees cold —struck it 130 feet deep.

344

Chadds Ford, Pennsylvania
June 2, 1911. Friday morning

Dear folks,

Three more completed *Treasure Island* pictures are in my studio, making the total thus far, eight, with *nine* more to do. Scribner's are intensely enthusiastic over the pictures. (Thank God! I can depend on the enthusiasm from these people.) The proofs of the first four pictures, although unfinished, are corkers and stand in such great distinction as compared to those *miserable smudges* printed in *The*

Long Roll. I'm utterly disgusted with Houghton Mifflin. They have done me considerable damage and I can't help but resent it.

345

Chadds Ford, Pennsylvania
June 12, 1911

My dear Ed,

It's 5:30. The numerous calves tied about the place are singing a morning serenade. They make the very air tremble!

I have a garden which is doing well, but needs attention; bean-poles put in, corn thinned out and hoed, lettuce thinned and set out, and third planting of radishes, lettuce, corn, etc. Well, I'll break the coming Sabbath.

Our little abode is a symbol of neatness and coziness. We have enjoyed the summer so far, as a family, more than we ever had time to do at the other house.

As to me, the fact of my studio being nearly a mile away, making four trips a day means very much to me. I've done better and more continuous work, not less than nine hours a day and often considerably more. This with other matters to watch and think about I've been gloriously busy and happy.

The house is coming finely.

346

Chadds Ford, Pennsylvania
June 16, 1911. Friday morning

Dear Mama,

The week is slipping by as rapidly as usual—*Treasure Island* lot of drawings (8) went yesterday, and my studio actually seems lonely. Before completing the remaining number (7) will illustrate a western sheep story for *Century.* Have the picture already started on my easel—and it promises mighty well.

Somehow, with all that's going on (I don't mean to say that I am busier than 9/10 the people today, but there is such a *distinct variety* of affairs on my mind), my art seems to hold a place in my mind perfectly isolated from all other matters. It is as though it were stimulated by radically different thinking and action. So it has been the past three months. My conceptions are fuller, more significant, besides being so much more ornate. Besides, I do things with more *authority*—put statements down with a clear knowledge and directness. My *Treasure Island* pictures you shall see, will show just this.

You ask for anecdotes.—It is for me to take Henriette to the closet in the mornings. This morning as she arose from her seat of action, after a very satisfactory séance—she remarked: "Papa—do you like green?" I said "Yes, very much." After a pause, she added—"Well, do you like 'hockey' green?" I looked and found the basis for her observations. I must admit she succeeded in changing my viewpoint.

The brick work starts today. The huge fireplace in the living room is laid out. All is doing finely.

347

Studio
Chadds Ford, Pennsylvania
June 24, 1911. Friday, 4:30 P.M.

Dear folks,

I am writing dangerously near to a fiendish bunch of Godless men scrambling over a stockade! It's surprising how quietly they are doing it too, loaded down as they are—first, with *rum* and all manner of arms, guns, pistols, cutlasses and knives!

Am busy turning down orders, which I am always sorry to do, because everything seems to present such great possibilities. Three mss. from Scribner's in my desk now, besides *Harper's* and *Delineater.*—*Century* story completed and shipped yesterday.

Some time ago I said something about a machine (an Oldsmobile). I had it a weekend and sent it back! Glorious machine! Glorious sport! but it dragged me away from the little things I love so much.

The week was one of real pain and suffering to me, until late one evening Carol and I were listening to Beethoven's Minuet, and I came to the end of my torment. In two days the machine went.

The idea and opportunity to actually have an auto at our command was overwhelming. We imagined ourselves refreshed and invigorated by delightful rides of an evening through these gorgeous hills. We fancied the pleasure and benefit 'twould be for the children— such an easy way to get them around. We saw ourselves enjoying life to the utmost—a home building, good work on my easel and auto riding!

The dream faded quickly.

I claim it a victory in a double sense.

Have three *Treasure Island* pictures started, four more, then I'm through!

348

Windtryst
Chadds Ford, Pennsylvania
July 7, 1911

Dear Mama,

I reckon there's no need to tell you what hot weather is, or how much of it we have had—judging from the papers, you too have had your share.

Men have been dropping over in the harvest fields like so many flies—yet they work, work, work. Carl Petersen suffered two sunstrokes in a week's time, yet today he is on the binder (I can hear it now; its clicking sound rising and falling on the hot humid wind that blows in my window). Such weather! 101 for three days! 90 is *cool* now.

Work is coming well. *Treasure Island* pictures all done but four, the last I truly believe to be stronger than the first (a rather unusual occurrence for me, as in a long series I am apt to tire or lose enthusiasm owing to repetition of subject matter).

The house is taking shape—the roof timbers being cut this moment. It's one of the most fascinating homes I ever saw, and promises to be just what I wanted exactly—practical, picturesque, and indigenous to the country. In two years, as soon as the grounds assume a natural look again, the house will look as though it had always been there. I make my second payment to the contractor tomorrow. To have actually invested $3600 in such an undertaking makes me feel substantial; it is a good stimulus. As much again and my home will be paid for; just think of it!

Chadds Ford, Pennsylvania
July 16, 1911. Sunday

Dear Mama,

The house is progressing rapidly and thoroughly. The architect is superintending the job, which assures me that all is done right and carried out to the letter. It is the greatest satisfaction to go over on the hill and to actually stand in the various rooms; to actually look from the windows upon scenes which will become so familiar to us. Although the interior of the house is sheer skeleton work, we know the exact placement of all the articles of furniture, rugs, etc. Often, while at the table, or in the evening up here in "Windtryst," one of us will make a chance suggestion that the big chair perhaps would be better located in such and such a corner—the quick answer comes back: "Oh, no! The cupboard door in that corner won't allow for that; we must decide to place it where we first determined." And so it is that we have a very vivid and complete picture of "our home" three months hence.

The word *"satisfied"* will never come into my curriculum of development, but I must go so far as to admit a feeling of real encouragement at the turn my work has taken just at the moment when one would expect the spirit of practicality and commercialism to prevail.

It is impressive to know that in the majority of cases, Mr. Pyle's pupils achieved quick and pronounced success in illustration. This fact is most singular when one realizes that the large art schools but seldom turn out *one* successful man. It stands to reason, however, that such *manufacture* of successful artists (and it is nothing more) cannot be based upon wholesome growth—there must be at bottom, a clever, practical receipt by which men are whipped into line—a shortcut to practical results.

For instance—what man of us can we name, not excluding Mr. Pyle, could make of a simple time-worn motif, an eminent picture. And still it is just this achievement which proves a man's power. The fact is that in every case we have been more or less journalists—news reporters—taught to grasp the unique, the obviously picturesque, the essentially dramatic, sifting out here and there striking and novel situations, queer and tragic events. We were taught to shut our eyes to the simple and glorious beauties about us, to seek the strange and unusual. My Oh! My!! What a distant call to the true realms of painting! The eternal sunlight is discarded for plunging broncobusters; the glint on the brooks is passed by for raring and tearing automobiles; the wind in the trees gives way to the diving airship!

To conclude, we were taught essentially the art of journalism, to be rendered in the *manner* of painting. Even though there were those of us who cared for the more usual phases of life, we were bound to interpret them theatrically, building up artificial semblances of nature. Of clouds? They were made great upheaved masses of unusual and freakish formations. Of mountains? They became great tortuous hummocks of nightmare shapes. Of a face? It was the extreme of characterization to the point of burlesque and the limit of facial expression.

350

"Noon" was Wyeth's first cousin, Newell Barker, son of his aunt, Amelia Annie Wyeth Barker.

Chadds Ford, Pennsylvania
July 26, 1911

Dear Mama,

Treasure Island completed! I write that as though I were glad.— In one way I am—to know that I pulled through the entire set of seventeen canvases (almost as tall as I am) without one break in my enthusiasm and spirit. The result is I've turned out a set of pictures, without doubt far better in every quality than anything I ever did. Scribner's have expressed their delight over them by wire and letter several times. All this gives the right to feel jubilant and with no little satisfaction from the illustrating viewpoint.

On the other hand, it was with regret that I packed the last canvas in the big box tonight. I so thoroughly enjoyed the work; I was for some reason able, throughout the series, to keep my pictures fresh and brilliant and striking in their variety of composition and color, dramatic incident and emotional quality. These features are what appealed to Scribner's, and which will, I am convinced, appeal to the public.

Soon (perhaps in a day or so) I'll have a partial set of rough proofs which I shall send on for you to see.

I shall take off the weekend with the kids and Carol and go down to the beach (Jersey shore—Beach Haven) only two hours from Philadelphia.

This will be a striking change for us, and I'm so eager to play with and watch the kids on the beach, and in the water. I shall take my camera of course.

The house proceeds rapidly and well.

The plasterers are booked to come in there to work in ten days.

Postal from Noon.—He has been to the Louvre.—I wonder how many times his cheeks flushed scarlet—for shame or for admiration.

N. C. Wyeth, Beach Haven, New Jersey.

351

Dear old Ed,

I've waited in vain for a promised letter from your camp but have concluded that if the spell is to be broken, it's up to me. If you were only *here* now, right in the next chair, I'd warrant a long noisy chat, if not an enlightening one. I'm in just the mood for it; and just this moment the clear bracing air is brushing through the studio, spilling papers, tilting pictures from the walls, and waving the big curtains like mad. Oh! it's great!! The leaves are rustling on the big chestnut tree outside the windows, and it makes me think of early autumn—the smell of dried grass and fall flowers, the closely cropped pastures, and cool, clear running brooks! The other day I walked over beyond "Sugar Loaf" down into "Heifer Run Meadow" and sat near the roots of a tree, under which we had all eaten a memorable supper—Mama, Nat, Babe, Gladys, Carolyn, the two children and myself. Rummaging around, I came across several gaunt corncobs, unmistakably those of "Black Mexican" (small and deeply grooved). What pictures and memories flashed through my mind! I have one of the fragments of cob, together with a bit of baked-potato skin, in a match box in my desk up at the house. I take it out occasionally and slide open the box—it works like magic; the genie places before me that pleasant afternoon and all its incidents, even to the sound of the running water.

I don't know just how to account for it, but do you know, those trifling matters (personally, I cannot say *trifling*) occupy a large and important place among the thoughts dear to me. I can connect and associate more poetry, more drama, more mystery, with these simple little matters that occur spontaneously, than with happenings obviously important and weighty.

For instance, I can concentrate on a tiny detail—say, the old signboard, "Green St.," which I remember was for years poked up in that cedar tree on the corner, nearly smothered from sight, and all gray and dirty. The mystery that used to surround that name-board—because in spite of the word "Green," people all used to call the street "Blind Lane"; and during my early school days when I dared not trust my own knowledge, but yet deciphered the sign to read "Green," I puzzled at the reason how it could be "Blind." Until I very gradually emerged into the full realization that it took years for the old (and much better) title to wear off and the new to take its place.

Beyond these mental problems, it is so impressive to think of the years that that tree, with its burden nestled in its branches, swayed in the storms, winter after winter; how it drooped and withered under the sun of many summers, and dripped the water of a thousand rains—how, four times a day, every one of us boys passed it by to school. It stood as a landmark, a guide at the turning point where our house was shut from view and we plodded through the short stretch of sand and on up the stony hill by the "pine woods."

Tomorrow, I run into Wilmington for shirts and stockings—if cool I shall walk in.

In two weeks I am due in N.Y. to go over the *Treasure Island* proofs at the engravers. I won't say what I may do when I get that near home.

My big canvases for the decorations are being made, and a month should see them well under way.

It may interest you to know that Scribner's have paid me $2500 for the illustrations for *Treasure Island*.

352

Chadds Ford, Pennsylvania
October 1, 1911

Dear Babe,

I have read with profoundest interest and affection, Frank Sanborn's study of Thoreau! The spirit of the book will never cease to haunt me. The subtle and glorious glimpse into the life and soul of Thoreau is *marvelous* and means exceedingly more to me than the Bible and the works of all other men, dead and alive, put together!

I believe Thoreau to be the prophet of the future.—I am aware that this is a very broad, unassuming statement. When I say this I refer to his fundamental philosophy pertaining to our attitude toward life.

The WYETHS

I came home to find Henriette sick in her stomach. She seems quiet now, on the big chair nearby. Her mind is so fresh, so impressionable, so imaginative; it seems as though she must needs thrive on it, and not rely on the material nourishment to any great extent. Perhaps it is because I feel so often that I could think better, and accomplish more, were I less heavy, with less of an appetite, with less blood in my body. For some reason I envy the thin body, the less sumptuous demand for food. I am inclined to believe this idea to some degree is true: that *flesh* is not conducive to spiritual thinking. I should never think of undermining my normal and healthy condition by imposing upon myself a too restricted diet, to force my body into unnatural submission. And yet I see no reason why this weakness should not count as one of my problems, and that it would be for the best to restrain and deprive myself of unnecessary foods.

Later in the evening: As I finished the last paragraph I realized that Carol was not bustling about as is her custom early in the evening, and went to the bedroom to find her very much depressed and quietly sobbing. She blames herself for "not being able," she says, "to give me that spiritual aid necessary for my work and development."

We talked in the dark for an hour and emerged feeling better and more determined than ever to carry out our ideals and aspirations.

I did not specify that it was the peculiar sympathy and belief from a fellow *man* that I craved in conjunction with the abundance of true sympathy which I get from Carol and Mama. The stimulant from our *men* sympathizers is distinctive (although no more valuable), but it *is distinctive* and plays its special and important part in our lives.

We must agree that it is impossible for a woman to enter into our special work and stand before us to lead—to take the *initiative.*

This power is not woman's, as the past ages in Art and Science testify. But they can bless us with a spirit of love and faith that supersedes all other stimulus or encouragement. In the proportion that a man and wife individually do their part well, in that proportion are they a *spiritual* aid to one another. And I believe this to be the *only* vital spiritual aid that can be transmitted between man and wife, or between man and man for that matter.

I have progressed well with my decoration of "The Fisher." I am really enjoying it, at the same time I appreciate my own severe limitations as a mural painter. It is a grand field of work and I hope to make some progress in it.

353

Chadds Ford, Pennsylvania
October 13, 1911

Dear Mama,

Carolyn is on the floor (bare floor, now that our rugs are in town being made worthy of their admittance into the *new* house). Wednesday or Thursday we move in!!

Carolyn is feeling mighty well except that she tires easily from the excessive weight. In fact she looks better now than under normal conditions. The event of going into our own home, and as charming and ideal as it is, will do much to offset the anxious period. I shall take great care that Carol will not do anymore than is good for her, you can bet—although this will be a hard matter, under the circumstances.

The painters will finish today and heat goes on immediately.

The studio is being finished rapidly and [I] will soon be in there to put final work on my decorations. These are coming mighty well I think—am enjoying them mightily at any rate.

354

Their first son, Nathaniel Convers Wyeth, was born October 24, 1911.

Chadds Ford, Pennsylvania
October 27, 1911

Dear folks!

It startled me when I realized how long ago I wrote home—and during these stirring times at that! Even now you'll not get much satisfaction in the way of a letter, I'm so bewildered with the hundred and one things that have happened in the past two weeks.

From moving, to the present moment has been pack-jammed with incidents of no mean order, I can tell you—to enumerate them would make it all seem incredible!

Old Mr. Stork tarried just long enough to allow us into our new home—so here we are cozily nestled in our own palace. We are pretty well settled now; in fact we were before the baby came.

Carolyn busied herself right up to the last hour and enjoyed it mightily. The baby's entrance into the world was without incident, the birth being very normal, of short duration, and left absolutely no bad effects—easier, in fact, than ever before. We find upon verifying the nurses scales that *9 lbs.* is right.

And the birthdays! So *many* of them! The letters and the box! Such rich garnishments! I don't know when I appreciated birthday letters so much; each one so individual, so meaningful. Babe's wonder letter came first, in all its freshness and vivacity. I traveled with him through that hallowed country [Concord, Mass.] and am determined to do so in *fact,* the very first chance I get. The grip that Thoreau and his country has upon me grows in intensity—so strong is it, that under the greatest stress of excitement of any distraction, I can suddenly give myself up to his spirit that so breathes of Nature. Sometimes I feel like flying to Concord to stay—to die in that glorious atmosphere! But immediately I know I am better here in these mellow, beseeching hills. It is as though there was some mysterious and constant communication between this place and Concord—in other words, that through the beauties of Chadds Ford, the mysteries of Concord are translated to me.

Then Nat's very sad and plaintive note came to me. His letter was so full of that yearning for the things we know he loves (and we all love), glimpses into the past, of our boyhood life. It seems to me that my standard of attainment in living is to strive to match those matchless days at *home,* when we were *all* there.

I telegraphed Chapin of Scribner's—"*Treasure Island* brought an eight-pound boy."—His answer was "Heartiest congratulations" (signed) "Capt. Bill Bones, Silver, and Hawkins."

Grandmama's birthday (the 21st) did not go by forgotten. *Treasure Island* lies here on my desk, already inscribed, but in the packing, was placed out of sight and thus out of mind for the time being. I shall send it tomorrow.

Aunty Guss once more graces our household and of course has charge of the children. She is the one person with whom I could leave the children and feel as comfortable as though they were asleep. Hilda is here and is doing capitally running the house.

And, I've said not a word about this beautiful home. I am so eager for you all to see it! I can say no more. It is positively ideal in every way. We look down upon the valley from every window—and now that the valley is one veritable pot of gold, it takes one's breath to cast a glance upon it—particularly in the morning as the low sun gilds the hill tops and the white mists follow the winding river path.

The new house.

355

Home
Chadds Ford, Pennsylvania
November 7, 1911

Dear folks,

The little *tout* upstairs is a corker! There was a time (but now it is past) that I wondered just what N. C. stood for. I was inclined to believe (until Oct. 24th) it meant *Never Could.*

Well, as you say, Mama, "October" is our eventful month, and I don't know but what that name would make a good title for our Homestead.

356

Miss Mary Glancy, referred to at the end of this letter was N. C. Wyeth's teacher at the Harris School in Needham.

Chadds Ford, Pennsylvania
November 14, 1911

Dear folks,

Well, I've been about all in this week. The news of Mr. Pyle's death came as an awful blow—far greater in fact than one could ever have made me believe. The sudden telephone call from the Associated Press almost stunned me, but as suddenly brought me face-to-face with the man in all his power, goodness and glory, shorn entirely of the many petty matters which I had held against him. This calamity has awakened a profoundly deep sense of gratitude within me which will be an everlasting stimulant—to really make myself worthy of his years of friendship and guidance. He is gone, there is nothing more to say—all concern now rests with us who came under his masterly influence, to carry on the honest impulses he awakened within us—to perpetuate his *beginning!* So, I speak about myself, my hopes and ambitions with a full knowledge that I am simply an instrument, fated to have learned from him the first steps, and left to approach as near as possible the *unattainable* in art.

With all my candid opposition to much of his theory in relation to an artist's development, I rest quite satisfied in the belief that I have come nearer to carrying out his underlying principles than he himself believed. I may go so far as to say that he practically said so the last time I saw him—a week before he left for Europe. Therefore, you, Mama, who may feel somewhat regretful of certain criticisms of mine, must remember that I was in reality following the path he had planned out for me the two years I was in his class, and that my opposition and criticism came only when he himself began to depart from his earlier golden thoughts.

If I can ever achieve any triumphs, my past behavior (referred to above) will be fully justified, and I will feel that any other course would have been either very weak on my part, or no more or less than sentimental hypocrisy! I was too entirely convinced by his earlier teaching to be misled by his later beliefs, which rested on nothing more than his own discontent and restlessness. His gradual decline, which gained terribly in impetus the past two years, exemplifies exactly what I feared in my own mind, and makes me cling more faithfully and reverently than ever to the grand and noble Howard Pyle of 1903–1906.

The cause of his decline—mentally first, then physically, I can see very clearly, in *generalities*. Were I not afraid it would bore you, I would attempt it here in writing. If sometime you care to listen, I believe it will be possible for me to make it clear.

I do not wish to dwell on his downfall, however.—His downfall was only temporary—he has risen to glorious heights and ever to remain there in the annals of art and education!

We experienced a gale the other night (Sunday) that kindly removed several roofs in the village and a number of trees, but our little domicile stood the blast without a quiver.

N. C. Wyeth's studio.

The studio is still being built, but ten days will surely complete it.

Treasure Island continues to excite my friends to write me enthusiastic letters. It has sold phenomenally.

Received a perfectly corking letter from Miss Glancy yesterday and have passed it on to the young energetic teacher in the little schoolhouse down the hill. Miss Glancy's ideas and beliefs exactly coincide with mine (or vice versa), and I will, to the best of my ability (against terrific odds in this community), try to adapt and carry them out.

Miss McKay is delighted that someone (meaning myself) appears to have interest, as no one has even called on her since her installment. As soon as I *seep* myself into the hearts of the other directors in the township I'll endeavor to act. But it's a long, crooked lane to follow. I doubt if a like community of schools and management exists on this continent. Worse than nothing. No discipline (teachers not to blame, but absolutely no cooperation on the part of the parents)—and considerable vice.

Miss Glancy's assertion that one's views undergo a radical adjustment as soon as one sends, or anticipates sending, *their own* children to school, is a bullseye! I am having that experience.

357

Chadds Ford, Pennsylvania
December 18, 1911. Monday

Dear folks,

Christmas! I don't believe it! Where even now it is possible for Henriette to wander through our lower field and pick dandelions— short-stemmed maybe, but dandelions just the same, quite large and yellow. And only last Sunday did I point out a large blue-black butterfly lazying his way through the soft air—as indifferent and blasé as you please. Oh! Yes—we are thinking of putting in some peas!

But tonight the sky looks wintery, sure enough; a fresh north wind which smells of snow has continued throughout the day. And now, although the wind has ceased, the sky is thickly stuffed with pregnant clouds, all looking as though their cheeks were puffed, ready to belch down some kind of a storm—let us hope for a white one.

The glowing logs are singing and purring softly like a simmering teakettle; the flames have died down but the great fireplace breathes out a fragrant warmth, so cozy and comfortable. It is all very quiet in the house. The one lamp upon my desk casts a dim light across the low broad room—the rafters are touched with the soft light and lifted out in delicate relief. The big clock adds the final touch with its slow rhythmic tick.

How I look forward to our life in this snug and compact little home—its utter simplicity, its beauty and quaintness of form and its perfect freedom from the yoke of pretension.

There is one deep-felt regret that goes with all this blessedness— (perhaps in a Xmas letter I shouldn't talk of regrets). It has all been won too easily. I regret that my own hands could not have placed the bricks and fashioned the roof. Whenever I hear of a man who built his own house, from the foundation stones to the chimney and fireplace, I can't resist the thought that he has attained one of the supreme gratifications of life.

There was something cold and unnatural in "signing a contract," then to sit by and watch the carloads of material come in (from where I knew not). Bricks, lumber and hardware. Squads of men sweating themselves out in the hot sun, plying their separate tasks like pieces of machinery—perfunctorily digging holes, building the walls, laying the roof like so many dummy engines. Instead of feeling myself an integral part of the proceedings, I was an outsider, almost an intruder, standing aside, my pocket bulging with a wad ready to pay when the work was done.

358

Studio
Chadds Ford, Pennsylvania
January 1, 1912

Dear Stimson,

A miracle happened Tuesday night—and Nat blew in! As all miracles hailing from New England do, it vanished as suddenly as it came.

The wind is rushing about the corners of this palace of windows, like so much water—like a freshet. It is soft and warm too—like spring. The sun is cheerily shining, made infinitely more sparkling and dancing by the myriads of transient pools spotted over the entire countryside, hills and dales. These pools look so clear and inviting, shallow and fresh—it is as though nature were preserving certain samples of her handiwork under glass for inspection. Every miniature pond is a crystal-lined cup; its saucerlike bottom is so smoothly coated with translucent ice. This morning I went toward Sugar Loaf —it was like meeting so many friends or, I should say, *relatives,* after a period of separation. The trees seemed alive and peculiarly alert to this near-spring day. They seemed to tiptoe awaiting the whispered word to *bend,* to break forth in dainty splendors. How sad I felt that they were doomed to disappointment; that many days of frantic waving of arms and branches, many nights of bitter cold and blackness, and weeks of snow and burdening ice would pit their strength against them. But after all—it is the struggle that makes the springtime dearer and sweeter.

Never have I been so keyed up, so *famished* for spring—! This does not bespeak the healthiest of attitudes. I *love* the winter in its most (so called) *dastardly* forms—the foggy, stiffling, mucky days, when the brooks teem with yellow water and slush, and the whole earth seems coated with a soft dirty veneering of slime, I am in my element! I seem saturated with the very elements of this globe of ours. I seem to be identified with it—an integral part. But—just now, the external worries, the interruptions of home building and the general upset atmosphere in the house, makes these pleasures of communion exasperatingly brief. At times I am quite disconsolate over everything.

However *practical* we might want to be, however, we must make Elemental Nature our basis of inspiration. Without this as a starting point, our aims and actions must needs be extremely limited in result.

I think of a hundred things a day that I would love to realize (on canvas). The process of mind, after grasping the purely *elemental* motif, quickly reduces it in rapid succession to a practical theme. (This process, however, is unconscious.) I can usually tell, yes, *always* tell whether or not it came from the right source. If a *failure,* the motif was born of external thoughts. If a success, it came of an inner perception, from basic thoughts born from close identification with Nature.

I am sure all this applies to every mind of creative tendencies.

I have very lately developed a craving to execute a series of pictures depicting "Pickerel-Fishing Through the Ice." My mind has brimmed with our experiences as boys on Cushing's Cove, Onion's Meadow and the Stone Bridge. I am now wondering if this makes any appeal to your pen, and if you'd like to rough out a true and intimate story of that marked phase of our winter life at home.

Tell me, how do you feel toward this particular phase of development. You have the feeling, profound and magnificent—and it will be a pity to see you pass it by. The total result of an artistic development, in *vital channels,* is of far more value to the world and vastly more embracing, than the most arduous and intense ethical career. Don't mistake this last meaning however; perhaps I haven't expressed myself well: the highest form of ethics is to exemplify them in your own life and to make notes thereof. To do this however results in true artistic development which is (artlessness). Thus it is that the man too intent on spreading good doctrine amongst his contemporaries is missing his greatest achievement in life, the development of *himself.* There is no worry lest people about him are unaware of his sterling qualities, his good influences.—Just keep a record of your thoughts, put them into presentable form, that they will be communicable.—That is all. Time will do the rest.

Personally, I'm getting stomach-sick of all this harangue we are hearing on ethical problems. "It is strange that men are so anxious to get fame as teachers—rather than knowledge as learners." (You can guess twice who said that.)

359

Chadds Ford, Pennsylvania
January 9, 1912

Dear Papa,

Last evening Henriette was repeating some of her nursery rhymes for the entertainment of a couple of visitors (sedate visitors at that), when she astonished us all with her powers of deduction—as follows:

> Goosy, goosy gander,
> Where will I wander,
> Upstairs and downstairs,
> In my ladies (great hesitation here) *water closet!*

Carol and I both shot questioning glances at each other and blamed one another for the moment, for teaching her such shocking variations of the good and pure old verse. I perceived in a moment, however, that she could not remember the word *chamber,* so substituted what to her was the true meaning of the word "chamber" as she knew it.

The incident is not wholly desirable for the opening paragraphs of a letter, but in spite of it all, it was comical—but furthermore, it shows how her little mind reaches out for *meanings,* and not satisfied with mere parrotlike memorizing of sounds. I am struck every day with the unusual quality of her mind—or (rather than exalt her beyond good taste), I should say, I am struck with her reflective powers, her logical attitude toward all she sees or hears. She lives in a world of imagination and when once started with Sis Carolyn playing with their toy dishes, she will lead the game of imaginary cooking and eating for nearly an hour at a time. Every untoward noise in the faucets, or subtle rumbling in the radiators, or the sudden cracking of an uneasy timber in the house, she immediately concocts a highly colored story about it, terrorizing poor Sis Carol with terrifying pictures of boogyboos or Brownies.

I do believe, though, that it is bringing out in Sis Carolyn that same phase. I am glad of this, for otherwise I believe Carolyn would be perfectly contented to sit before a plate of beans all day.

Last night the wind struck our northeast quarter full blast with the mercury 0/7, seven below zero. I walked to Sugar Loaf in the evening and came nearer to freezing certain protruding features of my face than ever before. When I got back, my face felt like a mask that I could take off and hang in the closet, perhaps. But Sugar Loaf was great!

360

Chadds Ford, Pennsylvania
January 22, 1912

My dear Ed,

Last week, by chance, I got in touch with a young landscape gardener. He is with one of the two important firms of Philadelphia.

I lost several trains, but caught hell when I arrived home a half a day late, owing to our prolonged discussion over the fascinating subject.

Although being a *modest* "argufier" (as you will testify—eh? no?)

"Blind Pew" from *Treasure Island*, 1911

I cannot help being convinced of certain points which I made, and have a sneaking idea that the opposition thought so too, however he differed on the surface. It seemed strange to him, no doubt, that I should invade his territory with assurance, and yet, when I explain, I am sure you will see the compatibility and justice of my presumption.

The arts of *Landscape Gardening* and *Mural Decoration* are closely akin, closer in fact than any other two arts you can mention. That is, the function of both is to beautify without intrusion, to elaborate without detraction from essentials. In decorative painting, to embellish the walls of a room without destroying the beauties of construction and the atmosphere of livableness—in gardening, to ornament without molesting the character of a place, or to destroy its naturalness and homelikeness.

Here we differed in the very beginning—it is my contention that the future development of landscape embellishment will abandon the traditional "Italian Garden." Its title bespeaks where it belongs and nowhere else. If a man demands a *toy* or a curio, very well, an Italian Garden, or an artificial geyser is permissible; but if he be a man of consummate taste, he will surround himself with those things which take their place naturally, which are indigenous, and which will add in *perfect harmony* their fuller and richer chord to the subtle orchestrations of the surrounding country.

Italian Gardens (I use this type as an example only) are soul-moving only in their own country (a fact recorded by *all* garden lovers who have seen them there). This is sufficient argument for anyone. Its characterizations are *not* copied from *any other* gardens; they were the result wholly of natural opportunities offered by that curiously formed part of the world.

Now *we* must evolve from the geographical peculiarities and characteristics of this country, decorative beauties compatible to them. A New England farm developed and elaborated must *remain* a *New England farm* to the end; a mountain hermitage must remain a child of the mountain, pregnant with the spirit of remoteness, a true offspring of the spot upon which it grew. (By the way, the *rustic,* in our usual understanding of the word, is to me absurd and always an *abortion* on the face of the earth) and so on—(I do not presuppose that you disagree with me; we have never discussed the subject so do not know whether we would come to blows or not).

Well, the other man's argument can be easily deduced by the reading of mine, so need not explain. His abhorrence of all that is modern and his worship of all that is tradition, irrespective of location, biased all his statements.

Further! Which is my concluding statement on the matter—(Rare wisdom this!):

To rightly handle a problem in landscape elaboration, one must become deeply acquainted with the grounds and surroundings before he can presume a remedy. This may mean months, or *years!* (I realize the idealism and utter impracticability of my statements, and yet it is in this direction one must strive.) One cannot influence another to a better mode of living or thinking until one has won the other's regard and confidence. So it is with Nature—one cannot learn her secrets and move her to greater beauties until real affection has been established and communion begun. Only then will Nature reveal her wants. No matter what training or vision a professional gardener may possess, it is utterly useless to *force* preconceptions upon her.

I am taking a particular interest in just this phase of the matter, and have concluded that I shall be very patient in the development of the gardening features of this little place. As the days pass, ideas slip into my mind, unperceived, just where such and such a feature will look well. The one step I have taken is the placing and laying of a flagstone flight of stairs. I merely followed the beaten path formed by the carpenters during their long summer's passing up and down the embankment between the house and the studio. Here, they had determined the line of least resistance, which has proven a most joyous and practical little flight of stairs winding its way between the trees and rocks.

All this corresponds perfectly to the features of mural decoration. We are both facing identical problems.

361

Chadds Ford, Pennsylvania
February 1, 1912

My dear brother,

I just came downstairs after telling Henriette some Brownie stories and coaxing her off into a sleep. She seems to be breathing quite comfortably and has no fever, but memories of that croupy bark at midnight last night are not pleasant. All this, of course, is in direct opposition to Christian Science—but when such disturbances come to those who are closest to you, certain profound truths come into one's mind (at least I feel them in my mind), that sickness is sickness and there is a *physical reason* for it, and all the minds in the world will not counteract a destructive germ that may have got a good start.

I am in perfect accord with Edison in his views on health and its protection. Science, to me, is becoming a factor, and will become in the end, a consummate religion, at once profound and highly practical. It is the perfect union of mental force and acquired knowledge. The Christian Scientists' idea that sickness is an *error* in thought is profoundly true; but to correct these errors we must use scientific remedies—the *big* point is, however, *not* to commit the *error!*

The old wind, Babe, is blowing harder and harder. The little glass fandangle which Mama sent on Christmas is jingling away at the northwest window; a slight draft is waving its red strip that plays the music. The tinkling sounds like the five bells on Grandpapa's old pung. What dreams it recalls!

This brings me to the matter of a letter I received from Miss Glancy last evening. She wrote a long letter, and amongst the many things she mentioned, the important message was regarding childhood days—that these were our happiest days in life, and how tragic that we would never, *never* experience them again. She also enclosed a poem to the same effect.

It is extremely sad to find people thinking thus! It shows a retrogression. Reminiscences are among the most poignant thoughts we have, most certainly—but should they be the happiest to the well-ordered life? I say *no!* If *"the nick of time"* is not the happiest moment, then a man is failing to do in life what he was put here for. I do not mean that the present moment is always the happiest moment, but there must be the tendency, yes, the *achievement,* of happier and happier moments. These moments may come in the midst of supreme struggle, or they may blossom in moments of utter relaxation. But they must come. What does it mean? Simply a bigger conception of the meaning of life and all its mysteries. So it is that all men of achievement in their most enlightened moments have said much this thought—Oh, to retain the *spirit of childhood* throughout one's life is the secret of steady advancement. Constable, the English master landscape painter, said in his last moments something like this: "The spirit of a child combined with the ability of a man is the greatest and most blessed of all endowments." So, to live, ever advancing, is to be wholly wrapped up in the blessedness of life at the moment, in the *nick of time.*

362

N. C. Wyeth made a trip to Utica, New York, to oversee the installation of his murals for the Hotel Utica.

Chadds Ford, Pennsylvania
February 22, 1912. Washington's birthday

Dear Papa,

Apropos of Washington's Birthday, I must tell you a little tale. An Englishman was entertaining an American friend at his London Club. Several club members were duly introduced and a sociable evening progressed. Suddenly, the English host (contemplating some fun at his American cousin's expense) said, "Why say, me boy, we've got a large picture of one of your presidents hung in our club here. Do you want to see it?" The American appeared pleased and followed the crowd downstairs. They led him into the toilet rooms and upon opening one of the water-closet doors, showed him the portrait of *Washington* hung there. The American beamed and said, "Gentlemen, you are wise, *unquestionably* wise—you have hung this portrait in the right place! If there's anything that will make an Englishman shit, it's a portrait of George Washington!"

Don't relate this to Aunt Hat!

Well, here I am; the Utica trip over, and I am decidedly glad, no mistake. I returned to find the children very much improved, which gave me great delight, of course. I left under stress of mind as baby brother had apparently added to his cold the morning I set sail—but I determined to go and have it over with.

My work up there is completed, although when all accessories are in place, I will go up there to take a final look. That will not be before spring, however. The decorations look better than I had hoped for, and I feel more or less gratified, of course.

I am returning to an immense accumulation of work before me

and hope to get it all out of the way by late spring. I have over $2000 worth of work to be completed before June first.

Reached Utica Monday night 9:30, got to work in an hour (all artificial light), worked all night Monday, Tuesday night until 1:30 without a break except for two meals. Day and night shifts were at work in the Hotel, so had electricians and decorators at hand all the time. In so doing I was able to return to the family Wed. afternoon.

Never knew such wind! Some fine barns were flattened in this township last night, besides windows being blown in galore. We stood the brunt of it, but our house is like a rock! Not a very cold wind thank goodness.

Well, I'm tired so will close. Thank Mama for letter and enclosed pamphlets. Give my best to Uncle Deny. I believe he and Washington chose the same date.

Chapter XIV

THE ILLUSTRATOR

"The occasion has helped me to understand and appreciate more clearly how fortunate I am to be able to illustrate."

Dear Mama,

Won't I be glad when I start to see my way out of the maze of work before me. I'm getting tired. The winter has been one grand rush, with little chance to enjoy that phase of nature I love so much.

Yes, I bought a *safe* horse, about eleven years old; looks ever so much as old Tom did, build and all. I bought him for $50. In fact, for $75 I got horse, harness, express wagon and Dayton covered carriage, besides two buckets, halter, etc. The poor old fellow was busted, and for cash I cleaned him out. I've got just what I wanted, and oh! how much I've enjoyed it all already.

You mentioned something in a letter about a pony. It's strange (unless Carol had already talked to you about it) that we are arranging to get one later in the spring. That's why I have contented myself with a farm plug to knock around with. I'm sure the pony and basket wagon will give Carol and the children *great* pleasure. With a few chickens my stock will be complete.

Our chestnut trees are bound to go! So say the tree experts. It makes me sick to think of it. I am wasting no time, however, and am arranging to plant maples, locusts, buttonwood, and so forth, as soon as the ground breaks.

364

Dear Mama,

All three children have had two sets of colds, both cases of which we believe to know the origin, now that we have learned from the medical world in general that most colds are caught from other people—that a small minority are contracted from exposure.

I cannot feel that the house is at fault, as we have been exceedingly

comfortable throughout this severe winter. From reports, I am inclined to believe that we got fully as severe a season as you did, if
not a little *more* trying, with our two cyclones which leveled four
barns (within two miles of us) and lifted several roofs. Actually
lifting Dill Hughy's immense barn off its foundations and setting it
three feet to one side—(a barn larger than on the Harvey place). It's
a curious sight.

Our little castle showed not a tremor, but Oh! the windows fairly
sagged! And yesterday, to add to the variety, we received a rain-
storm I will not soon forget. The Brandywine ran riot, and they tell
me that Ike Arment's cellar was the *one* in Chadds Ford in which
the furnace was not drowned out. The village this morning reminded me from our promontory here, of a lot of children's dirty
blocks floating in a pan of dishwater. I have not been to the village
today so do not know the exact state of affairs.

Our brook in the woods raged all night and reminded me so much
of that incessant noise of the waterfall we heard in Lowell, Vermont,
from our sleeping room. Remember?

A letter from Scribner's today eulogized a picture just received
from me. I worked hard on it and am gratified for practical reasons
that they made special mention of it. I also have on my easel the
cover design for *The Pike County Ballads* for Houghton Mifflin
Company, which stands for the most virile thing of the sort I ever
did—printing and all really have considerable quality and power. I
am doing my best to knock *Treasure Island* into a cocked hat, and
feel with this start that I have a fair chance to succeed.

My desk is choked with letters from everywhere—mostly flamboyant notes of praise for some work or other. Dorothy Canfield,
who wrote "The Artist" (the story I painted the old man and cows
for), writes from Tuscany that she thinks she has discovered the
master whom I must have studied, in the galleries there. She sees a
similar spirit in the *Masters* and my "adequate distances." If she only
knew that Sugar Loaf was the farthest I'd been (it is true I've been
quite a distance on that magic hilltop), I wonder what would be her
words.

Henriette, let me tell you, Mama, is *astounding* in her powers of
perception and her sense of logical reasoning, and you should see her
fight to help wipe the dishes, and brush up the floor, etc. She makes
a capital trailbreaker for husky little Carol, who is picking up won-

derfully in speech and understanding. Pencils and paper will keep them contented practically all the time. Henriette drew a picture of a Japanese lily bulb we have here, and it was fabulously well done!

Of course, she's an impulsive and strong-headed little imp, and it takes every resource and bit of discipline we've got to handle her. Carolyn is different: very sensitive, but very mischievous, nonetheless.

Playing in the brook.

The baby I am more enthusiastic over (as an infant) than I was with either of the other two. There's a certain pathos about the little kid that reaches me clear down.

I have decided myself unfit to take those pupils from Chicago (the number's growing too rapidly). Offers have recently come in to teach in N.Y., and also to undertake the establishment of a large school of illustration in Wilmington. All of which is by the point. The latter would degenerate into a veritable art *factory,* which would drive me to suicide.

How I yearn to find a sympathetic, resourceful friend. I am deadly tired of introspection, and can only care for philosophy which points out lucidly the true paths to follow. In writing, I have my worshiped friend *Thoreau.* Without him my life would be a half blank. But I need one in the flesh. I yearn for frank criticism—I *give* it, why shouldn't it be my lot to receive it?

I am busy, so must get to bed for the sake of the morrow. My card is joyously full of commissions:

> Mary Johnston's *Cease Firing*—4 pictures
> *Pike County Ballads*—8 large pictures, 30 small
> *Scribner's*—"Finnish Legends"—4 large pictures
> Civil War story for *Everybody's*—12 full pages
> Two Syrian stories for *Scribner's*—3 full pages
> Thomas Nelson Page—"Story of Christ"—2 full pages
> *Saturday Evening Post*—4 small pictures

Have done considerable landscape work this winter and have advanced.

365

Beside the brook
Chadds Ford, Pennsylvania
May 31, 1912

Dear Sid,

A thousand years ago I received a very kind letter from you, reporting, in one instance, the impression you received when you viewed certain *Treasure Island* illustrations. To be brief, I thoroughly agree with your comments, but do not consider you severe enough—in short, I am positively surfeited—I feel as though I never wanted to see or hear of the things again.

Well, very much has transpired since you and I last met. A retrospective glance dooms this thick pad under my pen (no! don't worry, the supper bell will be your merciful savior). Uppermost of course is the passing of Mr. Pyle. There is no need to relate my feelings when I heard of his death; we both must have been struck in very much the same way. In the same breath with this terrible news (from the Associates News, N.Y.) came the request for an interview over the long distance! Imagine my utter confusion!! I utterly refused to say a word but promised a half-column by the following morning.

Until 2:00 A.M. was spent writing and discarding until in utter discouragement, went to bed. Six in the morning I wrote a few lines which adequately expressed my sentiments, but which I knew did in no way satisfy the cravings of the press. (I mention all this as it bears somewhat on an attitude I have held to, throughout all this feverish and hasty scurrying to *write, talk* and *lecture* on Howard Pyle.)

The following, as near as I remember, is what was published:

> You ask me to say something concerning Mr. Pyle. I am at a loss. Words cannot express my deep grief or the sense of gratitude I feel toward this great friend and teacher. With the passing of Howard Pyle, the country has lost its greatest illustrator and art educator. To the world at large the loss will be keenly felt, but to the group of young men and women who for years were nourished and inspired by his teachings so profusely and generously given, his death is nothing short of a calamity.
>
> For years Mr. Pyle poured forth the richest of his thoughts for all those serious-minded who would listen, claiming only as his reward the deep pleasure and inspiration it gave him to help others. To have been reared and directed in the study and making of illustrations by his unfailing powers of tutorship was not only a glorious training in the profession, but one of staunch and healthful character building.
>
> He has left in all of us who were so fortunate as to come under his influence, an underlying and solemn desire to rise to the greatest heights of our capabilities, not only as artists but as *men!* What broader combination of teaching could there be!
>
> Throughout my life, I will reverence the spirit of his help, and endeavor to show my gratitude by rising above myself as a man—as an artist. In this I know I speak for all who were blest with his impartations.

Sid—this is *all* I feel competent to say at present—and yet it befell me to refuse several requests to speak and write. To mention, simply, one's grief is not for the lecture platform, and it is not within my powers or prestige to talk of his art and teaching with any authority.

Chase, nothing ever struck me in quite such a shocking manner as the news of Mr. Pyle's death. To this day, I am conscious of a sinking feeling inside whenever I chance to think of it. I do not for a *minute* claim to feel the loss any more keenly than many others, and, with others, I suffer an overpowering onrush of humility, and a religious desire to justify what that generous soul so graciously gave, and I am determined to do my utmost! Therefore, in comparison, the desire to write or talk for public consumption fades into obscurity.

Frankly speaking, I cannot believe that any of us are fit by experience or achievement to talk vitally or worthily on the man as a teacher or as an artist. Someday if my life grows rich enough I know that the impulse to express certain things will be irresistible.—I am sure it will be the case with many of us.

I am nearing the end of settling all payments due on my house, which has been an item of considerable burden; but how much more substantial I shall feel!

Here it is dark, Sid, and I intended getting it off in tonight's mail.

Supper bell hasn't rung and I must investigate—I'm hungry!

366

N. C. Wyeth was illustrating Cease Firing *by Mary Johnston.*

Chadds Ford, Pennsylvania
[*no date*] *1912*

My dear Miss Johnston,

I shipped to you on this morning's express, two canvases—the "Jackson" and "The Bloody Angle." I have directed them to Warm Springs.

Invariably I find myself hopelessly lost in a maze of meaningless "rough sketches," and rather than submit a misleading statement of an idea, turn to the *final* canvas, and then send that. And so in this case, you will receive the completed illustration.

Do not shudder that I have chosen "The Bloody Angle," for I believe there is the feeling of desperate struggle without cause for repulsion. Furthermore, a *design* was in order to be used as a poster and in this way I detected the opportunity to build up an effective mass. The great reduction requires that all details be reduced to marked simplicity.—They will regain their strength when reduced.

If the canvas is satisfactory, Houghton Mifflin are desirous of receiving it as soon as possible.

I also read in the *Atlantic* of your house-building. They neglected to record *my* achievements in that line!

Your kind invitation is one I am determined that we shall realize —sometime. I am very anxious to paint landscape there.

Sorry the boy is not on this card. I must complete the record sometime and send you his photo.

367

Chadds Ford, Pennsylvania
October 3, 1912. 8:00 A.M.

Dear Papa,

What weather! Those snappy mornings followed me from Needham (minus the frost, however). The fields are mellow, and here and there swampmaples are turning scarlet on their own hook, impatient of winter's scout and outrider to do the job. Corn is standing in shocks on every hand, and even now, if one will look sharply, one can detect some distant southern slope speckled with golden heaps—yes, husking has begun. Our own field is shining like old parchment, and the slightest breeze makes it rustle like satin. The old potato field has been pampered into a smooth brown table, and its tiny furrows are pregnant with wheat and broadcasted with timothy!

Day before yesterday, in scouting about for a new washwoman, our journey chanced to be near brother Faucett's of Dilworthtown. The bee-king you know. We gazed upon three tons of honey (extracted and put in ten-gallon cans) in one storeroom! It seemed incredible, yet there it was! In another room stood in tiers something over a ton of comb-honey. The odor was so delicious and languorous as to make one want to drop into an eternal sleep there. The latter form of honey—in the comb—interests me far more than in the extracted form, and yet the market demands most entirely the latter. Faucett claims this is his bumper year in 18 years experience. I cannot imagine a more fascinating vocation.

Yesterday was my only chance to see Christian Brinton (an art critic represented profusely in *Scribner's, Century, Harper's* and *The Studio*); perhaps you have noted his name. He too lives near Dilworthtown, about a mile the other side. He has just returned from Norway with most wonderful material and also many examples of their illustrated books which profoundly astonish me! We are years behind them in cleverness of illustration and decidedly so in process of reproduction. I was aroused to an intense point of enthusiasm and this morning feel peculiarly clumsy and unwieldy regarding my own talent.

Christian Brinton with his father.

Well, I cannot hope to express in words the pleasure of my home visit. Every moment was and is important. I could not have visited at a better time; it seemed that the moments chosen to be with you all were the *choicest* of the year! *Two* days, but stuffed with the spirit of a year.

Enclosed find the check for my *board!* Well, I wish I could send 50 times the amount every six months and see you constantly tending to your cow, chickens and garden.

368

N. C. Wyeth took his family back to Needham, Massachusetts, for the winter of 1913. The "tank house" he refers to in this letter was the vacant water tower connected with his grandfather Zirngiebel's greenhouses. Wyeth had made it into a studio.

Chadds Ford, Pennsylvania
October 15, 1912

Dear Mama,

For the past week my mind has in one respect resembled the aspect of the landscape around us. Here and there a bright red spot compelling interest, but on the whole a confused jumble, running from crimson to the dirtiest most dismal gray. The moments of peace, like the smooth shaded water on a river of restless ripples, come when my mind turns homeward—to the place where simplicity of living, thinking and doing is respected and protected.

There has been in my cosmos two factions warring ever since I can remember—as the years have passed, this struggle has grown. Until now I can hear nothing for the din they are making. The one faction is that of personal ambition and worldly gain—the other is the desire to live simply, serenely, morally, and to develop my talent to its highest state for its own sake.

The din of the conflict, as I say, is deafening, and I can hear nothing else for the noise; but I can surely detect that my better self is, at present, uppermost, for now and then the opposing faction subsides into low incoherent mutterings. At such times if I had but the courage and the consistent faith of all those I care for, with one plunge those mutterings could be choked into silence.

The children are all well and the baby is all but weaned.

And about the "Tank House" (an appropriate name, by the way, when I get in there)—I know what to expect in the way of estimates, it calmly. I know you are all doing just the right thing.

let me tell you, and if $200 had been the figure I would have taken

369

My dear Sid,

Wall read me your letter. I am responding to your effort to "start something." When you said, "Roosevelt for *me!*" I jumped clear out of my chair! That's a fact. I am deeply moved at your decision and congratulate you. I've gotten so much inspiration from him that my admiration has grown into affection.—I am not worshipping him like a fool, but have based my belief in him upon constant reading of his speeches and writings for years back, and feel that he represents, on the whole, the *kind* of leader we need. A letter from him not long ago, in answer to a very brief appreciation of my own, convinced me of his value to me. I am stirred to stronger manhood every time I read it!

I am coming up to New England for the winter and probably longer. Fixing up a studio at home now. All settled, and if nothing serious comes up we will all start in November to be there by Thanksgiving.

370

When the family went to New England, they left Mrs. Hanna Sanderson and her bachelor son, Christian, to live in their house.

My dear Mrs. Sanderson,

This unseasonable weather has put me all at sea. I know not whether we should pack and hie south to start our garden, or whether this is still early autumn and the long winter is still before us!

It has been a busier winter for me than ever, and I can see now where it will be difficult to clear up my work so that we can make the break for dear old "Chadds" the last of March.

The *Pike County Ballads* has brought me in endless commissions, but withal it proved to be a financial failure. The publishers are

Mrs. Hanna Sanderson.

kind enough to say that it went *over* the buying public's heads. However, whatever was the reason, I am not disappointed (it may be funny to hear) but am rather stimulated by the failure.

My mind's eye is forever looking over the valley which lies spread out before *you* and in spite of the glorious time I am having here in my own home, I yearn to see it again. Your last letter made me feel deeper than ever its significance and I doubt if I ever leave it again except on compulsion.

371

My dear Mrs. Sanderson,

We leave Monday evening on the through train for Philadelphia and will probably arrive in Chadds Ford on the 8:25 train in the morning.

We are *crazy* to return, and you will no doubt feel relieved to have us take the place off your conscientious mind.

372

Wyeth was illustrating Kidnapped *by Robert Louis Stevenson.*

Chadds Ford, Pennsylvania
March 29, 1913

Dear Sid,

In regards to your friend at the Normal Art school. It really seems unnecessary for me to repeat exactly what I know you are convinced is the right thing for her to do. It makes me very weary to see how students insist upon avoiding the *one thing* that will fundamentalize their work throughout their lives—that vital necessity of knowing how to draw. The designer (the most conventional designer) will be important in the profession only in proportion to his ability to draw. One's mental conceptions always exceed the power to express, so we are always limited by technical inability.

The last thing I can say is this: that there is no such thing as studying "decorative illustration." One must study the *truth,* and *not* the affectation of the truth. One's *individual treatment* of the truth can only evolve from knowledge gained from doing the thing as it is. To base one's study upon *another's* conception of "decorative illustration" is absolutely fatal (if one is serious and striving for individual development). If Miss Engle's drawing is weak, every other department of her work *must* be weak. Make your friend stick to drawing and she will bless you later, if not now.

Kidnapped coming well, considering!

373

Chadds Ford, Pennsylvania
April 7, 1913

My dear Mama,

It has been two weeks since we broke up our solid little settlement with you all, and as the time passes we look back more and more upon the past winter as precious months, to be cherished in the memory along with the most vital occasions of our lives.

Grandmother Wyeth in her garden with Henriette and Carolyn.

I recall almost every moment of my four months with you. Do you ever realize what unutterable tragedy it is to be always living in the past or anticipating the future, which inevitably signifies that the moment is tedious? How true this is in my work, or *any* work! How false it is to think to oneself: next year will be my valuable year, or next season I will paint the more interesting foliage of autumn, or next summer in my new environment I will improve!— when the value of the year forthcoming depends *mainly* upon how you are handling yourself at the *present moment* (or as Thoreau calls it, "the nick of time"). Can I drum this into my daily living I shall attain the best that is in me.

374

Chadds Ford, Pennsylvania
April 11, 1913

My dear Babe,

After I close this note to you, will pick up my book on Rembrandt and read it with less stress and pain than has been my experience of late.

The lesson of his life is powerful, and one is stirred to white-hot action one moment and then feels hopelessly incapable the next. His absorption in his work was nothing short of *glorious,* and amply justified all his failings, and almost convinces me that to throw oneself into work *requires* sacrifices unnumbered (sacrifices so-called by society and customs). I am also finding out that he based his art upon design (as the book terms it "chiaroscuro"); that he (Rembrandt) considered this phase of painting, if deeply felt, the key to painting. His feelings expressed in his own words about this matter coincide so with my own that I cannot but feel encouraged! Perhaps I seek flattery—whether or no, the instance is stimulating.

I worked until 1:30, and after lunch it closed in very gray and dark, so struck at another occupation. I rebuilt the worm fence in front of the house, making it smaller (less high) and moving it in places. The exercise was invigorating, and I enjoyed mightily handling the dry rails that still exuded the strong aroma of chestnut wood, although cut over a year ago. I shall dream of laying the *"worm" "rails," "poles"* and *"riders."*

About five o'clock Carol came out with several dishes (large shallow bowls) and the children and we went over into the woods,

422

dug and transplanted a full variety of blossoming spring flowers with plenty of buds. After arranging these in the dishes we carefully layed a beautiful carpet of fresh green moss about the stems. The miniature gardens are exquisite!

Violets
Spring beauties
Anemones (2 kinds)
Hypaticas (purple, lavender, and white)
Woods Buttercups
Blood Root
Quaker Ladies
Yellow Bells

Jenkins' working around the place adds serenity to the house. He's the most secure and comforting old character: always puffing his old pipe, intently interested in what he is doing, yet never so indifferent to other matters but what he can keep his eye on Sis Carol, untangle the pony from his rope or put up or take down the clothesline. It is fascinating to watch him set a sod or scratch around a shrub. He does it with that sort of rough kindness that I have learned to respect. You could never inveigle him into expressing himself regarding the beauty of a plant or flower, but you know by the way he attends to them that they are significant and appeal to him in some subtle way.

375

Chadds Ford, Pennsylvania
April 12, 1913

My dear people all,

The reason for my silence has been depression. I never can write, even the most commonplace statements, when depressed. But now I am emerging from the worst period of the "blues" that was ever my experience, and I am mighty grateful for the relief. Never in my life have I suffered such a total eclipse of optimism, and would have willingly swapped places with the sickest man alive. All week I was on the verge of flying *homeward*. I seemed to be eating my heart out just for a sight of all that grew so dear to me during the past five months. How often my mind followed the complete inventory of all that transpired, how vividly the faces and figures of every one of that happy family in those dear old surroundings came before

423

my eyes. Even with the children and Carol about me, I pictured them *there* with *you,* in a glorified state!

The week has been cold, detestably clear, and windy. The flowers withered and blew away, and the new grass turned a tarnished yellow. Robins and meadow larks whisked across the skies helter-skelter like flying leaves, and the trees shivered and withdrew their tender foliage. Such dreariness! and such loneliness!

The wind whooped and shrieked around the studio, and all the windows rattled noisily—the big north-light bellying in and out like a great sail—in and out, in and out, all day long with the same monotonous wheezing and squeaking, until almost frantic, I tried to brace it with a board. Yes, the wind blew a gale for four days, cold and penetrating, and as I would return to the house now and then, the bare, windswept yard and long slope to the valley looked bleak and lonesome, accentuated by an occasional glimpse of old Jenkins as he would dodge out of one barn door and into another, holding onto himself all over as though he would be rent asunder!

Then I caught a miserable cold. My nose got sore and red and my brain became heavy and unwieldy so that I sat and sulked like an old fool.

I was ripe for just such a "spell." Every night for the past three weeks I have been "soaking up" Rembrandt, word by word. The great story of his life has affected me tremendously. It has stirred up my profoundest realization how deficient I am in general characteristics and habits necessary to drive my capabilities to the limit. His life story inspires this shuddering thought—unless one drives himself to the limit of his powers, what use is there of doing *anything?* One is always aware, privately, of the true extent of his accomplishments, and must either immediately repair defects with a genuine remedy, or resort to subterfuge—the deception of worldly flattery with its material compensations.

I am fully conscious of the tendency of mine to listen to sweet applause, but must candidly admit that the temptation is a powerful one and constitutes one of the greatest struggles that confront an artist.

But I must stop talking—and *act!* My resolves would make you smile.

I have completed a cover for Heines and today got a promising start for a *Kidnapped* picture. This, with a letter from Utica, N.Y., have lifted me somewhat out of the mire of discouragement. This letter referred to advises me that C. W. Cameron of the N.Y. City Board of Education was impressed by my decorations in the Hotel Utica and intends to correspond with me concerning some mural work for the Washington Irving High School. I am eager to hear from him and already have a scheme to offer him—Irving's classic *Rip Van Winkle.*

This is, as yet, all in the air, but I hope to be able to state something more definite in my next letter.

Two portraits of myself (from a looking glass) comprise some rattling good study.

Now, with my own most important and recent history thus related and dispensed with, I will descend to other matters!

The children!! I have not appreciated them of late and am in no way worthy of reporting the inside story of their virile little lives. It has all been going on, *volumes* of it, but my eyes have been shut and my ears heedless. I do know, however, that they are at the zenith of blooming health and must surpass the mark and decline on the other side, as one mounts a hill and down again. Such exuberance of health and spirit one never saw!

If possible, Baby Brother exceeds them all at his age for alertness and enthusiasm. He seems even now, older than the rest, and so serious and responsible. He will leave them in the midst of play, indicating that his little mind has taken a definite turn, and will march stolidly to his new interest—no amount of calling or coaxing can divert him once his mind is set. His Napoleonic frown at a reprimand is almost sinister, but never a tear.

I write as though years had transpired—since you last saw him. Well, years *have,* in a sense, for his walking put him into a new era (to himself and us). It raised his social position, so to speak, and he is no longer an infant.

Sis Carol is as broad as she is long and her cheeks are like moons! She pounds through the days like a war-horse and seems never to weary. The moment before she closes her eyes is the liveliest of all! Her little burly figure pushing an old doll-coach retrieved from the dump, or dragging by the one leg a disemboweled rag doll, is a common sight between here and the brook.

Henriette is hard and tight all over: powerful and lithe as a tiger and just as graceful. Her manifold interests keep one in a constant

N. C. Wyeth, self-portrait, 1913.

state of surprise. To see her whisk into the big room from the wind, all aglow, pick up a book or magazine and immediately concentrate is superb! Or resort to the Victrola (the records of Joe Jefferson in *Rip Van Winkle* are her favorites now—they are truly inspiring), hold her head almost *in* the machine, watching as she fancies, the dwarfs of the Catskills slinking 'round in the dark depths of the machine. She keeps our numerous bowls and dishes abundantly supplied with flowers.

The other evening as Carol was putting Henriette in her bed, mention was made that the rag doll in her arms was the one An't Mama made. After reflecting at some length she remarked significantly—"I told you I didn't want to come home so soon!" It is easy to trace the train of her thought during those moments.

Sis Carol hilariously commented today on Baby Brother's new sandals as being "like An't Ma wears!"

So it goes, a thousand events fully worth reporting going on daily.

Our garden is ready for the seed and tomorrow Jenkins drops the potatoes. Mr. Stackhous was planting corn today in our lower east field. Our wheat is superb and the timothy has started well amongst it. Bought 10 qts. clover seed and will broadcast it the first thing in the morning when there is no wind.

I dream incessantly of Papa at home. I feel a happiness about it so acute as to almost make me cry sometimes.

376

Esther Bockius, a younger sister of Carolyn's, often made long visits to help with the children.

High Run Meadow
Chadds Ford, Pennsylvania
April 18, 1913. About 2:30 P.M.

Dear Mama,

What might have been a tedious day at home (with the plaster all torn down in the kitchen and the stove and water service disconnected) is proving to be one of the cherriest in this dear old valley back of "Sugar Loaf."

As I write (I am sitting in the auto, which stands facing the great sweep of the meadow), the two children and Esther are playing in

427

the brook—at present feeding crumbs to the "minnies." A little in front and to my right stands the swamp maple and our fireplace—the very ones used by that memorable party when Nat and Gladys were with us. Yes, *today* I found remnants of corncobs, those we ate from years ago (3 or 4). We have not boiled corn in this valley since, so I am sure of the identity of the cobs. You and Babe were with us too! What a glorious day that was! Who would have thought at the time it would become memorable?

Just back of me at my right, slung under two tender-leaved beeches, is the hammock. In it, Baby Brother fast asleep; alongside on a carriage robe, Carol asleep too, with Hawthorne's *Scarlet Letter* half-open in her hand.

Not an hour ago we were feasting on broiled steak, roasted potatoes and broiled Bermuda onion slices—bread, milk, and crackers. Then, a cigar, and an hour with Thoreau!

The prospect from my comfortable seat here in the machine is all that one could desire—*more* in fact than one can properly appreciate.

The valley ends on either hand with a long, low sweep of hill, the tops of a distant wood feathering off the view into a soft sky. From end to end "Heifer Run" twists and turns, glimmering every foot of the way to the southwest (against the sun) and flowing with a perceptible quiver and deep blue color from out of the northeast end of our valley. At the base of the great hills that lift from the opposite side of the flat, the gray line of worm fence wriggles its way, emulating the brook and disappearing with it into distant woods.

There is something deeply satisfying to be thus sitting here, with the sound of the brook in my ears and the staccato calls of the children as they frisk about. The light blue of Carolyn's rompers and the warm yellow of Henriette's dress flashing in the sun, and in both cases the tarnished luster of their blowing hair. It make me realize more deeply the significance of life and the perpetuation of life, and makes me grateful that these children of mine are being brought up on the right kind of stuff: natural surroundings, lots of sun and air!

It was *great* to hear the exclamation of joy when I suggested spending the day beside Heifer Run. Just the enthusiasm that one would hear if a *circus* were in prospect. They thoroughly enjoy it and I hope they always will.

Poor Sis Carol's spirit must be lifted to *great* heights, for she has grown oblivious to the accompaniment of an extra-heavy load in the rear, which she was very careful to deposit just as we got here. Although she runs with some indication of an impediment she is nevertheless the liveliest of the group. She has fallen in the brook only thrice.

[Letter continued]

Tuesday morning, 6:30 A.M.

(Baby Brother is still asleep, but in his own little crib upstairs.) As I reread the last paragraph I laughed at the poor kid's (Carolyn's) predicament myself, and Carol awoke from her slumbers and asked me what I was laughing at. Thence she too came into the machine and there we talked for an hour or more.—Yes, until the sun was getting low and we heard the distant 5:10 train winding its way up river from the "junction." (I can hear the distant whistle of the "7:07" coming down-river this minute.) We got busy immediately to make the children their supper (the rest of us were not hungry, although finally I could not resist making some pancakes).

We pulled out of the pleasure valley just as the coolness of evening was settling over the low ground and the hill shadows were bathing the brook trees and fenced in a great watery shadow. Out across the open field onto Sheatz's Lane, we coasted content and comforted clear to the "road to the village." We arrived home to find the kitchen done and the water service in order. A quick fire, hot water, the children bathed and abed, we were ready to turn in ourselves—and not a yip was heard from 8:30 until 6:00 this morning when Baby Brother pulled himself upright in his bed and called, as is his custom, "Hello! Hello! Hello!" He has dropped back to sleep again, however.

377

Chadds Ford, Pennsylvania
May 4, 1913. 9:00 P.M.

Dear Mama,

How much this night recalls those mysterious evenings four years ago when Halley's Comet blazed in the sky. A few moments ago as I stood on the front grass plot in my bare feet and felt the cool freshness of the damp grass, my thoughts suddenly reverted to the night that I routed you and Papa out of bed in the old house and we all made our way, very gingerly, over the gravel walk, to the west slope to look at the celestial traveler.

Every condition seemed singularly recollective of that memorable evening—the same soft, impenetrable blackness of that spring night, with a strong, pervading sense of growing things coming to you through the dark, and the sound of frogs from the river. The whole recollection seemed to jump at me, and for an instant I felt it all such a reality that I looked into the sky expecting to see the comet there. Then reverting to fact, my mind flew to all the details of that spring you and Papa were with us, and I came in the house feeling rather blue. Recalling all such glorious events that have passed in our lives makes me feel sad—the way beautiful music makes me feel.

And how that comet did impress me! I acquired a deep friendship for it in the brief time it was within sight. Night after night the sight of it did not fail to send an inspiriting thrill through my body. It hung, faint and still, in that western sky like a signal or an omen— perchance a *good* omen. I felt *infinitesimal* in the world, and yet in all its gigantic and terrible mystery the fast-fading ball inspired me, and helped me to do better.

I feel a sort of yearning and regret that I shall not see it again.

378

This letter to Stimson Wyeth on the eve of his graduation from Harvard University shows how involved N. C. Wyeth became with the characters he was portraying on canvas in his studio. At this time, he was deep in his illustrations for Robert Louis Stevenson's Kidnapped.

Chadds Ford, Pennsylvania
May 26, 1913. Monday night

My dear Babe,

I cannot resist a few words, on this the eve of your last day in college routine. Clear your brow, for this will *not* be an advisory note, although God knows, you *need* it—but also He knows that I am in no countenance to give it, and never was for that matter. How many hundreds of times have I transgressed!! You can bear witness!

The Class Day invitation and Mama's letter announcing Tuesday as your last regular college day started an undercurrent of thought which has consistently followed me in my work like a haunting accompaniment, subdued, and then swelling in volume until itself forms the theme; then it loses again in the mists and spray on my Isle of Earraid, and the form and features of yourself come and go as David Balfour stands there wet and disconsolate.

There has been a certain feeling in this, my conception of David, coincident with your position today. Not that you are disconsolate, or in any such dilemma as my hero; but, as the story unfolds to us, he was in truth standing upon the threshold of a long, arduous fight for life—a life, as it proved to be, worth living. I can follow David's struggle over the Highlands as a symbol of your own.

I can see your experience with the covetous old guide on the Island of Mull and the following encounter with the blind beggar with the brace of pistols in his pockets. Then you are a witness to the murder of Roy Cambell of Glenure, then the subsequent flight in the heather and your varied life with Alan Breck.

I hope you may meet with an "Alan Breck"—that marvelously courageous man whose frugal praise and stinging but vital criticism meant so much to David. When he admitted to the boy, after some very worthy action on the latter's part—"You show some rudiments of sense"—the boy was inspirited. I hope you meet such a man. But even *Alan* took advantage of his friend and gambled the boy's last money away while he lay delirious with a fever. And afterward David was big-hearted and strong enough to rise up and forgive Alan Breck, and they fought on together to the glorious end!

These thoughts, so clumsily expressed, have played through my brain since the receipt of Mama's letter, as I said. I am sorry not to give you a better account.

Your present transition from one form of development into another, its significance to those at Home, and the speculation on your future, all impresses me. As always, I wish you the best of everything with enough of the adverse experience mixed in to make you understand and appreciate more than ever, the privileges of your training and good inheritances.

Meantime, on comes a birthday! We all send congratulations!

P.S. I have written to the Commonwealth Trust Co. to find out what spoils are left. Then I'll see you through C.F. [Chadds Ford] and back.

The WYETHS

379

Chadds Ford, Pennsylvania
May 30, 1913

Dear Babe,

Whenever I finish housecleaning my desk, I feel like the man who is lost in the wilderness and tramping all day suddenly discovering himself at the point where he started. And so, for diversion, to shake off that feeling of "wandering without avail," I'll drop you a line or two.

Today comes as one particularly significant of peace and rest after a few hours (or *years,* was it?) of brand-new sensations yesterday.

It was "varnishing day" at the Academy [Pennsylvania Academy of Fine Arts]—a traditional term adapted, I believe, from the old custom in European galleries, to allow the *exhibitors* to view their works lining the walls, and to retouch or varnish out points that may need it. At one time, I believe, this was considered quite an event, but not now in these days of *clamor* and *rush,* when the *soul* of the artist is forgotten, and *subtleties* take a "back seat," in place of which is commercialism and ambition, to strike the clarion sound rather than the low throbbing sound of hidden mysteries. However, I must frankly state, if immodestly, that I was keyed to the highest pitch of eager anticipation: first, to see my own pictures on the wall, and secondly, to see what *others* had to say. I am confident that my eagerness to see *my own* was not the eagerness of one *ambitious* (this feeling I am inwardly proud of), but rather to study it from a fresh viewpoint and to note its carrying powers (technical and poetic) amid all the conflicting surroundings. As I said, my anticipation was intense.

I went into the galleries wildly anxious to discover my canvases. I swept through the entire building without a discovery.—I grew feverishly anxious that by some mistake they were left out, or that I had been misinformed! Finally, I calmed myself enough to sensibly resort to a catalogue (which had not occurred to me before), and in it I found my name with only one canvas credited to me. For the instant I felt a keen disappointment, but with calm thinking threw it off and went to the gallery where it was hung. The poor thing was stuck on the top row (*skied* is the term) and looked as weak and flat as a pancake. It is needless to say that I was disappointed—in *myself*. The course of my mind at this juncture I cannot possibly put into words—a confusion of blasted hopes, disappointment, *encouragement* and determination may perhaps suggest slightly how I felt. However, I soon calmed myself.

After reasonable consideration of "the first-born" I proceeded through the exhibition, which I enjoyed fully—(a salient proof of my equanimity).

(Of course I can't honestly say that my mind is entirely free of "personal ambition"—it is *in* me, only I believe I have that tendency in subjugation. You know, *Emerson* even writes somewhere that he dared not trust himself with Fielding because he—Emerson—was not pure enough to interpret his writings.)

This lengthy "treatise," this introspective analysis may make you ask, "What's it all about?" Well, to speak frankly, *I don't know.* I of course realize that the experience marks an important moment in my life—superficially that it is my first attempt to exhibit, as a *painter,* and then in the deepest sense, the impressions made upon me will in some way affect my work hereafter.

As to *this* day of peace and rest, I can speak more simply and to the point. I feel that a certain contentment has come over me, a feeling that another *hunk* of that weakness in my character has been laid aside for good—to *show* what I can do. (If I ever exhibit again, in a public exhibition, it will be because something I have is peculiarly adaptive or that "bread and butter" bids me do it.) Furthermore, in placing even this plaintive weak whisper in the company of 300 other expressions, my eyes seemed to become suddenly *cleansed,* as it were, so that now I come back filled with a clearer vision of my *purpose* in art (not of my art and manner of expression understand, but a clarified understanding that I am placed here in this world to interpret what *I* see, *for* myself, and *not* for that public that *demands certain things*).

The occasion has helped me to understand and appreciate more clearly how fortunate I am to be able to illustrate; in other words, to have a *practical* streak, that I can go through life, giving necessary comfort to those dependent upon me and to develop myself under normal conditions, which, made proper use of, should give me health and longevity, incidentally, *red* blood and *a* clear brain.

I can feel no evil pressure at present, and I bid fair to live decently and with some simplicity, for which I am deeply grateful.

Oh! how I like to talk about myself! And yet, why isn't it perfectly right to do so? Outside the burden it places upon the recipient of such letters, I believe it a proper and healthful action (providing it is not morbid and too self-condemnatory).

Your enthusiastic note gave us all the deepest kind of pleasure. I don't know how to tell you what it means to us to have you come down. Thursday stands out, a glowing symbol. I was immensely surprised when I read your note, for I fully expected (having read in Ed's letter something about exams being over with last week) that you would *"renege."* Happy Days!!

To add to our pleasure (I am confident it *will* be an addition) get your ticket to *Wilmington,* and if it is storming *hard* (a drizzle or snow flurry won't matter) get off at Broad St. and come the usual way; otherwise I'll meet you in the Wilmington R.R. station and I'll have a horse and buggy (from "Stackhous"). We'll have a good hot breakfast at Hanna's and drive out to the old Ford—what? This scheme may involve a few extra pennies, or a dollar maybe, but as I'm footing the bills, do as I *command!*

By carrying out this scheme, I leave here about 5:30 in the morning in order to be in Wil. on time. If by any chance you see real reason to countermand my orders, do so by wire (collect) sometime before Wednesday noon.

Should matters insist your coming direct to C.F. by train, watch your time schedule (if your train is late), and by getting off at *West* Philadelphia you may head off the Chadds Ford train, which leaves Philadelphia I think about 7:10.

380

The "large express box" contained several completed illustrations for Kidnapped.

William Engle, an admiring young artist, came to live in Chadds Ford to be close to N. C. Wyeth.

Chadds Ford, Pennsylvania
June 8, 1913. Tuesday night

Dear folks!

Let me see, in my last letter I was anticipating the New York

Trip. A fine trip it was: business, duty, and pleasure.

I reached Chapin's office just as the large express box sent from here the day before was being unloaded before their doors.

The exhibition that followed brought nothing but sincere praise and approval. Of course I felt very comfortable, and somewhat surprised. The things looked bad here, the last thing. Although the squad of half a dozen editors said everything pleasant that could be said, I felt insecure about the real value of the pictures until the morning after. I went down to the engraver's office (where the pictures were in the meantime sent) and I really felt encouraged. They looked virile and *progressive* (which is all I care for at present).

That's all I want! To keep flexible! To be always on the move, *morally, mentally,* no matter what the immediate consequences might be. *Ruts,* habits, customs, good or bad, are *all* bad! To move always until the end—and move then if possible. That is my slogan.

The process of growth I worship! Growth in its maturity is a tragedy.

I know how infinitesimal I am and always will be, but to feel the irresistible march of progress within, that is heaven—all the heaven I ever want.

A dinner at the "Dutch Treat Club" the first day in New York brought me in touch with most of my contemporaries in illustration. It was a dismal meal. Jolly? Oh! yes!!—but dismal in results. One's face must be kept in a continual state of grimace to respond with appreciation to the incessant flow of "canned humor"—which I *abhor!* You watched the face of James Montgomery Flagg as he flung some sally at John Wolcott Adams and heard the retort; you knew just what his packed-in-paraffin answer was to be. And so on for two hours—with not one word in *edgewise* about the profession. One could believe them all to be clerks or bookkeepers. How I would liked to have really *talked* with some of them.

I reached home 7:45. Carol met me with "Major" and the road-cart. It was a beautiful evening and the little home glowed in the fading light, and I loved it better than ever.

The Friday following we all spent a memorable day. About eleven o'clock we ate a light lunch and then piled into the machine and followed the Brandywine twenty miles up to Downingtown. The meadows and hills all the way were one better than the other,

435

and every village seemed older and more fascinating than the one before it. After this long jaunt we returned to Brinton's Bridge (just above here), stopping at Sinclair's on the way, and bought two quarts of ice cream. This we surrounded and demolished under the huge trees at Brinton's dam. Afterwards the children went in bathing and I fished.

At sundown we returned. The children browner and happier than ever!

Sunday blew in cold as March, and exceedingly clear. We drove over for Engle who was attending a reunion at Westtown. We spent a bully day in his company. He stayed overnight. Monday (that was yesterday) was colder than the day before, and so windy! This morning I started, and almost finished, my most impressive *Kidnapped* illustration! This evening we all went up to Brinton's Bridge again for wild strawberries. Tomorrow we will have wild strawberry shortcake. (Do you remember that wild raspberry shortcake in Vermont, at that farmhouse where was held that church sociable, Mama?) The best I ever tasted. Carol says she can beat it no matter how good it was!

381

Dear Papa,

The curtain has dropped on one spectacle and another is making ready, if I can judge by the ever-growing volume of rumbles and grumbles to be heard just west of us. We have witnessed this past hour one of the most spectacular electrical storms that I ever remember, after one of the hottest days I ever remember. The day opened clear and hot—that is, the sky was clear but a suggestive milky haze clung about the distant hills, veil-like. The sultry heat was stupefying and seemed to press down upon one and made it an effort to breathe if one stopped to think. About eleven o'clock, however, the whole sky became a moving pageant of cumulus clouds majestically moving in and out, weaving incessant patterns. They seemed to move so slowly, but even as one gazed, a cloud would transform itself from a solid rounded head of white into a diaphanous veil, emerging suddenly into delicate skeins threaded against the hazy vault of the heavens. It made one reel to look long into one place, the movement was so interchangeable and rapid.

From then on distant battles in the air passed us on all sides, and we would say, "That must be over Wilmington," or "They're getting that one in West Chester," or "Kennett." Meanwhile we *sweltered,* praying for a shower, not only to cool the air but to partly quench the hard dusty fields which were beginning to look like those in November. The corn was withering and the potatoes scorching. Cows pasturing in the upper fields left little wakes of dust as they walked searching vainly for a green patch.

John Weller was posing for me under my skylight of glass! He represented "Cluny Macpherson" playing cards with "Alan Breck." In his intensity he leaned far over the table, and would you believe it, Weller must lay a wad of cloth on the table directly in line with his chin to catch and soak up the sweat. He dripped, dripped all day like a leaky spigot. But he posed!—posed like a rock—and I put in as satisfying a day as I would boast of. I stripped to the waist, and my belt, that thick leather one, is black and wet, and is now strung over the stove like a drenched sock.

Once I came down to the house for a pail of water, and here I found Carol looking like a wax image encrusted with jewels—a million beads of sweat standing out over all visible portions of her skin. But she seemed happy and had a dozen things a-cooking on the stove. Steak on top and chicken in the oven—"cause they wouldn't keep," she said, "in this dreadful weather." Esther was also a walking jewelry shop, and the children out under the trees as happy as larks; but I noticed that all their little faces were redder than usual and that their foreheads glistened in the light. I asked Henriette if she was cool, she answered "NO! I'm soakin' hot!" Mighty expressive, I think.

The afternoon wore away without change or interruption, except once, Jenkins stuck his head in the studio door and asked if it was any cooler up here than down t' the barn. I fired the pallet at him and Weller cussed; then Jenkins descended the stone steps, shimmering and dancing in the sun-glare like a mirage.

Five o'clock came. Weller moved slowly toward the station and I changed my clothes (fourth change) and read awhile. The children ate cold milk and bread and cornstarch pudding, and then we all piled into the machine and went for the mail. The sky looked threatening, and before we were pointed homeward, sharp, nervous gusts of wind were driving clouds of dust up all roads. We hustled home in a whirl.

At the gate I got out and picked 45 ears of "Golden Bantam" sweet corn and six cucumbers, and tested the cantelope, but they weren't ripe, and in a jiffy we were in the house slamming down windows, pulling in porch paraphernalia, husking corn, and a dozen other things.

It got black, black as a pocket in the western sky, and the speckled village stuck out midst the livid green foliage like scattered bits of highly colored papers—red, yellow, white, green and orange.

Meanwhile the corn was boiling!

Suddenly Henriette said, "It's raining on Sugar Loaf!" Sure enough, that grand old hill, flattened in a sheet of driving rain, and groups of trees, as the storm approached, suddenly became gray, faint—and then *gone!* We watched, when suddenly about a dozen bolts struck in quick succession, it seemed, and with these the swish and seething of sheets of water against the windows. The house shook, and it sounded as though the Battle of Waterloo were being enacted all on our little roof. The trees within twenty yards were barely visible and they leaned way over, straightening their backs only once in awhile. Now and then a branch wrenched from their hold would slam onto our front lawn or porch. Gray streaks of leaves sped by the windows, and the water sucked in between the sashes.

The storm was terrifying, but as an example to the children, we sat down in our seagoing kitchen and ate 45 ears of Golden Bantam! The din and racket added zest to our ravenous appetites, and the sweet little ears vanished from the great dish in the middle like frightened birds.

After the storm, the air seemed as bracing as in autumn. I went out in the golden light of the after-glow and was attracted by the great booming noise of our brook in the woods. I went over through the long grass and tall weeds and flowers, getting well wet, but proud of it! In the dim light the brook looked enormous (as it really was comparatively) gushing its way through that dark little grove. It was too beautiful to see alone, so I helloed for Carol, and she soon joined me.

We stood below the first falls and watched in the dusk and over that turgid, foaming flood, the lightning, which I judged was then playing havoc over the city of Wilmington!

How's that for an impression of Tuesday?—*Hot* Tuesday, July 29, 1913!

There's a rain check in this letter with your name on it, Papa.

382

The end of this letter refers to the fact that "Babe" was about to leave for a teaching position in Kentucky.

The illustrator whom N. C. Wyeth knew from the Howard Pyle School days is Philip Goodwin.

Chadds Ford, Pennsylvania
September 1, 1913

Dear folks,

Labor Day afternoon. The day of Marblehead fishing excursions— the last day of grace before the depression of school days—the last fling, before imprisonment and the smell of blackboards, slates, cedar

pencils and musty books. Every year, the day takes on this significance. I even sadden under its influence.

My last group of *Kidnapped* created considerable enthusiasm, and
if I am to judge by the demonstration, were better liked than the
earlier ones. I am pleased, for it proved my power to sustain interest
and enthusiasm, and perhaps to create an even stronger impetus for
the last sprint! I am gratified that I "wound up strong."

Thursday morning Chapin and I spent making final corrections
in titles, subtitles to the illustrations, and other minor details. We
went to lunch at the Players' Club and thence to the engraving house
to spend three intense hours over the plates and proofs.

At 4:30 I left the city for Mamaroneck to spend the night with
[Herman] Wall. Did not find him at home so looked up John Cecil
Clay, a successful illustrator in the sentimental department of the
art, also a sketch portraitist of considerable note. He is now an in-
valid in a distressing condition. I found my way to his very remote
farmhouse tucked away in a big Connecticut woods. Pitchy dark
and met in the middle of a field by his watchdog. The house was
shuttered, and only one gleam of light from an upper window encouraged me to press on.

A woman (his nurse) let me in and after some hesitation on her
part led me upstairs.

It was a hot, stifling and sticky night and the low, dim rooms were
almost suffocating, and the rancid smell of oil lamps was almost unbearable.

His room seemed dimmer even than the rest of the house, and I
was deeply impressed by his long deathlike figure lying across the
bed, half-propped by a wad of pillows, his gaunt face shaded from
the lamp by a water pitcher.

We talked for two hours. I saw how hungry he was for a chat
with one of his own profession. His low, hesitating voice teemed
with enthusiasm as he expressed his ideas in art, but faltered perceptibly when that inevitable subject of conversation, the *conduct of
life,* which is after all the vital question in art as in anything else,
came to be discussed.

His tale was sad; in fact it was near to torture to listen to the end
of what was practically his confession to me. He probably felt my
genuine sympathy and I imagined as I left that he had relieved his
mind of a great burden. He appeared cheerier.

Briefly, he had debauched his youth (a handsome, manly looking fellow he was) and now he is paying the penalty. His father, Col. Clay, was in the Department of Justice at Washington for 35 years— a great hunter and intimate friend of Roosevelt's.

The nurse left us alone and I took charge of his medicine. To lift that almost weightless body, to hold the large cup of rather warm water to his palsied mouth, to watch him as he centered every ounce of muscular strength to swallow a pill was enough to make me want to fly from the room.

I shall write to him, but he will probably not live long enough for me to see him again.

I made my way back to Wall's home. I had left my hat, as a card, and they expected me. They are comfortably fixed, but to my mind in an *impossible* locality. Their baby has grown into a perfectly healthy and handsome child. One of the few babies that measure up to what I admire in a child.

Wall is very busy and they all seem happy.

Goodwin was within striking distance so I called on him early in the morning. He is the same old Goodwin that I knew twelve years ago. Even his work stands exactly at the same point of development.

The day before Chapin invited me in to meet Roosevelt. He was to come in on business at eleven o'clock. You can surmise my enthusiasm and excitement. When I arrived, Scribner's had my *Kidnapped* pictures hung on the wall and proofs of them spread on the table for R— to see.

Well he's *big!* It was *I* that got the reception, not he! That shows his caliber.

He bustled in, all sails set! Face aglow and teeth shining! He seemed to come half-trotting, on his toes, moving in and out among the office desks and chairs like something on tracks. His approach was, in a way, awe-inspiring, as though some magnetic influence preceded him as he walked, and made actual contact before he spoke.

Chapin had at sometime or other told him of Dunn's and my escapade in Washington during his Inaugural so his greeting was apropos: "I am *dee*lighted to at last meet the *only* and *original* cowpuncher!" His teeth clicked and a grin that almost rent his face asunder flashed throughout his bronzed features. Electric energy seemed to radiate from his whole body. Every look and gesture was fearfully concentrated, each having some very good reason for their being.

We talked some. He enthused over my "Alan Breck" and asked, as he flashed a glance at my cover design, "Where are Breck's side arms?" I pleaded that the picture was consistent with R.L.S.—that Breck had none on his flight across the heather.

"He *should* have had and *would* have had, and you should have strengthened R.L.S. with the correction!" Bing! *Bang!*

And that's the way the hour went, and no wonder I was fagged when the most wonderful of all men I have ever met stomped out of the office.

I dreamed of T.R. that night and again last night.

Well, now I'm ready for the coming month and a half when the three Bible pictures for *Harper's* and three or four pictures for Xmas *Scribner's* and one for *Century* are due. I'm fit as a fiddle and will enjoy the work. I never had so many friends comment on my healthy condition, color, etc. Even T.R. ventured to say that I spoke well for the Blood of New England.

Well, I must close. I have intended dropping a line to Babe, but have not gotten to it. However, he knows how much our thoughts are with him and how they will go with him to Kentucky.

Chapter XV

DEAR BABE

"Not a day, I can almost say not an hour,
*has passed, but what flashes of thoughts con-
nected with you and your work have come
into my mind."*

Chadds Ford, Pennsylvania
September 12, 1913

Dear folks,

Babe's departure had its effect on both of you to such a degree that your letters fairly throbbed with supreme sentiment.

Simultaneously with Babe's departure, the children, Henriette and Carolyn, started in at school! Mrs. Betts, the doctor's wife, decided some time ago to start a class of very young children—sort of a kindergarten—using the *Montessori* system which she is keenly enthusiastic over. So are we. The children go down to her house at 9:00 and remain until 11:30.

You are probably familiar with the Montessori idea—the awakening development of the senses. It is undoubtedly a great thing. Henriette rather astonished Mrs. Betts, however, by going through the entire apparatus of some sixty pieces, deftly and easily, doing the various problems of matching color, fitting various complicated geometric shapes into their slots, tying bows, lacing, and buttoning with ease, and then sitting down and drawing a house "where colored people live."

With no intention of boasting, the child has always shown an unusual power of perception and observation, and I am not surprised at her ability.

Baby Brother is picking up finely, and should be in the full glory of health when we come up next month. Carolyn, contrary to Papa's impression received from the photos, has squared up the most. She is *solid* and strong now, where before I had always felt a certain softness, almost flabbiness. Her sense of humor is remarkable and is showing singular development in certain departments of understanding. Her almost frantic concern, when a storm is coming, is that everyone is under cover, even the cat. Henriette sometimes plagues her and threatens to run out in the rain, and to see little Carol cling to her with a grapple hold 'round Henriette's waist is pathetic.

Our upper potatoes are dug and are super-fine. Not many, but all a good size and smooth. We got about 17 bushels against 22 last year. Below, the potatoes are rougher and don't run so even. Will send potatoes the last thing before we leave unless you would like them earlier.

384

Studio
Chadds Ford, Pennsylvania
September 19, 1913

My dear Mama,

This is an indoor day for the children—though not actually raining, it is soggy and wet with a heavy mist left from a steady downpour during the night.

An indoor day means *noise,* and lots of it, so instead of doing my writing at my desk, I have sought a place where calls and howls, knocks and bangs will not reach me—although even at this distance suggestive rumblings are coming up the hill. Henriette is attending the little class at Dr. Betts, but Carolyn's shyness, or rather, her determination not to be left alone without Carol or Esther, has eliminated her from the class, for the time being at least. In short, the *"big noise"* is at home. She's an enthusiast, anarchist, pugilist—and angel all in one! Baby Brother follows her like a shadow and, like the shadow, emulates every move of the original—his noise, however, is like a distant echo. He's a wonderful little spirit, well poised in spite of his great sensitiveness, and astonishingly alert to every sound and movement about him.

We are coming in the machine as I said, and will leave here, roughly, about Oct. 15, maybe before, depending upon the progress of a picture I am to do for *Century* the first part of Oct.

385

Home
Needham, Massachusetts
October 17, 1913. Friday morning

My dear Babe,

After an unusually splendid trip we arrived here last Monday afternoon in perfect weather, and just to suit *me* the night shut in black and threatening with a raw northeast wind sighing through the big spruces and rattling the windows in the spare room. And ever since, until an hour ago, a steady driving rain has constantly drummed against the east windows—a sound that revives the past to me even more than muttering wind. Everyone was saying "narsty weather," and I would nod a bare assent to sidestep an explanation of my true feelings. It could not have happened better. It fitted exactly into the scheme of things as I loved them.

To sit by this window, in the parlor, and to look through the slant of rain toward Grandpapa's, dreaming of the thousand dear events that have passed, and suddenly, to catch the stooping figure of Uncle Denys, abstractly plodding his way along the soaked path, fires my imagination into fact until my emotions are beyond control. This window has been my shrine these wet days. How well I know how you appreciate it!

I have been so anxious to take advantage of these beloved, inspiring days, that, even after two days of crowded emotional experiences, Carol and I drove our way in a persistent downpour to Concord yesterday. The trip adds one more notch to my record of red-letter days, and as we watched the trembling water of Walden through the streaming sky, a sense of remoteness passed over me that placed me beside that dear old prophet. For moments the present was utterly forgotten, and I could see that homely figure in his faded sack coat and brown cap, winding his way in and out the oaks and pine trees, stopping now and then to pick up a leaf or stick, buttoning his collar a little closer perhaps and peering out across the white water.

The spell of Walden prevailed, it set the minor key for the experiences that followed.

The hour and a half spent in Louisa Alcott's house has made its indelible impression on both our minds. Carol is completely carried away by the experience. We were both in fit mental condition to be responsive, as her life, letters and diary have been quite the important topic at the Ford for two months (a book which I place with the best things I ever read).

The house, although bare of furniture, carries out the spirit of varied experiences which that immortal family went through, to a remarkable degree. It is cut up into so many little quaint low-ceilinged rooms, and winding stairways. As I told the folks last night, one could easily imagine the sound of music downstairs, and could see that big-souled mother by the window, sewing; or perhaps could hear the soft sobbing of "May" or "Jo" in one of those dim rooms, and out through the small-paned windows, catch sight of the sensitive figure of Bronson Alcott coming up the walk. And all the time, in perfect harmony with our thoughts, like the haunting, rhythmic, accompaniment of a symphony, the rain dripped and dripped, now and then seething against a window.

Today it is clearing, and one of the grandest, most beseeching overtures to a month at home is done. We have been lifted to the summit of appreciation, and how I anticipate the coming pageant of glorious days ahead!

386

On this trip back to Needham, Mrs. Wyeth's two younger sisters, Hilda and Esther Bockius, went along to help out. Ida and Innez Frost, from Nova Scotia, helped in the Needham household on and off for years.

Cora Livingston was a family friend who painted dainty pictures and gave Wyeth his very first lesson in drawing.

Toward the end of the letter, Edwin Wyeth's fiancée is mentioned, Clara Moeller.

Home
Needham, Massachusetts
November 5, 1913

My dear Babe,

The ring of genuineness and conviction in your letter received today goes far beyond the homeside stage. I very deeply sympathize with you so cannot resist a few lines. It is late, very late, but your letter has stirred me, so here goes.

Personally, I anticipated this dissatisfaction, and would prophesy it for any serious-minded and sensitive person venturing outside of these nine or ten states up in this corner of the country. Mediocrity is damned evident everywhere, but here at least one finds an occasional oasis. I am sure that if I had not enjoyed the tremendous outdoor attractions during my Western experiences, and had not previously made up my mind to seek and revel in its very crudities,

I would have turned away with a hearty dislike for that end of our country. As it was, my slight contact with the citizens of Denver almost crimped my enthusiasm. However, I was more comfortably located than you are for I did anticipate an outlet. With all, I am positive that your present sufferings are more apt to leave a mark of real growth and advancement on your character than my experiences did on mine.

Your letters are, in themselves, full justification of your present circumstances. Your comments and conclusions are being brought to the surface plainly, and well spoken. And I feel most confidently that just such harassing experiences as you are passing through now are of utmost value to your point of view. In your more reposeful moments you should thank God that you were made *capable* of discrimination, and be grateful for the pain it gives you. It is just such misery that drives a strong man upward, and the weak man down—down into discouragement or pessimism. God help the man who finds himself in comfortable, smug surroundings, where he has but to turn his head to meet satisfaction on every side! To a healthy mind, friction is the mother of achievement.

One cannot lose sight of the blighting handicap you are laboring under, and to feel sad that the boys are losing a great deal that you might give them under favorable conditions; but there remains this inevitable feature—that you are gaining firsthand knowledge of certain conditions that will probably form the nucleus of valuable action later on in your life. A study of the growth of almost any life of real achievement reveals this phase of the struggle. That is why it takes health and backbone to survive it all—to come up serenely out of the muck and mire, still believing in the ultimate virtue of mankind. I cannot resist pointing to our living example, Roosevelt! To follow his course of public life: through the pettiness of minor politics; through the slime of police activities in New York City and the filth of graft and plunder as governor of his state; through the narrow, secretive offices under Cleveland, and then the forced obscurity as Vice-President; the assassination of McKinley and the following three stormy terms in the White House; and finally his plunge into Progressivism with the accompanying mauling and slander of the press. *Still* he bobs up as our most optimistic prophet! An ardent believer in the ultimate victory of the American people. When he fights he fights with passion, as every red-blooded man must; but he *always believes,* and for this quality alone I measure him as a great man!

Your letters constantly refer to the healthy glory of our common home, as well they should! And it strikes me that the rare fabric and texture of which it is made was created for nothing else than a superb background upon which to meet and solve the various problems of life.

One of the strongest features of our home and I believe the most unusual, as you no doubt highly appreciate by this time, is the power that Mama shows in bending and responding to the severe demands of our letters—those never-ending and fluctuating records of our ardent beliefs and impressions. This is a talent of the highest order, and requires infinitely more of intellectual balance and flexibility than we are apt to think or give credit for. I will never forget Noon Barker's remark to Mama after she had read one of my letters to him some years ago—"I do not call that a letter—it's an essay." One can easily see what the communications between him and his parents amounted to—simply a steady, unvaried stream of commonplace happenings, fearing always to venture into supposition or to trust in memories. This, to a great degree, is responsible for Noon's juiceless soul.

Well, I could go on indefinitely talking this way as you must, at times, sadly recall. Now I'll give you some idea of the four stimulating weeks that have just passed.

First off (as they say in Chadds Ford) let me assure you that Mama has lived on "easy street" since we have been here. With Hilda, Ida, Innez, and Esther, household duties and responsibilities have all but vanished, and have left Mama and Carol high and dry, and at the beck and call of all who care to entertain them. Today Ida and Co. leave for home, but Hilda, with Esther's aid, can swing everything—and twice as much if necessary!

The little dutiful Ford has done pleasant service for all, and hardly a day has passed, when I've been home, but someone has been whisked into Boston, uptown, Winchester or some such place. Mama has not used the trolley or train for a month, but Papa insisted now and then on returning to his old love—the Spring Street trolley route. I know now that he *enjoys* those jolting, stuffy cars with their inevitable loads of miserable inhabitants. It is probably a reaction and possibly a tonic which tends to lessen the gap between his life of a year ago and today. It is a constant joy to see him so content, which has been greatly heightened by the golden forecast in the sky toward Winchester.

After basking a few days in the contentment and peacefulness of home, I joined [Clifford] Ashley at Horse Neck, near Cuttyhunk, for a week's sketching. The experience was full and varied, and I feel fully repaid in everything but the results of my sketching. The magnitude of the terrific sou'easter' (which lasted one-half the time I was there), the general bigness and mercilessness of the country overawed me, and my work was as simpering and timid as Cora Livingston's.

Another week at home and then Carol and I left for Wilmington to attend the opening of the Pyle students' show. I was quickly winning the very unenviable title of *indifference,* so deemed it the psychological moment to forestall this precursory idea. The jury showed their indiscretion in bestowing first-prize money upon the indifferent one—but it helped out finely as Carol and I had to make several additions to our scant wardrobe.

The exhibition was only good.

Now we are on the homestretch of our stay here, which as far as the eye can reach seems to be studded with various pleasures, looming out of which Paderewski! We hear him tomorrow!

Sunday we drive to Segregansett with Clara and Ed, and I am planning a trip with Mama and Carol down to Cape Cod.

Meantime Heines demands a cover, and the old Tank House will nod its head once more in the wind, groaning and creaking under the terrible, *terrible* responsibility.

Christmas numbers of *Harper's* and *Scribner's* will reek with N.C.W.'s. Will send *Kidnapped* shortly.

387

The "Paxton" referred to in this letter is William Paxton, the Boston painter.

Chadds Ford, Pennsylvania
December 8, 1913. Temperature 68°

My dear Babe,

Your last letter home, or rather, the last letter I had the opportunity to read, made me feel so good! Your reference to occasions we have spent together make me glad—and proud, proud to be a part and of help in creating an inspiring atmosphere. Those hours in the "Tank House" will be forever hallowed.

Your resolve to change your surroundings seems complete, convincing, and wholly to be expected. You must know from past conversations that we have had, that it can be no surprise to me. Candidly I am pleased that your senses demanded the change.

No doubt there are two sides to this question as there are to any other, and it is nearly *easy* to convince oneself that "sticking it out," as Papa says, would be the most courageous and helpful course to pursue; but as Bill Engle adds, "It takes more courage to give up the proposition in your circumstances than to stick it out," and I agree with him. I am an ardent believer in *impulse*. Impulse is the heart and soul of real progress, and it behooves us to nourish that quality by giving it the encouragement of action. As you say, one can stifle one's impulses to the point where real desire is transformed into *mediocrity*—and God help us from that. I know no worse calamity!

The autumn visit home is over. It differed in character, in most respects, from the winter's visit of a year ago. In reality I feel that I have profited more in proportion to the length of time. I have returned in a more fighting mood and can sense that this coming year will mean much to me. The six weeks proved to be rather intense, both in pleasures and seriousness, and I have come away with many ideas firmly fixed in my mind.

The symphony, Paderewski, the flower show, the Harvard–Yale game, "The Blue Bird" by Maeterlinck, the Art Museum, and Paxton (in whom I firmly believe I've found an inspiring friend) made up a very full six weeks—also a visit to Segregansett, which I count as a big experience, and of course *Concord,* with Uncle Denys and the girls, Carol, Hilda, and Esther, never impressed me more! A dark lowering day: cold, penetrating and silent. Such spirit! To Louisa Alcott's, Sleepy Hollow, and to Walden at dusk, and around the sacred stone pile at dark!! Thoreau! My God!

Your absence from home, has changed the spirit of the household considerably, and I am glad for Mama that you are to return, and I hope you may locate where you can be in touch at least once a week. You are life itself to her and I am proud of you for it. She is one of the noblest women I ever expect to know. .

Dear Babe

One of the deepest experiences of my life is to find those of my own family, Carol, Hilda, Esther and the children, developing such love for her. She stands as a great light to them all and it makes me happy. I am really very much attached to the younger of the Bockius children and am deeply interested in their welfare. We have just taken little Nancy. She's a dandy, bright little kid, very responsive and the best kind of an associate for the children. It does not cost much extra to feed and clothe them, and I can't see them slamming around with no home. Hilda, I am so glad to say, is home with Mama again. The girl is dependent on her now for what she is to learn of the *right* ways of doing and thinking, for she got very little before, and I feel every confidence that she is the making of the kind of woman the world needs the most of—a faithful, energetic, and accomplished home-builder. In many ways she patterns after Carol, and I defy anyone to find a more remarkable type of mother and wife. In this respect no one can be better off than myself.

[Letter continued]

Monday morning, Temperature 20°!

Since I started this note I have had much and varied experience from "private views" of art exhibitions, down to the most depraved sights I ever expect to witness. In an opium den in Phila.! Such actions I never thought could exist! I shall say no more about it. It was an ordeal to go through—the sight of such things, but work for the publishers demanded it.

The wind is howling around the house, and the trees are swaying and tossing like mad. But it's great! I do not recall when I have so deeply appreciated this beloved country as during the past week. It is all so peaceful, so complete and remote. My only wish would be to have some members of the family at least located near me. I have dreams of it!

Well, Ed makes the jump on the twenty-fifth and I suppose you'll be there to help him out. I regret that I cannot attend too. It strikes me that their start is to be made in an ideal way. A dandy little house, all light and air, with Ed's wonderfully sympathetic work cut out for him right at hand. How often have I pictured you in that school too! Had you ever thought of it?

Well, I must get to work; it's 8:30.

[P.S.] *Kidnapped* seems to be well received in spite of bad printing —will see that you get one when I get my allotment.

453

The WYETHS

388

Edwin Wyeth, horticulturist, married Clara Moeller on Christmas Day, 1913.

Chadds Ford, Pennsylvania
December 23, 1913

Dear folks!

Christmas in April!! That's the way it seems. The rain is drumming on the house in a heavy downpour, and the lower fields are yellow with muddy pools! But we are hopeful, for the sky 'round the edges looks a tarnished yellow; and if one looks closely, one can see the clouds flying fast there—which means clear and cold in perhaps a few hours. Sixty hours is apt to make a great change, and it is very possible that the great fire in the living room will not crackle in vain Xmas morning.

The box arrived safely yesterday morning. Its weather-beaten boards added a charm that fit in finely with the dream that it had traveled from the remote corners of the universe, where "Old Chris" lives! At any rate, the children were carried away with the idea, and I believe they truly worship the very boards the box was made of.

The children happened to be with me when I got it at the station —and such enthusiasm you never saw. At length, after they had cooled off sufficiently and started to think of the box a little more materially (of its possible contents, I mean), Henriette sighed very complacently and remarked, "Well, there's no need to worry anymore anyway!" She was at last satisfied that Old Chris had not forgotten us.

I followed your directions (rather reluctantly, I must admit, for I did want to leave the mysterious chest sealed until Xmas) and opened the covers, at once removing the cake and wreath and quickly closing it tightly again.

In the wreath your letter, and under it the cake. But that letter! I have no words to tell you how much it means to me and how much deeper than you surmise I can feel just what pervaded your spirit in those dear woods which bore the laurel. I feel particularly blest, when I think that my life's work is built upon just such yearnings, longings, and spiritual communions, such as you experience so much; and to think that it is my most important business to nourish and protect those feelings. Those moments are intensely sad, but who would wish to lose them! Believe me when I say that more of your letter than you could possibly put on paper reached me—the thoughts of which will decorate every joy of my Xmas. Further, I have no words to say.

The right spirit of this Holiday is strong in this house and I am happy.

My strong hope is now, that you will get our box in time. As to its contents, they are all marked, I believe. There's one invisible object however, which perhaps is unnecessary for me to explain after all—the refuse paper wadded in the top of the box all means love and hearty good wishes from us all. You see there is a good deal of wadding—and a good deal of good thoughts!

It surely will be a memorable day in Needham, and I hope that all events will transpire with the true joy that should exist on a wedding day and Xmas!

A Merry Merry Xmas to all from everybody!

389

Chadds Ford, Pennsylvania
February 19, 1914

Dear Babe,

With a foot of snow on the ground and a pouring, steaming rain coming down, it is not hard to realize how dim the studio is and how difficult it would be to work. But there's a tranquility that affects me deeply, and I am moved to write you as I have intended doing for a long time.

I have waited, it seems years, for you to break the silence with a letter of some kind, until now I am well aware that it is deliberate on your part not to write at all, which plan I am asking you to explain.

I cannot conceive of such a sudden change in the relation between two people, who in the past have meant so much to each other (at least it is eminently so from my standpoint, and if not reciprocated I have been mercilessly misled). For one who is so keenly and so worthily responsive and sensitive to all associations of home as you are, and to realize, as you must, how *I* too worship the shrine of our home and depend so much upon it, it hardly lies within the meaning of generosity for you to cause me so much pain by your attitude.

It is a pain which I fear you do not understand, for if you did I think you would not sanction it. The reason for any disturbance based upon conflicting opinions or ideas is as vapid an excuse for personal antipathy as it is possible to find. On the contrary, the conflict of ideas should be the basis of deepest attachment. Passive relationship is most always scrupulously free from constructive inspiration—and equally free from deep feeling. To begrudge me your help on the grounds of contrasting opinion is pretty selfish, when you come to think of it.

When I look back over the past twelve years of my life and realize how anxious I have been to maintain a *constructive* relationship with those who are vitally attached to my life and feelings, and how every means within my power, spiritually and materially, has been used to sustain and nourish those relations, it seems strange that a break should come from where it hurts the worst. And all based upon minor differences of thinking!

You, who have been for four years in touch with acknowledged men of learning, who have talked to you enthusiastically and yes, pedantically, should be in finest mettle to parry any thoughts of mine that do not fit into your scheme of things, without becoming stupidly morose. You mistake my apparent cock-surety and enthusiasm for downright brow-beating, and you are emphatically wrong! Ask yourself, "How long could I stand Roosevelt as a near acquaintance?" and yet I have heard you *curse* the people who disagreed with him—on the same grounds that you object to me.

How I would like to hear from you, direct, some of the good criticisms you tell others. But coming, as they have, from the outside, I can but receive them with a taint of regret.

You cannot accuse me of saying to one of our family what I would not to another, and no doubt this diplomacy would have stood me well with Mama last fall; but her own startling franknesses inspired me to believe that at last I was exchanging ideas with one who could give and take.

I am very deliberately pleading with you to think it all over, generously. You stand as a pivotal point in my connection with *home*. You cannot fail to recall a hundred communions that we have experienced, which on account of our parallel understandings, have added greatly to our lives. This has not been my experience with Ed or Nat to any great extent (which is probably my fault and undeniably my misfortune). My relations with the father and mother are in an entirely different category and stand alone, beyond any possibility of disturbance.

I want you to understand this letter as the highest tribute I can think of to your value to me as a brother and real helper.

390

Studio
Chadds Ford, Pennsylvania
March 13, 1914. 3:30 P.M.

Dear Mama,

The snow stays with us, although heavy thaws occur the middle of each day. Just now the distant hills glisten like a mammoth confection, and dazzle the eyes. Sleigh bells are almost constantly sounding (as we used to call them years ago at home, *bakers' bells*), and when one listens, it is not hard to be carried away by the general romantic spirit of this beautiful country.

Just to *spite* a very nonproductive period, I went into Phila. Tuesday night and heard Josef Hofmann.

I sat beside a French musical professor during the recital, and toward the end, our mutual enthusiasm broke down the barriers and we sat and talked after the concert until an usher had to ask us to leave. I was particularly interested in his talk of Liszt, Rubinstein and Wagner, whom he knew personally, and for years he lived and studied in Weimer, Germany. All this I soaked into every pore of my skin, as I am to soon start on our interpretation of Liszt playing Wagner's scores while the latter is listening with the greatest intensity. This is to be hung in Steinway Hall, New York.

In all the excitement we did not ask for his name, so I do not know my valued friend. To know that he talked and smoked with dear old Liszt and Rubinstein is enough! He talked for all the world like Grandpapa, and I understood him perfectly. He said, finally, "Are you not a foreigner?" I said, "No—an American." He answered quickly, "Goot! I *congratulate* you!!" I looked at him (as is the habit of us down-trodden Americans) a little dubiously as if doubting his word. *"Oui, Oui, Oui,* I mean it, I *mean* it!" he continued somewhat exasperated. And I think he *did* mean it.

457

Chadds Ford, Pennsylvania
April 15, 1914

Dear Sid,

No doubt you will be shocked to hear from me. Well, *I'm* shocked at the attempt, for God knows I've nothing worth saying. How many times have I started letters—yes, *articles* too, by heaven! And after a few hours of effort have torn up the damn stuff, only too well realizing what an insane fool I am to talk about things and not *do, do, do!*

I got an awful jarring while in Boston last fall and it sent me back to Chadds Ford with the distress signals set—and so have they remained ever since. On top of this came various influences into my life, things that would take up too much of your time for me to explain; one of which, however (a lesser one, perhaps), the opening of the Academy show, which has further opened my unseeing mind.

I do not want to tire you with my thoughts, and furthermore it may give you a wrong impression for me to break out now after so long a period of silence.

But, anyway, here goes!

The modern painter, as represented at the Academy show in Phila., has *nothing* to say—in this respect he is a *farce!* But his technical powers are paramount, and just here is where *we,* you, I and all of the Pyle school fall down hopelessly. None of us knows the *semblance* of truth when it comes to recording an individual impression in drawing, color, and values; and moreover, we can readily be blamed for practically ignoring the importance of technique in all its branches. It is pitiful that the great awakening power of Howard Pyle was not substantiated by some appreciation of the meaning and *might* of the sheer *craft* of painting. Had it been so, the class would stand for something better than tolerable (and steadily weakening) magazine illustration.

I *know*, that with my intense love of life, my emotional sense of things about me and the power to sustain enthusiasm would have carried me well into the nobler realms of interpretation had I not *bitched* myself with the accursed *success* in *skin*-deep pictures and illustrations! I *know* this is so—and all the passive talk about being content with the really-noble-art-of-illustrations-if-you-are-doing-your-best, etc., etc., is emphatically wrong, when day in and day out I feel those insufferable pangs of yearning to express my own life as it is in this beautiful home and these hills.

It is so damned easy to sit down and play jack-straws with an author's work and fiddle and fuss out a picture by chance, good luck and receipts, and float it on the market. But when it comes to recording a heart-tearing, soul-moving phase of the dear life at your own table—when three beaming, healthy faces look over their porridge bowls, and the morning sun slants across the glittering dishes and white linen, Ah! one knows then that the *divine* brush must speak, the one that knows no tricks or receipts, the one that from sheer knowledge can profoundly grasp the truth of the scene with an *innocent* eye, *untainted,* undisturbed by the meddling property-man attitude of the dramatic or poetic *illustrator!*

Oh! Chase, what an abundance of life there is about me on these dear old hills! My eyes fill every day at some phase that almost asks out loud to be expressed. And I can't do it. I try and try, and I cannot! I seem to be fitted neither by training or professional habit to satisfy these Religious Cravings. I have wished many times that contentment in illustration were mine.

392

Studio
Chadds Ford, Pennsylvania
April 25, 1914

Dear Mama,

It's about two o'clock, and outside it's blowing an eastern storm. This morning I partly "laid-in" a fantastic picture for *Scribner's,* but do not feel capable of taking it up this afternoon to carry it on. It's dark and gloomy, and I feel kind of indifferent, for some reason or other, so will use a little time writing a letter or two.

The weeks are running along all spattered up with various interests—they *have* been all winter—but with no particular direction or progression. I have been thinking hard, but cannot boast of much good work. Carol has accomplished more than I have in every department, and in her *ideas of things* has reached some mighty sane and wholesome conclusions. I can feel underneath, however, that I am preparing for a decided step ahead in my profession, and all I need is that my power of concentration and the even more essential power of self-forgetfulness shall be brought back into play. These qualities have been taken from me for a longer period than ever before, but when I win them back this time it will be the last time I am caught napping.

The summer looks as though it would be a busy one, for with no end of commissions to select from, I shall spend considerable time outdoors; that is, sketching. I want, however, to retrench enough so that another year will find me in Europe. I wish to go there to see the country (particularly Switzerland and Germany) before my ardor ceases. The art too will have its great value, but not to such an extent as one might suppose. It is almost foolish, with the large number of great examples of the old masters which we have in this country, to simply go abroad to see others. To live there several years is a different matter.

I have had plans in my mind for years just under what conditions I would like to take this trip, and with whom. But I have had to decide to take it alone. This is a regret I may not be able to overcome. Carolyn is my first choice, of course. I could not imagine anything more to my pleasure; whereas a sound, vigorous man-companion in art would possibly wring more intrinsic value from such a trip. Neither Carol nor I could think of leaving the children without one or the other of us. My! When I think of those dear little kids, *Europe* has no significance whatever.

And let me say how much I am enjoying those children this spring. I can feel that my life will go over to them completely sometime and then I won't waste time trying to become a *bigger and bigger* artist. Sometimes these words strike me as being senseless after all.

Easter was truly children's day here. The day itself was glorious, sunny, warm, with just a tantalizing breeze blowing. The hidden eggs and fancy tokens (in the way of a little basket apiece with a "bunny" sitting in it) caused all kinds of excitement.

The package came from Ida. It touched me deeply, for it contained the little fork I used twenty-six or seven years ago. I remember it perfectly. A certain normality of shape and proportion of that fork and knife too always appealed to me. And I remember when Ed got his *silver* one, all embossed with scrolls and designs, I was still glad to have my wooden handled ones. What happened to the knife?

393

Chadds Ford, Pennsylvania
April, 1914

Dear Mama,

Look in *Harper's* May number, and in the frontispiece you will see a reminiscent setting. The table does not belong there, nor the dishes in the shelves; but the main feature—door and pantry no doubt you will recognize.

394

Studio
Chadds Ford, Pennsylvania
May 4, 1914

Dear Mama,

It is very hot and close, and one can almost hear the buds unfurling.

The day has been arduous, both here in the studio and down at the house, for Carol is completing her housecleaning. The children's calls have been in my ears all day, and I can hear baby brother's laugh and the splash of water as he throws stones into the brook.

Weller has *posed* until a few minutes ago.

The strain of work has never pushed quite so hard as these past weeks, owing to two commissions being suddenly *rushed* to suit customers.

With all the work, I feel happy. A letter from Babe cleared the air and I'm thankful!!

395

Studio
Chadds Ford, Pennsylvania
May 15, 1914

Dear Mama,

It's four o'clock and I'm about at the end of my string for the day, and quite a successful one has it been, too.

461

The WYETHS

Skipper "Roarin' Bill Higginson" is facing me, lashed to the wheel of his brig with a mountain of water rising behind him. It looks wet, is full of storm, and is otherwise quite the most compelling thing I have done in a long time.

This week has been colored by the arrival of the series of pictures I did in the Tank House studio, illustrating "War."

I say the event of the return of these pictures *"colored"* the week because they brought back so vividly the experiences of that wonderful winter we were with you.

I do not get near the pleasure out of the pictures themselves as I do from the memories they conjure up in my mind. Uncle Denys, about four in the afternoon, stealthily climbing the stairs, the slow lift of the trap door, and the gleam of that old straw-hat—and then the pleasant talks about things of the past. These pleasant conversations are dear memories now that rank with my choicest, and I shall forever feel richer that they happened.

And then the weekly visit of Papa's—the climb up the steep steps, which never seemed quite so significant and dangerous as when he would creak his cautious way to the summit! But it was always worth the risk. And then his pleased countenance, when I answered that I thought I was doing good work there in that little room, was encouragement of the most genuine sort.

I can see Babe's "desk" with the paper-shaded lamp, where for a brief few weeks he plied his night hours. I recall how often I would look, of an evening, through the thin spruces, to see if his light still burned; and once I walked over there in the moonlight and sat on the doorstep for a long time. My reflections there, while Babe labored by the lamp, burned themselves on my brain, and I warrant that I can recall every thought of that evening.

I have thought often of that swaying, creaking building, and wish so many times, that I could hear the Minuet or the Provençal Song in that little room again.

I am feeling particularly fit, and everyone, whenever I go anywhere, comments on my healthy appearance. I have always felt and looked well, as you know, but I have improved matters by a consistent stunt I've been doing of recent weeks—chopping wood. From five until six-thirty *every* morning, I have hied to the woods where several large trees lay prone on the ground, blown down by last fall's storm I have told you about. I have cut with an ax every bit,

462

which is *some job* when you consider the wood to be black oak, and the largest trunks averaging 20 inches.

I also have dropped to 228 which is 20 lbs. lighter than the winter we were with you. But I do eat and can't help it.

396

My dear Babe,

It's a long time since I've written to you, and I do so now hoping that we can forget the exchanges of last winter. The entire incident, it goes without saying, made me suffer very deeply. Perhaps I am the cause of it all; I do not know. However, I am going to ask you to patch up my deficiencies the best you can. We all stand in need of that charity at times.

I cannot bear the severance of our communications, as slight as they were. They meant too much to me. Not a day, I can almost say not an *hour*, has passed, but what flashes of thoughts connected with you and your work have come into my mind.

I have subjected myself to the severest discipline of restraint, and have done my best not to let the dribblings of an agitated mind come to the surface and molest others.

397

The whooping cough was believed to have been brought to the Wyeth children by Mrs. Wyeth's sister, Elizabeth Bockius Sargent.

"Cousin Caroline," Caroline Peart, a first cousin of Mrs. Wyeth's, was married for a short time to the art critic, Christian Brinton.

Chadds Ford, Pennsylvania
July 10, 1914

Dear Mama,

There's a congestion of facts, emotional experiences and surprises to relate, but I will only give you a bare outline of the week's progress.

The bronchitis sure enough turned to *whooping cough*. The three of them have it and I am authorized to say that in all probabilities the worst of it is reached and we can expect a gradual change for the better from now on.

It is now two weeks since Carolyn showed the first signs of what we thought then was a bronchial cold. We do not doubt but what Elizabeth brought it here, and we are very much concerned about her condition now, for her baby is only a few months old; but we hear nothing from them in Swampscott. Warn Hilda, for if she took it, and you or Papa contracted the cough, it might go hard with you (unless you have both had it, which I never heard you admit). Of course I've not had it but seem to have no fear of getting it.

For three days and nights Carol and I were up every minute. The paroxysms were fearful (at least they sounded and looked fearful to us), and it was hard on Carol particularly—it did not have so much effect on me. However, we couldn't have stood it much longer, so we got a trained nurse from the hospital in Wilmington and she will be here until we see a marked change for the better. She is a wonder with the children and they take to her as they do to you. With her resourcefulness and experience we feel almost happy. She thinks the children a remarkable group to manage in spite of their distress.

An instance of their good sense can be illustrated by an incident which I have witnessed several times, and which has stirred me deeply. When any of the children break into a fit of coughing, the nurse forces their arms straight in the air, which induces an intake of breath. During the day the youngsters are playing out of doors, as usual, and often are scattered here and there about the place. Little Baby Brother will start to cough and the nurse will call to him, "Hands Up!" and *up* they will go, and he will stand, his face almost purple, reeling with the violence of the cough but his hands in the air until relieved.

Now, they do not need to be told, and one can see their little arms shoot into the air before the cough is upon them—signals of distress showing above the tall grass and from behind the low bushes.

Enough about the whooping cough. The yellow quarantine tag on the kitchen door and lower gatepost looks queer to me. I am inclined to let the lower one remain all summer; it's more useful than "Beware of the Dog."

Last night Alan True and his sister Catherine arrived in Chadds Ford, stopped overnight at the Hotel, and spent this morning with us. I took them into Wilmington this noon where they boarded the train for Phila. and home. True has been working with [Frank] Brangwyn in London since early last winter. His sister joined him there this spring and they saw considerable of Europe and are just returning. Their few hours' stay was inspiring and particularly encouraging to me, as True claimed my development and ideas were in accord with the best men abroad. This, in the matter of the true junction of painting and other ideas too technical to explain here.

I might hint here that I can sense very strongly that I am on the threshold of the biggest gain yet, and will be deeply disappointed if the next year or two does not very materially strengthen my hold on the kind of art worth something to the world.

Last week a Madam Lans au Parenti? (I can pronounce the name but can't spell it) visited us. She teaches French at Columbia besides being efficient in all known tongues. Cousin Caroline brought her here for my edification and pleasure as she is well acquainted with Rodin, Zuloaga, Sargent and practically all the important painters abroad.

Her reputation (for languages) preceded her visit, and it did not look promising to me. Well, she came—one of those Sarah Bernhardt types, right out of the pages of a Parisian fashion book. Intellectual snobbishness smeared all over her face, fairly sputtering like water in hot fat, with all sorts of repartee, clothed in all languages, from defunct Hebrew to Bowery slobber. I listened, interrupting her at every foreign word to explain herself. (Impertinent maybe, but damned satisfying.) After twenty minutes of this, she turned her analytical searchlight on me and gave one of the most amazing pictures of the world I ought to live in. "Ho! You are not American. No! No! You should have lived during the revolutionary period in France! Ah! *Mirabeau!* Now we have it. You look like him. A New England accent with your head! Nonsense!! This charming *"petite* home! These sensitive children! This fascinating flagstone walk to your *atelier!* It's all perfectly astonishing and ridiculous!!"—and then a long, rippling divine Sarah laugh!

Then I gave her an awful *bump!* The word came freely and easily, and what I left of her ideas were only a few shreds. Poor Cousin Caroline stood aghast to think one so provincial, so *American* as I, should presume so much before Madame Lors au Poop te dee.

465

The rest of the afternoon was perfect, and the Madam and I got down to brass tacks (as Nat says) and had a talk worth publishing a *tract* about. I broke through the "stuff" she feeds Fifth Ave. high-brows, and she admitted it. She's a woman, I now believe, well worth knowing.

I have a dream of a trip to Milan and Venice this fall to see Segantini's collection and the great autumn show in the latter city. My French friend insists that I visit Rodin and she will arrange it. I cannot reconcile myself to presume upon his time and am loathe to take advantage of the chance—heaven knows how I would like to though!

But I am an *American!* and Madam Lors au Purente knows it now. I do not weep every time I see the stars and stripes—no I'm not that kind; but, my God, I was born here and nourished on this continent's soil, and no one can sob over my misfortune and get away with it!

The devil! I could go on forever.

398

Chadds Ford, Pennsylvania
July 17, 1914

Dear Mama,

Hot as hell!

On the way to the city to get some "Pripussin" [Pertussin], a wonderful discovery by a noted throat specialist here for whooping cough.

It may be that we will all go down to the shore for a week or two as soon as certain work is done. Just now it looks less possible as poor Mr. Jenkins is in a bad way. Urine poisoning threatens. I've been at him for a year to listen to what reputable doctors have told him, but he has stuck by the "quacks" and is in a sorry plight consequently. I feel it deeply as he is one of the family and one of the nicest, most honest and faithful men I ever knew.

Christian Brinton has done much for me this summer. He's a critic but he's all right.

399

Dear Mama,

The day's work is over. The wind moans and sighs under a heavy rolling sky, and it sounds tremendously like fall. Here we are, making arrangements for three weeks in a cottage at Beach Haven, and this wind distracts me with its message to "stay at home, roam around in its autumn kindness," and incidentally stock the cellar with wood and winter provisions. But I suppose another day will turn on the summer's scorching heat again, and we'll all be glad to be on the beach.

One can't help being influenced by the weather conditions, and Carol and I both feel this strongly today.

However, another week and we will be in Beach Haven. I have rented a cottage there for a month. It's going to be a great thing for everyone. Particularly the children, who are all over the worst and decidedly on the mend, although coughing quite severely now and then.

We've got a woman to go with us (Atwater's housekeeper who would like the few weeks change), so Carol will be relieved of household responsibilities. The cottage is not large, but roomy and is two squares from the surf! and a wonderful beach.

I went down Saturday and made arrangements.

We will go down in the "old Henry" (Ford car), and I shall remain a week, when I will return to complete some work due in August. It is at this juncture that I am planning that you can join me here in Chadds Ford and return with me, in the auto, to the shore and remain there with us as long as you can. There will be lots of room and nothing to do but soak your feet in the brine— and enjoy the children. Can't you come? Get here, and expenses need not worry you from then on.

Let me know as soon as you can.

400

Dear Mama,

The final rush to get things shipshape all 'round before we abandoned the little house in Chadds Ford prevented my writing a letter to you before we left. Then, when we arrived, there seemed to be so much to do to get things shipshape before we could begin living in our adopted quarters.

The trip down, in the machine, was comfortable and just as we had planned in every detail. It was wholly a pleasure. We left home 8:30 in the morning, Tuesday—through Wilmington, boarding the Ferry to Penns Grove (across the river from Wilmington) at 9:30. We covered the remaining stretch of 125 miles in the easy time of five hours, so that we were all quite fresh when we got here.

Beach Haven is like all other American beach settlements. Everything looks more or less ramshackled and badly in need of paint. Its few spare trees constantly nodding in the unceasing sea breeze, their leaves dry and rustling like paper. Few people moving about, but a general rush of delivery wagons and autos, marked "Central Beach Store," "New York Market," "Cranes Ice Cream Co.," "Vienna Bakery," "The Engleside," "New Hotel Baldwin," "Ocean View House," "Beach House," "Ocean Spray," "Sea View," and a hundred other *ingenious* and novel titles painted on buses, trucks and carry-alls, in big flourishes. A dozen residences within view, their front porches transformed into show windows full of cheap toys, windmills, balloons, boats and a thousand varieties of stain-colored toys and jim-cranks. Skinny children standing 'round with violent red all-day-suckers sliding in and out of their thin, tanned faces—and over all the wail of fretful babies and the peevish cries of children.

Opposite us happens to be the town's pumping station, and its incessant, muffled chug, chug, chug is having its effect on me, and I know from now on, when I hear a water pump and the muffled wheeze of its engine, I'll always think of shadeless Beach Haven.

And this is where poor Bill Engle was mostly "raised!" God must have helped him!!

Of course the beach is fine and the ocean is enchanting. We all took a fine swim before dinner—but the children's whooping cough has not improved "immediately" as everyone enthusiastically assured us. Their coughs are decidedly easier, and we feel sure that the worst is over; but we had hoped that the *miracle* would happen as it has in dozens (?) of other cases.

Chug-wheeze-chug-wheeze-chug-wheeze———

That horrible condition of affairs abroad has given my system a jolt. I am somewhat surprised, for I believed myself too much of a kid to be anything more than stirred over such events. But this makes me feel almost sickened, and my confidence in humanity's good sense and character has been outraged. For a country of men, such as Germany possesses, to force hostilities is inconceivable. I cannot comprehend why, in God's name, with such advanced intellect, such superiority as Germany has exhibited in almost every line of development for fifty years, why they should drop back into veritable mediaevalism.

The Kaiser's last speech to the nation (in today's paper) is worthy only of a *hypocrite* and *general damn fool!* Well, enough of this. I hope you'll get this before Sunday.

Chug-wheeze-chug-wheeze-chug-wheeze.

401

James B. Connolly was the author of many stories that N. C. Wyeth illustrated.

Beach Haven, New Jersey
August 17, 1914

Dear folks,

Old Chadds Ford never looked quite so good to each and every one of us. A week has filled our bellies with the summer beach offering, and we are going back to God's country tomorrow.

The children constantly talk of home, although during the bathing hour they are happy; but all in all we are eager to return.

The beach and the ocean are very impressive, but too glaring and hot for comfort. We eat little bought food, for our appetites are quite satisfied by the swarms of mosquitos that plug one's eyes, ears, nose and mouth. Big fat ones. The children's legs look like ears of corn.

But then we've enjoyed it. The deepest pleasure I've found is the strong desire of all for the little brick house on the hill.

So direct mail to the same old place.

P.S. If James B. Connolly ever turns up, give him a glass of milk, some doughnuts, and show him the swimming hole.

402

Chadds Ford, Pennsylvania
September 17, 1914

Dear Babe,

I see that the kind Kaiser's heart bleeds for Louvain, and for the horrors of the war generally, and he is ready to talk peace! Pish! Tush! Likewise Piffle! Does he think he can convince any man, much less an entire nation, that such language is any other than mendacious *cant?*

We've got to watch out how we believe in his sincerity.

Why did he not consult his heart before he let slip the "dogs of war"? Why didn't he hold parley with that Supreme Being of whom he speaks so familiarly (not to say jauntily). His heart did not *bleed* until the tide seemed to be turning against him, and until he realized that that "scrap of paper" stood for something!

All our hearts bleed for the domestic and home-caring, peace-loving people of Germany, Belgium, France and England, who have all been rushed or dragged into this catastrophe by a mad Kaiser and advisers—a damned false prophet!

403

Chadds Ford, Pennsylvania
September 20, 1914

Dear Mama,

Sometime this coming week I will come home. Just when I cannot say. I must start an important commission Monday, Sept. 28th, sure! And as I am at the call of the Washington Irving High School Faculty in regards to a mural competition I have entered, which appointment will be in the mid-week, I am tied hands and feet as to my disposition of time.

We had half-thought of letting one or both the girls join me, but everything considered—the rushing around in N.Y. and the necessary nocturnal traveling—it would not be a wise thing.

A burdensome problem is bothering me just now, in spite of my conclusions not to accept the offer. A request from the Hearst, Doubleday Page and *Century* Magazines that I join the Cossack regiments in Poland, in company with two writers, to furnish pictorial material.

404

Studio
Chadds Ford, Pennsylvania
September 30, 1914. 4:00 P.M.

My dear Babe,

My thirty-hours-at-home has been much on my mind; consequently it is hard for me to avoid saying something about it. You, probably, cannot realize just how distinctive and *golden* that day was for me. No doubt foregoing and succeeding events in N.Y. had much to do with brightening the hue of that glorious Tuesday. I refer to that abominable war proposition, which, I can say now, proved a bigger tax on my powers of decision than I thought possible. The money offer soared higher than I would care to remark, and I saw in it a possible chance to carry out my painting ideals, if all went well during the 18 *months* in Poland (and perhaps Germany). But then the visions of my family life and of my beginning in art *here,* both of which I have worked so steadily for, would be sacrificed—and my conclusion was that *nothing* in the way of a fortune earned in such a manner could tempt me.

The value of war experience would of course add something to my repertoire in illustration; but I am lessening my *variety* show in art, and hope in another ten years to boil it down to one *good act.*

405

Studio
Chadds Ford, Pennsylvania
October 1, 1914

My dear Sid,

The summer has been a jangle of more or less serious problems.

The WYETHS

The three children with the whooping cough upset all my calculations of a reposeful, progressive season. Then this damned war has made me feel the utter frailty of a profession which I believed was helping to create a moral and spiritual stimulus that would make such a huge calamity as this less probable. To see Christianity, Art and Science, where it was in its highest form of development swept aside like chaff, and devastation and carnage take its place, is a terrific shock, and I for one feel about as infinitesimal as one's mind can conceive.

Then, on top of my intense loathing of it all, comes a huge money offering to join a Cossack regiment in Poland, and produce vivid pictures of the absurd tragedy!

Flying cavalry! barbaric dress! glitter of clashing steel! roar of cannon! rattle of musketry! the cry of victors!—all these enticing descriptions poured into my ears—my God! Sid, I've got an old fellow working out in the sun in my truck garden, just as picturesque and a damned sight more vital to me and the world than all the crazy Cossacks in Russia.

At any rate, the proposition was almost an ordeal to handle in spite of an emphatic decision made the moment I received the offer.

Let me know when you reach Lathrop's. Will come up to see you and talk things over.

Chapter XVI

EXPERIMENT AND INVENTION

"Experiment and invention, invention and experiment! The real nourishment of progress!! for the man with a message."

Chadds Ford, Pennsylvania
October 10, 1914

Dear Sid,

Two solemn, drizzly days could not have come at a better time—
so conducive to retirement and reflection, and following, as it did, so
closely upon the heels of that wonderful day and night in New
Hope.

Like everything you do, it seems to me, your plans bear fruits for
others besides yourself, and I have no way of thanking you for the
rare opportunity your visit to Mr. Lathrop's brought to me. The
experience came at a perfect time!

I'll ask you to take the Segantini book back with you to Mr.
Lathrop.

Chadds Ford, Pennsylvania
October 15, 1914

Dear Papa,

Tonight, we expect Mama, and the children are all on tiptoe
awaiting the event.

Carol has completed her fall housecleaning, which adds more than
ever (for her) to the event of Mama's arrival.

Spent Tuesday with W. L. Lathrop who lives up the Delaware
River. Lathrop is one of our big landscape painters and modeled in
stature, habits and productions very closely to Thoreau. The day
proved to be one of the most valuable and inspiriting I ever spent.
The pleasure was mutual, however, and I think it the beginning
of a rare acquaintanceship. He is 55 years of age.

Finances are tied up in N.Y. in the magazine field, and find it a
slow job collecting from all but *Scribner's* (who are even willing to
pay in advance if necessary). Various publishers are withholding

$1200 of mine, which makes me fidgety, to say the least. However, I'll get it in time, no doubt. Work comes in, however, and I see plenty to do ahead.

The War still preys on my credibility, and I find it hard to turn the matter from my mind.

N. C. Wyeth with W. L. Lathrop.

408

Chadds Ford, Pennsylvania
October 24, 1914

Dear Babe,
A wonderful day—Mama leaves tonight.

The week ending today has been one I shall not forget. Every shade of experience seems to have been touched in the seven days, and I feel, as I'm sure Mama feels, that the visit has been a most complete one. Her close identity with the children touched the highest mark in my estimation, and I know she has clinched her personality and the role of grandmother on their little minds for the rest of their lives.

It may please you to know that Mama's spirit has been almost *jubilant,* which may sound something like an exaggeration; nevertheless it is so.

Your letter brought with it other pleasures than the one of hearty birthday greetings. It contained one or two paragraphs that show your power to depict deep feelings and graphic pictures in a few words. I could wish you would write much oftener—just *snatches* on the cars or by the river, in the barn, under the apple trees, where emotional impulses stir you. Keep a pad and pencil in every coat pocket and create the habit to record your passing thoughts—which is the only time to record them, for when they are once passed you cannot conjure them back. Send them down here for my pleasure. Let me respond—not critically, but sympathetically— just enough to keep up the spirit.

Please give my suggestions a test; a fair trial will mean more to you than a protracted dose of the Boston Library.

409

Studio
Chadds Ford, Pennsylvania
November 19, 1914

Dear Babe,

Your bully letter came yesterday morning and has done me good! I cannot express to you how pleased I am to hear of your new resolve to write often. I am convinced that you are undertaking a *constructional* exercise with no *possible* ill effects, and that in a comparatively short time you yourself will begin to appreciate its tremendous value as one who has had *actual experience,* which is infinitely more significant than to appreciate it theoretically. (A damn platitude, but how often we complacently accept a theory *without* practicing it. The older we grow the more we know this

477

failing to be true. It marks the division between the non-productive dreamer and the man of accomplishment.)

I am prone to make too many radical, generalizing statements, which in many cases I believe are really sane and with a certain breadth of vision, but not having the care or inclination to seek fact and details in subjects outside my ideas or actions with tangible reasons. Thoreau towers head and shoulders above Emerson (in my mind) in just this particular, and I confidently predict that his works will long outlive the word-playing of his older friend. Thoreau's words *live,* they vibrate, with a singular virility. And there is no accounting for it except that he *lived by his spoken words.* This ability measures a man's strength and it is a prayer constantly on my lips. It is the life of my art and of tremendous importance to my family, and would create a noble respect for me if I could best live up to it in my relations with the world!!

Your experience with the gun some ten days ago coincides so with my feelings toward the shooting of wild animals, that I thought much about it the following days. The annual event in these hills (the hunt for rabbits) is becoming a source of sorrow to me. So much so that I wish that I could avoid the last two weeks in October while the rabbit season is in its "glory."

Thank heaven, I never liked the sport. Two rabbits and a few rats, some chickens and a "beef" on the round-up is all the killing I ever did. All else I admitted was a fabrication. To kill does not turn my stomach; it sours my sensibilities.

A little sop has just been handed out to me in the shape of an invitation from the Fine Arts Commission of the Panama Pacific Exposition to exhibit a group of eight canvases. I seem to be the favored one of the illustrators outside of Howard Pyle, whose works will occupy an entire gallery.

(I should not call this sop—it is really an honor that I appreciate.)

If you will consistently carry out your plan to write, it will give me an outlet of expression that I've longed for. I starve sometimes for someone to write to. Writing cannot be supplanted by talking. There's an intensity about writing that the best conversation lacks.

You are strictly my contemporary. You fill a place as contestant in plain speaking that even Mama cannot fill. Many times I write things to her which I should not, mainly because there has been no place else to send my ideas. Accept my ideas as those firmly believed in for the moment at least. I am always willing to abandon them as I have done so many, many times.

410

Chadds Ford, Pennsylvania
December 10, 1914

Dear Mama,

Packing cases have been busy for the last two weeks. I have contributed seven pictures to three Emergency Fund Exhibitions, and have already derived the satisfaction of winning for the Belgium sufferers $350. Tonight I shall send one more—the stage in the moonlight (*Pike County [Ballads]*)—to the Mrs. Harry Payne Whitney Exhibition, N.Y.; sales to be evenly divided. Five large canvases went to the Panama Exposition yesterday and two to the traveling show, St. Louis. So I am cleaned out of my best work.

The task of writing over 200 personal letters to owners of H.P. originals is completed with ridiculously small results. Roughly figuring, I estimate that these two hundred art lovers hold four hundred paintings of Howard Pyle's—and I only succeeded in winning the promises of 22 for the Panama show. Either the people cherish his canvases to an unusual degree, or else they do not realize the great honor bestowed upon the master by the Panama Commission. I don't know. At any rate it is a great disappointment to me.

And now, there arises a new difficulty in prevailing upon the Wilmington Society to loan their collection of Pyle canvases. Without these the whole matter, as far as the Howard Pyle exhibit goes, will fall through. I attended two meetings of the Society last week and find a strong prejudice against the idea, extending even to Schoonover and Arthurs (who are trustees).

Personally, I believe this *no* time to recognize such petty annoyances, but to do everything and overlook such hindrances with an effort to give Mr. Pyle his just due before the American public.

We had an intense meeting. I sensed that the spirit of the entire meeting was against the movement so said nothing, not thinking it worthwhile. But just before we adjourned I felt the injustice so strongly that I got up mad and said what I had to say, and lo! what a transformation!! There were dozens there who were as timid as I was but who were of my mind, and they gave me a great hand

479

clapping; so instead of clinching the matter then and there we are to hold a special meeting in two weeks. I think the matter looks promising.

Schoonover rented an auto and paid me a visit on Tuesday. He feels desperate about his work and seeks advice. It gave me courage and satisfaction to see him brush aside all of the subtly contemptuous spirit he has flaunted at me for years and get down to utter earnestness. I do not infer *gloating* satisfaction, understand, but the kind that makes me appreciate the apparent justifiability of the course we have taken (Carol and I) in the past five years.

But everything isn't on my side by a long shot, and I feel that my problems have only begun. Thoreau is my springhead for almost every move I can make, except in the intimate matters that transpire between a man and woman. Here he is utterly deficient, as is Christ, on account of his lack of experience. Some say that Christ had *vision* and did not need *experience.* A *word* from Tolstoy, Goethe, Roosevelt—derived from *experience*—is worth more to me, infinitely, than a chapter from Thoreau on "love" or from Christ on sex relations. But when Thoreau talks about "simple living" and "high thinking," and Christ on Faith, Hope and Charity, then I will listen and *thrill* with understanding.

411

Chadds Ford, Pennsylvania
December 17, 1914

My dear Sid,

The three gifts were very gratefully received and arrived in due season—and will be handed out to the joyous trio on Xmas morning! We wish that you could be here! It's the most wondrous day of the year for us, Xmas is, and is so *packed* with high-spirited and emotional pleasure, that we always feel sorry that all our dear friends cannot be with us to receive the tremendous stimulus that fairly bulges out of our little home.

We carry the beautiful illusion of "Old Kriss" as far as possible, and have succeeded already in tracing a fascinating mystic pattern on the minds of the two older children, which in time will become an everlasting source of uplifting reminiscence and inspiration. The "pain" of disillusionment is a *myth,* from *my* experience as a child, and later observation—providing the parents can always enter into the fairy spirit of Xmas traditions, and become for awhile, children themselves. This we do. So much so, in fact, that the excitement of impersonating Santa Claus and acting stage-property-man at the same time have set me *crying* in pure and exultant joy as I straddled the roof in the dark morning hours, thumping and stamping, ringing a great loop of bells down the bedroom fireplace chimney and calling out in a rumbling voice; and then quickly sliding down the ladder to take my next position inside the house by the fireplace in the big room. The dazzled and bewildered faces of the children, who in their ecstasy and in the dim light of the candles are unaware that I am cautiously escaping.

"I will send tomorrow a picture of 'your boy'."

I quickly return after depositing my buffalo coat, mask and red tuke behind the cellar door. The miracle has been perfect! And as the dear little kids slowly sense that their dad is in their midst, they excitedly tell me all about "Kriss," and their eyes grow big as saucers!

The spirit was so strong last year, that those few who were with us admitted that they too were almost completely rapt in the strong mystic atmosphere. It was glorious!

And now "Baby Brother" is added to the ranks of the uninformed. His initiation will add a wonderful zest to the erstwhile Santa, I can tell you!

I will send tomorrow by *"parcel post"* (and I am meditating whether it will arrive to you by the hands of the *American Express,* which will tally consistently with the transformation which took place as your packages came south, for we received them via "parcels post"! despite your word) a picture of "your boy." Perhaps you will wonder if he is asking the flowers if their "wheels are underneath." With the photo goes our best Xmas wishes—Carol, the children and myself to you and your mother.

412

The first mention of the murals N. C. Wyeth did for the grille room in the Hotel Traymore, Atlantic City, New Jersey, was made in this letter. The murals have since been destroyed.

Chadds Ford, Pennsylvania
January 18, 1915

Dear Babe,

The children are rapidly putting their colds behind them. Everyone is cheerful and happy in the house, and I feel free now to write on matters apart from health and practicality.

Yesterday was a great day for me, and like all fine experiences I could wish that you had shared it with me.

A week ago George Harding asked me to meet him on Sunday noon at the home of Chas. H. Stephens (better known perhaps as the husband of Alice Barber Stephens of magazine fame). "The meeting," he said, "is to discuss the possible decoration of a luxuriant hotel now building in Atlantic City."

I gladly accepted the invitation of course, and so, in the downpour and almost summer's heat of yesterday's storm, slopped my way to Rose Valley—the home of Mrs. Stephens near Philadelphia.

The event of the few hours in Stephens' home was as full of charm and stimulus as one could well assimilate, but which was overtopped by the visit we payed to William Price, architect.

If ever a man emanated that electric force and energy of Roosevelt, Price is the man! Such enthusiasm, such virility, such exquisite taste and refinement perfectly mixed with a wholesome manliness I have seldom seen, except, as I say, in Roosevelt, and, I imagine, in such men as Riis, Phillips Brooks, Rabbi Wise and all those where we feel that the force of the animal, the *brute,* has *not* been dulled but finely directed.

Well, to my tremendous surprise I found him to be one of the leading architects of the country—designer of the Pennsylvania Terminal, N.Y.; of the new Union Station, Chicago; of the Marborough-Blenheim Hotel, Atlantic City; John Wanamaker Building, Phila.; and numberless other structures famous in this country for individuality and distinction.

It goes without saying that I felt lost in the atmosphere of such heights of achievement; but how quickly his magnetic power dispelled my discomfort, and in a jiffy we were exchanging ideas and sympathies relating to life and art that brought us quickly together on a rich, wholesome basis of understanding. Music was an early subject, and a few choice pieces on his Victrola, varying from Bert Williams' classic, "Turkey in the Straw" and "Nobody," to Dvořák's "Boat Song of the Volga" and Wagner's "Tristan and Isolde," gave the afternoon a flushed start. From music to his astonishing collection of Oriental rugs, temple hangings and various other fragments of marvelously colored and decorated fabrics (from the land of the *"poor heathen"*) was next in order. I never was so stirred by Eastern color in my life. It goes to show what a value it is to enjoy things with others who know their subject deeply. One sees through their eyes and mind, as it were, and gains a glimpse of a new field of beauty and thought which for all time tantalizes one's sensitiveness into constant activity along the new lines.

With all this fabulous mosaic of music, philosophy and Oriental art as a background, we went into Price's sanctum (in itself a temple and place of worship), and there he unfolded his scheme for the interior design, furnishing and wall decoration of the $2000 hotel at Atlantic City.

With his back to the window, and seated cross-legged on a broad divan, he built up for us a prodigious mental vision of the vast structure. His ringing, insistent, keynote was *modernity, modernity!* A beseeching appeal to us to face our modern spirit and customs unflinchingly, and to cease thinking that unless a building resembles the Pantheon, or a mural decoration resembles Angelo or Donatello, that it is "rotten." That we *must* recognize that our life today, from the frenzied circus-ridden antics of Billy Sunday to the spendthrifts and money gluttons who patronize the hotels of a resort, are *realities,* just as much as Nero and his extravagant retinue were realities, feasting their eyes on a gladiator's battle, or gloating over the sacrifice of Christians in the arena. That to paint, sculpt, or design classically is merely to be true to your era.

On this line he talked for an hour and drove and redrove home his arguments with pointed analogies.

To all this I am extremely sympathetic. It is what I profoundly believe, and with the stimulus of an older, stronger man than I am behind me I should be able to escape the shackles of tradition and evolve something modern.

And now I have an opportunity. A gorgeous underground café, stark in its simplicity; a great black marble dancing space dropped below level, upon which are coral-colored tables and chairs; huge pillars, four of them supporting a glass ceiling which is in reality a lake filled with Japanese goldfish! From the dance floor one gazes at the sky through the water and the flashing goldfish. The great flat walls and pillars are to be painted in blues, emeralds and whites, interpreting the feel of the deep sea! Such a chance!! Mermaids, flying fish, seaweed, spume and glittering bubbles, rising, rising, like champagne in a glass!

Last night, I couldn't sleep, but I evolved my scheme, and unless something unheard of happens, the scheme will go through with a rush!

The banquet hall is another matter: 65 × 80 feet, fountains, huge glass globes with goldfish magnified as big as shad!, illuminated jets of water like running gold and jewels, Chinese rugs of pumpkin yellow and jet-black pillars!!

It's a brand new chance, Babe, and may be the beginning of something worthwhile for both Harding and me. I feel the deepest gratitude that I was invited into the work. "Treasure Island" and a few other pictures did it.

Experiment and Invention

How you would have gloried in the fullness of that atmosphere. It made one feel *fat* with the desire to express. It gave the mind a nourishment at once hearty and productive of strength. It made me religiously resolve to let myself out *sumptously* on any work that I tackle, whether it be painting, writing, talking or living. We haven't time to be anemic, to dribble out our thoughts in meager mouthfuls, to half or only *quarter* express ourselves. If we say anything, say it fully, say it fatly, serve it with juices and garnishments. This does not mean to overload, to burden with sickening sweets or seasonings, in no sense is this art; but to leave a statement unrounded, thin and full of cavities like a skull, is stingy and of no additive value to human records. It would be better to say nothing.

No one can realize more than I the tremendous distinction between that which is well said or well done and that which is over said or done (and one is as great a crime as the other). The power of discrimination and selection is the creative man's *genius;* herein lies the secret of profound expression.

Within what I have said lies a suggestion to you, and one which you must recognize no matter what line of expression you are following. Simplicity is not *meagerness.* To cut a sentence down from ten words to five is not necessarily a simplification, it is more apt to be *starvation.* The desire to be direct in expressing a thought must not descend into frugality. Frugality is terribly tiresome.

There is a common notion amongst laymen that any demonstrative action or word expression is an *affectation,* an untruth! They forget that expression is 1/10 idea and 9/10 emotion, that to use a dead vehicle (such as a vocabulary or a scale of colors) one must use them sumptuously, with reckless abandon perhaps, in order to conjure up in the mind of the reader anywhere near the vision that stirred the writer.

For instance: your last letter about your fishing trip with Ed and Andy Lloyd was intensely interesting to me, but I will venture to say that to one who did not know the Charles River, the meadows near Needham and the old red windmill, the real message of your expression would have been lost.

Your writing was a brief, a shorthand account, almost a code letter which to me was perfectly understandable, but to others a cold, unmysterious relation of a few facts. I knew the weather, the wet ice, the feel of the fire, the hotdogs, the spirit of brotherhood, the reclaiming of boyhood days, the triumphant return and all that. I

485

read between the lines—I built my emotional story on your inventory of facts.

Richness of garnishment, more *gravy*telling analogies, poignant stimulus, the reaching high up for *glorious, dreamlike* symbolisms to express those experiences that played such fascinating, alluring music on your heartstrings.

Create your impressions at all costs. Art knows no propriety, no prudery, no notions of restraint when it desires to be *convincing* in its impression. *Impression* is the thing! I have nourished a thought or have experienced a sensation. I want to convey it to you. I must do it by hook or crook. Stevenson did it with enchanting rhythm, perfect euphony, gliding sentences; Whitman fired great chaotic chunks! great *gobs* of thought—fairly *hurled* his ideas in heavy masses, so that your brain *reels* with the power of his meanings. And along comes Thoreau, the master of them all, with ideas expressed and reinforced by analogies and descriptions that keep one's brain on tiptoe, perhaps wrapping it all in a little parcel of five words at the end! But he knew that a demitasse of black coffee could only be appreciated after the sumptuous meal.

When my friend tells me it's a nice day, I want to see it on his face; I'm not content with the words.
P.S. Your letters are sketches, I know, but even so they must imply completeness.—Don't you think so?

413

Carol Wyeth was expecting her fifth child.

Henry Zollinger, a great uncle to N. C. Wyeth, was the husband of Mrs. John Denys Zirngiebel's half-sister, Friederika.

Chadds Ford, Pennsylvania
February 8, 1915

Dear Mama,

The days are squeezed full—of duties and professional activities; and when not of these, my mind labors with the thousand thoughts and concerns dealing with the expected events of the near future. All this makes the time go fast.

Carol is well and as comfortable as can be expected at this time.

Babe's awakening interest in the techniques of creative art is a good omen, and will, if persisted in, lead him into that soul-satisfying power of compelling expression. Once he acquires this, his force (both ethical and dramatic) will grow with an ever-accumulating impetus. With his sensitive and emotional nature as a groundwork, nothing but the *craft* of writing can stand between him and prolific production. This lesson I am only learning after 12 years of intense experience. It is a basic principle which I shall always feel to be my duty to impress upon those who stand on the threshold of any creative specialty. The prevalent idea that real genius *"will out"* in spite of a lack of technical knowledge is without foundation. Some acquire the facilities one way, and some another; but the point is that technique must be studied and loved for technique's sake, not, of course, to the exclusion of the vital interest in life, the source of all art, but in the manner of the fine cabinetmaker who knows and loves his tools. Only after the development of such affection can he instinctively and deftly use the tools to accomplish his will. Apropos of "cabinetmaker": how often, and with what pleasure, do I recall, from the few experiences I was privileged to enjoy with Uncle Zollinger in his workshop, how caressingly he handled his beloved wood-files, his queer-shaped planes and keen-edged chisels. I can hear now that heavy breathing through his nostrils, and can smell that fascinating aroma of new lumber, orange shellac and glue, with a poignant tang now and then from his strong pipe. The memory of the z-z-z-zing! from the circular saw, shrieking down from a high piercing treble, cutting the air like a knife!!

There he stood, this cabinetmaker, patternmaker, within arm's reach of a thousand tools, every instrument different in shape and size, and perfectly fit for their work. Ah! so must the artist, writer, speaker stand within reach of a million turns of expression in color and form, phrase and analogy—and what is more he must ever invent, contrive and fashion new queer-shaped tools, subtly adapted for the special need. Experiment and invention, invention and experiment! The real nourishment of progress!! for the man with a message.

The sketch for the hotel decoration came fast and hot! and I feel that I have struck something unusual. However, I'll wait until I've cooled off before committing myself definitely.

Poor Jenkins has typhoid. I saw him today and his appearance and condition were a shock. The poor man is scared clear through, which is of serious detriment to his power of resistance. I felt his fear of death as though the fear were my own (although I boast of absolute indifference to the "experience" that must come). He has been brought up on that hideous, morbid interest that all the people of this section of the county take in dead people and the stupid, crazy speculation of the "great beyond," and is paying the awful penalty now. He has enjoyed (I use this word in a measured meaning) the emotional and exciting sensations of many a funeral, and now the visions of his own terrible thoughts as he gazed upon cold, waxen faces come to him like a retribution—they make him sick at heart.

When will the blot of public funerals and the attending barbarous customs be wiped from the experiences of civilized people? In my mind it is one of the *crimes*.

All is well. We are waiting—watchfully waiting!

414

Chadds Ford, Pennsylvania
February 22, 1915

Dear Mama,

Mr. Jenkins is back on the job again, apparently pretty well; an improvement brought about by a severe dosing of drugs. It is a great relief to have him here, but it will only last until April 1st, for then he intends to quit work altogether—to be "loose-footed for a while," as he expresses it.

415

Chadds Ford, Pennsylvania
February 28, 1915

Dear Mama,

Weather is delightful; children are in excellent health all 'round; and Carol is well, although slighty depressed. The doctor made a bad guess as to time and it looks as though Carol was correct, as usual.

416

Chadds Ford, Pennsylvania
March 12, 1915

Dear Mama,

Everybody well, and expect something to occur daily. It seems to be a long drawn-out affair. Carol is quite uncomfortable and I wish it would take place.

Am *deeply* elated over my headway at the studio and feel confident that I am at last nearing a real ability to *paint*. Would give a great deal to have you all see my large canvas, "The Fence Builders" —with all of the old valley behind them.

Hotel matter hangs fire. May fall through, don't care. Am having hell of a good time in the studio.

417

Chadds Ford, Pennsylvania
March 16, 1915

Dear Mama,

Well, the event is over, and so much easier and better than I anticipated that I can hardly believe it. Somehow, this time, I had a foreboding feeling. Don't know why.

Saturday Carol, the children and I went into Wilmington in the machine and did the marketing. Sunday her mother came down and they spent a pleasant afternoon together. Carol was feeling unusually well, being free of the indigestion which has bothered her of late weeks.

I went to bed rather late (11 o'clock), and Carol was then complaining of gas in the stomach—at 12:30 I got her some soda and hot water, privately surmising that there was something more than *gas*. The doctor arrived at 1:30 and dumbfounded us both by saying that a stranger would arrive within the hour!

The pains started, mild ones.

Jim Baldwin kindly drove to Wilmington in his auto for the nurse. At 2:25 *Ann* was splitting the air with her cry!

Carol kept saying she was afraid it was all a dream. But it's not— about as healthy a little chunk of humanity as you ever saw.

The children are *wild!* and when we went for the mail this morning, they hailed all the town's folk as they passed and told them the news. The whole village was in a broad grin.

But around the corner Herbert Jenkins lies dead (Mr. Jenkins' oldest son), and yesterday the doctor buried his youngest child.

How I hated to drag him out at midnight after his day of sorrow. But he came, perfectly poised, and handled matters in his usual cool, jovial, collected way. He's a sterling character! and I'm deeply indebted to him.

The house is sailing along perfectly smoothly and I was able, even without a wink of sleep last night, to put in a hearty six hours of work at the studio.

We are all sleepy now, however, and will retire right after supper.

Say, but what a rut we are in—*seven* granddaughters with poor little baby brother marooned. Perhaps will have to wait for *Babe*. - Carol's birthday next Monday.

418

Chadds Ford, Pennsylvania
March 31, 1915

Dear Mama,

I am making an effort to get off a few lines to you. I seem to lack all the spirit necessary to write letters. I seem to have slumped into one of those periods of stagnation (which followed so closely a few weeks of exaltation over the condition of my work). My large canvas, "The Fence Builders," has progressed favorably, and herein lies the trouble. In this canvas I am following the truth as closely as I am capable of—going directly to Nature for my inspiration and details. In every case I am putting things down from *knowledge* of *fact* and not of fancy. Suddenly I must turn and do an Italian artist of 1750 and his model in the Milan Cathedral!—a subject that must be made up out of the whole cloth, with nothing to refer to but a few photos and costume sketches.

I cannot explain to anyone, so that they can sufficiently appreciate, what a shock such a change produces on the mind. Figuratively, a jump from white to black.

My last cover for Mr. Heines easily "topped" anything I ever did for publication—this too was done from true sources, which has also added to the contrast.

However, I realize it's merely a matter of readjustment and that the opportunity at hand is really a fine one. It has taken two weeks thus far to "transform" and "adjust" myself to the new conditions, and only two hours ago I got a bare hint of a start.

It is to meet just such "blank spaces" that one must have a strong body and a well-balanced "top piece." It is well that aspiring art students do not get a taste of these *intermittent bitters*—they'd drop art like a hot potato! To an outsider, and even to one's own friends and relatives, the painting of a picture is one grand and glorious *cinch*—canvas following canvas with equal ease and alacrity. How little, how *absurdly* little they understand of the hideous hours, night and day, that almost always precede the *visionizing,* the conception of a picture! These preparatory periods vary in length, and oftentimes the best motives are born after short labor—however this is indeterminate as anyone of experience can testify.

Here I am, discoursing on a subject I am loathe to touch upon lest it appear as a vainglorious parade of one's difficulties. Now that it's down, I'll let it go. It has loosened my pen, at any rate, and that is something accomplished, please believe.

Everyone is very, *very* well. Baby Ann has gained ½ pound the second week and did not lose an ounce the first. Carol has been absolutely normal in every particular and looks younger than ever.

I carried her down to Sunday dinner, and am doing so daily.

Baby brother is looking rugged with very fat and red cheeks.

The other two look like *thugs!*

Your letter about the Swiss entertainment was fine, and I appreciate exactly the rest and pleasure you derive from the atmosphere of that noble little country—a heritage we boys are all proud of.

Although I receive a steady flow of inspiration from the circulation of Swiss mountain blood in my veins, I also get tremendous help from my thoughts of this astonishing country of ours, and particularly from my home in Needham.

It is right that dear old Switzerland is *your* background of romance and idealism; it is right that my essential background is faith in and love of my natal country. The tremendous idealistic advances of the United States in the course of 140 years are astounding and cannot be matched by any other country on the globe.

Our very close contact with the innumerable details of government, social and ethical upheavals and the endless exposures in our voluminous press, are apt to deprive us of a true perspective, and consequently we lose the true status—our true worth.

Your understanding and conception of Switzerland is from the most favorable standpoint—and, moreover, a very just one—and it gives one the hint just how one should withdraw from the noise and dust of our own machinery in order to understand and appreciate it.

It is strange that not a month ago I picked up a book in the library by a Swiss statesman, which went into strict details of social and governmental affairs of Switzerland; and although in the greater part, one felt the nobility and the justice of their viewpoints, there were several matters which no self-respecting person would tolerate on this side of the water.

We have like blemishes and many of them perhaps, but it only goes to show how easily too close contact with inevitable details can absolutely kill one's love and faith in a country and its men.

Here it is mailtime and I *must* close. Hotel job is OK.

419

Chadds Ford, Pennsylvania
April 1, 1915

My dear Sid,

Sid, I have cast off the habit of postponement and am *painting*—along with illustration, to be sure, but painting is getting the big doses. I have spent a solid month on a large canvas which I call "The Fence Builders" and have made some decided advances, some of which I really feel are entitled to be called "painting."

I have kept busy with practical work despite the hard times.

The winter has been an intense one for me. Have made very little money, which leaves me quite strapped; at the same time have given my ideals a boost with some actual accomplishment in that field.

Attended the reception at the Academy in February, which is an important event for me, and have since had several landscape men down here on visits, including [Daniel] Garber, whom I like very much.

Disappointed in most of them though and find that they have no particular lines of advancement laid out and seem to be trusting to luck just what progress they can make. Painting, as in anything else, requires intelligence. No man, be he ever so much a genius, ever slammed at his work haphazard. A thing done right is done with the authority of *knowledge* (coupled with temperament). One has difficulties only when one lacks the knowledge of *truth*, which includes the knowledge of craft as well as of nature—a clear vision is absolutely necessary before the creation of a piece of art is undertaken, and the power to *execute* said piece of art with precision and fluidity is just as necessary.

Experiment and Invention

Please read technical treatises on the works and workmanship of Leonardo, Velasquez, Rembrandt, Vermeer, Constable, Segantini, and learn the great underlying lesson of the value of technical knowledge. Every one of those men were adventurers and *discoverers*—as great as Columbus, as profound as Newton. First and last they had *love* of course, but to do justice to their love they sought means; they sought it definitely and with *precision*. They knew! Damn it they knew!

By Jove! how paltry are my puny efforts, but by the heavens, I'm going to *accumulate, accumulate,* accumulate my forces and see if, before the end, I can't register one solitary feeling I have toward this dear old life of ours. It's too great not to try!

420

Chadds Ford, Pennsylvania
May 1, 1915. Sunday morning, 6:30

Dear folks,

Chadds Ford lies in the gray white shroud of her own smoke. In one place I can faintly see the blackened end of a chimney, but all else is concealed under the pale sheet that has spread into the entire meadow.

I have just returned, after almost five hours of hard hot work with the bucket brigades and the lifting and moving of numerous showcases, drawers and chests—and from the dwellings the usual variety running from pans to pictures.

Baldwin's store, their house, the building containing the barbershop, restaurant and hall, and Arment's homestead (next to the wheelwright's shop) are destroyed. Out buildings, garages, a stable, etc., were consumed.

A quiet night saved the other half of the village.

It was a stubborn fight, and the persistency and courage were good to see.

What hurts me worst is the destination of the old Arment house. Mrs. Arment, 93 years, is now, at this very late period, without a home. It is very sad.

[Dwight] Howland did great work, and between us I believe we were the means of saving the old wheelwright's shop, and more too, for with the burning of this, Brittingham's and Jenkins' house would have gone for sure.

Two fire companies from Wilmington and two from West Chester got in action about three o'clock (2 hours after the fire started) at the east end of the blaze and saved the hotel and barns. (How I wished the Arment Home could have been saved instead.)

10:30

The depression is strong throughout the countryside—a large number are viewing the ruins, and feeling runs high against Dick Baldwin who built the "firetrap" within three feet of Arment's walls.

Still too tired and depressed to write further.

421

Chadds Ford, Pennsylvania
May 6, 1915

Dear Mama,

It is bedtime, but, as is my custom, I went out on the front porch and took my last look across the dark valley before "turning in." One of the rites of this little ceremony is a thoughtful gaze directly over "Sugar Loaf" toward *Needham*. This has so long been a belief in my mind that I am convinced were one to follow the direction indicated by my gaze that 'twould not be long before the tops of the old spruces in front of the house would loom into view. I love to think of this.

By this time Hilda must be with you. At least I *hope* so. She accomplished her mission here *perfectly*. Affairs in the home moved along smoothly and with precision.

The whole event of the coming of Ann transpired with almost no confusion or undue intensity and so far has provided us with perhaps our healthiest baby, weighing 11¾ *lbs.* now (gaining ¾ lb. last week). She's a buster, no mistake.

The Norwegian waif in the kitchen is doing her best and improving. She is thorough although not apt, but with Esther who is patient and mighty efficient we are getting along fine.

It is amusing to glance into the kitchen and watch the frantic sign language and exaggerated facial articulations. Martina Thorolson will either learn or bust!

Henriette, Carolyn and B.B. are tough as nails, and about the color of rusty ones! They keep the woods full of echoes and are up to something all the time.

The mural work I consider about half done.

The worry has not been so much the actual accomplishment as the *huge* problem of collaborating with [George] Harding. It is absurd to think of *collaborating* in art unless it is with the builder or architect—but to *compromise* with a fellow painter is hell, and I wouldn't undertake another job under the same conditions for love nor money. We have not seen any of the latter as yet. I'm not worried for it will come sometime, but expenses are particularly heavy on this kind of work and keeps a fellow busy as a financier.

Four parcels are to be shipped Saturday; five more must be done to ship the *25th.*

422

Studio
Chadds Ford, Pennsylvania
May 21, 1915

Dear Mama,

The day is dark and wet.

I cannot say that I have given myself up to the muse of the fascinating weather conditions of this particular day—mostly because of this mural work, which, as it nears the end, seems to weigh heavier and heavier as a burden—and the consciousness of an enormous bare canvas to be covered (the *last* one thank goodness) takes all the subtle glory out of the wet skies and dripping leaves.

This morning I sat here and rewrote a rather long treatise, in which I am endeavoring to express clearly, comprehensively, but not dogmatically, my feelings toward the Bible and its function for the good of humanity.

Right out of the clear skies it may sound strange to you to hear of such an occupation, but down here, a good deal of pressure has been brought to bear upon everyone who doesn't hold up Billy Sunday and his teachings. Several local friends of mine have pressed me hard for a complete explanation of why I do not believe the Bible to be infallible, etc., etc. The new progressive ? minister here has pushed me the hardest. He seems bent on dragging me into the church, so to treat him with due respect (and I do have respect for him) I feel it a duty to my own peace of mind to be somewhat complete in my explanations and conclusions.

495

It is difficult to make one's position clear, when one's adversaries have not or cannot understand Darwin and the inspiring mystery of evolution; or who ignore the history of science and the diabolical set-backs and threatened extinctions it has suffered at the hands of absurd preachers of the Bible. The mystic, and I claim myself to be one, derives his inspiration from all natural phenomena, and can be moved to superior motives by the magic of the birth of his own child, but must needs smile at the stupid myth of the Immaculate Conception of Christ. Christ would mean infinitely more to me, had I been taught from the first that he was a human being begotten as I was begotten, and not placed among the people of the earth from supernatural causes. This robs me of all incentive to follow Christ (as the majority of churches teach it [*sic*]).

To see a man who is fallible rise and overcome a weakness, an evil, is the supremest example for a young fellow. To live and actually *know,* and to *touch* the hand of Roosevelt have produced more than I have ever gotten from the Bible or the church.

The serene, unblemished life of Thoreau, the stirring appeal for artistic democracy of Walt Whitman and the urgent stimulating force of Tolstoy comprise about all I can handle at present. These men have all said sacred words. They are not to be found exclusively in the Bible!

But here I am fumbling around again. I shall send you my more complete attempt.

423

Hotel Sterling
Atlantic City, New Jersey
June 3, 1915

Dear folks,

The old surf is pounding the beach with one long continuous roar! The rain is hissing against the black window and the wind is weaving a weird siren call throughout it all. As I peer through the wet glass into the night the gently winding boardwalk glistens under the lights like a great serpent rolled up from the seas—lying prone against the bank of lighted store windows.

At home—I wonder what the dear little kids are dreaming about, cozy in their beds, and if the rain is beating on their windows too.

Perhaps Henriette is sitting upright this moment gazing into space asking if I'm home, then snuggling down from her delirium again. She does this often.

After a long day in that fabulous room before the huge frieze of our fantastic dreams of the sea, my mind is curiously alive to my strange surroundings, and the visions of the people and country I love stand out in striking relief against this exotic background. It makes me uncommonly happy to think that I have built up in my life such precious relations—have been so constant in my cherishing of a limited scope of attachments. I know by so doing that my appreciations have run deeper and are firmly rooted to a source of inspiration which will ever increase in force.

We are arriving at quite remarkable results—Harding and I. The Hotel itself is attracting nationwide attention on account of its size, cost, completeness and numerous *features,* the most talked of being the "submarine cafe." With the room only ½ done, *7000* people visited it on Sunday! and the manager had to sign away and publish in the local papers that admission into the café would be prohibited until completely done.

We are spending every hour our energy will stand to finish by Friday, midnight. Saturday a banquet for 400 hotel managers from the principal hotels east of Chicago will be given in this room. A remarkable advertisement.

The architect has handed me over an astounding commission to build and decorate the interior of a great dome on the top of the hotel for a child's playroom. A marvelous opportunity for imaginative creations—a brand-new scheme which will astonish the public. I'm too tired to tell you about it now in detail—I would spoil it.

Besides, it will pay handsomely and refund what for the time being has been quite a severe loss.

The *Shelburne,* a fastidious hostelry owned by John Wanamaker, is to be torn down and rebuilt on a grand scale, and the management has spoken to me about some mural work to be done there—so you see the "advertisement" has already begun its work.

Aunty Guss is home with Carol, which makes me feel better. Baby Brother's sharp cold is better—the baby is in fine shape (the last I heard)—the others are fine as usual.

It occurred to me that I forgot to remark Babe's birthday—and Nat's too! It's my first slip-up if I remember rightly, and I'm sorry.

497

Those annual recurrences mean much to me. However, extend my best regards and wishes to Babe.

I shall try to make a trip home (Needham) within the next four weeks if all goes well at Chadds Ford.

424

Chadds Ford, Pennsylvania
June 22, 1915. 3:00 P.M.

Dear Babe,

Though only in the middle of the afternoon, it is so dark that Hoffman's barn is indistinguishable. It looks as though we're in for a violent storm.

(I wish you could see how black the sky is—it is incredible! Have just moved things in from the porch and Carol has lighted the lamps. It is almost pitch dark; we cannot see the village. It's the darkest daylight hour I ever remember!)

I am outgrowing the idea that it is *your* fault for not writing.—I feel sorry that I am not big enough to compel your impulses—there's the blame absolutely.

How many times have I begun a belated letter to some acquaintance with the words: "This is the first opportunity I've had to write to you, etc., etc.—" when it's short of nothing but a damned lie. Had that friend held a vital place in my thoughts, if I felt necessary to him, or him to me, I would have written quickly, spontaneously. The mild, ladylike, excuse of "no time" has no place where productive relationship of spirits exist.

I am hoping that I can command yours sometime.

Spring ends today, according to the almanacs, and I can guarantee that it has been a full season for us all. And yet I have not arrived anywhere near real efficiency as far as *amount* of *production* is concerned (I never expect to reach full efficiency in quality of production). I receive warnings from here and there not to expend too much energy. I'll tell you those are words very unfortunate for one to hear (unless one happens to be a frail person of distinct physical handicaps—and I'm not that). The momentum of production is one of the strongest aids we have toward our goal. The process of fermentation works better under pressure. Had Stevenson conserved his energy, he might have lived ten years longer, but he probably would have produced twenty books less—the world can better lose his ten years than his twenty books.

The clouds are breaking. The sun is bursting in the windows and the lamps look a dull orange. There is general elation throughout the house now that the fearfulness of the thundering storm has passed.

Baby Ann weighs 14 lbs. and is a rugged, happy, lively little bunch. To me, she is the most interesting baby of all. She looks quite like us kids when we were small.

425

Chadds Ford, Pennsylvania
August 3, 1915

Dear Sid,

The house is quiet except for the low conversation between Carol and Baby Brother upstairs—his bedtime story. The rest of the children are asleep.

I feel that an unusually long period has passed since I last saw you —a far longer period than actual dates would say. A great, great deal has taken place.

You will remember that "your boy" was not feeling "scrumptious" when you left us in May. Two weeks later (the very night I completed the Atlantic City job) he was taken seriously sick with bronchitis and a severe attack. His fever mounted to 103 to 4½ and *stayed* there nearly a week. It was a hard seige and I shall never forget it. We of course got a trained nurse on the job, and as soon as our home doctor broke up this trouble I got the best child specialist in Phila. Much to our joy, upon rigid examination he found no organic trouble except that his digestive apparatus was in a very weakened condition (the results of the strain of whooping cough). The diet list contains surprising articles of food which, to our untrained minds, would seem outrageous.

I do not usually dwell on these subjects at such length, even to my home people, but I felt somehow that your particular interest in Baby Brother demanded it.

Frankly speaking, I'm damn sorry that you feel it such a sense of duty to hunt up that class of work to do when you ought to be digging after the great big things that *I* know and *others* know are down in that big heart of yours.

I feel sure that you've got enough to keep you in oatmeal and shoes, so why not throw your whole energy, even to robbing the days set aside for rug hunting, into ripping good work?—I mean the *experimental constructive* kind. You work; no one on earth can accuse you of anything else; but there's only one kind of work that counts, and that's the *constant, sustained* effort.—*Drive,* drive, drive, in the one direction, *painting!* without a break. It is the only way any man ever accomplished anything worthwhile.

Have the courage to shatter into a thousand pieces the multitude of duties you have assumed. You've got a profounder duty than any you would shatter, and that is to give your talent the *best* chance. If it isn't worth the *best* it isn't worth a damn.

I mentioned *rugs* in particular for I caught in an *instant* the concern and useless worry you were throwing into the matter of *rugs.* No doubt you would make a far better bargain than I would in buying rugs today, but by heaven, Sid, I bought mine in five minutes and have enjoyed it thoroughly for three years and don't know today whether its "doped" or not and don't give a damn, and don't give a damn for anyone who thinks I'm *stung,* or might be. I *do* know that I wanted it because the color was dang beautiful and was tickled that it cost $250 instead of $500. The dog pissed on it yesterday and the color didn't run, so I guess if it can stand that it's *some rug!*

426

Chadds Ford, Pennsylvania
August 13, 1915

Dear folks,

This is a day of rest (loafing). Yesterday I spent in Atlantic City with Christian Brinton and wife for the specific purpose of seeing the decorations at the Traymore, apropos of their being published in the *Studio* of which Brinton is now their active editor and critic. It was more of a surprise to me than it will be to you to know that the day was intensely enjoyable and beneficial to me, not more from the trip itself (by motorcar) than from the stimulation received from Brinton himself. I feel that in justice to myself and to him I must recast my impressions of that man and recognize the sound intellectual forces that exist and work under that external superficiality.

Experiment and Invention

I realize more and more my inability to bridge my prejudices and judge a man beneath his cloak. If I meet one of my own strata, so to speak (i.e. unconventional, democratic, free and careless of formalities, contemptuous of restraint, and with a wayward enthusiasm), I can usually size him up and judge his spiritual worth. In such a character there is less obstruction to a glimpse of his soul. On the other hand, I am very apt to allow trifling traits and customs, born of a dozen generations, to stand as a barrier between me and a man's true worth. I am apt to be too satisfied that my own free way of manner and dress, my prodigality of enthusiasm, etc., etc., is the one and only solution to vital accomplishment. History sings a different song many times.

How often have I placed a new acquaintance on a pedestal built of the frail stuff composed of an insignificant action or two—actions that fitted my *fancies!* And then was forced to suffer the reversal of opinion built upon the solid substance of association and experience!

On the contrary, to be foolish and silly enough to consign a man to the eternal bow-wows because he wears a wristwatch or pronounces the word neither, *neyther!*

This might be a slight exaggeration of the case, but not so much. The habit is *small,* to say the least, and is a terrible obstruction in the path of one's own development.

I must confess that there has been considerably more than a "wristwatch" or a few fancy pronunciations for me to overcome with Brinton. Many of his fallacies are dangerously near his *Soul*—but even those I am managing to sidestep. His messages to me this summer have been a *Godsend.* I say this with full meaning of the words. His remarks have not been the profoundest I ever heard by a long shot, nor were they intended to be; but they have come, I feel, at the crucial moment. I am balancing on a point and needed the impending jump directed, and I am getting it. His influence has been technical, but not without a fine sense of the deepest desires of an artist, which latter consideration give his technical criticism immense prestige in my mind.

So it came to pass that yesterday's trip was sort of climactical, and gave a final, vigorous impulsion to the summer of suggestions.

The WYETHS

Wyeth had taken on a few students for private lessons. One of them, Clark Fay, is mentioned in this letter. The others were Dwight Howland, Leo Mack and Pitt Fitzgerald.

The relics he took to Birmingham Meeting House belonged to Christian C. Sanderson, a local historian and schoolteacher.

Chadds Ford, Pennsylvania
September, 13, 1915

Dear Mama,

It's outrageous that I have let so many days (almost *weeks*) slip by without writing you some kind of a letter.

On my easel stands my most ambitious and successful technical effort. I feel quite certain now that a few years will see me at least in competition with the *painters*. This is no idle boast, for I feel quite definitely just where I stand, in spite of Brinton, Garber, Lathrop, [Edward] Redfield and others telling me enthusiastically that I am easily eligible to exhibit now.

In a way I am; I could *"put it over"* now (to use the popular term), but there is no earthly sense in that. I don't want to be rated as an *illustrator trying to paint,* but as a *painter* who has shaken the dust of the illustrator from his heels!!

With the atmosphere of my studio *electrified* with artistic zest and zeal, the outer atmosphere has been electrified with various thrills and distractions. Two circuses (immensely picturesque)—one drowning fatality—the Battle of the Brandywine memorial celebration, and a wicked little fight back of our hill (in which I was forced to play an active part) are some of the events of the last ten days.

Clark Fay, one of my pupils, dived three times in fourteen feet of muddy water for the drowned colored lad, and helped me out on the fateful noon with an ugly drunken Irish family.

But somehow, it all gave me zest, especially the fight; for after all, to test one's ability and power to land a telling blow after a few years of artistic dissipation is damned stimulating and digs up one's faith in his physical manhood again. The worst I got was from an old sheepdog who rightly thought I was trying to annihilate his master, and promptly jumped on my back, ripped my two shirts to shreds, and gave me some ugly teethmarks on the fleshy part of my side to nurse. These worried me at first but are entirely healed now.

I took a lot of Sanderson's relics (besides some of my own) to the Meeting House Saturday morning before daylight. I spent an hour in that grand old place of worship while the morning mists were slowly curling back off the hills. With only the faint sounds of distant cattle, a dog or two and crowing roosters. I stood over the great bloodstain in the center of the oaken floor (the spot that marks indelibly where the operating table stood, in this erstwhile hospital during the battle) and thought, as I gazed at it in the dim light, of the patriots who bled for us just 134 years ago! The impressions I received in that wondrous hour were overwhelming, and no inducement could make me attend the services and speaking in the P.M. with 6000 people, not even the appearance of Ambassador [Jean Adrien Aubin Jules] Jusserand. It would have all been spoiled.

Mr. Atwater entertained Jusserand, Murrough O'Brien (military attaché from England) and some others at lunch. It was a great day for this section. But as I watched the scores of autos and carriages from my studio window winding up the crik road, I did not reproach myself for not going—I was, in truth, sorry that all of the 6000 could not have experienced the tremendously inspiring sensation that I had that morning.

Baby Brother seems to gain. A new diagnosis of his condition reveals nothing abnormal, but has brought the specialist round to believe that *rest* is what the boy needs, physical and mental.

Henriette enjoys her school hugely. Her drawing is improving astonishingly. Carolyn is a *staver* and keeps us all guessing, and laughing. Baby Ann is a corker and seems to be weathering the inclemencies of the season with "benign indifference."

428

Studio
Chadds Ford, Pennsylvania
September 22, 1915. Tuesday

My dear Sid,

Your brief account of a momentous plan to actually own a spot of land on the Maine coast has aroused me *dreadfully!!* That is, it makes me burn inside to do likewise.

Can't we, this winter, take a run up to Port Clyde? I do so want to see it! I still cling to the glimpse of winter in Ogunquit as one of my most cherished memories. I never hope to repeat just that, but I want more of that stirring coast in my system. Tell me more about it, and if you can, send me some photos to soak up! I'll return them.

The early autumn is bringing to a close, the most industrious, arduous, and intense season I ever experienced. Playing on the somber background of Baby Brother's ominous condition of health, my efforts in living and art stand out livid and clear. I shall not dwell upon the wonderful boy's fluctuations between ecstatic life and low ebb—it is too painful. God knows, his brain is *perfect*. His spirit, his disposition, his understanding are positively *uncanny,* and so *many* times during moments of utter bodily weakness his brilliancy and power of feeling and of determination have lifted us all to exalted heights of understanding. To him I feel supremely grateful for my unquestionable growth this summer. We will keep him, I'm sure— we *can't* get along without him.

429

Chadds Ford, Pennsylvania
October 11, 1915

Dear Mama,

I returned from New York Wednesday evening after a very eventful two days stay.

My visit *bulged* with intense interest outside the field of art, yet in *no* way irrelevant to it.

I left home Tuesday on the first train with two canvases for *Scribner's,* which completed the Xmas story I have been at work upon for two months. The work represented my best achievement to date and I had every reason to make the journey in a pleasing state of mind. Furthermore, all at home were well, and happy with the consciousness of my evident satisfaction. I moved out of the valley with mingled feelings of delight and sadness.

I was comfortably settled in the rear seat of a "smoker" on the New York Express when I noticed, directly across the aisle, an old gentleman in the modest uniform of a G.A.R. veteran. His resemblance to Grandpapa was quite striking, except that he was built on a smaller scale. His whole being radiated energy and alertness, and his eyes twinkled. He was, to all appearances, an unusual specimen of rugged health for a man of his age and experiences.

It was quite impossible for me to keep my eyes from wandering to his face as we passed through the shifting lights and shadows of bridges, terminals and open stretches, and once I detected a faint smile on his face that indicated sociability.

Meantime a large puffy individual—another veteran—(they were evidently returning from the Washington reunion) made his way back from somewhere in the middle of the car and held a short conversation with my virile, unknown friend across the aisle. They swapped ages and regiments, and I was astonished to hear the little fellow confess to *84*. So was the *comrade* astonished. Their ages reversed would have exactly fitted.

After the larger man returned to his seat my friend came from across the aisle and sat by me. He radiated from every pore; he was as alive and enthusiastic as a boy, and with eyes flashing and hands waving told me the story of his life, from his birth in Breslau, Germany, to his present comfortable home in Watertown, Mass.

He needed little urging to unbury the minutest details, and he began with his first consciousness of life when he realized he was left an orphan at eight—his severe but perfectly trained apprenticeship in cabinetmaking at the orphanage, his supreme delight when he was graduated at 14 years (his diploma he has framed in his home), and then in glorious detail, the long tale of his wanderings over the face of the globe, beginning with his attempt to get through the Prussian lines and join the cause of the Hungarians in 1848 or thereabouts, his return to Breslau, and his subsequent voyage to Honolulu on a merchant ship. His desire to come to America and his escape from the German ship to an American whaler, the *Young Republic* (the hulk of which Ashley has a photograph). The wonderful story of whale hunting in the Bering Strait, the eventful journey via Cape Horn, and his landing in New Bedford in 1852.

Then, at the advice from the captain who favored him (18 yrs. of age at the time), he sought his trade (cabinetmaking) and soon located at Corn Hill, Boston. He married the boss's daughter finally and then to war, where he spent the entire four years.

"Then," he told me in his excellent English with the slightest accent, "I made a radical change in my life due to a new line of acquaintances." At Beverly he worked in a cabinet shop beside an American who never laughed at his somewhat ribald jokes, and who finally took him to see his pastor of the Baptist church. This seemed to awaken him to a renewed understanding of life, and the heritages of his home country, the *sentiment* of life, inspired him. He continued, "I left the cabinetmaker's trade and become a horticulturist. I have greenhouses in Watertown!" I hurriedly asked him, "Did you know Denys Zirngiebel?" "*Did* I know Denys Zirngiebel? *Did I* ——he was one of the best friends I had!—I look like him! I have often been taken for Denys Zirngiebel—with my hat on, see?"

"He was my grandfather!!!" Such looks of incredulity, astonishment, amazement, and final comprehension of the truth—(for he could see by my face how it affected me).

We fell to shaking hands and slapping backs until the whole car was interested.

Then we passed into the Hudson tunnel. It offered a few moments for reflection. I had been carried around the world—a twenty years' experience packed into 80 minutes. I had followed him through his life of cabinetmaker, husband, father, warrior, widower, again a husband—and then to my own doors on South Street to my grandfather, where he has been many, many times. *Robert Lassman.*

It is useless to say of what terrific value these experiences are to me. They mean infinitely more to me than concise, adaptable lessons in any of the forms of culture. I can only say that I am infused with an energy that comes as near being Holy as it is in my power to conceive.

To continue briefly, the chain of phenomenal experiences—I stopped in a flower store on Fifth Ave. to use their directory. I noted that it was owned by Thos. Galvin. I asked a middle-aged man standing near me if this was the Boston firm. He answered, "Yes," and that he was apprenticed there when a boy. He knew, and remembered so well, Grandpapa, Farquar and a dozen others whose names were so familiar to my ears years ago.

Had not this little incident followed the other so closely I might have passed it by.

Then my experience with Adolf Hanfstaengl, junior member of the big German art print store on Fifth Ave., and his older brother, I will never forget. We shall talk of it later. I had hoped to have spirit enough to write of it in this letter, but it fails me. There is too much to say. To admit that my appreciation of that profound spirit so characteristic in all who come from the continent has been more intensified, is only a trifle of what I would like to say. The grave crisis that is bound to come from the ever-increasing lack of that *earth love* which so envelopes the *peasant;* the *death* to any chances to make this extraordinary country of ours produce great things in economic idealism, scientific and artistic achievements is fast growing. I am suddenly and keenly awakened to what this nation lacks as a whole. I have *always* felt that I knew what it lacked for the development of art and music. Now I see that the same foundation of that religious love for *earth* and the *things that come out of it* is just as necessary to the farmer and craftsman as to me. To think of one's field of corn in terms of prayerful gratitude instead of jingling dollars is *imperative* to the success of Posterity.

I am sending you by express a memento of the trip in the shape of a framed proof of my most ambitious canvas—"The Fence Builders in Chadds Ford." I will see you all next Saturday A.M. if all goes well.

Chapter XVII

THE FAMILY

*"They, my children and the mother, are an
incorporate part of my body and soul."*

430

Chadds Ford, Pennsylvania
October 28, 1915

Dear Mama,

The birthday box arrived on Monday and not until then did it really seem like "birthday week."

The Swiss book I shall take up and try to get as much out of it as possible. I cannot expect to win from it the reverencing thrills that you have received, but to know that *you* did, from those very lines, will mean a great deal. This, added to a not inconsiderable old-world love which is inherent in me, I may get more than you think.

Birthday week was bitterly slashed into by another bad spell of Baby Brother's. Less violent than the previous attacks, but very depleting to his little body. The result was another rigid examination which uncovered not a single organic weakness except the upper intestine which is sensitive.

Henriette wrote her letter before the box arrived and wants me to say that she will write again soon.

She feels vitally attached to you all and the home up there, even though her visit was so brief. She forms indelible impressions so rapidly! I cannot but feel that she will do something in the way of creative work some day.

431

Jefferson Hospital
Philadelphia, Pennsylvania
December 3, 1915. Friday A.M.

Dear folks,

It is useless for me to conceal the fact that this has been a heavy week for all of us. The idea of the *hospital* is grim always, and to isolate one who has been under our constant and minute supervision is an extraordinary strain, to say the least.

The fact that this is the very best thing we can do to come to some definite conclusion and treatment of the case does not relieve the

511

pressure of apprehension, as much as I try to think it should; and until the diagnosis is complete and the treatment specified I must live in that suffocating condition of fear.

Esther is here with him, and is doing admirably of course. I have come up every day but Wednesday, when Carol came in my place. Today I arrived early as they are to take a series of X-ray photographs of his stomach to help determine the trouble. Thus far Dr. [Edwin E.] Graham believes it spasmotic pyloris, which is a nervous contraction of the stomach's exit which forbids the normal passage of food residue. This, he believes, will be curable by medicine and diet, but which if malignant is only remedied by an operation, which heaven prevent! There also seems to be some difficulty with his heart action which misses a beat three or four times a minute.

Upon his arrival he was immediately given a large meal. Instead of showing ill effects, he seemed to thrive with normal passages and all—the second day the same, and for a time it was hinted that maybe we were giving him too little to eat. Tuesday afternoon, however, he developed trouble and has been quite sick ever since, vomiting (something unusual for him) and quite weak.

Today he is all in, but has managed to hold down the "opaque food" given him for the purpose of photography. This series will be taken a number of times between now and tomorrow afternoon, when we will return home, I hope.

The folks at home are OK. Baby Ann doing exceptionally well.

I shall let you know any details of significance immediately as they come to light.

Babe's perfect visit hangs like a gem in the full gallery of my memories. As to digesting it and truly enjoying its benefits I must confess that I have been in no state of mind to do so. Its savor will last however, and when the air is cleared of the cloud that now dims it, I shall take up that tonic and make the most of it.

Will you pass on my very best wishes for Ed's birthday anniversary on the fifth. It is likely that I shall not write.

[Letter continued]

3:30 P.M.

As I have part of an hour left before I start for home tonight, I will add more of the day's history.

At one o'clock we studied Baby Brother's stomach by the aid of the X-ray. The opaque food (a barley paste as far as I can make out) had not left his stomach except a very small amount. It was a fascinating thing to see, the shape of his little stomach and the coil of the upper intestine leaving it, the stomach practically a silhouette and the dark spots in the intestines indicating the passage of residue.

The black room, with its hopeless maze of wires, coils, switches and great black mystery cabinets and cells, was impressive enough without the terrifying cracking and banging of the blue flashes from contact points—and underneath all, the heavy drone of dynamos. With this sensation in one's ears and brain, and add to it the miraculous event of actually watching a stomach at work, it was more than I could comprehend, and I am still living in the vague impressions that border more on the supernatural than on intense realism.

On a small scale this examination was in the form of a clinic, and the chief constantly talked of what he saw, etc., and then in that black hole I heard him say the only remedy is to cut a new hole in the stomach! I never felt so awe-struck in my life!

It sounded so final that I gave myself up to that conclusion. For the ensuing two hours I was stupefied, then the *grand old man,* Graham, removed the ten-ton weight by saying that he had not even *thought* of an operation and that he felt confident of correcting the case otherwise. Such conditions only call for an operation 1 out of 50 so I feel there is only 1 out of 50 chances that that will be our bad luck.

Tomorrow noon winds up the examination and by evening we and the boy will once more be at *home,* God bless it!

432

Chadds Ford, Pennsylvania
December 8, 1915

Dear Mama,

The diagnosis is complete, which claims the case to be in the main nervous trouble together with a too small pyloric passage of the stomach. We start in tonight on the treatment, mainly diet and certain postures.

513

433

Chadds Ford, Pennsylvania
December 16, 1915

Dear Mama,

A wonderful storm hit us Sunday night and left us the following evening with five inches of snow, a driving wind, and the mercury well down in the tube.

Henriette is here in the studio with me, playing the Victrola and drawing. She is great company, no mistake. Such an abundance of interest for a child. She actually creates an atmosphere wherever she is. (Just now she is playing *Ave Maria* by Elman.)

434

Chadds Ford, Pennsylvania
December 20, 1915

Dear Mama,

Baby Brother seems well as usual and we all think that we can see an improvement already. Even his weight has increased this week.

It is right in line for you to mention Christian Science.

I must confess myself to be so enamored with the mighty theory of evolution, the survival of the fittest, and the utter *equality* of all things from the human brain to the pebble at your feet, that I could never embrace the teachings of C.S. One of my most stirring interests in existence lies in the *fallibility* of nature in *all* or *any* of its forms, and in my most reposeful and reflective moments, the withering of a leaf is as tremendous a bit of phenomena as the passing of the nearest human associate. This may seem cruel, but I maintain that by so thinking and feeling, I am not lessening the importance of humanity but I am lifting the passing of a leaf up to the same importance.

What would happen if I actually saw a *miracle* transpire—a bone heal, a cancer cured, a broken back mended, I know not. I would probably *believe,* just as I would believe in *ghosts* if I could meet and talk with one, and plunge a knife through its filmy form without damage.

But to cease *worry* is another matter, and I am in full *accord* with the principle. It is sane, comprehensive, and decidedly practical. But this is *not* Christian Science.

435

Aunt Hat was sending to N. C. Wyeth a portrait of his great-great-grandfather, Noah Wyeth.

Studio
Chadds Ford, Pennsylvania
December 28, 1915

Dear Mama,

Xmas passed off *splendidly!* Baby Brother seemed to profit rather than lose by the spirit of the day, and has held his own since—so the *foundation* of Xmas day was quite complete. The glamour and excitement, so characteristic of our other Xmases, was held in check perfectly in spite of the prodigal generosity of all our dear relatives and friends. We were overwhelmed with remembrances from all sides. It seems hard to believe that we have a right to so much expressed good feeling. It has all given me an added vim—a new *urge* to make the very best of all departments of my life.

As good as my memory is for details, it is hopeless for me to thank each one in particular, nor do I think you will demand that of me. So all I can say is Thanks! Thanks!

Of course, the symbols of home, those things that express even more than the spirit of the sender—such as the *wreath,* the photographs, the cake made by you and browned in the stove that baked and boiled for all of us so many years—stand out with especial significance.

When the package—

(Two hours and a half have elapsed since I layed down my pencil —one of the boys came over with a couple of canvases for criticism and I had to take advantage of the fast-fading light. Since then, the chores had to be done, fires fixed for the night, mail gotten, supper eaten, an extemporaneous Santa-Brownie story for the children and a cigar smoked.)

When the package arrived it was in a ragged condition, no mistake! But nothing, I'm sure, was lost from it. The top was almost free from wrapping paper, and exposed through the squares of cord (which, with heaven's help, saved the complete disintegration of the bundle) was the photograph of the dear old "front gate," embraced by its appropriate and rightful garnishment—the wreath!

These two articles we removed immediately and hung the greens in the usual place of honor in the center of the panel over the fireplace. The photograph I placed on my desk, and in the evening, after all had gone to bed, I dreamed over every detail, seeing, smelling and hearing again, a thousand of the cherished remembrances of that spot.

I peer into this silent surface-image. It begins to live, and I can hear, as I stand in that velvety shadow of the "spruces," their soft soughing, like the distant sound of summer surf. The familiar, delicious fragrance of the "needles" and their pitchy limbs reaches my nostrils, and *instantly* all my senses are atingle! Every twig and grass blade lives—the shadows on the ground move, gently, like seaweed moves in deep water. I squint my eyes to look through the drenching sunlight beyond, and slowly my sight pierces the dark house shadow. The piazza in all its detail, the narrow windows of the parlor and those of the "spare room" above. My eyes do not stop at the windowpanes but continue on into the dim room. I scan all its furnishings carefully, I feel the carpet under my feet, and hear the bookcase shake as I walk past it into the "sitting room." And so I search every nook and corner of the old house.

Once, I saw Mama, sitting by the sewing-table window—a letter in her hand, its paper slightly trembling, the other hand in a characteristic pose spread over the lower part of the face—so much like Grandpapa. She is looking out over the river toward Burgess's. Her glasses are somewhat crooked. Her eyes moist.

And then I move through the pantry and inhale the slight fragrance of clean dishes, preserved pears, and bread smell. Over the warm threshold into the kitchen, and as I round into the "back room" I look out of the east window and catch a fleeting glimpse of Papa. The sunlight on the milk pail dazzles my eyes for the second, but I have caught the impression of Papa's back, arms lifted and crooked a little, head forward and to one side. He disappears behind the corner of the barn.

Again I am looking in the front gate. I can hear footsteps—about every third or fourth, a slight scuff. Through the pales of the fence

I define a figure of a man, somewhat stooped, head bent, left arm considerably crooked and held a little back. Passing behind the sliced lights gleaming between the pales, the figure trembles along as though behind a rapidly opening and closing shutter. Although indistinct I recognize Uncle Deny. He moves down the driveway and I lose sight of him behind the bank—and then I listen for the even, dull staccato as he mounts the back steps. I can hear the sound of the screen door as it slams.

I could go on infinitely with these word pictures; could reverently dwell upon such trifling details as the sound [of] the front gate "chains," as from my bed I used to hear Papa loop them over the post as he left home for the "early train." The Lilies of the Valley that grew, timidly, in the corner on the right—and *always,* behind all this lovable pantomine, the sprinkled glisten of the river! It's all too wonderful!! I cannot write with dry eyes.

And so you see, the soul of that glorious Xmas box was the photograph of our beloved "front gate." It has made me rich in gifts.

But have I a right to thus transcend the really great joy we experienced from the many attractive parcels marked "Henriette from A'nt Mama," "Sis Carolyn from Aunt Hat," etc., etc.? I am living my pleasures in the imagination, and the imagination was nourished and stimulated by the little packages. So I pay my deepest tribute after all to the packages!

The photo of Stimson is singularly fine and by a long way the best portrait yet. I say with full meaning that I am proud of his countenance—it is inspiring! This photograph implies somewhat the richness and significance to us of his last visit, which I shall never forget.

Please, if Aunt Hat is there, tell her how much I will treasure that fascinating portrait of Noah Wyeth. I am so happy to think that Aunt Hat has learned to respect my deep love for these keepsakes and heirlooms, to trust me with them. No one will ever quite know how *necessary* the *associations* of just such mementos are to me. It is a big *chunk* of what I profess to be my *religion*. I thank her deeply.

The letters, too, meant so much. Ed's sparkling note indicates that time will ripen him into a real "wit." It is a happy tendency!

The photo of his twins shows them to be sturdy little youngsters,

517

and although we too can easily pick out the "Moeller" baby and the "Wyeth" baby, I see marked resemblance to Ed in both of them. To Clara and Ed we send our thanks for their kind thoughts so fully expressed in gifts.

Stimson.

Amongst many useful presents, I received *Winslow Homer* by William Hans Downes from Carol. This adds book No. 6 to my growing set of the finest books published on the masters. Vermeer, Rembrandt, Segantini, Rodin, Ingres and now *Homer.* I also received Charles Kingsley's *My Winter Garden,* which I must insist that Babe should read. It is short and *fat* with inspirational motives. Not morality preaching however. Will mail it someday.

The Legend of Robin Hood was offered to me to illustrate, the day before Xmas. What a wonderful opportunity! I trust that the scheme can be put through.

Now I shall not attempt to do any more Xmas present gossiping. To do it completely would be an *appalling job,* as I look at the mountain of gifts on the piano, table, and about the *tree* in the corner. I must let each one speak for himself, and save my energy for the two canvases I expect to "lay-in" tomorrow.

I will end this rambling letter with long and loud cheers for a Hearty and Happy New Year to *all!*

436

Chadds Ford, Pennsylvania
January 28, 1916

Dear Mama,

The composition lectures every Thursday are creating a stir, but it is keeping me busy scheming to keep fellows from the art side (Phila. and Wil.) flocking in. It would be too much. The four fellows, Howland, Mack, Fay and Fitzgerald, are very sympathetic and about all I want.

437

Chadds Ford, Pennsylvania
February 1, 1916

Dear Mama,

Baby Brother is coasting down the steep bank from the barn. I am sitting by the kitchen windows and can see him. Mr. Jenkins has just given him an extra good push, and he is yelling his delight all the way down.

Mr. Jenkins!! He is back with us again apparently as well as ever. I can never express the relief it was to have him take up his duties again. I wish, for himself and for us, he would last forever. He's the most comfortable man I ever knew. I never realized what I lost when he left us a year ago. He looks exactly the same.

438

Wyeth was illustrating The Mysterious Stranger *by Mark Twain.*

His grandmother Zirngiebel's half-sister, Friederika Zollinger, had one child, Marianna, who married Henry Holzer. The Holzer's three children, Marguerite ("Gritly"), Henry and Albert, were the second cousins who grew up with N. C. Wyeth.

Chadds Ford, Pennsylvania
February 17, 1916

Dear Mama,

Although it's but 3:30 in the afternoon it's all I can do to keep my eyes open. Shocking!! Last night the boys and I (five of us) went into Wilmington on the 5:30 train, had some supper, saw a moving picture and at 10 o'clock walked to the Ford in the wonderful moonlight. Of course, this was the real reason for going. We came by way of Rockland & Beaver Valley—a long way, making it a 15-mile jaunt. We arrived here at 1:10 which, you see, proves that we did not loaf on the way. The night was unusually charming and the old valley radiated romance under the extraordinary conditions with greater effusion than ever before. But today I'm dead tired, and my eyes close in spite of everything if I start to read—this being my present duty in preparation for my next picture.

The first Mark Twain picture reached *Harper's* yesterday and I am eagerly awaiting a word from them.

It's a picture of three boys of 1590 in the Austrian Mountains in winter. Feathered caps, leather jerkins, tight breeches and swaggering boots or leggings. They are by an icebound brook, shooting at a target with a *bow-gun*. Snow-laden firs, distant Alps, and conspicuously rising on a rocky pinnacle in the middle distance, a great turreted castle.

Much of the spirit of the scene I have built upon the spirit of, and memories of, my boyhood in the Holzer family. One of old Uncle's homemade bow-guns, that Albert and I used to use, plays a prominent part, and I feel sure you will feel the romance of castles and mountains as related in German legends and fairy stories, particularly as Bertha used to tell them.

The whole series of eight pictures will be created from that same source, the impression gained during the visits to Clarendon Hills. Then follows the big contract of the year, Stevenson's *Black Arrow* (to be done like *Treasure Island*).

A fine letter from Scribner's today suggests that they give me still more to do, that is, come nearer to keeping my time filled so that they can count on monopolizing my output. This sounds good to me as there isn't a publishing firm in the world better equipped, financially and with better mediums to reach the public. I am deeply pleased that they feel stirred to this action. We (Scribner's and I) have passed through several squeamish moments, and in each case I have turned things in their favor, thus I feel that they hold implicit faith in anything I promise to do—thus no written contracts have ever existed. Personally, *contracts* are a blight on my artistic ardour, and turn me into too much of a machine.

439

Chadds Ford, Pennsylvania
February 26, 1916

Dear Papa,

The New York visit was pregnant with fine experiences. Delivered two of my best works to Scribner's; saw ten of my originals installed, permanently, in the children's reading room of the New York Public Library on Fifth Ave.; witnessed the delightful and thrilling presentation of *Treasure Island* on the legitimate stage at the Punch and Judy Theatre, N.Y.—thrilling in particular to me, for they have followed my types and costumes almost exactly, and the scenery where possible.

I noticed, amongst the photos in the lobby of the theater, a picture of one Ferguson, an actor I had met 15 years ago in Reed's studio, and on the strength of this sent up a note to his dressing room, was subsequently invited behind the scenes, and we all, Long John Silver, Black Dog, Bill Bones, Jim Hawkins, Ben Gunn and the rest, in the flesh and blood, had a lively time.

Thursday I spent some of the time in the library looking up medieval data concerning my forthcoming books, and then, much to my enlightenment and extreme pleasure, visited the Swedish art exhibition in the Brooklyn Museum.

Am feeling more and more the weakness and insincerity of Amer-

ican art, its lack of individuality, and the rusticating content of the
artists to rest on past traditions. I am most ardent to come abreast
of the modernistic spirit and *will do so* if my *caliber* is equal to it.

440

Chadds Ford, Pennsylvania
March 3, 1916

Dear Mama,

The Medieval period is gradually drawing me down into its tremendous confusion of customs, costumes and its singular spirit. I
feel all pent up with the crowding impressions of an age rich in
picturesqueness but black with infamy. The history of those times
is after all rather suffocating—that is if one goes deeper than the
mere panoramic pageant of events. So, as I say, my mind feels
stultified and perverted, and will be until I blow off steam by producing a few canvases on the subject.

Excuse this thin note; my head is dogged with long-bows, spears,
solets, doublets, mail, quarter-staffs, jousting bouts, ferries, skerries,
and moats—and Lord knows what!

441

Chadds Ford, Pennsylvania
April 19, 1916

My dear Sid,

Will celebrate Lexington Day!

Although I am just returned from a very tedious, laborious twelve
hours in Phila., haunting the recruiting stations, arsenals, government commissaries and a dozen other dismal offices called headquarters for picture data, I shall scribble off a note to you. It will be
a refreshing relief.

This has been the busiest winter, and I daresay the most progressive winter I have experienced in my short career.

There has been so much work offered to me that it has been a
constant problem what to take and what to leave. I am doing *The
Black Arrow* (Stevenson's) in the same format as *Treasure Island*.
Am also carrying along Mark Twain's "The Mysterious Stranger"

(a posthumous story which begins in the May number of *Harper's*)
—also Col. Cody's autobiography for Hearst's magazine. A wonderful chance to do a 30 full-page edition of *Robin Hood* in color I had to turn down. All this besides two problems for private mantel decorations—one a landscape and the other a hunting scene in the making.

Mrs. Skinner, the poet, has been here since Jan. 1st and left only a week ago. Painted a decoration for her "Wild Woman's Lullaby" for *Scribner's,* which came out unusually well (meantime she fell violently in love with me and I had to send her home!! sh! Will tell you about it sometime—'tis a very humorous yarn to listen to, but it was hard on us here).

Then I've had four boys with me since the first of the year. Composition lectures once a week, Thoreau readings Sunday night, sketch class Sat. afternoons. They have made big strides and have given me tremendous impetus. Howland appears with three full pages and ten vignettes in *Scribner's* June number. College rowing illustrations. Clark Fay is illustrating a book for Chapin, has done three covers for Heines and several stories for *Sunday Mag.* Mack has just sold a cover to Heines and has bright prospects of placing a subject picture with Chapin.

Fitzgerald, the fourth boy, is here just to study and is starting right at the beginning on close still-life and out-of-door study. He has money for two years. He's going to make good. Fay drops illustration for one year, beginning in June, and expects to do solid study. Little by little I'm getting them shaped round to a healthy method of attack.

Two weeks ago I spent the day and night with Alden Weir and Gari Melchers—Christian Brinton and a young fellow by the name of *Tack* [Augustus Vincent] who is making some wonderful discoveries in the science and system of color, which is stirring up the bigger men tremendously.

There is no doubt in my mind that Segantini and the Duisionists hold the solution to the color problem. To retain strength of color and values we must give up this *mixing* proposition, i.e. in the slightest degree mess color together on the pallet. Every color manufactured by the color chemists is a separate and distinct unit or organism; by mixing any one with another the *force* (i.e. the carrying power) of both colors is dissipated, even though it is heightened

N. C. Wyeth, 1916.

with white. If you mix white with blue you raise the *value* but lessen the *color* strength in greater proportion. Now instead of mixing white with blue, put down a spot of pure cobalt or ultramarine, as the case may be, and surround it with the necessary white which by *refraction* will lighten the value.

T. [Tack] works over a white impasto (with lights only) and uses neither pallet nor brushes, but applies his paint direct from the tubes! Now don't think for a minute that I condone this stunt, for I *don't*. I admire *surfaces* too much for that; but I'll tell you, Sid, I never received such a good demonstration of the *direction* a man should go in the management of his color! Since then I have heightened the brilliancy of my pictures 50%.

In contradistinction to all this (as I said, with the atmosphere enhanced by Weir and Melchers) I got into a genuine nest of post impressionists of the rankist kind. Duchamp—the-nude-descending-the-staircase man, and all the other nuts. I've kept my mind entirely open to this movement and have struggled to derive some benefit, and if possible to sympathize with their viewpoint. I spent a night at one of their clubs on Madison Ave. Enough! They are entirely without aim or principle—a motley lot of charlatans, most of them, with no head nor tail to their endeavors unless it is to be *different*— goddamn the word. I *worship* individuality, but one can't *manufacture* it!!

But my God, how I admire Segantini, and I was so happy to hear Melchers declare him to be perhaps the biggest man of the century and the father of one of the most potent influences in the art world today.

Brinton comes down here in June with all his wonderful lantern slides of Scandinavian, Spanish, French, and Russian art. Will have a treat. Wish you could be here.

Passed another glorious hour with Roosevelt in N.Y.—and never laughed so hard in my life. His account of the "whiskered bird" and the way the papers assailed him for the "discovery" (which he never claimed, giving full credit in almost the first paragraph written the night he saw the queer creature—ms. of which I saw) was without doubt the most humorous monologue I ever heard!!

I am glad I have lived to come in contact with that man.

442

"Sancho" was the Wyeth's Irish setter who held the distinction of appearing in Ripley's "Believe It or Not." The dog lived to be twenty-four.

Carol Wyeth's sister, Elizabeth, was married to Ralph Sargent.

Chadds Ford, Pennsylvania
April 21, 1916

Dear Mama,

It's just seven, and to settle my breakfast will get off a line to you. I am in the sun room. The light from the entire eastern sky floods in upon me. Although the sun has not emerged from a cloudy sunrise it is nevertheless brilliantly lighted by the fiery edges of the cloud forms. Birds are singing at a great rate, the woodpecker keeping perfect tempo for the combined symphony with his steady beating. Blood roots, great starry ones, are spattered over the bank before me, looking more than ever like the constellations. "Sancho" darts hither and thither, aroused and excited by the birds and an occasional rabbit.

Baby Brother has just arrived from the breakfast table to take his accustomed one hour lay-down on the couch here. It's a wonderful place for him to pass this quiet period. As he lies on his back, he watches the flights of birds, and occasionally a sparrow lights on the glass roof or even on the sill by his side. The waving of trees in the wind seems to fascinate the little fellow too.

Henriette and Carolyn are tuned *way* up. Brown as mulattos and active as goats, they're a team! When H. isn't picking flowers and singing at the top of her lungs, she's contrastingly silent and deep in a book. *Alice in Wonderland* is receiving its 3rd reading in her hands; *Robin Hood* has passed its second; *Grimm's Fairy Tales* gets a spasm regularly. It will astonish you to hear her read out loud to Carolyn—fluent and understandably, gliding over long sentences and big words with expression and full meaning. It seems remarkable to me.

Carolyn is also a bookworm, feasting on pictures. To hear her fake reading, inventing the tale as she goes along, is killing. She does a *heap* of cutting out too. Her eyes seem to be improving.

Ann, I'm particularly anxious to have you see. I have no words to describe her. She interests me as an infant more than any of the others did, on account of her sense of humor and good fellowship. Honestly, you can bang her 'round and really jar her severely in rough and tumble, and she'll laugh it off. Wait till you see for yourself. I call her my "joker." So rosy and round-faced too!

Hilda has gone with Elizabeth—just now in West Chester for a couple of weeks, then to Perth Amboy for a few months, and thence to Virginia where Ralph is to build. We will miss her like everything. A girl of marked ability and integrity in certain directions. I just hope she finds a good, simple, wholesome man. It will be her Salvation.

One of the stiffest "drives" in work has just come to a close, with a series of seven pictures, all large ambitious attempts, done one right after the other without a letup of a day between. I just heard yesterday through Schoonover that Chas. Scribner said that he never in his experience with illustrators for 50 years knew of anyone who could catch the spirit of a theme and push it through with such vim and consistent strength as I can. A rather modest remark for me to pass on—however I am pleased that a man of his experience can say that of me. It bodes well for the future. Now, I've got a couple of pictures to do for *Collier's* and then I'll come up home. I plan to leave Friday night.

Celebrated Apr. 19th by having a long reflection on the times down at Leach's corner, watching the bicycle race.

443

Chadds Ford, Pennsylvania
May 19, 1916

Dear Mama,

Wednesday morning I dropped Mack from the group here. It created a stir but I find all the boys approving, or at least sympathizing, with my action. He was not industrious enough and was letting the girl question and other affairs interfere too seriously with his hours and his energy. I was giving too much and getting no return.

444

En route to Pittsburgh
June 27, 1916. 6:30 P.M.

Dear Mama,

Tonight I am off to see the annual exhibition at the Carnegie Institute, Pittsburgh. The directors have gotten together a fabulous show of all the European moderns, inclusive from Bastien-Lepage period up. They claim it to be as good as three trips to Europe in point of quality and representative selection. Of all times that I should *not* leave my studio, *this* is that time, but it would have been an incalculable educational loss not to have gone. So I'm on my way. I shall return tomorrow night. I have letters of introduction to the director of the Institute, Beatty, also to a Mr. Stimmel of Pittsburgh who owns 12 canvases by a young Russian I'm deeply interested in. There are 800 pictures in the show!

Out of three applicants to fill Mack's place in the class I have accepted Owen Stephens, the son of Alice Barber Stephens. Perhaps you remember my remarking a year or more ago how much he resembled Babe in appearance. I'm glad to have him, for I feel he will be a virile addition to the group.

445

Chadds Ford, Pennsylvania
June 3, 1916

Dear Mama,

My trip to Pittsburgh was wonderful!

The exhibition far exceeded my anticipations, and gave me tremendous added admiration of the French artists. To anyone who, even though only half-intelligent in the judgment of pictures, would look at the retrospective group of 200 canvases, they must inevitably be struck by the indefatigable energy and sustained integrity of that nation's painters. It is a severe commentary on the transient, puerile efforts that are masqueraded as art in our annual shows (made up mostly of grotesque, sensational stuff flashing mere whims of shallow brains and shallower emotions). One can stand before any canvas there and criticize it with justice from the point of view of our modern discoveries in the matters of light interpretations and air, etc., but one cannot gainsay the fact that any or all of these works represent thought, feeling, and sustained zeal which should be added to the pea-soup strength of the present day output.

The English section was indifferently good, the German bad with two notable exceptions, Italy ditto. Belgian mediocre and the French contemporary examples brilliant but very uneven. Henri Martin's "Lovers" is magnificent.

Mr. Beatty, the director of the Carnegie art museum, treated me royally—in fact he practically spent the day with me.

I've got the capacity for a good deal more work than I'm doing even now, and I figure it's a big mistake to relax one whit if one is feeling well and buoyant—and I *am* all the time. To know, as I know now, what other men have accomplished (that is, the important men), and to recognize their strict economy of time and *long* hours and great variety of achievements constantly stirs me to greater activity. Of course it *takes* from one, but what one loses of longevity he gains by momentum. There is no one of my contemporaries to whom I can turn as an example; they all, as I do, waste time and give in too quickly to the tired feeling, or which is more likely to be the case, to feel that we have done our share and *deserve* relaxation or rest. Roosevelt, as one of the older men, is extraordinary they say, but I believe it possible for *anyone* with a good stomach and decent habits to get near to his standard of activity.

446

Enclosed in this letter was a faded Fourth-of-July paper cone from a sky rocket.

Studio
Chadds Ford, Pennsylvania
July 5, 1916. 3:00 P.M.

Dear Papa,

One tiny incident that came to my notice early this morning swung me completely away from any desire or power to work. And ever since my thoughts have soared and suffered by turns, until now I must write for the little satisfaction there is in it.

Yesterday was a glorious day for the children. They had some firecrackers, some paper balloons and, in the evening, a few fireworks.

The WYETHS

I cannot *bear* letting the day pass without this form of celebration, as much in memory of the boyhood experiences *I* always enjoyed, as for the national reasons. Although I worked until four in the afternoon I joined the kids there and we had a high old time for six hours. Well, this morning the children were enjoying the *leftovers,* in the way of a few stray firecrackers and the empty shells of Roman candles, pinwheels, etc. Henriette and Carolyn wandered down into the field below the house and picked up four of five of those paper heads, shaped like dunce caps, that are fastened on the ends of rockets. Carolyn had one of hers filled with wild raspberries! This was enough!! Visions of the old home on the "Fourth" and after *avalanched* into my mind and I have been overwhelmed ever since! How many times did we boys hunt the cow pasture over for these little pink, blue, green or yellow caps!!—found days after the celebration perhaps, the pasteboard cones faded by the sun and rain to delicate shades of lavender, nile green and near white—and then to fill them with those few choice dwarf blueberries that grew in the thick curly grass somewhat near the grafted tree. The vision of those heavenly blueberries, dusted over with sky dust! Their fragrance in the sun-warmed rocket caps!! and the thousand memories that it all brings up! My God, what ecstatic *joy,* what exquisite pain it is to dream these things over again. I am writing this with wet eyes, but through the blurred sight I can see the dear old Charles silently moving by, screened by the alders, and flecked with myriad crumbs of sunshine. The lone elm is slightly waving back and forth, back and forth. The lay of the land across the river, the dark sentinel cedars along the "New Road," the glimpse of Burgesses' black and white chimneys—and the rumble of a team over the "iron bridge," and under the bridge the river weeds moving, beckoning— beckoning to me.

Papa, my heart is too full, but I thank you and Mama for all the wonderlife that you gave me in my boyhood!

447

Chadds Ford, Pennsylvania
July 17, 1916

[To his mother]

530

A Memory

Evening, just after dusk.

The Lay of the Land from the Cowyard
    down to the River.

The uneven, heavy-sodded turf, the long
    black line of Arbor Vitaes, the low-
    hanging apple trees and through
    their arch a glimpse of the soft
    sheen of the River.

The smell of damp earth, fallen apples,
    mouldy boards (piled under the
    evergreens)—a whippoorwill
    calling rhythmically, incessantly.

Shapes hang in festoons, heavy and dark;
    the black hedgerow like sentinels
    in close formation casts a brooding
    spirit over these acres and gives
    to it an air of seclusion, of great
    remoteness.

This little tract always held a singular
    and strong fascination for me. I
    often wandered over its uneven
    surface wondering at its varied
    mounds and hollows (places
    where rich loom had been removed,
    and the hummocks of spent earth
    dumped from the greenhouses). Here and there
    a faint trace of
    an apple tree stump.

A primal spirit hovered about this place
    —it seemed a little grim, out-
    lawed as it was from its
    neighboring fields of flowers and fruit,
    just a place to dump things or, on
    occasion, to pasture an animal. I
    sympathized with it because it
    was ostracized, and lonely.

I will close this jotting while I am still lingering under the early apple tree by the cowyard gate. I am listening carefully, and methinks I can hear old Lizzie munching her oats in the barn. The whippoorwill has stopped.

448

Chadds Ford, Pennsylvania
August, 1916

Dear Mama,

The birthday gathering at Holzers must have been *great*—how all things that have anything to do with Switzerland appeal to me!—it is a feeling that of late has developed rapidly. The Swiss dinner is *genuine* celebration—it has a universal meaning (not the fact that it is *eating,* understand) but it symbolizes something *fundamental;* it embodies the *essence* as it were, of the Mother country. The costumes would have spoiled it for me (putting myself in "Aunties'" place). It's sort of dragging in a superfluous *material* detail that is too close to allow one's fancy and reminiscences full sway. The odor of an old home-dish will bring marvelous thoughts of the past into one's mind; the sight of characteristic wearing apparel on a household member thrusts all suggestion to the rear. I doubt if Aunty enjoyed this phase of the celebration as did the wearers of the costumes.

449

Studio
Chadds Ford, Pennsylvania
August 11, 1916

Dear Mama,

Sky thickly curtained with one great cloud blanket. Light pours into the studio like a liquid, soft and strongly luminous. Nature seems to be completely relaxed, silently idling after her debauch of a month of torrid heat and fierce spasmotic rains.

The summer seems to be heavy with problems, some of them menacing. Against the gray, thundering background of the great war across the seas, one deals with the oppressive heat and the ever-threatening contagion; and meantime one must watch so closely the business of progressive living and doing—the *doing* that brings in the monetary returns, the *progress* that means so little to the practical world and yet the most vital to ourselves.

The boys here have added great zest to the working spirit. Their response to what things I can teach them has been highly satisfying and inspiring. In fact the whole atmosphere seems to abound in reciprocal energies. A genuine feeling of affection is growing, one for the other, and all for Nature.

450

Chadds Ford, Pennsylvania
August 18, 1916

Dear Mama,

Ann is walking—has been for 10 days. It is strange that each one of the children walked at 17 months. She is, to my judgment, the most attractive baby of them all.

On Wednesday our new Hudson arrived. The worst part of it all was the passing of the old Ford. The folks had quite a time quieting Henriette—she was so affected by its loss. I am pleased she feels those things, for I did and the memories are dear to me.

The glamour of the new car helped Sis Carol and Baby Brother over the period.

451

Chadds Ford, Pennsylvania
September 8, 1916

My dear Sid,

It is very possible that you were writing your note to me while I was talking to Ivory [H. Pyle student] about you last evening. He was interested in what I could tell him of your Maine retreat and seemed to appreciate with more than his usual feeling the glory of such a program as yours.

Your account of the work accomplished at Port Clyde sounds bully!

This has been the biggest working summer I ever put in—from the standpoint of practical work accomplished, and of constructional work along the lines of painting—and *living*. The record of 17 canvases for *Black Arrow,* 7 canvases for Mark Twain's story, 4 large and several small canvases for Buffalo Bill's autobiography, besides two magazine stories for Chapin—a subject picture and a Pierce-Arrow ad (which netted me a sum I could in no justice to my bigger ambitions refuse)—and several *Collier* stories—all since May 1st.

The Harper things have won me several new friends and there has been quite a call for the originals, which signifies something. *Black Arrow,* I believe, is considerably more mature than my other Stevenson books. I am anxious to know what the public opinion will be.

But today I have a canvas on my easel, the culmination of many studies and the deepest consideration I was capable of, regarding all its expressive phases—dramatic, poetic, cosmic, decorative—besides careful drawing and construction.

The boys are driving me to it, that's a fact! A more earnest lot you never saw. The strong bond of real attachment for one another is deeply affecting, particularly as it is based upon the rock foundation of candid intercourse. The types are *so* different too! Clark Fay, an adventuresome, boyish but intense character from Denver— Pitt Fitzgerald, a highly refined and sensitized lad from Ohio— Owen Stephens (the son of Alice Barber Stephens), the product of cultured circles, with high ideals and a faultless character (with the blemish of conservatism to fight).

Poor Howland at present is out of running, owing to his marriage which I'm afraid will permanently hurt his progress.

Our composition class, although composed of only four members, is just as intense as the best of the old H.P. classes, and the arguments that follow the lecture proper are corking!

I've missed putting a question to you we've had in mind all summer. What chance is there at Port Clyde for a cottage or something, where we could get our meals out, for say, July and August. We are determined to hit the Maine coast next summer. We have a new Hudson Super Six and the trip in itself will be great. Besides, we could realize one of our dreams and spend some weeks together sketching.

452

Chadds Ford, Pennsylvania
September 15, 1916

Dear Mama,

Thousands of blackbirds are making use of our skeleton chestnuts (the last honors to these noble trees) and are creating a great racket discussing and cussing their voyage south, I suppose.

453

Dear Mama,

The American Art Student, a monthly magazine published in
N.Y., appeared last month with an interview given by one of the
magazine editors of *Collier's.* The conversation was mostly regarding my work and methods, which were presented in a false and very
damaging way—damaging to the art student; so I deemed it my
duty to answer the article with one of my own, dealing at length and
in detail with the question of art education. I shall accompany the
article with a series of reproductions of my *studio*—out of doors,
portrait and still life—in order to substantiate my argument. Now I
shall want that self-portrait I sent home Xmas. Will you please remove it from the frame, put sufficient pasteboard around it and
mail it as soon as possible by parcel post or express, as you see fit?
I shall return it immediately after the half-tone plate is made.

The paralysis scare came near last night, at Brandywine Summit.
A sister of the little girl who was a victim of the disease the summer
Henriette had it. The child died 9 o'clock last night, 14 hours after
inception.

Carloads of horse manure (for mushroom houses) are unloaded
daily beside the house, which adjoins a siding. There is no doubt
that from there came the germ. The manure comes from New York.

The physicians in general essay to howl at the "absurd quaran-
tines," "undue alarm" and "paper talk"—nevertheless, I can say but
one thing—their howlings and protestations sound like so much
babble if "all this bother" has but saved the life of one child!

Were the doctors on the track of a cure, or even knew from
whence comes this dreadful scourge, they would be more in a position to be listened to.

454

My dear Papa and Mama,

I am in the maelstrom of a period of intense home sickness. My
recourse to pen and paper is not always a method of relief that I

permit myself (and not always one that I have even the courage to follow). These periods seem to come so often, following directly upon a spell of concentrated labor usually, and lasting anywhere from six hours to several days. At such times the very piers and pillars of my life's work and ideals crumble to dust—into heaps of refuse, and in their places stand the visions of a lost life or, God grant it, a life to be reclaimed—those cherished threads of existence that I broke twelve years ago when, in my eagerness to achieve, I lurched into a new country. I doubt if you can begin to realize how many, *many* times I have looked back at those dangling threads, always with covetous eyes, ever in the firm belief that had I continued along *that* road of destiny I would have found myself today at least equally happy in my work plus that incomputable glory of lifelong associations with my father, my mother and my brothers!

It indeed seems almost senseless, in such moments as I am experiencing now, to forsake the intimate relationships, to break the sacred associations that one has been born into, to shatter the actuality of family unity, for any calling whatsoever. My art vanishes into the merest speck when suffered comparison to the one Divine and tangible sensation bequeathed to us, parent to child, child to parent.

The irresistible forces of Destiny arrange plenty of lives to do the drifting and scattering, it seems, lives that have from the beginning been deprived of congenial surroundings and even of homes—so why should those of us who were blessed with both be drawn asunder? For me, I cannot conciliate my feelings, and as the years are slipping by I rebel at the thought of driving a tap-root into this adopted country, but cherish with almost a frenetic fervor the belief that I will eventually draw all my nourishment from those beloved spots of my birthplace, which my searching memory recalls with uncanny vividness, from the broken niches in the cellar concrete to the evanescent gleam on the dear old river.

It must be taken for granted, however, that in giving expression to these intense feelings I in no way disassociate myself from my family, even in the wildest eerie of emotional dreamland. They, my children and the mother, are an incorporate part of my body and soul. I write these thoughts with their hands helping to guide the pen.

Dear Mama,

Yesterday we took a ride—3:30 to 5:30, and went over into the Mt. Cuba county—just south of us. The trip was brought to some high spots for us older ones by several of the comments by the children, two of which I must tell you—comments that attested to the fine power of observation the children seem to be blest with.

We passed a snug farmhouse nestled close to the road, and framed in the vines that all but concealed the lower story sat a farmer—an unusual type with high forehead, dark brooding eyes, a dark drooping moustache and iron-gray hair pushed back in impressive fashion. He looked at us passing, from under his brows, and Carolyn piped up in that eager impulsive voice of hers—"He makes me think of 'Paderooski.'" Sharp on the heels of this Baby Brother piped still louder, "No, the game of Authors!" and Henriette with an air of finality said, "Bret Harte!"

All in a flash this was, starting with an impression and gradually driven into a corner and *"nailed"* by the maturer one. And they were *all* correct.

Then, later on as we were passing along a comfortable single-track road all filigreed in the shadows, Henriette reminded me that it looked so much like New England. I asked her reasons, for there were no trademarks of stone wall, frame house or evergreens to tell the tale—and yet it *did* look like N.E. to me. She quickly determined that it was first the color of the road (which was unusual at this place—that colorless gray so suggestive of granite dust and gravel) and also the colored blackberry vines along the level border to the fences on either side. She hit it exactly.

I'll tell you, these things are significant to me and offer me great relief, in that they show an ability that will always give them a foundation reason why it is worthwhile to live, and secondly, as they weave the textures of their lives the background of memories will give them untold pleasures, and *perhaps* be the basis upon which they can build an important life work.

I lay great stress on this tendency—to *observe*—and they are responding to it.

I received Babe's bully letter.

I intended to write him in particular as I am anxious that he read what I consider my greatest discovery since Thoreau, in the realms of wonderful expression. Robert Frost's book called *North of Boston,* published by Henry Holt Co., N.Y. Any good bookstore will have it as it is the literary sensation of the times. I've known of it for two years but postponed getting it for various reasons, mainly because I had so much else to read.

Ask him to first read the lines on the title page—a bit that, read in serene mood, makes me almost sob with joyous anticipation. Then "The Mountain," "The Wood Pile," "Blueberries," "Apple Picking." Then the rest—I have no words to tell him how vividly and exquisitely these wonderful themes appeal to me—and I know will to him.

And then a superb critical study of Thoreau by Mark Van Doren (pub. by Houghton Mifflin). He has cleaned up points in Thoreau I never knew another man could touch, especially in the fourth essay, "The Specific"—and also "Position." He will linger over the study with intense delight.

456

Chadds Ford, Pennsylvania
October 16, 1916

My dear Sid,

There is a strong undercurrent of sadness prevailing here today due to Wm. L. Price's death yesterday. He was the architect of the "Traymore" at Atlantic City, and the work we did together there brought us in very close touch with one another. I considered him one of my very vital friends in art as otherwise. We had planned so much ahead. His death has stirred this whole section of the country as he was greatly loved and admired. He was a tremendous inspiration to me.

457

Chadds Ford, Pennsylvania
October 28, 1916. 6:40 P.M.

Dear Mama,

Henriette and her school adds a new and important topic to the family discussions. Her robust enthusiasm is inspiring, and the secure and calm way in which she accepts the new code of life, from extra early breakfasts, the trip on the eight o'clock train, until she is met and escorted to school from the Wilmington station by *Sarah* (a reputable colored woman, for years in the employ of the Friends School)—the long hours there with its story telling, singing, gymnastics and the three R's, and back again on the 4:15, and home just before dark. Her life is full, no mistake.

Her main concern just now is the mastering of the long a's—sta-a-f, ca-a-lf, da-a-nce, etc., promulgated by the bevy of Wellesley College teachers and a sweet cluster from Framingham! This makes me smile (inwardly) as I realize it's a case of hands off! But it sounds just short of absurd to hear a child say, "It's ha-a-alf-p*a*st seven and I ca-a-n't take the p*a*th through the gra-ass because it's d*a*mp."

The past two weeks has filled my cup with sadness and then happiness, beginning as it did with the passing of dear Price, and ending with the festivities involving four birthdays, all of which was, in my mind, permeated by the thoughts of a fifth that took place under the shadow of the beloved Swiss Alps years ago.

I have attended not more than five funerals in my life. All were impressive of course, and although in every case I came away with firmer resolves and more serious intents, I don't know that I ever experienced the sensation of positive exhilaration and constructive desire as I derived from the services last Tuesday.

Price was a Quaker—naturally the services were Quaker, that rare spirit that one finds in its original genuineness only in a few communities, such as Rose Valley, Pa. This little home on Tuesday was the mecca for the best of them and a remarkable spirit prevailed.

There were no flowers to speak of (not enough to be depressing). There was no official speaker.

When the time set for the services had arrived there was perfect silence. This lasted say ten minutes. One could feel veneration and prayer vibrating through the rooms. Then out of the silence in another part of the house spoke a voice, gentle but very audible, in a cheerful conversational tone; it said something like this:

"I knew Will Price from early manhood. The first meeting was in a railroad station and I was late for a train. I had two heavy satchels and Will Price grabbed one of them and said, 'Come on!'

and ran, holding the ticket gate open until I got there. He has run ahead many and many atime since, with our heavy satchels, and has held the gate open for us to enter. Some of the satchels were too heavy, or else he ran with too many—"

And so it went on. Then he (Dr. Holmes of Swarthmore College) stopped and there was an eloquent five minutes' silence, and still another voice from a different part of the house spoke in those same kindly, sincere tones, once in a while breaking, but regaining poise would begin again.

Henriette with Nancy Bockius.

This lasted an hour and then we all went away to our homes. There was silence with all the moving of people and of carriages, and so the event floated into my mind, became fixed there forever and I moved away undisturbed, but *fiercely illuminated, stimulated, resolved* and happy—yes happy, that I had known, even for only two years, such a *man!*

I dropped myself into my work the next day with ease and became a part of that evolution that led me into the glory of birthdays.

Then the box came!

It is difficult to tell you, I may as well say it is impossible for any mortal to interpret into understanding terms, the whirls of dreams, memories, and aspirations into which I am precipitated when a "box" from home is opened.

You see, there is not only the sight of familiar objects (even to the shapes and the color of cakes that are so particularly yours), but there is that miracle worker "Fragrance" who gets in his marvelous work on one's brain.

The smaller cakes were taken to bed by their respective owners and on the natal day they were burdened with 5, 7, and 9 candles apiece.

You know best about coming down, but we should love to have *both* come, not at once of course, for you couldn't arrange that. If you will come I'll promise to keep my mouth shut, except to laugh. You may be a little afraid of my, "insistent German ways," as Carol calls them.

458

Chadds Ford, Pennsylvania
November 3, 1916

Dear Mama,

I have dropped Clark Fay from the class—a most regrettable affair. He was one who got closest to my heart during our relations the past two years, and at the same time in a most exasperating way inclined toward and really carried out most emphatically a disintegrating code of ethics outside the hours I actually had him under supervision. His inherent weakness was his susceptibility to low standards made palatable by the kind of people he has been thrown with most of his life.

459

Chadds Ford, Pennsylvania
December 20, 1916

Dear Mama,

Two snowstorms in a week! and another one brewing!! That's going some for Chadds Ford, and we are all hoping it will stretch its whiteness and cold over Xmas day at least.

The WYETHS

The spirit is rampant in the house. Added to the usual glamour is that of gift making and buying by the children this year. The excitability of Sis Carol in particular amounts to almost an obsession. She's so anxious to remember _everybody_. Henriette's Xmas spirit has been considerably broken into by her school, which keeps her from home from daylight to dark, Saturdays included—to make up for the delay in opening this fall. (Education, it seems to me, cannot be _made up_—a child's growth proceeds in spite of a column of spelling words lost, or a page of examples to be done—I'm somewhat out of patience with this ironclad 200-days-a-year rule).

But she's busy as a bee and enjoys it to the full. Her days home are "packed to the doors" with a thousand things she planned through the week—with duties of the household thrown in, _don't worry._

460

Stimson Wyeth had fallen in love but was having doubts. He decided against marriage at this time.

Studio
Chadds Ford, Pennsylvania
February 28, 1917. Wednesday noon

Dear Babe,

Your last letter took firm hold of me, to say the least, and I have considered its main contents deeply.

I must confess to have hovered between the propriety of saying nothing, and the duty to say something, but as the following will testify, have concluded to speak.

If you have, since writing, concluded that it will be best to work out your problem alone, you will do me a great favor to destroy this letter at this point. Otherwise minded, accept it (as I know you will) as the most thoughtful advice I am capable of.

Your confession to a "growing indifference" to Amy throws a radical new light on the entire situation. Let me remind you that when a basic love ends between two people, it is folly for anyone to attempt a critical analysis of one to the other, and the only right thing to do is to dwell upon the obvious points of virtue and deeply believe and hope that upon these the structure of a happy, well-rounded life can be built.

542

The Family

For a steady diet, for the diet that brings out the best in us, fervency and zealous warmth are indispensable to our natures. Enthusiasm and vehemence, although even lacking in maturity or capacity of understanding, are tremendous assets. The more rugged and robust a man is mentally or physically, the less able he is to stand the impoverishment of people who cannot rise to dizzy heights of ambitions and hopes on occasion, no matter how wild these schemes may be. It is the *sympathy* that counts, a contagious sympathy that goes *beyond* faith (that faith of the King-can-do-no-wrong variety is not enough), for although we may still swing to dizzy heights, we must swing alone, with the faithful ones standing below with hands clasped and a believing smile.

We are essentially (I speak of you and me) beings who are constantly in a state of impetuous fermentation. We may dream of contentment that comes through the channels of passivity, but herein we are wrong, for our greatest contentment will come from the greatest constructive activities.

Your deep-rooted attachment to Mama would not be near so vital, so firm (outside of sentiment I mean), were she not the impetuous, "stormy petrel" that she is (in addition to the eminent mother qualities and practical substantiabilities). Without disrespect, an *Aunt Hat* or *Aunt Annie* would have been utter failures in Mama's position as *constructive inspirators* for four boys with big bodies and just as big enthusiasms.

I have found that a woman is something more to a man than a warm lap to lay his head against to be rubbed; that she must, besides the duties of children raising and its million demands, be inspiritingly alive to her husband's labor and ambitions, with also that extra spunk to be combative when necessary.

All this takes a large degree of mental buoyancy (rather than intellectuality) and physical vitality.

And now, the inevitable parallel that we must accept (no matter how strong our aesthetic beliefs may oppose it), is that fundamental matter of sex. What we demand in spirit we demand in sexual intensity. Our bodies are too big, too healthy, to overlook this phase. We are neither Thoreaus nor Brownings in this respect (thanks to the red blood of our parents), and it is easy to prophesy that our blood will continue to inhabit the earth for sometime yet.

Considering your temperament, and your plans, which include the indispensable and noble consideration of keeping together the old home, with inevitable age coming upon the folks, I should say that you must think well before you make the final move.

You are the last and the youngest, but it strikes me that you are shouldering the biggest and most exacting problem in this matter of marriage.

Whatever you do, Babe, you've got my faith and deepest wishes for the best.

"Their arrows flew together . . ." from *Robin Hood*, 1917

Chapter XVIII
WORLD WAR I

"The mantle of supreme evil must be lifted from the age-old shoulders of the King of the Huns and placed upon the living shoulders of the Emperor of the Boche, the arch-tyrant of history!"

Studio
Chadds Ford, Pennsylvania
April 16, 1917. Monday

Dear Mama,

The feverish excitement you show regarding the war is entirely uncalled for, because it can be of no earthly value to a soul on earth, in fact reacts terribly on you and in turn upon us who look to you for your strength which is so clearly manifested in your *composure*.

Your feelings about the war can bring you to the same unbalanced state that Aunt Hat holds toward the Irish and Catholics. There is not a *whit* difference between the two motives, *Irish Catholics* and *World War*. The point is our strength lies in composure. To feel that this war is ready to drop on us like the knife of a guillotine— to take our heads, or some other Americans' heads, is absurd.

No international acts of bloodshed within the U.S. shall we see, mark my word! All this damnable jingoism may be doing the dull masses a sight of good, if only to get their blood going, but it takes it out of the supersensitive ones, no mistake.

The children ask every day about your coming. Do try to do so soon while the wild flowers are here. Carol is naturally eager to see you. Everyone is in prime condition.

462

Carol Wyeth was expecting her sixth child.
Henry Reuterdahl was one of the outstanding World War I artists, especially noteworthy for his paintings of naval battles.

Chadds Ford, Pennsylvania
May 3, 1917. Wednesday

Dear Mama,

The persistent sadness created by a night fraught with subtle but stirring dreams has clung about me all day. I seem to be walking in a cloud of misty vapor through which I can see life as it is but dimly, the vague shapes taking on strangely different appearances, some reminding me very vividly of the past and others revealing to me an unfamiliar life I *might* have lived. It is a singular state of mind which no doubt you have experienced after a climax of especial effort.

I must confess to a certain impressive pleasure gained during such periods. It is as though I were eaves-dropping on the Fates I did *not* follow, or peeking into the future, or renewing contact with a vanished past!

How desperately I cling to memories!! They are shrines to which I constantly attend! They bring to me more vividly than by any other means of contemplation the significance of the eternal past, the eternal future—and our place between the two eternities. As I look back over my experiences, from the recent sharp and defined ones and follow them as they recede in the rapid perspective of only 34 years, it has the effect of precipitating my imagination down the countless ages of *all* experiences!

The most evanescent grasp of the phenomenon of eternity is the source of my profoundest inspiration. I feel that the greatest power of expression will come in proportion to my ability to read this fathomless mystery into any object the eye rests upon; whether it happens to be one of my own children or a withered leaf lying in the snow, *both* should arouse the same sensation, thus every stroke of my brush will become charged with a *cosmic* truth—the *universal message of the ages!*

But here I'm trying to *write* the things I cannot as yet coherently express with a *brush*—absurd! But Beethoven's *Fifth Symphony* has been playing steadily and the thoughts just had to be put down.

This has been the most unsatisfactory two weeks, and the most feverish I've experienced in many a month. The publicity department of the U.S. Navy has asked for work—it must be *rushed* to be of service, and it is so out of harmony with my other work. However, today I completed a large mural poster, 6 × 10 feet, of the call of *Neptune* to protect the freedom of the seas. The canvas has at least the virtue of being compelling. Tomorrow I must plunge back into the lovable tale of *Robin Hood* for which I have completed six pictures with 5 more to do. *King Arthur* title page done. Wonder just how I'm going to get it all done on time.

The children are looking so well it hurts! Brown as berries and full of the devil!! Carol looks better than she *ever* has, although she always *has* looked well at these times. She beats her best record.

We feel very deeply the blessing (as well as the responsibility) of the new member to come, but how could we feel differently with the group of four, which I feel cannot be beaten, about us? Baby Brother's steady improvement alone is a victory and Godsend, and my heart goes out to the thought of another little brother or sister. The war has depressed Carol considerably and very naturally it would. I know how she must feel. Of late the war spirit has come into the home more than I like. Constant communications from Lieutenant Bennett and [Henry] Reuterdahl spurring me on in the poster work, war letters from *Collier's,* etc. All of them smacking of *jingoism,* I feel, and not counted to set one's feelings to rest by any means! I'll be glad when my share of this work is done, for I must keep in a passive state of mind at all hazards. There is *so* much I want to do.

I feel it is a major crime against oneself, his country and the world at large to allow *speculative excitement* to clutter up his mind and pursuits. Even in the matter of business, strict normality of conduct must prevail.

I was astonished to read of Mr. Shepard, of Shepard, Norwell Co., Boston, advising the Boston merchants to "Go slow in buying, *very* slow." The worst economic crime he can commit in these times, especially as it comes from such a conservative and influential man. But, by Heavens, these *conservative* people! When they go crazy they go the limit!! I think the state of feeling regarding the war, in New England at the present moment, in business, educational, and even artistic circles, is absurd to say the least. It's all so disrupting. If a storm breaks we must be ready for it with tremendous *composure.* It's a pity that the wheels of preparedness can't be moved without demoralizing the entire country to accomplish it.

I appreciate very deeply your sympathy for your German friends, and they deserve sympathy. Remember, Mama, this Germany let loose today is *not* the Germany you know. I'm afraid you are wrong when you try to cover up their enormities by claiming like enormities in all wars. No war in history has ever given us the faintest parallel.

I too sympathize with the German people—but *France!* by God, how about her? How Grandpapa would feel!!

But here! I wanted to talk about the children all through this letter for my heart has been full with them all spring—the most glorious little kids that ever lived!! But can't you *possibly* come down for just a few days, please! You would see for yourself—and Carol wants you so bad—please do. Can't Papa take care of his chickens alone by now? How I would like you both! Alas, only a dream.

463

Esther Bockius was engaged to Myron Files, professor of English at Dartmouth College.

Studio
Chadds Ford, Pennsylvania
May 19, 1917. 3:00 P.M.

Dear Mama,

I've just laid-in the *King Arthur* cover design and have a little while before the composition class which meets at 4 o'clock. Thursday is the regular day, but McKay came down yesterday to look at the *Robin Hood* drawings so had to postpone it.

Tomorrow Prof. Zug, Professor of Modern Art at Dartmouth, stops off to see me on his way from Washington to Hanover. He has always been quite interested in my work, in fact has lectured on it, and together with Files' enthusiasm has determined to call.

I suppose the studio rafters will rattle tomorrow with highbrow art talk—*maybe!*

Carol, although always well during pregnancy, is healthier, stronger and better in every way this time. I have a feeling that she will retain much more weight permanently than before even.

464

Studio
Chadds Ford, Pennsylvania
May 24, 1917. Friday

Dear Mama,

The aspect of the canvases I am now finishing presents a mighty fitting prelude to the event of your coming. Next to the satisfaction derived from the anticipation of your arrival, comes the satisfaction of some of the best pictures I have ever done, being accomplished in the midst of a merciless time schedule, not mentioning the depressing influences of the world conflict. The sunny color of medieval England, its fairs, festivals, and contests in archery, quarter staff, jousting, etc., with dear old *Robin Hood* smiling his crafty way throughout the many adventures—all this has asserted itself with precision of late, and it is always with a shock of surprise when I confront myself with the present terrific conditions.

As I understand it you will leave Wednesday evening on the Washington Express. If this is so get your ticket right through to Wilmington. I'll meet that train there. This will avoid any possible long wait in Broad Street in case your train is late and misses the C.F. train.

This will make a *bully* early morning ride for the whole family in to meet you and won't in any way interfere with my day.

Wish you'd use a little chloroform on Papa and ship him on the same train—as baggage if necessary.

Grandmother Wyeth with Carolyn, Nat and Henriette.

465

"Uncle Frank," Dr. Frank Freeman, was related to Henriette Zirngiebel Wyeth by marriage, being an uncle to her sister-in-law, Etta Zirngiebel.
"Uncle John," John Barker, was Andrew Newell Wyeth II's brother-in-law, married to his sister, Amelia Annie.

Studio
Chadds Ford, Pennsylvania
July 3, 1917. Forenoon

Dear Mama,

I spent yesterday in New York—there to deliver three *King Arthur* drawings. Today I am recovering composure and impetus to go on with the remainder of the book.

To pick up my correspondence will be a healthy relaxation, so the first off, I'll write to you.

The trip to N.Y. was highly satisfactory in that my drawings were very much liked. The trip itself was extremely uncomfortable due to the extreme heat, which was partly compensated for by the sensitively cool and brief wearing apparel displayed by the women on Fifth Ave. The sight was exhilarating, to say the least, and I well nigh forgot the perennial streams that coursed down my back and which topped the breakwater of my belt and down, down into my shoes! The sight would, I verily believe, have made Papa totally forget his feathered variety of *chickens* at home had he been there with me. (I know I am shocking your admirable sense of modesty and propriety, but confession, once in awhile, is good for the soul, they say.)

Of course N.Y. is afire with war as well as in the two ways above mentioned and my susceptibility responded deeply. The result is I am on the verge of creating a reeking cartoon—a bloody commentary on Emperor William. The idea came to me as I was on the way home, digesting the fruits of the day's impressions.

I had the privilege (or misfortune) to look over a hundred or more photos, besides numerous other documents recently brought here by a high official of the German government who, having sickened from the violation and sacrilege of all human rights as perpetrated by the *Ruling Juggernaut* of Germany, has managed to escape and seeks refuge in America. Names I cannot give, and the photos, etc., the public will never see, for they would in all likelihood spread such a horrible spirit of vengeance throughout our land as to drag us down into an equally abysmal mire of cruelty and barbarity. Enough to say that I feel impelled to express in some manner my *loathing* of the leader or at least the approving head of such diabolical infamy.

The Abdication of Attila is the legend for my cartoon. I will depict a throne, mountain high, built of human dead and dying (women and children conspicuous). On the summit of these writhing bodies the throne chair, which Attila the leader of the Huns is abdicating in favor of Kaiser Wilhelm. Attila, the fat, bloody monster, stands to the right center (with his generals) humbly proffering his crown to the new "Scourge of the Human Race." Wilhelm in bigoted ostentation is accepting it, his eyes lifted to God, his acclaimed *accomplice!!!* Behind the Kaiser and to the left the admiring ghosts of Bismarck, Nietzsche, Frederick the Great, et al., with the very real and gibbering likeness of the Crown Prince, heir to all the conditions wrought by his father—monstrosity, pillage, devastation, orgy murder, incendiarism, violation and sacrilege, coupled with perfidy beyond compare.

Back of this tableau of diabolism the lifting smoke from the ruins of cities, hamlets and homes.

History has been pleased to hold Attila as a symbol of all that is ferocious and depraved. His brief comparative record as against the German Kaiser was humane, generous, a suckling babe or innocent novice in that which we call tyranny and horror.

The accursed hypocrisy of William II, he who at every occasion invokes "Alter Gott," he who has profaned beyond comprehension, has actually burned 2000 houses of the Almighty, murdered priests and sisters, aged men and little children. The mantle of supreme evil must be lifted from the age-old shoulders of the King of the Huns and placed upon the living shoulders of the Emperor of the Boche, the *arch*-tyrant of history!

But to return to the scenes of peace and plenty.

We are all well, and although the heat here was excessive, also it rapidly cooled after two heavy showers late in the afternoon. Today is comfortable if a little "muggy," but we are in no way suffering.

Aunty Guss has been with us for nearly a week, helping Carol preserve currants, gooseberries and raspberries. Her presence is distinctly enjoyable, and as I heard Henriette say: "I enjoy Aunty Guss next to Aunt Mama," meaning you of course. And I don't blame her. Even with her 77 years she is as quick-witted, sympathetic and substantial as ever. I truly believe with Henriette that she comes nearer to filling the place you leave than any other woman I know.

This brings me to the matter of the girls' visit to you this summer. I am planning to do so about the twenty-fifth of this month. You see, August, we figure, will be the eventful month; it may be late in August. Now if we sent the girls too soon I *know* we would get so homesick for them as hardly to stand it for so long. It would be that way with me at any rate. But sending them the last of July, you will be assured of having them a month, and we would be assured of a contiguous distraction which will bridge over the period very well. I don't want to seem selfish for I know you are anxious to see them up there, but I can't help my own sensitiveness to family separations, even if only for a few days. It has been the incessant distractions of my restless profusion and the constant panorama of family duties that have made it possible for me to bear the separation from my home and people in Needham. The following analogy is absurdly inapt and misleading in a way, but I can but think of David Harum's assertion that, "fleas is good for a dog 'cause they make him fergit he's a dog" or something to that effect. The value of distractions is incalculable sometimes!

I was extremely sorry to hear of Uncle Frank's death. His utter serenity and peaceableness were outstanding traits that always impressed me even as a boy—much like Uncle John. He made an indelible impression on my mind as one of the party that used to go fishing from the rocks of Marblehead every Labor Day. I remember one Labor Day he could not go, and how I missed him. He always reminded me of Longfellow, that same genial, soft-spoken air about him that the photographs of the poet seem to stand for. I could wish that I had a photo of him and Uncle John (taken about the time of our Marblehead expeditions) to go with my collection of Cambridge folks' pictures. There must be some extant.

466

Dear Babe,

A gold and silver morning after days of heavy rains and foggy nights.

So once again the kind hand of fate has moved in our favor and brought the mother through safely—and with a boy! One hears so many ominous tales of increasing difficulty (as a woman gets older) to bring children into the world, of shattered nerves, and spent body, etc., etc. But this morning Carol lies in her bed as composed and as youthful as ever, and as far as any of us can judge, the mother of a perfectly healthy and normal child.

Never has a period of nine months gone so quickly and with less physical distress, which even *normally* occurs, and never did she show such good balance and general optimism in spite of the intensified atmosphere of war, etc. I have been blest beyond all deserving and I feel the impulse throughout my whole body to rise nearer to the high level indicated by the gifts of wife and children and home.

The new baby, Andrew, looks almost indentically like Ann as I remember her the first day. So you can judge that in stature he is not unlike his grandfather for whom he is named. I think he will be dark; he has the wide eyes, short straight nose and square shoulders (with a goodly chest) which coincide with our sturdy dad. Won't it be strange if he resembles his granddad as nearly as Henriette does her grandmother!

The children are delighted. None were conscious of the arrival of the new member but Baby Brother. He awakened and felt the event so intensely as to lose his night's rest. He slept most of yesterday.

Now lastly, about the children. I'm going to ask you if you can come down within a few days and take Henriette and Sis Carol back with you. I'll pay your R.R. fare. Then when they are ready to come back I'll come up and get them and make *my* little stay.

467

Mrs. Wyeth's youngest sister was Nancy Bockius.

Studio
Chadds Ford, Pennsylvania
August 3, 1917. 5:30 P.M.

Dear Mama,

You don't know what a deep sense of pleasure the thought of the children being with you all has been.

Henriette's letter received yesterday stirred us all. If it was all her own it was wonderful in its narrative power as well as smacking so strongly of herself.

Also the urgent spirit of little *Sis* Carol. She is always so eager to do, and to think of others. I can vividly realize her pestering—*divine* pestering, to send messages. Even as a wee, incoherent child, how many envelopes she padded with meaningless scrawls and intended pictures—this to send to A'nt Mama or Nancy or somebody she felt the impulse to communicate with. She's a character, no mistake, and will bear watching.

Work is coming finely and tell Henriette I'm now making Lancelot carrying Queen Guenever off on horseback (her escape from burning at the stake).

468

Studio
Chadds Ford, Pennsylvania
August 21, 1917

Dear Sid,

"—And then they were married and lived happily ever after."

Today Esther left us, the wife of Myron Files, professor of English, of Dartmouth. The climax of three very intense days, for on Friday there was no plan of marriage owing to Files' pledge to serve in the present war; but as the moment of his departure came near, with France only six weeks away, the flood gates opened; so the ceremony was quickly arranged, and now it is done. A touch of war-time romance within my own home! Three days of surging emotions, of decision and indecision, from hot to cold, from joy to grief—and then joy again, such as I shall never forget!!

And also, not many weeks ago, *Andrew*—who came July 12th on Thoreau's birthday! Nine pounds, a facsimile of Baby Brother, blue-eyed and all. And with all this the accomplishment of *Robin Hood* and *King Arthur,* Navy posters, Red Cross posters, etc., etc.—and the damned hot weather!! Some summer!! But we are all happy!

Poking its insidious nose in amongst it all, an *invitation* from the government to accept a First Lieutenant's commission and go to hell for a few rare tidbits in the way of *subject* matter. Told them I thought 'twould save time if they would send me out to Armour's or Swift's in Chicago. I wouldn't mind a crack at a Boche or two, and would be tickled to death if I could disembowel their divine leader, but no war on canvas for me!!

Yes, the summer has been jammed full of everything. One other new development, which I shall dare to offer your gloating soul, is the one of "New Englanditis," which has assumed ominous importance, bidding fair to move us *all,* body and soul, to that glorious land of my birth, of healthily progressive people, and invigorating atmosphere.

I feel more or less *bound* to tell you of our plans so rapidly nearing a final decision, for it was your father who predicted certain things which, in the enthusiasm of my love of this country, I could not see. His sense of the practical, pertaining to the up-building of a family, was of course far beyond me—but he was right. However there are other equally urgent reasons.

Both Carol and myself are starving hungry for the closer contact with my parents. With me, my spells of yearning and homesickness are becoming too frequent. This is the strictly personal and selfish phase of it. Secondly, we want the children to enjoy and profit by the tremendous privilege of associations with their grandparents, and equally so, to give my parents the joy of grandchildren, something deprived them, except for a few days in a year. And then, I may, by carrying out these plans, obtain my grandfather's home adjoining my father's property, and perpetuate still longer the old homestead, hallowed ground to us all!

The question of a cooler climate for the boy I believe is imperative, the hot weather here sets him back, as it has this summer. And then the educational problem is really serious in this section. The bewildering question of help inside and out is beyond me for successful solution; and the cost of same, of *everything,* for that matter, has been made impossible by the influx of the duPont millionaires who are hemming us in on every side. But it's the old home and its people primarily that is making the call. It has been growing slowly and surely for two or three years. I foresee the final struggle when we pull up stakes, for I have a very deep love for the soil, the trees, the brooks and the sky here. Carol has also her attractions, not less intense. It is the greatest question that ever confronted us. But I am not afraid; I've trusted my impulses many times before and I shall do so again.

Our disappointment in being unable to carry out the Maine Coast idea this summer would have been very great if it had not been overshadowed by the coming of Andrew. Next summer, however, we are considering the season in Maine as a necessity. We have thought of you often facing those ocean breezes and have seen you in our minds' eye moving round on the rocks with canvases and a box. You are very lucky.

The two oldest girls are now at my mother's and are having the time of their young lives. They have been there since July 18th. Both have learned how to swim, I believe.

Eastertime marks the last of my sketching out of doors, sad to relate, but there is satisfaction in the fact that my three last sketches are the nearest to good things I ever did. I will enclose photos (which Prof. Zug took for lantern slides for his American Illus. lectures this summer. They are rather black and contrasty for the sake of lantern work). The moonlight of cows I am still working on from observational studies only. I hope to send this to Wilmington in November.

(By the way, I'm on the jury of selection in spite of my abortion of last year!!??!)

Well, I must close now, though I've lots I could say apropos of a new acquaintance *Jonsen,* an Icelandic sculptor, whom fate brought to my studio 3 days after he landed in N.Y. Anatole France calls him "the only competitor of Rodin in Europe," although strictly different in work and aesthetic point of view. He has pumped new virus into me, I think. His virility and astonishing naturalism have been an eyeopener to me. He is located in Phila. for a year, having won the competition opened to the world of sculptors to do an Icelandic sea rover for Fairmount Park. His sketch is tremendous!

P.S. The account of our maturing plans related in this letter I would

558

prefer you to keep to yourself. At least let no news-spreading artist get hold of it.

469

Dear Mama,

Henriette started in at Friends School, West Chester, on Monday. It's a stunning place for her to go and I wish she had attended last year. Large grounds and almost real country—somewhat near Cousin Carolyn's.

Carolyn is pressing us hard to let her go and I think I will. She got a strong inclination from Miss Glancy to *learn,* which seems to have counteracted all feeling of timidity, etc.

Andrew is developing very rapidly and is proving to be a very good baby to care for. That is, sleeps regularly, etc.

470

Dear Mama,

Carolyn starts into school on Monday and she's happy, let me tell you! I'm so glad that she has apparently overcome that exaggerated shyness so evident last year. Took her to West Chester last evening, in fact all the kids, and fitted them out with winter shoes and hats.

Poor Fitzgerald answered the draft call Monday morning. It has disturbed me more than I imagined it would to see him go. I realize more than ever now what a sterling fellow he was and his great value as an associate. It seems a pity that he should be torn from his work in its crucial stage, and it has brought home to me how many thousands of young fellows will probably be thrown off the track of a cherished destiny into strange fields.

There are only the three of us now, Howland, Mack and myself. Mack is really developing finely, but he isn't quite the wide-open nature I'd like to have him. He's a wee bit selfish. His work is surprisingly growing. Howland, well meaning and honestly attached to us, is "rough-locked" hopelessly. I see no chance for him to swing free. This eliminates him from my deepest regard. Cold on my part perhaps, but I haven't time to be sentimentally interested in mistakes.

I don't know whether I told you or not that I'm scheduled to speak at a banquet to be given to Book Sellers Organization in Phila., Nov. 14th. Chas. Scribner is giving the dinner and Henry Van Dyke is the other speaker!!! God knows that I'm aching in every joint over the prospect of such an ordeal. I would have refused in a second had it been any one but Scribner's. How I wish they'd let me alone with my canvases and paint.

471

Jefferson Hospital
Philadelphia, Pennsylvania
September 28, 1917. Wednesday morning, 6:15

Dear Mama,

Passed a very restful night after having that ambitious piece of geography removed from the back of my neck.

It had grown quite large of late, as round as a half-dollar almost, and rising like a young mountain. It was absolutely painless to me of course, but for some reason I felt demoralized with that on my neck. It's humiliating, to say the least, to even have the Good Lord build an ell on your neck, for no other purpose on earth than to make you carry it 'round!

The operation took an hour and under local anesthetic, which made it next to painless. Of all the stabbing, pulling, cutting and sewing you never saw! The surgeon, Warren Davis, said I had the thickest hide he's had to get through in years! I never realized what a laborious effort it is to cut the skin.

Here I am, gracefully reclining, swathed in white linen, on a white bedstead, in a smooth white chamber with a white table and mirror. I feel for all the world as though I were incarcerated in one of Jordan Marsh's sanitary refrigerators!—especially when I am eating delectable viands from a large white tray, assorted foods arranged immaculately on a dozen little dishes—with even the lump sugar done up in hermetically sealed packages labeled "Jack Frost Sugar Lump"!

Withal, I have enjoyed myself by feeling silly—think of your colossus-in-flesh of a son being wheeled down the long white cor-

ridors, in and out of elevators, then more corridors by a little wheezing spindle-shanked nurse thus:

I felt like the proverbial elephant with a violet in his buttonhole!
I'd like the job of writing the libretto, for a comic opera entitled,
"Convers in Confinement," or, if that sounds paradoxical or in danger of being misconstrued, call it "Newell and His Neck" (I'm
strong for alliterations!).

No, seriously speaking, I am tremendously relieved and the above
silliness is just a little effervescence coming off the top.

Left everyone at home in good shape, and shall return this afternoon.

472

Chadds Ford, Pennsylvania
October 3, 1917. Wednesday night

Dear Babe,

Sometimes I feel certain that no one can appreciate how utterly
isolated I feel and how I yearn for someone capable of giving me a
lift now and then. (I refer particularly to matters dealing definitely
with my profession.)

I realize keener than I ever have before (and never has the realization been sustained for so long a period!) how much of a craftsman

I am and how little an artist. This self-reproach, if most who know my work could hear it, would cause a din of expostulation and they would say something like this—"Nonsense! Look how much you've accomplished and how *young* you are! Why you're one of the leading illustrators!" as if there were compensation in *that*. And herein lies the real tragedy of my friendships, that not *one* has had the perception to note my exact position as an artist, or (which is far worse) if they *have* the perception, do not take the trouble to batter down my ego, my air of self-sufficiency which I carry so openly.

I am certain of a rich power in my system somewhere. I know it from the fact of the constant flow of intense emotional experiences. In spite of all these sensations (many of them as worthy of artistic expression as have ever been done) not one has yet emerged on canvas in its pure state! *Hints* of these feelings, yes, mere ghostly shadows of the live, vibrant experiences of the heart.

The fact is, Babe, I'm facing a problem in its actuality which I vaguely foresaw years ago when Pyle used to say that "Illustration is the legitimate stepping stone to painting"—a theory easier said than done. The difference in viewpoint is so vast as held by the illustrator as against the painter.

You and I often relate to each other the experiences of the spirit which mean so much to us, such as those you wrote about in your letter anent my visit home—the chores in the evening, the sound of the wheelbarrow on soft grass and crunching gravel! It is this nature of things that appeals to me too, but do I paint them? No! I use the divine fragrance of these inspired moments to garnish a pirate picture, an Indian scene, or some meaningless fantasy. Ah! I've had long drilling in thus diverting the golden stream into the gutter. Can I stop the leak? I *must!!*

Perhaps you wonder why I do not seek further for professional friends. Judging by their work they are not worth looking up—at least in the field of painting. Not a painter in America today that I have found is answering a bonafide *impulse of his own*. Each one following in the tracks of another, giving exaggerated importance to insignificant changes in rendering or choice of subject matter but in no case reflecting their strictly personal impressions. Winslow Homer (besmeared and beslimed by such nincompoops as Paxton, Hale, etc.) was our last vigorous *individual* in painting. The peeling criticism hurled at his "uncouth color and clumsy handling, don't ye know," cannot obliterate the great enveloping feature of his stark honesty to himself in painting the sea for the first time in history as it really looked. Even though he does not measure up to the craftier technical demands of today, the sterling lesson of his integrity of vision will always live in posterity. Walt Whitman is another of the real masters—almost a Beethoven in writing. Robert Frost, one contemporary (and this may seem a far jump), has at least got a grip on himself, rather frail perhaps, but genuine, and if masculine and physically vigorous enough may yet blaze a new and glorious trail.

Every mother's son of us is born with that supreme gift of individual perception, but the sheeplike tendency of human society soon makes inroads on a child's *un*sophistications, and then popular education completes the dastardly work with its systematic formulas, and *away* goes the individual, hurtling through space into that hateful oblivion of mediocrity. We are pruned to stumps, one resembling the other, without character or grace, shaped to produce standard fruits, easy to pick and so many to the box!—and with flat flavor at that!!

It does not make me flinch to admit myself as one of the peaches or *prunes,* as the case may be. I may be a little more ruddy, a little juicier than some others, but nevertheless I am one of the cratefull. I do not flinch because I am gratified to be able to see myself in the true light, which is the first step toward reconstruction and perhaps —victory! But it is high time to make the move—I am thirty-five this month!!

I'm crouching low and gathering all available force to start my 36th year with the best that's in me.

473

Studio
Chadds Ford, Pennsylvania
October 10, 1917

Dear Mama,

I'm not in the calmest state of mind today by any means—for that matter I've not been exactly myself since my return from those glorious days spent with you all. A period of growing dissatisfaction seems to have me in hand to a greater degree than I ever remember, and for the time I seem unable to accomplish much.

Don't read any other meaning into the above assertions than the one outstanding fact that the entire problem lies within myself and must be gone through with. It is, I trust, a restlessness toward some good, an internal upheaval that in the end will eliminate what I consider to be serious stumbling blocks in the way of personal progress—and following, the progress of the whole family. That this restlessness will be to my advantage I have perfect faith, provided I carry out its dictates. This will take courage. Nietzsche's formula that "he who lives peacefully does not <u>live</u>" always struck me as being true, as proved by my own experiences. Of course aimless restlessness is an abomination and can create nothing but unhappiness. That deeper restlessness inspired by idealism, although distressing, is divinely so, to the extent that it becomes an ecstatic spiritual joy. That suffering and supreme spirituality go hand in hand is expressed in all *great* art, as for instance in *Beethoven*. Even sadness has its light.

To express through the medium of sadness the exquisiteness of life is my great desire, because I feel Nature in her *glory* that way. The more beautiful an aspect of nature the more I turn in upon myself and live deep in sober reflections. The brilliant sparkle of a sunpath across the water does not make me jubilant and happily excited, but creates an intensely reverse feeling of solemnity, almost of austerity. This embodies my true point of view.

As you realize, I have indulged myself freely, my habits being generally good. I have been saved the pain of any serious errors. The sense of *economy* has never been strong enough to temper any plans which I had any reason to feel more reasonable. My prodigality in the disposition of money has in no sense been because it came easily. Lots of people are perfectly benign to this belief and take great pleasure in saying "Come easy, go easy." The real reason lies far deeper than that which in short is this. An artist's only real compensation for his work is in the *doing* of it. That payment in pleasure is well nigh consummate. The money received is an *excess* payment, as it were, or perchance a gift. In spending a dollar the artist can feel it in no way related to the labor extended in a picture. On the other hand, how differently the man who earns his money by the hour looks upon the silver in his hand before he spends it. It represents so much life blood to him to be used sparingly; he thinks of his money in terms of toil—the artist, in terms of remembered joy!

Thus it is (partly, at any rate) that I have surrounded myself with too many of the pleasures which, although healthy, are dissipating my efforts. I want my strength to flow like a river between walls of rock. I am living too well, too luxuriantly for the proper disciplining of my nature. Our home is too richly appointed with large grounds and accessories that demand attentions which I should not divert from my work, besides the cost of upkeep. Furthermore the school problem is becoming serious on two counts—cost, and the time and energy expended in getting the children to school. There is not one detail of the above objects but what I enjoy doing, but I know that it is all taking me away from the altar which stands supreme to me. I do not have the time to dream, to commune, to sustain my "true point of view." In short I am too happy (in an external sense) and too unhappy within. These conditions must and will be reversed!

In the above, I seem to have excluded almost all consideration from the family point of view. But let me say quickly that Carol is even more intensely aware of the necessary change that should be made and also has her own personal reasons in addition.

Although she seems to me to be unusually capable to stand alone, I can see at times that she feels almost overwhelmed by her responsibilities as a mother of five live wires and wishes deeply for at least a sympathetic background into which she can retire on occasion for advice and reassurance. You offer her just that, of which she is more than ever convinced since the return of the girls, who seemed so to thrive both mentally and physically under your care.

"The luxury of frugality" is an invented phrase of my own. Paradoxical and perhaps trite, it rings with a truth I am bound to follow if I am to *proceed!*

I've come to these beliefs through the very slow process of evolution, and if you were to look back over my letters you would detect little spatterings of these thoughts pretty well back. I've been very headstrong in my prodigal ways and no one else is to blame for it. I have exhibited qualities of persistency in a few directions which have proved of inestimable value, but the virtue is a misfit in this department of my nature and it has taken me a long time to find it out. All is, I *pray,* that this "spell" of truth revealed will cling to me long enough to make the necessary reforms and to launch my-self well into the second lap of my life in which I expect to accomplish much better things.

P.S. I write these things (with many repetitions of thoughts I have expressed before, no doubt) with the idea of keeping you and Papa and Babe in touch with any transitions that may take place. I need your faith, but without a perfect understanding on your part I could not expect it. I shall keep you always in touch as events move along.

474

Studio
Chadds Ford, Pennsylvania
October 24, 1917. 2:45 P.M.

Dear Mama,

This has been a fitful day for working, every hour checkered with brilliant sunshine and black shadows from great rainy clouds rushing from southeast to northwest. A "line storm" perhaps. Last night was wild! Wind, rain, flying leaves, and now and then the crash of a falling tree branch. But we were all cozy, warm, and dry, and really enjoyed going to bed in the tumult.

Today, of course, is Nat's birthday. He is celebrating his continued good health. He is really looking fine.

I am sitting near the open fire in the studio. Four great chestnut logs are crackling away, throwing a ruddy glow throughout the room, turning to gold the gray silver light so begrudgingly given by the dull wet clouds. I have had to stop painting, and the natural inclination is to communicate with those at home. An open fire invariably inspires this.

How well I remember a sermon on "The Home Fireplace" preached by Chas. W. Eliot's son (Sam Eliot, I believe). I could only have been twelve or fourteen at the time, but his words so well divined the deeper value of the open fire, not alone as a source of heat but as a source of family strength and unity. He mourned the passing of the great fire on the hearth, for with its going there has also passed the good old days of family gatherings and good conversation.

How true it is! To be sure, every "portable bungalo" has its fireplace now, but only as a faddish accessory; not enough of practical value to make it a part of necessary living, but only as a dead ornament, a useless hole in the wall, gapping foolishly with its two or three dusty sticks laid across its shiny andirons.

I have feelings of exasperation sometimes, that I have had to live in a period when so many of the old customs, so fundamental in their appeal, so substantial in their usefulness, have been casually cast off as worthless for "modern conveniences." It seems to me that the primitive methods, although more clumsy, a little more bother, and perhaps a little less sanitary, offered a *spiritual* help in the very problems they presented. Is there not a deeper appreciation of heat when one must cut the wood, carry it in, light it with the hand and *watch it burn!* than when one blows down the tube and orders the janitor to send up more heat! Does not the experience of *contact with every detail,* even to the removal of ashes, automatically add to one's deeper understanding of life. I'm sure it does.

Even the argument, always given with an air of finality, that one *wastes time* with the old clumsy methods strikes me as absurd; for what are we doing with the time thus saved? A few good things, no doubt, but in the main we are becoming pathetically artificial, using the spare time in search of excitement and pleasure or—what is by far the worst offense—trying to gather in extra dollars!

Deep down I *pity* our race of today. Almost every hour I see signs of modern disintegration, and the deepest roots of the disease firmly imbedded in the *family life!* How slight the spirit of family reverence —almost a lost art to many. What an oasis in the desert when one *does* happen upon a person who feels the deeper significance of life —of *family* life.

Perhaps I've not seen enough of other people and therefore have not the right to censure. But I do get terribly lonely at times for that rich communion, to find someone who can also understand and feel those things that bind you in Needham and we in Chadds Ford together.

With *all* the time-saving *Modern Conveniences,* how few people find time to live.

It is very dark, although only four o'clock, and Carol asked me to come down to the house for some tea and rolls. How glorious it would be to find you and Papa and Babe down there too!

But before I close this letter I want to express our appreciation (the depth of which you can conceive easier than I can tell) for the box containing the three cakes! and the arbor vitae! There is still some left, enough to bind together with the *Home* spirit the entire week of birthdays.

Carolyn is delighted with her magazine subscription and expressed herself as being more worthy of it than ever, after Henriette had stepped on one of the cats this A.M. Henriette of course deeply enjoyed your letter.

The first copy of *Robin Hood* arrived the A.M. and I signed it over to Nat. The poor little kid was delighted beyond anything I expected and has carried it around under his arm all day.

Friday night I'm going to rig up a sort of Halloween table in my studio as a surprise, and the children will eat their supper here. We will have some little favors, etc. Chicken Pox and Measles are rampant so will have no other children.

The bread must be delayed in the mails, for we never get it twice on the same day. Its all right, just keep on with the same program.

The coal and sugar famine is serious. Although I ordered my coal last April, I've only 1/3 of what I need. Have lots of wood, thank heaven! Sugar we have 40 lbs. of, also a barrel of flour. Harvested 3 bushels of onions and about 30 bushels of potatoes from the garden, the latter in yesterday (about 1/2 crop).

P.S. Tell Papa his letter meant a great deal to all of us, and to remember that he (and you too, Mama) have built yourselves very deeply into the hearts of the children, including the boy, who asks continually to go to Needham again!

475

Chadds Ford, Pennsylvania
November 1, 1917. Thursday morning, 6:15

Dear Mama,

The birthday week passed with great success. There were no elaborate gifts, but I arranged a combination Halloween and birthday party in my studio. I built up a large framework on the model stand and leaned great stalks of field corn about it, making a sort of tepee. Inside I piled pumpkins and golden ears of corn upon which we put the birthday cake with its 24 candles, $6 + 8 + 10 = 24$, and suspended above, a blood-red Chinese lantern. Through the interstices of the corn it was a handsome effect. We had some horns, rattles and whistles and ice cream, and had a high old time in the light of a big fire on the hearth. It was a total surprise, which helped.

476

Chadds Ford, Pennsylvania
November 25, 1917. Sunday evening

Dear folks,

It is clear, still, and cold outside. The moon is bright and icy looking. The first real touch of the frigid season to come.

In here it is cozy. The children are all busy with one thing or another. Nat is playing the Victrola. Ann is cutting paper dolls, Henriette is reading, and Carolyn is in the kitchen listening to a story being told by her mother. Andrew is asleep.

What a strange state of mind it puts me in tonight! Mingled happiness and sadness, inspiration and depression. To forget, to cease knowing anything of the frailties of human life—of that archweakness war! My God, how it does bear down on one's head!

And yet I can't rise up in wild, indignant protest against any single nation. I do, of course, express myself about the Germans (those whom we are fighting) but I get no satisfaction in doing so.

Tonight, I gazed long and lovingly on a beautiful photograph of "Buigen on the Rhine." A marvelously appealing little town crowned by its ancient castle, and across the Rhine, the thousand terraces of grapevines and fruit trees. My heart went out to it. It seemed as though I had always lived there. I could see my ancestors roaming about the hills, or moving down the clean-looking little streets. I could smell the good old fragrances of substantial cooking, of sawdust from the woodworkers' shops, of leather from the bootshops, the variety of odors from the dwellings, each with a "foreign" *tang,* resembling those I remember having smelled at Klausers', Holzers', in Grandmama's, etc. It seems as though sometime or other I must *have* lived over there! France, Switzerland, Germany or Austria, or even in Scandinavia. My heart goes out to the world's people, who will *not* be *left alone* by the damnable spirit of *greed!*

477

Chadds Ford, Pennsylvania
December 7, 1917

Dear Mama,

Today Babe writes from the Christian Science Church in New Rochelle—also gloriously courageous and terrifically inspiring!

Of course my mind has been mainly on Babe and his new adventure. This will be a tremendous experience for him of course, and no doubt but what he will acquit himself as successfully as ever. He's too well grounded and *rounded* to do anything else.

How grateful we should all feel that he has been able to enter that department of service. How I dreaded to think of his going to the trenches. It is a relief to think that his work will keep him at *headquarters* whether it be here or abroad.

One matter struck me immediately. Did he get extra spectacles? If not will you order two pair from his last prescription, silver rims; have them put in strong cases and sent to him as soon as possible! Send the bill to me. I have an idea he may have forgotten this. Tell him to sew a pocket on the inside of his coat jacket and another under his O.D. shirt and sew a pair into each.

Also, as soon as you receive an address which will find him, drop a postal immediately.

478

At the kitchen table
Chadds Ford, Pennsylvania
December 27, 1917

Dear Mama and Papa,

Carol is washing dishes, Henriette is putting Ann to bed for her afternoon nap, Nat is already asleep, Carolyn is building with blocks at the base of the Christmas tree, and Andrew is lying contentedly in his coach kicking his legs to pass the time away before his meal.

At 5:30 Christmas morning it was still raining a wet, warm sprinkle. Low dark clouds could be seen moving from the southwest. Had not the ground been considerably covered with snow and treacherously slippery ice, one could have well imagined the time to have been early April instead of December. As I came down from the studio, bundled up in that prodigously ample and clumsy Eskimo suit of mine belted with a scarlet sash (one Babe gave me years ago), half-suffocated behind an "Old Kriss" mask, with my heavy boots garnished with red flannel tops and hands cased in Arctic Seal mittens, I could not but think of the striking incongruity of all things that morning. Here I was rigged out in a costume befitting the brilliant, frosty and ringing clear weather associated with the thought of Santa Claus, and yet a spring drizzle poured upon me as I groped my way in the murky dark down the precipitous stairway from the studio to the house, and down my back streamed honest summer sweat. Then, in sharp contrast to my outward appearance were the tremendous feelings within that were so difficult to suppress—that consciousness of the world debacle and its shameless indifference to that ancient and honored thought "Peace on Earth —Goodwill to Men."

It was extremely difficult, to say the least, to assume the role of One who brings cheer and good tidings. In fact I am fully aware that the pantomine lacked the usual vigor and spontaneity I am accustomed to give without stint and with so much personal pleasure.

I was distinctly relieved when I repaired to the cellar and deposited my "camouflage" in a black corner near the coalbin, where it lies at this moment. I have not even enough spirit left over to perform the coldly practical duty of returning the next year's masquerade to its private closet in my studio.

The excitement of the lighted tree and the distribution of gifts was as keen as ever and in no way suffered because of the very noticeable practice of economy on our part. The spirit of the occasion was certainly enhanced by the timely recovery of *all* from the measles.

479

Studio
Chadds Ford, Pennsylvania
December 29, 1917

My dear Sid,

Your box, so full of things for the children, came this morning!— so I hasten to write. I am sorry of course that it was so delayed (for it is marked the *20th*), but do you know it created a new furor in the household, so that as I left the house for the studio this A.M. the big room rung with shouts just as it did Xmas morning! It all made me come to my workroom with more vim than ever! So many thanks to you!!

It is now 3 o'clock, the mercury stands three below zero and the wind is blowing about thirty miles an hour. The air is hazy with fine snow which is slowly and patiently drifting here and there—thin, hard, frugal little drifts, but Oh! it is so cold.

My big window is all but covered with exquisite little engravings in silver frost, and every now and then the great sashes bend in and creak from the sudden pressure of a heavier blast—then occasionally the fine sandy snow hisses softly like steam. It is truly a soul-moving day.

This Xmas we were *particularly* grateful, for on Thanksgiving Day *four* of the children were taken down with the measles, but were able to be up for the first time Xmas morning! Andrew did not get it.

Nat is undoubtedly stronger than ever and bids fair, I think, to eventually overcome his weakness.

Little Ann is as striking in her way as Nat—we call her "Beethoven" because she has such a broad, strong countenance with an astonishing amount of sternness in the set of her features for such a little kid. Andrew is another Baby Brother, with a larger and huskier body. He also glows with good nature. Henriette and Carolyn are very industrious.

We have all been deeply and strangely stirred by Beethoven in recent months—years I should say, as I can detect the force of the man and his music in the regulation of our lives almost two years back. The youngest have actually developed a veneration for the master, which I am deeply proud of, and so love his music as to stop everything almost anytime his music is played. It is tremendously thrilling for me to hear little Ann as she lies on her bed before dropping off to sleep to hum the melodies from any of a dozen of his symphonies or sonatas!

Apropos of Beethoven, I wonder if you have read that astounding novel by Romain Rolland—*Jean Christophe?* If not, I most earnestly suggest that you let no time slip by before you *immerse* yourself in its pages!

572

480

Stimson Wyeth was in training for the army at Fort Oglethorpe, Georgia.

Studio
Chadds Ford, Pennsylvania
January 26, 1918. Saturday

Dear Mama,

It has been a busy, busy week. In the past eight days I have all but completed two pictures (of a set of four) for the *Red Cross Magazine* depicting the British occupation of Jerusalem, trying to bring out dramatically the sharp contrast of the new as against the old. For instance, my first picture depicts a group of shepherds on the hills outside the Holy City, gazing wraptly and with astonishment at an English reconnoitering airplane. The second shows an advancing column of British infantry descending the Mount of Olives, with Jerusalem spread out before them in the afternoon light. The third, a sentinel standing in the moonlight before the "sealed Golden Gate"—and the fourth, a regiment of British soldiers—or possibly a "tank" (if I can find out authentically that these modern leviathans *entered* the Sacred city) passing under the *Arc de Ecce Homo,* the arch under which Christ passed bearing the cross!

Meanwhile I have received orders from Scribner's to take up the work of illustrating *The Mysterious Island* by Jules Verne. This I have been reading closely. It's a long, long book, and although offers *splendid* material for my brush, I must say that I am laboring through the tale. Verne was no artist and was endowed with very little imagination, in spite of all we hear regarding his imagination. The author of *20,000 Leagues Under the Sea* was rather ingenious than imaginative and conceived of an infinite number of experiences and situations upon which he floated an abundance of scientific data, by which he rescued his actors from inexplicable situations, giving them the power to concoct and invent all manner and kinds of solutions, to the amazement of the reader. I suppose, strictly speaking, it takes imagination to do this, but the higher quality of imagination he certainly lacks, that of conveying to the reader a profound realization of elemental beauty and power. In other words, the sense of gripping reality, that quality, *par excellence,* which abounds in the spirited writing of Stevenson.

Nevertheless, I must do my best to supply this quality.

Everything is going finely in the house. Dr. Wales put his finger on the error in Andrew's case. Carol has not had as much milk for him as she had for the others so we resorted to the bottle (in part) sometime ago, as you know. Carol was advised by Dr. Betts to mix the feedings—i.e. allow the baby to nurse five minutes and then the bottle for ten. Dr. Wales maintained that either the bottle or the mother's milk was not agreeing with him. "*Separate* the feedings so as to determine the trouble." The fact is, the mother's milk is at fault, partly because it flows too fast for his digestion and partly on account of quality. By skipping feedings the breast milk is disappearing rapidly and another 3 or 4 weeks will probably find Andrew on the bottle entirely. Last week he gained over ¼ lb. and is ever so much better. What slight changes cause great improvement!

Last night I had the most vivid dream which, as usual, has pervaded my mind today. I heard Papa's voice calling up the stairs that it was ten minutes past five and if I didn't hurry he'd miss the ten-minutes-of-six train. I labored out of the warm bed, got into my clothes, passed through the kitchen where you and he were sitting at the table. The tall lamp we used to have was lighted, shaded with a paper shade, and the aroma of coffee and doughnuts filled the air. I passed through the kitchen and down the cellar stairs taking the lantern I found lit there as I went.

Then everything was blank until we stopped in front of the pumping station and called to Charlie Mitchel, asking the right time. We were told that we couldn't get to Needham up the New Road on account of a big fire (which was the reason Mitchel was pumping so early), so we left the horse there and cut across, straight towards where the old gentleman Eston and Mr. Lyman lived. The Boulevard had just been put through and I remember the deep sandy walk which made Papa puff. We stopped and looked at a great chestnut tree that had blown down near Lyman's house, then suddenly it became Chadds Ford, and we saw the fire here, although it seemed to be on Great Plain Ave. too; however it was, we saw "Tug" Arment dash into the burning house to rescue his little girls, whom we could see roaming around the flaming rooms looking for their dolls.

Then the train pulled out—Conductor Storey was standing on back with his lantern in the crook of his arm (so characteristic of him), and I hid under the yellow blanket in the buggy because I remembered that I owed him a quarter which I borrowed (and this is based on fact, and I never paid it back)! The horse started home and I fell asleep.

It is seldom that I have such a consistent and reminiscent dream. It all seems like yesterday to me.

Yes, I've heard three times from Babe since his arrival at Oglethorpe. The first note merely told of his arrival, the second gave more detail, and the last one, Monday, told of the receipt of the pen with a few words of the Camp doings.

A bit of conversation I overheard the other day between Henriette and Sis Carol will amuse you. Henriette, during my "crusade" to Jerusalem, has been reading parts of the Old and New Testament—result, she is bubbling over with Biblical expressions.

Sis Carol had just swiped a piece of candy from her mother's sewing bag. Henriette looked at her eat it and said, "Don't you know Carolyn that stolen fruit does not taste good?" Sis Carol answered in a flash, "Oh yes it does, only you have to eat it so darn fast!"

"Self Portrait," 1918

Chapter XIX

SIMPLE EXPERIENCES

"We make a great deal of these simple experiences."

Chadds Ford, Pennsylvania
February 8, 1918

Dear folks,

I am on the 3 o'clock train bound for Philadelphia to take up two canvases for an exhibition. The train was late in leaving C.F. so that now even as we pull out of the valley the sun is striking long shadows across the fields, and the trees, bushes and brook-banks are a rich rosy brown.

Now comes a request to paint a poster of American troops going "over the top" for the N.Y. Treasury building (outside). This will be worked up large by sign painters to the size of 15 ft. by 30 ft. long. The right to do this must be passed by the N.Y. legislature first though. It's likely to go through, so they say. [Henry] Reuterdahl is to do a Navy Battle on the other side of the building, I believe.

Andrew is gradually becoming seasoned to cow's milk, although we will not feel satisfied until he shows more gain in weight. He lost almost a pound during the weaning. Carol is indefatigable in carrying out every detail and even talks in her sleep of nipples with the right-sized holes and sterilized bottles! No wonder the children are such fine specimens of color, size and temper. Their care seems to me perfect.

A long letter to Owen Stephens sent in December went down, according to reports from his folks who sent letters and packages at the same time.

The sinking of the transport *Lusitania* is, I suppose, a forerunner of what we are to have.

Studio
Chadds Ford, Pennsylvania
February 22, 1918

Dear Mama,

Back of me, on my easel, stands a self-portrait which (I wonder if I dare say it!) is the most virile and alive study I have seen in *years.* This is a terribly daring thing to say, and yet I am calm in doing it. I am highly elated over my success, which, besides being a result worth having, indicates a decidedly stronger grip on the fundamentals of realistic painting and shows me conclusively that I have been growing steadily in the power to see things truthfully and with *life.* In the subtler points of finish, exquisite color, and choice design, there is plenty lacking, yet I would be willing to place the study alongside any work of the modern portraitists. It rings the bell, no mistake!

Andrew has lost ground during the past 10 days, losing half a pound. But Carol claims to have found the trouble (which was an error in mixing the food). I was so sorry that Carol was to blame, as she suffered bitter pangs of self-reproach, and has not been herself for several days. In all her eagerness to do just right, she slipped —her very *over*eagerness did it, I believe. But he is on the turning point again and is coming around nicely. The weaning has been a problem with him as it was with Ann and Nat.

The war situation is of course acute, but I feel perfectly confident that the next month will bring a great victory for the Allies—possibly the final one needed. Reports of conditions within Germany are leaking out—genuine ones, and their state indicates much.

483

Chadds Ford, Pennsylvania
February 28, 1918

Dear Mama,

I'm sitting in the glass house. The sun is pouring in as warm as in summer, although a high wind is making a stir outside—a warm wind with indications of its quickening into cold before many hours. The smell of dinner is on the air; even now Ann is calling, "Dinner weady." So I'll go in now and take this note up directly afterwards.

There now! My belt's unbuckled and I feel more comfortable.

We are all through dinner but Ann and Nat, who are still lingering over their tapioca pudding. Carol is feeding Andrew with the bottle. He has really picked up remarkably in the past two weeks and apparently Carol has struck the right program. What a difference it has made in him! Vigorous and hearty—he bids fair to follow in the footsteps of his husky sisters, I do believe. The utmost care has still to be used however. Nat's condition remains uniformly good and continues to show gains from the olive-oil massages. I feel positive that this treatment is giving definite aid in giving him weight at least.

Mrs. Wyeth standing in the "glass house."

I spent Wednesday in N.Y. The two main reasons for going were to deliver the "Jerusalem" pictures and to see more definitely just what I am expected to do for the 3rd Liberty Loan. I'm not sure that I have told you that I am supposed to paint a large picture of a land battle featuring the American troops in action—"Over the Top" is my chosen motive. This is to be placed in the gable of the sub-treasury building on Wall Street facing Broad, N.Y. The opportunity is really exciting. The space for each sketch will, I judge, approximate 15 ft. by 30 ft. Reuterdahl will do the Sea Battle. At the foot of each extreme column will be an heroic-sized figure of Uncle Sam and Columbia respectively, with an arm of each indicating, on a barometerlike board set up to one side, the progress of the Liberty Loan receipts.

An amusing feature of the scheme will be the moving pictures taken of us fellows painting the pictures, the putting of it in position, etc, etc. These pictures will be shown at all the movie houses as a phase of advertising. So you may see your bulky son on the screen after all!

The time to do this mammoth canvas (which it is determined we should do instead of making just a small sketch for others to work from) is the one serious factor. But it's just *got* to be done, that's all.

It is next to impossible to find editors, these days, who are willing to *think* when they look at a picture. On the contrary they want a canvas to bowl them over with obvious sensationalism in both drama and color. One has but to study their faces as they look at one's pictures, and one finds not a *trace* of contemplative expression.

I have been aware, for years, of this shallowing process that is vibrating the art departments in the publishing houses, and blame it mostly to a false conception of the functions of painted pictures. They are confusing art with moving pictures. They are trying to do the impossible, and that is to create that obvious and striking sensationalism of the cinematograph in their magazines!!

As a glorious antidote to all this (only the antidote was taken *before* instead of after) was the accidental meeting and a long conversation with Edwin Markham (poet). This happened on the train between Phila. and N.Y. He had given a reading the night before and was on the way to Holyoke to do the same at the girls' college there.

Howard Pyle he knew well, both being enthusiastic Swedenborgians, so my old teacher's name was the open sesame to an inspiring conversation.

Markham looks for all the world like Longfellow, particularly as you study his face closely. He was exceedingly picturesque in his old greatcoat frayed and worn, his long gray locks tangled over his collar and bristly white beard. He sat there in the car with his "congress" shoes off, his lap heaped with newspapers.

During our talk he referred to a poem "to Howard Pyle" and thereupon opened his old alligator-skin satchel which gave me a glimpse of the confusion within: mostly books, a collar or two, some used handkerchiefs, and a package which contained "Limburger" (I knew this without verbal proof on his part).

Best of all (which opened the doors to the very inner chambers of riches) he is an ardent and enthusiastic student of Thoreau. Our conversation on this subject was the feature of the meeting for me, and I feel that much more convinced of Thoreau's vitality and greatness.

This will interest you. Mr. Markham referred me to several books of recent appearance dealing with Lafcadio Hearn's teaching in Japan. To Lafcadio Hearn belongs the honor of making Thoreau one of the best-known authors in the English language, so that the Japs as a nation are more vitally concerned with the doctrines of Walden's sage than we are. Does this not dovetail well into the striking evidence which you witnessed on the shores of Walden last year?!!

There are certain thoughts expressed by Thoreau which Markham was not familiar with, so I very fortunately have an excuse to correspond with him, to send him excerpts from the journals.

To look into his face, to note the perfectly unselfish, detached and thinking way in which he answered every question I asked, was not a compliment to me so much as a fine manifestation of his habit of contemplation, a quality that is tragically rare in these tragic days. The contrast of my short relations with Edwin Markham and the rest of the day in N.Y. stand out vividly.

484

Studio
Chadds Ford, Pennsylvania
March 1, 1918

Dear Mama,

Andrew is pegging along again nearer the way he should. I think he's the most sensitive and spiritual little body I ever saw. Henriette said last night, as she was looking into his face, "He looks as though he were going to be a great composer or artist." That's just it; even as young as he is the power of reflection in his eyes is astonishing.

Andrew.

485

Carol Wyeth's two brothers, George and Richard (Dick) Bockius, were both in the navy.

Chadds Ford, Pennsylvania
March 25, 1918

Dear Sid,

Carol's father was blown to pieces in an air raid in London last week sometime. And I have just received the news from a Wilmington newspaper office that George was lost on that last destroyer which was blown up a few days ago.

584

I'm almost sure there is an error, for at last accounts George was head draughtsman in a government shipbuilding plant in Texas. We've not heard from him for over a month, which is a little ominous to be sure, but then he's not one to write much anyway.

I have already telegraphed to trace down the facts and will endeavor to get the matter certified one way or the other before Carol returns from Phila. where she has gone to see her brother Dick off. He starts on his tenth trip (this time as 1st officer) through the war zone to Bordeaux (merchant marine). He was on the *Orleans* when she was torpedoed, on the *Kroonland* when they tried to get her three different times, and the last trip (on the *Satsuma*) had the pleasure of a timebomb in the hold, which gave them a fire to fight for two whole days 400 miles off the Azores. He's thin, but full of vim and developing into a phenomenal character. He is unusually striking to look at, and this morning I made a portrait sketch of him which turned out quite well. We cannot help feeling depressed at his departure.

486

The two speakers at the Third Liberty Loan rally on April 6, 1918, were Martin Vogel, assistant Treasurer of the United States, and Joseph Hartigan, Commissioner of Weights and Measures for New York City.

N. C. Wyeth's uncle, Denys Zirngiebel, had lived in the old Zirngiebel house since John Denys Zirngiebel's death.

Chadds Ford, Pennsylvania
April 22, 1918

My dear Sid,

I came in less than two hours ago soaked to the skin, laden with sprays of peach and cherry blossoms, and the pockets of my old coat bulging with muddy balls of earth wrapped about the roots of violet plants laden with blooms!

The last week in March and the first few days in April were spent on that sub-treasury poster. During that time I came in touch with a good many of the New York artists and architects, and of course we talked and talked. Several were interested in my points of view on various topics concerning illustration and this flattery led me on, and to put the last straw on the camel's back what must I do but

585

deliver a *speech* from the sub-treasury steps to thousands of people—eight thousand, they say! This at the unveiling of our poster. Reuterdahl spoke too of course, also Martin Vogel and Joseph Hartigan. It was the most terrifying experience I ever went through and I have resolved that the speech shall stand as my *swan song!*

I got a great "hand," which proves nothing in a wild N.Y. crowd, but this did not offset a horrible feeling that I was standing in the very tracks where Washington delivered his inaugural address!! What desecration!!!

The entire experience in N.Y. was extremely novel but very wearing, and I am still suffering from the feel of it.

The 92 ft. canvas (8 oz. duck) was stretched on the scene-painters' frame in the Manhattan Opera House. It was the only one of sufficient size in the city. We had to stand on a six-foot iron "bridge" which is suspended five stories above the stage floor. The great canvas hung against the wall and was lowered or raised as we desired by pulleys and weights. There was no railing of any kind to prevent one from falling seventy or eighty feet into the black abyss behind —i.e. down onto the stage below!

Most of the time we were there (and one night we worked until 4:30 in the morning) the great cavernous building was as black and silent as a tomb. To glance back from the bright glare thrown on the canvas by the battery of spotlights, one could see nothing but myriads of gray ropes disappearing down into that black well.

Twice the stage was in use, however, and the contrasting sensation was startling, to say the least. One afternoon a ballet appeared for rehearsal and at another time the opening performance of "An American Ace"—a wild thrilling war drama depicting, as its main attraction, a section of "no man's land," with trenches, tanks, and airplanes in full action!!

Imagine if you can what my sensations were as I painted away on my mammoth picture of "Over the Top," to look behind me and down, through the slits between the "drops" and "wings," at the flashing of roaring shells, the spattering light of stuttering machine guns, the moving grotesque tanks and airplanes across a chaotic groundwork. Hundreds of figures dodging here and there, some in action before the audience wildly yelling and gesticulating, others (stagehands) sneaking and stooping behind the "sets," but all giving the most vivid impression of real conflict! And then the curtain would go down (I could see its great dusky shape lowering beyond the mass of ropes and scaffoldings) and there would come up to us a queer sound as of rushing wind, or hard fine rain beating on a tin roof. It was the sound of applause from the thousands who packed the auditorium!!

The ballet rehearsal, although less spectacular, was deeply impressive. I was able, from my remote vantage point, to look down with a strong sense of detachment, at the same time feeling to a full degree the sense of *tragedy*. I watched those tiny whirling figures, dusty pink, dusty yellow and drab gray, moving in geometric groups across the smooth surface of the great, gaunt floor—sliding noiselessly as though moved by some concealed mechanical device, starting and stopping suddenly, coincident with the nasal rattle of the piano out in the orchestra stall—and all punctuated by the gruff staccato of the dancing master! Thus suddenly I was made to realize that these little gliding spots of color were flesh-and-blood girls—jumping about that gloomy old floor spending their young lives, giving the most cherished period of their womanhood to puppet dancing! in order to amuse, for a few months, the thoughtless multitudes. It was extremely affecting.

I really started out to write you reassuringly about George. Although we all felt that a mistake had been made in the report, it was a fact that no one had heard from him since he went to Texas at the government's request to take charge of a group of ship draughtsmen. But we found him safe and sound, and somehow the rumor got started in Wilmington that George was on a torpedoed destroyer; it was really *Dick* who had been torpedoed months before on the Orleans, and some news gatherer had just picked it up and built thereupon a fairy tale.

So much is going on these days that one is bound to feel apprehensive of the wildest rumor.

[Harvey] Dunn is across the water now serving as captain (special duty as Gov't. Artist). He's about the best man in the country for the work and in the end will no doubt turn out some valuable pictures. The immensity of things will bowl over even Dunn, I think, and I do not expect him to do big stuff for sometime after the excitement has subsided.

The plan to reclaim New England as our home is stronger than ever and I am bending every effort to push the deal through whereby

I can come into my grandfather's property. The place was officially placed in the market this spring, which relieves me entirely of the awful feeling that I might be forcing my uncle out of the old home. The fact is the place is a burden to him (the uncle that listened to your story in my improvised studio), and the family have at last decided to sell. His wife's family is very dollar-hungry and are trying to interest some "house lot speculators" (God forbid!) and thereby gain a fancy price.

His grandfather's house, Needham.

I am moving in the matter, incognito; a friend of mine in Needham, a real-estate man, is dickering for me and is using a friend as a dummy, so you see it's rather exciting. It keeps me on edge though, for if that dear old place (every foot of which is *sacred* to my mother and us boys) should fall into the hands of strangers, and for *house-lots!*

588

But count on it, Sid; we'll be up there sometime in the next year or two, just as soon as arrangements can be made. The move fairly *bulges* with advantages for us all, and will be a *boon* to my parents. They need the children and the children need them. Also, I will at last be within reach of intelligent people!

My first group of pictures for *The Mysterious Island* were delivered Thursday. Scribner's were very enthusiastic. For this I am thankful.

487

Chadds Ford, Pennsylvania
May 2, 1918

Dear Mama,

A "celestial blue" haze, as Thoreau calls it, envelops the whole valley this afternoon. The wind is talking away at the east end of the studio and I look for rain within twenty-four hours.

One reads that *now* is the time of all times that the world needs the best the artist has to offer, but they forget that the artist—the creative spirit in all lines—is the mouthpiece of *conditions* and no one can dodge the preponderant influence pervading the air today.

This dear old valley is suffering slow torture in many ways in the hands of the moneyed people (principally from Wilmington). They are not only ruining its natural physical aspects but they are paying huge prices for everything from hash to help.

Back of us, right near the "twin bridges," came the rocking reports of 5 or 6 huge blasts which spelled finis for that wonderful stone barn and house of Barney's. Papa may remember it, as he always liked the view of that farm coming down the hill road on the other side of the Brandywine.

Holiday, one of the duPont "bigguns," has already erected great buildings on the place, out of keeping, ugly and impractical. He will, like the rest, do *fancy* farming, which will amount to a very expensive plaything for him. This is the worst thing that can happen to the small American farmer, who lives in the same community and who has to make a living. He can't compete with the prices his rich neighbor pays for help and all other accessories, so in the end must go under. This very thing has happened several times within four miles, and will happen again and again.

589

The Barney place from Pyles hill.

Damn *money*, damn the people who slop it around like hogwash!
It does evil to all!!

The children are all fine. Andrew is hustling right along now and
gained 9 ounces! last week. I'd give anything to have you see him.
He's a wonderful little chap and gives promise that he will live up
to his name.

488

Dallas Lore Sharp (1870–1929) taught English at Boston University from 1900–1922. He was a naturalist and author of A Watcher in the Woods, *published in 1904, and* Beyond the Pasture, *published in 1914.*

At the kitchen table
Chadds Ford, Pennsylvania
May 24, 1918. A.M.

My dear Sid,

The arts as they stand today are *humbug*—there is no art *only* where it claims no right to itself and considers only its duties.

Winslow Homer, [George] Inness, and Gari Melchers are three that give me some satisfaction in this line. The rest, except in sporadic outbursts of rather sentimental and flimsy poetry, such as in [J. Alden] Weir, [William L.] Lathrop, [John] Twachtman, [Willard] Metcalf, et al., are distinctly ephemeral and shrink to mere whispering sweetness when compared to the epic forces of master paintings.

[Edward] Redfield, I know now, works at his art like a carpenter, and when exchanging thoughts with him one is constantly distracted by his sawing and nailing!

There are a few men, Oh! so few!! who, in their maturity, are big enough to be interested in the promise of the younger generation. Their interest seems to be mainly concerned for the *completed* art about them rather than discovering and stimulating the potentialities in the younger men.

No longer does the heart speak, no longer is there frankness and candidness, but only the revealment of *surface;* a beautiful surface may help, like enamel, vitreous, impenetrable. The secrets of the personal equation of the master be always hidden; the facts of the student's personality lie untouched, ignored!

I am not declaring a demand for art *secrets* from these men, but I beg for human intercourse, warm, rich, sympathetic understanding and interest.

I have watched with keen interest what such men as [Daniel] Garber, Lathrop, [Charles] Rosen, [Charles W.] Hawthorne, [Robert] Henri and others are transmitting to their students, and 'tis the same old story. No attempt to cultivate the powers of individual conception, but merely the handing out on a platter the regular stock of tricks and stunts that tickles the palate of the aspiring boy and which in the end leaves him marooned and starving on Garber's Island or Rosen's Reef!

Oh! for men the size of "Jean Christophe," when at the pinnacle of his fame yet found the time to interest himself vividly in the newer men! To the last giving, *giving,* not from his copybook of craft and cunning, but from his deeper wisdom won of sincere living and yearning!

And so New England calls!

I am aware that even Massachusetts does not teem with such greatness but there are a few there whom I know already, which make the change well worth the while. I am anxious to see more of Abbott Thayer, who has written me some wonderfully inspiriting notes, and also Dallas Lore Sharp and Robert Frost are men I think much about. The two last are *very* potential, I feel. Mr. Thayer is quite old and not well, but to be nearer to him will mean something.

I must go where I can tune myself up to the standards of better minds and better lives, where friends will be friends to my virtues and so stimulate me to truer labor—a labor which will call art my real energy—that I will not fear danger. And this is just what I am doing now!

I have seen the growing gravity of my situation and the moment for action has steadily drawn nearer.

Early financial success started me off on the wrong foot. I never counted the dollar (an offense which is a part of my blood, I fear). I made money easily, at least it was the fruit of a constant round of pleasure before the easel, and although I have always worked steadily and hard, I have never suffered the thought for a moment but what I could go on indefinitely. No one, not even Carol, could argue me to the contrary. In this I have been wilful indeed.

But now in the rush of this great war, when I am pushed to the limit to get things done, not only my own work, but for the government, Red Cross, etc., I seem to see in a clearer light how far I am missing, even in my best, the thing I dream of day and night.

In short it is costing too much to live out here. Our place is too valuable for me to keep and the cost of education for the children (the *right* education) is getting to be prohibitive.

Wealth is turning this beautiful valley into a place where only rich men can afford to live, besides destroying its charm of remoteness to the point of disgust.

But I *could* stay and see it through by opening the doors of my studio to a grade of art which brings in rich returns. The temptation stares hard into my eyes sometimes and I catch myself saying, "Oh, well, with such returns I can save enough to paint more, etc., etc." But I am beginning to see that it is not in me to do it that way.

I look forward to the fight ahead with the greatest eagerness imaginable and with particular more pleasure that I have determined to do the job amongst my old friends and in my native land!

489

Ruth Bockius, like her twin sister, Esther, often came for prolonged visits to help her sister, Carolyn Wyeth, with the children.

Chadds Ford, Pennsylvania
May 30, 1918

Dear Mama and Papa,

I am going to make a confession. After you have read it through I know you both will understand and forgive me.

My two telegrams wired to you yesterday, one announcing that I would be home today, and the second (within four hours) reversing the message! It has caused you unnecessary disappointment, I know, and in these days one should be careful to cause as little regret and worry as possible. I am deeply sorry that I could not have forestalled it.

I am going through one of those spells of depression which are bound to overtake one every so often. Carol, being very naturally sensitive to my state of mind, has felt it all deeply. Yesterday seemed to bring everything to a sort of climax, and to relieve it, a visit to you and Papa seemed the only thing.

At noon yesterday we concluded that I should go. The first question, and the most important, was who could we call on to remain with Carol for the two or three days I would be away. It happens that there is absolutely no one here in the village available but Mrs. Sanderson, and so Carol thought she would prefer her own mother; consequently I called up Cousin Carolyn and received the most insulting tongue-lashing imaginable for interfering with other people's business, etc., etc.

Finally, we urged Mrs. Sanderson to come down, also Christian if he wished. She agreed, but could not come until late, some hours after I would be gone.

Well, the afternoon wore away. The children picked a large box of flowers, packed them in moss and wrapped them up. At five I was getting into my clothes, and took leave of the little family at just six o'clock. They all felt pretty lonesome to see me go out of the yard, and the great black storm grumbling on the horizon added to the feeling. However, on my part I fought the feeling with the anticipation of seeing you and Papa the next day and so managed to get on the train. As we pulled out of the valley, there they all were, Carol and the four children, waving towels and handkerchiefs, and back on the porch I could make out the little form of Andrew sitting in his coach, and I could imagine his wistful countenance regarding the puffing engine, little realizing the meaning of the frantic towels or that his dad was off on a trip! Had the train been going slower I would have jumped off then and there! But I stuck it out, believing, as at other times, that the yearning would be overcome as I progressed on my way.

The storm broke and lashed the old train fiercely. Lightning was livid and the thunder crashed far above the rattle and roar of the cars. Thoughts of Carol alone with the brood of little children, and she in a state of mind inevitably saddened by my own depressions of the past weeks preyed on my mind, so that when I reached Philadelphia I was all in. I immediately called up Carol on the telephone and amid the cracking and banging of the storm's effect on the wires I made known to her my change of heart. To my delight she could not suppress her joy that I was coming back, in the same breath, however, urging me to go on! But I just could not do it, and so here I am in the studio this gray, coolish morning after the storm. I can hear the children calling to each other, and I am not sure but what it's all a dream.

Now, I shall not attempt another start, no matter how my soul may crave it, until Ruth gets back from the West. I cannot tell just when that will be, but it must be soon, say another week perhaps.

The box of flowers which the children so enjoyed packing will not reach you. Henriette soaked them so well with water, that by the time I arrived in Phila. the box was ready to fall apart. I made every effort, however, to get them to you and got a fellow in a drugstore to place the box within a box, and after it was reasonably well packed for shipment, found the parcel-post branch office closed and I did not have time to go way downtown to the P.O. I returned to the drugstore and gave them to the very pleasant but pallid man behind the counter. He admitted he lived on 10th street and has seen nothing green from the woods this year, and I felt that the flowers were well disposed of.

What I am going to say now to you and Papa, and I request that it go no further for various reasons, is only the logical conclusion to tendencies which you both have read in my letters before and have probably taken only half seriously. It is fast shaping its way to complete action however and only the fates can stop it.

Conditions in this section of the country are getting intolerable, out of all proportion to most other sections, due mainly to the colossal accumulation of wealth by the duPonts, not mentioning the several other gigantic industries all within eight miles of us—Worth Steel Co., Intervale Steel Co., Remington Arms Co., the great shipbuilding concerns and a dozen other varieties. The flood of money therefrom in inundating us. Not that we get it, but that we must live up to the terrific cost of every single thing which this wealth has stimulated. Is it not absurd that I cannot get a day's hoeing for less than $3.25?— and this is the least of difficulties. Even we who are in constant contact are extremely sensitive to the changed temper of the inhabitants, their feverish thirst to get their share of gold, and every phase of their lives dominated with this thought. So much for the "atmosphere" of the place.

Then the wholesale dismantling of the dear old farms, and in their places hideous new concrete and iron barns, "abatoirs" I call them, and great palatial residences topping every sacred hill—like Babylonian brothels! No longer does the wind come sweet and pure from the remote and innocent vales and valleys behind "Sugar Loaf" or Forsythe's Hill. No longer does "Heifer Run" meander its musical way, but must needs splash over concrete structures, its silvery surface prostituted with iron grills and swinging fences hung across to prevent trespassers!!

Personally, I am beginning to feel the need of a greater stimulant in the form of thoughts hot from the tongues of men who are thinking beyond me, and, in no less degree, the *atmosphere* created in the past by the men who have meant so much to me in their books. And then what is most important of all, to reclaim the remaining years of contact with my mother and father and to stand for the rest of my days on my native soil!!

I have had Ernest Thorpe keeping his eyes open for a possible place for us within easy reach of you.—I have watched the developments concerning Grandpapa's place for a long time and learned months ago that it was in the market.

It will be sold sometime, that's pretty sure, and my plan is to wait patiently for that moment to come, for I am the logical owner of the old homestead.

Meantime this place has been put into the hands of Robert Gauze and Bro. of Wilmington. They are not working on the sale aggressively, but are holding it in mind for any special customer which might come along. When plans are definitely made as to where we will go in N.E. then I'll lift the restraint and they will take up the matter aggressively.

490

Studio
Chadds Ford, Pennsylvania
July 5, 1918

Dear Mama,

We all passed a very quiet yet impressive Independence Day. The one note of celebration was a flag-raising, or rather unfurling, which we enacted at 12 o'clock. As chance would have it Dick, now lieutenant in the Navy, was granted a 48-hour furlough, arrived here about 11 o'clock, which gave to the little ceremony the very appropriate touch of the military. Mrs. Bockius and Nancy completed the party.

On Wednesday I went into Wilmington and bought a 7 × 9 foot flag, a really fine grade of heavy cotton. That evening after six o'clock Henriette, Carolyn, Nat and Ann joined me in a search for a pole in the woods. We found a perfect poplar (tulip poplar so plentiful in this section). I felled it, trimmed off its branches, and with ropes tied around the butt end dragged it way from Cleveland's peach orchard down through the woods, across the brook to the barn. It is seven inches through the stem, tapering perfectly to a height of 35 feet. Everyone wonders how we moved so heavy a green stick so far. Before dark I had it neatly "skinned" with a draw knife and the few knots carefully hewn down smooth.

After supper, in the dark, we arranged the pulley and placed it for immediate planting in the morning. Harrison (the fellow who works for me) had dug a five-foot hole in the location we had chosen—in the center of a spur of raised ground to the left of the winding stone steps leading to the studio.

It's a perfect location in relation to all the buildings, which we decided would be the better consideration instead of trying to make a countrywide display which a 7 × 9 flag would not suit at all.

On the peak I used an old flush box copper float and gilded it with gold paint.

We moved the Victrola out onto the lawn and at the appointed time played the "Star Spangled Banner," all singing while Nat gave the halyards a twitch which released the flag done up in a ball at the peak. It all meant a great deal, more so than I have ever felt toward the flag before. Following this Henriette recited a narrative poem she found in *St. Nicholas* this month about Lafayette, and Nancy read "Barbara Freitchie."

After snapping half a dozen photographs we sat down to dinner. The camera results I will send you.

About five o'clock Uncle Gig and Aunt May turned up. They stayed for supper and then we had some ice cream (which Carol made) and cake (which Ruth made) out under our little grove of locusts right back of the pumphouse. We hung a dozen lanterns in amongst the leaves, brought out the porch chairs and really had a delightful time, more delightful as the whole thing seemed so reminiscent of the gatherings on Sunday afternoons at Home.

Uncle Gig and Aunt May thoroughly enjoy these little visits, as do we.

Around the dinner table we listened to Dick's most picturesque and vivid narratives of his experiences and what he saw on his last trip through the war zone. His ship was "commodore ship" (the first in line) for a group of 80, I think it was (all cargo ships), and on their return three in the convoy were sunk by submarines, one directly back of his boat which he saw lifted clear from the water by the explosion. So you see his narrative was highly seasoned.

However, his thrilling account of the way England and France are showing their feelings of gratitude and astonishment at what this country is doing should have been told from a pulpit.

There is no doubt but what Nat will give a handsome account of himself—as handsome as he looked in his uniform mayhap. His visit here was richest in his relation to the children, which was the finest I ever saw. I shall never forget it. Of course the children are Uncle Nat crazy!

I suppose by now he is on the other side—he must be. I shall write to him periodically.

Just now I am trying to aid Stimson in obtaining his transfer into the intelligence department, in his rightful place as an interpreter.

I was astonished and sorry to hear of the frost damage in Needham but was of course thankful that Papa was so fortunate. It was cold here too and made us think of the *possibilities* of frost, but nothing happened and vegetables are doing wonderfully. We have pulled about 80 ears of "Golden Bantam" this week and they are delicious. Of course that's the potted corn Uncle Gig gave me, and do you know I'm going to do the stunt next year on a larger scale? He gave us only 25 hills (5 plants in a hill) and its surprising what this has produced.

We have had a dozen or more heads of cabbage, lots of cauliflower, peas galore, beans, and now our tomatoes are just turning yellow. It's the best and earliest garden I have ever had. Also summer squash. The noon meals these days are great besides being inexpensive.

Raspberries are abundant and delicious. Gooseberries *loaded*. Currants are now all picked. Carol has jellied 50 or more tumblers of currants and about 12 qts. of raspberry jam, which will be the extent of the sweet stuff (no! peaches later on).

Wheat is being cut on all sides of us now and it's a handsome sight. Across the valley a large binder with four horses is at work, "manned" by a woman.

491

On the porch
Chadds Ford, Pennsylvania
July 24, 1918

Dear Mama,

I spent from 12 to 5 yesterday in Babe's company, almost every moment of the time! It was a glorious privilege for which I have no one to thank but my own audacity and fools' luck.

To begin at the beginning: I received the same kind of a telegram as you did; I immediately wired back that I would start in an hour for his camp. In so doing I fortunately escaped his second wire *not* to come. I got his message at 5:10 Monday afternoon; at six I was off to Wilmington in the little Ford and toward midnight caught a belated train to Cape Charles. Arrived at this place 6:30, connected with a boat for Old Point Comfort (two-hour ride). From Old Point took a trolley to Newport News, arriving about 9:45.

At this point the real circus began. To begin with I found that there were two camps, Camp Stuart and Camp Hill. As there was no address on the telegram I received I had to guess, so spent a long time around the outskirts of Camp Stuart questioning cavalry guards and various soldiers. Finally one fellow advised me to go to a telephone and call up Casual Headquarters for instructions. I did so and was advised to go back into Newport News to Embarkation Hdqtrs. At this point I got desperate so captured a nigger with a Ford and retained his services for an indefinite period. We hustled back to town (5 miles). The *Port Surgeon* fortunately gave me Babe's exact location, to the number of the barracks, before he told me that it was impossible to see him because they were *quarantined,* even during the naval visitors period 4 to 8 in the P.M. I could have slammed that officer, I felt so mad. My plea that Stimson has seen none of his family in 7 months only made him more emphatic.

However, I went directly out to Camp Hill, my "chauffeur" leaving me within walking distance of the camp. I wandered aimlessly around the outskirts and when one of the cavalry guards moved to his furthest point away from where I was I quickly ducked inside the lines. No other guard once questioned me. I found the "Casual Headquarters" of the camp and there established

a winning friendship with an orderly from Texas who knew my
work, and when I told him my story of Babe, etc., he suddenly
said, "By Gawd, I'll find your brother for you!" I wrote a message
on the back of a photo of Andrew and he left the building. He
hadn't got twenty yards when he fairly bumped into Babe and in a
few seconds we were shaking hands. Stimson was on orderly duty
himself and was delivering data to Casual Hdqtrs.

"Babe," 1918.

Babe went immediately to his Col. and asked if I could stay with
him awhile. The Col. shot a glance at me and asked, "How did you

get into camp?" I replied that I had just floated in like an old ferry boat. He smiled a short smile and said that I could stay around for a little while, keeping strictly within Babe's restricted zone (about 50 yards about barracks. He added, looking at me, "I don't know what luck you'll have getting *out* of camp." (Later on, Capt. Rutledge offered to see that I got out OK.)

From 12:30 on we had a corking visit together, frequently interrupted by short duties of various kinds. One of many of the rigid physical exams taking place while I was there. It's very sad to see two fellows turned down for signs of a reactionary sexual disease which they had 10 years ago. The comments on this examination were side-splitting—the boys call it the "short-arm exam."

The spirit of the unit is overwhelming and made me feel tantalized beyond description that I could not go with them. Babe beyond all seemed the most spirited. His relations with the bunch far exceeds anything I expected—the feeling of respect and real attachment they have for him is apparent in every sound of voice. "Stimmy" is what they call him. His eating abilities have gained fame there as elsewhere. His judgment on many matters is sought for, I could see in the four hours with him, and the way he spoke to the men that were turned down was very significant and they felt his earnest sympathy. It was all so obvious.

Babe never looked so well, and this I realize is saying much. He is not as stout but seems so much better set up. His neck is larger and strong and with his close cut hair gives one the impression of great strength. His skin and eyes are as clear as a bell.

It was strange that Monday morning I received printed blanks and a letter from Washington—the machinery to start Babe toward the Intelligence Department. However, he *may* remain in Camp Hill long enough to have them forwarded. They will follow him to France at any rate and the scheme will move on there as well as here.

492

Chadds Ford, Pennsylvania
July 29, 1918

Dear Mama,

I have just finished the last drawing for the Jules Verne book! Go to N.Y. in the morning. There are some dozens of pen drawings to make right away so will return immediately. When these are done will try to skip home.

If it is possible to do it Babe says he will cable to you when he lands.

493

Chadds Ford, Pennsylvania
August 14, 1918

Dear Mama,

We got the card from Stimson on Monday morning notifying us of his safe arrival. It made us all feel good of course. Yesterday I finished my 51 pen-and-ink drawings!

494

Chadds Ford, Pennsylvania
September 20, 1918

Dear Mama,

Nat is sure enough *boy*. He's up by daylight and before every morning partakes in the chores: going for the milk, early mushroom expeditions and nut-gathering.

This morning we were picking mushrooms way up in Cleveland's meadow when it was barely light enough to see them. He was all over that great field with his basket and got more than I did. Sometimes I could barely distinguish his little figure in blue overalls, gray sweater, and Boy Scout hat in the dim morning light.

The mushrooms stood out bright and clear like stars—a sort of inverted effect of the constellations.

My N.Y. trip was highly satisfactory. The *Red Cross Magazine* placed about $4000 worth of work in my hands for the coming year. All war stuff.

They are very anxious to get me across for a few months to gather material in general for the abundant pictures to be done in the future on War subjects.

I feel it stronger every day that I should have at least a glimpse of

Europe under war conditions, not only to meet the demands in the field of illustration for the coming years, but to get that *something* into my blood which all vital painters of this generation will have to have. It's a matter of deep physiological significance which defies definition, yet I know it exists.

495

Chadds Ford, Pennsylvania
October 7, 1918

Dear Mama,

Although Ann is upset at present, due to playing under the damp corn shocks newly cut and stacked in our lower field, we are OK. The epidemic is raging all about us and it is dreadful. Wilmington is quarantined so that one can go neither in nor out of the city. The report is that near ⅓ the people are down with it there.

There is a growing list in the immediate vicinity, and West Chester is hard hit, so you see we are quite isolated on the hill here.

The children stopped school just a week ago today—that is *I* stopped them, preferring not to wait for the official notice. Three days later *all* schools were closed.

I must go to West Chester this P.M. however for some things we need, but feel no particular danger in doing so, as we have had a heavy rain which has laid the dust which is the principal menace, I believe.

I am hoping every minute that neither you nor Papa expose yourselves needlessly, and that he has cut out his Boston trips.

The distraction of so much sickness takes the gloom off of the war news in spite of its importance. However I *am* gloriously elated over the turn of events, although do not hope for too quick a peace which will let Germany get away without sufficient punishment, and by all means not to allow those damnable Prussian leaders to get away with their necks! Everyone of them ought to be shot from the Kaiser down, and I have a hunch they will be. Certainly Germany knows how to squeal when something goes unfavorably!

496

On the way to New York
October 18, 1918

Dear Mama,

We are just passing through Trenton. I have finished reading the continued great good news in the morning papers and it puts me in fine mettle for the day's work ahead.

It certainly was not my wish to make this trip but was unable to avoid it. The retirement of country living is more to be cherished than ever and this autumn has been exceedingly handsome—more so than ever. I have thrust enough of my practical work aside to put in every afternoon at landscape painting—this for three weeks now, and I have profited immeasurably from it, both in actual artistic results and spirit, not mentioning the health feature. I am as brown and clear-skinned as though I'd worked outside all summer.

Ann seems entirely straightened out again. She's a wonderful specimen of happiness, alertness and physical vigor in spite of recent upsets. She's a vivid little character. And Andrew, you'd love him to pieces! He's growing rapidly and already says Mama and Papa and shows an uncanny interest in the auto, which throws him into an ecstasy of delight whenever he sees it.

Sis Carolyn is still our "farmer" and of late has had much to do with the pony—driving him all about and crawling over and under him. Yesterday Carol saw her prone on her back with the pony's nose next to her face while she tickled it. He seems to understand her so well.

The *no school* edict has suited me just right (all but the reasons). These fine days are too glorious to shut children into a schoolroom and both Carol and I are delighted that they have been home to take advantage of it. We have all been nutting several times and how the kids enjoy it!

Then of course it is "birthday week," and although there will be little in the way of gifts, I always arrange some sort of surprise for them in the way of Halloween decorations in the studio with the fireplace going, etc. They rise to this sort of thing tremendously.

604

497

Dear Mama and Papa,

The above sketch embodies the motif I have been doing the afternoons of the past week on a canvas 4 × 5 feet. It has turned out unusually well and marks another distinct step ahead in that most cherished of all departments of my work.

You no doubt recognize the dear old barn. I quake many times when I hear rumors that it is to be torn down!

The children have been abed some time now, having wound up a full day in a flurry of enthusiasm over a sheet of those *transfer pictures* which we boys as kids used to get in Needham at "Mrs. Higgins"—put them on the back of our hands, wet them and then lift off the blank paper. You know.

How I wish Nat would write to me, but say *not a word* to him please, he will "come to" after a while. He's a boy that nurses a grudge and I expected it from him. It may or may not have been my harangue that stirred him to his true self in regarding to keeping well in touch with you all at home. I take absolutely no credit for creating in him any new feeling. I rather stimulated to new action that which he has always had abundantly, but which was becoming dulled by the confining and exacting distractions of a scientific atmosphere.

I'll warrant had he run into a "Howard Pyle of mechanics" he would have been stung out of countenance in short order and would have left in a huff! How Pyle did reach *in* and *down* and fairly <u>tore</u> at one's weak spots! It was like salt on an open sore, but it cleansed and healed!!

But old Babe! What scraps we have had! What scraps we *will* have! But what a great spirit he is!!—like the huge well-rounded hulk of a ship, he rises high on a crest, heaves low into the valleys with the bare topmasts indicating that he still floats, then *up* again facing the far horizon with all sails set!!! His life is my life and I am following him in France in my dreams.

Now for the birthdays!

The cake came on time. The usual excitement prevailed as the ceremony of unpacking progressed, and as board after board was pried off, the wonderful fragrance from Home filled the room! The sweet hay! The apples! The mincemeat (for the cover was just loosened enough to add to the chorus), the spruce cone and the redundant cake!! And even the barberries, somewhat crushed against the caketop, seemed to exude a delicate aroma. The fern too created a phantom impression of moist black earth and tangled roots.

The apples disappeared without my getting a taste! The mince pie was served as a "piece de resistance." The cake was cut under the blaze of 27 candles (to add *36* for my birthday would have been an imposition—to the cake) on Wednesday night in the studio, where, as has grown the custom, I had the room decorated with corn stalks, lanterns and grimacing pumpkins; we all gathered for an hour's real fun. Nat reached the pinnacle of excitement with his new watch and chain (Ingersoll); also he donned his new corduroy suit for the first time. He's an exalted being these days and certainly appears to have turned a milepost.

N. C. Wyeth painting the "old barn."

Carolyn got a little sewing case with scissors, needles etc., and Henriette a kneepad for writing letters, which she can take with her on her ramblings to the brooks and hills.

Ann could hardly be left out of the list of recipients for she would surely have felt herself the victim of calculated partiality, so she got a little two-wheeled cart which has ground out its doleful wheel-squeak ever since! Halloween favors were at each place, and with the smirking and ogling pumpkins peeking through the ranked cornstalks and the fire on the hearth flickering over it all, another valuable impression has been registered on these children's minds—and *ours!*

The interest these past two or three days seems to be hovering about the henhouse, which is being built as an extension of our wagon shed. It is about 10 × 12 feet, with large windows and concrete floor, and promises to be a real attraction for *laying* hens.

A yard 30 × 40 feet will be put up, which will include four of our six plum trees.

Now when Papa feels inclined, ask him to make me a schedule of his diet table—the kind he uses to inveigle 4,247 eggs in 224 days, out of his hens. I have an idea that I can put it over my neighbors a little with the right feeding propaganda. I will follow him to the letter, providing the tarts, pastries and pies of hendom can be procured in our village. Screenings, middlings, scratchfeed and "mill offal" are easily procured, and I have fifty bushel of corn which I raised myself.

498

Chadds Ford, Pennsylvania
November 19, 1918

Dear Mama,

We got our first egg yesterday!! The commotion it caused in the household would have made you smile, and today the poor hens have been pestered to distraction by spying eyes, so much so that I had to place a "war zone" around the barn; so this afternoon if any biddy felt so inclined she has ample opportunity to swell our larder with another seven-cent donation (for we are paying 85¢ a doz.).

The pullets are last of April and early May productions. We have two old hens, four roosters, and the balance (21 in all) are pullets. Three of the roosters I am fattening for the table.

499

Chadds Ford, Pennsylvania
December 21, 1918

Dear Mama and Papa,

I am sitting in my shirttail in the warm kitchen. It is only 5:45 Sunday morning. I am down here to warm Andrew's bottle. Feeling quite wide awake with no inclination to return to bed I'll start this letter. It is raining and a thick mist all but obscures the lights in the village, and as the fire is burning brightly and the oatmeal steamer is singing merrily I feel snug and cozy even with "my-mother-doesn't-use-wool-soap" shirt on!

Your two dandy letters came yesterday—the box on *Friday!* The suspense is over, for we all consider the box from Needham, with its customary wreath and other good things so fragrant of that home so significant to all of us, the key*note* to our Xmas. It gets us off on the right foot, so to speak. Without the ceremony of placing the Home wreath over the fireplace, Xmas eve would not be Xmas eve, and the day following would be like a king without his crown.

Late Friday night Carol and I opened the box, but the first sight of the spruce spray was so suggestive, so enjoyable, that we both reproached ourselves for disturbing the box until *all* could enjoy its unpacking Tuesday evening. I stole a glance into the internals of the box by lifting one corner of the covering paper to see if all was well and that nothing had broken its bonds. Everything looked as snug and peaceful as the moment you finished packing it, so the deep pleasure remains to be dispensed Xmas eve!

We make a great deal of these simple experiences; with you I believe them to be the real foundation of one of the most profound ethical ideas in regard to early training, to obtain the utmost of pleasure and inspiration from the simplest and homeliest events of the life about you. I cannot but recall the passage in Thoreau's diary where he writes—in substance, "When I am asked why I do not go abroad and rub off some rust—to gain in a worldly sense, I fear lest my life lose some of its homeliness. If Paris is more and more to me, Concord is less and less, and yet it would be a wretched bargain to accept the proudest Paris in exchange for my native village. I wish so to live here that I may derive my inspiration from the commonest events, and the conversations of my neighbors may inspire me. A marsh hawk flying over Concord meadows is more to me than the entry of the Allies into Paris. In this I am not ambitious. A man may acquire the taste for brandy and so lose his love for water, but should we not pity him for it?" etc., etc.

This is poorly quoted for I have no memory for the sequence of words, but it is the gist of his thought and embodies to me one of the simplest and profoundest bits of wisdom I ever heard. It is a perfect antidote to all the glaring and hideous mistakes of modern life which has so lately blossomed forth in ghastly form. It is also a hunch for the so-called *public educators!* Schools are a *menace* to

all children who are by natural ability above the hopelessly mediocre
—*all* organized schools and colleges too. I could easily become a
Bolshevik on this question! (The children will finish this term, then
quit absolutely—they are uneducating them faster than we can patch
them up!)

[Letter continued]
9:30 Sunday evening

I took the warm bottle up to Andrew. He reached out for it in
the dark and immediately suckled away at a great rate. Carol turned
over and said, "What time is it?" I answered, "Six o'clock, and time
for breakfast." "Poach me an egg and make a nice cup of coffee and
I'll come down and eat with you before bedlam turns loose!" The
suggestion sounded good to me, so I turned from the pen to the frying pan, and in no time we were enjoying some oatmeal, coffee and
an egg apiece! Yes, *eggs,* by God!! We were still talking at daylight
(the longest night of the year) and rain was beginning to patter
against the east kitchen windows. But soon the second story began
to *roar* and the morning idyll came to an abrupt end.

We have seen little of each other as I [have] spent it all but the
dinner hour in the studio—to finish a picture I am very much interested in, and after early dusk to do some more work on a miniature
barn I have been making for Carolyn. It is about three feet square
and two feet high—an exact replica of our old barn on the Harvey
place, even down to broken boards, etc. I have actually shingled it,
and when the weatherbeaten colors, even to the manure stains, are
put on it will be fascinating to look at. This will be her principal
gift and I have a notion it will make a hit. Carolyn still has a mania
for barns and farm animals. The hill directly back of the house resembles a countryside with its half-dozen farms and fenced fields in
miniature.

We have bought various little china and wooden animals in proportion to the building, and I shall give it all a setting in a large
shallow box with moss for grass, young trees and a looking-glass
pond.

Several amusing things have happened lately. Nat has, for a week
or more past, been agitated by the calendar. As Xmas grows nearer
the figures grow larger, which seems to ruffle his feelings in spite of
the fact that he readily understands the explanation. The other day

Carol discovered in his room a carefully made calendar (the one-sheet-to-a-date kind) made in reverse order thus:

Thurs.	Fri.	Sat.
7	6	5

etc., etc. This was neatly tied at the top with red cord and hung at the foot of his bed.

There was something very humorous, ingenious, and highly suggestive of his impressionability in this little stunt, wasn't there?

The following might be considered by some to be potential of bad, but not to me, for I recognized myself so clearly in Sis Carol's story-telling, which had, I am bold enough to say, so much ingenuity that the lie justified itself!!

She lately saw a gift down in the village store which she wanted very much to purchase for someone (her mother, I believe). It cost a dollar! In her paper bank (to be given to a Santa Claus Club for poor children) was a dollar bill which I had given her in exchange for the handful of pennies, nickels and dimes she has saved up throughout the summer and fall.

Day before yesterday she suddenly called to the other children that she had captured a wet dollar bill from the *cat* who was carrying it in her mouth—yes, you could even see the teeth holes! "She must have found it up by the rock, dropped by a hunter perhaps, or Mr. McVey!" Everyone swallowed the story hook, bait, and sinker, and the rest of the children envied her mournfully that whole dollar which she had the perfect right to spend for Xmas presents!

The following evening we set to work to send the accumulated money in the three banks to the Santa Claus Club, and lo! Sis Carol couldn't find her bank! She got real excited about it and blamed first one then the other of the children for mislaying it. I smelled a mouse, and when things quieted down a little suggested that she send the *cat's* dollar in place of the missing bank, and when she found it again she would still have her money. Reluctantly she fished the crumpled dollar out of her blouse pocket where she had it safety-pinned in. This ordeal over, I noticed that she took no further interest in the search for the lost bank. Then I questioned her about the cat and all the details of how she rescued the dollar. "I saw Timmy comin' down through the bushes. I thought he had a bird or somethin' in his teeth, and then I saw it was a dollar. I was afraid he would choke on it so I took it away!" I asked, "How did he come down the hill, fast?" "No, he just runned along with his paws up this way, bouncing the dollar along just like he does when he plays with a ball, and I picked it up." Then I said, "I thought you picked it out of his teeth!" It was all over then—she saw the trap she had fallen into and broke down. But she has revived since and haughtily claims that the cat brought her that dollar.

In the Xmas tree there will be a stuffed cat with an imitation dollar bill pinned to his mouth!

Oh! She's a schemer!! She and Nat did their shopping last week in Baldwin's store. Nat made all his purchases but didn't have quite enough cash to buy what Sis Carol said *she* wanted, so she chipped in and helped pay for *two* things, both of which (Nat divulged to me) Sis Carol demanded she should play with *before* Xmas, which accounts for a new iron horse and wagon out in a soapbox barn near the nut tree!

Last night she went out in the dark to retrieve the premature present so that Nat could wrap it in white tissue paper and wind it with yards of gay cord and speckle it with varied "Ole Kriss stickers," as the children call the holiday stamps. Last night was one great wrapping bee. We had just gotten our allotment of white tissue and string which accounted for the activity.

Oh! how I wish a thousand times over that you and Papa could see these children Xmas morning!! They never looked so well in their lives, which is saying much, and the excitement of Xmas has added a super-quality to their appealing faces. It is a *shame* beyond words that we can't *all* be together. How many times have Carol and I repeated this wish.

I have been exceptionally busy, but not too busy to give sufficient time to the Xmas spirit.—It is more important than my work for the simple reason that it is the *source* of my work. Of course what little I've done has been mostly concerned with the children.

We got Henriette a secretary desk for her room. She deserves and needs one. Also two of Barry's books (author of *Peter Pan*).

Carolyn: A small theater (pasteboard, with magnet to move characters on stage), barn and animals.

Nat: More track for his electric engine, Boy Scout suit, stone building blocks, and machine gun.

Ann: Doll, wicker cradle and chair.

Andrew: Blocks, and music roller.

For Carol I got a set of "Spode" (I think you call it) china—dinner set. She will now have a set for "best." And for Ruth a Brownie camera.

I've got a nice tree and the children and I made a second pilgrimage in search of trailing evergreen and found lots of it! Not as large and vigorous as the New England variety, but fine nevertheless.

Today (it has poured a warm rain all day) the children spent in weaving the mass of evergreen into long strings and have made a really beautiful job of decoration in the big room here. Tonight they demanded the *piece de resistance*—the wreath, so I robbed the Home box of that trophy. It holds its accustomed place of honor in the center of the mantel!

The spray of spruce, you will note, is on the mantel. I get a singular thrill when I look at that spruce branch together with Grandpapa's portrait (in the black oval on the right) and to reflect that he was responsible for that very spruce evergreen which at this moment, nearly 60 years after he planted the baby trees, is adorning his grandson's mantel in Pennsylvania, placed within a few inches of his portrait, taken, I should judge, about the time of the plantation!

Uncle Gig and Aunt May will be with us Wednesday.

Esther and Myron and little Myron will stop here over Xmas day on their way north (Myron was discharged Thursday). Nancy and her mother will complete the party. The little house will fairly burst. But if *you* both were only here I wouldn't care if the whole state of Pennsylvania blew in—as it will be I will feel periods of sadness which will often make me go out of the house for awhile, as in other years. I shall look in the direction of Needham, just over the top of Sugar Loaf, many times that day!

I shall also think of Stimson so much. He's too fine a specimen to be wallowing around that pigsty, Germany!

500

Chadds Ford, Pennsylvania
December 26, 1918

Dear Mama,

The Day is over—a gloriously happy one, everybody proclaiming it the happiest in years!

There were fourteen at the dinner table. They included Uncle Gig, Aunt May, Mrs. Bockius, Nancy, Esther, Myron, Dick!

The latter sailed in about 11:30 (a 20-hour leave of absence), which made the party particularly complete from Carol's point of view, and meant much to me also.

Remembrances poured in from all sides and the big room for once seemed *small*. With people, children, tree, floor space for machine gun, miniature theaters, farm buildings and other sizable gifts, one had to "watch his step." We had music, singing national songs and the familiar old "College songs," and Uncle Gig gave us a really thrilling repertoire of Swiss yodles, etc., which were tremendously enjoyed and which stirred me to my depths as a vivid reminder of the past. At such moments he completely justifies himself and I could excuse him for all things which at times bother me. He fairly reeks in appearance of so much of Home—looks so much like you, Stimson and myself, his face beaming exactly as young as of yore, that in the moments of music or in the short periods of his finest side, he stands as a demigod, a vivid symbolism of that which is the most internal of my soul—the haunting vision of my first and profoundly loved Home. The day (socially) centered about him—all felt the magnetism of his joviality and responded with vim. His behavior was unmarred, and all went to their homes that evening with a strong, pleasant flavor of his personality in their minds.

In a different way Dick was, of course, a hero of the hour, and his sea tales and warm stories of France, which he has come to love deeply, found an ardent circle of listeners.

Christmas morning, 1918.

501

Chadds Ford, Pennsylvania
February 27, 1919

Dear Mama,

Henriette is reading *Little Men* by the center lamp, chuckling aloud at irregular intervals at its humor. As I turn to look at her face she shows distinctly her utter detachment from everything about her, completely immersed in the surroundings created by Louisa Alcott.

615

Henriette is indeed an ardent and constant lover of those wonderful books and has reread all of them so many, many times.

Yesterday, she and I spent a most interesting day in Phila. mainly to see the annual Academy exhibition.

She is just as satisfying to go with to such things as an older person of recognized intelligence. Her appreciation and judgment of pictures was so genuine, judgment which was based upon so much basic understanding, that I felt upon leaving, that keen gratification one feels after spending time with a mature, unsophisticated and sensitive mind. No prejudices, no assumptions, no palaver. Whatever limitations of understandings she exhibited were the inevitable intellectual restrictions due to her youth. *Infallibly,* she caught the big fundamental strength or weakness of this or that canvas. The impressions I gained only went to verify my conclusion that any painting which depends so much upon the intellect (allegory or reference to legend, etc.) for its appeal is robbed just that much of its importance; and that the appeal to the inherent senses is the only true test of a work of art.

Whether or no it is because I am not an intellectual that I could never consider Milton, for instance, a great artist, I do not know, but it has always been my contention that if to appreciate a work of art one must depend upon a wealth of knowledge of the classics and history, then great it cannot be. In contra-distinction, Shakespeare makes his greatest claim to his supreme position as an artist because he deals entirely with the fundamental human emotions, which the human family will understand for all time. One's enjoyment of Shakespeare is limited only by one's limitation in human interest. The great gamut which lies between *humor* and *tragedy* is played upon by this master without ever cluttering up the appeal with historical or literary references. Nor even do too exotic customs or costumes ever mar the *universal* quality—at least none but what will always be understandable and accepted.

It seems that I can never reconcile myself to the mere demonstration of the mechanics of the brain, no matter how prodigiously it works, unless the sound of its grinding wheels is completely lost and *smothered* in overwhelming *feeling—that feeling that amounts to bodily sensation* rather than mere mental perception!

Yesterday I was offered, by one of the wealthiest advertising houses in the country, the sum of $20,000 a year!! to work *exclusively* for them. I *refused* the *instant* the word was out of the man's mouth, so *emphatically,* in fact, that the three men in the party looked at me with that startled look of men who had unintentionally offended. But like a vivid view of a landscape in a flash of lightning, the full consequences of such an arrangement stood before my eyes—no more books, no more free time for painting, and very much suffering while doing a hundred subjects distasteful to me to one good one! It has passed from my mind like a silly dream—and best of all Carol said when I told her all about it, "What a terrible thing it would have been if you had accepted!"

502

N. C. Wyeth was illustrating The Last of the Mohicans *by James Fenimore Cooper.*

Studio
Chadds Ford, Pennsylvania
March 17, 1919

Dear folks,

We are all elated over the opportunity to get Mrs. Dunn's house for the summer and hasten to ask you, Papa, to give her the final word that we will be on deck the third week in June to take it off her hands.

What little experience I have had in renting furnished houses for part of a season, I think $100 for ten weeks is reasonable.

Your kind suggestion to come to the Home for a short time before occupying Dunn's will be taken advantage of, I think, perhaps for only a week, for as my plans are now I hope to finish up the Mohicans before we leave, which will use every moment of time up to the 10th or 12th of June.

You can't imagine the spirit of anticipation running throughout the household. Particularly Carol, who is deeply touched by the definite chance at last to see you all again and to be able to drop in often to have those talks and visits which she so many many times speaks of!

The snow stopped my ploughing with one field almost done. I shall break up all the grassland this spring, putting corn on all but 2 acres which will go into potatoes. Am doing it on shares as last year.

The children are fine and little Andrew is delighting us these days by singing with phenomenal ability the "Marseillaise." When I first heard him on Saturday I could not restrain the tears.

503

Studio
Chadds Ford, Pennsylvania
May 6, 1919

My dear Sid,

As an opening gun, I might announce that we all of us will arrive in Needham the third week in June to stay definitely until September —(have rented the house) in the meantime seeking a home for the winter and longer, at least long enough for us to decide where we shall establish new roots *permanently*. So you see, the first step back toward my native soil has practically been taken, and some step it has been too! You are hardly in a position to realize what a problem it has all been, to know just what to do. Through it all, the *desire*— yes, the feeling of *utmost necessity* that we *must get back to New England*—has shown like a star, steady and far off, but the attractions and attachments of a home where the children were born, the appealing loveliness of the country and all the other subtle entanglements of sentiment have made the ultimate decision very difficult to come to. However, it is over, and we are coming. We are happy in the decision albeit there will be heart-burnings in the process still.

It has been as severe a winter as I ever put in in my life. I have had mountains of work to do but none of it has come easily; most of it falls short of any real advance, while some little of it shows distinct promise.

In January I determined to launch into purely illustrative work with no turning aside to tease the muse along. The time had come for me to build my *finances* into a firm foundation, so that when the moment for the great change came I would be ready for it. I have accomplished my purpose fairly well and the outlook seems particularly bright to me. New England, with its greater intelligence, with its deeper appeal, and its greater honesty, seems to offer me the needed help.

504

Simple Experiences

Dear Mama,

The European muddle is *so* unsatisfactory that it gives me a feeling of unrest to take part in victory celebrations. Italy worries me; she has developed a strangely new covetous spirit that does not forbode good. Feeling in N.Y. and everywhere running high—not outward but under the surface.

505

Dear Mama,

Last night I returned from New York after delivering an address before the American Institute of the Graphic Arts, so today I've done very little but loaf around, thoroughly enjoying the gracious contrast offered me here.

However, the evening proved especially satisfactory to me, as well as a great surprise, for my paper aroused the greatest enthusiasm in spite of a formidable array of speakers eminent in the art world and in New York particularly. Charles Dana Gibson, George Bellows, and Edward Penfield, three whose names would mean anything to you, were amongst the speakers.

Without carrying an account of my satisfactions to the point of objectionable immodesty, will say that an enthusiastic and unanimous vote was taken to have my paper printed and distributed to every member, and also entered in the records of the organization.

I can only account for it all with this reason—that the constant talk and discussion that goes on amongst the New York men (who see too much of each other) leads them into hair-splitting argumentation which finally becomes the means of throwing them away off the track of fundamentalisms. They subdivide their thoughts and then get lost in a single subdivision which in the end becomes painfully irrelevant and useless. So, with my platitudes, clearly spoken, they were swept by a renewal of the truth which proved refreshing.

I cannot but liken my situation (on a very tiny scale of course) to Roosevelt's situation in Berlin and at the Sorbonne, where he was openly and contemptuously accused of fatuitous and platitudinous speechmaking—which nevertheless provoked discussion for months following!! (And woe betide Europe that she did not act on his advices!)

506

Chadds Ford, Pennsylvania
June 11, 1919. Wednesday

Dear folks,

The actual date of our coming up must be left until the last thing, owing to the great confusion of my own professional program. About the first of July, I should judge, or in that week anyway.

507

As a very young child, Henriette was surrounded with various aunts. It was so natural to call someone Aunt Ruth or Aunt Nancy or Aunt Hilda that she called her Wyeth grandparents Aunt Mama and Aunt Papa.

Chadds Ford, Pennsylvania
June 26, 1919

Dear Aunt Papa,

Henriette started this letter but I had better explain matters.

We are coming Tuesday next on the train leaving Wilmington at ten o'clock in the morning, arriving in Boston the same night, 8:05, at the South station.

I trust that we can get into Dunns' house immediately, or if you and Mama think well of it perhaps it would be better to spend the night with you, as bedclothes and a certain amount of food for the kids, particularly Andrew (milk and cereal), for the next morning would be difficult to get right off the bat.

Chapter XX

MAMA AND PAPA

*"I know of no moments in my life here
rarer than these. You both know how I feel
and love you."*

The Wyeths remained in Needham through the first week of September, returning by car to Chadds Ford, September 7th.

Chadds Ford, Pennsylvania
September 14, 1919

Dear Mama,

One of those mornings so bracing, so ineffably charming that one almost suspects Nature to be held under some sudden mystic spell—a suspense, a pause in the season's vicissitudes—a breathing space between seasons, the dying summer's hush with her ear to the ground listening to the distant trample of oncoming winter. It makes one feel like moving about on tiptoe lest he disturb the exquisite calm, lest by loosening a stone or ruffling the trees he may precipitate the elements into ever-increasing movement and clamor!

So keenly poised do I feel this morning!

As I face the big north window the lush tops of the peach trees bank up on the east side, and on the west the grayer green mass of a wild cherry rises well against the sky. Between this arboreal setting the prospect of the valley shines like a colossal gem in the golden sunlight; the checkered fields of buff stubblefields, green cornfields and greener meadow pastures, struck into life by the thread of emerald water, all lie before me like a paradise—a paradise unappreciated, a miracle of forces turning and changing, massing up wealth upon wealth for our eyes and hearts—and all in silence—and mostly in vain.

It seems as though I would *burst* in the effort and passionate desire to assimilate *all* of the beauties of sights and feelings that have come into my life. Life at times seems almost too good, too rich for my spiritual digestive apparatus to cope with. Were it not for my slight ability to vent my feelings through the medium of paint and, in a lesser degree, through the spoken and written word, I *would* burst. Production is my salvation, it is the one thing that keeps me on a reasonably even keel. The process of fermentation is vigorous within me. That is good. But I must just as vigorously keep the doorways of expression cleared of accumulations. Cloggage is the bane of most of us; with passages kept clear, body and brain will function with ever-increasing value to oneself and the world. This is self-evident.

We have been home a week.

Your letter, received yesterday, was a particularly appealing and beautiful tribute to the summer we spent together. Of all your letters I remember none that impressed me as this one does. Clearly, lucidly expressed, completely done, neither too much or too little. One fairly throbbing in moving sentiment and yet finely poised—in short, consumate. I feel in it the quintessence of the *great* qualities you possess, the greatest any woman *can* possess, those qualities which symbolize *motherhood*—sympathy and understanding upon a foundation of earthiness—a real shepherd to spiritual and bodily welfare.

Last of the Mohicans proofs are *terrible failures;* a strike among engravers ruined the whole set and the books are going to be put through in that condition! just because Scribner's must live up to their announcement.

509

Chadds Ford, Pennsylvania
October 5, 1919

Dear Mama,

These are indeed turbulent days, and although we have cut ourselves down to only an occasional newspaper (and that a conservative one) the distant roar of the breakers seems to come in upon us by one means or another. Even my reading, which I have been carrying on steadily, reading which I had chosen with little thought of its relevance to strictly contemporary affairs, has fanned the embers of certain reflections into white heat, and I find myself in a veritable tempest of wonderment and doubt.

Two books have absorbed my attention tremendously since the return to Chadds Ford. *The Passing of the Great Race,* by Morrison Grant (Scribner's) and *The Saturday Club,* by Edward Waldo Emerson (Houghton Mifflin). Both of these are momentous books for any serious-minded person to read.

The former volume I shall not attempt to describe except to say that it is a deeply studied, exhaustive and scholarly presentation of the inevitable direction the races of the world are taking, particularly

624

our nation. A book which, by the way, aroused the deepest attention of the Great Roosevelt (the loss of whom I'm feeling more and more is a calamity to the whole world!).

The other book is like a great light shining behind modern life, throwing its huge, restless and ominous silhouette in bold, black relief. I refer to *The Saturday Club.* A wonderfully charming account of immense flavor, telling us with keen description and trenchant anecdote of many of those men of New England that made up the "Golden Age" of intellectual America. Agassiz, Emerson, Longfellow, Hoar, Dana, Hawthorne, Lowell, Motley, Holmes, Felton, Henry James, Norton, Sumner, Adams, Wyman, Lowell, and a dozen others less familiar to me—these all shine and glisten in brief but *throbbing* interpretations or, I should say, *translations* of their characters. The book makes one's heart ache for the company, or at least the living existence, of just such a group of men. To know and feel that in one's country there thrives an oasis of true understanding, an atmosphere of spiritual understanding and sympathy, where strong minds can and do come together, face one another in real battles of wits, each powerfully entrenched in his point of view but willing to give and take, sustaining all the time deep friendship and attachment. Is there anything more heartening, more inspiring? I think not. It is one of the few phases of human relationships that gives one courage and faith.

One so often reads in Emerson, Thoreau, Channing or Parker of the "vast and hurrying encroachments of commercialism." What would those men say, could they see the stifling mess we are in today?!!! The overwhelming surge of materialism almost makes me despair at times—but enough of this. I must send you *The Saturday Club!* My heart yearns toward dear old Agassiz and Longfellow —and always I think of Grandpapa. I feel even proud that when my little article appears in *Scribner's* next month (November number) the divine word *Agassiz* will appear in it!

Another strata of new interest is taking its place in my life— Henriette's daily study hours in my studio. I can only say that her work is remarkable. Certain fundamental knowledges such as perspective and proportion seem to be instinctive to her. Perspective alone is so perplexing that in my experience I have observed very few who understand it. It relieves me much to know that this usually stubborn stumbling block will not impede her to any extent. Perspective is and should be a delight not only to the artist but to the observer of his picture.

Carolyn's hens are doing finely considering the time of year. Five eggs today, and running from 3 to 7 right along. A little excitement lately because signs of egg-stealing are apparent. But we are blaming it upon a droll old raccoon that lives under a rail pile near the henyard.

Westward Ho! by Kingsley (my next book probably) I've already started to read (at least Henriette has been reading it to me). It's a robust story of the period of the sea rover, Drake—a hunt for treasure.

Often as I look through the wonderful autumnal haze of these glorious days, directing my eyes northeast, just a little to the right of "Sugar Loaf," my imagination projects my vision over vast spaces until it reaches the familiar country of Dover, Charles River Village, and the slides between Burgess's and the new bridge, thence onto those dear acres of ours—that gentle slope of land rising from the River to the giant hedge of "spruces." At this moment of mental projection I always feel as though I could dream on forever. I think of every stone, tree, path and building, every window and door, and then inside to every nook and cranny of that dear old house; and, as I have told you so many times before, I discover you, Mama, doing one of the hundred duties that mean so much to all of us; and then from the kitchen window near the "box," I watch Papa come up around the barn and disappear in the gloom of the big door— with a basket perhaps, or a rake or scythe. I know of no moments in my life here rarer than these. You both know how I feel and love you.

510

Chadds Ford, Pennsylvania
October 12, 1919. Sunday night

My dear Mama,

The close of a wet, cheerless day—the kind of day and the time of year that never fails to recall those thrilling and familiar lines of Longfellow's which I have so often quoted:

> "The day is cold, and dark, and dreary;
> It rains, and the wind is never weary;

The vine still clings to the mouldering wall,
But at every gust the dead leaves fall,
And the day is dark and dreary."

It has been a day of ruminations, interspersed with fitful reading, and attending now and then to a few home duties. Looking back over the ten or twelve sober-colored hours, I am aware that most of the meditations were along the lines of my own life, its past, present, and future.

It is seldom, in these days, that I can give such an unbroken period to such reflection, and it is probably well that I cannot; retrospection breeds a potential sadness, to say the least; introspection creates dissatisfaction usually; and prospection is often baffling and always flimsy. To deal with tangible problems of the moment with force and precision is my salvation, as it is with most of us. I usually suffer in proportion that I fail to do this.

The book I have been reading, and just finished, *The Saturday Club,* has had much to do with my frame of mind of late and particularly today. It revives the spirit and recalls vividly certain realities of the surroundings and atmosphere of New England, which existed when I was a boy. What arouses me particularly are the accounts given, and the dates, of the passing of certain prominent men of that glorious circle of Concord, Boston, and Cambridge men. Not that their *deaths* impress me inordinately, but that my memory has been cleared, in some instances *perfectly* cleared, to a positive remembrance of the occasions. For instance, Oliver Wendell Holmes—what a stir it made—"The last of the famous group!" I heard it said. This was in 1894. And then there was Whittier in 1892, and at that time I can remember somebody (it may have been Miss Glancy) telling of Emerson's death, "Just ten years before" (my birth year, that was). And of course the name of Agassiz was still warm with life as it came from Grandpapa's lips, or yours, although he died in 1870, I think—and then Longfellow's passing was also in 1882, the same as Emerson's. All this may sound dismal to you, this recounting of demises, but not so to me. I feel a subtle but deep stimulation from the fact that I have lived when some of these men were still standing on the planet with me; that I was at least *conceived* when dear Longfellow and Emerson were of the living, and I am especially grateful that it was my good fortune to have such a virile connecting link between myself and Agassiz—that is in Grandpapa.

627

And then to feel through all this, the more remote, but with cameo clearness, the distinguished figure of Thoreau, a man who more than ever today towers above the others, as great as they were!

I have just finished work for the day. Yesterday was brilliant and cool, the autumn leaves sparkling like clustered jewels. I put in my third painting on a large canvas I am doing in the meadow—a spot I can see from the window here.

I am becoming more encouraged and have sufficient reason to believe that in time I will emerge into the painter's field. I am looking forward to this with all my heart. I am not covetous of gallery honors in this new and superior department of art. It is wholly a desire for more personal and therefore more powerful expression that I seek. This is a point which I wish Papa could grasp. If he once saw the distinction between illustration and painting, and would compare the idealism which lies behind these arts, he would understand my eagerness, which appeals to him now, I'm afraid, as a mere manifestation of impractical restlessness.

As one self-evident measurement of values, let me say this: that illustration has existed from the beginning of the history of art; in fact, early painting amounted to illustration and nothing more—these early examples remain with us today as a matter of historic interest and not artistic. But since the development of the painter's art into the higher forms of expression, as in Michelangelo, the result [is] of one fundamental trait—an uncontrollable desire to express one's personal feelings toward life. This constant "welling up" within one can no more be ignored nor suppressed than the feelings of hunger or thirst.

I suppose the bottommost mistake of all is the prevailing attitude that art is a form of entertainment—a passing diversion.

I seem to have launched (and very clumsily too) into the midst of the intricacies of an art talk. I foresee the possibility of endless pages given over to this topic, with not much achieved in the end either, so I'll stop it here.

Am sending sugar for some birthday cakes—you may be short. Was afraid you would have to miss making them.

511

Mama and Papa

My dear folks,

"Carnival Week" is upon us, suitably and impressively ushered in by our grandmother's and great-grandmother's birthday anniversary. In memory of this I am mailing and presenting to you a copy of *The Saturday Club*. It is the one I have read, and read with the deepest enjoyment, and now on this appropriate occasion hand it on to you. I hope all at home will derive pleasure from it.

As Jean Louis Agassiz is the colorful figure in the volume—the *hub,* as it were, around which the others circulated—it seems especially fitting as an offering in the memory of my Swiss grandmother—also as it deals with the men who were living very deeply and nobly, almost within Grandmama's sight, often passing by her very gate while she was struggling within her home to heal a broken heart. How Agassiz would have felt for her had he known!

What a busy week we have had! I say *we,* but it is *Carol* who is really busy these days. What a marvelously virile little body she is! Never has the home moved along so smoothly and so efficiently. It seems as though the more she does the more she wants to do.

Andrew is *splendid* and has made extraordinary gains in the past weeks. You would hardly know him—his cheeks full and blazing with color, and the most active kid and the most rowdy you ever saw. He keeps Henriette in a gale of laughter most of the time. Henriette is very quick to catch the humorous or whimsical side of any situation and Andrew offers her much variety.

512

Studio
Chadds Ford, Pennsylvania
October 24, 1919

Dear Mama and all,

Now that it's over I'll confess to a disagreeable headcold for the past week, which made me feel very dumpy; so much so that I did nothing but sit around and read, finishing that remarkable book of Kingsley's, *Westward Ho!,* my next Scribner book I guess. *Robinson*

Crusoe looks to be on my list this year too, for the Cosmopolitan Book Co. They are very enthusiastic and have arranged very liberal royalty payments paying me $1500 in advance when I sign the contract. They expect at least to sell 20,000 copies before Xmas (1920) and I shall receive (minus the $1500) 25¢ on every copy sold.

Scribner's, I suppose, will go up in the air, but it is stupid of me to sacrifice the large field that seems to be opening up for me in holiday editions.

Yesterday I was startled and flabbergasted to receive a visit from Hugh Walpole, the famous English novelist.

He blew in here like a breeze of wind and promises to call again in January. He is lecturing throughout the U.S. now and will remain in this country until April. He is very fond of my work and insists that he will force Doubleday Page to have me illustrate Conrad's sea books. Conrad is his close friend, and advisor, I should judge, from his remarks. He was much attracted by the children and Carol, and caught us all red-handed in our work—Carol with her house, me with my paint. It pleased him. Big fellow, deep-chested, and extremely genial and unpresuming. I feel much elated and invigorated by his visit.

513

Studio
Chadds Ford, Pennsylvania
October 25, 1919. Saturday

My dear Sid,

The week your letter arrived my brother Stimson returned *at last* from the War. It was a great and stirring homecoming and I shall never forget it! That boy is a blessing to me, as he is to all of us, but to me in particular he has become well nigh indispensable to my life.

The least I can say is that my Home in Needham stands as a bulwark to us boys, particularly in these days when one's faith in the genuineness and sincerity of much of the life about us crumbles on every hand. The unconscious and utmost simplicity, the ever-increasing spirit of affection, and the practice of our economy which in these days of wilfull extravagance appeals to me with spiritual significance!!

And so we have returned to Chadds Ford for another season, inspired and strengthened.

We arrived in Needham the 3rd of July, took up our abode in a house situated on the edge of the town proper and within a few minutes' auto run of my house. We immediately fell into a program which was of necessity carried out consistently throughout the following two months.

I had planned last winter to be almost entirely free of contracted work when July and August came 'round, but my good scheme fell through so badly that I found myself in Needham with thirteen canvases to be completed by August 25th for *The Last of the Mohicans!* Preparatory work, trips to the Adirondacks—the country of Hawkeye and Uncas—and prolonged study of the book had absorbed so much time that I was almost in a state of mental panic when I realized that the time for moving to N.E. had arrived.

July 5th found me at work with a vengeance in the improvised studio in the tower, and for six weeks, including Sundays, from 7:30 until, in many cases, dark, I smashed through the series and turned out what I believe to be the best set of illustrations I have done. It's the longest and most sustained period of concentration that I ever accomplished and I felt rather proud of it.

The *bitter* part of it all came afterward, when the N.Y. engravers practically ruined the colorplates, so that there is very slight resemblance to the original canvases.

The 25th of August found Massachusetts tied up in an express strike, my last five canvases (all 32 $\times$ 40) ready for delivery, and Scribner's clamoring for them—so what must I do but take them on to N.Y. in my Ford.

The remaining ten days until Sept. 7th I spent with the family in Concord, Plymouth, nearby beaches, and visiting a few relatives. The swiftest two months I ever remember.

During my working period Carol and the children joined me in the automobile every fair morning to spend the day at my mother's, returning with me in the evening. After Stimson's return I would often return later at night, after the children were abed, and my mother, father, Stimson and myself would sit on the porch or out under the trees in the dark and talk. And such delightful talks we had! As I look back upon these conversations they appeal to me almost heroically. The quiet strength of my father, the rich maturity and repose of my mother (an almost exalted repose won from her vigils for over a year while Nat and Stimson were in France). And then the perfect relaxation of Stimson, with his fascinating tales covering a wide range, from the fighting front to Cambridge University.

I spent one day in the Boston Studios amongst the crowd that stand for Boston Art. My impression is too dismal to relate—suffice it to say that in my mind they have become a castrated group of bloodless pedants, their pitiful emasculation being rapidly completed by Christian Science, which seems to have swept them like a plague. (I'm not so narrow as to declare C.S. of no value—for the successful bourgeois, the noncreative class, all right—but God help the artist who breathes in its spirit and emotion-withering fumes!)

Now that I've related the bare outline of our summer's history, you can readily imagine how much we left undone of the many things we had planned. Cape Cod, the Maine Coast (via Haverhill), the White Mountains, besides days set aside for me to wander about Concord, to roll in a blanket and sleep at night on the shores of Walden—all this and more for my Thoreau book and the *Miles Standish* pictures for Houghton Mifflin.

My outdoor painting I have taken up with a vengeance this autumn. I haven't a lot of canvases to show for it but the two finished are large ones, ambitious in motives and a distinct shift ahead.

There is much work ahead for the year. *Westward Ho!*—Kingsley (Scribner's), *Robinson Crusoe*—Cosmopolitan Book Co., *Thoreau*—Houghton Mifflin, *Courtship of Miles Standish*.

At present I have 18 canvases (Stevenson illustrations) at the Carnegie Institute, Pittsburgh, and the prospect of sending it [sic] to the John Herron Art Institute in Indianapolis.

I have managed to do some reading—Homer taking precedence since I started to read him this spring. I feel that these works have added a great deal to my life.

Butler's *Way of All Flesh* and his notebooks are certainly most stimulating, and for an antidote (if I needed it) *Amiel's Journals*. These latter are rather melancholy but exquisite, but probably you've read them.

The older I grow the more I feel the need of *message* rather than *manner* in literature, and although I am aware that the best writing embodies these two qualities, style is ofttimes too much the soul of a book, covering its tracks so prettily that one does not miss *substance* until later when comes the sudden realization that the book remains in the mind as a title and not much more.

The Education of Henry Adams interested me much, and *The Saturday Club* (both Houghton Mifflin) is reading of a fascinating flavor to anyone that is susceptible to the spell of that wonderful New England group of the 50's. The photogravure portraits alone are well worth looking at. The Longfellow, Whittier, Agassiz, Forbes and several others are remarkable.

The Passing of the Great Race, Morrison Grant (Scribner's), has impressed me much (perhaps because I agree so heartily with his deductions).

The children are in superb condition and are tremendously fascinating just now; Henriette's natural ability to draw is so astonishing that I hardly know what to do about it. Carolyn has developed a love for animals which is almost an obsession, and her drawing of them is admirable (if I can find one of her cows I'll enclose it). Nat (Baby Brother) is large and strong now, as happy a boy as ever and very active. Ann is as distinctive as can be, and Andrew reminds everyone so much of Nat, although he's ever so much more a *rowdy!*

514

Chadds Ford, Pennsylvania
November 3, 1919. Monday evening

Dear Babe,

There is nothing, it seems to me, so irksome, so discouraging and depressing, as the reconstruction of one's business relations, particularly when it encounters bad feeling and unwillingness. To cut a long story short I have broken the long custom of confining myself to Scribner's Sons in the matter of illustrating juvenile Xmas books. This move has caused the "feeling" above mentioned, but it could not be helped.

For several years I have recognized that Scribner's has been getting the very best of my work very cheaply (that is, as compared to what other publishers are willing to pay for the same things). I have turned down outside offers persistently until now I see the danger in isolating myself from all but the one house, a house of wealth and prominence, to be sure, but one which seems to me is losing ground for the lack of enthusiasm and speculative energy. They are increasingly playing the *conservative* game, which has its deadening effect on the younger workers, men within their office staff as well as the outside contributors such as myself.

The juvenile book field has opened very wide for me, offering splendid opportunities from half a dozen directions, so attractive, in fact, that I am unable to further refuse such tempting propositions. Result: I have contracted to do *Robinson Crusoe—twenty* pictures, with originals back, $1000 down when first three drawings are delivered, and 25¢ royalty on every book after the $1000 has been worked off at the same rate. This book is for the Cosmopolitan Book Corporation, who are going to advertise it lavishly, devoting editorial space, personal interview articles (with me) and newspaper full-pages all over the country. With no advertising to speak of, Scribner's have sold (advance sale) nearly 10,000 copies of *The Last of the Mohicans* —the Book Corporation claim that they will easily *double* this at least, which will mean $3000 extra, besides the advance payment. And I get the originals back! An item of great importance which Scribner's would never agree to. They have made a mistake, for with originals back, as I have vainly requested in each contract, I think I would have stuck by them.

And then *Rip Van Winkle* for McKay in 1921, with *originals back* —price to be paid outright not decided upon yet.

I seem to be talking a lot about *remuneration,* but the trouble is I haven't thought of it enough before. After all is settled I shall think of it no more. *Westward Ho!* (Kingsley), which was practically agreed upon at Scribner's as my next book, I have read and have already schemed my layout. Scribner's have withheld their contract for so long, and now with this last *bomb* of mine I don't know whether I'm to do it or not. It's a wonderful story, almost the richest in interest and color I ever read!

The children are in splendid condition, and Andrew is a case! Carol is accomplishing wonders in the house. Never did I expect to see her swing everything with such smoothness and pleasure. It's a greater pleasure than ever to come down at four o'clock and have "tea" in the kitchen—only this afternoon we both thought how wonderful it would be with Mama and you (I can't fit Papa to a tea table!) at the table with us. It was lowering and gray outside, and quite cold. As we sat looking out between the curtains we could see all the children coasting in their carts down the steep bank from the barn, Andrew and all—cheeks fiery red, and eyes asparkle. Sancho dashed in amongst them at intervals, and the pony tied nearby would join in with his heels! We sat there until almost dark.

515

Chadds Ford, Pennsylvania
November 14, 1919

Dear Papa,

I've given Carol a day off, the first time she's been out of the house for over an hour at a time since Ruth left. She and Henriette have gone to Philadelphia, primarily to fit Henriette to a coat, or cape-coat. It will be a pretty problem. Carol will also get a new winter hat—a real event for her—besides odds and ends for the rest of us to complete our winter's outfitting.

While I was thus busy this morning, Nat, Ann and Andrew played about the studio. The distraction was not so serious, as the work was more of a cleaning up around the edge of the canvas and such labor.

It is probable that Stimson has told you of my recent aggressiveness in my business relations with Scribner's. It took much courage, for I hated beyond words to take any chance of destroying a fine relationship which we have maintained for over a dozen years. However, I took the bull by the horns, put it at them straight and solid, and this morning received a letter which relieves the suspension [*sic*] tremendously. In fact, they are so square and generous in their understanding of my situation that it makes me feel almost guilty.

I demanded two concessions of primary importance—all my originals back, and freedom to do one other juvenile book for someone else each year.

The trouble is, they are getting old and need new blood; Chas. Scribner, Jr. is a mighty agreeable chap, but no pusher, and far more interested in a good time and in society than anything else. The outlook for the next generation in the Scribner house does not look very good to me.

And yet I get a letter back deeply appreciative of my frankness— and on the side, in pencil, Chapin says, "You hit the nail on the head!"

It is the first instance where I have taken the initiative in price-fixing, which is a pleasant commentary on all past relations with publishers. I am not taking a gloating pride in the victory of my first skirmish, only thankful that it is over and that there is no wreckage left to stumble over.

At my left, pinned and hung over and about the fireplace, are a dozen or so pictures—all of Xmas flavor, and depicting everything from "Ole Kriss" leaving the moon, to children playing with their new sleds in the snow. Some of the drawings in color are mighty clever, and I look at the *freedom* of conception and rendering with no little envy. How wonderful it is to do things with no traditions or sophistications of the past to bother one! Why, they draw things in absolute defiance of the laws of perspective, color, tone, construction, etc., and yet they convey to the observer clear, sparkling, living truths, unblemished impressions, virgin impulses!! And this embraces all there is to Art!!!

The men are finishing the corn-husking and it looks as though my share will be about 180 bushel. Farmed on half shares. Most of it is excellent. I shall sell all but 50 bushels immediately. Fodder is bringing a good price too—6¢ a bundle. I will sell all but 300 bundles of this too.

516

Chadds Ford, Pennsylvania
December 27, 1919

Dear Sid,

A sudden divergence! But I must tell you, before saying anything else, that your last letter before this one at hand furnished a clue to a fact which I am at last glad to find out. A letter written to you shortly after Xmas, last year, must have been lost! It was a long one, as I remember it, and had quite an assortment of photos of the kids, interiors of house and studio, and what else I do not remember. The "clue" lies in the remarks you make concerning the *little theater,* particularly, that I had not mentioned it in my letters and you wondered if I understood, etc., etc. Now, I recall *vividly* my great pleasure in spending perhaps half the above-mentioned letter in telling you of my deep appreciation of it and continuing with a graphic account of the many Sunday afternoons at home when we played *Robinson*

Crusoe to the muted strings of my uncle's violin, and his very affecting rendering of "Misereri," played tremulo during the scene in *Pocahontas* when the Brave steps up to dash Capt. Smith's brains out!

The fact is that the appearance of your little stage sent me into a very stirring reminiscent mood, and during the many "shows" we had last winter my only regret was that the rest could not possibly get the richness of the emotional pleasure *I* was experiencing as the familiar old pasteboards slid into "right center" or "advance to left center," perchance falling on their noses at a most critical juncture in the dramatic proceedings!

Around the nucleus formed by your very precious gift, I have built hundreds of vivid recollections of Home. For a long time the facsimile of your little theater was the center of attraction in that Home nearly 30 years ago! The grownups were as much interested as us boys. With many ingenious sunlight, evening and moonlight effects, we achieved quite a reputation within our family circle at least. The struggling battleline in "Bunker Hill" finally became charred to a crisp from the flare of gunpowder sprinkled on a tin trough set directly behind the cardboard—and the red glow from a ruby-colored "Bullseye" lantern *glorified* that wonderful little scene in *Pocahontas* where Powhatan passes down the river in his birch-bark canoe!! And then the setting in old Crusoe's cabin! When the beautiful little ship slowly passes on the distant horizon. The glimpse of those sails through the open doorway and window always thrilled me through and through—and does to this day!

I think you have placed this memento of your youth in good hands. I wonder a little that you let it go.

Amongst the many letters received this week came one from *Bill Aylward,* and following it a German infantry rifle which he found in a dugout in France. Mrs. Aylward has just passed through what I presume was a serious operation. She has not been at all well for years. Bill's letter was very cheerful, although I hear from other sources that he is having a struggle of it.

Did you know that I painted at Mystic one spring about 18 years ago and received two criticisms from Mr. Davis? I can remember it all so vividly. How charming he was! The sketches I made hang on the walls in Needham now, and give me much pleasure to look at them.

How sorry I am that [Alden] Weir is gone. His influence, mainly spiritual, will be sorely missed.

517

Chadds Ford, Pennsylvania
December 30, 1919

Dear folks,

My *Miles Standish* cover is done, and I'm highly pleased with it! *Westward Ho!* cover is drawn in and ready for color and looks very promising indeed.

I feel that this work is all going to come along with real swing and gusto. I want to make Houghton Mifflin the best Xmas book they ever had!

518

Edward Gleason Spaulding was an educator in Boston.

Chadds Ford, Pennsylvania
January 2, 1920

Dear Mama,

I have just concluded a rather lengthy letter to Nat.

There was an amusing enclosure in his letter in the shape of a "questionnaire" asking some dozen questions about the particulars of my life. This, from a nephew of Spaulding's—a list of questions given to him by the school. What a shame to jam the fact of my *notoriety* down my brother's throat!!

Although the work in the studio is coming along in really fine shape, it has been a worrying week. Andrew does not pick up as he should, although the little fellow is astonishingly happy, bright and extremely active. Isn't it strange that the two boys should be so much less vigorous physically than the girls? But Andrew shows a real vitality in spite of all, and I am confident that with patience he will spring into his own as Nat has. Nat is most assuredly a tough, wiry specimen, muscular and daring in his rigorous play out of doors, and yet just as gentle, homey and comfortable inside as one could wish.

You would be immensely pleased to see the way Henriette swings her share of the household duties these days. She is extraordinarily capable in a purely practical sense and works with a real conscience. The way she makes her four brothers and sisters step around is almost too autocratic, but very useful.

638

Carolyn, besides her school, and animal duties, is getting to be another book fiend. She has a remarkable little library of a dozen animal books (some I got through the *Geographic*) besides all my own Nature books. She is picking up her reading rapidly, and one can see her poring over animal descriptions an hour at a time. And best of all, she illustrates what she observes and reads about.

I've saved a lot of drawings, which I must send up to you, which show a power of characterization, be it armored knights on horseback or just a plain white bunny, that is nothing short of phenomenal —at least to *me*.

Ann is following suit with brush and pencil. She got her own paint box Xmas, and she keeps it immaculate. She's a foxy little minx, for every chance she gets she uses the other children's paints so as not to dirty her box!

Even Andrew is shaping his pencil lines into true enough automobiles! It's all so amusing and so wonderful.

519

Studio
Chadds Ford, Pennsylvania
January 21, 1920

Dear Mama,

On Tuesday the 13th, Kinsey, for whom I am doing *Robinson Crusoe*, came down. He was delighted with what I had to show him. He feels very confident of a big success. Then there was that Thoreau paper, which I seemed unable to get started until Friday. I finished this by Sunday noon and read it in Wilmington that night. It was quite a long paper and took me over half an hour to read it. Got the rich dilettantes considerably stirred up—struck at them pretty straight from the shoulder, and drew nothing but an ominous silence when I sat down. Soon discussion began to grow louder and louder, and I left them at midnight still talking. Since, I've received several letters from the members "coming back" at me, but asking what of Thoreau should they get to read, etc. I feel less begrudging of the time I spent on the work now.

And then today comes a letter from a prominent firm of New York architects, asking me to make an appointment with them to talk over some mural paintings for the Missouri State Capitol Bldg. in Jefferson City, Mo.!!!

Except that the subjects are historical (probably dealing with the early history of the state), I know nothing further. I shall report to you as soon as I know more. This *looks* quite important.

And last but not least, Henriette has just completed a second Beethoven masque head in charcoal, which is nothing short of phenomenal. Such freedom of execution, such surity of drawing, I haven't seen for years! What is it all coming to—and at other spare times she is deep into *Plutarch's Lives*—a set of books Carol got for me recently —and is all enthusiastic over them, discussing them with a depth of thought that stirs me deeply. And all the time her ability in the house is second only to her mother's. She has, to a great extent, the charge of Andrew, and attends to the dressing and undressing of him and Ann morning and night. She is, as per plans this noon, helping her mother make doughnuts this P.M.

Sis Carol is excited over the anticipated event of a litter of white rabbits; also the 'possum is becoming quite tame, which pleases her so much. Her evenings are spent, without variation, drawing and painting, and we fairly have to drive her to bed, causing no little sadness on her part. She just *loves* to draw. We've got hundreds of specimens of the most original and remarkable creations of hers. She wrote a long story the other night about a reindeer ride in the Arctic, which is so full of her passion for animals that it is hard for me to read it. She ended it with these words, "and when we got near our house made of ice we could smell the nice seal cooking." At this juncture we just had to force her to bed (it was after ten), and she pleaded for just five minutes more. Well, we let her have it, and this is what she added at the bottom of the paper (as near as I can remember it) "I can't tell you any more about my trip because I hear polar bears coming. Don't you hear polar bears coming? We must go to bed."

And all this she was writing out all alone (some three closely written pages of it) in her quaint phonetic spelling. As I looked over from my chair again and again, I marveled at her intense face aglow with enthusiasm, doubled over the pad on her knee. She must have been at this an hour and a half at least.

I am going to get her to rewrite it with a *little* better spelling and send it to you.

Andrew is in fine shape again, but still thin. He's eating well though and should put on weight slowly.

Ann and Nat are forever out of doors and, for the last three days, coasting incessantly. We have had so little snow—and now it is raining a nasty cold sleet.

520

Chadds Ford, Pennsylvania
Feburary 5, 1920

Dear Babe,

With a foot of heavy icy snow, badly drifted and solidly packed, and more of the same kind beating against the windows for all its worth, we are experiencing our *first* real winter storm. The little house rattles and whines as the nor'easter whistles by!

I had a hunch that you wouldn't be on this week (I suppose the storms made me think of interrupted train service). I have been holding seven canvases of *Miles Standish, Westward Ho!,* and *Robinson Crusoe,* hoping you would get a look at them before they went. And then there is the Academy reception Saturday night (where my first landscape submitted will be hung—guess I told you). The Boston men will be there, and I thought maybe you'd be interested to go. And also Yeats, the British poet, I expect will blow in here Saturday afternoon, who would prove interesting to meet.

Oh yes, you will miss an extra-large batch of doughnuts made for your coming. Be sure and let us know a day or two ahead of your arrival so that Carol can fill her bread and doughnut cans!

I feel very happy over a commission which was brought to a conclusion yesterday, which gives me two large Civil War mural panels to do for the Missouri State Capitol Building—lunettes, 18 × 10 feet. I feel particularly pleased that the job *came to me,* instead of scrambling for it with hundreds of others, as is usually the case. It is indeed deeply encouraging to know that one's work is sufficiently worthy to be sought out. It is a wonderful opportunity and I shall try to make the most of it—not to be delivered before Jan. 1st, 1921.

The folks in Needham are certainly getting some hard old winter weather these days, and it makes me feel very thankful that they are so comfortably fixed and in no way forced to get out in too much of it. I do miss the extra reassurance that comes of your being there with them. Sixty-seven seems quite an age for Papa to be walking uptown with the milk, but it is at the same time darned inspiring to know that he does it with almost a boyish pleasure.

Tell Nat that his little windmill is keeping up an incessant prattle in the engine house, bobbing this way and that (the spindle is worn a little), whirling like mad trying to beat the wind at its own game.

521

Chadds Ford, Pennsylvania
February 26, 1920

Dear Mama and Papa,

Carolyn's hens are laying to beat the cars, and the old rooster is getting more arrogant than ever!

Went to Phila. last Sat. night to meet Charles Frey, a very well-known advertising man, who is trying to inveigle me to work for him (as an advertiser) exclusively—that is to only give him one month, two months, or a restricted number of pictures a year, but to exclude all other advertisers. Says to name my own figure. Don't know just what to do about it. If I could make it highly worthwhile financially, I'd be willing to tie up for a couple of months a year in order to give myself the freedom to paint 6 mos. in the year without having to consider the dollar. I am going to meet his representative in N.Y. Friday to talk the matter over.

522

Christian C. ("Sandy") Sanderson lived with his mother, Hannah, at Washington's Headquarters. He was a much-loved schoolteacher and an authority on the Battle of the Brandywine.

Studio
Chadds Ford, Pennsylvania
March 5, 1920. Friday, 11:30 A.M.

Dear Mama and Papa,

It is raining in torrents, and the sky is so overcast and the light so feeble that work is impossible except for occasional periods at a time. *Saturday, 2:30 P.M.*—Although it still continued to rain, there came sufficient light to paint. The darkness referred to was really the forewarning of a very severe storm: wind, torrents upon torrents of rain, and then at eight ó'clock last night it became translated into a furious blizzard which raged into the middle of the night. About three thirty yesterday the fog lifted sufficiently to show me the whole valley inundated. It was so startling that I thought most certainly some dam-breast above us had burst. I immediately went to the house, donned some old clothes, and by walking to the east through Murphy's farm and over onto the railroad grade made my way to the station. The village itself was entirely flooded; all the houses (except the hotel and Baldwin's) were completely surrounded by water and ice and their cellars *full!* Lin Baldwin was plying his canoe between the station and his store, with the mail and with a few passengers who dared to venture across the open water which was whipped into whitecaps by the northwest wind. All the fences between the village proper and the station were out of sight, the wagon bridge which we pass over, right near and almost under the railroad bridge, was out of sight, and over it all a formidable current passed, full of logs, trees, lumber, boxes and God knows what, reeling and lurching, looking weird and dismal in the muddy water and churning ice.

As a sporting proposition (for in reality there was no real need of my going) I paddled over with Jim. It was quite exciting. I got there just in time to see Sandy wading out of the water, holding his green schoolbag over his head, and like a frozen rat made his way up the concrete road toward home. You can imagine my astonishment when within forty minutes, back came Sandy (Sanderson) in his finest toggery—dress-suit, patent-leather shoes and all the fixin's—on his way to some damn banquet in Phila. Lin agreed to ferry him to the station. I was given the stern seat, Sandy next, Frank Oakes third and Lin in the bow. We embarked in a deep ditch in front of the hotel, the whole village looking on. No sooner were we launched than Sandy got nervous, grabbed the rails of the canoe and over we went! It was not deep, as we had swept somewhat out of the ditch, and at my end I was lucky enough to be able to reach a shallow knoll as she sunk, so I didn't even get water into my boots. Sandy got wet up above his knees, Oakes got in nearly all over, and Lin had hip boots which saved him except for the splashing.

The audience on the hotel porch *roared!* Sandy got mad, and when I yelled at him, "Stick to the ship, Sandy!" he bellowed, "God damn the ship, give me a Tin Lizzie!" and away he went in a Ford for Brandywine Summit to catch the train. *Think* of that fool, soaked to his middle, attending a banquet in Phila. without changing a stitch.

I heard this morning that he went to a friend's house in the city, stood over the register of one of these pipeless heaters and dried out, attended the banquet, returned to Brandywine Summit 3 o'clock this morning (midnight train 2 hours late) and walked the three miles in the blizzard, which even at that time was blowing hard and very cold! Sandy is reputed to have only one lung, and we *know* he hasn't any teeth, and I'm sure not much blood, but he rarely has a cold, is never sick and is out every night and never misses a day of school. He is indeed a super-Ichabod Crane!

"A super Ichabod Crane," Sandy Sanderson.

The crowd gathered about the dry spots, porches, roofs, etc., was a ribald and motley outfit, but I wouldn't have missed it for anything. Some of the comments, although not exactly *distinguished,* were hilariously funny—such as were excited for instance by the antics of a colored fellow, Bill Loper, who tried to cross from Gallagher's store toward Green's drugstore with an armful of groceries and one of those big canvas advertising umbrellas used on wagon seats. In trying to jump a ditch he miscalculated and landed square in the middle; the wind wrenched the colossal parasol from his hands and it went sailing across the flood. Scrambling out he set his groceries on a marooned cake of ice and started after the umbrella. Almost instantly a fierce gust of wind slid Mother's Oats, Royal Baking Powder, crackers and sundry packages into the water and away they went like scattering ducks. Old Bill caught the humor of the situation, stood there up to his knees in water and laughed long and loud. In the din and tumult of wind and rain we couldn't hear a sound, but the pantomime of that gesticulating nigger, his great open mouth and flashing teeth, I'll never forget.

We watched the umbrella, its black letters staring out of an orange background, "Harrison's Town and Country Paint," until it blithely sailed under the railroad bridge and made off toward Wilmington, all sails set and before the wind!!

But it all has its serious side and I think of all the dirty wet cellars and the possible bad health that will follow.

This morning we are drifted in. Not very much snow fell but it has piled high wherever the formation of the ground lent itself. My whole drive and lane is clogged full and it looks as though the old Ford would get quite a rest.

It is cold and very windy, and instead of the rare promise of spring of Thursday, with the grass actually greening under the soft warm showers and the song of two woodpeckers down in the woods, here we are at grips again with hoary old winter and his confederate Boreas.

And this brings me to the thoughts that have been uppermost in my mind since I left you on that clear, crisp and magnificent Wednesday morning.

Never in my life did I ever experience such a singular sensation such as was given me by the startling change from Chadds Ford's mild, semi-springlike appearance to the violently contrasting facts of ponderous winter in all its beauty and glory. This was made even more impressive when I returned 9 o'clock Wednesday evening as walking from the train must needs remove my coat, and all about me heard the soft free purling of the brooks and draining roads, and crossed the pasture sinking inches-deep into the softened turf. This

645

experience in contrasts has whetted my memories and imagination beyond the usual, so that at all times, whether during subconscious moments before the easel, or listening to music, or just before dropping off to sleep, clear pictures and impressive thoughts come to me of that snug and contented snowbound homestead, nestled in behind those towering bulwarks of black spruces—glimmering and warm in the flashing sunlight of day, and wrapped in the tangle and mesh of deep moonlight shadows at night—and at all times—*silent.*

It seems as though I had lived *years* in that few hours at home. It seems as though I had been in touch with all the life I had ever known about the old place, and yet it is astonishing for me to realize that I wasn't out of the house, not even in the cellar, the twenty hours I was there! I can hardly believe the facts.

Although I have reproached myself a dozen times for not going out to the barn, to the henhouse—to follow the deep paths through the snow that Papa shoveled, to walk over to the house, to come back by the road and a dozen other little excursions, yet I feel everything so keenly. Papa brought the spirit of the barn into the house so vividly, Uncle Denys revived the imaginations of all that I associate with him so sharply (including an eloquent glimpse I got of him through the parlor window as he trudged his way over in the moonlight through the deep-cut path), and then Miss Glancy brought in with her such a vigorous gust of memories (rather suggested by her ever-familiar voice, manner and hearty laughter than by the conversation) —and Cora in her quiet pathetic manner was no less eloquent of the atmosphere of the "Livingstons," as I remember it.

One incident seems to lack vitality, which fault lies not in any prejudice on my part but simply because it is genuinely exotic to our home atmosphere of wholesomeness, genuineness, deep sentiments and honest affections—I refer to the visit of the young people across the way. How little I recall these few moments, and yet every other instant spent with you and Papa is indelibly stamped on my mind.

As I left you and Papa on the porch that morning and wound my way up through the narrow pathway—still, frosty and brilliant, the morning sun just tipping the low woods on Fanny's lot—I almost burst into tears, and would have if the burly figure of Mr. [Charlie] Mitchel hadn't loomed up. How happy I felt to see him, and I thought of what you had told me about his growing knowledges of Indian lore, and I told him then and there to get it down on paper, I'd edit it, illustrate it, and we'd publish it together!

I was reluctant to leave him and envied him so, that he could travel in *that* direction!

After leaving the old school I felt myself leaving the sacred haunts as I knew them. The coasting tracks from the school steps down under the big oak and over the steep bank into "Colburn's" field brought a lump into my throat—but as I said, from there on I moved into a strange land, for I shall never get used to "Birds Hill Station" and that awful cut through Gay's pine grove. To be sure, before I descended into that dismal crevice to take the train, I had one long look at the spires of those dear old spruces and I thought of you and Papa moving about in the house snuggled behind them!

From this point on, my experience and feelings were mixed ones, two incidents standing out prominently: first, the enthusiastic reception of my pictures at H. M. Co., and second, the running smack into C. W. Reed at the terminal station.

I wish so that I could have avoided the last event. The impression of a broken old man, still arrogant and overbearing with that queer admixture of strange generosity and fierce impulsiveness.

Mrs. Reed died in September—an acute sufferer for some months. He cursed God bitterly, damning the church, ministers, doctors and what not. He wandered into a long involved discourse on his religious philosophy, much of which brought back the days in his West Street studio. I had ten minutes to catch my N.Y. train. I broke into his harangue and said that I must catch the train to return to my wife and five children. With a bitter look, which I got to know so well, his parting comment was, "Didn't know you were in the incubating business."

I can see that his tendencies, strongly developed even years ago, have overwhelmed him, and I'm afraid he stands a pretty lonely old man today. I wish to heaven I could have a change of heart and do something in genuine spirit that might prove pleasant to him, but first I despair of the necessary change of heart, and secondly, I question whether it would be possible to do or say anything that would not arouse his "spleenetic" nature. No one, even you, will ever realize what I went through with him at the last, and how seriously my interest, gratitude, and respect was shaken. He is tremendously pathetic to me, and yet I feel it is entirely his own fault. He has wrenched much pleasure from life (as some men see it) and has been, in a deep sense, very selfish in his methods.

I know that you consider my whole attitude in this matter somewhat reproachful—and from certain angles I do myself, but there
seems no way to correct it.

I wish you would read this letter over again sometime *up to* this
last incident to get the taste out of your mouth. The *"second movement,"* which so often sounds the richest in a musical composition,
is the best part of this letter, that part which tells of and relates to
my visit Home.

523

Chadds Ford, Pennsylvania
March 10, 1920

Dear Mama,

Architect [Richard Clipston] Sturgis of Boston wants me to see him
about two panels for the new Federal Bank in Boston. A man by the
name of [Frederic] Curtiss is president of said bank and has summer home in Needham; who is he?

How we are all looking forward to Babe's being here this summer.
He'll have to learn to drive a Buick, for I'll have one by May 1st
to 15th.

The "Buccaneer Room" at the new $3000 Hotel Flamingo at
Miami, Florida, is mine too to do next year.

524

Chadds Ford, Pennsylvania
April 14, 1920

Dear Mama,

I am alone tonight. Carol, Babe and Henriette have gone into Wilmington to see *Romeo and Juliet* as played by Walter Hampden.

How glorious it is having Stimson with us. He is busy every minute
of the time and I guess he finds life pretty full.

There is no need for me to dilate on the old, well-known theme of
his deeper value to us, apart from his physical help. You know this.
Only last night, while he was away (to see this same wonderful
Hampden in *Hamlet*), how we all missed him. How richly he plays
his part! Such simplicity and yet such depth! We are all enjoying
every minute and I can see that it will be so all the time he is here.

He is very contented and gets very little time to brood. The children hang around him like a swarm of flies, and every time he uses the machine they flock into it so many coattails of his own.

Today he spent in hauling cow manure from Cleveland's. Tomorrow he plants 12 replacement trees in the orchard: 3 apples, 3 pears and 6 peaches. (No matter what may take place I want the orchard in complete and good shape.)

Babe has scoured the place from one end to the other, cleaning up accumulations of boxes, rubbish and all sorts of things "saved" by Jenkins; consequently everything shines like a new dipper.

The weather has remained aggravatingly cold, which has held us back from the planting, but the ploughing and harrowing are done, we've got all our seed, and we are ready to start right in.

The Wilmington Art show claimed some of my attention in the past few days (late afternoons and evenings). We attended the reception, Carol, Babe and I, and enjoyed it much. The waiters' clothes did not arrive in time, but all went well, as many were in Sack suits. However, perhaps Babe may find other occasions to don the "soup and fish" regalia. Thanks for so promptly responding to his wire.

Andrew is as lively as a cricket, with rosy cheeks and perfect habits and functions all 'round. The truss seems to be doing well now since Carol, after considerable experimenting, found out how to adjust it. It is doing so well that we shall not take any action for awhile at least. We will wait and see how things progress. It's a great relief all around to be able to postpone at least any radical action.

The rest of the children are in fine condition.

Well, I expect a telephone call any moment from the folks, which will mean that I shall start for "Hunter's Corner" (about 5 miles from here) to meet them at the trolley from Wilmington.

525

A historical pageant was being held in Needham. Stimson Wyeth portrayed the Indian Nehoiden who had sold the first settlers a five-mile-square tract of land. This area eventually became the township of Needham. His second cousin, Gritly Holzer, also took part in the pageant. A blanket was borrowed from a neighbor across the Charles River, Miss Onion, and beads from his first cousin, Jessie Zirngiebel.

Chadds Ford, Pennsylvania
May 15, 1920

Dear Babe,

I'm a little late in mailing costumes, but they left this morning (Tues.) parcel post. Wish you would have Mama or Gret catch on the loose wampum on Squaw dress. This wampum is quite valuable and I don't want to lose any more if possible. I have been offered $175 for the buckskin shirt (show it to Charlie Mitchel—"Crazy Horse" made it while in captivity, strung with quite a number (not all) of Apache scalp locks), so keep an eye on it. The beaded moccasins are some I sent Carol before we were married, so ask Gret to see that they are strong enough for dancing. They have laid away so long that sinew threads may be rotten.

Use shirt for dance but not very appropriate for Nehoiden. Strip to waist for latter; get several strings of large beads for neck (Jessie must have loads!); get red flannel blanket (Miss Onion perhaps); use leggings and beef moccasins I sent; get colored chalk, red, green or blue and white, and mark simple device on top of foot.

You really ought to have Indian wig for the night.

526

Chadds Ford, Pennsylvania
July 27, 1920

Dear Mama,

We have had to postpone our start until Monday morning owing to the fact that the Missouri Art Commission have requested me to meet them Sunday in New York. This would mean that to follow original plans I would no more than get home before I'd have to hike right back to N.Y. on crowded weekend trains, so decided to hold over the rest of the week.

My sketches for the capitol turned out exceptionally well I think, and [Egerton] Swartmont, the architect, to whom I delivered them on Monday, feels very enthusiastic about them. Of course the commission has not seen them yet so the final decision is yet to come.

527

Chadds Ford, Pennsylvania
August 1, 1920

My dear Sid,

All leave for Needham tomorrow morning if nothing intervenes. We will go by motor. Although the trip will be in the nature of a vacation, its principal feature will be to decide upon a New England home. We have several plans to look over and hope by all means to come to some decision. Several things make it imperative that next summer will find us located in Massachusetts.

I (and possibly we) will make a brave attempt to wedge in a short visit to Port Clyde. My books are done—three of them. There are 43 originals in all and constitute the best work I have done, I feel sure.

The *Miles Standish* book is the best. My sketches for the Missouri Capitol decorations were passed upon and accepted Sunday last. This will add real zest to my two or three weeks layoff.

528

Needham, Massachusetts
August 15, 1920

Dear Sid,

The folks have just gone to a Symphony Concert and I'll get off a line or two.

We arrived home about 8:30 Sunday night after an uneventful trip and no one the worse for it. In spite of the 228 miles it was very enjoyable. The heavy traffic from Lynn, through Revere and Cambridge delayed us most exasperatingly, otherwise daylight would have lighted our way into Needham.

We are all tremendously enthusiastic over the great week spent in Port Clyde and feel so happy that arrangements assure us of future summers there. We all deeply appreciate the part you played in making everything so enjoyable. You certainly had your hands full, and I hope that by now you have recovered your customary equanimity. You indeed gave of yourself without stint!

You must realize how pleased we are over your success with Capt. [Norris] Seavy. Personally I am ever so much pleased that the dear

651

old man is satisfied with the price and I would willingly sacrifice any possible advantage for his sake. Even now I feel as though we were desecrating the very thing that makes Port Clyde what it is. My memory of the old Captain heading his dory into his little beach under full sail, then slowly and soberly unstepping the little mast, will ever remain in my mind as prophetic of the great change in his life my contact with him was to cause.

However you and I will both approach our opportunity with real reverence and we shall cherish the charm and historic appeal of the little storm-beaten homestead. In this lies real satisfaction.

Your letter was received this morning. Just as soon as you say so I will remit my check for $1500 and my share of any further expenses.

I leave early in the morning for Chadds Ford. Had a memorable dinner in the Tavern Club with certain moguls of Boston. Also got the commission for two 10 X 13 foot panels in the Federal Bank.

Captain Seavy's house, Port Clyde, Maine.

Chapter XXI

BACK TO NEEDHAM

*"The time is drawing near for us to migrate.
... It appeals to me as the dawn of a new and
better era for us all."*

Studio
Chadds Ford, Pennsylvania
September 7, 1920

Dear Mama,

It does not seem possible that a week has gone by since we left Needham. It has been a week chock-full of various duties and interest, and it is only tonight that I can really say that everything is set for unbroken work in the studio.

To be sure, I have already set up one of the big canvases and have the outlines of the Wilson's Creek Battle scaled up and ready for the paint. This was no small job, but was more or less mechanical and tedious, although before I got through I had made some new changes in action and grouping which smacked of real emotional effort.

I have just finished blowing fixatif over the charcoal lay-in with a spray pump and, as I said, this is the first moment that I have really felt ready.

It seems but yesterday that we were all at home with you. It was certainly a corking visit in spite of my wild running about. But I am glad I did it. It's so much accomplished in the direction of home hunting. I must say that the prospects do not look very promising, at least for the kind of place we have dreamed of. Perhaps a miracle will happen and just the right kind of opportunity will turn up. The romantic side of the proposition is extremely important to me as it is one of the most valuable assets possible in connection with my work. Unless I can find this in conjunction with reasonable facilities for schooling, etc., I would not dare to make the change. We have the romance here of a very rich kind—a real asset to me, but hardly practical when considering the growing family.

We at least have a foothold in Maine, which will give us a rare change and comfortable weather for the summer, which includes a couple of short stays with you, on the way there and back. Also it will give you, Papa and Stimson opportunity to enjoy the seacoast at times. Sid and I have bought the property I spoke of, which will offer the finest chance in the world to camp a few months in the year. Of course we'll rent the cottage I spoke of next year. This will give me the proper chance to get the Capt. Seavy place in shape for the following summer.

530

Dear Sid,

I am really quite fagged out after a long steady day before one of the Missouri canvases. I am drawing it in to scale from my small sketch and it is some job!

Can I bother you to take some photos of "our property"? Especially four of the house, giving me the four sides. When you take the main end of the house (i.e. the western end), will you tack a piece of white paper 6 feet up from the floor sills; and when you take the front or back, take a piece of paper 6 feet from the corner. These are so that a friend of mine—an architect who is daffy on Cape Cod architecture—can scale up the building and submit some rough sketches for an added ell. Also, can you make a rough floor plan showing location of doors and windows, with stepped-off dimensions of the interior, if you happen to call on the captain? This is asking much of you, and will further bust up your time, but it will save me a trip to Port Clyde and also give me a long start in arriving at something definite regarding the changes in the old house.

I must mention the fact that I made a special trip to the Brooklyn Museum to see a large canvas by Segantini. It is without the slightest doubt the most stirring canvas I have ever seen!! The canvases of the old masters and the marbles of the old Greeks most certainly stir me too, but in this marvelous canvas of Segantini's he has brought together all the power of modern brilliant color, has so perfectly handled broken color, and withal has sustained such decoration and such rich, throbbing tonal qualities plus a powerfully poetic message, that I feel that he has stepped above and beyond anything that has ever been done! Perhaps this sounds like overstating, but never before in my experience have I been enthralled for almost two hours steadily. It gripped me and hung upon me like overwhelming music.

656

I feel that I got more from that painting, more real constructive teaching, not technical but *moral* and *spiritual* teaching, than I have received from all the pictures I have ever seen. It represents the most concentrated essence of virtue in art that I have ever beheld! How I wish you could see it! It's one of two canvases of Segantini's that we will ever see on this side of the water. The others are to be left forever in the stone castle built for them near St. Moritz.

How I teem to paint that wonderful water and shore next summer! I can hardly wait. Sid, you and I are going to do some thundering big stuff there in the next few years. You are getting a strong foothold on *essentials,* but now we must dig deep for the loftiness, the majesty, the sublimity of that wonderful shore. I only wish I had your experience and associations with it back of me.

531

Joseph Hergesheimer, the writer, lived in the nearby town of West Chester, Pennsylvania. Introduced to Wyeth by Christian Brinton, he became a lifelong friend.

Chadds Ford, Pennsylvania
October 11, 1920

Dear Mama,

The program these days is quite reconstructed. The children are off to school 7 o'clock and return via Lenape at 3:30.

This sending the kids to school has been a sad affair to both of us. It has made me feel quite "homesicky" throughout the day, realizing as I do how both children dislike it. They make no objections at all but all their conversation on the topic is about "getting home," and then when they do get here how happy they are, and how hard they try to make up for lost time, playing out of doors until bedtime—8:30 and 9 o'clock Saturdays and Sundays are a treat to us all, particularly to watch Carolyn. She's up at daylight, even *before* sometimes, and she crowds every minute with action that brings her in closest contact with Nature—shocking corn, picking grapes, pears, apples—even digging potatoes, which she enjoys to the utmost! She says, "I love to see them tumble out of the earth—I could just eat 'em up!"

She saddles and rides the pony a dozen times a day, and often one sees her walking about with some favorite hen or rooster in her arms, holding its head close to her face and talking to it as though it understood every word she said. It is truly remarkable how content they seem, and drawl out a contented cackle, like a crooning almost. I loathe schoolrooms when I see her thus.

And Nat! It seems as though he were growing more thoughtful, pleasant and lovable every day. His enjoyment of every little thing is extremely touching. He clings, even at this early age, to traditional things connected with his home, and it's quite usual to hear him reminisce and talk in the most astonishing detail of you all in Needham. He never tires talking of Stimson, and tells of many incidents which seem indelibly impressed upon his mind. Even the coarse, rough men in the village mention him to me and speak of his geniality and pleasantries.

It is a good trait and will mean much happiness to him, I should think.

Amongst those at home, Andy is the sensation at present. You would hardly know him. He has gained *pounds* in weight and looks actually fat and chubby. His color is marvelous and his spirit beyond description. He's an entirely different boy, and it is a great temptation to make a weekend run up home with him just to show you. I should so much like Mrs. Bleidorn to see him now, who so often said with such hopeless sympathy, "The poor little frail fellow." I always felt that suddenly Andy would hit his stride and become as rugged as one would wish for. To date he is!

Ann teems with irrepressible life and devilment, and is on the go from early to late. I am often awakened at dawn to the music of her humming—and then to find her lying on her stomach under the quilt, drawing, *Drawing!*—that's the outstanding stunt in this house, and to see the whole five around the lamp at night, each one seriously bent over a tablet of paper, recording all sorts of facts and fictions of Nature, one would at least guess it were organized night art school —or that all were nutty in the same way!

Henriette—it may be better for me to talk of her lest I seem to overstate the facts. Her expansion in feeling and expressed thought is no less than a miracle to me, for she seems to gather good sense and wisdom from the very air! When I say she leads me in honest responsive feeling and sensing, I speak the utmost truth. She comes as near as anybody I ever knew personally to candidly, and without affectation or prejudice, reflect and respond to the experiences she meets with. This is saying a very great deal, I am fully aware, but

I am thoroughly convinced it is so and will ever pray that the inevitable and encroaching disease of sophistication and partiality will touch her lightly. This human trait is the dominant menace to the individual, and it seems to me that our true strength is measured by just this quality, or the lack of quality, of honest responsiveness, uncolored by petty influences or sophistries.

She is reading steadily and soundly. Like myself she is inherently a romanticist, so that at present is filled with the spirit of Hergesheimer, W. L. George, Walpole—and the present English school of writers she is reading avidly. Some might say that she should not waste her time on second-rate novelists, but my feeling is that as her interest is hot, let her suck the marrow (if there is any) while her enthusiasm runs high. What is chaff will be swept away in time. She is benefiting from the strong wave of her personal interest in the men, particularly those whom she has met (Hergesheimer and Walpole) and is stimulated toward George because Carol and I have talked of him so much. She also seems suddenly awakened to the sublimities of Nature (at least some of them), and I am relieved and happy to note it.

I am beginning to think that people of today are divided into two classes: those that accept elemental Nature casually, as a mere accessory to the important business of *trivial living;* and those who sense the perfect amalgamation of elemental nature and human life, that *cosmic relationship* which if not felt leaves us superficial, and at bottom, *useless* to ourselves and to the world.

The bibliography of Howard Pyle has been prepared by the Society of Wilmington and edited by a well-known bibliophile whose name escapes me now. I have been selected to write the introduction to this volume—and quake with the subtle responsibility of the task. However, I shall try it. It's a sad commentary that of all the pupils of Pyle it has come to the point where they must ask me to do these things, not because I deserve it of my own strength of position, but because the Pyle School has flunked so horribly, and in their sinking have left me a little higher than the rest. But (not to be too modest) I do not despair of rising *myself* sometime to reasonable heights.

Oh! Mama, the world is so full of things to do that one hasn't much time not to be pretty happy. But I wish there wasn't any such thing as money.

532

Chadds Ford, Pennsylvania
December 3, 1920

Dear Mama,

It is a few moments after six, and I must try to get this note off to you before the circus begins—i.e. before the children get out of bed!

I am sitting at the kitchen table in my bathrobe. The room is cozy and warm with the perceptible murmur of the tea kettle on the stove. The morning outside is clear and cool but not frosty. It promises a sunny day, which will be the second one in nine days.

Today the big canvases leave my studio. Carol will help me in the delicate task of rolling them and packing. I hate to see them go, for I enjoyed the work immensely. If they are received half as well in Missouri as they have been here by the fifty or more who have seen them, I shall be pleased. The task has been highly suggestive of what I might do in this line. It has opened up a new and wide horizon.

533

Studio
Chadds Ford, Pennsylvania
December 22, 1920

Dear Mama, Papa, and Babe,

It is after nine P.M. The children were going to bed as I left the house, somewhat disappointed that I would not remain to tell them a promised Christmas story. (This must be left until tomorrow night.) Also they are much chagrined about the weather. Yesterday morning the thermometer registered 16° above, and then about noon it began to warm a little and grow slightly hazy. It surely looked like snow. The same night a huge ring appeared about the moon, and we all gazed upon it with anticipation for a snowy Xmas. Today it grew warm, and tonight it is raining a hard, steady, almost summer's rain!! I feel sorry for them—in fact I am quite keenly sorry myself. However, two days might work wonders.

Day before yesterday we all went down below Cossart to gather evergreens and brought home a splendid lot. The children set to and made some handsome wreaths of it and also braided a lot for festoon decorations on the windows and fireplaces. The room looks fine! and one can faintly detect the green-earthy smell of the fresh vines.

The spirit, as is usual at this time, is running high. All shopping is done and packages have been wrapped and re-wrapped a dozen times. Each of the children have their private corners in the upstairs rooms—corners inviolate by special arrangement! One can hear at almost any time of day or evening the crinkling of paper, the soft monologues of discussion or expostulation of some clumsy-shaped gift that just won't stay tied—or stickers that won't stick! Rain may dampen their spirits for the moment, but only to rise again with greater intensity, obliterating weather and all else but the thoughts of Xmas morning!

Today I took Mrs. Sanderson and Henriette into Wilmington to see *The Last of the Mohicans*—the moving picture is wonderfully good, and tell Babe to see it if he gets a chance. It was particularly fascinating to me, as the producers very obviously followed my pictures with marked fidelity, even to the selection of facial characteristics and certain poses and postures I represented. At times I felt as though some of my pictures had suddenly come to life. The sensation was singular indeed.

Today, however, I spent my time in the library looking up *Rip Van Winkle* material and called for Mrs. S. and Henriette after the show. They enjoyed it tremendously.

534
Mr. Puffer, a family friend, was the Unitarian minister in Needham.

Chadds Ford, Pennsylvania
January 1, 1921

Dear Mama,

Here I am! The middle of the afternoon, *writing*! My conscience troubles me not a little for doing it, but nothing else seems quite so congenial just at the present moment, and as I am a confirmed and humble servant of moods, write I *must*. Perhaps the piano is responsible—but then, why should I be playing the piano at this time of day?

The morning was brimful of good intentions, but as the day wore along it became less and less sympathetic until the early afternoon dispelled all desire to work. It was a dull morning and beautiful, a thin sandy snow blowing from the northeast. In this I sketched with great pleasure. My results were only so-so, but not discouraging because I feel confident that if I had prepared better and had worked on a larger canvas, and for a longer period my efforts would have been justified. As it was, I had the subject within my grasp, but quick changing light made me hurry, therefore the work appears careless and weak.

This afternoon it is clear but raw. Narrow, uninteresting strips of slaty clouds are stretched across the horizons. The distances pop out as though magnified by some great glass—they lack mystery—I am dragged into the commonplace and almost vulgar details of distant barnyards and bare, uninviting hills. The sky drops behind them, a sheet of cold unsympathetic metal—it lacks *quality*.

These days always strike me so. I can almost remember the dates of similar days during the past year; they seem to mark vacant spots on the calendar.

It used to be that a clear "slashing" day symbolized and inspired vigor and ambition, but not of late years—I seem to crave wet clouds, mists and all degrees of the so-called dismal and dreary weather. It is not dreary to me—on the contrary, it fills my heart with an indescribable *yearning*, a deep-lying affection for *all* Nature.

I wonder if I am understood? My letters to you are the only ones from which I get any real satisfaction, i.e. the only ones that I write from genuine impulse. I try to express in them what lies deepest in my own meditations. I feel in you that responsive attitude. Of course, there is much that I say which is intangible, partly because it is poorly expressed and partly because my ideas are oftentimes hazy and vaguely formed in *my own* mind. However, I feel your sympathy and cherish it, and as time goes by I know I shall cherish it still more.

If I could only find a *man* to whom I could write, or to whom I could talk and discuss. One who is in perfect sympathy with *Nature*, who looks upon her from a vastly higher standpoint than I do. *Then* I feel my soul would be filled, my progress would continue well nourished, and in this short life I could accomplish so much more! To be sure, I have met but few men, but of the hundreds I know, not *one* has in him that quality which I *crave*. There are plenty who are superior to myself in a moral sense, but where is he who looks out into the world as one who is *thankful* for his being, in the biggest sense of the word. They all have nails to drive, axes to grind in one direction or another, which precludes them from seeing life as *something* to be *thankful* for merely, and creation exquisitely beautiful to live in and to look upon. It is true that many men realize these moments intermittently—but these periods are decidedly subordinated to other interests—their little deep rut that runs toward a set target is the prime motif in life—perchance, to earn money, to attain some personal ambition.

There is Mr. Puffer's type, you would say. Admirable as one can find! As noble in purpose as he is, for me, he lacks sympathy, he's too practical. His efforts are in one direction, most certainly a great and important direction. He is undertaking work of incalculable value to humanity; at the same time, he is dealing with a *detail* of human life. *My* effort is a summing up of life.

The man constructing the rock foundation of a building can be of little interest (other than appreciative) to the man carving the decoration on its portal. One is an invaluable asset to the other, but their lines of thought and action, although parallel in principle, are too widely separated to be mutually inspiring.

My last letter to Mr. Puffer, and his in answer, are clear examples of what I mean. I talked to him of the real pleasure of living; he talked to me of a method to reach it. *Vital* absolutely—yet I cannot be concerned deeply with the training of wayward youths if I am to make a serious effort to tell of the crowning pleasures of living.

At the same time we are working in each other's behalf—he, to give men and women a strong, healthy, moral start in life, and I, to elaborate their understandings that they may enjoy still more their awakened interests.

The following answers, to some extent, that article by Mr. Downes:

The Arts—music, painting and writing (and I place them in what I consider their relative order)—are mankind's highest and most profound methods of expression.

True art is absolutely *personal*! It is an expression of personal gratitude—a tangible form of reverence and love for the blessings of existence! It is not created, like parables, to teach a lesson, to give a moral; it is an abstract manifestation of divine appreciation.

The highest expression in art should not deal with humanity as life's most important detail. In the *great* vision, humanity should be no more significant, should hold no more of his love and adoration than the trees and rocks, the flowers and birds—than the light of the *sun itself*! When an artist confines himself to the emotions and problems of human life, he ceases to be an artist in the highest sense; he is a reformer, a preacher. He is talking to an audience. The true painter talks to *himself*, and the world listens as a matter of course.

To the divine painter, these expressions are painful to part with, they are sacred to him—yet, one has to live, and under the conditions of this epoch, it is the only conceivable method of sustaining one's life with food and shelter—to sell.

This ideal painter, composer, writer, in consistent form, is not known; yet this is the aim. The greatest expressions existent today were created under the influence of this spirit—of utter unconsciousness of any *particular* details of life, under the spell of abstract life in all its beauty and mystery.

Now as to interpretation with the religious or dramatic appeal. There is no doubt as to its value; it is helpful and enjoyable. There are many who are content to remain in that stage of artistic interpretation. But if one has once caught a mere glimpse of that *higher* conception, has for *one second* experienced that profoundest of sensations, a glimpse of the infinite, no calling, however practical, however obvious in its direct help to the masses, will attract him.

However, one should in no way slander or treat lightly this work with its moral appeal. It has its value—we do not slander the work of the road mender—his efforts render the public a benefit—does not that fully justify it?

To revert to myself—these ideas are not visionary; they are as unfanciful as eating and sleeping. To carry them out requires an exalted state of thought and living. A few precious men have come close to it, and why shouldn't I?—Is it presuming to say so? No! It is a profound duty to believe in yourself and *try* to do it.

If once a man rides its current, nothing can stop him from making the effort unless it is the bodily sacrifice of those dear to him.

I guess I've said enough.—I believe that I have expressed myself, in part, quite clearly. I want you to read carefully, and if any point is not clear, please ask me to explain.

You may be moved to think, "How selfish!" But when you think of it, it is one of the most unselfish things a man can do. He is giving, not money, not titles, not futile words of transient value—he is giving *himself*, his *soul*, which in time takes its relative place among the everlasting, helpful, inspiring things, to humanity—but this is not the *ultimate aim*, understand—it is but a natural consequence.

535

Dr. Greenleaf Whittier Pickard was an inventor and popular orator from Missouri.

Chadds Ford, Pennsylvania
January 12, 1921

Dear Mama,

I returned from Missouri Monday afternoon and found everyone well except for slight colds, which really started before I left. Andy is also suffering from four back teeth coming through all at once. He has lost a little weight, tho' his color is good.

The Missouri experience was very satisfactory and enjoyable indeed.

I arrived there, after an uneventful trip, Tuesday morning, Jan. 4th. I got right to work on the borders, laying the gold and painting in the color phase of the formal design. The work was under difficulties (of bad working light, and from ladders), and I became a little apprehensive that I had not allowed enough time to finish before the unveiling on Friday. So I worked until 2:30 the following morning. The next day, Wednesday, I started about 9:30 and worked till midnight, and on Thursday until three the following morning, and on Friday till noon—and just barely finished! So you see it was close figuring.

Friday afternoon they held a joint session of the House and Senate, the governor presiding—also attending was the governor-elect and the new Speaker of the House. Dr. Pickard delivered quite an elaborate oration in true spread-eagle style, which seems to be the kind of speech-making that goes in such a place. He said lots of good things and unquestionably aroused enthusiasm amongst the thousand or two visitors, as well as the legislators, and succeeded in committing the governors and speaker to very favorable action on new appropriations. There is much in Dr. Pickard that is unbearable to me, but I must give him credit for shrewdness in pushing this decoration scheme along practical lines.

665

The WYETHS

After he had extolled each artist, telling of his birth, history, etc., etc., and winding up with a general eulogy of American artists, a senator made the motion that each artist be asked to stand and be introduced to the assemblage. After this ceremony, what should Pickard do but single me out to speak in behalf of the artists. So another one of those horrible experiences was forced upon me. Nothing in the world is so painful to me as public speaking, and it is made tenfold when called upon unprepared. However, I got through it OK and caused some amusement by declaring that had I known that a speech was to be included in my contract with the state, that I should have turned it down flat!

It is probably my enthusiasm which causes me to talk volubly in a pure social way that leads me into these occasional *traps* of public speaking. I shall never get used to it.

The governor's reception followed the same evening, which was made interesting by the spirit of the early West which prevailed in the architecture and setting of pure early Victorian character.

The governor's mansion was built in the 60s—a huge structure with mansard roof, spacious rooms and ceilings high enough to kick football in. Old and very ugly (but quaint) portraits adorned the walls, with heavy lugubrious red plush furniture all about. The informality in spite of evening dress was rich, to say the least. Punch "with a punch" was served, and various "talented" guests displayed their powers on the big square piano, and the governor's wife whistled us "Swanee River."

About 10 o'clock I noticed a sudden shrinking in the number of menfolk, and becoming alarmed at my sudden predicament of being marooned in a desert of women, endeavored to solve the mystery. Making my way downstairs I found a lone "nigger" butler and asked him where the men had gone. He significantly pointed to a small door which when opened lead to a narrow descending stairway. Following this I soon came upon the governor, lieut. governor, justice of the supreme court, a senator or two and nearly all the artists sitting in at a game of "stud poker!"

I was immediately asked to "sit in" and proceeded to play a game I have not indulged in for years and years. The stakes were high (for me) dollar ante, but nevertheless I played. With newcomer's luck I was $26 ahead about midnight, but slid into the hole by 2:30 and left $8 poorer than before the game. The governor, they say, lost over

666

$50 and the big winner was the judge. I thoroughly enjoyed the experience but was pleased that our train pulled out for St. Louis at 3:15.

536

Studio
Chadds Ford, Pennsylvania
January 19, 1921

Dear Mama,

The children started in with their tutor last Monday, and it is quite evident already that they are going to make great headway. Mr. [Kirk] Meadowcroft knows his job, I should judge, and Henriette says she has learned more this week than in weeks of ordinary schooling. They work only three hours a day for four days a week, but they surely work intensely for those hours. My only hope now is that Meadowcroft will be able to stick to it. It's a Godsend to us. The young fellow graduated from Harvard in 1916, served as an ambulance driver throughout the War, and on his return met Dr. [Arthur] Cleveland's daughter, Ethelwyn. They were secretly married and have located in the west half of Washington's Headquarters. The fellow is somewhat of an artist and ekes out a little living by designing batik, and I should judge that the 12 hours a week spent here comes in pretty handy to him. He has taught in prep schools for two years.

This new scheme started, I next had to go to Washington regarding the Legion picture. There has been much lobbying in opposition to my doing that job—and not very worthy methods used either—by my "fellow artists." I sensed that something was going on by certain delays in maturing the arrangements to go ahead, so I forced an interim with the Legion chairman of the Legislative committee (a brilliant young lawyer and army officer) and went down with the purpose of fighting for the commission. Had proper and manly means been used I would most willingly have abided by the commission's decision, but certain developments got my blood up—thus the expedition!

It was a little difficult to arouse the commission, as I could see (and as afterward they explained) that they were very much befuddled and confused as to just what move to make. The fact is none of the men seemed to them artistically capable. As the chairman (Taylor) said, "Not one of them had anything to offer in the way of suggestions except that which is purely illustrative—and we want a work of art *first* and local truth second."

I brought with me several color proofs including all my past war pictures and also enlargements of the Missouri pictures. I got them thoroughly aroused and went into the broad dramatics of the World War and the particular features of the American in the War which should be recorded. For instance, their settled conviction was for a trench picture, "over the top" or something similar. I told them that every other canvas in that room (which will contain a picture from each Ally) would more than likely show trench warfare, and why not immortalize the one characteristic of American fighting that thrilled the world, as happened when the "doughboys" took *Chateau-Thierry* —fighting in the open, revealing the spirit of audacious youth and athletic ability, thus shattering the tradition of four years fighting under the ground.

The thought struck them solid. Their enthusiasm mounted, and I left three hours later with an order for a preliminary sketch—the first definite move they have made.

The thing that holds them back a little is the fact that I was not across to see the fighting, but I reminded them of St. Gaudens' Shaw memorial, one of the greatest works of art dealing with a war subject —and he never saw war in his life. Also that literality has always stood in the way of real art as depicted by the great masters of battle painting, Meisonier, Detaille, etc., who we realize now are great failures (from the art standpoint). However, I'm off now, and will do my best to nail the commission with a damn good picture. There are many chances to slip up, for my jury will be army men who know little about art but who retain vivid memories of the struggle. This is a colossal impediment to overcome—but you know me—I have sufficient self-assurance to face our Savior with a portrait of God!

537

Studio
Chadds Ford, Pennsylvania
January 31, 1921

Dear Papa,

It is snowing, and coming from the northeast, but we cannot take it seriously. The ground is slightly covered—upon a soft, springy foundation of almost summer earth—but old Mother Nature has slipped up so often in this department of her winter's duties that even the children have lost faith and little enthusiasm is apparent; yet I imagine that I can detect a smouldering alertness ready to burst into a flame of active interest the moment there will be assurance of coasting!

Indeed it has been a disappointing winter, for in spite of the hindrance and discomfort that snows bring to everyone, I am not sufficiently charitable and considerate not to wish for it. The stern character of winter is a necessary ingredient to my complete enjoyment of a year's round of weather—and I warrant that most healthy-minded men feel the same way—even those to whom heavy weather means a fight.

The snow is driving at a significant slant from the "right" direction now—may it continue!

I started this morning on my cover design for *Scottish Chiefs*. I have spent almost two months now (i.e. evenings and fragments of the daytime) absorbing data of all descriptions, embracing most of the authentic history of the early middle ages in Scotland (11th to 13th centuries) and renewing and augmenting my knowledge and dreams of the "Hielands." I could wish that I had what Babe has stored in his memory of his glimpse of Scotland.

It really seems a pity that one isn't given the time and sufficient money to do a book like this romantic tale of Scotland *thoroughly,* and with knowledge substantiated by facts as far as is possible—and above all else after a personal investigation of the country. However, I feel encouraged when I hear, as I did recently, that *Kidnapped, Robin Hood* and *King Arthur* are almost popular books in Edinburgh! Several Scotsmen have complimented my highland interpretations in *Kidnapped,* especially the Isle of Erraid. And yet the interpretation was purely imaginative, built upon accumulated and composite knowledge gained from photos, drawings, and descriptions.

I was impressed by the possibilities of creating convincing pictures upon research yesterday afternoon when Hergesheimer read his new story, just completed, of revolutionary Cuba—a romance and tragedy of 1875. It is superbly done, and one could not imagine but what he was listening to a story told by the actual people of the time and locality. Hergesheimer has surpassed himself in this story (*The*

Bright Shawl), and I predict it will create quite an impression.

There were twelve of us there (Carol was with me). We were entertained at lunch and heard the reading in the P.M., which lasted from 2:30 till 5:30 (40,000 words), and not a soul stirred or showed any signs of weariness in that long stretch of time. The story was very engrossing.

With all my defense of purely imaginative picture-making and story-writing, it is a far cry from that which is inspired by one's personal contacts with life, and here the argument ends!

The children are all well. We had a good talk about you and Mama this noon, and I told them of various stories of the childhood of you both, as they were told to me. Your cows and dog, Mama's mule she rode, and various other incidents. I shouldn't doubt but what extra mail will leave here by tomorrow.

538

The forty-two canvases referred to were eight for The Courtship of Miles Standish, *seven for* Buffalo Bill's Life Story, *fourteen for* Westward Ho!, *and twelve plus the cover for* Robinson Crusoe.

Chadds Ford, Pennsylvania
February 3, 1921

Dear Sid,

It seems extremely difficult these days to find sufficient time or the necessary energy to do a lot of those things that add so much to the joy of living—I refer particularly to letter-writing. Reading, good music and an occasional good play is about all we can manage—and these come only after the shrewdest arrangement of plans. Our lives are jammed-full of action: Carol with her really colossal task in the home, and me with many irons in the artistic fire—too many to be comfortable—besides the duties about the place. These I have had to assume for the past year, help being utterly impossible to get. However, I enjoy these occupations hugely. I derive from them much that is indispensable to my painting. Not only physical exercise, but the physical *contact* with the fundamental if ruder phases of existence—heavy ash barrels, the stable, wood-chopping and other chores. Most of the time I get a genuine romantic reaction from this work, except when it overflows and threatens my studio hours. I presume to say that with me, at least, these things play a definite part in my creative efforts, and eventually I feel certain they will become important—if I dare use the word!

I was very much interested in your comments on various of my last book illustrations. I would like so much to have you see the entire collection of forty-two canvases. It's an old, old story to complain of reproductions, but it is undeniably true that my pictures are suffering more each year from poor color reductions. The outstanding reason for this is that I am putting very much more color, *subtler* color, and *brilliancy* into them than in years back. I am depending so much more upon color arrangements and transitions. These qualities muddle and confuse the engravers ridiculously, the problem of color versus values, and with the very limited three-color process, it's a wonder they get any results at all.

Let me remind you that the same three colors—a red, a blue, and a yellow—are used to print the infinite varieties of a complete set of 16 pictures! So, where one design depends largely upon an area of turquoise blue, thin and brilliant, and another may feature a velvety night-blue, both must be achieved with the same blue ink—the first made bright by relieving the area of its red plate and some of the yellow, the other *deepened* by the inclusion of the yellow and red plates, plus the black key-plate.

The books have been too successful from the sales point of view to hope for a more expensive process of reproduction.

One obvious alternative for better results in printing rests with me —i.e. to restrict my palette to what would amount to a monochromatic scale. This I shall not nor can I do.

Do not give me too much credit for my "imaginative" sea painting. I made careful studies for most of the glimpses of the ocean used in the last books. These were made on the Jersey coast, and in Cohasset, Mass. The studies were as literal in color and construction as I could make them; however, as used in the final canvases, they were purely adaptations, subordinated to the schematic arrangement demanded by the subject and setting. What these final canvases may lack in conviction and charm is unquestionably due to my lack of fundamental knowledge, but their shortcomings must in no way reflect upon this method of willfully departing from literal truths. Expression painting must be interpretive in every sense, color, drawing and spirit, departing from the actual as much as need be to win emotional force.

Your own honest efforts in sea sketching (which I respect very deeply) are brought to mind. I think you should force yourself to work more from emotional impulse, even though your easel stands before the rocks and sea, and avoid too many facts. You have gathered in quite a supply of these latter in the past years, and it is time that you should indulge in more *privileges*—privileges of color adaptations, of distortions and exaggerations—in short, literal untruths, and by these tell the deeper truths.

If one can translate the sublimity of the level floor of the sea and its arching sky, it is quite unimportant as to his manner of doing it, how he draws it or whether he uses brown, blue, or black to achieve the end, provided his result is homogeneous and he projects the sense of cosmic relationship of land, water and sky. (This argument may flavor of "old hat," yet it does no harm to repeat it.)

Speaking of color—I recently saw a landscape by John Constable hung in the same room with a very handsome Hassam done in his best manner—shimmering light, fresh-washed color and all. Constable's, on the other hand, was painted mostly in browns, earth colors, green, gold and silver, very low in tone—and heavily handled. Yet for color appeal, and the sense of light permeation, Constable's canvas made Hassam's very frail. Furthermore, for projected force, for poetic subtlety and for color qualities there was no comparison at all.

Naturally I approve of the higher-keyed and brilliant surface of modern color, but I was more-than-usually impressed by the infinite color range an artist has at his command and how much depends upon schematical painting, and how literality is almost entirely subordinated in the creation of a great work of art.

And yet downright knowledge is the true harbinger however it must be concealed.

How ineffably charming is *My Friends' Books*. Pure music! I have nothing but praise to say and have been thoroughly captivated by it!

The reading of it followed a very full-blooded afternoon spent with Joseph Hergesheimer. The contrast, although in no way reflecting upon Hergesheimer, lent added charm to Anatole France.

We had listened to a reading (Carol and I) of his newly completed story, a Cuban romance.

I wonder if you have ever attempted to read anything of his. He has written much that is unsatisfactory, yet it all bears the stamp of potentiality. He is known mostly, in this country, for *Java Head*. His most recently published book, *San Cristobal de la Habana,* has made a mark and has created considerable interest here and abroad.

It will be especially interesting to you to know that he received a magnificent letter from Anatole France anent the above-named book, also one each from Conrad, Galsworthy and Edmund Gosse.

I am having H— autograph several copies and I shall take the liberty of sending you one. It is a short book and I'd like you to read it sometime. It is colorful, very gorgeous in spots and exudes a spirit of courage to implicitly trust and record one's own pungent impressions.

I have had to do a great deal of reading during the last ten weeks, gathering data for my next Scribner book, *Scottish Chiefs*. The work has led me into several fascinating byways of literature which I have enjoyed thoroughly. The poems of James Hogg (contemporary of Scott's) and *Metrical History* by the ancient minstrel "Blind Harrie," also Chaucer, whose work I had never been tempted to read before.

There is a flavor to Scotland and its people that stirs me very much. There is a certain appeal of the "Hielands" that makes me almost ache with the exquisite and yearning sense of romance. There is a relationship of mountains and men that drives the blood into my face. That country stands for the superb spirit of *masculinity*.

[Letter continued]
Wednesday night, February 10

I judge that the above was written about the first of the month. Now I will finish it and get it off.

Much has happened in the meantime. I have consummated a deal with my father for two acres of land (just west of my old home), and will build there either this coming summer or the following summer—probably 1922, on account of prices, etc. Say nothing of this on the outside as I want nothing of it known about here until the last thing. I am telling you because I know it will be of especial interest.

Now that the die is cast it's a tremendous relief to all hands and we are exceedingly joyful about it. Amongst the many advantages that I am counting on is the one of being where I can see you occasionally; I mean this very deeply. Another event of far less importance was the opening of the Academy show. It's a damnably empty affair and very discouraging to anyone hoping for much from American artists.

The WYETHS

Artists are not living hard enough is, I think, an important view of the matter. There is too much consciousness of what kind of things can be painted *strikingly* and what sort of an impression they will make, and little or none of the "lover of life" spirit which *compels* expression from sheer inward desire.

Even the old standbys—Redfield, Emil Carlsen, Garber, Simmons, Hawthorne, et al.—appear weak and perfunctory. I am speaking conservatively, and I'm sure anyone looking at the exhibition seriously and with the future in mind would approve of my words.

As I wandered through those "empty" galleries yesterday, I thought of how refreshing and invigorating it would seem to come upon a group of *expressive* canvases—a good Homer, a Segantini, a Henri Martin, a Millet, a Twachtman, an Inness!

It is of course unfair to pick out such a string of "winners" to contrast with a catch-as-catch-can show. However, a significant fact would be made obvious—that each canvas of the above-mentioned group would ring clear, first and last, with drama and poetry (*besides* color and design). To be novel or bizarre (and artificially so) is as near dramatics and poetry as the modern painter allows himself to go.

From my firsthand knowledge of several of the painters and what I hear of many others, much of the fault lies in their superficial living, in not accepting the humble duties (those that lie outside the distractions of brush and paint) with keen interest and enjoyment. Inspiration must come from the fundamental experiences of everyday life. This, as a source, will produce something besides insipid nudes, girls combing their hair, blue fans and interesting landscape "motifs." Every enduring work of art is a testimony to this.

I do not mean of course that because one earnestly wheels out ashes of a morning that he must necessarily *paint* such a subject, but by wheeling ashes, by lifting, by hearing the scrunch of the wheel along the path, by sweating, by squinting into the sun, and *enjoying* it, one arrives at certain profound understandings, certain *bodily* understandings which are bound to *demand* more solemnity, majesty, and mystic beauty in his artistic expressions.

Perhaps I seem to dwell too much upon the severely physical side. There are countless physical experiences running the gamut, from the stroking and smelling of an apple warmed by the autumn sun, to violent fisticuffs—all equally important in the creation of enduring art, providing they are thoroughly enjoyed.

674

Finished my *Scottish Chiefs* cover today.

539

Studio
Chadds Ford, Pennsylvania
March 9, 1921

Dear Mama,

I arrived home after a very comfortable trip 8:25 Saturday morning. Found everything OK and all in good health and spirits.

I have already written at length to Mr. Sturgis concerning the new house, and in all likelihood you will see him out there soon to look over the location preparatory to making the first rough sketches.

I can't express to you what it all means to me and to all of us. It will be one of those moves that goes far beyond adventure, but rather constitutes something precise and meaningful. The action will unquestionably rank as the most important in my life, and I look forward to its marking the turning point whence I shall advance into really important work. In various degrees it will mean the same to the whole family.

Andy's appetite has not been good of late, so we took him in to Wilmington to see Dr. [Joseph] Wales who finds nothing wrong with him except that his stomach needs tuning up. He also gave him a preparation containing cod liver oil, but we think it too rich for him, for last night we could smell it on his breath.

540

"The old place," meaning the Zirngiebel house, was being sold by John Denys Zirngiebel, Jr. ("Uncle Denys") and his wife, Etta Freeman Zirngiebel ("Aunt Etta").

Studio
Chadds Ford, Pennsylvania
May 13, 1921, 6:15 A.M.

Dear Mama,

It's early to be in the studio, but as this is my sleeping quarters for the present, it is easy to roll from the bed to the desk. Yes, Ann has whooping cough, so the doctor says, though I am still clinging to the hope that it is only a rather severe cough which seems prevalent around these parts. However, we are endeavoring to keep Andy from contracting it. We may be too late, for Ann coughed slightly for three days before we suspicioned anything extraordinary, so the infection may have taken place already and no good comes of moving Ann, bag and baggage, into the studio. It would be a pity, now that Andy seems to be getting such a fine start, to nip it with a siege of whooping cough. I hope by all means that we will succeed in saving him this trouble just at this time. We will know how successful we have been in about a week.

Ann seems perfectly well and hearty, except for two or three attacks of coughing through the night (which do not "whoop" as yet) and intermittent but less severe coughing in the daytime. She plays around outside, the other immune children taking turns in being with her. Andy is quite distressed to think that he cannot see her or come to the "toodio." He and Ann are great cronies. He is looking splendidly now and is one of the most attractive-looking little kids I ever saw.

All this has taken a little edge from the immediate responsiveness to your glorious letter regarding the old place. It is years since I have risen to such heights of joy. I feared so much that you at home might think me so impractical that the real glories of the transaction would be for the time, shadowed. Eventually, I felt sure all would be understood. But when your letter came I felt overwhelmed, and so thankful! The accepting and enthusiastic attitude of you and Papa have doubled our zest. It is a satisfying thing to accomplish that which one feels is necessary to their own welfare and comfort, but it amounts to a real ecstasy when the rest of the immediate family circle derive the same pleasures. Tell Papa how much I enjoy his "anticipated participations" on the place, and that I will be strong for any arrangements that will enhance his farming plans.

The contract stipulates (as they demanded) the right to sell the greenhouses, but if so these are to be cleared entirely away. Nothing else is to be touched.

I received a very nice note from Aunt Etta, which I will answer soon, which indicates that they feel very pleasant about it all, which helps a lot.

541

Renovations on the Seavy house at Port Clyde, Maine, took longer than

N. C. Wyeth anticipated. Not until the summer of 1930 were they completed. In the meantime, the Wyeths went to Port Clyde for short vacations, staying at a summer boarding house, The Wawenock, run by Captain and Mrs. William Harris.

Chadds Ford, Pennsylvania
June 30, 1921

Dear Sid,

I apologize most ardently for leaving you in the dark for so long, regarding the present whereabouts, the activities, and the future plans of this family. I did not wonder at your graphic inquiry. No doubt you have learned by this time never to be quite sure what the Wyeths will do next. However, the impulses of the heads of this family have always been sincere, but we are forced many times to renounce the most attractive plans when we come face to face with the unforeseen considerations demanded by a sizable family, and the exigencies of my work. You know somewhat of these things and must appreciate how much more complex my problem is than yours.

Thus it is that the glorious summers in Maine must be postponed one more year.

I do not remember when I last wrote to you (which indicates a lamentable lapse of time), but think that I told you of plans being drawn for our New England home. Just as these were under way, my grandfather's homestead came onto the market. The situation was tense, to say the least. On one side I had invested $500 in architects' fees and had bought land from my father; on the other, there was that grand old place on the verge of being sold to a man who was going to demolish the old house (built about 1760) and cut up the five acres into three places. To cut a long *harrowing* story short, I bought the place, and will be settled in it by October 1st if nothing of any serious nature interferes.

I shall not discourse upon the feelings we are all experiencing now that we are set to go. It has greatly intensified the summer for us all, and the topic is constantly uppermost in our conversation. Stern application to my work has left less time for me to think about it, but at odd moments throughout the day and night I experience a turbulent throbbing inside. The change will be a momentous one and will not be without its heart-wrenchings, but the future fairly bristles with promise.

The WYETHS

I must say that I am tremendously relieved of the ordeal of going into a *new* house; I detest them. [Richard Clipston] Sturgis's design was very appealing indeed—a perfect example of New England colonial architecture, but as Sturgis answered, after I had apologetically asked him to cease work on the plans, "If I could buy an interesting *old* house for a home, you couldn't *give* me a new one."

Fortunately for my work, I will be able to drop into the new surroundings (which are old to me) without making a ripple, and in a month's time sail fluently into my painting.

My studio is being built now and will be complete in September. You know what all this means, Sid—an occasional visit from you and to you, within a day's run of Port Clyde, one hour from the ocean, half an hour from Symphony Hall and the Museum, a ripping school within a short distance of the house, and innumerable advantages of associations for Carol.

It may interest you to know that I am arranging to study a part of my time from February on with George Noyes. His color knowledge is superb and I think he will give me much help at this juncture.

As soon as it was settled that we would move to N.E., I had to give up Mrs. Maxwell's cottage, so advertised it in the Transcript, and dozens of inquiries piled in, so had it taken off my hands.

My plan regarding the Seavy house is to have it cleaned and painted inside next spring so that we can use it for "camping out" next summer, and board at Capt. Harris's. Money will not be plentiful enough this year to spend the necessary $2500 to fix it up as per plans, so will make it do for one season. I am looking forward to the summer's painting at Port Clyde, with the belief that it will be infinitely valuable to me, besides the benefit to the rest of the family.

The opportunities in the work ahead of me are glorious. The Missouri decorations have brought much inquiry, and pleasant to hear, considerable praise. I have had to turn down a handsome proposition in Florida on account of the Boston Federal Reserve panels. These latter I shall not begin until I get north, and hope to be able to accomplish something of real mural distinction. I am featuring Hamilton and Washington in one, and Lincoln and Chase in the other. It is a privilege and stern discipline to work with Sturgis.

Have had a number of callers here recently (tourists going through

678

Chadds Ford on what is now a part of the Lincoln highway). Two art museum directors from western cities and a collector from Worcester were amongst them. It is singular—and encouraging—that I could have sold four of my large landscapes and the little one I sent to Lawrence. On the verge of leaving this valley I have determined to keep the few canvases I have left of it.

Scottish Chiefs and *Rip Van Winkle* are nearly done. A month more will clean them up. I think they are probably the best I have done in that line.

I am also preparing an exhibition of 50 canvases to be held in the Art Alliance Galleries in Phila. in October. All in all, I'm somewhat busy!

The two youngest children started in May with the whooping cough. Andy had gained in fine shape this last winter but the cough took him down. However, he is in splendid condition with high spirits and fine color all the time. I think he will regain now that the cough is subsiding. The rest of the children are in fine shape. Henriette's painting is nothing short of phenomenal to me. Her color is charming, and she can draw considerably better than I can. Something should certainly come of her ability, although this is something that I say nothing to her about.

A review (by request) which she wrote of a juvenile history of England, which is being published by the Yale University Press, was so large in grasp, so discriminating and so entertaining and so true, that I could hardly believe my eyes. The editor sent me a copy of her notes, as I studiously avoided rendering any influence and did not read a word of what she sent week by week in letter form. Her interest in Ibsen at the present writing, her enthusiasm over Anatole France, her enjoyments and criticisms of George Sand's *Consuelo* and innumerable other books keeps us all alive. She is rapidly becoming a most vital helpmate to me.

I can't account for it.

Well, Sid, I must stop. It's dark and I've got to go on an errand to West Chester.

Your pictures at the Wilmington show were admired by a lot of people—I took the pains to find out—but nothing sold except a sort of a hysterical spurt at the end bought a [William M.] Paxton for some $2200. It would make a good Schlitz Beer ad.

542

Dear Mama,

Whether or not the intensive reading I have been doing on the subject of Abraham Lincoln, the weather, or both, has affected my feelings these past few days, I do not know. I am certain, however, of the sensation of depression and a general disorganization of my forces. Perhaps it is due to the tenseness that usually comes with the final work on my books. Just at this time I invariably suffer and am tormented with the doubts of the artistic value and usefulness of what I have striven for. In retrospect it appears all so common-place, inadequate and hurried—and yet would I *ever* feel that I had sufficient time!

And now ahead of me are the two momentous subjects to paint for the bank, as great subjects of that kind as ever a man could be faced with. I must confess to a feeling of utter feebleness when I think what *ought* to be done with them.

I have recently read three of the ten volumes of Nicolay's and Hay's history of Lincoln, also several other books dealing with his domestic and official life in the White House, besides numerous accounts of his appearance, personality, etc., all particularly related to the early Civil War period. Have studied numerous photographic portraits of the man, and also of Chase, so that now I feel fairly *saturated* with their physical appearances, the sound of their voices, their complexions and their characteristic movements, both bodily and facial.

The surrounding data, such as the details of the "cabinet room" in the White House, must still be found, and this looks as though it will be a task indeed.

I still have seven more canvases to do for *Scottish Chiefs* and *Rip Van Winkle*. When these are done the vast hulk of the summer's work will be out of the way. There will be one or two other things to paint before beginning to "pack up." This matter looms up like a dream so vivid, that one must believe it, and yet with that underlying admission that, being a dream, it can't be true. It will be a happy moment when all is settled in our new and glorious home.

The weather continues to be *intolerable!* Hot, wet, and excessively sticky. One feels almost desperate at times. I know though, that if I were outside *painting* this weather, which has indeed been superlatively beautiful in its dreamy and misty haziness, that I would more than likely take an intense delight in the very features I call insufferable now. To paint a landscape, wherever one is endeavoring to represent with passionate emotion the hot molten gold of sunlight, the heavy sultry distances and the burning breath of soft breezes, one returns home in the evening proud and happily sympathetic in sweaty clothes and burned arms and neck. To feel thus completes one's sense of identification and unity with nature. But how different it is to stand in a studio almost completely detached from the prevailing spirit of the outdoors, tearing one's mind away from the miraculous and stupendous beauties all about, in a futile and nonsensical effort to identify oneself with the twelfth century in Scotland or the colonial period in the land of old Rip. If it wasn't that I was enabled to pour snatches of sunlight and shadow, storm or moonshine, into my canvases I could never stand the strain. And after all, it is just these little loves of mine that find me a few patrons.

The children are all well except that Andy seems unable to put on any weight. The doctor blames the weather and the aftereffects of whooping cough which has left him with still considerable phlegm in his throat, which we are inclined to think affects his stomach a little. He has grown quite tall, so his "skinniness" is a little more apparent than it was.

543

Chadds Ford, Pennsylvania
July 21, 1921

Dear Mama,

It has given us all a great deal of pleasure to hear of your happy and successful trip up country. I can well imagine how deeply you enjoyed it all because of your predisposition for mountains. I must inherit this from you, for the outline of a mountain against the sky is enough to set my heart throbbing every time.

Well, now that it is probable that those delightful places will be within reach of us all, we will enjoy them too. To think that Carol has never been in the mountains—only to view the Catskills at a distance! I want to be present on her first trip!

The children enjoyed the postals, and even to this morning I saw your card to Andy, "Agassiz's Pool," on his pillow by his head—crumpled and quite worn—however he took it to bed with him.

544

Arrangements were made for the move to Needham. Newlin Arment, the village mail carrier, was general caretaker. Carol Wyeth's brother, Logan Bockius, rented the house for the summer, and a neighbor, Jack McGinley, rented the fields.

Chadds Ford, Pennsylvania
July 28, 1921

Dear Papa,

I am delighted to hear the good reports of the progress on the studio, also that it is looking so well.

Andy is picking up some. He's had a slight attack of bronchitis and his liver has been a little sluggish, both of which are in better shape now. Doctor advises the seashore for a week or so, which he thinks will put the finish on the effects of whooping cough, so Carol leaves Monday for Ocean City (Jersey coast) and will stay there as long as conditions dictate. I shall run down there on Friday (tomorrow) to arrange room, etc., if it's possible to do so at this time of year.

Henriette will run things here, which she can do very handily. She took her lesson in scrubbing the kitchen floor from her mother yesterday.

You have beaten us on corn. I think I can get a mess today. The long dry spell set us back and I saw corn in the West Chester market Tuesday selling for 60¢ a dozen!! Eggs are down again, selling for 35¢. Carolyn's hens have just recovered from a siege of setting and are laying quite heavily. Sis Carol is just now thoroughly wrapped up in the event of four bantam chicks which she says a hen hatched in a stolen nest in the woods, but which we have concluded she is entirely responsible for. A Rhode Island Red hatching four bantam eggs without a confederate looks a little suspicious. They are a lively bunch and I can hear them peeping from the spare chamber window where I am writing.

Back to Needham

The time is drawing near for us to migrate. It seems impossible. I awake sometimes in the night and it strikes me as the wildest kind of dream. The full realization of it in the daytime, however, sets me atingling. It appeals to me as the dawn of a new and better era for us all. This has been a remarkable 15 years in this valley, and I shall of course always cherish every experience here. However, I think it is a matter of self-congratulation that we were able after such a long period of intense living to have the courage of our convictions to make the change when we saw it necessary. It took quite awhile for the transitional stage to culminate into action, but it is done now and a great relief is felt all round.

The village is making it a little hard to pack up and go, by constantly referring to our leaving in deeply expressed feeling. It's hard for me at times to keep back the tears, when some old farmer to whom I never more than passed the time of day will stop me on the road to tell me how sorry he and his family are to know that we are going.

I have not given out the impression that we expect to stay away for good; in fact I plan to return alone occasionally (perhaps a few weeks in the autumn or spring) for a period of landscape painting. This lets me out from telling a downright lie.

I have arranged with Newlin Arment to look over the place twice a week, inside and out, and keep a close watch on the condition of buildings, etc. In April, Logan will come here for the summer, paying a rent which will meet the expense of upkeep throughout the year. McGinley, my neighbor, is to rent the three fields under cultivation.

This morning I finish the last of the *Rip Van Winkle* color drawings (I still have the pen drawings to do). Three more *Scottish Chiefs* will finish that up.

I am awaiting word from President Harding, giving me permission to make some studies of the Cabinet Room in the White House. I have asked for that privilege next week, so half expect to visit Washington sometime soon.

I have always admired Lincoln—it is an American boy's natural heritage to do so, but I have never admired him enough! During recent months I have read quite a number of volumes dealing with the various aspects of his character—personal, political, religious, etc., etc.—and I can only say that I feel completely overwhelmed by his colossal proportions from any view one takes of him.

The WYETHS

One occasionally meets a man who lightly says, "Oh, Lincoln is overestimated" or "Look at the mess he made when he freed the black man"—or some other detracting comment. I think if I hear such drivel again I shall be tempted to strike. This type of man is a damned fool or just a common defamer, nothing more nor less.

Well, the children are stirring—the locusts are singing and a hot red sun is striking across the bed in this room, so I must close.

I must mention Miss Onion however; I have often hoped that she could live until we were settled up there. She, one of the old landmarks, to still be there would help tie over the lapse of nearly 20 years away from home. At her age we can hardly expect a recovery now. I often thought of her and am glad that I have several mementos of her in my studio. It is singular that I have been using my memory of old Mr. Onion for the last pictures of *Rip Van Winkle,* and will complete the portrayal this morning.

545

The New Willard
Washington, D.C.
August 5, 1921

Dear Mama,

Just a note for the weekend. I'm down here looking up Lincoln matter. It is intensely interesting and have found much valuable help.

Carol and Ann and Andy are still at Ocean City. The weather there was so bad on Monday, Tuesday and Wednesday, and Andy did not seem so well, that they threatened to return, but Thursday opened up fine, so Carol telephoned that she would stay the week out. Of course I'm anxious to know how Andy is now and am eager to get home.

546

"Frank" was Frank Zirngiebel, son of Uncle Denys.
Henriette had been enrolled as an art student at the school connected with the Museum of Art in Boston.

Chadds Ford, Pennsylvania
September 10, 1921

Dear Papa,

Your stray letter came tonight. I started to worry about the noisy silence and conjured up all kinds of wonderments regarding the truck and its (precious to us) load of furniture.

We loaded very carefully, but the last thing I detected the men with a bottle of "hootch" and I became apprehensive. I am relieved that the load is there and I hope the chairs are not badly hurt. There was no reason why this should have happened, they being on top. Of course one must expect *some* trouble, as you say, but $225 *should* bring a load like that in pretty safe shape.

If Wendel Hassenfus will sew and put down the carpets upstairs, by all means let him go ahead.

First, have Bryer take out that partition in Frank's room—the one that makes the passageway. I will have these rooms (walls and ceilings) done over soon as we get up there, but the rooms are so small that the carpets can be easily protected with canvas while the painters are at work. I want Hassenfus to lay first the two large chambers, hallway (*up* and *down*) and stairway. (Stair carpet came with load of furniture.) I want all carpets to be well padded with regular cotton-filled paper (something like sample). Ask him to cut out parts that are too worn (and in one case a large ink spot), or else if he finds he must use worn portions, to place them where they will be least used and observed.

After the above-mentioned areas are carpeted, start with little east room and work west (of course he will not start a room with insufficient material to finish).

I am having some large sketches (for my bank pictures) sent by freight sometime this week.

Have got the Bank sketches well along and I think I've something very promising. Expect to ship them next week early.

The house is barren indeed, and if Carol and I weren't as busy as it is possible to be, we would be blue indeed. Henriette is keeping a stiff upper lip, but it is hitting her hard and will do so until she is busy with her studies in Boston.

547

Wyeth wrote his mother that he would be returning to Needham "18 years to the day (within a few hours) after leaving home for Howard Pyle's classes." His arithmetic was incorrect. Nineteen years had gone by.

The WYETHS

Dear Mama,

Friday slipped by me during the night sometime. I fully intended to get a note off to you yesterday, but the day being somewhat "irregular" for me, I forgot. The trouble is we have all been fighting off colds. Andy started the fireworks last Monday, and one by one we "caught on," but we have succeeded in breaking up the invasion, so it is only a matter of a few days when we will all be straight again. Whooping cough has left Andy's bronchial tubes sensitive, so every little cold he gets, down it goes. Flax seed seems to head it off O.K. if taken in time.

We think now that it will be better for Carol and Andy to make the trip home by rail. If we should happen to run into any unusually snappy weather (and riding) it might do some damage.

The plan now is for those of us who go in the car, to leave Wed. morning, the 19th. Carol will spend Wed. and Thursday with Logan in Wilmington and take the night express to Boston that evening. This allows me to get home Thurs. night (two days for the trip) and then I can meet her at Back Bay, Friday A.M.

If possible I don't want you to undertake *one single thing* in preparation for our arrival. It may be that a couple of the children will sleep in your house the night we blow in, but with carpets down it will be only a matter of a few moments to set up a bed or two, so we will be O.K. A pot of oatmeal from your stove, some milk from Papa, and a few eggs are all we want.

Well, I'm doing lots of wondering about how Jewett is getting along. I do hope that he can get everything done by the time we get there. I'll warrant that the old house looks pretty fine inside, and am so anxious to see it I can hardly wait. The whole event of getting back home with you all, and in those beloved surroundings, looms even greater than I really thought.

I'll tell you, I can't imagine how it would have been at all possible to have carried through this gigantic move without Papa on the job. He has indeed done it surpassingly well.

Do you realize that I am returning just 18 years to the day (within a few hours) after leaving home for Howard Pyle's classes? It's something to think about.

Chapter XXII

DEATH OF HIS MOTHER

"You and Mama will ever be the most vivid in the endless procession of mental pictures."

Homestead
Needham, Massachusetts
November 30, 1921

Dear Sid,

We were mighty glad to hear from you, albeit your letter made my conscience smart that I had not written to acquaint you with our arrival.

A great many events have taken place which I am eager to tell you about, but the best I can do now is to briefly skim over the top with the hope of amplifying them later on in person.

You can well imagine how we have all been more or less overwhelmed with the great change. The pressure and confusion of new impressions has surprised and baffled even me. I had credited myself with sufficient imagination to forecast much that would transpire and just how it would affect us emotionally, but I fell ridiculously short of a reasonable conception of it all, for I find now that I am experiencing all the lights, shades, and shadows sensed by each member of the family due to the change. I am so much a part of them that this is inevitable, and the purely personal equation has been thrust into the background—very far into the background.

Gradually, I suppose, we will each emerge and come to the individual understanding of our new surroundings and undertakings.

I now realize (as I never have before) how intensely I have been living *through* my family. You see, I felt the Chadds Ford environment—the home, the hills, the valley and the people, through the feelings and reactions of Carol, Henriette, Carolyn, Nat, etc., all in *addition* to my own view apart. It was as though I had six live points of contact with life instead of one, from which I have profited beyond words. So, coming back here, to a place that I knew all about, a place which is a very part of my blood and bone, I was unprepared for the distinctly varied reactions as represented by the other members of the family who are being transplanted from the land which is a part of *their* blood and bone.

The WYETHS

To be sure, we have visited here several times, and once for a whole summer, but the realization of absolute transplantation for good and all has galvanized their deepest sensibilities into a new conception that strikes into the vitals.

I do not mean to convey to you that there is any feeling of dissatisfaction, or that there is anything but the greatest interest and hopefulness for the future. I have been merely dealing with the normal process of acclimation, which is having its interesting effect upon me.

The physical conditions are just what they should be. My grandfather's house was built in 1738. It has modern improvements such as electricity and plumbing, etc., and, so far as we have restored it inside, is a perfect beauty along the lines which I love most—the severe but chaste frugality of a farmer's home in the early days. Completely comfortable and cozy and a home which I will never feel is more than I should have. (I have cherished and developed a truth which has become of the utmost importance to me—that I am indigenous only to the working middle class, that my attachments and true enjoyments emanate from this strata of human activity, and there I must stay. The heights of expression are, most certainly, just as attainable from this source, perhaps more surely so.)

The extension of the old house has been badly treated in the last sixty years. But it can all be brought back to much of its original beauty. If it were not *that* I am so anxious to see you, I should say wait until next fall before you get your first glimpse of the old homestead (you know how first impressions on another count so much to us artists). But I must waive this pleasure for the far greater one of seeing you as soon as you feel able to come down.

Work stands before me mountains high. I do not see how I shall even be able to accomplish it all. Just as soon as our trunks were in the house, the dishes in the pantry and my palette in the studio I was at work, and it has been nip and tuck ever since, jumping from one kind of duty to another.

My Boston show has eaten into much valuable time, yet I do not begrudge it, for I have received encouragement which I never expected. The show has been especially well attended (over three hundred visitors one day), and the notes from artists and picture appreciators have been numerous. Also the reviewers were good to me. The exhibition closes on Saturday next.

Then of course there is the matter which is uppermost in my mind at the present time—the Bank murals. This work is entailing much study along various lines, including the great problem of the interior (color-scheme) decoration of the rest of the room. Deep coffered ceiling with much rich ornamentation, marble and plastered walls to be considered, hangings, etc.

N. C. Wyeth working on the Boston Federal Reserve Bank murals.

A striking incident has transpired, which I know will interest you, in connection with this work.

As soon as I arrived in October I was called in consultation on the general color scheme for the banking lobby. I was directed to a studio on Beacon Hill, somewhere between the State House and the river. It was difficult to find and after much wandering I discovered a delightful little courtyard called Bellingham Place. On approaching the end of the court, a door opened and there stood *Robert Chase,* our old friend at Pape's—pipe in mouth, blue smock, slippers, a shiny, smiling countenance—as of yore!!!

Chase is doing the ceiling!!—and so we have been brought together again after twenty years or more, during which time we had lost entire track of each other!

We must plan to visit him together. He's the same fine fellow as ever, and has not changed in appearance at all.

He has decorated a large number of interiors from floors to ceilings, carving and designing furniture, making wall paintings, etc. I had seen various photos of his work in the *Studio, Architecture* and various other architectural publications, but had never associated Robert Chase with the old Rob Chase of Pape's!

To return to the subject of our new surroundings, there was grim irony in the devastation caused by the ice storm. I stood on my studio steps, which command a view of the valley and its river, and literally watched the old trees, which I had played under as a kid and which I have longingly planned for years to paint, fall to pieces before my very eyes. Every crack, wrench and shriek as great branches crashed to the ground seemed to tear at my vitals. I don't know that I ever felt more depressed than for four days last week. Now that it's all over and the poor remnants of trees are hopefully lifted again, one is instinctively lifted also and somewhat relieved. But oh! what irreparable damage has been done! And my dear Concord with its elms 150 years old mangled beyond recognition. It was an ordeal for all of us who count so much upon this historic, natural, and serene beauty of trees, their symmetry and skyline—but it seemed especially hard to have such ruthless destruction take place just as one steps upon the threshold of his old home to greet the dear familiar scenes.

549

Needham, Massachusetts
August 3, 1922

Dear Sid,

The pace has been terrific since the week we arrived in Needham, and my little trip to Haverhill marks the longest period I have been away from the studio (or at least from canvas, for I *have* worked in the bank finishing my decorations there). I can be severely criticized by almost everyone for working too hard and too steadily; it is neither good for my art or for my body—and too, it's hard on the family. But it had to be done or to *flunk* on some important commission.

I have illustrated, since Feb. 25th, two books, *The White Company* and *Patriotic Poems*—i.e. *34* canvases. I have also done 6 other story illustrations and two portraits, besides a rather elaborate sketch for a decorative panel for a school in Penna.

This bank job has also stirred up the new First National, which is just being erected, and they have several spaces which they seem anxious to have me fill with Landing of Columbus—Landing of the Pilgrims, etc.

All this is some distance ahead fortunately, and I will have a breathing spell. I even want to get abroad before tackling these very large spaces.

I've spent a good deal of time this winter amongst the artists and writers, etc., in Boston. Through Sturgis, the architect, I was enabled to meet a good many of Boston's "cultured" nabobs; so many evenings were devoted to this form of diversion. I shall tell you more of these experiences when I see you.

[Charles] Hopkinson is the one man from whom I have received any truly constructive help. He is now in the struggle to pull himself out of the suffocating atmosphere of the "intellectualists," spending much of his time, of course, with his relatives—Chas. W. Elliot and his cousin, John Sargent—both of whom I can see (although he will not admit it) pall on him. His struggle, which is a real one, is very exhilarating to me, for in the process of fermentation Hopkinson radiates a most inspiriting tonic.

He is very hard on me at times, but the virility of his attacks are what I thrive on.

Some of his recent works are astonishing, which to me, with all their failings, make the slippery slicknesses of cousin John and the pusillanimous realism and drynesses of Tarbell and Benson look like hell.

On the whole Boston is a mighty stupid place. The people there know infinitely more than I do on almost every subject, but they have lost *completely* the exhilarating joy of living and the greater joy of transposing that enthusiasm into their pictures. This it never enters their heads to do!

The WYETHS

I spent one Sunday going to Chatham, Cape Cod, and back. Was much impressed and would like to know it better, but it can't take the place of Port Clyde—ever!

Port Clyde! Not this year, except for a few days there myself.

Next year we will fix it up, and from then on our regular rendezvous.

Carolyn, Grandmother Wyeth, Mrs. Wyeth, Nat, Henriette, Ann and Andy at Nantasket Beach.

I am thoroughly stirred up over *Moby Dick,* which I read this spring and again just recently. I shall do no more books next year, but in two or maybe three years I want very much to do the above-mentioned title, not as the regulation Xmas book such as I have been doing for years, but different in format and quite different in dramatic approach.

Even the powerful Conrad fades before the colossal power and profound mysticism of Melville. And to think that *Moby Dick* has passed through my hands for years and I never read it!

I'm also reading Scott and have read through one following the other in quick succession. Boyhood reading of Scott meant little or nothing to me. After closely studying Conan Doyle's *The White Company* (the title I've just illustrated) *Ivanhoe* makes Doyle awfully thin, except in the latter's depiction of the "lower class" people for whom I feel Doyle's sympathy and understanding is warmer and more genuine.

The reading of the Chronicles of Froissart (all of them) was a very bright spot in the preparation of *The White Company*.

And for poetry Henriette and I have been enjoying some wonderful hours with Shakespeare's sonnets. Most of these books and things are "old hat" to you, I suppose, but to me they represent what I missed in my younger days. I've spent too much time on ephemeral moderns, and excepting Hardy, France, Conrad, Hamsen and one or two others I may have forgotten to mention, the modern author is poor nourishment.

We have all been well except that Andy does not take on weight as he should—due to bad tonsils, we feel convinced. Sometime this month this little crisis is to be gone through, i.e. to have his tonsils out. A small matter to the surgeons, but to us a nervous moment.

550

Needham, Massachusetts
September 15, 1923

Dear Sid,

Port Clyde is a delicious memory. I consider those few fleeting days there one of the most exhilarating experiences of late years. I am looking forward with the greatest eagerness to the next occasion of a whole summer there *with the family*. I missed them more than I dared let myself think at the time.

The family is very enthusiastic about the nine canvases I brought home, and they have revived their enthusiasm to a high pitch.

I have done several landscapes since I returned, and have Andy's portrait well along. Preparing for a show at the Boston City Club and one in Milton.

Hope you've been able to carry your work on at home. I think this procedure will mean ever so much to you. Paint a colorful still life once a week, spend no more than two days on them, don't worry about too careful drawing but get some emphatic color-scheme *interpreting* of the groups. Call one "The Green Bottle" and make every other object and color patch serve that bottle. Make another arrangement in *blue and gold* and play with the color until it plays a gorgeous symphony of these two colors, using your grouped objects as suggestive matter. A poet rhymes beautifully and tenderly of the milk herd winding its way through the evening shadows toward the home pasture, but he does not mention the litter of cow flaps dropped by the way.

551

Needham had changed during the nineteen years that N. C. Wyeth had been away, and since Chadds Ford had become home to his children, he decided to move back.

Chadds Ford, Pennsylvania
November 10, 1923

Dear folks,

Electric lights just turned on and everybody is excited! Adds much cheer to the home.

Arrived home tired but happy. Trip Home was most enjoyable from every angle possible.

552

Studio
Chadds Ford, Pennsylvania
November 12, 1923

Dear Mama,

It is indeed a case of an "embarrassment of riches" these days, i.e. as applied to the opportunities in my field of work. Each project seems to transcend the last until now I am beginning to feel them to be a menace to my proper and slower development.

Mr. Robert Winsor, as I understand it, is the big gun in the Kidder, Peabody & Co. of Boston. He is also an ardent and active Unitarian. Dr. [Charles H.] Thurber is a great personal friend of his. Through the latter, Mr. Winsor has asked me to create a handsome book for him, putting into pictures some forty parables from the Bible. This book is to be made the best money can buy, and an edition of 10,000 to be printed to be *given away* to all the Unitarian churches and various active organizations connected with the church. He is willing to spend $15,000 on this project.

553

Henriette had become a student at the Pennsylvania Academy of the Fine Arts in Philadelphia.

Nathaniel Jarvis Wyeth, a collateral Wyeth relative, led two expeditions to the Oregon territory between 1834–1836, establishing Fort Hall on the Oregon Trail.

On train to Philadelphia
December 12, 1923

Dear Mama,

How many times have I promised myself to write to you the past ten days, and every moment seemed to have its distraction.

When hard at work, *then* is the time I could write *pages,* and often think I would like to try dictation to someone who could take it in shorthand. I seem to do my painting subconsciously, for every moment before a canvas my mind is occupied with all manner of things —*unless* the picture is giving me trouble, then I can think of nothing else.

There is nothing extraordinary about this subconscious working; it is not only common to most, but is the only way fluent work can be done.

Henriette is working hard and doing excellent work. Every morning I hear that alarm go off at ten minutes to six. It means a good deal, I think, for a girl sixteen to do this six days in the week, get up without a miss, get her own breakfast and get the seven o'clock train—returning at 5:30. But she seems to have lots of vitality, energy and enthusiasm.

The exhibition opened Monday night (Howard Pyle Memorial, by his pupils) and I can say without any question that "The Giant" was the canvas of interest. We had a big crowd there, the picture was given the place of honor and created quite a sensation. (This statement is for family consumption!)

Another mural order has been offered to me. A high school in Highland Park, Illinois. If all arrangements can be made satisfactorily (price, time, etc.) I shall do Nathaniel Jarvis Wyeth leading his train to Oregon. His first trip was from Pittsburg, you know, and straight through Ill. to St. Louis, passing not far from Highland Park.

The big National Bank panels are ready for the color now. Today I am delivering the first three pictures for Legends of Charlemagne. They look well and are quite different.

The folks are all well. Andy has recently gained 1½ lbs. He's looking splendidly and is one of the keenest and most joyful little chaps I ever saw. His constant flow of conversation fairly scintillates with unusual observations and comments.

Nat's benchwork is quite remarkable to me. When I come up I'm going to bring his latest boat, a skiff, also Andy. As true and fine a model as one could wish for. How I would like big Nat to see it.

554

Chadds Ford, Pennsylvania
December 22, 1923

Dear Mama and Papa,

Just a word of final greeting before Christmas day breaks upon us.

It is early in the morning—almost 6:30. I am in the studio. The din of an easterly rain on the roof makes me feel quite alone and remote. It is easy for me to project my senses into the Home with you all. The vision is exceedingly clear. I can hear, see, taste, smell, and feel with almost perfect completeness any object I chance to think about. Last night Henriette played the Victrola for an hour or more just before going to bed. The music stirred my mental pictures of Home into startling vividness. We had just unpacked the box, reverently. It had come badly broken, but *everything* apparently in *perfect condition*. We unwrapped nothing. This will be done Xmas morning. The wreath I held in my lap as the surging tones of Beethoven and Tchaikovski filled the room. The fragrance of the green boughs rose to my nostrils like an incense more wonderful than the pomp and presumption any church could possibly make of it. The spell of *Home* enveloped me completely and I finally went to bed, memory intoxicated. My head reels with it this morning; I feel myself in a semi-stupor. The rain is beating on the roof. I'm in a state of profoundly sad ecstasy.

I intended to write more, but I cannot.

With the deepest and most solemn thoughts of love and gratitude to you both.

555

N. C. Wyeth's great-grandfather, Job Wyeth, was captain of a privateer during the War of 1812.

Chadds Ford, Pennsylvania
December 26, 1923

Dear folks,

Christmas eve and the following day were perfect as to weather. A full moon, clear, and quite sharp.

We have an unusually beautiful tree. As chance would have it, the decorations and their arrangement on the tree seem more significant in their symbolism than I have ever felt them before.

Somehow the haphazard arrangement of the tinsel and exotic ornaments on this tree suggests more than ever the strange gifts brought by the Magi—the Persian Wise Men—to the Christ child. The typical offerings of subjects to a King. The glitter of gold. Spicy, Oriental odors seem to fill the air. Frankincense sends up its pungent perfume —and there is myrrh, bitter as life, and as old to the fancy of the East as the ceremonials of Death. The singular shapes of the glittering and many-colored baubles suggest incense burners, chalices, shining vases of rare ointments, and a thousand gifts offered by the sages out of the East.

There is a mystic look to the tree this year that has impressed me deeply.

Together with this reverential feeling toward the tree, just as reverential and yet more sweet are my feelings when I think of the Home Box, with its familiar odors and its characteristic touches— and as if to paint the lily were added mementos of the vanished past. The tinderbox! Grandpa's Freedom vest! Capt. Job's epaulets! and as a sort of connecting link, the braided rug and the Nova Scotia mittens. You can only *begin* to realize how I cherish all these things, that the older I grow the more ecstatically I cling to those subtle but acute suggestions of family traditions and realities.

The little baskets of cookies were *so* good, the coffee rolls so homey. The wreath-spray of evergreen with its cone and berries occupies the place of honor in the room, and shall until it falls to pieces.

New Hampshire, which I had already learned to love, was a most appropriate gift. It shall occupy Carol's reading table near the bed, where we can both get at it during those delicious moments of reflection before going to sleep. My original copy is here in the studio. (Frost's "grace notes" in this book are marvelous to me.)

It will not be long before I shall come up again—possibly in two weeks. I may decide to ship the first panel up there to study its effect in the Bank. The *City of Tyre* is almost done.

556

Studio
Chadds Ford, Pennsylvania
February 1, 1924

Dear Papa,

This note can't be any more than a few words, to send you our profound congratulations on your birthday. Some of the children have written and all the rest join me in this. Andy is at my shoulder as I write. He has spent the P.M. with me in the studio—his mother enjoying the day in the dentist's chair.

Could you and Mama continue just as you are for all time; it would be—well, it's foolish to say what it would mean to us all. The background of happiness and stimulation which you are giving us is worthy of infinitely more than we are capable of doing, but know that (and I speak for all four) we appreciate everything and are striving.

557

Mrs. Wyeth, his mother, had cancer.

Studio
Chadds Ford, Pennsylvania
December 21, 1924

Dear Papa,

I have thought of this as yours and Mama's wedding anniversary.

I'm so glad that I saw Mama, and I'm so happy that I was with you. The disaster is beyond any expression of words, but the glory of lifting sympathy, feeling and understanding cannot be overesti-

mated. My heart is with you both every minute. I know that I am
expressing just what Babe, Nat and Ed would say too.

I may or may not write before Xmas. The children are going to,
as I heard them say.

558

When Mrs. Wyeth was told she had cancer, she fell into a deep de-
pression.

Chadds Ford, Pennsylvania
December 26, 1924

Dear Papa,

The children's Xmas was a joy to them, of course—just as it should
be. Naturally it lacked its appeal to me, but at least I did not let myself interfere with the spirit which you and Mama taught us so well
to revere.

We all talked much of you and Mama at various times of the day:
of the old Xmas's in Needham, of Mama's birthday and all.

Could I have felt certain that Mama were in good mental condition
I think I should have come up—but I dared not do it.

Keep me posted (it is absurd to ask you this, for I know you will)
and tell me if Mama's rational periods increase.

My thoughts are with you and Mama always.

559

Chadds Ford, Pennsylvania
December 31, 1924

Dear Papa,

The night letter and your own following are like dreams to me,
and I am not able even yet to fully grasp their significance. I do not
think that, as a rule, I am one to lose hope, yet I must confess that
this time my courage and faith were at low ebb.

By all means see Mama all you can and carry out any plans you
think wise.

On *Friday* I shall be in New York and between one and two
o'clock I shall call you up. Be prepared, as far as it is possible, to tell
me at that time what condition Mama is in, and if very favorable I
shall come right up and see her on Saturday.

If this is imprudent, according to your ideas, don't be afraid to tell me so when I call up.

We all wish the best there can possibly be for Mama and yourself. May 1925 bring us all the desired blessings I am sure we deserve.

My deepest love to Mama.

560

Chadds Ford, Pennsylvania
January 30, 1925

Dear Papa,

This letter is being written with the thoughts of your birthday in mind. As I look back at the date Feb. 2nd, 1853, it seems quite a long time ago—when I look at, or think of *you,* it does not seem such a long time. All I can say is, and I mean every word of it, I do hope that I shall be allowed and able to carry 72 years on my shoulders as gracefully and manfully as you do.

I am sitting here in an upstairs room. Andy is sleeping just now beside me in his bed. He is having the grippe, as did Nat the first of the week. As I had several letters to write I thought I could be useful by staying with Andy and so give Carol a little change from the confining cares of the last few days.

The fine letter to Henriette from Mama arrived this A.M. I haven't felt so much calmness, collectedness, repose, or whatever you wish to call it, in Mama's state of mind for, I might say, several years as is indicated in her recent letters or, for that matter, in my two splendid visits with her last week. My state of mind upon returning here last Tuesday was some improvement over that experienced just before Xmas.

In this matter of *gloves* for your birthday—remember it is *Mama's* thought, and this, to please her, is more important than your "economic" point of view. At least I'm going ahead from that angle.

You will probably receive a package by Monday morning (I hope), which I wish you would take up to Mama *unopened.* Let her open it and present the gloves to you. I would send direct to Wellesley, but Mama's orders, based upon her belief that mail does not reach her, *must* be obeyed!

702

Death of His Mother

Carol Wyeth had undergone abdominal surgery in 1923.

Port Clyde, Maine
July 26, 1925

Dear Sid,

A silent and gray Sunday—the wistful color of pearls in a subdued light. A gauze of dry warm-colored mist is suspended before every object. Even the bayberry bushes at my feet seem subtly shrouded with gossamer. Distant Monhegan alone is gently eliminated from the familiar prospect.

The harbor water lies like moulten glass that has cooled, its glint slightly dulled by a faint trace of dust—sky dust! Upon its surface are many colored boats—toys set about as though left by children at play.

It is a day for solitude and reflection, and I am reluctant to disturb it with letter-writing. Letters, as I am able to make them, are such blasphemers of the desire behind them.

Furthermore, this letter comes from a very unpracticed hand. Outside of required business letters and the burdened letters to my home in Needham, I have written less than a half a dozen others in two years.

Starting with Carol's illness in 1923 we have passed through a succession of intense worries: the greatest of these (the pressing weight of which is upon us now) is the slow passing of my Mother, who is bearing up heroically under the doom of a fatal cancer. It is just a year to the week that the knowledge of her affliction has been known to us, and in that year we passed through with her what must be worse than death—a complete nervous collapse which rendered her completely helpless both in mind and body. For a time we looked for the end almost daily, when, to the astonishment of all the doctors, my mother made an emphatic turn for the better and on April 1st was able to return home from the sanitorium completely restored in her mind and miraculously resigned to meet the inevitable.

Her physical strength was naturally considerably reduced, but she embraced the few months of grace with a demonstrative thankfulness and enthusiasm which has impressed me as a miracle might do. To take part, as I have, every two weeks, in the resurrected life of my mother and father—and they with supreme composure facing what so surely lies ahead of them is the most awe-inspiring, the most moving experience I ever had!

But yesterday a letter from my dad tells of an obvious failing, and I shall leave here Wednesday with two of the children whom my mother has not seen lately, to visit her.

In September last, in the midst of the most depressing period of my mother's illness, little Ann was suddenly operated on for appendicitis. Her rugged health pulled her through peritonitis, but not after a torturing struggle of nearly seven weeks.

You will excuse, I know, my relating of these matters. It is hard for me to do it, yet I feel that you should know the dominating circumstances of an almost silent two years.

Of course my work had to go on, not only on account of promises and contracts, but for relaxation.

I have almost a feeling of irreverence when I say that my work, in spite of all, has advanced, and that the future is offering singular opportunities if I can but rise to them.

The two years represent much work accomplished; a little of it augurs well, some of it resulting indifferently taught me a great deal, and the balance pretty much a failure.

Besides the usual amount of illustration, I have painted eight large panels averaging 15 × 20 feet and one of them 15 × 30. Five of these are in the First National Bank in Boston—those three others in the Roosevelt Hotel, N.Y. They have brought me, besides much helpful criticism, an embarrassment of opportunities which I have had to turn aside ruthlessly. I am, so far, rather pleased with my courage to preserve my time and not submit to overwhelming commissions.

The apotheosis of Franklin for the Franklin Bank, 42nd St., N.Y., will occupy me the coming year, starting Sept. 15th.

So much for me.

The children are developing rapidly. Henriette has stepped ahead consistently (and, to me, rather phenomenally). This year she captured the Penna-Academy School first prize for "Imaginative Composition" and "Academic Progress." To substantiate her Academy work she has painted several very successful portraits of Wilmington people, including the District Attorney of Delaware and his wife—also Christopher Ward (parodist), and now has in prospect Herge-

"The Giant," 1923

sheimer and his wife, also a Wm. Laird of Wilmington and a Mr. Patterson. In fact Henriette returns to C.F. next week to start some of this work.

She is fairly certain of a traveling scholarship next year and is saving the proceeds from these portraits against an eight months' stay abroad (the scholarship is only for three).

Henriette, 1925.

Her development has been a great prod for me, urging me into a greater desire for color, abstraction and flat painting.

Carolyn, although showing unmistakable talents in drawing, is thoroughly taken up with animals, especially horses, and has developed into an intrepid rider, taking part in the fox hunts and jumping contests, many of which take place within easy reach of Chadds Ford. Her homesickness and yearning for her animals have forced her to return with Henriette to C.F.

Nat has grown very strong and rugged. His talents lean very strongly to handicraft. He's a happy youngster, courageous and full of life. His high diving off the pier railing here amuses the rest of the boarders immensely.

Ann and Andy are in fine condition—two very normal and happy youngsters.

The mother never looked better in her life, and is thoroughly enjoying her stay here.

Last week for five days there were four very large Gloucester fishermen in here, icing and baiting up at the "cold storage."

At the same time there were three lumber schooners and one loaded with salt fish, all moored inside. What with the coming and going of a number of large pleasure yachts and launches it has been a fascinating and lively place. As I sit here now, two sizable schooners (one a stove boat with wide-set masts) are moored the other side of "Raspberry," all sails set, rising majestically from the glassy water like images that would never move.

I am happy to report that there are still nine lobster sloops still in use here, but am sad to say that John Teel has his for sale (wants a power boat), and that poor old Raymes Davis died two weeks ago, and so now *his* sloop is for sale.

Harris has started work on my house—has rebuilt the east wing and repartitioned the whole house according to plans.

He expects to have men to work on it soon again to shingle it in and get the plastering done throughout before cold weather.

Port Clyde is meaning a great deal to me and will mean increasingly more as time goes on. As soon as I can outgrow the *picturesqueness* of appeal of the country and its inhabitants, it may be I can someday strike at something bigger in the painting of it.

The work that I've done already this year is better than before, but it rises not a whit beyond the "pleasing scene" stage and misses the heart of the subject.

Not long before coming here I had the good fortune to see about

15 of Homer's watercolors I had never seen before. More than ever I was made to realize that he alone, of all who have attempted the Maine coast, has risen above locality (yet sacrificing none of it!) and has presented the sea, land and sky for everybody and all time.

We have made several excursions to places you first took us to, such as Mosquito Head and of course the cove, etc., and they mean more to me than ever. I desire no farther exploration of Maine to fill my soul and body with sea, sky and sun. If I could translate into color and design the deep note of mournful joy I experienced from lying on the grassy slope in front of our old house, listening to the soft rush of the water on that stony beach, and feeling the soft, salt-laden air "moaning in the hollows of my face," I would feel quite happy, I'm sure.

It is the *ex*traction of *ab*straction that I want to get out of this beloved spot. Every spot on earth is potential of great interpretation by someone, if he but gives himself up to its underlying beauties rather than to its scenic sensations.

I'll close this interminable letter now with the hopes that your "letter muse" will treat you better than mine does. But, mark you, I do not expect an answer just because I am the last to write—I may even start another before this one is in your hands.

562

Henriette Zirngiebel Wyeth died August 11, 1925.

Port Clyde, Maine
August 27, 1925

Dear Papa,

We plan to leave here on the morning of Tuesday, Sept. 1st, and expect to arrive in Needham that evening. Just when will depend upon how early we start.

Things have been going on as usual here. The weather has been especially fine—clear and cool.

The girls H. and C. are at present out sailing in a sloop with two boys from Weston (friends of Robert Winsor). The rest of the children are down on the shore playing.

Carol is here reading.

My canvas is completed and I believe it marks an important epoch in my painting—with one lash I have cut my moorings to certain old habits and feel free now to develop along a much larger line than heretofore. I feel that the intensity of the past weeks with you and Mama played a tremendous part in sustaining my courage to carry on this work. That is what it should be, and Mama would have been the first to glory in it.

When I walked into the parlor that Thursday morning and looked upon her powerful face, at last calm and serene, I resolved in words, which you would have heard if you had been near, to carry on for her sake into a more important field, an approach nearer to the great possibilities which she and you gave to me.

I feel that I have taken the first definite step.

"The story of my mother . . . ."

563

Chadds Ford, Pennsylvania
September 7, 1925

Dear Papa,

We made the trip very comfortably, although we passed through considerable rain in western Massachusetts. We got as far as Montgomery, N.Y., Thursday evening about seven (about 40 miles this side of the Hudson). An early start Friday put us on our own doorstep at 4:30 P.M.

It was a severe pull to leave you on Thursday morning, and my mind was crowded with many wishes and yearnings.

Plan just as soon as you feel you can, to pay us a visit. Perhaps you can arrange to return with me sometime this autumn.

A summer of great portent has, I feel, come to its official ending. Its intensity and stress must, on all our parts, be turned into triumphs. I feel, personally, that I must come much nearer to justifying Mama and you.

We all send great love to you.

564

Chadds Ford, Pennsylvania
September 13, 1925

Dear Papa,

The weather here is stifling hot, and has been steadily. It's just as though we were being given to understand that we did not, after all, escape the "rigors" of summer.

We had to take Andy out of school; the hot weather and the excitement were telling on him fast. We may wait until next year before starting him. Nat starts in next Monday (not tomorrow) at Swarthmore Boys' Prep school. We think it an excellent place for him. All men teachers and he will have to get under the weight of his work a little more.

Henriette is still in New Jersey painting. Carolyn starts in my studio on her drawing about the 25th. Ann and Carol are very well.

Was pleased to know you and Babe went to the Cemetery with flowers.

565

Chadds Ford, Pennsylvania
September 25, 1925

Dear Papa,

Henriette returned Wednesday night and brought back with her a successful portrait. Today she goes to Mrs. Hergesheimer's to arrange for work there beginning Monday. She will remain at Mrs. Hergesheimer's house until her portrait is done. Henriette's school opens about Oct. 6th.

Your last letter meant a great deal to me. How often do I follow you around the dear old place in my imagination. Especially in the autumn, my mind seems especially alert to memories and visions of Home. You and Mama will ever be the most vivid in the endless procession of mental pictures.

Don't forget to call on me when you want to.

566

Stimson Wyeth's wife, Constance Twigg Wyeth, made the traditional birthday cake sent from Needham.

Chadds Ford, Pennsylvania
October 30, 1925

My dear Papa,

Another week has spun around almost before I knew it. I have never passed two weeks more permeated with thoughts of home and all it ever meant to me, and yet it seemed impossible to get at pen and paper. The fact is I have been feeling everything *so* deeply that the idea of writing was repugnant unless plenty of time and energy were at my disposal—and, I'll tell you, they have not been.

The truth is I am beyond the point of saturation and I am simply stuck with the number of things I am doing. I am really having a glorious time in it all, but do regret a lot of things I cannot do.

As I write it is snowing hard, and it has been since 2 o'clock (it is now five). It has made the studio exceedingly cozy to work in, but it does make me feel queer, to be plunged into winter so suddenly.

I can hear the children coasting; they sound very hilarious and I know just how they feel.

Well, the box with the cake, a symbol this time with a double meaning—in memory of Mama and of the birthdays here, and I might add, of course, Grandmama's anniversary. The little box arrived the night of the 21st, and its interior was in perfect condition. The fragrance of the hay and the spruce twigs plunged me into intense memories which seemed to increase all the next day, so that when I returned to the house about 6:30 Wednesday evening and found the big room full of friends (an absolute surprise), I just couldn't stand it but hurried upstairs and wondered how in the world I could see the evening through. I had to do something desperate, so I hit on the plan to dress up grotesquely, which I accomplished with a soft shirt and a pink hair-ribbon for a tie—dress-coat and vest—golf knickers rolled up my thighs as high as I could force them—heavy golf stockings displaying bare knees. My face ludicrously painted, a hideous false nose, and hair thoroughly soaped and plastered like a skull-cap onto my head.

I never looked worse, and no one could accuse me that evening of vanity!

But it saved the evening for me. I succeeded in smashing the bulk of emotion which was pyramiding inside—"and a pleasant evening was had by all."

The cake was very splendid, and tell Constance, was commented on by all—only it was too small!

But above it all hovered the spirit of Mama, and my mind flew back again and again to my vivid imaginary pictures of 43 years ago and what might have happened in the early hours of Oct. 22nd. What an increasing wealth of vision concerning Home has Mama's passing left me. I cannot suppress my thoughts. They teem so that I have resorted to the idea of writing—The Story of My Mother—I have made many layout notes and wonder what will come of it. A vivid and honest picture of our whole family is my purpose. Can I but do it half-right it will be worthwhile.

I appreciated so much the home letters—yours and Babe's. I received one day before yesterday from Ed—written the day after you and Nat were down to see him.

I so want to write Nat soon. I get so much satisfaction from the thoughts of his being near you again. How I hope that he can reconcile himself to his new undertaking, and I think he will if he can carry on *something* of his own on the side. This will be necessary— it is his lifeblood.

The WYETHS

The panel ("Apotheosis of Franklin") is shaping up toward completion—at least the lower half which contains the 23 figures—the upper half (both panels are 15′ × 15′) is mainly architecture and sky and *should* not be so hard.

The problem of 20 portrait figures was some job and each figure a heroic size (7 ft. each). Here is the list: Franklin, Washington, Lafayette, Hancock, John Marshall, Hamilton, Jefferson, Sam and John Adams, Morris, Tom Paine, Robert Treath Paine, John Jay, John Paul Jones, Aaron Burr, etc.

Chapter XXIII

TRUE IDENTITY

"I realize definitely now the penalty one pays in one's effort to discover one's true identity, that is, what it is that makes one sense and feel things differently than any other mortal ever did *or ever* will.*"*

N. C. Wyeth coming from his studio.

567

Colyan Robinson was a young student asking for advice.

Chadds Ford, Pennsylvania
February 9, 1926

Master Colyan Robinson
My dear friend,

I think your sketches show real ability. Go to school a little longer, say until you are sixteen, then if possible go to a reputable art school and draw, draw, draw.

Forget the commercial aspect of art; your work will inevitably bring you returns in proportion to the "heart and soul" you put into your efforts. No artist of any permanent achievement ever thinks of the money one bit more than is absolutely necessary. Remember, there is no such combination of words as *commercial art*—commercialism and art are as far apart as the two poles.

568

Chadds Ford, Pennsylvania
February 26, 1926

Dear Papa,

You would have smiled at something I saw yesterday. Walking down around the barn in the P.M. I came upon Sis Carol sitting on her pony—full Western rig—very patiently learning to "roll her own." She finally got one made, pulling the *Bull Durham* bag closed with her teeth, in true cowboy fashion. To see her light up and puff away was really so picturesque that I did not disturb her. She is doing good work in the studio and is certainly an interesting character to watch unfold.

"I came upon Sis Carol sitting on her pony."

We've had another "flood" which was quite exciting. I helped in getting school children across the high water. These little events keep one in touch with primal experiences and I hope they will always exist in some way. Canned life is not agreeable to me.

569

Dwight Franklin, an authority on period costumes, worked closely with Douglas Fairbanks on the film, The Black Pirate. *William Beebe was the famous American naturalist and explorer.*

Toward the end of this letter, reference is made to Henriette visiting "Pete's people in Boston." This was her fiancé, Peter Hurd, who came to Chadds Ford from Roswell, New Mexico, in 1923 to study under N. C. Wyeth and who later married Henriette.

Chadds Ford, Pennsylvania
March 24, 1926

Dear Papa,

They tell me that this is Good Friday. Well, I know no better way than to open it (it is only 9:30 A.M.) with a letter to yourself.

There is so much to tell about and of such variety that I could wish a visit home were in order so that we could have a chat together—but I guess I'll have to be contented with a pen and paper this time —and you, with the usual darn bad writing.

I shall go back to when we concluded to sacrifice the very splendid plans made by Walter Brown for the addition to the house on account of their cost. When we finally got the bids in and actually faced the expenditure we quickly concluded that to proceed would mean too much sacrifice in the future, i.e. the curtailment of necessary leisure and the comfortable margin which would allow both Carol and me to do *some* of the things necessary to health and progress.

We turned back to my original scheme, which we have since improved into a very modest and attractive solution of our problem. This will cost us less than half of the more ambitious plans, and I feel sure now that it will give us just about enough room and the extra accommodations needed.

The engineering problem has worked out almost perfectly, as luck would have it, and I'm having a young fellow (William Price, son of Will Price who did the Traymore Hotel) work out the details right here under my direction.

We hope to break ground in three weeks.

That's that.

On Monday last, I had to go to Baltimore to serve on an art jury for that city's annual show. A Mr. Meryman (who recently completed a portrait of Coolidge's boy, which you may have seen reproduced) was a member of the jury, also Chas. Morris Young, well-known landscapist. We had an interesting session, but it was hard work to cull from 300 or more canvases and assume the responsibility of choosing those of the greatest merit. The other two members were fiendishly anti-Jew and anti-modern, which made it difficult for me, as I felt their attitude so unfair; and yet being the *junior* member, and a less experienced one at that, I felt at considerable disadvantage. We had to make several compromises and although I won my point in regard to showing a representative group of modernists, I lost in the support of the Semitic artists.

They must have been K.K.K.'s of the rabid kind, which is the reason that I cannot tolerate groups of that sort.

I arrived home Monday night, midnight, and left for N.Y. on the following morning at seven.

The main reason for going to N.Y. was to put the final wax varnish on the Franklin decoration. This I accomplished by one o'clock. I joined a friend of mine, Dwight Franklin, who accompanied William Beebe on his Sargasso Sea and Galapagos Island trip last year (and who took my place working with Douglas Fairbanks), and we attended the showing of the picture *The Black Pirate*. This was upon invitation of Douglas Fairbanks. After seeing this gorgeous and stirring spectacle of pirate life (in full and glorious color—a perfect monument to the legends and traditions of pirates) we went down to Fairbanks' apartments at the Ritz and spent a thrilling couple of hours.

I found Fairbanks a regular and splendid type of man and mind. Even Mary Pickford, his wife, has the simplest and most winning personality. We talked of everything imaginable concerned with art and life, and I hope he got one half the stimulation out of the meeting that I did.

He very graciously gave Ann (of whom I told him of her enthusiasm for all his pictures) a beautiful and large portrait inscribed to her. You can imagine how the event has stirred Ann.

True Identity

Franklin and I went to the Coffee House (an artists' rendezvous on 45th St.) to get something to eat (we had had nothing since morning). But even here we did not eat, for we met Robert Flaherty, the moving-picture creator of *Nanook of the North* of several years ago, and the current *Moana of the South Seas*. Both these pictures are conceded by all picture critics as the greatest accomplishment in the cinema world.

Flaherty is an enthusiast, no mistake! During the conversation, I asked him why he didn't do the *Hudson's Bay Company* epic before it was too late. It struck him like a thunderbolt! We started to talk of its possibilities, each one in turn contributing new ideas and suggestions. Just at the right moment it seems, Jesse Lasky, the great promoter of moving pictures, came in. He was drawn into the talk. Flaherty, in his great enthusiasm and intensity, tried to arrange a company then and there, making *me his assistant director*. Then I got scared. I didn't want to get into such things, so I bolted. But Flaherty insists that I'm his meat and I'm afraid I'm not through with him yet.

Otis Skinner the actor, who started in on the conversation, faded out of the picture. Even his exuberant spirit paled in that maelstrom of enthusiasms and hopes.

This incident makes me feel that moving pictures are headed in the right direction and that time will redeem them and make them of true artistic worth.

About seven thirty, Franklin and I wandered toward that singular community in N.Y. city called Greenwich Village. We stopped in various printshops and bookstores, fabulous in riches of that sort. We wound up at the apartment of Don Wickerman, the genius and proprietor of three prodigious and much-heralded eating places in Greenwich Village. They are called respectively "The Pirates' Den," "The Blue Horse," and "The County Fair."

At his apartment we regaled ourselves with two delicious Scotch highballs and four drinks each of a concoction for the *gods!* called *"Silver Fiz."* This latter is made of rum, gin, eggs, cream and several other ingredients. Such nectar I never tasted, and never expect to again.

By this time our tongues were hung in the middle and we owned N.Y.! How we got down to The Pirates' Den, I don't know, except that the walking was floating, and the scenery beyond compare!

The WYETHS

I don't know how I can describe The Pirates' Den.

It was originally an old warehouse that had been gutted by fire. It is four stories, the floors being narrow and very deep.

We entered by a small but heavily bolted oaken door—a pirate, "6 foot 6" in great coat, cocked hat, heavily belted, bristling with flintlock pistols and a cutlass at his side, let us in.

We crept along a long narrow hallway dimly lighted by flickering candles in ships' lanterns. At the tunneling end of this passage came the sound of a brawl, yells and clashing steel. Through the dim light we could make out the kaleidoscopic movement of figures, the flash of metal and an occasional report of a pistol.

We entered through this bedlam, so it is that all patrons are received. As we groped our way up twisting stairways, along ships' balconys, captains' walks, and such-like paths, we reached a large room stacked with guns, racks of cutlasses and hundreds of pistols. Ropes, tackle of all description, boarding irons, culverines, brass cannon, cages of parrots and monkeys—all lighted with ships' lanterns!

In the large elevator shaft (which was) was arranged the pirates' orchestra. The stand, upon which they sat, rocked and gently moved up and down, which amongst the rigging, rattled shrouds and ships' gear which one looked through, gave the impression that the whole floor moved like a ship's deck.

We sat to long narrow tables and were served by swaggering buccaneers. They called the orders to the galley in loud rough voices; they were carried down the line in repeated calls until one heard them disappear into the distant kitchen. For instance, my order for rare steak was "Beef—cripple the beast and drag her in!"

Throughout the building the calls of the watch were periodically sounded, the first coming from the hurricane deck, the top-gun deck, second-gun deck, and the muffled cries from below the hatches. And always in the dim distance somewhere, one heard the gutteral singing of "Yo! Ho! Ho! and a Bottle of Rum" and raucous laughter.

While we ate, a monkey played about the table. Once he snatched something from my plate; again he took my fork. He was a long-tailed variety from central America and he would wrap his tail about my arm, swing under my chair and appear between my legs and so on to my lap. Then, on occasion, he'd sit on my shoulder or on someone's head.

720

Above us was a parrot that incessantly cried, "Pieces of Eight, Pieces of Eight." Then yell to our host (Don Wickerman, the owner), "Damn your black soul, avast there!" Just as plain as though I had said it. While all this was going on, I happened to turn to look at a patron on my left, who had several times laughed long and loud at our antics at the table, and lo! it was *Clarence Darrow*, of Bryan and Evolution Fame. We swapped yarns, it seemed for hours, and had a great time.

It was a crazy night!

I got to bed at 2:30 Wed. morning.

Retiring at such an hour was not conducive to early rising. Nevertheless, I had an engagement to breakfast with Robert Winsor at 8:30, also at the Ritz which, fortunately, lies right opposite the Roosevelt Hotel on Madison Ave. where I was staying.

This interview, with its strawberries and cream, poached eggs on toast, coffee and rolls and mild cigars, was a strange experience after the night before. From the curses of pirates to the Parables of Jesus was too much of a shock for even me, for the babble and futile chatter of *reform*, as the soft words fell from Winsor's lips, sounded almost senile.

The fact is, upon the soberest reflection, R. W. is getting revoltingly *soft* in his Christian uplift interests, and he almost turns my stomach. His suggestions are almost puerile, as, for instance, the suggestion that we publish a book called *A Day Book*—a quotation for each day of the year on each page—"so that a man may read in the morning and obtain a Christian viewpoint thereby, which would aid him in his day's work and play," as R. W. said. To tell him that such books were on the markets by the *hundreds* and were a *pest*— to agree that not one man in a thousand ever bothered to *open* a book like that meant nothing to him.

The work on the Parables, which I shall continue, *must* be done through Thurber. I must see Winsor as little as possible.

It's too bad.

The man in his later years is floating in an atmosphere of moronic religion, of honeyed spirituality, which to every strong man turns his stomach!

Thursday was concluded with a talk with the Roosevelt Hotel managers and it looks as though I will make another panel for their dining room, and two portraits—of Peter Stuyvesant and the first governor of N.Y., whoever he is.

At home the Easter vacations are on. The weather has been unsettled but today is clear and windy. All are well.

The Wyeth house with the new wing.

Henriette had planned to visit you this week (incidentally to visit Pete's people in Boston), but I've been pretty insistent with Pete lately regarding his work, and he has postponed visiting his Aunt and Uncle until the last of May. Then, I suppose, you will see H. and probably Sis Carolyn or Nat, as the case may be.

Carol has mentioned time and again about writing to you, and doubtless you will hear from her soon. We all enjoyed the eggs so, and Carol was much moved by your birthday card, which was the only one she got outside the attentions we gave within the home. You carried on a custom of Mama's. Mama never seemed to forget Carol's birthday.

I am wondering if you and any of the boys will get an opportunity to visit the cemetery Easter. I hope so.

Mama was quite moved by Easter, I always felt.

I do hope that the back of winter is broken and that you will be able to carry on your garden work with unbroken pleasure. Don't go at things too hard, and remember that the *pleasure* derived is very important, which cannot be if you undertake too much.

570

Chadds Ford, Pennsylvania
April 18, 1926. Sunday night

Dear Papa,

I'm just winding up affairs before leaving for N.Y. on the early train tomorrow. Carol will go with me. We will attend the unveiling of my decoration in the Franklin Bank.

This trip will *obviously* celebrate our twentieth anniversary which occurred last Friday. We celebrated it quietly and thoughtfully then.

It is hard to realize that so much time has passed since that day when you and Mama made that hurried trip to Wilmington to attend the little wedding. Frankly, I did not at all look forward to a married life so replete in experience, running the gamut from supreme joy and satisfaction to moments of darkness. But the bright side certainly dominated and I have no reason to think but what it will continue. It is marvelous to realize what a vigorous family has grown from that rather frail slip of a girl of twenty years ago.

My garden is plowed, harrowed and rolled and ready for first plantings, but will wait for a few warm days.

The orchard is sprayed and pruned and I had a fellow wheelbarrow between the trees.

We break ground in a week. The new plans are perfect and enthuse me rather than worry me as the others did, so don't worry about that.

571

Chadds Ford, Pennsylvania
May 18, 1926

Dear Papa,

I have just received my contract to do five panels for the Hubbard

Memorial Bldg. in Washington. With the contract came a letter from the president of the Geographic Society telling of the plans for an unveiling in January, at which will be Pres. Coolidge and his cabinet—diplomatic representatives, etc. So there seems to be some chance that I will meet another president—and one whom I admire too.

But this seems very soon to talk of such plans. The panels in the meantime are to be done, which means that a great deal must pass before my mind and eyes before January.

I went through another and final siege with the Insurance Company a few weeks ago. I took out a little more insurance and also had a $10,000 policy changed into liability insurance. All my policies now are liability, so that if anything whatsoever would ever happen to me which would interfere with the carrying on of my profession I am fixed as long as I live for $250 a month.—This in no way interferes with the death benefits. So now I feel very secure.

But the physical exam was very severe, and on one score I had a difficult time to get through—i.e. my weight and its effect upon my kidneys. Finally, they sent their expert from N.Y. and after giving me some very sound advice he passed me as being in unusually good condition for a heavy man. I have not touched meat for three weeks and don't miss it at all. I have a harder time not to eat too much, but have already dropped 12 lbs. The reducing will go slower after the first ten, they say.

I am planning to make use of the excavation earth and build a tennis court just west of the house. The men are figuring out the cost this afternoon. If not too expensive I shall go ahead. I may have to wait till fall but I *do* need the exercise.

572

Chadds Ford, Pennsylvania
July 13, 1926

Dear Papa,

Andy celebrated his 9th birthday last evening. As it happened, about 8 people dropped in during the evening just by chance, and he felt highly honored. I hope to get up home before long.

573

Chadds Ford, Pennsylvania
July 23, 1926

Dear Papa,

Yesterday morning I had to go to N.Y. on business.

I don't know that I told you that I met and talked with Commander Byrd (of North Pole fame) in Washington last week. Yesterday I went to the Pathé News building to study a showing of all the movies of his trip, which were run off for my benefit (in preparation for one of the panels commemorating Byrd's flight for the Geographic Bldg.).

I enjoyed the extra excitement of viewing these pictures with [Vilhjalmur] Stefansson, the Arctic explorer, who happened in just at the time to view some *dancing-girl* films! I said to him that I could imagine nothing more incongruous or unique than to meet Explorer Stefansson on the twelfth story of a N.Y. skyscraper on a July day registering 103°, and he *looking at a picture of dancing girls!* He made a wry face and I think only half-liked my crack.

I was glad and relieved to get your favorable report of matters concerning the burial of Uncle Gig. I received another letter of very warm appreciation from Aunt May, thanking all here and in Needham for their kindness. She's got a battle ahead to work out a scheme of living and self-support.

574

Chadds Ford, Pennsylvania
August 1, 1926

Dear Papa,

It's pretty lively around the place with 7 to 9 men on the house and grading the new tennis court. It seemed a poor time to start a court with everything else to watch and pay for, but I feel it a necessary detail for my own physical benefit. I need more concentrated exercise, and the court handy by the house will be conducive. Of course the whole family will derive pleasure and benefit too.

Peter Hurd's father was here yesterday. Interesting type of Boston lawyer transplanted into frontier life. Veteran of two wars, one eye, bad hearing, but genial, shrewd and humorous.

725

These days, their bearing upon events a year ago, make me think and recall so much.

The oak-paneled dining room.

575

Joseph Brinton was Christian Brinton's father.

Chadds Ford, Pennsylvania
August 10, 1926

Dear Papa,

Well, I suppose the prospective plans, as recorded in your last letter respecting Nat's visit, panned out about as you had hoped. You know now of course that we enjoyed 5 or 6 hours of his company here, sending him off about midnight with a belly full of "golden bantam."

I was certainly surprised to get the phone call (as we were feasting at old Joseph Brinton's table, celebrating with him his 92nd birthday) that Nat was in Wilmington. Fortunately little Nat was able, in company with [George] Whitney (a fellow studying here with me), to go in for him.

Nat looked well, and it was good to hear him talk "his stuff" with renewed enthusiasm again. It would have pleased Mama could she have heard him.

This time a year ago is vividly in my mind. Mama is with me in my dreams almost every night.

576
Charlie Sedgwick replaced James Jenkins as handyman.

Chadds Ford, Pennsylvania
September 17, 1926

Dear Papa,

I have just put the finishing touches upon a piece of work for the Forbes Company (a calendar to be used by the Edison Mazda Company). It is an elaborate piece of work and has taken a solid month to do. It will be called "The Carvers of the Sphinx"—a night scene: torchlight revealing King Chedren and his spouse seated in their golden double-chair, supported on the shoulders of 8 eunuchs, watching the carvers at work on the huge stone face.

It is very closely done and is exceedingly dramatic. The border and other design around the picture is very elaborate and all Egyptian in motive.

I have an idea that the picture will make quite a hit. They are to pay me $3500, which is nice to think about now that it is done.

The building is nearing completion; the plasterers start Monday. It is a splendid job so far and I am very proud of it as it represents my own design and I have watched every detail.

The two youngest will not start on their schoolwork until we are moved into the new part.

I am making pretty definite plans to go to Maine just as soon as my next two jobs are done, which will be in February, I judge. I want ever so much to see and, in part, live that life on the coast in mid-winter. I'm looking forward to it even more than though I were going to Europe.

Fruits of all kinds are in quantities this year and Carol has put up some 250 jars of everything. Our apples are marvelous looking and I wish so you could see them. The trees are bent to the ground. For awhile I thought we must pick some of them to relieve the boughs, but thanks to proper pruning they are holding the loads perfectly excepting two very small breaks. It's a singular sight.

PICS HERE

Grapes are loaded and Charlie is preparing to make another 25-gal. cask of wine. Last year's "brew" is splendid, almost like a champagne.

I shall send you within a few days a package of honey in combs. It is locust honey and especially good, I think.

I am enclosing a couple of photos I snapped of Nat last week at work on his galleon model. He is doing a remarkable piece of work. His bench is in the entrance room of my studio and now that he is at school I miss him greatly. The brig in the photo is one he did last winter.

Nat at his workbench.

577

Dear Papa,

New Years! 1927!! By God, these days fairly tread on one's heels, they come so hurriedly!

We had a very quiet but very delightful Xmas day. Just us, no visitors even, and one had time to really enjoy the significance of it all.

Books seemed to be the order of the day. Andy got soldiers, Ann a miniature circus and the inevitable doll.

I'm getting a good start on my "Ships of Columbus" for the Geographic series, and have completed "Balboa."

578

Dear Papa,

Just a note to say that outside of some slight colds, all are well. The children are enjoying some fast coasting after a very blowy and cold storm. Heavy snowing and eight above zero don't come together so often! Snow not heavy but badly drifted.

Tell Babe that I am deeply stirred by [William James] Durant's *Story of Philosophy,* which I have just concluded. W. H. Hudson's *Far Away and Long Ago* is also a recent reading which appealed to me deeply. *Esqueruelling,* that classic of pirate days, and a remarkable treatise on Chinese Art (for which I have always had a strong but vague affinity) are before me now. It is strange how closely the Chinese aesthetic point of view resembles our own. I have heard it conceded many times, by authorities, that this was so, but now I am finding it out firsthand. I feel that it will mean much to me in the future.

I'll conclude with the news that we are announcing Henriette's engagement to Peter Hurd in tomorrow's papers (Phila. and Wilmington). It's been an old story for us for a year, so it's no shock.

The terribly urgent and recent attentions of John Harriman of

N.Y. (grandson to E. H. Harriman of railroad fame) drove the matter into the open. Harriman got quite a jolt, I guess, for he's supposed to be the "catch" of N.Y. just now, with his social standing and millions, but I was happy beyond expression to see Henriette put genuine attraction before the blinding glamour of superficial glory.

Peter Hurd and Henriette at the time of their engagement.

Chadds Ford, Pennsylvania
March 4, 1927

Dear Papa,

I have spent the last 45 minutes looking through one of Mama's scrapbooks and the little curly-maple box of her trinkets and jewelry. I shall not tell you the state of my mind now; you can realize for yourself. I chanced to open one of the lockets (not expecting to find anything inside) and what was there, on either side, but a head of Carol and one of me, taken, I should say, about 10 years ago.

There is a fragrance in that maple box that I hardly dare let myself be conscious of—a mixture of faint violet and rose, the same fragrance I associate with all her boxes and dressing bureau drawers that contained her laces, collars, handkerchiefs, etc. I cherish the captured aroma in this little box and take care not to leave it open and so lose it. To smell it is ecstatic pain!

But I *must* leave this subject.

You don't know how happy I was to get that photograph of Noah Wyeth. I have always been fascinated by this uncle of yours, although my knowledge of him has always been meager. Perhaps his name alone conjured up something in my boyish mind years ago; possibly I felt a kindred spirit in his wood carving and whittling—the creative spirit; but impetus is greatly added now by the fact that I look so astonishingly like him in this photo. Did you never notice it? To place one's finger over the mouth, the upper part is strikingly like me, and no one who has seen it but what exclaims.

You couldn't have sent anything that would please me more. These old keepsakes, these *miracles* which clear my vision into that hallowed past, have become almost fetishes. During periods of depression I but *think* of these tokens and in turn of the dreams they bring to life and I feel it worthwhile to go on.

It seems a far drop to speak of my Washington trip. It was all successful from the angle of the Geographic Society. Extremely successful, I can rightly say. But I returned somewhat oppressed with it all, because, when a job like this is out of my studio and off my mind I realize how far I have fallen short of those rumblings and agitating forces within me. In short, how little I have expressed *true me,* and how much there is of *me* to express.

The WYETHS

I tore into a canvas of my own upon my return, and made a *definite, incisive* advance. It is so different, so much more virile than my other efforts that it is difficult to believe I did it—and terribly difficult to think that I can produce still more of the "picture-pictures" that are demanded of me. But I must.

Noah Wyeth.

580

Dear Papa,

It is not easy to write legibly on a train, but it's the only chance I've got to get a letter off to you today.

The weather is clear, cool and crisp, and I hope it stays this way long enough to retard the extraordinary start everything has gotten in the past warm weeks.

The hills are a pleasurable sight to behold. The rich patches of ploughed areas contrasted with the greening fields and the still greener meadows all fringed with the misty gray of the woodlots, the south sides of which show the faintest blush of swelling buds. The glistening silver of the water courses give the final touch to a scene of beauty and promise.

It is quite difficult to know where or how to begin a letter these days, for my life seems more than ever submerged in the purely personal equation. And once this becomes released in conversation or a letter, it is apt, like a cloudburst, to inundate all surrounding territory.

I realize definitely now the penalty one pays in one's effort to discover one's true identity, that is, what it is that makes one sense and feel things differently than any other mortal ever *did* or ever *will*. It is only when we reveal this individual reaction to life that art becomes creative; all work up to this point (although it has its practical uses) is bound to be transient and ephemeral. And this term describes almost *totally* what is being done today.

It has become (what I have yearned for for years) an obsession with me now, to uncover *something* of the vast amount of accumulated emotional experience which it has been my keen pleasure and ecstatic anguish to have gathered. It is as though the bloodline from both houses (from yours and Mama's) was rising near to the surface in me, clamoring for expression. It is not presuming to admit this, for all of us feel the urge more or less, and it is a mere incident that one is constituted to be more articulate than another. I have said previously that I am paying a *penalty* for this effort. The penalty is that every ounce of my energy is being directed into one channel, which means that I am receding more and more into myself.

At the same time, never have my thoughts been so sharply focused on all those who are dear to me. Day and night my brain teems with intense vibrations of love and the appreciation of the sublime.

The safety valve which will preserve sanity and nominal health lies in the increasing ability to accomplish genuine expression. Pent-up desire becomes a fury which merely burns up one's body and soul.

I have felt for years, and continue to believe, that Mama burned up much of her physical vitality by her inability to put into more satisfying and coherent form the intense agitations of her emotions. As I grow older and observe men and women, it is rarely that I have encountered others, men or women, who manifest the enormous amount of emotional fermentation that she almost constantly displayed. It was largely misconstrued as the result of bad health or aggravated querulousness. With no constructive and progressive method of relieving this pent-up spirit, it is bound to reveal itself in abortive ways.

And so it is that I have felt the necessity of cracking open a new and progressive phase of development. And I am convinced that I am on the trail! Two recent canvases prove to me beyond the shadow of a doubt that I have gained a footing, and that it is only a matter of good health and perseverance to achieve something. What for? I don't know nor care. One does not produce a bowel movement to fertilize the land. It is simply a physical, an organic relief. And so is the accomplishment of a true piece of personal expression.

In the meantime I am gradually eating a hole in the "cordwood" of practical illustration and paying my bills. Perhaps someday I can turn my back on this and devote my whole time to the bigger theme. But just now it succeeds in putting an amazingly keen edge on my appetite to really express *myself* every chance I get.

And not a word yet about the family. All are well. Carol survived her 40th birthday and looks younger than ever! She appreciated your card so much, especially as no others came from her family. (There are so many, I guess they lose track.)

We had cake and ice cream, and today I may get her a little remembrance.

Andy is showing phenomenal ability in drawing, which is beyond doubt more than a phase. I may establish a man Wyeth in my studio to carry on after all.

Nat is doing splendidly at school, and so is Ann. She too appreciated your card, and no doubt you will hear from all soon.

Henriette just completed a very successful portrait head in charcoal (of our neighbor Joe Luke), and Carolyn has taken a big brace in household duties, which pleases Carol and me, for she has always been a little weak in this direction.

581

Chadds Ford, Pennsylvania
June 7, 1927

Dear Papa,

Well, the Lindbergh event swept us all off our feet, and I'm sure it did you too. You made a derogatory remark in a letter about the *uselessness* of it all about the time he flew, and I was about to scold you then for it, but I guess you feel as we do now that that remarkable young fellow has served a world that needs it, with something that goes infinitely further than to prove the worth of his courage, the endurance of his machine, the possibility of overseas flight. He has given the entire world a lesson in modesty, and the power to resist commercialization, which thrills me more than any other phase of the whole matter. It's bound to have its splendid effect upon the impressionable youth of the world, and has probably helped the feeling between nations (although I haven't much faith in the enduring qualities of this latter influence).

582

The schoolhouse located just below the Wyeth home was purchased by N. C. Wyeth for the future use of his daughter Henriette and Peter Hurd. For several years after their marriage they used it as their studio. Later, they added a living wing and moved in. In 1940, it became the first home of Andrew and his bride. Today it remains the studio for Andrew and his son James.

Chadds Ford, Pennsylvania
June 17, 1927

Dear Papa,

I expected to have plenty of time this afternoon to devote to letter-writing, especially to you, but about 1:30 a man rushed up here to tell me that the painter I have giving the schoolhouse a coat of paint fell from the scaffolding and was unconscious.

So, the afternoon has been shot to pieces attending to the poor fellow, getting the doctor and taking him to his home in Kennett Square.

He's a man of 55, stockily built, and of no age to fall fourteen feet to the ground. He was knocked unconscious and was badly bruised and shaken up, but no fractures as far as Dr. Betts could discover. What his internal condition might be is something else.

This has been a week fraught with happenings of that nature, the worst one happening last Saturday when a Lincoln touring car skidded on the wet concrete right into that little brook where you and Mama and Carol were grouped, when you were washing up after our lunch the first time we all visited Chadds Ford together, 22 years ago. I took the photograph, which shows Mama down on the bank, you standing and Carol perched up on a fence in a white dress.

Well, that charming, pure and innocent little stream drowned the two women who were in the car. You see the car turned turtle, holding the women down, and the brook dammed up and covered them with water. One man, the driver, was crushed and killed, the other is not expected to live. New York people and strangers.

An incident of this sort shakes a small community.

An old landmark—a Mr. Wicks, some 80 years old—overworked in his garden and was found dead there. So all in all it's been one of those tragic weeks here, such as seem to happen every so often.

Mr. [Joseph] Chapin spent the day with us last Friday, viewed the *Strogoff* pictures (which are now done), rode over the country with us and returned to N.Y. the same evening. He was highly pleased with the pictures, as I felt sure he would be, because they are the best book illustrations I've done since *Scottish Chiefs*, I think.

583

Chadds Ford, Pennsylvania
September 12, 1927

Dear Papa,

Yesterday (Saturday) was one that I shall never forget, and only wish that all of you could have been with us.

"Portrait of My Mother," 1929

True Identity

The 150th celebration of the Battle of the Brandywine.

The sham battle was superbly done, in a setting unsurpassed in the world!

Not far from the Birmingham Meeting House, in a rolling field and amongst the towering woodlots, between which the distances of the marvelous valley spread out for six or eight miles, the advance of the Redcoats and the retreat of the bedraggled Continentals took place.

As the "company fronts" emerged from a woods, halting to fire, the rattle of musketry echoing across the hills, the moving forward, the halt to load again and then another volley from 200 rifle barrels! —was a sight and sound that made me tingle to the point of tears. As the Colonials in ragged order retreated to the worm fences and rail piles, here and there the wounded dropping into the tall grass, it brought back more vividly than I ever thought possible that day 150 years ago.

The reason mainly, I think, was the fact that nothing has changed in the surroundings. Perhaps a few less woods, perhaps a few new farms in sight since that old day, but almost all the original farms in that vicinity are still there! The worm fences are there, and the swaybacked farm wagons (of which a number with four-horse teams were on the field) are identical with those of Revolutionary days.

The day itself was a miracle. One of those hazy, dreamy kind with low silvery clouds festooned across the sky, moving slowly, here and there illuminating the near or distant hills with a bright sheen as on old silver. Under this dripping silver light and on the undulating hills of variegated greens and soft browns, the British, the Hessians and the Colonials moved in serried ranks, hidden here and there by the smoke of the muskets or the artillery, the blue and buff darting into a deep woods on the left, a scarlet stream of redcoats emerging from the right. All of which was punctuated with that deep round booming of old cannon and black powder.

And later, as the impressive ceremony of laying wreaths in memory of the English, the Americans and the French who fell there (done in the old time formation of twelve Continental rifle men and the fife-and-drum corps, who went through the old manual of arms, playing the dirge and firing the salute of three over each wreath) was going on, the great dirigible—the *Los Angeles*—came out of

737

the clouds (just like poking through a mass of lace curtains of filmy texture), dropping messages as tributes to the dead of 150 years ago.

Another *blimp* and two airplanes sailed around, going through battle maneuvers, overwhelming the crowd of 50,000 people (assembled to see the spectacle) with the crushing contrast of the old and the new.

Well, you can imagine Andy's reactions. The boy is lost today in drawings of cocked hats, guns with bayonets, Hessian miter helmets!

It created a wonderful effect upon us all. We had expected nothing of the sort; in fact we expected to be bored to death with the usual pageant stunt. But this was great!

584

Chadds Ford, Pennsylvania
October 20, 1927

Dear Papa,

Tomorrow is the anniversary of Grandmama Z's birthday. I believe I never failed to make note of it with a letter or little gift to Mama. So—I feel better that I have mentioned it to you.

The following day we will celebrate four birthdays—Henriette's, Carolyn's, Nat's and mine.

You may know how much Mama will be on my mind the next few eventful days. It will be her memory I'll be celebrating all the time.

585

Henriette Zirngiebel Wyeth saved most of her son's letters. After her death, the letters he sent to Needham were not so carefully kept. This was the last letter found to Andrew Newell Wyeth before his death on July 29, 1929.

Harl McDonald, director of the Philadelphia Orchestra, had become a close friend.

Chadds Ford, Pennsylvania
December 20, 1927

Dear Papa,

We are joining you in a thoughtful anniversary of your wedding day—the 21st.

I thought of having some flowers sent but decided upon Xmas day—Mama's birthday. These should reach you on Saturday the 24th.

Carolyn has just finished a close drawing from the bust of Lafayette, which is good too.

Nat's *castle,* which he has been making for Andy for Xmas, is really stunning, and after all is done I shall photograph it for you.

Saturday afternoon we all go over to the [Harl] McDonalds' for a Xmas eve dinner (four o'clock in the afternoon), then some music. We will all sing a few carols and then their tree will be lighted. We will leave early, about 7 o'clock to get ready for our own celebration Sunday morning.

Xmases will always be, from now on, subdued but enriched for me. It is an acute combination of ecstasy and depression. We all send deepest love and Christmas greetings.

586

This letter was written to James Boyd, the author of Drums, *during the period N. C. Wyeth was gathering facts to begin his illustrations for the book. Johnny Fraser is a character in* Drums.

The WYETHS

Edenton, North Carolina
December, 1927

My dear Boyd,

Some tower in the brilliant moonlight has just rung out the hour of two. I have tried to sleep but the crowded hours of the day are racing through my mind at such a pace that sufficient composure for slumber seems out of the question. Perchance this letter will invite sleep—if not to me mayhap to you.

For the last two hours, lying by the open window, I have listened to the night sounds of this little town and have contrasted them with those Johnny Fraser heard so often, and by doing so have enjoyed revealments which, for moments at a time, became very poignant and very moving.

At this instant a dog is barking somewhere on the edge of the city; there is also the faint muffled staccato of a small power-boat out on the sound. Occasionally, the sudden angry grind of a Ford, new-starting in the cold, shatters the quiet. But the silence following becomes the more pregnant of the echoes of the past.

I am actually not many feet from the cubic areas occupied by the boy Johnny and his dad in their candlelit room at Hornblowers. My window faces the harbor and I too can look upon "dim shapes of fences, walks, houses—" some of them identical with only the changes of roof coverings. Dimly bulking against the glow of the moon on the water I can see the angular shapes of three warehouses. There they stand as Johnny Fraser saw them!

This afternoon was spent wandering in and about these relics of 1770. My heart went out to them, because you, Boyd, have made them live for me. The oak timbers, whose adze-marked surfaces are still crisp on their protected sides and smoothed to gentle undulations where the sun and rain of years have touched them, thrilled me like music.

While I was sitting in one of those large empty storerooms, with a sharply cut square of the sunlit bay before me, a roof timber creaked, a slow, weary creak, as though it were changing its position. I was greatly moved. It was a privilege, I thought, to have heard that. There was no wind, the sun was low, the old building was talking to itself, and I overheard. I imagine that I know what it said—and that's one reason I can't sleep.

740

There is a man here in Edenton whom you did not meet—Dr. Marck Boyd. He is not a native but has lived here some time and is now secretary of the Historical Society. He has interested himself especially in the waterfront and has arrived at quite a complete idea of its appearance (based upon extensive research) of the original docks. We went over the ground quite carefully, and he pointed out the few remaining original fragments, which included the three warehouses referred to. Even the half-hidden piles of ballast stone slowly settling into the earth tribute from far away and strange shores. Mute Romance! A shrieking silence!!

I arrived (very thankful to you for the use of your motor and pleased with the careful but not dull driving of Calvin) at Plymouth this morning. Impassable roads from Williamstown to Edenton changed our route. From Plymouth the passage lay over rails to Mackeys, where I shifted to the ferry for the sake of sensing Albemarle Sound from the deckline of a boat. Not before a short trip up the Roanoke River over narrow sandy roads in a coughing "flivver."

The Spanish moss was dreadfully beautiful to me, as were the swamps and treacherous-looking shores.

Approaching Edenton on the ferry the waterfront became monstrously enlarged for a few moments by a mirage—a "loom," as the Maine fisherman would call it. It affected me queerly. It was as though the little port had stood up from a seated position, open-eyed, to view with alarm the impertinent coming of another man to reveal her past when one had already accomplished the job. That no other one of the twenty passengers in the boat made a comment on this phenomenon, I am convinced that it was a personal affair!

Well, I am going to try some sleep, but not before I express my warmest thanks to you and Mrs. Boyd for your kindnesses. You have given me a wonderful start in the new adventure *Drums*—and I do hope I succeed.

587

Peter Hurd married Henriette Wyeth, June 28, 1929. For over ten years they chose to spend several months each year in Chadds Ford. Not until 1940 did their ranch in San Patricio, New Mexico, become their permanent home.

The WYETHS

Studio
Chadds Ford, Pennsylvania
October 16, 1929

[To Peter Hurd]
My dear Pete,

While awaiting the arrival of Dr. R. W. Rogers who seems intent upon seeing the *Odyssey* originals (all of which I have on hand for a few days), I'll write you a few lines.

I hope he may prove a contrast to the three young squirt art students who blew in here this A.M. and silently sniffed and sneered at The Cyclops, Calypso, and Company until I flew into a rage and lashed them with my tongue within an inch of their lives! My candid attack finally cracked them into making what amounted to the most naive confessions of their tiny, insectlike art-student points of view, and you bet your bottom dollar I didn't leave them with a leg to stand on! I refused utterly to show them anything more (having shown only three of the *Odyssey* canvases). Until, just before leaving (after an hour of *robust* argument), I turned the canvas of my mother for them to glimpse, and they figuratively began to bootlick, craving to see more of such. But I closed the show, being careful to insinuate that I had dozens such efforts facing the wall (which I haven't of course!).

I know that I said a number of things which, if they could but expand a hair's breadth mentally, would help some. Outside of its being a setting-up exercise for my chest and larynx, the whole hour or more was absurd and futile. The next bunch of bowel-running art stoodents that approach this studio will be shot down in cold blood—for they haven't any warm blood anyway.

Henriette's two canvases and mine ("The Barn and Old Albert") left for Chicago last Thursday. That show opens Oct. 24th and it will be interesting to learn the fate of the two submitted canvases.

Harl [McDonald] was here last night, and the most stirring part of the evening was his playing over and explaining his orchestrated *Mexican Phantasy*. I am thoroughly convinced it is splendid! (Incidentally, Harl has presented the original ms. to you and Henriette—and also is to present me with that of his last trio, which is dedicated to me!)

By the way, Carolyn has just done an excellent piece of flower-painting—living, fresh, sober in color but with real qualities.

Your last letter, Pete, was very bright, charming and graphic. I felt an unusual concentration behind it.

Your letters (yours and Henriette's) have given me quite a vivid glimpse of your life in and about the cabin, but I would so like to see some snaps of the place! Haven't you a camera?

Grandfather Wyeth with his sons: N. C., Nat, Stim and Ed.

Dower was here last week. The McCall Company are taking over the *Red Book* and *Blue Book*, determining to build in order to beat Hearst. I have an idea that there will be work there you can do. Dower was much interested in you, and I know he's looking for new talent. I feel there's a possibility there, and mostly "he-man" stories—and they will publish in full color later.

743

The WYETHS

Don't favor Henriette traveling in present condition alone—would
prefer to contribute funds if necessary to ship your motor—try to
realize that you naturally cannot realize how dangerous the period
of first pregnancy is.

588

*Ann Wyeth had begun her serious study of piano under William
Hatton Greene of West Chester, Pennsylvania. Showing an outstanding
ability at composition, she completed her training with Harl McDonald.*

In December of 1934, her composition for full orchestra, Christmas
Fantasy, *was played by the Philadelphia Orchestra, Leopold Stokowski
conducting.*

Ann.

True Identity

My dear Babe,

Ordinarily, this would be called a disagreeable day—it is dingy-gray, very little light, coldish, with a slight but continuous spatter of rain. The suppressed tattoo on the studio roof sounds like a distant, muted hand-clapping—a celestial applause, as it were. And to me, it is just that! It is not personal, however!! I certainly have done nothing to call for heavenly approbation.

It is happier that I say, perhaps, this gentle din from the skies is more the expression of a mutual feeling of inter-appreciation and gratitude between Nature and Man, that life is life and that it is possible for the mind and heart to be conscious of its amazing completeness and variability.

The leaven of some extraordinary music has crowded my capacity for reverent enjoyment and exaltation. I feel for moments that I must burst for the need of greater understanding and expansion, and the glory of it is that it is not the ego which is dominant, albeit alive to the uttermost, I believe and hope.

Food that is best for the body is that which is keenly relished by the sensory faculties—that high consciousness of flavor, texture and the miracle of its being. Physical and being follows. So will the spirit more certainly thrive upon one's keen consciousness of every light and every shade of every kind of experience. Life faced and accepted in this manner becomes distilled into the bloodstream of our aspirations.

At times it seems as though the inspiriting atmosphere is almost too thick to breathe. I feel ecstatically overwhelmed with the rapid and kaleidoscope passing of the simplest scenes and events that I must stop it all that I may more adequately reflect. Every passing moment seems so worthy of permanent record!

We *all* heard Rachmaninoff yesterday. He played every type of composition—from Beethoven through a heart-burning Chopin group, to a number of those notalgic expressions of emotional Russia.

But these musical experiences are most cherished because of their bearing upon our lives in the home.

Ann's exciting progress, plus her great expansion as a character; Nat's aliveness and increased success in his studies, plus his impressively appealing personality; Sis Carol's new grasp of a very mature effort in painting; Andy's incessant aliveness and eager efforts in drawing; Henriette's superb existence as a wife, mother and intense painter; and lastly, the bulwark of Carol with her interest and activities, without which we would all fall to the ground.

The stimulation from all this is tremendous, and my yearning is of course to sum it up in a few good canvases.

Like a great solemn backdrop suspended beyond it all, like the miracle of a great sky of towering clouds are the vivid memories and searing thoughts of Home. I dare not let myself go on what has become the painfully searching and beautiful obligato of my life. Its remote yet immediate strains persist like the sublimated rumble one hears from the bowels of Niagara.

589

The reference to Jesus was in connection with the triptych N. C. Wyeth was working on for the National Cathedral in Washington, D.C.

Studio
Chadds Ford, Pennsylvania
June 18, 1934

Dear Kids!

It is hard to believe that you have all been away for five days! On the other hand, the comparative emptiness of the little brick house seems to have been going on for a long, long time. It is really very hard to reconcile oneself to it, but I guess I'm very much spoiled after all these years of close and complete family living. I am conscious always of an uncomfortable hollow feeling in the pit of my stomach, and a hundred times a day my mind questions this discomfort and I have to say, "Oh! it's because Ann, Nat and Andy are away up in Maine!"

Today makes one full of yearning and homesickness. A stern, gray day, quite cool and a persistent rain out of the north. The drumming on the studio roof has been continuous, and the heavy foliaged trees on the south and west sides of the building are weighted with water and bend, sway, and drag their great green hands across the weather-boarding and roof shingles, as though repeatedly wiping off the drenched building.

What delight your letters and postals have given us. The flavor of Port Clyde has reached us without losing a drop.

You were *magnificent*, Ann, to write the very day you arrived, and being so tired out and all. But your message meant so much to us. It came on the last mail Saturday night.

Then Andy's splendid letter came today. It had lots in it, much more than the actual statements made, which is always proof of a full mind and heart. Nat's postal came also.

Ma is writing and will tell you the news (if any), so with very little time before mailing this, I'll wind up this note by saying that Jesus is behaving very well and I'm beginning to get a real kick from the experience. I shall write to each one of you (in rotation) more at length soon.

590

Port Clyde, Maine
July 20, 1935

Dear Henriette,

I'm sitting at the very edge of the piazza in a comfortable green rocker. It's a luminous gray day and the sea and sky are a flashing and shifting silver. The stretch of grass between me and the shore is a lovely golden green. A fresh easterly breeze is flowing about my face and arms like soft cool water.

We groped our way into Port Clyde Wednesday evening about 8:30 through a thick fog. In a surprisingly short time our unpacking was accomplished and everyone promptly fell into a deep unbroken sleep until 8:30 the next morning.

The fog still hung about us like unnumbered layers of gray white gauze. Looking seaward no one could imagine that a shoreline had ever existed. The damp green grass became swallowed in the white shroud within twenty yards of the house. A vast emptiness! No trees, no birds, no sounds! Perhaps the faintest call from some distant complaining gull, but that was all.

As we later found out, this was the fifth day of impenetrable fog. All life had been suppressed and silenced by the vast power of obscurity.

By noon, and in a moment's time it seemed, the baffling pale curtain lifted, and spread out before us in the most lavish display of

The WYETHS

color and brilliance possible, lay the blue jeweled water, the familiar green islands, the moving flecks of white, yellow, and green boats. From the depression and gloom of a dozen hours we were suddenly set into the center of a gorgeous and dazzling world. The arch of the heavens loomed stupendously and the twinkling floor of the sea stretched into the infinite. No greater miracle ever happened!

For hours we but sat and gazed!

The trip up was especially enjoyable. The country everywhere was fresh and opulent. The Connecticut River Valley through northern Massachusetts and up into Vermont and New Hampshire was superb. We had spent the night in the magical town of old Deerfield. Andy, Nat, and I wandered about the old town late into the night. The moonlight on those old houses was beyond expression!

591

Ann Wyeth was engaged to be married to John McCoy of Wilmington, Delaware. Taking his senior year from Cornell abroad, he studied art first at Fontainebleau and then in Paris. Returning to Delaware, he worked briefly as a draftsman and designer for the duPont Company and met Ann on Christmas, 1933. This led to the opportunity to study under N. C. Wyeth. In the late fall of 1934, he started training in Wyeth's studio with one other student, Andrew Wyeth.

Port Clyde, Maine
July, 1935

[To John McCoy]
Dear John,

The time is slipping by too rapidly for all of us but Ann!

The family as a whole have been thoroughly enjoying themselves, with now and then a little letdown in the direction of homesickness and other yearnings. This is as it should be. Without the capacity for such feelings one becomes nothing but a stuffed shirt.

Outside of Ann and Andy, not much is being done to startle the art world. Considering everything, Ann has done pretty well with her new composition, and I notice, as the time draws nearer to your arrival, her ability to concentrate improves. Two weeks ago she was quite blue, and with the price of train fare in her pocket nothing would have held her back. But I remained hard and unrelenting—so here she is—waiting!

748

Her composition is really coming along now.

Andy, free as a bird, has been doing a lot of canvases and is succeeding in exploring considerable new territory in the field of moods and technical devices. He strikes me in his present state of mind, character and habits, as the ideal student in art, and with an unmolested preoccupation of life, will go far.

"Andy, free as a bird, has been doing a lot of canvases."

How he'll manage it when he is tripped up by some designing and beautiful girl, or if he meets up with some other unforeseen obstruction, no one knows. That's when he will test his metal.

Nat too has been doggedly working on his boat in the face of the fascinating distractions of the place. The *White Whale* is coming splendidly and the development of details is quite exciting, even to me, who is supposed to be especially dumb along these lines.

But, I'm going to *insist* upon another summer for him up here. I guess the General Motors Corporation can wait a few months longer for him. I feel sure he can't complete his project this summer.

As I'm sitting here on the porch, with all my letter paper, sheaves of unanswered letters, etc., weighted down to keep them from sailing off, a snappy cool easterly breeze is flowing over me like delightfully cold spray. The sky is cloudless, the water a deep-pulsing blue flecked with twinkling sunspots of diamond brightness.

A few moments ago two porpoises were playing just beyond our mooring, and at this moment a thousand gulls, in one vast cloud, are gathered around the "cold storage," where undoubtedly a fisherman is in with herring.

592

Ann and John McCoy were married October 26, 1935.

Henriette had painted a portrait of Stimson Wyeth's son, John. Her portrait of Miss Katherine Flaherty won first prize at the Delaware Art Center. Andy sold his watercolor to Mrs. Ellen Meeds, a wealthy patroness of the arts in Wilmington, Delaware.

Studio
Chadds Ford, Pennsylvania
November 4, 1935. Monday

Dear Ann and John,

Your splendid letters came in this morning!

The time, since you left, has been strangely vacant and strangely full to repletion. We all go around with a hollow feeling and yet our thoughts, and actions too, fairly teem! We seem to be vaguely seeking to pick up the loose strands and in some way to seek a new combination that we may tie them together again to start anew. At the same time our lives are actually very full and each one is accomplishing something.

The canvas I thought sure was a failure has turned into one of my good ones. Andy has done his strongest landscape as well as several superb life drawings. Carolyn has come out of the dark woods with a powerful still-life and her bust. Henriette painted a corking portrait of John Wyeth and on the side captured first prize in the Wilmington show with her "Miss Flaherty" (and Andy sold his "Seiners" to Mrs. Meeds). And Ma has been turbulently busy in the home and making many dashing visits to your homestead beyond the brook.

Back of it all are the resurgent echoes of the wedding, memories of which will never fade. It is all a massive dream to me, real and unreal as all dreams are.

As John truthfully said, the procession of events on that evening of the 26th left a deep mark on most of the friends who were here. There was a poignancy about it all which I believe transcended the vast majority of similar occasions. The surroundings were indeed happy and felicitous, but the important ingredient was the great sympathy and the great faith in you two—in you, as individuals, and together as builders of a new generation. To sustain the integrities which you are both generously endowed with, to keep alive that sense of charity toward one another, to be sensitive with a purpose, and with vast energy and deep-laid ambitions, you two will go far—and by this I mean you will go far into the realms of human happiness. All else, by comparison, is nothing.

I am sorry, of course, that the fog has persisted. Perhaps Nature herself has conspired to give you privacy on your honeymoon!

But if I know you two, even persistent fog will not be lost and it will always take on a certain hallowed beauty and character which never existed before.

Our weather here has been dark, wet, lowering and commonly called *lousy*. But no! It has been like a great gray curtain dropped after a magnificent "third act." It has given us a remoteness—a chance to get our emotional breath. It has been gorgeous!

751

John McCoy.

Chapter XXIV

ANDREW WYETH'S FATHER

*" 'By God, are you the father of Andrew
Wyeth?!!' "*

This letter, written from the Wyeths' summer home, "Eight Bells," was sent to Henriette, who was spending the summer in Europe. She left her infant daughter, Ann Carol, in Chadds Ford and her son, nicknamed "Chucki" or "Little Peter," at Port Clyde with his grandparents.

N. C. Wyeth at Port Clyde, Maine, 1936.

The WYETHS

Eight Bells
Port Clyde, Maine
July 24, 1936. Friday

Dear Henriette,

How strange it all seems with you abroad, Pete in the southwest, Nat working in Pa., your baby with her nurse in C.F. and little Peter with us here! It is all quite upsetting to me and it's going to be difficult to lose myself in the atmosphere of Port Clyde.

The press has kept us apprehensive with the reports of conditions in Spain, yet I felt sure that you would *use* your good judgment and switch your tour. My main concern now is that the mess in Spain will not spread into France and catch you there. We'll count on your own perceptions and wisdom there too.

Chucki is continuing in health and behavior 100%. He seems to know how to adapt himself and so enjoyed his trip up with us immensely, the stopover at Stim's, etc. He spent yesterday afternoon with Andy on Raspberry Island, playing on the shore while A. made three watercolors. Last night Peter ate potatoes, peas and *fish* with gusto. After he finished I said, "Well, you enjoyed the fish, didn't you?" The scamp answered, "I ate it because I knew it was all I would get!" He followed this with a fine large doughnut.

Andy's trip up (with Carolyn) was quite an eventful one. The Homer watercolors at Worcester, Cambridge, Boston and Prouts Neck were almost all new ones and he went wild over them. I saw them too, later, except the Worcester Museum. They arrived at Prouts Neck the opening day, and Andy evidently made a hit with a Mr. [Lloyd] Goodrich (who is at work on the definitive life of Homer and is to reproduce every known drawing and painting) and also Homer's nephew, a Chas. Homer, who looked exactly like his famous uncle and had the same crusty characteristics, but evidently was attracted to Andy and Carolyn and told them many episodes and details of his "Uncle *Winnie*," as he called him.

It all is resulting in a lurid flow of watercolor over many sheets of paper, here in Port Clyde.

My pictures went well at Houghton Mifflin Co. and will be reproduced by that good offset process.

756

Andrew Wyeth's Father

594

*A new wing had been put on the schoolhouse studio in Chadds Ford,
and Henriette would make that her home on her return from Europe.*

Port Clyde, Maine
August 9, 1936

Dear Henriette,

If I let my reflections run away with me this moment I'd go *nuts*,
or else *you* would! Before me, on this brilliant and cool Sunday
morning, the harbor of Port Clyde spreads out like a great irregular
blue rug encrusted with myriads of flashing diamonds. The sky is
bright and dazzling, and as if to prove that light can be even more
intense, the flying gulls swoop and dart, flashing their pristine whiteness like silent explosions of incredible incandescense!

Behind me, powering out through the screened door, in clear but
wavering volume, the staccato and gutteral announcements by the
German Olympic Officials in Berlin! These are followed by tremendous and reverberating cheers by the vast multitude packed into that
concrete bowl! Remotely, but with acuteness, I feel your nearness to
this mammoth event, as though you were just around the corner, as
it were; I can almost see your diminutive figure moving up some
ancient street, walled in by tall, queer houses, arched gateways and
vistas of pointed towers and turrets. It is a singular medley of feeling
—but I must shunt it off and get down to what you are really interested to hear.

According to Nat, your furniture is all moved and your new living
quarters very near done. I have given orders to do nothing about the
interior painting of the big room until my return, which I take it
will be several weeks in advance of yours. Also nothing to the floor,
for they want $60 to sand it. It will take this much on account of its
bad condition, so my suggestion is to paint it, perhaps that nice color
Haskell has in his house—an olive green, as I recall it. I can find this
out and get the same stuff if you say so. In fact, in your next letter
tell me what color you want the trim to be in the large room. White?
Cream white? Gray white? Or what have you in mind? The painting *ought* to be done before you move in. The room is entirely re-
plastered (except the ceiling). I ordered this done and I shall pay the

extra cost. It will solve your wall problem and will look well, I think —the white plaster, I mean.

All are thriving here. The problem of too luxuriant appetites seems much more under control, although no one has lost any weight. Andy leads the field by a big margin in accomplishments and has done some superb watercolors and a few strong oils.

But with my mind inevitably reaching into the far horizons, East and West, in an effort to satisfy myself that all is well, I find myself quite out of contact with the kind of thing I love to contemplate here. It is gorgeous, but I feel quite unproductive.

595

Port Clyde, Maine
August 19, 1936

My dear Henriette,

Your magnificent letter to Ann, from Florence, just arrived this morning.

You can't imagine what a deep pleasure and satisfaction you have given us all, and as I read your vivid and sensitive account to the entire family (gathered about the long table at lunch), the tension grew to unbearable proportions. How much you are extracting from the experience! What a gorgeous experience to find all those old towers, the great buildings, and the art within them to exceed in beauty and appeal what you and we all had vaguely dreamed them to be. Your letters are the first I've ever read that haunt me with a compelling desire to see those wonderful things. Besides the very personal and felicitous way in which you express yourself, I am conscious that your unusual powers of discernment and your extraordinarily good taste in matters of artistic judgment weigh greatly, and make a pilgrimage to Florence irresistible.

Andy is bounding along in his painting and shows, still more, those indications of big work ahead. His rapidly maturing grasp of matter and mood, that goes to make up highly vitalized expression, is very astonishing to me. He will have some splendid watercolors to show you—lots of them.

The wind is whistling its way into every crack and crevice of the house. It is blowing directly from Europe and my imaginings of its passage from where you are to where I am are, in spirit, akin to that remarkable paragraph in *Eyeless in Gaza*, when Anthony lies sleepless and listens to the waves of cock-crowing coming across the remote reaches of France.

596

Eight Bells
Port Clyde, Maine
September 3, 1936

My dear Ann,

This is the second of a pair of good soaking rainstorms since you and John left. At the moment it seems to be brightening, and as I sit here at our bedroom windows, facing the water, the whole room has suddenly become luminous with silver light. A dozen gulls or more as spasmodically flying in circles, dipping down, then zooming up, and I know Andy must have just dumped some garbage at the shore.

Yes, there comes a Pilot Cracker box and a coffee can passing on the incoming tide. Soon they will ornament Miss [Mary] Fields' front yard!

The tides are exceptionally high just now of course (full moon), and the banks look hardly capable of holding the crest flood.

Andy and I have been spending a good deal of time on the Cannibal shore lately, both day and at nights. The effects have been especially moving due to the fantastic moonlit-cloud effects, which have strangely prevailed the last two nights. Great ghostly arms of clouds reaching directly up from the sea, the moon peering between the rifts in sharp golden splendor.

The other night I sat on a sizable ledge within a few yards of the advancing tide, watching the curling of white spume and green water as it played under the sprayed light of the moon. As the rollers broke on the outer reefs and burst into fanlike fountains of gray heavy spray, their force would send great drafts of dank sea air into my face. The smell of the ocean depths was almost overcoming; one could almost call it a stench, so avid and strong it was of kelp, rockweed, clams, fish, lobsters and a thousand unknown animals of the sea. It was a different, a more intense smell than I had ever experienced before. I felt that I were being allowed a more intimate sensing of the sea's odor, a very private one, like the heavy musk from its armpits, so to speak.

Lost in dreams and reflections, I had not noticed the advancement
of the tide. Suddenly, the convergence of two waves centered upon
my stronghold, and in an instant the boiling water rose up and over
it, submerging me to my heartline. It's the greatest physical surprise
I've experienced in a long time!

Gasp! was all I could do. Andy was down the shore somewhere,
and in the dark and the fickle light of the moon, I felt more alone
than ever before in my life. It was several minutes before I could
return to high and dry land, for a series of heavy waves continued,
which kept me marooned. And was I cold! but with no ill effects,
even though I could not change for an hour.

Andy and N. C. Wyeth on Cannibal shore.

We have also been up to the Glenmere church in the moonlight. It
is stupendous in spirit, that simple little edifice!

Work has begun to come better. Andy continues to improve and
has done some of his best work lately. We have plans for several
interesting painting expeditions—one of them to Teel's Island, for
a couple of days.

597

Nat was engaged to Caroline Pyle, the niece of Howard Pyle.

Eight Bells
Port Clyde, Maine
September 9, 1936

Dear Henriette,

We were all spellbound again last night by your letter from Switzerland, written the last day of August.

I haven't yet fully realized the *fact* of your adventure in Europe—it all seems so much a dream. Although your letters, for the moment, bring its reality into sharp focus, I quickly slip back into a nebulous state of mind regarding it. Last night, just before I fell asleep, my thoughts full of your letter and experiences, you merged back into my mother and grandmother amidst a fantastic pageantry of Swiss Alps, mountain peaks, little chalets, cattle and steep hayfields, and even village streets and the sound of thin-toned bells. All of these things seemed to be moving about you in a circle. I was on the outside and yet I witnessed the spectacle from the inside, and saw to my painful astonishment the transfiguration of you into my mother and thence into my grandmother. The horrifying part of it was that you were eliminated from life in this metaphysical process, and I awoke with a start and it was some time before I could allay the sharp agitation and believe again in the factual things.—This vivid hallucination was inspired, no doubt, upon your own expressed feeling that it was so right that you should be in Switzerland.

Everything here and everyone here is in good order and good spirits. Nat and Caroline are with us for a week, arriving last Saturday night. It is Caroline's first visit away from home and under the circumstances especially, she was quite homesick for the first two days, but has chirped up considerably and seems to be thoroughly enjoying the novel and contrasting experience.

The duPonts are going to place Nat in their mechanical engineering department (the developing of new machinery).

Of course it may mean Kansas, Tennessee or some such place—or it *might* mean near home.

It has taken me all this time to break through into a semblance to advanced effort. I think now, however, that something has happened and things promise better. Andy has been a great stimulation and is pounding along at a great rate doing some really fine stuff.

Unfortunately "8 Bells and Studio" is becoming too well known, and a more or less steady flow of visiting so-called artists are dropping in to and fro Monhegan. We've got to pass a law! Andy threatens to move over onto Blubber Butt.

598

Port Clyde, Maine
September 15, 1936

Dear Ann,

The next major objective, so to speak, is Henriette's return from abroad and her arrival in N.Y.

The short two weeks remaining seem no time at all in the face of all Andy and I are planning to do. Work is going on apace and I have one canvas that I do believe hits my high mark, if not better. Andy's Glenmere church is superb!!

I am terribly eager to hear the "Island Funeral" composition and am especially pleased that you have attempted it. Your creative urge, like mine, seems to be on the move again. Keep it going!

On Sunday Andy put his last hours on the Glenmere canvas. We wondered whether he should work on the picture while the services were going on, but finally he decided to risk it. After he returned I asked, "Did anyone object to your working in the churchyard?" "No," replied Andy, "I felt no concern about it, for, when I got up there, I asked the old bellringer, Mr. Barton, if he thought there'd be any objections to my painting during services, and he burst out with—'Cehrist, no! Work all you damn please!'—I had no compunctions after that."

599

The Wyeths' eldest grandson, Peter Wyeth Hurd, was spending the summer with them at Port Clyde.

Port Clyde, Maine
June 26, 1937

Dear Henriette,

As I hinted, the voyage up through the heart of the Green Mountains exceeded all expectations, which is saying a great deal. I hit upon a route which is exciting every mile of the way from Williamstown, Mass., to the intersection of the Maine boundary. The high spot, sentimentally, was the revisiting of the little and very remote village of Lowell, where I found things practically unchanged—even the cheese with the screen fly protector was in the same place in the old general store, over which my mother and I had a room. It astonished me to find how vividly I remembered many of the details —and that was 42 years ago!

I was unusually keyed up, emotionally, during the entire journey from Williamstown, Mass., to Newport on Lake Memphremagog. Besides the scenic beauty, which, *to me*, cannot be surpassed anywhere, I was swept into an intense and sustained mood made up of reflective memories and revived youthful ambitions. I was brought to realize again how strong the call and romance of "up country" flowed through my father (who rarely went there but who dreamed intense dreams of Vermont as the paradise of farm life) and so into our hearts and minds, including my mother, who never ceased talking about the "people of Vermont."

Whether or not this tendency to nostalgic meditation, which I think is the strongest sensation I have, is conducive to enduring artistic expression is a question. However, it is a personal experience I hallow as another might a religion.

The sweet smell of new-cut grass, the gleaming farmhouses as well as the weathered ones, the huge barns and the winding fences and stone walls. The sparkling clear and rushing mountain streams and the occasional glimpse of a sugar house peaking out of a maple orchard—and always the sound of cowbells and the poignant fragrance of birch and maple wood-smoke!

Peter is a splendid traveler and when tired of looking would retire to the back seat and carry on a long pantomime with his iron man and the iron ax. Sometimes he would nap.

He was quite appreciative of our overnight stop in a tiny mountain village called Pittsfield. We walked in the evening, holding conversations with the natives, followed up a brawling stream and spent some time in an ancient graveyard, reading the glorious Saxon names and studying the curious carvings and sculptures.

The "Hotel" was an experience in itself, but the beds were good and we slept well. My car was stored between two rows of feeding cows, and the delicious smell of sweet grass from the hay mows and from the clean Jersey cows themselves stayed in the car for hours.

All is OK here. Too many people, but the middle of the week some of them leave.

600

Henriette Hurd came up to join her son and parents at Port Clyde, bringing her young daughter, Ann Carol. The confusion of two grandchildren in the household led to a temporary disagreement and she returned to Chadds Ford. The visitors, Ed Seal and his father, Howard Seal and William Miller, were neighbors in Chadds Ford.

Port Clyde, Maine
August 12, 1937

Dear Henriette,

The day after your departure, the thickest fog I ever saw settled down upon us and remained for five days! It seemed to descend upon us as a kind of retribution for the poor management and the failure to adjust matters pertaining to your stay up here with the children. We have all been considerably agitated about it and still are, especially Ma and me. The murky hot fog completely discouraged the desire to write.

The very core of the whole problem is, of course, the fact that this place has taken on the increasingly tenuous atmosphere of a workshop; and now with Andy's added passion and zeal the spirit of the place seems definitely pegged.

Nevertheless, I feel a deep personal regret and disappointment that between all of us some plan could not have been devised to solve and save the situation, some projected willingness on the part of each member to offer help; but a spirit of selfishness, I fear, prevailed.

I have known for a long time, theoretically, that selfishness has its definite uses and is justified by those who can use it for noble accomplishment. In spite of this, when it is manifested by myself or by others, to the detriment and unhappiness of somebody else, it always distresses me.

The human family (as I have been fated to observe it in my period) continues to pile up one miserable failure upon another, carrying one rapidly on toward a state of complete disillusionment. My present personal feeling amounts to this: that no accomplishment, however fine and noble, is especially necessary, and is not worth the sacrificed happiness and discomfort of others. This leaves out, to be sure, the factor of inherent urge and burning ambition— but then we get right back to *selfishness* again.

One of the most doleful things imaginable happened last Sunday morning. The fog was as thick as a blanket; the house seemed actually dark in full daylight. We were all sleeping late when suddenly a loud rap at the door awakened Ann, who called down to me that Ed Seal was here! Well, you can imagine my state of mind! I hastily dressed, as the rest did too, and found not only Ed Seal but his father and Mr. [William] Miller (Paul's father) standing like so many disconsolate-looking barnyard hens in a group up by the barn. One could only see a few yards, so all they did was look at spots on the ground within sight, and talk in a spiritless and bedraggled manner about the heat, the fog and the bad food on the road, and each were bemoaning their "sour stummicks."

I led them into the house, offered them breakfast, which they refused with wry faces, and they continued to stare with unseeing eyes at spots on the floor.

We groped our way to the wharf but could not even see the boat at the mooring; we walked into my studio, which looked dismal indeed in the dim light, and after a little desultory talk of mileage and routes they pushed their way into the milky obscurity and departed.

What their impressions of Port Clyde were one can only guess. They were all pallid and heavy-eyed with not a glint of life or interest, and undoubtedly retreated from the famous Port Clyde wondering why in hell we ever came to such a forsaken place. Undoubtedly they never caught a glimpse of the Maine coast on all their trip because fog prevailed.

601

Andrew Wyeth was preparing for his first one-man show at the William Macbeth Gallery, 57th Street, New York City.

Chadds Ford, Pennsylvania
September 26, 1937

Dear Andy,

Well, I've had a great feast on your mounted watercolors! They look *magnificent,* and with no reservations whatsoever, they represent the *very best* watercolors I ever saw! This remark from your old dad may not mean much to you, but I believe what I say and I'm certain I'm right.

You are headed in the direction that should finally reach a pinnacle in American Art and so establish a landmark for all time. I am extremely happy over it all, and for the first time in my life I am beginning to feel secure in the belief that certain fundamentals which I have always stressed, to those who would listen and absorb, were sound and potential. You had the good sense to accept and apply them, and now you are proving to have the personality and talent to emblazon them. There are certain phases of your destiny which are largely in your own hands, and *these* it is my prayer that you control. First, your health; second, your sensible judgment regarding the arrangement and organization of your affairs, both material matters and those of the heart. I can say no more. I am very happy.

Rather than risking the express box of your pictures hanging around an express office over the weekend, I'm going to ship them Monday morning. I shall notify Macbeth to this effect.

I often try to visualize just where you are and what you are doing many times a day. How I wish I could have seen the surf with you on the back shore. Am so sorry however to hear that the fishermen have lost so much gear.

As I told you I would, I am placing a number, small and in ink, on the back of each watercolor, and will make a corresponding list, each with a title (I will *not* write a title on the picture but will confine this to my written list). These will serve to identify your different pictures at least. You can always change the titles if you wish. I'll make them simple and to definitely identify each one, if possible.

There's one thing you must prepare to do at Macbeth's when you next come face-to-face with your works. Sign them.

602

Henriette had joined her husband, Peter Hurd, at their ranch in San Patricio, New Mexico.

Robert Macbeth was the owner of the William Macbeth Gallery at 11 East 57th Street, New York City.

Andrew Wyeth's Father

Studio
Chadds Ford, Pennsylvania
October 16, 1937

Dear Henriette and All,

As Andy might roll in from Maine at any moment I'd better well get after this letter to you.—The distractions during the next few days will be many and I do want to get a birthday word to you.

You see, Andy's show opens Tuesday, and of course we are all going to make the trek up to N.Y. to see it.

The past month has sped by alarmingly fast, and yet when I think of you and Andy it seems a long long time indeed.

Affairs in the home have gone along splendidly and Ann Carol has been well nigh perfect, in both health and behavior. She's one of the sweetest and most appealing little kids I've ever known and we've hit up a real friendship. But it is her grandmother who is *queen,* and it delights me beyond words to see how much Ma is enjoying her renewed duties and the attachment Ann Carol has for her. We've just packed a box (mostly of sentiment) which I trust you will receive before Friday. A part of the contents may strike you as "coals to Newcastle," but the crop has been so fine (of apples) that I sent you a dozen or more specimens, which I hope you will pile up in a bowl and so occasionally recall the autumn hills of Chadds Ford.

Macbeth's unqualified enthusiasm over Andy's watercolors is another heartening thing for me to know. He's certainly giving Andy a great send off. You'll receive a catalogue. I note that this week's *New Yorker* notifies of the coming show.

I hope the exhibition will be reasonably successful and I have a feeling it will be.

603

Chadds Ford, Pennsylvania
October 22, 1937

Dear Henriette and Pete,

What better thing could I do Henriette, on our birthday anniversary, than to write you the phenomenal news that Andy's exhibition of twenty-three watercolors were completely sold out before the close of the second day!

And the type of purchasers!! Mrs. [C. V.] Whitney herself, for the Whitney Museum ("The Lobster Trap"), two art dealers in N.Y. and McClees of Phila. (bought for speculation), several collectors and other private buyers. The rush for them on Wednesday was just unbelievable—the word passed so quickly that here at last were some stirring watercolors. And it all leaves Macbeth wondering what to do about his best clients who hadn't as yet even seen the show.

Dr. [Robert] Harshe was there, picked out a group for a Chicago showing and was much stirred by a big egg-tempera portrait of a fisherman (with his wonderful house behind him). Took notes about it, especially about its freedom of handling and smashing effect and superb drawing.

Doll and Richards of Boston have booked a show for next year, also other galleries, which I forget for the moment—so much happened!

Macbeth is holding back a few in reserve (a selection of those not hung), preferring not to give a false impression that there are many more papers to be had. He is insisting that only the very first-grade paintings be shown and to continue this policy toward the right kind of a build-up in the future. I am much impressed by his ideas and feel that Andy is in splendid and honest hands. And he formally passes into his hands this next week, by contract. We will study it carefully.

The praise from the other dealers (all the galleries attended!) made even me blush.—"The first watercolorist since Homer."—"At last, a man who has the guts to present nature honestly, powerfully and beautifully."—"A much-needed spirit in a New York sick with unmeaningful, unsightly and unsalable moderns."—etc., etc.

And the critics—Jewell sent his understudy Tuesday morning; two hours later he came himself. All he told Macbeth was, "I guess I better handle this show myself." Royal Cortizzos, very rarely at shows these days, whispered to me as he left, "Don't tell the boy, but let him read it in the paper (*N.Y. Sun*) that I think it a corking show." And all the other papers came.

Sunday is when the press reviews appear and will send on any that are exciting (either one way or the other). (I wonder what the critics would have said had they seen the red stars on every picture the second day!)

Well, we were all in N.Y. with a dinner for 14 at the Algonquin that night. We all had a most wonderful time but wished so much you both were there.

Andy stayed up and returned last night. He went down to see Pete's landscape at Miss Sullivan's [Associated American Artists] and is raving about its beauty of color, great distance, luminous water, etc. Thinks it's a major American landscape, etc., etc.

Well, now all this does set me up! God dammit, Chadds Ford has started something—now let's finish it!

604

The Maine book N. C. Wyeth refers to is Trending into Maine.

Chadds Ford, Pennsylvania
November 11, 1937

Dear Henriette,

It's the end of a day, and a long one it's been, having started work very early this A.M.—and now it's dark.

[Letter continued]
November 12

I was stopped in my tracks by other duties, so will start again. Again it is dusk but raining a driving storm from the east. Andy and I have just returned from a foiled afternoon of outdoor painting. The wet came just as I primed my palette, so all I brought back are the cockle-burrs clinging to my stockings—and how they itch!

The days are full to overflowing and work is exciting. The string of ten or twelve gesso panels for Ginn & Company and for the Maine book done since you left are, I firmly believe, my tops in illustrative painting. It has been intense work and I'm driving myself to the limit —but I'm thriving on it.

Andy is well into a period of searching study, drawing at present, but preparing in addition to undertake some portrait study in egg tempera. It is gratifying to me to see him embrace the task of learning more about construction, with almost feverish desire. The wild

N.Y. experience seems to be well behind him. I feel very proud of this trait in him.

The contract from Macbeth has arrived. It seems highly just and even considerate, nevertheless we intend going over the matter with a legal mind before signing up.

Andy doesn't know yet just how many of his watercolors were sold —between 25 and 30, we believe.

You may have heard that Carolyn took the first award with "The Jones House." It's a splendid thing and looks handsomely in the show. I didn't realize how advanced and mature the little canvas was until, splendidly framed, it was hung amongst others.

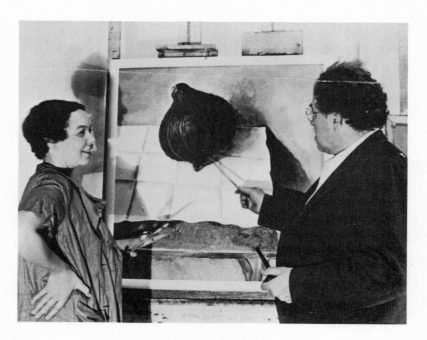

Carolyn with her father.

The award came at a most fortunate time, for Carolyn is in better health and state of mind than ever she was, and is decidedly on the up and up in her painting. Even riding is very much in second place, although her care and watchfulness of Clavelle is gratifying.

Nat's official report from duPont Company is so good they want him permanently in the industrial engineering to be in Deepwater another year anyway. Ann's string concerto is on the rehearsal list of Stoky's [Leopold Stokowski], so that's promising anyway.

605

Cat Island lies off Georgetown, South Carolina.

Chadds Ford, Pennsylvania
December 1, 1937. Wednesday

Dear Henriette,

It seems so long since I've seen you that every once in awhile an apprehensive feeling comes into my mind that I may never see you again. Of course this sounds either sentimental or foolish, I know, but so much has happened in the past year, so many subtle changes are taking place—in short, time is constantly accelerating, and with it, personal, family, and world transitions are shifting so rapidly! It all becomes very disconcerting.

I have been working very steadily and with considerable intensity. It has been mostly illustration, as you know, but there is the satisfaction that it has reached a higher level of workmanship and feeling. Occasionally I have plunged into my own painting, but there's little time for that just now.

Andy is at present down at Cat Island. He left the Friday after Thanksgiving and will be there two weeks. We've not heard from him, of course, but undoubtedly he's enjoying it thoroughly. It has been hard for him to settle down after the N.Y. excitement, but he has done some very strong drawings from life, showing a definite gain in his draughtmanship and sense of form.

However, he weathered the exhibition experience perfectly. His reactions seem to me to be very sound. I've succeeded, I think, in keeping well out of his natural fermentations following the show, and I feel that he has already made a happy landing in what was truly a solo flight.

I got what was really my first taste of a certain experience yesterday, which I pray may be repeated increasingly. I went to N.Y. on business and incidentally was introduced to a fairly young and brilliant color-engraver. I was to confer with him on some work he's to do on the Ginn plates. The meeting was casual, until the end of the conference he showed me a watercolor he had done, in the Cats-kills, which was to be reproduced as a Xmas gift print. It was an unusually interesting paper and I asked him if he attended the water-color shows in N.Y. "Yes," he said, "all of them." Did he see an exhibition at Macbeth's by one Andrew Wyeth, I remarked. "By God, are you the father of Andrew Wyeth?!!"—At last he knew who I was, and I had difficulty in shaking loose from him!

I might say right here that I saw the show at the Whitney Gal-leries. It is distinctly an exhibition of paintings that are superficial, political, vaporous in mood, with the vacillating mood of a period which seems to me too ephemeral to admire. This work has no place whatsoever in the future. There is no faith and no love in the spirit behind the work. There is plenty of the *excitement* of propaganda, but no warmth, no glow to indicate, or even hint, that there is any depth of spirit. Everything seems to spring from reason and cal-culation, and so obvious as to inspire nothing but derision.

One feature which appealed to me was the definite advance in the richness and substance of color. Disagreeable color mostly, not leav-ing the opportunity for a stinging dissonance; but nevertheless a certain built-up throbbing quality which shows that brilliant color can be arrived at in oil, plus weight and body.

606

Chadds Ford, Pennsylvania
May 18, 1938

My dear Andy,

Your letter, received this morning, has stirred me very deeply be-cause I know, so acutely, just what you are passing through. My thoughts have been with you constantly all day; I have felt at once very sympathetic—and very proud of your reactions and your will-ingness to write me about them.

Feel triumphant, rather than ashamed of your present experience. Anyone as sensitive as you are is bound to run into just such a men-tal and emotional upset sooner or later. The conditions being right, it's bound to come. It would be quite a disconcerting worry to me if it didn't.

Andrew Wyeth's Father

Intense nostalgia constitutes a very definite form of growing pains and is the truest barometer in the world of your spiritual and emotional potentialities. You have always had these qualities in abundance, of course, but as one swings into maturer years the reactions are more intense, more glorious—and more difficult.

Nostalgia is no joke, but I am counting on you to ride it out. Throw yourself into work of some kind, even if manual labor.

Don't worry for one instant about the ultimate recovery of your spirit and directed energy in Port Clyde—it's just around the corner and will crack down on you with surprising and relieving swiftness! As you know, if you were to follow an impulse to come home, the reaction would again be an unhappy one. Just think, it's only 20 days and Ma will be coming up, and the rest of the folks.

Your feelings toward Chadds Ford, under the circumstances, are just as they should be. This experience may be just the one that will crash through the passing phase of dulled interest caused mainly by great familiarity. This happens occasionally to every artist who ever lived. Thoreau was one of the rare exceptions who consistently hit through the commonplaces of familiar scenes and lifted them into extraordinary experiences—emotional and intellectual. So, seemingly, did Rembrandt.

But in spite of what you say, Maine has opened certain secret pages to you which are *vital,* and you will never permanently lose, or forsake, her magic appeal. The work you have already done is wrought with too deep an understanding to ever be called superficial, and it will continue to grow and expand. Your present shadowed feelings have obscured this for the time.

Oh! if only more American painters had the capacity to suffer the pangs you write of, how much less we would have to be bored with the work of the "journeyman" type of "sketchist" who blithely travels from place to place, annually returning to market with a bundle of trifles, brilliantly executed perhaps, but as bloodless as so many empty paper bags!

I hope all this hasn't bored you too much. However, take the best care of yourself—watch your eating.

There is no one I'm counting on more than you. Give no thought to money-making, you can always do that.

The WYETHS

607

Ann McCoy was waiting for the birth of her first child in Chadds Ford.

Eight Bells
Port Clyde, Maine
August 11, 1938. Thursday, 2:00 P.M.

My dear Ann,

It is a dark, gray, and wet day.—A driving easterly rain slants across the window, etching all beyond it into fine right and left lines like delicate scratching across a glass negative. The steady wind quietly moans and whistles about the little house, and the pine logs on the hearth crackle and blaze fitfully.

The home is very quiet. Ma is reading, lying prone on the couch. Alice is moving about the kitchen completing her after-lunch duties. Carolyn is napping. Peter is looking at books and Andy is down in his studio at work on his "Walter" panel.

I am at the round table facing Homer's "Eight Bells," but my gaze passes to the left out of the window and up toward the barn. I have a fragmentary glimpse of the lilac bush, two of the weathered apple trees, a bit of stone wall and the tangle of spruces beyond—also a patch of the deep yellowed grass trembles and undulates in the wind.

This is, to all outward appearances, an extremely modest and commonplace vista, confined as it is by the four sides of the window frame and cut into light exact panels by the window sashes; it is a scene that might be almost anywhere on earth. It is stripped of any glamour whatsoever; not a detail is outstanding or sensational; in fact, it is a glomeration *steeped* in utter commonplaceness and seems doomed to eternal oblivion in its own estimation, or in the memories of anyone or anything else. But a resurgent gust of wind sweeps across the tiny area! The lilac leaves shudder and fold themselves back into broken heart shapes of new-wet luster, then frantically restoring themselves into position to be swept again and again into bright-varnished and twisted shapes. The tawny patch of long grass bends and leans into agitated motion, and the gray thin limbs of the spruce trees sway up and down in a ghostly slow dance. The deep gloom of the forest beyond remains still, like darkness.

774

Andrew Wyeth's Father

My imagination is suddenly whipped into an almost exalted appreciation of the magnificence of the little isolated and unrelated scene before me, and I am astounded at its vast beauty and its sublime importance, and am made to realize in one poignant spasm, that before my eyes exists the profoundest beauty, the greatest glamour and magnificence possible for human sight and spiritual pleasure. The limitless ocean itself, the mountains and valleys of the *world* are of no greater importance in appearance or significance.

In this flicker of wet leaves and waving grass lies the touchstone which connotes and inflames my love of life, which is primarily the love of my family, the air we breathe together, the winds we face and the warm sun we absorb into our bodies. All else seems relatively dull and of not much importance.

The spirit of the world, even from our own familiar townsmen, is too selfish, too evil, and too ignorant to be anything more than an obstruction to that vast nostalgic, prayerful appreciation of primal simplicity and the cosmic sense of things.

This is the strangest "coming to Port Clyde" I ever experienced. There is no reason to touch upon the reasons, for well you can imagine them. Needless to say, it is your own situation back there in Chadds Ford that dominates the moody color of my feelings. Perhaps this foolish illness of mine makes me feel this way.

I am still convalescing. I'm doing well, but this insidious "bug" is stubborn. It was a pneumonia germ and totally unrelated to a cold picked up from exposure, but picked up because perhaps my resistance wasn't what it should have been at the time.

I *did* feel rotten the night I telephoned you from Winsor, Vt. I guess I had quite a temperature, for the next morning, until I checked up on my hotel bill, I wasn't sure that I phoned you at all.

We had run into a thunder and lightning twister that evening, right in the mountains, and a whole pine tree just about the size of the main wing of "Eight Bells" was lifted and blew right over the car and smacked into the forest with a horrific roar. Electric wires were torn helter-skelter, and sparks were spluttering in half a dozen places. A bus, right ahead of us, was caught in fallen timber, so we waited an hour when swarms of woodsmen and linesmen swept in there and, by the aid of searchlights, plied their double-edged axes and had us out and on our way in a short time. But I think the excitement didn't help my fever.

The WYETHS

I've been getting a great reaction from Andy's work, of course. His watercolors are richer and more brilliant than last year. They lack, at the present stage, a certain variety of motive, but the boy is throwing himself so heart and soul into tempera panels of intense motivations that he needs his watercolor less. But, make no mistake, he has made a dozen *masterpieces,* not speaking of dozens of others which may be just as good. *I* don't know.

I do want to mention your last letter. One, by the way, which I wish dozens of people could read. Fresh, vigorous, hopeful and so completely stimulating. No one but you could have written it, and I'm looking forward to some of your great soundness and fundamental strength and classic beauty (with which you abound) showing up in future compositions. You've got *lots* of time and your spirit has never ceased to build and build. It just can't stop.

608

Andrew Wyeth was working on a tempera painting. The tempera colors he used were in powder form and sometimes gritty. His close friend, Walter Anderson, helped grind the colors smooth.

Off Port Clyde, Maine
August 17, 1938

On Little Caldwells
facing south and
overlooking the
beach and clamshells
where we've all picnic'd.

Dear Ann,

I am ensconced in a deck chair, which I was professionally advised to take along if I insisted on a day with Andy on the island. I'm still not supposed to do much moving around so that all energy will be used to throw off this cough and infection. But I'm definitely getting better, although the period when I can actually work is still some time off. Isn't it all fantastically silly?

It's a hazy but sunny day, and from where I'm sitting the water is a beautiful modified blue, almost a Delft blue. The breeze has kept the surface of the sea in a brilliantly twinkling state since morning. Andy has worked steadily on his tempera painting and all I have to do is turn my head to the right to see him and his panel silhouetted against the sky. Walter, his man Friday, is hunched up beside him mixing color, preparing egg, and whatnot.

This noon Walter visited the surrounding traps and brought in 14 lobsters, cooked them, besides baking potatoes, etc., and we had the finest feast of sweet lobster meat I ever expect to have! We had milk, chicken, cake, and lettuce sandwiches too, but small lobsters and lettuce sandwiches were my fare!

Just now I can hear the dim blast of the foghorn out on Monhegan. The horizon is very hazy and I wouldn't be surprised to see it creep in on us before we start for Eight Bells. (I don't know how long Andy will work.)

609

Little Caldwells, off Port Clyde, Maine
August 17, 1938. Tuesday, 2:30 P.M.

My dear Henriette,

The bulwark of my stay here this summer will be Andy's accomplishments. His watercolors have so definitely advanced into an impressive maturity. They rely less and less upon dramatic subjects, or even pictorial attraction, but are becoming so purely watercolor in beauty of color, design, and idiom. Some that he has done in the last few days are acutely abstract; their impact upon anyone whose sensitiveness lies beyond romance and drama makes it hard to hold back tears. What magical power that boy has! I am at once stimulated beyond words to new, purer effort, and plunged into black despair.

610

Port Clyde, Maine
August 19, 1938

Our dear Little Annie Roonie,

What with the glorious news and all the attendant excitement, coupled with the terrific feeling of frustrated plans—that we cannot rush to see you, has left Ma and me in a cockeyed state of mind, to say the least. It all seems so strange and queer that I feel as though I were wandering around in a trance, or even behind prison bars. And I know that Ma feels likewise, if not worse.

777

The WYETHS

She has gone over, a thousand times! just how you must be feeling, translating into your experiences all her own (which were rich indeed). Ma's vividness of mental projection has left me with the conviction that, after all, we *have* been with you, and *have* seen the baby, have talked with you and John and all. I had fragmentary dreams all night, of you and your baby, of you *as* a baby, of Ma as you, and every conceivable combination; and when I awakened into full consciousness early this morning I could not believe, for a moment, that I could possibly be in Port Clyde. It has all left me bewildered.

John's telegram arrived about 10:30 yesterday. I hope that you received ours sent early in the afternoon, and that flowers for yourself and Jean Denys arrived in due season.

Incidentally, I am very much moved and gratified beyond words over the selection of the name. To know that the feeling and tradition prevailed in your own heart, that at last my greatly revered grandfather has been honored, and all accomplished without discussion or outside pressure, but simply that *you* had remembered and *cared* to perpetuate his name. If we, as a family, can claim that important heritages have come down to us, to our benefit and help, certain it is that an important spirit and urge came from my grandfather Zirngiebel. His sense of the sublimity of life, his worship of the beautiful through the things that grow, was a living flame, and I do believe that some strain of it has come to us.

It makes it completely happy and satisfying to know too that the name signifies in a dual capacity and that the baby carries his father's and grandfather's name too. There is no name on earth better than John.

Well, we are waiting for details, rather impatiently, although we realize how full John's time is and how his energy is flowing out in other and more important channels.

Mr. & Mrs. [Robert] Macbeth and Mr. & Mrs. [Charles] Homer (Mr. Homer is Winslow's nephew) rolled in yesterday long enough to spend a couple of hours in Andy's studio and stop here for drinks. Macbeth is greatly impressed with Andy's new work and sees in it an unexpected advance and maturity. Bought eight of them for himself (which he offered Andy immediate payment for if he wanted it). This selection was to assure his gallery of a group to have on hand, also it was a shrewd business move on his part, and also a splendid way to show a practical and supporting interest in Andy. People are dropping in more and more, asking to see Andy's work, and in some cases are making reservations to be bought from Macbeth later. All this is exciting to me in that it shows how definitely Andy's reputation is percolating amongst a sizable and widespread public.

Andy, Charles Homer and Robert MacBeth.

779

611

Nat and Caroline were married January 16, 1937, and were living in New Castle, Delaware. Nat was employed in the engineering department of the duPont Company.

Eight Bells
Port Clyde, Maine
August 23, 1938

Dear Nat and Caroline,

Doubtlessly you have wondered why some of us haven't written. Certainly the splendid letters received from both of you rated quick and enthusiastic replies; but you must believe that with all that has been taking place of late—we, up here, have been considerably bewildered, to say the least.

As grand and exhilarating as the arrival of "Jean Denys" is, both Ma and I have felt so frustrated that we could not have hurried back to Wilmington when the warming news came, that it has been rather depressing. We feel thoroughly disgusted with ourselves that illness should have stepped in at such a critical time. Ma awakes in the night and the little room becomes crowded with profanity (mixed with coughing), and it takes an hour of the most diplomatic argument and reasoning to lull her back to normal. Of course, I catch hell for exploiting the "bug." But today looks brighter, for Ma is up for the first time without fever nor ache nor pain.

There is more or less bustle down on the dock at the moment, while Andy makes preparations for a day at *Little Caldwells* to continue work on his ambitious tempera panel. His painting paraphernalia is already aboard, and I see him now passing baskets and thermos bottles to supply the day's need of food. Walter Anderson is with him, of course, also Peter, who has spent the day on the island several times and seems to enjoy it.

We so often talk over, Nat, the new era of your work! We get enormous pleasure in this and feel very, very proud of you. We realize the amount of work and the hazards that lie ahead of anyone in any ambitious undertaking, but we are confidently betting that your star is in the ascent. Remember, Nat, that depressions and discouragement are a definite waste of energy, especially if that discouragement is kept concealed. Blow up occasionally, but don't fret or become self-pitying. Self-pity and whining is the surest road to unhappiness and general failure. You've got everything ahead of you. Watch your health, keep your balance and poise in all domestic affairs, and success, or at least *advancement* (which is so much superior to success), is certain to be yours.

612

Mr. and Mrs. Wyeth, with Andy, visited Marjorie Kinnan Rawlings and the area surrounding her Florida home to gather material for the illustration of Mrs. Rawling's book, The Yearling.

Ocala, Florida
February 5, 1939

Dear Ann,

This is Sunday morning and I'm sitting before the east window of our room. We are on the fifth floor of this modern hotel, which gives me quite a prospect of the town and the wide rim of the out-laying wilderness called "the scrub."

The town itself is quite thrifty looking—a clean, swept-up appearance, which I must say is a relief from the usual dowdy southern towns we have been through. But it is horribly characterless and it could be a new town in the middle west as well as in Florida, except that one is struck by the tropic appearance of the shade trees and gardens.

Ma is by the north window reading a fascinating article on *home-cooking* in the *Pictorial Review*, and with her smacking of lips, her "Ohs and Ahs," and her excerpt readings to me, it's hard to get this letter going.

Andy is in the next room doing a watercolor, something based on notes he made yesterday, I think. You see, while I was trekking through "the Scrub" with my bear-hunter guide yesterday and day before, Ma and Andy took a trip to the Gulf-of-Mexico side of Florida, thinking it might be of special interest, but it wasn't. However, they did stop on the way and Andy made two corking water-colors of inland scenes.

The trip down was *not* interesting and was pretty much of a chore. We may, if it can be done, get onto a boat at Miami (on our return from Key West) and sail to Charleston; this would eliminate a good chunk of boredom on the way back. Food has been undistinguished except for the fruit, which is delicious. No one, fortunately, is over-eating, which is pleasant to relate. "Marge," as everyone around here calls Mrs. Rawlings, is not especially interesting nor prepossessing in appearance. She's a bit younger than we expected, and although weather-beaten and tough-fibered looking, she looks not very happy, pretty nervous and at loose ends. It may be it is because she's divorced. But she has given heartily of her time and interest and has put me in contact with just the types of backwoods people I wanted to see, and the experience has been quite thrilling. I have saved the account of the excursion into the scrub for Henriette's letter, so supplement this one with hers.

Yesterday evening Leonard, the guide, a youngish chap that Danny Boone would have surely selected as a buddy, took me about forty miles into the wilderness to see some captive bears (belonging to Frank Buck, a young fellow was in charge), so I saw all I needed to help me in the picturization of old Slewfoot. They all know *The Yearling* and are extremely fond of it, and so many places and things are named after the features in the book. So in this case they had "Old Slewfoot" in captivity. He's blind and about 24 years old, but is large, weighing about 400 lbs., and according to the keeper, "as gentle as a kitten." He is kept in a circular corral about 30 yards across and very high, with the few tall yellow pines standing in the enclosure covered part way up with sheet zinc. This was to prevent a large panther, who occupied the same space, from climbing the trees and making a desperate leap to freedom.

We went to the door of the corral, scratched the bear's head through the wire, then I was invited to come inside to take my photographs. As I walked in, assured in the meantime that the panther was shut in his house cage with the sliding door, the huge old bear caught the scent of a stranger and by means of his keen smell followed directly after me. Well, it may have been perfectly safe and all that, but it was a queer feeling, and the keeper must have felt a little dubious about the bear's action because he headed him off gently with a small stick tapping him on the snout. In the meantime I was quickly snapping some photos. Suddenly old Slewfoot made the quickest pass with that great paw of his you can imagine, and caught the top of the keeper's leather riding-boot and ripped it to his instep, belching a growl and showing his teeth with all the approved fixings. Leonard was in there too and grinned broadly to see me step slowly but steadily toward the door—but I noticed he followed me. The young keeper's nerve was fine though, for he cracked down on the bear's nose with his stick and in five minutes had him sitting dog fashion and scratching his head with his fingers.

As if this weren't enough excitement for the time—we stood by the closed door, discussing the incident, when we were astonished to observe the panther walk out from behind some scrub growth at the other side of the corral! He'd been lying there all the time! The glances that passed between my bear hunter and the keeper were significant enough. In fact, the keeper asked me not to mention the incident to anyone in Ocala or Silver Springs as he might lose his job.

This panther is native and is very large, almost as large as a Great Dane.

Night before last, standing in a swamp with a vast tangle of Bay trees, live oaks, pines, palmettos and heavy vines, all swaying in the night breeze and writhing with the ragged festoons of Spanish moss —and the full moonlight pouring through it all, we listened to the distant shriek, as from a frightened woman, of a panther. It chilled my blood for an instant. Leonard said I was lucky to hear it, he hadn't heard one in years. It seems that they rarely make a noise of any kind.

I've seen a number of "gators" slither into the murky streams and have watched the scuttling of fox squirrels, handsome black animals, have seen a number of deer and caught the glimpse of a bear rolling his way through the scrub.

I feel ready to tackle *The Yearling* in pictures and wish I were home and at it now.

But we go to Key West, leaving Monday morning. I can't tell just what day will arrive back.

613

Ocala, Florida
February 5, 1939

Dear Henriette,

I feel quite thoroughly impregnated with mood and character of the wilderness surrounding this nondescript but rather clean little town. And, let me tell you, it *is* a wilderness. I've been forty to fifty

miles into the scrub country, an invariable flat terrain of scrub pal-
metto, black jack (small gnarled oaks) and tall gaunt yellow pine.
These unending spaces are broken occasionally by "bays," so-called,
groves of live oaks, cabbage palmettos and some palms. And as a rare
stream or swampland occurred, the forestations would thicken into
fantastic jungles of all kinds of tangle, including cypress, magnolia,
many species of bay trees, and great thick vine-like growths, all
festooned with the inevitable Spanish moss. In the dry portions which
comprise three-quarters of it—the white sand gleamed through the
scrub and a million lizards darted like silver shadows in all directions, and with almost equal fleetness small deer bounded in gray
ghostly streaks and in an instant disappeared. Once we saw, at a
distance, a lumbering rolling bear, head down his rounding back,
lurching amid the scrub like some mammoth turtle. And he too
miraculously disappeared. No shooting was done, as we were over
the line and in the Government Game sanctuary.

Miles apart we would come upon "*clearings*" or "*islands*," as they
are called here (*hammocks* is another name) upon which would
stand the remains of an early settler's log house and farm buildings,
with the frayed skeletons of a few fences surrounding it all. One of
these was "Baxter Island," and it was quite an emotional experience
to sit on the old broken porch and dream over Ma and Penny
Baxter and Jody. As one deer flitted through the outer rim of the
farm it could be no other than Flag, of course.

Long, sandy trails, gleaming and treacherous, crisscross this wild
land, so I was able to see a lot of it from an expertly driven motor,
an old, old contraption, but about as tough and fibrous as the bear
hunter who drove it—one Leonard Fiddio (pronounced Fiddy).
This chap, about 38 years old, comes closest to the early Boone-period
type I ever saw. His lingo is stirringly early American and his entire
point of view, that of the hunter and trapper. We wound up at his
home, thirty miles from any other habitation, and there, in the most
primitive but cleanest cabin you ever saw, were his old wrinkled
mother of 84 years, a young, pleasant Irish wife, and a handsome
flaxen-haired little daughter of five. As we approached the cabin,
there, in unbelievable storybook fashion, nailed on the west end of
the log house, was a 9-foot bearskin, a number of fox squirrel skins,
and a "gator" hide.

It was a hot day, and the breeze that swept through the covered, open-porchlike connection between the two cabins where we sat and chatted was welcome indeed.

The one living room, with its clay fireplace built over a mesh of cypress sticks, was sparsely furnished with a table in the center, the top of which was made of one thin section of a cypress log beautifully polished with age and use and all its two or three hundred year-rings as clear as the veins in marble. One wall was devoted to shotguns and rifles, and amongst them was an early Winchester, which I bought for five dollars. Leonard had repaired it years ago for an old neighbor of his, but he died, so he let me have it. A huge "gator" skull was on a special shelf. "Yiso," says Leonard, " I kept that skell, cause it's the fust gater Mindy and I see when we was frashe married."

Well, I could go on and on, and if you're interested you can read my letter to Ann which goes into other details.

Except for the oasis of Charleston, the trip down was a dreary affair of endless miles of scrub land and miserable habitations—without a spark, hardly, of picturesque interest. Food is good enough but utterly nondescript, but we *are* enjoying the oranges and grapefruit. No one is putting on weight!

The orange groves fascinate Ma, and Andy finds some relief in an occasional weird-looking stream. He has one paper of this subject which is very telling and beautiful.

We have dinner with "Marge Rawlins," as they call her here, tonight, and tomorrow we start for Key West—some 600 miles.

614

Chadds Ford, Pennsylvania
February 19, 1939

[To Robert Macbeth]
Dear Bob,

I've been cogitating a letter to you for some time, regarding certain phases of Andy's development.

Naturally I have been fairly sensitive to every move he has made from the beginning, and although I have been careful at all times not to clutter his mind with irrelevant and complicated argument and theory, there are fundamental principles which have been stressed and which so far have proved their value.

The WYETHS

The habit of self-conscious picture-building is one phase I have consciously in my teaching tried to avoid. From the time he started regular study in the studio at the age of 13, I have endeavored to make every phase of academic procedure exciting: from his first studies in perspective, the application of it to cubes, spheres and pyramids, through cast-drawing and still-life painting, and finally figure study and landscape. All this was strictly *objective* teaching—purely representational study, free as possible of mannerisms or stunts. The exciting memories of this succession of his studies are very much alive in my mind, and I am especially happy to say that he can still turn to a pure and simple academic problem with great intrinsic and sustained enthusiasm. This faculty, if kept alive, will, for all his life, be the source of progressive artistic development and unfolding.

From this long training and contact with factual things, he has not only learned to draw them as they *are,* but has learned to love them for their spiritual values. The factual knowledge of the shape and proportion of a jug has unlocked a fascination for that object, which reveals to him the shape of its insides as well as the phenomena of its hollowness, its weight, its pressure on the ground, its smell, its displacement of air.

To my mind the aliveness of all our senses at every moment will produce virile expression in art. So you see the training, as he received it, was exciting. The shift from Andy's academic period into creative painting was hardly a shift at all; it was a natural and almost imperceptible transition.

No one knows more precisely than I do that Andy has only scratched the surface and great problems lie before him. He knows that too, down to the bottom of his feet!

But here is what I want to get at.

You have been marvelous in the way you have handled the boy. I cannot imagine anyone else who could do the job better, but there is one matter which you might possibly lose sight of. You must be patient and trust him as still very much the student in his work, and accept what he radiates on paper or panel as a succession of irregular and varied phases of his unfolding. Candidly select from his production what is worthy and marketable, but do not discourage any specialized endeavors (last summer's work, for example) which as a group fall short of being well-motivated compositions but which *do*

786

embrace an infinitely important sequence of sustained and specialized study, which he hungered for at the time.

Andy eats, dreams and sleeps with a deep faith that watercolor has infinite possibilities of power and beauty which have never been touched. He has an unmovable right to this belief, and his search to prove this truth will be, of course, a long, arduous one. The road he travels will doubtlessly be cluttered with variable results.

Andy's roots are in the ground. I feel exceptionally secure in his emotional potentiality—the quality which gives art its only valid reason to exist.

As long as I live or just as long as my influence lasts, I will encourage anything the boy wants to do, in any way he wants to do it, providing it promises to forge a link toward greater knowledge and greater power.

His spirit runs too high to miss doing something every once in awhile in the nature of a fulfillment of a good picture, but these must come like words underscored in a letter, only occasionally.

615

Chadds Ford, Pennsylvania
February 25, 1939

Dear Bob,

My words about Andy's work and development, which I sent you the other day, were not intended as criticism at all, but in the nature of a suggestive discussion which might possibly prove of use as time goes by. Your personal attitude toward his work has been exceedingly sensitive and appreciative.

I write these thoughts of mine to you principally because you are about the only one I know who has a large, sympathetic and intelligent viewpoint and a grasp of what is potential in American painting. Also, because you have for us here in Chadds Ford become a key man, as it were, both in a practical and spiritual sense.

I know very well the danger that always lies before me of being too zealous, perhaps, in considering and expressing my ideas regarding procedure of my children's professional adventures. After all these years of active and intense relationship with them, it is not easy, I suppose, to taper off, so to speak, and fade to a discreet and serene silence. Perhaps I never can.

The WYETHS

I suppose the reason I stressed the need of Andy's occasional adventures into fragmentary study phases of his painting was because of the number of comments that have been made about the lack of motivation of numbers of his past year's work. Perhaps I have magnified the worrying effect it seemed to have upon him. I am so eager to see him continue to unfold, as he has in the past, with that natural but inevitable expansion commensurate with accumulated knowledge and enlarging sensibility—to feel no undue pressure of what is expected of him, but only the pressure of the natural urge for expression.

A great artist once said, "The style is the soul." This is true, but the *emotional content* is the real measure of "style" after all, and I look to see this content increase and manifest itself only in the degree that knowledge is accumulated for knowledge sake.

Chapter XXV

RETREATING DREAMS
AND HOPES

"All sense of serenity and security has crumbled away, and all I can do, when I think about it all, is to gawk stupidly at the retreating pageant of my dreams and hopes."

Clyde Stanley was a lobsterman from Port Clyde and part-time care-taker of "Eight Bells." Bill Belano from Staten Island, New York, was a young friend of Andy's.

Port Clyde, Maine
June 28, 1939. Wednesday, 6:45 A.M.

My dear Ann,

The distractions of our trip up here and the hours since our arrival have made the time evaporate like mist in the morning sun.

It was one of those scintillating and sparkling blue afternoons when we arrived, and as we rolled noiselessly out onto the soft grass-covered driveway, above the little house, the great expanse of water seemed bluer and purer than I had ever seen it before. The fresh-painted boats floated at their moorings like luminous white paper shells lightly dropped on a sheet of indigo glass. Gulls flashed and gleamed in the sky, swooping in long curves, then suddenly swallowed behind the black barrier of pointed firs.

Carolyn had the house in good order, but of course Ma could not enjoy herself if she did not find a hundred things to do, if it were only to push a chair two inches this way and that lamp slightly to the left, and give a rug a twitch. Then there was all the counting to do! But that's all to the good. Ma and I may always be carelessly free, but I can always count on her to see that things are kept and in good order.

Since our arrival we've heard so much of the great run of pollock off little Green Island, which lies between Metinic and Haddock Ledge.

Yesterday, we left at four in the morning. Clyde, Walter Anderson, Bill Belano, Andy and I. We were well on the fishing grounds as the sun lifted from the sea, and a marvelous sunrise it was.

The water was smooth and the great, oily rollers of the deep-sea swell passed silently under our boat, and we rose and fell in perfect rhythm as though resting upon the heaving chest of Nature herself.

The WYETHS

The sky was cluttered with flying white fragments—thousands of gulls, for all the world like torn scraps of paper spasmodically blown through the air. Occasionally a group of these would fall to one point on the smooth water, frantically diving and fluttering and suddenly rising again, each with a herring snatched from a school driven too close to the surface by the marauding pollock underneath.

We idled the boat's motor to a slow walking pace and dragged astern our trolling lines baited only with a large flat-leaded hook and a piece of scarlet woolen rag tied on it for bait. The excitement began at once, for some one of us five would always be in frantic action with a fourteen- to eighteen-pound pollock fast to our lines. A swirl in the water, sometimes the flash of the fish itself, and the tussle would begin! Darting right and to left, up and then down, the great silver fish would be hauled gradually but steadily toward the boat. A heave and he would be swung aboard—deep blue-silver to black on the back, a flashing white belly, a streamline body, a killer's head and jaws, large luminous eyes alive and burning, sunk to the degradation of an ordinary fish box upon a gasoline power boat! What excitement, but what a pity!

We brought back 300 weight of almost exact uniform size. Sold them at the cold storage except what we kept for our own use. Last night we had pollock steaks! As delicious as swordfish with an added flavor of clean salt water and rockweed hard to describe.

617

Port Clyde, Maine
July 28, 1939

Dear Nat and Caroline,

I feel very guilty for not writing long before this, but time has sped by unmercifully.

Through the long winding panorama of our journey in Vermont, I look back upon our stay with you as something very far off, yet as clear and defined as crystal. It was a most pleasant experience and one which is more important to both of us than you might imagine. I will not attempt, in a brief letter like this, to explain it except to say that personally I feel as though I caught a vivid glimpse of both of you in a transition state, so to speak, on your way toward inevitable advancement, greater fullness of living, a permanent home, and finally, security—or as near security as we humans are allowed. The glimpse, indelibly impressed on my mind's eye, is not unlike a single film cut from a moving sequence showing the hero and heroine in the motion of going forward but with strangely projected arms and legs caught in arrested motion.

Nat and Caroline.

The problem of "getting going" in this job of adult living is not easy for *any* of us. We are bound to meet unexpected difficulties to be overcome, in the most unexpected places, and at the most unexpected times; difficulties common to both and strictly individual ones too. But with both pairs of eyes kept upon a single high target set at a fair distance ahead, the chances are more than favorable that a man and wife will hit gratifyingly close to the bullseye.

The pilgrimage through fascinating Vermont (and it was a pilgrimage) was tremendously impressive. I shall always be thankful that my life has never been cloyed with too much travel and sightseeing, and that today, at my age, I am as excited about a few hundred miles in modest Vermont as though it had been with Aladdin through China and Persia!

618

Nat and Caroline were living in Pompton Lakes, New Jersey, where Nat continued to work for the duPont Company.

Port Clyde, Maine
August 7, 1939. Sunday

Dear Nat,

We were all excited when we received your wire telling of the success of the new machine. This news made us forget the postponing of your coming.

I am eager to hear some of the backstage history of your latest venture.

I'm on the last two *Yearling* panels!! I've never worked more intensively nor more smoothly than on this task. I think the work is pretty well done too. Everyone here enthusiastic, but really that doesn't count. It is natural to favor the "old man," you know.

We all enjoyed Caroline's letter so much.

619

Port Clyde, Maine
August 27, 1939

Dear Henriette and Pete,

Ironically enough, this day has blazed forth into brilliant sun, jewel-blue sky and water, with a "westerly" pouring over us from Caldwell's Island like some crystal liquid. I say ironically, because Nat and Caroline vanished from our doorway yesterday in a thick murk of fog, a condition which dominated their two weeks with us. However, we all had an unusually splendid time, and every hour of clearing weather was used for exciting explorations of islands, events usually garnished with clam bakes or lobster boils—and in one case the return to "Eight Bells" in an impenetrable fog cleverly mastered by Nat with chart and compass so that we landed within thirty yards of our wharf.

Retreating Dreams and Hopes

Four days after Nat's arrival, I completed the last vestige of work for *The Yearling*. This included two extra drawings for the special edition, besides the thirteen panels in color. Three others, of course, were done at home, as you know.

It's a long, long time since I've written a letter and I seem to have lost what little I had of spontaneity and free flow of expression. Your own letters are full to bursting of truly "winged words," and they have given joy to all who have read them—and many have! You will never realize what pleasure they've given.

When I think of the gamut of experiences that Pete has gone through since he left Chadds Ford, I feel hopeless to express my own reaction to it all, except to say that I have followed it all like a small boat tossing in the wake of a ship, rising, falling and rising, but exhilarated in the end over an experience based upon life, energy and enthusiasm.

This watching of the unfolding of all the younger members of the family is a glorious episode of my life. As you both know I am asked interminably, "Aren't you proud of it all?" Of course I am, beyond the expression of any words. But my answer is always restrained because I am still in the battle myself, in spirit at least, and I still have a fairly clear vision of what lies ahead to be done before a real mark is achieved. I believe, as I never believed before, that we, as a group, *have got something* and that there is a real promise of sound achievement—of *major* achievement in the offing. Based upon the sound and constant seeking for the truth, and out of this the gradual unfolding of personal spirit and mood, and all based upon intensive and simple living, the possibilities are limitless.

You will like to know that John has made *extraordinary* progress in his watercolors, and under the stimulation of very busy people around him, has done a quantity of work.

Andy's results are to me astounding. Just at the conclusion of his summer's work he went starry-eyed over a *very* attractive young lady. She's really a splendid person, very handsome and very sound. Betsy James is her name. She hails from northern New York. Her family are, or at least seem to be, solid, sensible people. As long as such an event must happen, it is deeply gratifying not to have to worry about *what is a girl's background*.

Earlier in the season there were some very lurid distractions here in P.C. which can be told you better by word of mouth. That's all over now, thank heavens.

I start tomorrow on my first tempera panel for myself. I shall have a full month to do what I want. I hope it goes well.

The European situation is the only headache. I believe the present crisis a colossal bluff, one which conceals a very ominous one of the economic tie-up between Germany and Russia which, if allowed to progress through the years, will enslave the world in a terrible manner.

We may stay on here into October if my painting goes well. My first spell of freedom from commissions in a long time.

620

Charlie Stone, a fisherman from Port Clyde, often posed for N. C. Wyeth.

Andrew Wyeth had begun his courtship of Betsy Merle James, who spent summers on her parents' farm in Cushing, about twenty miles away. She was attending Colby Junior College in New London, New Hampshire.

Port Clyde, Maine
September 16, 1939

My dear Ann,

I'm on the wharf.—Charlie Stone is this instant going by—returning from hauling. The afterdeck of his power boat is loaded high with water-soaked traps, and as he passes me he is busily working with his hands, cleaning out bait bags or some such thing—stooping, standing up, stooping again, but always his eyes alert, casting glances in all directions, seeing everything. His motor purrs quietly as the boat glides through the brilliant sunlit water. One looks at him and wonders if, after all, his life doesn't represent about the best solution in this agitated world. Perhaps not, but I derive great solace and inspiration as I watch his passing.

Happily, Andy has done a beautiful large panel in tempera—an early morning thing. It was gratifying to me to observe that after those hectic weeks in Cushing he could gather himself together and land with his two feet on the ground and still hold his head in the clouds.

Doubtlessly, his ability to see things through, in the creation of a picture, is to a large extent dependent upon his thorough preparation

796

for the task. Morning after morning he was out before daylight, so when he came to doing it he was prepared with knowledge and feeling.

Of course we missed you all very much indeed. This goes without saying. But it is beyond my pen to express that subtle yearning which persists, to see Denys somewhere about. I can see him vividly, this moment, "crabbing" his way down the path, varying his speed according to his changing technique of locomotion and punctuated with sudden stops and a *sit down* to view the prospects or the distance he has traveled. To this day, I find myself depressing or lifting a door to avoid squeaks and whines that it may not wake up Denys. And I *do* miss your early morning activities, the set breakfast table and the fresh fire blazing on the hearth.

Denys McCoy with his grandfather.

Andy has decided to attend his N.Y. show; I'm glad for this, because I think he should. He wants to get home in ample time to get things settled before going to N.Y. Also he will call on Betsy in Keene, N.H., on Sunday, Sept. 30th.

621

Port Clyde, Maine
September 27, 1939

Dear Pete,

Joe Chapin died last Friday, and after 34 years of association with him the news gave me quite a jolt. Pneumonia it was. Heroic measures were taken to pull him through; the new drug, oxygen tent and all, but I guess the poor fellow was in pretty poor shape and offered very little resistance. He was working with me on *The Yearling* right up to the last.

A slashing nor'easter is driving by the windows in lateral streaks. The gut is afoam, and now and then a gray-white specter of a gull wheels madly through the murk. The old house moans and whines like something being whipped.

We are about packed, and tomorrow Andy pulls out about eleven to spend the night in Winslow Homer's old studio. It seems fitting indeed!

622

Chadds Ford, Pennsylvania
Monday, October 30, 1939

Dear Pete,

This is a very hurried note to ask of you a great favor: I have suggested, and Macbeth has approved, a plan to have you write the introduction for the catalogue of my show in his gallery.

I cannot think of anyone more fitted than you are for the task. There are several others who were under consideration, no one of whom would I trust to undertake the job, for the simple reason that they know so little about my painting or what lies back of my aspirations in this field.

You know, better than anyone else, these things, and although what you may write may not deal particularly with this phase, a sympathetic and intelligent knowledge of background is necessary.

The show opens Dec. 4th.

The show will be built around the "Island Funeral." Three new Maine temperas you haven't seen deal with the lobstermen, and one a back-country landscape. The others are:

"The Three Fishermen" (figures back to)
"Blubber Island" (the low sun one)
"The Red Dory"
"The Fox" (Thoreau endpaper)
"Back Shore" (breaking seas)
"Deep Cove Lobsterman" (Academy purchase)

623

Betsy James.

Andrew had driven to the home of his fiancée, Betsy, in East Aurora, New York, to announce their engagement.

William E. Phelps, a close family friend of the Wyeths, lived a few miles away in Montchanin, Delaware.

The WYETHS

Dear Henriette and family,

This is practically Christmas Eve. It is growing dark—one of those clear cold evenings when the stars will pulsate brilliantly and seem so alive and so near.

This is a strangely different Xmas. With you and the children away, with Andy in East Aurora, and Nat not to be here until tomorrow afternoon, and therefore, an entirely new program for the first time in many years. But I'm not complaining in the slightest. There's so much to be grateful for, especially that we have all had more than our share of these festivities together, which gave us time to build a grand tradition.

A week after Christmas, the whole family gathers together—for the last time.

"Springhouse," 1944

I shall close this now, get down to supper and afterwards we will trim the tree. We go to Ann's early tomorrow morning. She is, as usual, brimming with the spirit of Xmas, keeps running back and forth between her home and ours, has decorated our big room, beautifully, with holly sent up by good old Bill Phelps, and hung the wreaths at the windows. She is, in short, doing her best to fill the gap we all feel.

Incidentally, it was a trying moment Sunday night when Andy said good-bye. He was quite broken up; I've never seen him quite so emotional. But he's doing the right thing and we all urged him to go. Perhaps next year they will be here.

624

Chadds Ford, Pennsylvania
March, 1940

Dear Henriette,

I spent a couple of hours studying "The Birth of Venus" yesterday (in N.Y.), which has shocked me into a new realization of the direction tempera painting should take. I have never been quite so stirred by a painting. It is *beauty* carried into the realms of abstraction so far that it circles upon itself and becomes intensively personal and burningly dramatic. One of the few paintings I ever saw to completely rise out and above time and place and still remain a tangible, intimate and familiar experience to every sensibility.

625

Studio
Chadds Ford, Pennsylvania
April 3, 1940. Late afternoon

My dear Henriette,

Carolyn has just completed the Keats' mask still life, and both Andy and I believe it to be an *astounding* canvas. If she never painted another thing, this will record a truly important talent. This may sound florid, but I'm sure of what I'm saying.

626

Andrew and Betsy were married May 15 and went to Port Clyde for their honeymoon.

Chadds Ford, Pennsylvania
June 10, 1940

Dear Andy and Betsy,

How many times a day I think of you two in Port Clyde. It is always a tonic to my spirit, but it is also very agitating and induces a deep restlessness.

It is extremely beautiful here this early summer.—I cannot recall anything to equal it in recent years; but with it I am building up an inevitable tension, the tension of exacting work done under pressure of time and the added oppressiveness of that incessant trembling and rumbling of that horrifying nightmare abroad—that approaching and dreadful shadow which I believe can only be stopped when unity occurs and the world of sanity puts an end to it.

One of my great and blessed relaxations is to concentrate upon any chance detail associated with remote Port Clyde and the sublime sea that bathes its shores—even the imagined sight and sound of a small ordinary wave, glass-clear and jewel-green, gliding over the smoothed surface of a gently shelving ledge, laving its surface as with a magical and luminous lacquer, then finally cresting into the delicate complications of incredible silver lace. I feel desperate at times to be there with it and with you both, and to feel that air moan in the hollows of my face. It all seems, from here, so free of stress, which we are all feeling so intensively.

627

The outstanding primitive artist, Horace Pippin, lived only a few miles from Chadds Ford in the town of West Chester, Pennsylvania.

Chadds Ford, Pennsylvania
June 15, 1940

Dear Ann,

We all have been blessed with cool, bracing weather (only three really hot days since you left). Personally it has affected me strangely, so unseasonable has it been—more like certain early- or late-summer days in Needham, and it has been very nostalgic, to say the least. This weather experience has been responsible, I believe, for an unusually long sustained series of boyhood memories. It is as though, suddenly, everything became sharply focused, resulting in many sharp-etched visualizations of people and events I had totally forgotten. Could I devote myself to my "autobiography" I would have lots to put down, but I'm not in the mood at *all*.

I've had an astonishing time with Horace Pippin. I can't possibly tell you about it adequately now; I'll only tell you that after looking at many of mine, some of Andy's, and Henriette's, he looked at Carolyn's "Keats" with real excitement and wonderment, blew a long low whistle and said, very slowly, and solemnly, "Now, *that there's* a sensible picture!" It affected him deeply.

628

Chadds Ford, Pennsylvania
July 8, 1940

Dear John,

It's so long since I've seen Andy! With all the diabolical things that are going on in this cockeyed world (and trying to work harder than ever before at the same time), I seem to see him as through the big end of a telescope, a little miniature figure, in sharp detail, but so far off. What a strange summer! And Betsy? With all her aliveness and attractiveness, she is still to me an "academic" daughter-in-law. How eager I am to renew her acquaintance and to really establish ourselves as members of the same family.

629

Port Clyde, Maine
July 27, 1940

Dear Henriette,

Our journey up was *very* enjoyable. The stop at Nat's was really the high spot. His home is especially delightful in its spirit and warmth, and is furthermore most tastefully furnished and arranged. Ma enjoyed every minute of it and was loathe to leave. My own excitement culminated in my visit to the plant, where I saw Nat's wire-stripping machine in action. It's a marvel of simplicity and positive in its functioning, and the deep regard this design has won for Nat amongst his superiors is thrilling and impressive.

I'm the only outsider who has been issued a pass to that plant in years, and so I was taken into the fraternity of the executives and they talked freely to me about Nat and his work and his great promise for the future.

He is already singled out as one of the *three* men in creative automatic machinery who top this department in the whole company.

They say that his ability to strike at the heart of a problem, quickly and unerringly, and his great and flexible ingenuity to mechanically solve the most complex situation are astonishing. And, of course, they never failed to stress their delight in his personality.

I could tell you so much! And I came away from there with a feeling of pride and gratitude that will last me a long, long time.

His superiors are advising him to buy land in Chadds Ford, convinced that in two years he will be permanently located in Wilmington.

630

Port Clyde, Maine
August 16, 1940

Dear Henriette,

Everything in the home here is going OK. All are well, the weather is perfect and all immediate things and circumstances seem in order. Nevertheless, there seem to be so many and deeply disturbing vibrations that flow in upon us from the outside that I find myself writing this brief note to you simply to ease my conscience that I have at least communicated.

My brother Nat's condition worries me very much indeed. Like my father, he conceals so much concerning his physical and emotional disturbances and holds out to the last ditch. It seems to be, almost entirely, a nervous and mental collapse. He has terrific spells of depression, although he remains rational.

God knows, he has every reason to at last falter under the depressing load he's carried for years—it must be close to fifteen.

Again, I'm in my favorite spot on our wharf. The day is cameo-clear, and a fresh sou'west breeze is whipping the blue, blue water into a vast tabletop of sparkling diamonds. Gulls are cruising up and down our little coastline, now and then dropping like a plummet into the water for a crab. The tide is pretty well in, and the crabs venture into shoal water. Below me, to my left, Andy's gray and green dory is floating so lightly, and at ease in the lea of the wharf and mothering the little skiff which seems to nestle under her starboard quarter. The larger boat lies outside, facing the breeze with nonchalant steadiness. The subtle overtones of the breaking surf on the shores of the outer islands float in a rising and falling monotone.

But all this is maddening when one's imagination and heart-tearing sympathies plunge back into the thoughts and mental pictures of the beloved isle of Britain. That mangled and bloody land fairly rises out of the sharp line of the sea as I look in her direction! The thought is devastating! And then I peer over the edge of the silver planking at my feet and I see, through the glass-clear water, a miraculously patterned mosaic of smoothed and rounded stones and shells, shifting and wavering under the surface of the undulating tide. Again my mind crashes, and everything else for an instant, seems so unimportant!

Betsy and all of us are getting along magnificently. It started badly, for we noticed a sharp recoil from Ma and me right at first, and it worried us sick. I had almost planned to return to C.F. immediately, rather than destroy a summer for them. It's as though someone had embittered her against us. But it's all over completely, and through association and many pleasant and revealing conversations, everything promises well. They are certainly a happy pair!

631

Chadds Ford, Pennsylvania
November 18, 1940

Dear Henriette,

These are terrifically crowded days. Don't worry, I'm putting in no more than my usual hours of painting, and physically I feel splendid; but the intervening hours are so congested with the distractions of other things that I find *weeks* slipping by with never a pen to paper.

The dreadful world affairs dominate, of course. Then there's Nat and his pitiful state. I am really fearing the worst.

The constant concern to know the outcome drains me of much ambition to write letters.

Then there are Andy and Betsy getting settled. Nothing depressing about that, for contrarily, it has been very exhilarating, and Betsy's energy, good ideas, and Andy's greatly aroused interest in it all have meant a great deal. Yet it all uses up extra time and energies.

And John's show, which opened in Boston last week. All of these things are distracting. Then the opening of the Wilmington show, where Andy captured first prize, and where we as a group took up so much space and really made the walls quite thrilling. Andy's superb tempera sea panel, one of the most distinguished and truest examples of painting I've seen in this medium, then Carolyn's sensational Keats still life (which few grasped but were much impressed by). My "Island Funeral," "Road to the Jones House" and "John Teel with his Wife and Granddaughter." John's unusually fresh and strong "South Thomaston Seascape," which got the purchase prize, and then your own very poignant and beautiful portrait of Ann Carol.

To return to your portrait. It's hard for me to judge it (not that you crave my opinion!) because it overwhelmed me in its mood, besides reaching me in other personal ways. It is beautifully disturbing.

I went into the Gallery the other day, removed it from the wall and looked at it by itself. It impresses me deeply—but perhaps this can mean little to you, coming from your Pa who is steeped, these days, in a sense that the great shift in his life, so familiar and glorious to him for so many years, has at last taken place. Even the world has shifted with it, and the chasm between the past and the future yawns astonishingly.

632

N. C. Wyeth was working on a series of murals for the Metropolitan Life Insurance Building in New York City. These murals were completed after his death by his son Andrew and by John McCoy. His fifth grandchild, Ann Brelsford McCoy, was born on September 26.

Studio
Chadds Ford, Pennsylvania
December 7, 1940

My dear Henriette,

My hands are terribly sticky with Toch varnish which I have applied to the murals completed for one wall (46 feet long, 10 feet high). This section is to be hung on the walls Dec. 16th. I am proceeding, of course, with the others.

Everyone is well. Ann's children are splendid, and little Ann Brelsford is growing like a weed and seems very healthy.

806

Andy is just completing a series of a dozen dry-brush drawings of the Brandywine Valley for Henry Canby's book—one of the Farrar-Reinhart series of Rivers. Andy has done a *magnificent* job, and the effort has got him all stirred up about the landscape here, which is as it should be.

He and Betsy are getting well settled. She's a capable girl, no doubt, and the way she's fixed things up, painting woodwork, furniture, making curtains and drapes, is a pleasant revelation to us all. While thoroughly enjoying the transformation of the little schoolhouse into a place of living identified with Andy and Betsy, I shall always sigh a little when I recall your own magic hand in those same surroundings. If this be "sentimental"—make the most of it!

633

After Robert Macbeth's death, his cousin, Robert McIntyre, became the owner of the William Macbeth Gallery in New York.

Studio
Chadds Ford, Pennsylvania
February 12, 1941. Lincoln's birthday

Dear Henriette,

I have waited vainly for the normal and spirited desire to write to you. But I have been too distracted and too highly keyed this past month to attempt it.

The tension of these mad and terribly uncertain times affects me every moment I relax from work. Were it not cowardly I wish I could, by some magic, pass into unknowingness for the next six months. How I dread its terrible unfolding! How hungry I am to know the outcome!!

I'm on the third 45-foot panel for the Met. Life Ins. Building. Two are up and they have made a decided impression—so much so that the "powers" are now considering the proposition to commission me to go right on with a continuation of the series for the new unit to be built in five years—considerable additional footage, but how much I don't know. This is all rather reassuring personally; besides there is the larger significance of an existing and active faith in our world which may not crumble after all.

On the credit side there is, apparently, the steady pull toward the recovery of Uncle Nat. I naturally felt very apprehensive about his condition and I am enjoying the marvel of his nervous and mental reinstatement.

Betsy suffered a miscarriage, about which you may have already heard, but is well out of it and back to health again. Incidentally, she and Andy have left, within the hour, for New Hampshire (Colby), where Betsy will revisit her friends, and Andy with ambitious plans for a week of snowscape watercolors.

[Robert] McIntyre is encouraging him to do this as there may be possible sales for this character of watercolors. Sales, so far this year, have been slim indeed, and Andy is beginning to feel the ruthless pressure for funds. He sold only two from his Boston show and one or two from Macbeth's this season. In fact, picture sales seem to be at a new low everywhere in the East.

634

Studio
Chadds Ford, Pennsylvania
March 11, 1941

Dear Pete,

It is near the close of a singularly weird kind of day. With most of last Friday's ten inches of snow still on the ground, it has become just warm enough to cause a milk-white fog, dense yet luminous, with the nearby steel-colored tree stems rising sharply from the white spread of snow, and lifting quickly into limbo an impressive hush prevails, and for the time one feels deliciously apart and remote from this mad-dog world.

This has been, I believe, the busiest winter I have ever put in. Just what the expended effort will represent in accrued knowledge and painting progress is impossible for me to even speculate upon. My main enthusiasms are, as always, it seems, in the *next* thing to be tried, or in some less tangible dream in the future.

Both Andy and I have submitted panels to the Corcoran (no word yet of our luck). I have two shows of illustrations opening today—twenty in Phila. and fifteen in Clearwater, Fla.

Several possibilities to dispose of the *Children's Anthology* pictures, also *The Yearling* set, are in the wind, but expect nothing to come of it.

The *nobility* of an artist's personal effort which is springing from the discipline of truth, the richness of understanding, and unmistakably reaching toward the stars, seems only to affect the majority of current commentators—first with suspicion, and thence with boredom.

Doubtless there are many discriminating people who love the painter's art, who do not recognize or are not bothered by press and art magazine reviews; yet I cannot but think that a sufficient weight of professional opinion, based upon broader understanding, sounder knowledge, and greater vision, with intent to seek out *potentialities* amongst the works of contemporaries, rather than the clever accomplishments of the moment, could not only be a stimulation to the artists themselves but would clarify, for a badly befuddled public, a very muddy situation.

635

Peyton Boswell was editor of the magazine, Art News.

Chadds Ford, Pennsylvania
April 15, 1941

Dear Henriette,

Met Peyton Boswell lately and he is certainly strong for what we are doing and standing for. Believe our direction will have much to do with a real trend in American painting. *Eh what?*

636

Studio
Chadds Ford, Pennsylvania
May 21, 1941

Dear Henriette,

Andy is in N.Y. today trying to drum up some trade. Pictures are not selling *anywhere*—at least in the East—but on top of that he feels Macbeth Gallery is letting him down. Not even acknowledging his truly remarkable temperas when he sends them up.

I dare not try to express my feelings about world affairs. I'm too bewildered and dismayed to utter a word about it. All sense of serenity and security has crumbled away and all I can do, when I think about it all, is to gawk stupidly at the retreating pageant of my dreams and hopes. I am working furiously; that is my one salvation. I wonder how long I'll be allowed that.

637

Studio
Chadds Ford, Pennsylvania
August 3, 1941

Dear Ann and John,

I've been over to your place three times and all is spick-and-span. We've had corn from the garden twice, besides beets, lettuce, cucumbers, and a few tomatoes. The beetles are still holding a convention in the corn, and I found a few on the zinnias, but otherwise nothing seems to be bothered. The pool is full and the lawns are right green except on the knoll between the house and the studio.

But apart from, and beneath, the objective reasons for visiting your home, I am poignantly conscious and deeply stirred by unsuppressible feelings that cling to me for hours. The emptiness and frozen silence, in and out of the house, creates a mood so heavy, so strong, that I can almost touch it with my hands. Every object, a chair, a table, an iron toy left in a corner, conjures up visions that almost speak, and in remaining silent, they shriek! To suddenly see the gleaming head of Denys, to catch a glimpse of the recumbent little body of Ann Brelsford with bare legs lifted in the air would be such a release to the tension!

Yesterday, in the still vacancy, I suddenly answered an impulse to sit before the piano and crashed out a sequence of my well-known and undisciplined chords. The sound fairly smashed and surged through the house, and I felt a regret like that of years ago when, as a youngster, I would irresistibly toss a large rock into the mirrorlike surface of Haskell's Pond and shatter its perfection into a million fragments. A wave of self-reproach, almost remorse, would flow over me. It shouldn't have been done! That remoteness and silence should have remained inviolate!

What a bewildering and marvelous web is contrived by the flood and flow of our sensibilities. How terrible they are sometimes, and how magnificent too. Life without them would be barren indeed.

638

N. C. Wyeth arrived in Wilmington, Delaware, October 19, 1902, three days before his twentieth birthday, not his twenty-first. The date of this letter would be thirty-nine years later, not thirty-eight.

Retreating Dreams and Hopes

Caroline Wyeth was expecting a child. He was born November 14, 1941, and named for his grandfather, Newell Convers Wyeth.

Studio
Chadds Ford, Pennsylvania
October 23, 1941

Dear Nat,

And so the evident rash of birthdays is upon us again! So be it—but I'm getting a little sensitive about the blasted speed with which they return upon us. It seems but a couple of months ago that birthday ice cream and cake were being passed around the long table.

It's hard for me to believe that I'm in my 60th year—that you are 30, Henriette 34, and Carolyn 32!! Holy Smokes!!!

Just 38 years ago this afternoon I walked from Wilmington to Chadds Ford—my first glimpse of the valley which was to be so important in my life. You see I left home, Needham, the evening before my 21st birthday (just for a short course in illustration under H.P., although my mother broke down under the premonition that I would never return to Needham permanently), landing, via the Colonial Express, in Wilmington the morning of my natal day.

With complete directions from Clifford Ashley in my pocket, I took the 8th Street trolley, getting off at Adams Street and repairing to his boarding place—managed and run by one Mrs. Simpers at the corner of 10th and Adams. I took possession of Ashley's room (all the class were in Chadds Ford).

The next morning I started for Chadds Ford, one of the richest autumn days I ever remember. Mrs. Simpers gave me a lunch and I remember eating it at Adam's Dam. I had a trout line in my pocket and baiting up with bits of meat from a sandwich, fished a while in the run. Outside of a large minnow or two, I had no luck. Arriving at Chadds Ford about three, I went directly to the Harvey house (where Harry Pyle lives now) and met the dozen or more students there. That night it was frosty and clear and we took a ramble up through the vast cornfields back of the place (then the John Sheatz farm). It was all magic to me and tremendously romantic. The next day, a Sunday I think it was, we all went up to Howard Pyle's (the Alwater house) and attended a composition lecture.

It is all as clear to me today as can be, and it does not seem very long ago in spite of the passing of 38 years.

But how much has happened! How full all our lives have been, and spangled with a fair share of highlights, with sufficient shadows to set them off.

We are going to miss you and Caroline not being with us. Well, *this* year Henriette will fill a chair; that's something.

Allow me to say that Ma and I derive great and deep satisfaction from the life you are living and the energy and purpose you are putting into your profession. The years are accumulating, to be sure, but so are the satisfactions.

Naturally, we are all thinking of the great and impending event.

639

Chadds Ford, Pennsylvania
March 4, 1942

Dear Caroline,

Up to now, I had left the privilege of writing you on your birthday anniversary to Ma. She had requested this. But today, she's nursing a cold and feeling generally miserable, and I fear that this evening's mail will leave C. F. without any word from her. On the other hand, she *might* get it done after all, so you'll have to take a double-barreled greeting!

I don't intend to be sentimental (but probably I am, so instinctively, that I know not when my shirts are clear of it!), but to proceed—a birthday to me is first and last a memorial anniversary to the mother of the celebrant. And with this thought I send you my love and best wishes.

We think often of "the little feller," as my father always called us as infants, and feel so grateful over the good news that has consistently come from Cedar Road.

640

Ellen Lawrence was Caroline Wyeth's sister.

Studio
Chadds Ford, Pennsylvania
July 24, 1942

Dear Henriette,

The suffocating pressure of these mad days! Every hour is shot through with ominous reverberations. At the same time there is the imperative need to concentrate and so escape into that world of ours, of memories and imaginative projections.

In common with countless others, I suffer mainly from the oppressive sense of personal inadequacy, of my inability, in this time of supreme crisis, to be really effectual in *anything*. Even the qualified satisfactions gained from having accomplished a certain job over a period of forty years seem to have vanished. One covets the thought that a record so arduously and eagerly made must have some permanent and effective values—that an artist's tribute to the mysteries and forces of life, slender as they may be, has some valid meaning, some enhancing significance. But truly, these times banish the dream, and the pageant of my painted pictures dissolves into the misty nebular from which they came.

Andy and Betsy are still here, but there's a bare chance that they will get off to Maine soon. Andy has just completed a 25′ × 30′ panel in tempera. A stunning and vivid thing it is too, a very intimate glimpse of a fragment of a Brandywine bank: a leaning tree trunk, great fronds of leaves hanging over the water, and a most telling and beautiful bit of quick-running water purling by. Sunspots flicker throughout.

For two weeks Andy has been perched on a tall stool in the middle of the stream (between the railroad bridge and the big roadway bridge). He made fascinating studies in ink and also watercolor.

Andy feels it necessary to do a group of watercolors for a Boston showing this fall. Doll and Richards seem very insistent, feeling that they have a reasonably good market set for him this year.

I'm glad, of course, to see Andy carry out any plans beneficial to his work and prospects, but how I shall miss him! He's been a tower of strength to me this past year, which is meaning so much to the definite improvement of my painting.

A living is not easily come by for us artists these days, and Andy must scratch, as do we all; so whatever will be the best procedure for him must be done.

Nat and Carolyn with their "Moo," as they call him, spent a week recently with Ellen Lawrence, visiting us twice during the few days. Newell is prodigious in health, disposition and appearance. Caroline holding him makes me think of that picture of Segantini's called "The Child of Love"—the woman sitting in an apple tree, holding the large rosy-cheeked infant—remember?

Nat has been made a supervisor for the duration. A tedious job and a taxing one. Three thousand workers under him! How strange to think of our little Nat in this capacity! But naturally he's embracing the task with patience and, I hear, considerable skill. He also got a boost in his salary.

641

Chadds Ford, Pennsylvania
August 15, 1942

Dear Andy and Betsy,

We've had two solid weeks of violent storms, floods and humid heat, with hardly a glimpse of the sun in all that time!

The flood last week (Aug. 9th) was sensational and dismal. In two hours after rising—water started, an ice chest, a doghouse, boxes, and fencerails floated down within a few feet of your entrance!

A torrent, like a rapids, flowed through the village almost to the level of Gallagher's porch and of course filled every cellar in Chadds Ford and rose half up the windows in Jesse Tyson's barn and the Jack Harris' group of houses.

At eleven o'clock Jesse Tyson (preparing to leave for the West the following day) moved most of his belongings; at two his home was inundated.

Old George Kipe (Horace's father) was taken ill during the flood (probably induced by it), and they rowed Dr. Truitt right to his porch. Mr. Kipe died Wednesday. Thus another of the old timers here passed on.

This deluge was caused by a tremendous cloudburst near Coatesville.

Then, on Tuesday, came a nasty and bitterly intensive electrical storm which battered away at this valley like some prearranged celestial "blitz." It came very suddenly and I was caught here in my studio with two youngish fellows (en route from Florida hoping to see *you*) who were in deadly fear of lightning and very nearly surrendered to hysteria—one of them became sick in my fireplace. It angered me to witness such a diabolical display of craven fear, and I gave them a tongue-lashing during most of the fireworks! The impression of their visit to my studio will remain in their minds for some time!

You will never completely realize how much we miss you, which comes with it the sense of great good fortune that we enjoy your nearness for most of the year. I, personally, feel this is an inestimable blessing at this particular and critical time of my life when so many in like circumstances slip into a state of desuetude, or even worse, perfunctory action. I wish always that I may wind up in a real crescendo!

642

Chadds Ford, Pennsylvania
October 1, 1942

Dear Henriette,

I had thought this summer, when Andy left for Maine, and just before the great reality of the impending draft loomed upon us, that I could carry on a short series of letters to him which might prove of some interest to him and some pleasure (in the writing) to me.

We had concluded what seemed to be to me a very rich and constructive winter and spring, and this together with considerable constructive work going on in both our studios made a fine background for further exchange of thoughts and feelings.

Then it was that I found myself writing out of a sentiment and emotion and quickly realized from a letter or two from Andy that I was of more disturbance than help, so stopped in my tracks.

We have corresponded of course, but entirely of objective matters and practical affairs.

643

Chadds Ford, Pennsylvania
November 10, 1942
Monday evening, just before mailtime

Dear Nat and Caroline,

The photos created a furor of enthusiasm. The color ones of Newell are almost overwhelming in their appeal and magnificent in color quality.

How he has changed! And I must say, I see so much "Wyeth" in him now. This naturally tickles me to death! The closeups of his head and certain expressions of his eyes and mouth are *haunting* in their warm and alive charm.

The WYETHS

You have both done a superb job, from the beginning right up to now, and there is every reason to expect the best is yet to come.

Betsy and Andy.

Chapter XXVI

DEATH

"I am impatient and indignant for the lack of time left to accomplish what I feel now is within my power to do."

644

Dear Henriette,

Until the afternoon before the 25th I was miserably dull and depressed in spirit and felt entirely incapable of rousing myself to meet that high level of enthusiasm and excitement so necessary to do homage to the blessed tradition enjoyed by this Home and Family. But Andy and Betsy, carrying on the appealing custom which you so charmingly and spiritedly established, had us all to a Christmas Eve supper served, of course, in their big room which was beautifully decorated and crowned by an impressive tree. Memories of your own highly personal eloquence in delicious food and decorative ornamentation on similar occasions heightened the new and different expressions of the younger generation, with a keen and constant flow of nostalgia, much as the aromatic scent of an unseen flower or hidden shrub will glorify the entire landscape prospect before one's eyes.

So it was that I was snapped out of my lethargy and into the hallowed groove I yearned for. From then on the true spirit mounted and the great Day dawned in all its glory—or *almost* all.

How can any human being schooled, as I believe I have been schooled, to emotionally respond to every event and circumstance, large or small, turn off those vibrations as one would a radio or even reduce the flow of aroused feeling to a lesser stream. Many years of utter submission to the impacts of life weaken the power to stop, or even the *desire* to cushion, the emotional force of experiences. And particularly now, just at my time of life when the faculties of the spirit are most at work, when (to all men who have turned sixty) the time left seems so scant and so precious. Add to this the sudden rush of diabolical events which loom up in such portentious proportions!

These events are affecting something infinitely more than my personal ambitions in the field of creative expression—they bear down so cruelly upon the chances of fulfillment of my great hopes and aspirations for Andy's future. He is carrying now, in such full stride forward, the fundamental study and discipline I *should* have followed, and is so acutely building a very potential and sound foundation toward important expression that I cannot modify by argument or philosophy my bitter disappointment.

The argument that the experience of war cannot be but an enriching experience for an artist is the purest nonsense ever uttered. The greater the potentiality of the artist, the more damaging to his career. And knowing Andy as I do, I affirm with all the confidence I am capable of, that he will be, in time, and with luck, a very much needed force in this era, an era starved into bewilderment by floods of unbeautiful and uninspired rubbish, which is criminally inflated and given publicity and prominence by ignorant and short-sighted critics, and kept alive by the senile babblings of superficial and self-exploiting snobs.

Andy has been called by his draft board and is still awaiting the first physical test.

645

Chadds Ford, Pennsylvania
February 4, 1943

Dear Henriette,

Briefly, I'll tell you of Andy's situation to date. The boy has certainly passed through an odyssey in the past weeks.

The army examination, which he went through a week or so ago in Baltimore, emphatically turned him down. Principally on account of his feet and the twisted condition of his right leg which is affecting his hip. There were two other weaknesses, the significance of either we do not yet understand—one lung has something wrong, and a derogatory comment on his spleen.

The feet and leg condition are already in hand, and the bone man says it will take three years for a correction. The other matters will get attention promptly.

Betsy is again pregnant, which added to the tension all 'round, although everyone faced the situation silently and with as much courage as possible. She seems to be very well so far.

Andy is in Phila. today to get his special shoes and will take in the Academy show. I half-expected to go with him, but considering that

I will join him next Tuesday and attend the opening of the Museum of Modern Art show, I could not spare the time away today. I am very curious to see how Andy's and Pete's panels will look, and will report to you later about it.

646

Chadds Ford, Pennsylvania
February 25, 1943

Dear Henriette and Pete,

The show at the Museum of Modern Art was beautifully presented, hugely attended by members the opening evening, and the cocktail party given for the exhibitors and friends was a very pleasant and warm affair.

The display itself is puzzling to me. It runs the gamut from just damn bad eccentric painting up to Pete's and Andy's—and I use this sequence advisedly, for their two groups were the most enjoyed by the crowd that attended that night.

[Edward Alden] Jewell has said practically nothing about the show, and one of the half-dozen artists he mentioned was Pete. Today, [Royal] Cortizzos comes out with a very intelligent critical commentary, speaks of Pete's appealing landscapes and lays great emphasis on the feeling and the craft of Andy's group.

[Edward] Hopper was there that night, and he and Andy spent a couple of hours together. H— was quite bowled over by Andy's panels and told me so.

My main impression of practically all painting today is that the grand mass of painters have nothing to say but take great pains in saying it.

647

Studio
Chadds Ford, Pennsylvania
April 4, 1943. Sunday morning

Dear Henriette,

The tense season has in no way interrupted Andy's march ahead in the force and ecstatic beauty of his painting and draughtsmanship. It is all amazing to me!

He's at work upon quite an ambitious panel now (although almost two months' work have gone into it I haven't seen it yet! but from what the folks say it must be impressive). The motif is based upon a farm sale in Lancaster county which he attended with Bert Guest. After a couple of days up there Andy returned very dramatically stirred by the sad and sober mood of the event. I know nothing of his approach to the motif in color or pictorial design.

He recently did a very successful jacket in color for Farrar and Reinhart—a "Western" of all things!—about 1870.

I'm glad he was successful because it is very possible he will have to turn to this kind of thing occasionally, with the new responsibility looming up before him. He will always use discretion in accepting such jobs, I'm sure, and he's too firmly rooted in his personal yearnings as a painter, as well as fortified by an unusual amount of training and discipline, to be led off the track of his ambitions.

Andy has started on the job of correcting his left leg and feet. It's going to be a tedious affair, I'm afraid. I can see a job of constant urging and watching that he carries out instructions. He is so utterly unmindful of anything to do with his physical self!

Ma is in fine fettle! Most active and busy every hour of the day, both inside and outside, I never saw her looking better or in better spirits. What a bulwark of strength and support she is to me! With no help outside, she is doing a lot of cleaning up around the place, and it's beginning to look shipshape indeed. I help some, and Carolyn is doing surprising things in spurts.

648

Studio
Chadds Ford, Pennsylvania
April 4, 1943. Sunday morning

My dear Caroline,

The month of March is reaching back with her cold windy arm to push and shove us around just to prove that she's not done with us yet! But the day is lens-clear—and that's something. It's below freezing this morning, but the spring blushes of warm green and pinkish sap colors are bravely taking possession of the valley, getting off the sharp-cut geometric patches of winter wheat fields—that enchanting color quality of turquoise-green, slightly dusted! The divine harmony of it all!!

Do you happen to recall these opening four lines in a poem by Emily Dickinson?

> The skies can't keep their secret!
> They tell it to the hills
> The hills just tell the orchards
> And they the daffodils!!

By the way, what unending satisfaction I have derived from E. D.'s verse this winter! Their incisive and piercing beauty has never failed to cut through the thick miasmal gloom of these three terrible months. Creative work of such magnificent stature is infinitely more than a means, or vehicle, of temporary escape, but rather becomes luminous radiation which marks a course to steer by. By the mere glancing at one of these verses, crowned with its glowing nimbus, one's faith is refreshed and made vital again, no matter how dismal the spirit or prospect.

It has been a growing revelation to me to gradually awaken to the dynamic power of this frail girl's art and so meet face-to-face the consummation of what had been merely a theoretical belief of mine —that a woman's art, kept strictly and untarnishedly *feminine, could* rise to ecstatic heights. I had never met it before except in an in-completed degree. I am aware of no other woman's art, be it litera-ture, music, or painting, that amounts to anything more than "man's art drawn across her fan." *This* woman's creation is pure gold.

Hardly a day has gone by that I haven't, at some moment in it, lingered over the desire to write and ruminate upon some of the things I wanted to say. Each time would evolve *new* sequences of thought, and, as I suspected from the first, when the moment came to touch pen to paper I swung off on an unexpected tangent. One inference from all this is, of course, rather appalling—that had you been here in person I would have rambled on and on in a never-ending stream of one-sided conversation! You don't know what you've escaped!!

I do yearn for new adventures in conversation with fresh minds. Discussion based upon hearty and mutual willingness to exchange thoughts, to balance and weigh ideas and opinions.

So few are willing to do this, or are unable to, or just become bored to death. It is highly possible that I am fundamentally at fault, that I may parade an unconscious chip on my shoulder! I've been blamed for this, but I think that those who feel this way about me mistake my enthusiasm for egotism, or whatever else it is they feel.

We as a family do talk a lot together, and some of it has been enjoyable and profitable, but after forty years we've all become a little bit "old hat" to each other. At any rate, *my* cards are all on the table. (At least that's what the rest think, but I've still got some up my sleeve!)

Well, to get down to mundane matters let me say that everyone is well—especially so. There's an enormous amount of work to accomplish, outside and in, and Ma has been the busiest person imaginable! The amount of raking and cleaning up she's done outside is astonishing, and she thrives on it! Besides, of course, keeping a perfect house *inside*.

When we were married, Ma was such a frail little thing, about a hundred pounds, with a countenance that sparkled with Oriental luster, framed as it was in luxuriant and wavy, warm, black hair. Her eyes were very large and very dark.

I know full well that many of her friends looked at us, as a couple, with considerable sympathy and pity for *her* as they viewed my 200 lb., six-foot-one hulk looming beside her. I paint this brief picture because, ironically, I feel today that Ma is the bulwark, that I actually lean upon *her*, and in that stocky, strong figure of today, I enjoy a real sense of security. I never would have believed it!

649

Chadds Ford, Pennsylvania
April 19, 1943

Dear Henriette,

A forty-mile gale out of the northeast is roaring by. The old studio shudders and creaks like an antique craft on the high seas. It's a nostalgic sound for it conjures up such contrasting memories of fifty years ago when on this anniversary day of the Concord Bridge fight, we would all go down to the corner of South St. and Dedham Ave. to watch the 20-mile bicycle race go by. Even my father would be there, and all the neighbors—the one day in the year we would see them. Charlie Haskell and his mother and father, the Hassenfuses, the Smiths, Bowens, Suttons, Newberrys, Fullers, Downers, Blackmans and a dozen others and their families. What characters they were! Like people out of an old book on back-country New England.

Then we'd go back home to a characteristic meal of my mother's —and ice cream or sherbet. It was one of the few holidays my father had.

650

Studio
Chadds Ford, Pennsylvania
May 19, 1943

Dear Caroline,

I have just returned from lunch, and my white shirt is plentifully freckled with large silver splotches of warm raindrops which caught me before I reached the cover of my studio.

The sound of the rain on the roof, so like the subdued long roll of drums, is at once relaxing and stimulating to the spirit.

The unceiled and accoustical roof of this studio is one of the many features of this building which I have come to love very deeply. It is so sensitive and eloquent of so much that happens outside. Even the soft, scraping sound of falling leaves in autumn becomes audible on its pitched roof sounding-board; the fragile hopping of birds and the sound of the impulsive scratchy running of investigating squirrels fire the imagination into a singularly intimate relationship with these wild visitors. I always thrill with a subtle sense of pride when they thus honor my roof. They signal and communicate with me in code.

Am I getting too sentimental? Well, I *am* sentimental anyway and not at all ashamed of it!—but doubtlessly these lurid times we are living in are making this trait too obvious.

I wish at times that I could shut myself away from the terrible agitations, but it seems impossible to resist the morning paper or to listen to the radio broadcasts and so expose oneself to the glut of stupefying facts and frightful portents. And so it is, I suppose, that one surrenders to all the romantic and nostalgic faculties one is capable of, for relief and release!

This spring has been desperately intense with a fierce hunger and thirst for restfulness and mellowness of living. As I look back across the years, how generous life was to us in just these qualities. The past is irreturnable, I know that. And yet, blessed, or cursed, as I am with abundant nervous energy and teeming desires, I really refuse to accept this truth and constantly dream of renewed youth and to face again its glorious complications and its fascinating problems.

Were *all* the family here at least in this neighborhood! That would be the solution!! But how silly to rave.

Your letter of April 27 (we call it your Easter letter) was most poignant and beautiful. It was so true that it gives me pangs to read it—but I am completely grateful for it.

Yes, we have come to know each other. Perhaps, as you say, distance has enriched and hastened this mutual understanding. Nevertheless, I feel very depressed whenever I dwell upon it that I cannot enjoy more frequent contacts with you, and especially that circumstances have deprived me of the deep satisfaction of watching your boy grow and develop; and no one will ever know how increasingly I miss the steady light from Nat's radiating and spirited personality and his potential strength.

We are both lucky, of course, to still have Andy and Ann close to us. Andy offers me, in particular, great encouragement and stimulation. But I need the rest of you so much!

The storm is passing, the light is flooding the studio and I must pick up my brushes.

651

Chadds Ford, Pennsylvania
July 23, 1943. Thursday, 3:30 P.M.

Dear Caroline,

My recent letters seem to be borne of storms—the storm labors and brings forth a mouse! There's one now, and the heavens seem to be falling about our ears.

The old valley is steaming like a hot house, and the smell of new-wet vegetation and earth is precisely the same as that I used to enjoy as a youngster as I stood behind my grandfather as he watered down the long benches of potted plants and cuttings. Only the aroma from the long twisting garden hose is needed to complete the memory.

652

Peter Hurd was sent by Life Magazine *as a war correspondent to England and the Middle East.*

Chadds Ford, Pennsylvania
July 30, 1943

My dear Henriette,

It was very exciting to see the new group of Pete's paintings in *Life*. To my mind he is the only one, in all who have assayed to paint war activities, who has captured a definitely rich and authentic mood. I can't help feeling that Pete was very fortunate in being assigned to what one may call a modified phase of war—the threshold, so to speak, to finalities. From this vantage point the creative mind is far better able to extract the true poignance of mood and drama which is, very obviously, denied to those who penetrate the climaxes. The abnormalities of war experiences overwhelm and suffocate the creative faculties.

Peter Hurd, war correspondent for *Life Magazine.*

I have always felt that the very limitations and the brevity of Tolstoy's military experience in the Crimea *preserved* the potency of his imagination for his great creation of "Austerlitz" in *War and Peace.*

Certainly from out of all the vast military history of the world there should be some record left to us by some actor in it, which could be enjoyed as great art—but we have nothing of the kind.

653

Chadds Ford, Pennsylvania
October 19, 1943

Dear Nat and Caroline,

The memories of last week with you all are not dimmed as each event stands lens-clear. The beautiful and powerful little figure of Newell dominates it all however. His personality, for one so very young, is truly astonishing to me; the clarity of it remains in my memory, as does his blond face and figure, cameolike—in sharp preciseness and ultimate delicacy. I like to think mostly of the glow of his hair and face in the cavernous gloom of that cathedrallike woods of "the grotto." I shall never forget him there.

Obviously he is blessed with a quick and attentive spirit. Nourish these traits by every means you can think of. This will comprise his greatest and profoundest education, no matter what imposing institutions he may encounter later on. To keep alive and to intensify his sense of wonderment and his curiosity about the simplest things— these will become and remain the most potent factors in his life, no matter what he is destined to do.

654

Studio
Chadds Ford, Pennsylvania
November 14, 1943

My dear Newell,

Almost sixty years of time stand between us. To me they seem such a brief span of adventure—a mere hint of life and its vast possibilities. To you, such a parade of years must appear never-ending as they stretch far into the blue distance of infinite time and exciting promise.—This is just as it should be, of course. It is your birthright, your privilege, and your duty, to *dream* your way into the conscious significance of life and living, and then, through the alchemy of experience, good and bad, arrive at your own conclusions and solutions.

The high degree and richness of your youthful dreams will determine the quality of the gratifications to come.

You are blest with parents who have a sharp consciousness of this
—so it is that your grandfather, upon your second birthday, feels very
happy for you, sends his love, and a small remembrance for your
bank account.

655

Chadds Ford, Pennsylvania
December 5, 1943

My dear Ed,

I am apologetic for having had to resort to a last-minute telegram,
which I hope reached you this day. Birthday telegrams are officially
ruled out, but I presume you got the significance of the message anyway.

The days are not long enough to accomplish the things I have set
myself to do. I refer mainly to my own personal expression in painting, which is my one refuge in these days of killing intensity (commissioned work, although plentiful, I am relegating to a secondary
consideration, and am only doing enough of it to pay expenses).

Your birthday letter of Oct. 20th was an especially gratifying one
to me. It was so complete and full. I thank you for it.

My thoughts and feelings go out to you and Clara very, very often.
There's no blinking the realism of a son in the war. All the phi-
losophizing in the world, all the ostrichlike determination to create
diversionary interests in order to forget the truth are just so much
Pollyanna bunk!

All around me are my relatives with boys in the thick of it. Fate
has spared us the ultimate experience, with Nat ranking very high
in the creation of automatic machinery to make munitions, and Andy
definitely ruled out by a Washington Board of Physical Examiners
just ten days before he was to leave for the Solomon Islands as an
artist correspondent (a bad leg and hip dislocation which is proving
to be quite a serious, stubborn condition which the doctors say will
take years to correct).

Trained, as an artist must be, to be keenly sensitive to all the conditions and circumstances of his times, I cannot now turn off the flow
(as one would a spigot) of these disastrous days. But it is all building up overwhelming feelings of nostalgia within me, and I am painting like mad to release them. I am impatient and indignant for the
lack of time left to accomplish what I feel now is within my power
to do.

And this brings me to a few words of advice to your young artist acquaintance Metcalf.

From what you say, I fear that his work is so good that he will not listen to the only advice worth giving, advice that the great masters of all time would give him could they do so.

If he is serious, he must make up his mind to absorb every iota of academic training he can possibly get. There is no shortcut to fundamental training, as the sorry condition of art today proves. If, at 45, young Metcalf wishes to still be in a position of *growth* and artistic potentiality, then he must lay a sound foundation of truth. Only out of truth can be born a valid personal expression. All the "natural" talents of youth cannot take the place of *disciplined training*. Beethoven was a prodigy as a boy pianist, but witness the infinite and painstaking training which followed his initial flowering. Without this exhaustive discipline we would never have had the Beethoven of the nine symphonies.

The theory that a successful and productive artist makes an extraordinary good teacher is entirely wrong. I realize that this point of view contradicts what we used to believe at Home was the truth. I have learned, through hard experience, to know better.

The obscure and *academic* teachers have always, as the history of art proves, been the important ones. These teachers teach only of the literal truth and do not try to inoculate personal and pet theories into their students, for the simple reason that they *haven't* any.

Personally, I am spending the remainder of my life in an effort to undo what Reed and Howard Pyle infected me with. (I do not say this with malice for they were extremely generous men.) What I got from both of them, especially Pyle, enabled me to win a living and some fame (neither of which interests me very much now) but denied me the opportunity to release my own personality.

You might say that my own boy Andy's success and promise is a contradiction of what I have just said. But that would be entirely *wrong* for I never, for a *moment,* attempted to step out of the field of strict academic training in all the years I disciplined him in cast drawing, life and landscape. Of course he profited, I like to think, from the constant influence around him of the best music, the best prints, the best books, in the field of emotional expression, *plus* the sound living of a normal life of duties and experience within the home here in Chadds Ford.

Art schools, where they dispense *sound* training, are hard to find these days—this is a dreadful thought to contemplate. It's like saying that there are no true teachers of the pianoforte or of the exacting knowledge required for musical composition. What would happen to music if this were so!

N. C. Wyeth writing a letter at his desk.

656

Studio
Chadds Ford, Pennsylvania
February 13, 1944. Sunday

My dear Caroline,
 This is a winter's day of diamond clarity, and of diamond colors!

The WYETHS

In spite of the hypnotic majesty of the weather and the countryside, a disturbing note prevails in my mind at present, especially when I'm here in the studio. On Wednesday, three hours of film was projected here: the uncensored pictures of Tarawa. You see, I'm to do an interpretation of that horrific battle in the South Seas to publicize the value and need of blood plasma, and so it was that a special government release of these films was granted for the purpose.

The young chap who projected them was a Guadalcanal Marine veteran, badly wounded, but a graphic talker, and his conversation added tremendously to the vividness of the moving pictures.

The *blood plasma creators,* of Sharp and Doehm, were here too, but I was not allowed to invite anyone else to view the film. But it's just as well! I was near the breaking point several times myself and within an ace of losing my lunch several other times!

What has lingered with me since this showing is the most profound sense of gratitude that fateful circumstances have, so far, saved Nat and Andy from such hideous experiences. So many of the young soldiers looked, walked and talked like the boys, which made the film terrifically poignant. These films (with the soundtrack too, of course) recorded conversations including the idle and staccato cursings in the foxholes and behind barricades. A couple of shots from Burma were injected, one showing a "Fuzzy-Wuzzy" reporting to headquarters with five Jap heads in his hands, held by the hair. He received his stick of candy for each dead Jap and retreated happily! (He rolled the heads to the ground like so many coconuts.)

Yesterday I made my first rough layout for the picture poster. It has possibilities.

Newell, that gleaming child of color and spirit, is an obvious manifestation of your transcendent instincts of a mother. From that divinely intangible achievement of producing a supremely beautiful child, you are perpetuating his health of body, most rationally ordering his sense of discipline, and ornamenting his imaginative potential with those subtle benefactions which only a devoted, a right-hearted and reflective mother can accomplish.

657

Nicholas Wyeth, the son of Betsy and Andy, was born September 21, 1943. The three were visiting with Betsy's parents in East Aurora, N.Y.

"Nightfall," 1945

Death

Studio
Chadds Ford, Pennsylvania
February 16, 1944

Dear Andy,

There's a slow billowy wind coming down the valley. It comes in great round intermittent puffs and piles up about the studio ever so like some engulfing and invisible surf. One can almost hear it pouring off the back roof, cascades of spume spending itself in foamy eddies among the orchard trees and tangled grass.

The day is somber and gray, and I am reminded of Thoreau who found the drab days of winter so inspiring. These dreary winter colors which depressed other people suggested to him the high spiritual traits that constituted his concept of beauty.

The week has been, to me, a singular mixture of ineffable sadness and inspiration—two moods that often happen together. But there is a persistent melancholy which I seem unable to shake off.

To circumvent these feelings I have devoted most of my spare time to reading, especially at night when sleep eludes me.—Thoreau, Goethe, Emerson, Tolstoy—all have struck me, as always, with incisive vitality and freshness. My ruminations have again been vividly stirred.

These great men forever radiate a sharp sense of that profound requirement of the artist, to fully understand that *consequences* of what he creates are unimportant. "Let the motive for action be in the action itself and not in the event."

I know from my own experience that when I create with any degree of strength and beauty I have had no thought of consequences. Anyone who creates for *effect*—to score a hit—does not know what he is missing!

This period of unprecedented distractions and overstimulation constitutes a fierce antagonist to the accomplishments of the spirit. Whatever is worth discovery in one's heart and mind can only rise to the surface among quiet conditions, in which one thought grows beside another and one has time to compare and reflect. Periods of bleak thinking and austere feeling, that kind that cuts to the bone, are imperative. Experiences which so often masquerade for cultural influences are so often merely cozy and sociable.

The WYETHS

I was struck with a quotation from Michelangelo: "It is only well with me when I have a chisel in my hand."

How stimulating is the company of generous minds (I am thinking of the four masters named above) who overlook trifles and keep their minds instinctively fixed on whatever is good and positive in the world about them. Truly magnanimous people have no vanity, no jealousy; they have no reserves and they feed on the true and solid wherever they find it. What is more, they find it everywhere.

There is little doubt that the modern mind is opposed to the romantic mind. The modern mind is mainly content to ask and seek causes and consequences—whereas the romantic mind seeks the *significance* of things. The romantic mind must be restored to its necessary place of leadership. If things have no *significance* things are hollow!

The greats in all the arts have been primarily romanticists and realists (the two canot be separated). They interpreted life as they saw it, but, "through every line's being" soaked in the consciousness of an object, one is bound to feel, beside life as it is, the life that ought to be, and it is *that* that captivates us! All great painting is something that enriches and enhances life, something that makes it higher, wider, and deeper.

"A great painter is a great man painting."

Sound feeling can only exist in a man who is living on all sides the life that is natural to man. Only through this experience can he sense his times and avoid that ever-lurking pitfall of egocentricism. Someone, uncommonly wise, said, "Nothing is so poor and melancholy as art that is interested in itself and not its subject."

To live, to keep one's eyes wide open in wonder, to be surprised by things!

Here's a quote which I think will interest you—"Great painting like Bach's music, in texture closely woven, subdued like the early Gobelin tapestries, no emphasis, no climaxes, no beginnings or endings, merely resumptions and transitions, a design so sustained that there is no effort in starting and every casual statement is equally great."

But of course such depth presupposes another mode of feeling. One has to be a Bach before one can paint in his power and richness. Depth of style can only spring from a deepening of our emotional life. *That* is what we really demand and look for!

834

Betsy with Nicholas.

There's a real task on our hands, Andy. Modern art critics and their supine followers *like* the flat and the shallow. They like it as they like soft drinks and factory-made bread.

Intensity, distinction, fire—those elements of mature sincerity, these they loathe. They fear disturbance!

Ma's very well; we all are. Remember me to everybody, warmly— and give little Nicholas a special pat for me.

[Letter continued]
Monday, 7:30 A.M.

P.S. In reading this over I am impressed by the fact that none of the thoughts expressed are new to you. We have, together, gone over these matters again and again. But it is good, I think, to repeat fundamental truths and, if possible, bring them into new and fresh focus.

A great truth is like a mountain that one walks around, and the changes of its contour as one moves his position only emphasize and revivify its majesty.

658

Chadds Ford, Pennsylvania
June 8, 1944

Dear Henriette,

Well, Andy and Betsy got off to Maine on Monday and arrived Tuesday night at Broad Cove Farm. As always, it was a tough pull for Andy to wrench himself away from the scene to which he has devoted himself so intensively for the last two years.

I do not remain unscathed when Andy pulls out—his companionship and stimulation are enormously important to me these days. And especially since Tuesday I have had every urge to pack up and go immediately.

"The Spring House" is probably my best effort to date. At any rate, Andy feels so beyond question.

Little Nicholas is growing like a weed and is developing into a most appealing child. He was in the "pink" when he left for Maine.

659

Chadds Ford, Pennsylvania
July 4, 1944

My dear Caroline,

It most certainly has not been for the want of *desire* to write to you that has kept me silent these many weeks past. Perhaps never before have I felt the craving so intensively to either talk with you, or by letters, to communicate some of the many sharp delineations of feelings that rise and fall these days with such excruciating force.

Doubtless you have at times reflected upon the character of some of the letters I have written to you and have subtly wondered at some of the personal sentiments expressed in them. Also, those endless and ponderous dissertations on so many topics must give you doubtful pause. Well, it is hardly necessary to remind you that you hold a growing and unique place in my heart and mind. So, in spirit and person, you have become a shining mark which draws my fire—a very beautiful, resilient, live target it is which resounds with a clear ring if I chance to hit the bullseye, and equally eloquent in retaliation to a miss!

It may be, and probably is, some fault of my own, a hidden and quite unconscious trait of personality, that I am able to point to so few with whom I can freely exchange expressions of the mind and spirit, without leaving some trace of damaging reaction.

Perhaps this is an inheritance from my mother. If so, there remains to me the deeply compensating knowledge that so much of what she said and did was true and right. I yearn to believe that some remnants at least, of her superior intuitions, will prove to be mine too! I can definitely point to just a few.

It is so obvious as to be trite to blame one's reluctance to indulge in matters of personal speculations and hopes, upon the ugly and perfidious state of the world. But it is true. One's thoughts are so dominated by the oppressiveness of events and the colossal shadows they are casting before them that matters dealing with the simple and fundamental considerations of normal living seem vain and futile.

The principal release for pent-up feelings, which I turn to, lies in the shadowy world of memory—that blessed state of nostalgia, sweet melancholy in which dreams come nearer to attainment than life itself can provide.

Such a declaration sounds like a confession of advancing age, but this is definitely not so in my case, for as early as I can remember, the magic spell of remembrances played a precise role in the reflective capacity of my ego. The chance discovery of my grandfather's worn straw hat hanging in an obscure winter closet to await a new summer would move me to sudden yearning and recollection. My mind's eye would vividly see that familiar hat, resting lightly on my grandfather's head, move through his beloved sun-drenched greenhouses, the thin shadows from the close-spaced sash bars above him, flickering in quick succession across the shining straw dome of the hat. Not yet emotional enough to actually burst into tears, I would feel a sudden surge of acute sadness and exhilaration and I would be plunged into a momentary surrender of voluptuous ecstasy!

(Just at this instant I hear the distant sound of a Reading train whistle. On this significantly silent "Fourth" it is an especially eerie

837

and poignant voice—a call from great distances, in space *and* time. It also speaks of the future; it punctuates the moment between the two eternities.)

But I must shift from this mirror key of personal gropings and mumblings.

I have tapered this quick letter away from the personal intricacies which threatened to usurp all the pages, but let me tell you that I could go on and on, spurred by memories common to us both and heightened by the strange and haunting quiet of this holiday, which, next to Christmas, was always a stirring experience. The shadows of Nat and Andy dart in and out the trees through the haze of clustered skeins of blue smoke. The crackle of firecrackers—the occasional booming bash of a "Dago Bomb"—the deliciously acrid smell of burnt powder—it is all sharp in my senses now!

660

Port Clyde, Maine
August 20, 1944

[To Christian C. Sanderson]
My dear Sandy,

As I write this in my studio here (which is connected with our boathouse and the wharf), I can hear the sound of the incoming tide chuckling and muttering its way through the maze of tall spiles that support the dock.

And *now,* just as I am talking to you, the shuddering sound of distant cannonading, target practice at sea, rumbles up across the Bay of Maine from outside Portland, where daily, at this time, salvo after salvo roars across seventy miles of water to us here. The little studio trembles, and its floor, which is so close to the level of the sea, actually vibrates like the taut sheepskin under the rattle of the long roll.

The lyrical and mystical dream of the sea is thus shattered. (I am reminded of what is to me one of the greatest of dramatic poems, "Channel Firing" by Thomas Hardy. By all means look it up sometime.)

661

Caroline and Nat's hopes of moving back to Chadds Ford were dashed by a change of plans within the duPont Company. Later, these were re-

838

*versed and they did move back in the early spring of 1945. Their second
son, Howard Pyle Wyeth, was born April 22, 1944.*

Studio
Chadds Ford, Pennsylvania
October 12, 1944

My dear Caroline,

Penetrating the warp and woof of all these recent distractions, there
has persisted throughout a sharp consciousness of you, Nat, and the
recent hopes you had both embraced and the final disappointment
that came and made you suffer. My sympathy for the plan, and my
hopes too, were lifted very high, and I dreamed with you. But the
shock of disappointment was somewhat lessened for me by a prevailing realization that certain important considerations were sure to
present opposition.

To hold a potential relationship to one's job, especially one which
requires unusual alertness and acumen, it is so necessary that a man's
background of *home* be at hand—a live, tangible and ready factor in
his daily program. The spirit, and the actuality of the family, no
matter what vagaries of experiences or problems arise—even those
which may seem insuperable—are vital and necessary ingredients to
any man of character and promise.

I can understand your periods of loneliness, the hunger for more
enlightened and understanding neighbors and your burning desire
to return to your native land, to old friends, and to the warmth and
stimulation of family members. This is all so superiorly human and
so desirable! We yearn for it too!!

It would be tiresome to you, and quite inconsiderate on my part,
to launch upon you, just at this juncture, the protracted story of our
earlier experience (Ma's and mine). Experiences that were along
very similar lines to your own.

For, be it remembered, that I brought a provincial, young, and
timorous Delaware Avenue girl out into a strange country which, in
spite of its charm and beauty, was in those days, forty years ago, an
inaccessible and lonely place for any town-bred girl.

Ma faced just your problem, but we had burned our bridges and
we had to see it through. Children came fast, problems of all kinds
came and went, and several near-fatal illnesses were faced and beaten
back. Certainly the social atmosphere, for Ma at least, was nil. Only

839

twice a year could Ma venture, for part of a day, to shop in Philadelphia, and Wilmington was almost equally inaccessible. There were
no motorcars, and trains were very few and so impracticable.

Admittedly, I can see now that I was very selfish in my determination to carry through a protracted program of study and work alone
in the country, but I accepted the sacrifices which were being made
for me, and we all eventually profited, I think, from those years
which were difficult.

Without my growing family at hand—under my very eyes—and
without that sense of sustained responsibility and care, I would have
failed to establish a professional foundation which would have encouraged later growth and added strength.

As I glance back over the foregoing "discourse" on profession and
family, I'm wondering if you will accuse me of dull and insufferable
pedantry. The thoughts expressed restate in a large measure things
which you already know. I am sufficiently familiar with the character of your searching mind to appreciate this possibility.

The day will actually come, sooner than you realize, when you will
all be located here. There's lots of time and we will be ready for you.

As I have said time and time again, we hold a very deep and abid-
ing faith and admiration of your superb accomplishments as a mother
and wife. You top the list of all others we know. Your methods and
your serious integrity promise exciting results. You are an unusually
intense and sensitive person, and your feelings are bound to swing
the pendulum of emotional experience in both directions—from ecstatic and grateful moments to those of despair and frustration. That
is the penalty one pays for being so richly constituted. You have produced an outstanding pair of sons, you are caring for and training
them with understanding and shrewd foresight. For the family foundation which you and Nat have already constructed so solidly, we
here are deeply grateful. You have so much more reason than most
to look forward with confident hope.

662

In the Big Room
Chadds Ford, Pennsylvania
October 24, 1944

Dear Henriette,

You will be pleased, I know, to hear that since listening to Dewey's campaign speeches—and Bricker's—I have turned increasingly toward Roosevelt, and now I shall, most emphatically, vote for him. What a childish campaign the Republicans have put on—such small-town arguments! Foreign policy is, I realize, the predominant issue, which makes my dislike of a fourth term relatively unimportant.

I am worried about F.D.'s physical condition—his blurred enunciation and strangely new talking voice bothers me not a little—and I'm not at all sold on Truman if he should take the president's chair.

Andy is, I know, gloating over my change about.

663

Maude Robbins McCoy was born March 9, 1944.

Chadds Ford, Pennsylvania
December 17th, 1944

My dear Henriette and All,

Andy is well into his work again with astonishingly poignant watercolor of frozen deer hung in open barn door against snow hillside (up at Karl Kuerner's). Very moving!

Ann's family is fine. Robin is growing rapidly—quite an individual.

664

Chadds Ford, Pennsylvania
December 27, 1944

Dear Henriette,

Your high-spirited Xmas letter conveyed to us the most luminous spirit imaginable of that beloved day! At the same time it has created in the minds of all who read it a memorable and most vivid picture of Xmas in your New Mexican home. *Everyone* was deeply moved by your story and it became one of the major features of *our* Xmas week. Your spontaneity and the "hot-off-the-griddle" reporting of the impressive and charming sequences I shall not forget! No need to say that such achievements in the homes of our children are deeply gratifying to Ma and me. How deeply significant such experiences have been to me!

Nat and family's stay of three days was splendid and we all enjoyed it greatly. The kids behaved wonderfully, which gave us a real chance to enjoy them. That Newell is something! He's really got stuff!

Well, I've put the last day I'll have for some time on my "John McGinley." It makes me feel quite sad to quit it. I don't think I have ever enjoyed doing a picture so much, nor have I ever concentrated so intensively. The days have gone by like hours!

665

Chadds Ford, Pennsylvania
February 20, 1945

Dear Pete,

I am reminded that it will be your birthday in a day or two, and while waiting for the studio to heat up (it's just 2° outside) and perched as close to the heater as possible, I'll scratch off a few lines. There's a foot of snow too—a fresh downfall which came Saturday night. We are having what I would call a New England winter!

Thanks for your last letter, a highlight of which is the passage regarding mechanical warfare which might eventually teach us tolerance and meekness—"mystic humility as we face the wonder of life and the episode of human existence."

That of course is the sweet and salvation of the human being, it seems to me. As cold and scholarly as Chas. W. Eliot of Harvard appeared, he said many wise things during his last years, the substance of one I will never forget. When asked what he considered to be the essence and foundation of education he replied, "To awaken in a child the sense of wonderment."

In my mind it's a question whether the sensational development of mechanical powers of destruction can ever nurse the spirit of man back into the realms of wonderment and reflection. When the world becomes truly aware that we are accomplishing our own annihilation by scientific means, it may, through reason alone, take steps to stop it. But this will be a far cry from accomplishing a spiritual reawakening.

Doubtless, there will always remain a few who will understand and cherish the great truth of life and its magical significance, and the yearning hope is that from these will rise a great and dynamic leader who, as Christ did, will stimulate a rebirth of spiritual understanding.

Something must, it seems to me, take the place of the church before a virile recrudescence of man's spirit can begin again.

The present and increasing spread of the cult of ugliness and crude sensationalism in the arts is one of the symptoms of our crumbling sense of true values.

Let me wind up this early morning diatribe with the following from Jim Boyd's poems recently published. I think you will enjoy it.

> If poets are not listened to, the blame
> is theirs. They speak unclearly,
>   and are lost
> In their own psychic maze and
>   the intricate game
> Of words. In a twisted world
>   what matters most
> Is simple statement, open to
>   the least
> Of men . . .
>   . . . the obscure
> Is powerless over violence. Each
>   word
> Must be inevitable, urgent, pure
> If people are to hear, above the roar,
> The voice of those who know
>   what speech is for.

Written by Romain Rolland some time ago: "The integrity of the arts are declining under the pressures of competitive industrialism. The artisan and the craftsman are going out and the machine coming in, and men and women, not having leisure and quiet to cultivate their souls, are seeking amusement to compensate for their inability to think."

666

Port Clyde, Maine
September, 1945

Dear Henriette,

My head still rings with the impressive and exciting broadcast of Churchill's! He laid out the whole diabolical pattern in such heroic terms that at once lifted everything into sublime and portentous music.

The evening church bell is ringing. The waters have quieted after

843

a day of brisk succession of boisterous white caps on our shelving shore.

The prevailing color right now is an inwardly burning golden-pink, with the snuff-colored islands lying athwart its luminosity like quietly sleeping monsters.

Gulls are beginning their flights "homeward"—to the southeast, in groups of varying numbers, after their long tiring day seeking food in the slapping blue chop of the bay and amongst the glistening wet rocks and twisted and glazed ribbons of kelp heaped up on the shore. As I write, three shags are leaving the water in their heavy and laborious struggle to "take off." They are headed toward Caldwells.

Andy showed me two or three papers recently done. I note a startling maturity. He is revealing a spirit of penetrating sadness. This means to me, if controlled, enormous potentiality. Behind Andy's very free badinage and raillery, and almost swaggering carelessness, is a remoteness of spirit that is very moving. It stands clearly revealed this summer.

On October 19, 1945, exactly forty-three years from the day that N. C. Wyeth had stepped off the train as a young man arriving in Wilmington, Delaware, from Needham, Massachusetts, his life ended.

With his grandson and namesake, Newell Convers Wyeth, on the seat beside him, he turned his car down a road less than a mile from home. Alongside that road lay a field of corn, and his keen eyes spotted in the morning light two figures husking. He stopped the car and, taking his grandson by the hand, walked over to the scene. The last words anyone heard him say were, "Newell, you won't see this again, remember this." As they drove away they both waved back. Minutes later, perhaps distracted in his mind by the golden heaps of corn, a train he did not see nor hear came bearing down. Death came instantly to them both.

INDEX

Works of art by the Wyeths referred to in text will be found listed under artists' names.

INDEX

INDEX

INDEX

INDEX

N. C. Wyeth was one of America's greatest illustrators and the founder of a dynasty of artists that continues to enrich the American scene. This collection of letters, written from his eighteenth year to his tragic death at sixty-one, constitutes in effect his intimate autobiography, and traces the development and flowering of the "Wyeth tradition" over the course of several generations.

The opening chapters deal with N. C. Wyeth's days as a raw young art student under the exacting tutelage of Howard Pyle, his enthusiastic journey through the Far West in search of "material," and his gradual awakening to his own distinctive talents as an artist. The following pages tell of his determined courtship — in face of his parents' wavering opposition — of the girl he loved, and his subsequent struggles to support a rapidly growing family and to establish a home far from the clamor of the marketplace. N. C. Wyeth's middle years were a period of feverish and frequently inspired activity, crowned by fame and financial success, but not untroubled by domestic anxieties and self-doubt. During his later life, changing fashions in art tended to obscure his professional prospects, but he was to find deep satisfaction in the continuous evolution of his own work and in guiding the artistic development of a small group of young painters that included his son Andrew Wyeth and his future sons-in-law Peter Hurd and John McCoy. In the final chapters of this book we catch a glimpse of an extraordinary gift being passed on with wisdom and tender concern from teacher to pupil, from father to son.

N. C. Wyeth was a compulsive letter-writer who wrote out of an urgent need to communicate his innermost thoughts and needs to those he cherished. These letters reveal him to have been a man of sharply contrasting moods and temperaments, but of

N. C. Wyeth, Self-Portrait

constant enthusiasm and deeply rooted devotion to his art, his family, and to the rural American countryside from which he drew vital spiritual refreshment. His delight in the homely occurrences of country life (the little rituals and festivities that punctuated rural domestic routine during the early decades of the century), combined with his painter's eye for colorful detail, make these letters a nostalgic celebration of a rapidly vanishing way of life. This book is a masterfully executed group portrait of the artist and his family set against an American scene such as only a Wyeth could paint.

Betsy James Wyeth, who edited this collection of letters, married the author's son, Andrew Wyeth, in 1940. The Wyeths have two sons, Nicholas and James, and live in Chadds Ford, Pennsylvania.